New York City
Restaurants
2012

EDITORS
Curt Gathje and Carol Diuguid
COORDINATOR
Larry Cohn

Published and distributed by
Zagat Survey, LLC
4 Columbus Circle
New York, NY 10019
T: 212.977.6000
E: newyork@zagat.com
www.zagat.com

ACKNOWLEDGMENTS

We thank Jason Briker, Phil Carlucci, Leigh Crandall, Mikola de Roo, Lynn Hazlewood, Karen Hudes, Bernard Onken, Steven Shukow, Ian Turner and Miranda Van Gelder, as well as the following members of our staff: Danielle Borovoy (assistant editor), Anna Hyclak (editorial assistant), Brian Albert, Sean Beachell, Maryanne Bertollo, Reni Chin, Larry Cohn, Bill Corsello, Nicole Diaz, Kelly Dobkin, Alison Flick, Jeff Freier, Michelle Golden, Matthew Hamm, Justin Hartung, Marc Henson, Aynsley Karps, Rus Kehoe, Cynthia Kilian, Natalie Lebert, Mike Liao, Vivian Ma, Caitlin Miehl, James Mulcahy, Polina Paley, Josh Rogers, Emily Rothschild, Amanda Spurlock, Chris Walsh, Jacqueline Wasilczyk, Yoji Yamaguchi, Sharon Yates, Anna Zappia and Kyle Zolner.

The reviews in this guide are based on public opinion surveys. The ratings reflect the average scores given by the survey participants who voted on each establishment. The text is based on quotes from, or paraphrasings of, the surveyors' comments. Phone numbers, addresses and other factual data were correct to the best of our knowledge when published in this guide.

JOIN IN: To improve this guide, **ZAGAT.com** or any other aspect of our performance, we need your comments. Just contact us at **nina-tim@zagat.com.** We also invite you to vote at **ZAGAT.com** - do so and you'll receive a choice of rewards.

Our guides are printed using environmentally preferable inks containing 20%, by weight, renewable resources on papers sourced from well-managed forests. Deluxe editions are covered with Skivertex Recover® Double containing a minimum of 30% post-consumer waste fiber.

SUSTAINABLE FORESTRY INITIATIVE

Certified Sourcing
www.sfiprogram.org
SFI-00993

ENVIROINK™

The inks used to print the body of this publication contain a minimum of 20%, by weight, renewable resources.

Maps © Antenna International™, except for p. 308 and front panel of foldout map copyright Zagat Survey, LLC

Contents

Ratings & Symbols	4	Private Rooms/Parties	355
About This Survey	5	Quick Bite	356
Key Newcomers	7	Quiet Conversation	356
Most Popular	9	Raw Bars	357
Top Ratings:		Romantic Places	358
Food	9	Senior Appeal	359
Decor	21	Sleepers	359
Service	22	Stargazing	360
Best Buys	23	Sunday Best Bets	360

RESTAURANT DIRECTORY

		Tea Service	360
		Theme Restaurants	360
Names, Locations, Contact		Tough Tickets	360
Info, Ratings & Reviews	27	Transporting Experiences	360
		Views	361

INDEXES

		Visitors on Expense Acct.	361
Cuisines	284	Waterside	362
Maps	306	Winning Wine Lists	362
Locations	309	**Wine Chart**	364
Special Features:			
Bar/Singles Scenes	333		
Breakfast	333		
Brunch	334		
Buffet	335		
BYO	336		
Celebrations	336		
Celebrity Chefs	336		
Cheese Specialists	338		
Chef's Table	339		
Child-Friendly	339		
College-Centric	340		
Commuter Oases	340		
Critic Proof	341		
Dancing/Entertainment	341		
Dessert Specialists	341		
Fireplaces	341		
Gluten-Free Options	342		
Green/Local/Organic	342		
Group Dining	343		
Hipster	344		
Historic Places	345		
Hotel Dining	346		
Hot Spots	347		
Jacket Required	348		
Jury Duty	348		
Late Dining (1 AM or after)	348		
Meet for a Drink	350		
Newcomers	350		
Newcomers on Tap	352		
Noteworthy Closings	352		
Offbeat	353		
Outdoor Dining	353		
People-Watching	354		
Power Scenes	355		

Ratings & Symbols

Zagat Top Spot	Name	Symbols	Cuisine	Zagat Ratings			
				FOOD	DECOR	SERVICE	COST

Area, Address & Contact

🅉 **Tim & Nina's** ◗ *Deli*   ▽ 23 | 9 | 13 | $15

W 50s | 4 Columbus Circle (8th Ave.) | 212-977-6000 | www.zagat.com

Review, surveyor comments in quotes

Nina's grandmother's "hobo stew" and Tim's mother's unfrozen casserole "à la cheap" make for "endless lines" at this "dismal dive" deep down in the Columbus Circle IRT station; service is about "what you'd expect from the MTA", and the tableware is of the "Dixie Cup" and "plastic utensils" variety.

Ratings   **Food, Decor** & **Service** are rated on a 30-point scale.

0	–	9	poor to fair
10	–	15	fair to good
16	–	19	good to very good
20	–	25	very good to excellent
26	–	30	extraordinary to perfection
▽			low response	less reliable

Cost   The price of dinner with a drink and tip; lunch is usually 25% to 30% less. For unrated **newcomers** or **write-ins,** the price range is as follows:

| I | $25 and below | E | $41 to $65 |
| M | $26 to $40 | VE | $66 or above |

Symbols

🅉   highest ratings, popularity and importance

◗   serves after 11 PM

🅂 🅼   closed on Sunday or Monday

⊄   no credit cards accepted

Maps   Index maps show restaurants with the highest Food ratings and other notable places in those areas.

About This Survey

- 2,111 restaurants rated and reviewed
- 41,604 surveyors
- 135 notable openings, 68 closings
- Meals out per week per surveyor: 3.0
- Average meal cost: up 4.1% to $43.46 from $41.76 last year
- Average meal cost at 20 most expensive restaurants: $163.34
- Winners: **Le Bernardin** (Food, Most Popular); **Asiate** (Decor); **Per Se** (Service)
- No. 1 Newcomer for Food: **Ai Fiori**

SURVEY STATS: Thirty-two percent say they're spending more per meal, 54% say the same and only 14% say less . . . Restaurant group buying discounts leave surveyors cold: 43% never use them, 25% say rarely . . . At places that take no reservations, 62% will wait no longer than 30 minutes for a table . . . Service remains dining's top drawback (cited by 60%) followed by noise (24%) and prices (8%); all other complaints aggregate 8% . . . Favorite cuisines: Italian (32%), French (14%), American (12%), Japanese (12%) . . . On a 30-pt. scale, NYC rates 27 for culinary diversity, 24 for creativity, 16 for hospitality and 15 for table availability

ABCs: More than four out of five surveyors approve of NYC's new restaurant letter-grading system. Thirty-five percent of respondents say they would dine only in A-rated places, while another 53% indicated they'd go to places with A or B grades. Only 1% would patronize a C-rated establishment; 11% say they pay no attention to letter grades.

HOT NABES: West Village (**Buvette, The Darby, Fedora, Jeffrey's Grocery, RedFarm, Tertulia**); Williamsburg (**Betto, Isa, Mable's Smoke House,** plus spin-offs of **La Esquina, Meatball Shop** and **Momofuku Milk Bar**); SoHo (**B&B, David Burke Kitchen, The Dutch, Imperial No. 9, Osteria Morini**)

BIG-NAME OPENINGS: Mario Batali (**Birreria**); Daniel Boulud (**Boulud Sud**); April Bloomfield (**John Dory Oyster Bar**); David Bouley (**Brushstroke**); David Burke (**David Burke Kitchen**); Andrew Carmellini (**The Dutch**); Jeffrey Chodorow (**Bar Basque, FoodParc, RedFarm, Tanuki Tavern**); Tom Colicchio (**Riverpark**); John DeLucie (**Crown**); Todd English (**CrossBar**); Sara Jenkins (**Porsena**); Danny Meyer (**Untitled**); Michael Psilakis (**FishTag**); Marcus Samuelsson (**Red Rooster**); Sam Talbot (**Imperial No. 9**); Michael White (**Ai Fiori, Osteria Morini**); Geoffrey Zakarian (**The National**)

TRENDS: Southern cooking (**The Cardinal, Gravy, Hill Country Chicken, Lowcountry, Red Rooster**); retractable roofs make for all-seasons dining (**Birreria, Hotel Chantelle, Salinas**); on-site gardens provide ultralocal ingredients (**Bell Book & Candle, Colonie, Riverpark**)

TOUGH NEW TICKETS: Crown, The Dutch, Red Rooster

New York, NY
October 5, 2011

Nina and Tim Zagat

KEY NEWCOMERS

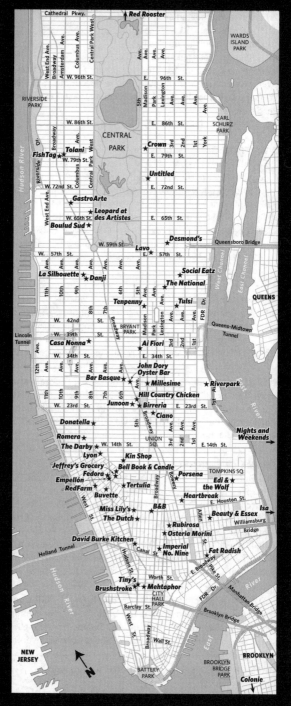

Red Rooster

WARDS ISLAND PARK

Cathedral Pkwy.

West End Ave.
Broadway
Amsterdam Ave.
Columbus Ave.
Central Park West

W. 96th St.

E. 96th St.

RIVERSIDE PARK

W. 86th St.

E. 86th St.

CARL SCHURZ PARK

CENTRAL PARK

Tolani ★
FishTag ★
W. 79th St.

Crown ★
E. 79th St.

Hudson River

Broadway
Riverside Dr.
Columbus Ave.
Central Park West

W. 72nd St.

Untitled ★
E. 72nd St.

GastroArte ★
W. 65th St.
Leopard at ★
des Artistes

E. 65th St.

Boulud Sud ★

West End Ave.

W. 59th St.

Desmond's ★

Queensboro Bridge

Lavo ★
W. 57th St.
E. 57th St.

Social Eatz ★

La Silhouette ★ ★ Danji

The National ★

QUEENS

11th
10th
9th
8th
7th
6th
5th
Madison
Lexington

Tenpenny ★

Tulsi ★

W. 42nd St.

Broadway

BRYANT PARK

Lincoln Tunnel

W. 39th St.

Casa Nonna ★

FDR Dr.

Queens-Midtown Tunnel

12th
11th
10th
9th
8th
7th
6th
5th

W. 34th St.

Ai Fiori ★
E. 34th St.

John Dory Oyster Bar ★

Bar Basque ★
★ Millesime

Riverpark ★

Hill Country Chicken ★

W. 23rd St.

Junoon ★ ★ Birreria
E. 23rd St.

Ciano ★

Donatella ★

Romera ★

Nights and Weekends →

The Darby ★

UNION SQ.

W. 14th St.
E. 14th St.

Lyon ★

Kin Shop ★

Jeffrey's Grocery ★
Bell Book & Candle ★

Fedora ★

Broadway

Porsena ★

TOMPKINS SQ.

Edi & ★
the Wolf

Empellón ★
RedFarm ★

Tertulia ★

Buvette ★

Heartbreak ★

E. Houston St.

Miss Lily's ★
The Dutch ★

B&B ★

Beauty & Essex ★

Isa ★

Rubirosa ★
Osteria Morini ★

Williamsburg Bridge

David Burke Kitchen ★

Holland Tunnel

Imperial ★
No. Nine

Fat Radish ★

Canal St.

Tiny's ★
Brushstroke ★

Worth St.

★ Mehtaphor

E. Broadway

Pike St.

Manhattan Bridge

CITY HALL PARK

Barclay St.

FDR Dr.

Brooklyn Bridge

West St.

Wall St.

East River

NEW JERSEY

Broadway

N

BATTERY PARK

BROOKLYN BRIDGE PARK

BROOKLYN

Colonie ●

6   Vote at ZAGAT.com

Key Newcomers

Our editors' picks among this year's arrivals. See full list at page 350.

BIG NAMES

Ai Fiori
Boulud Sud
Brushstroke
Ciano
David Burke Kitchen
Donatella
Isa
National
Osteria Morini
Porsena
Red Rooster
Tertulia
Untitled

SCENES

Beauty & Essex
Birreria
Darby
Dutch
Fedora
Lavo
Miss Lily's
Nights and Weekends
Rubirosa

SOCIETY WATCH

Crown
Desmond's
Leopard at des Artistes

CULINARY INNOVATORS

GastroArte
Mehtaphor
Romera

STRIKING SPACES

Bar Basque
Beauty & Essex

Darby
Leopard at des Artistes
Riverpark

NEIGHBORHOOD STARS

Buvette
Edi & the Wolf
Empellón
Heartbreak
Jeffrey's Grocery
La Silhouette
Lyon
Tiny's
Tolani

FARM-TO-TABLE

Bell Book & Candle
Colonie
Fat Radish
RedFarm
Riverpark

ASIAN/INDIAN ACCENT

Danji
Junoon
Kin Shop
Social Eatz
Tulsi

FRESH CATCH

FishTag
Imperial No. 9
John Dory Oyster Bar
Millesime

CROWD-PLEASERS

B&B
Casa Nonna
Hill Country Chicken

PROJECTS ON TAP (See page 352 for a complete list)

Three new Russians, **Café Pushkin, Moscow 57** (Midtown) and **Onegin** (West Village), plus outposts of London's **Hakkasan** (Midtown), Beirut's **Al Mayass**, Lima's **La Mar Cebicheria** (Flatiron), Copenhagen's **Aamanns**, Seoul's **Jung Sik** (TriBeCa)

Galen Zamarra works the wood grill at **Mas (la Grillade)**, likewise **Floyd Cardoz** at **Danny Meyer**'s Battery Park City seafooder **North End Grill**

Parm: the deli counter/sub shop at **Torrisi** finds a new next-door home

Tribeca Canvas: Japanese-fusion comfort fare from **Masaharu Morimoto**

Branches on the way: **Empellón** (East Village), **Lucali** (LES), **Meatball Shop** (West Village), **Momofuku Milk Bar** (UWS), **Quality Meats, Veselka** (Bowery), **Socarrat** (Turtle Bay), **Ippudo, STK** (Midtown), **Toloache** (UES)

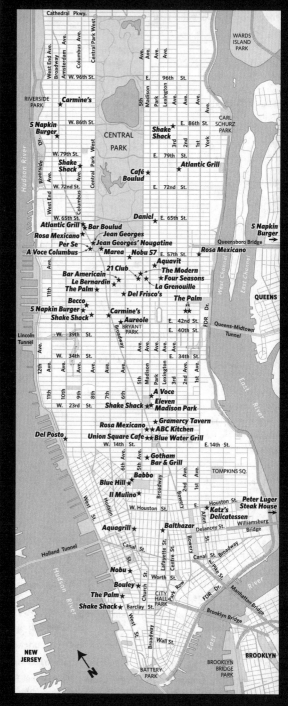

MOST POPULAR

Vote at ZAGAT.com

Most Popular

A more extensive list is plotted on the map at the back of this book.

1. Le Bernardin | *French/Seafood*
2. Gramercy Tavern | *American*
3. Peter Luger (Bklyn) | *Steak*
4. Union Square Cafe | *American*
5. Eleven Madison Park | *French*
6. Daniel | *French*
7. Babbo | *Italian*
8. Gotham Bar & Grill | *American*
9. Jean Georges | *French*
10. Balthazar | *French*
11. Del Posto | *Italian*
12. Bouley | *French*
13. Atlantic Grill | *Seafood*
14. Per Se | *American/French*
15. Café Boulud | *French*
16. Nobu | *Japanese*
17. 5 Napkin Burger | *Burgers*
18. ABC Kitchen | *American*
19. Aureole | *American*
20. Four Seasons* | *American*
21. 21 Club | *American*
22. La Grenouille | *French*
23. Blue Water Grill | *Seafood*
24. Modern | *American/French*
25. Palm | *Steak*
26. Del Frisco's | *Steak*
27. Marea | *Italian/Seafood*
28. Becco | *Italian*
29. Rosa Mexicano | *Mexican*
30. Il Mulino | *Italian*
31. Aquagrill | *Seafood*
32. A Voce | *Italian*
33. Shake Shack | *Burgers*
34. Jean Georges' Nougatine | *Fr.*
35. Blue Hill | *American*
36. Carmine's | *Italian*
37. Bar Boulud | *French*
38. Bar Americain | *American*
39. Aquavit | *Scandinavian*
40. Katz's Deli | *Deli*

Top Food

29 Le Bernardin | *French/Seafood*
Daniel | *French*

28 Per Se | *American/French*
Bouley | *French*
Jean Georges | *French*
Eleven Madison Park | *French*
Sushi Yasuda | *Japanese*
Annisa | *American*
La Grenouille | *French*
Peter Luger (Bklyn) | *Steak*
Marea | *Italian/Seafood*
Gotham Bar & Grill | *American*

27 Blue Hill | *American*
Gramercy Tavern | *American*
Tratt. L'incontro (Qns) | *Italian*
Roberto (Bronx) | *Italian*
Del Posto | *Italian*
Danny Brown (Qns) | *European*
Mas | *American*
L'Atelier/Joël Robuchon | *Fr.*
Picholine | *Fr./Med.*
Scalini Fedeli | *Italian*
Milos | *Greek/Seafood*
Café Boulud | *French*
Saul (Bklyn) | *American*

Jean Georges' Nougatine | *Fr.*
Il Mulino | *Italian*
Degustation | *French/Spanish*
Momofuku Ko | *American*
Gari/Sushi | *Japanese*
Grocery (Bklyn) | *American*
Masa/Bar Masa | *Japanese*
Four Seasons | *American*
Babbo | *Italian*
Ai Fiori | *Italian*
Sushi Seki | *Japanese*
Union Square Cafe | *American*
Torrisi Italian | *Italian*
Al Di La (Bklyn) | *Italian*

26 Modern | *American/French*
Aquagrill | *Seafood*
Totonno Pizza (Bklyn) | *Pizza*
Scalinatella | *Italian*
Lucali (Bklyn) | *Pizza*
Telepan | *American*
Nobu | *Japanese*
Tomoe Sushi | *Japanese*
Pearl Oyster Bar | *Seafood*
Tanoreen (Bklyn) | *Med./Mid.*
Blue Rib. Sushi (multi) | *Japan.*

* Indicates a tie with restaurant above

BY CUISINE

AMERICAN

28 Per Se
Annisa
Gotham Bar & Grill
27 Blue Hill
Gramercy Tavern
Mas
Saul (Bklyn)
Momofuku Ko
Grocery (Bklyn)
Four Seasons
Union Square Cafe
26 Modern

ASIAN

25 Asiate
24 Buddakan
22 China Grill
Wild Ginger
Tao
Zengo
21 Blue Ginger
Purple Yam (Bklyn)

AUSTRIAN/GERMAN/SWISS

26 Wallsé
25 Seäsonal
24 Heartbreak
Café Katja
Zum Stammtisch (Qns)
22 Edi & the Wolf
Café Sabarsky
Blaue Gans

BARBECUE

26 Fette Sau (Bklyn)
23 Daisy May's
22 Smoke Joint (Bklyn)
Dinosaur BBQ
Blue Smoke
Rack & Soul
Hill Country
21 Fatty 'Cue

BURGERS

24 Burger Joint
B&B
23 DuMont (Bklyn)
BareBurger
Black Iron Burger
22 Corner Bistro

67 Burger (Bklyn)
Go Burger

CARIBBEAN

23 Cuba
Victor's Cafe
Sofrito
22 Havana Alma
Café Habana/Outpost
21 Don Pedro's
Negril
20 El Malecon

CHINESE

25 Pacificana (Bklyn)
Shun Lee Palace
24 Wu Liang Ye
Wa Jeal
Mr. K's
23 Chin Chin
Xi'an Famous Foods
Spicy & Tasty (Qns)

DELIS

24 Katz's Deli
Mile End (Bklyn)
Barney Greengrass
23 Ben's Best (Qns)
Mill Basin Deli (Bklyn)
2nd Ave Deli
22 Carnegie Deli
Liebman's (Bronx)

DESSERT

25 Chocolate Room (Bklyn)
24 La Bergamote
L & B Spumoni (Bklyn)
Veniero's
Bouchon Bakery
ChikaLicious
23 Momofuku Milk Bar
Ferrara

DIM SUM

25 Pacificana (Bklyn)
23 Lychee House
Oriental Garden
22 Ping's Seafood
Chinatown Brasserie
21 Excellent Dumpling
Shun Lee Cafe
Golden Unicorn

Excludes places with low votes, unless otherwise indicated

ECLECTIC

27 Traif (Bklyn)
25 Mehtaphor
   Graffiti
   WD-50
   Good Fork (Bklyn)
24 Carol's Cafe (SI)
   Tolani
   Public

FRENCH

29 Le Bernardin
   Brooklyn Fare Kitchen (Bklyn)
   Daniel
28 Bouley
   Jean Georges
   Eleven Madison Park
   La Grenouille
27 L'Atelier/Joël Robuchon

FRENCH BISTRO

26 La Silhouette
25 Tournesol (Qns)
   DB Bistro Moderne
   JoJo
24 Le Gigot
   Capsouto Frères
   Raoul's
   Bar Boulud

GREEK

27 Milos
26 Taverna Kyclades (Qns)
   Pylos
25 Avra
24 Thalassa
   Periyali
23 Elias Corner (Qns)
   Agnanti

HOTEL DINING

28 Jean Georges (Trump Int'l)
27 L'Atelier/Joël Robuchon
   (Four Seasons)
   Café Boulud (Surrey)
   Ai Fiori (Setai Fifth Ave.)
26 Adour (St. Regis)
   Gilt (NY Palace)
25 Mehtaphor (Duane St.)
   Locanda Verde (Greenwich)

INDIAN

25 Tamarind
24 Amma
   Dhaba
   Saravanaa Bhavan
   Chola
   Dévi
23 Junoon
   Dawat

ITALIAN

28 Marea
27 Tratt. L'incontro (Qns)
   Roberto (Bronx)
   Del Posto
   Scalini Fedeli
   Il Mulino
   Babbo
   Locanda Vini/Olii (Bklyn)
   Ai Fiori
   Torrisi Italian
   Al Di La (Bklyn)
26 Scalinatella

JAPANESE/SUSHI

29 Sasabune
   Soto
28 Sushi Yasuda
27 Donguri
   Sushi Sen-nin
   Gari/Sushi
   Masa/Bar Masa
   Sugiyama
   Sushi Seki
26 Jewel Bako
   Nobu
   Tomoe Sushi

KOREAN

25 HanGawi
23 Moim (Bklyn)
   Kang Suh
22 Cho Dang Gol
   Mandoo Bar
   Madangsui
   Kum Gang San
   Gahm Mi Oak

KOSHER

26 Azuri Cafe
23 Ben's Best (Qns)
   Mill Basin Deli (Bklyn)
   2nd Ave Deli
   Tiffin Wallah
   Prime Grill
22 Liebman's (Bronx)
   Le Marais

LOBSTER ROLLS

26 Pearl Oyster Bar
25 Mary's Fish Camp
24 Red Hook Lobster (Bklyn)
23 Luke's Lobster

Brooklyn Fish (Bklyn)
Ed's Lobster Bar
22 Mermaid
20 Ed's Chowder House

MEDITERRANEAN
27 Picholine
26 Tanoreen (Bklyn)
Il Buco
25 Little Owl
Convivium Osteria (Bklyn)
Alta
24 Taboon
Red Cat

MEXICAN
24 Calexico (Bklyn)
Itzocan
Pampano
Mexicana Mama
23 Toloache
Maya
Crema
Fonda (Bklyn)

MIDDLE EASTERN
26 Tanoreen (Bklyn)
Taïm
Azuri Cafe
25 Taci's Beyti (Bklyn)
Ilili
24 Taboon
Mimi's Hummus (Bklyn)
23 Balaboosta

NEWCOMERS (RATED)
27 Ai Fiori
26 La Silhouette
25 Mehtaphor
Riverpark
Rubirosa
Ciano
24 Osteria Morini
Heartbreak

NOODLE SHOPS
27 Donguri
25 Ippudo
Totto Ramen
24 Momofuku Noodle Bar
Soba-ya
23 Great NY Noodle
Soba Nippon
22 Bo-Ky

PIZZA
26 Totonno's (Bklyn)
Lucali (Bklyn)
Di Fara (Bklyn)
Denino's (SI)
Roberta's (Bklyn)
25 Keste Pizza e Vino
No. 28
Franny's (Bklyn)

RAW BARS
26 Aquagrill
Pearl Oyster Bar
Jack's Lux. Oyster
25 Esca
Blue Ribbon
24 Oceana
Fishtail
BLT Fish

SANDWICHES
(see also Delis)
26 Num Pang
25 Meatball Shop
24 Defonte's
Porchetta
23 No. 7 Sub
22 Nicky's Viet.
Peanut Butter & Co.
Press 195

SEAFOOD
29 Le Bernardin
28 Marea
27 Milos
26 Aquagrill
Pearl Oyster Bar
Jack's Lux. Oyster
Taverna Kyclades (Qns)
25 Esca

SMALL PLATES
27 L'Atelier/Joël Robuchon
Degustation
Traif (Bklyn)
26 Zenkichi (Bklyn)
25 Graffiti
EN Japanese
Frankies Spuntino
Sakagura

SOUTH AMERICAN
24 Caracas
23 Chimichurri Grill
Buenos Aires
Churrascaria
22 Empanada Mama

Pio Pio
21 Via Brasil
Rice 'n' Beans

SOUTHERN/SOUL

23 Egg (Bklyn)
Pies-n-Thighs (Bklyn)
Char No. 4 (Bklyn)
22 Rack & Soul
21 Red Rooster
Amy Ruth's
20 Tipsy Parson
Lowcountry

SOUTHWESTERN

24 Mesa Grill
19 Agave
Canyon Road
18 Cilantro
17 Cowgirl

SPANISH/TAPAS

25 Casa Mono
Txikito
24 Tía Pol
Sevilla
23 Las Ramblas
Socarrat Paella
Bar Jamon
El Porrón

STEAKHOUSES

28 Peter Luger (Bklyn)
26 BLT Prime
Sparks Steak
Wolfgang's
25 Del Frisco's
Strip House
Keens
BLT Steak
Palm
Morton's

24 Benjamin Steak
Old Homestead

THAI

26 Sripraphai (Qns)
24 Thai Market
Erawan (Qns)
Kin Shop
23 Kuma Inn
Joya (Bklyn)
Jaiya Thai
Kittichai

TURKISH

25 Taci's Beyti (Bklyn)
23 Turkish Grill (Qns)
Sahara (Bklyn)
22 Hanci Turkish
Turkish Kitchen
Sahara's Turkish
Beyoglu
21 Pasha

VEGETARIAN

26 Taïm
Dirt Candy
25 HanGawi
24 Saravanaa Bhavan
Candle 79
23 Candle Cafe
Pure Food & Wine
Tiffin Wallah

VIETNAMESE

23 Má Pêche
Omai
22 Bo-Ky
Indochine
Nicky's Viet.
Pho Viet Huong
Nha Trang
21 Pho Bang

BY SPECIAL FEATURE

BREAKFAST

27 Jean Georges' Nougatine
25 Locanda Verde
Maialino
Clinton St. Baking Co.
Norma's
24 Prime Meats (Bklyn)
Katz's Deli
Barney Greengrass

BRUNCH DOWNTOWN

26 Aquagrill
25 Clinton St. Baking Co.
Blue Ribbon Bakery
24 Balthazar
22 Five Points
20 Cafe Cluny
Fat Radish
Bubby's

BRUNCH MIDTOWN

24 Colicchio & Sons
   Blue Water Grill
23 Artisanal
   Water Club
   Atlantic Grill
22 Cookshop
21 Brasserie 8½
   Penelope

BRUNCH UPTOWN

26 Telepan
25 David Burke Townhouse
23 Square Meal
   Atlantic Grill
   Community Food
21 Good Enough to Eat
20 Sarabeth's
   Nice Matin

CELEBRITY SCENES

23 Minetta Tavern
   Spotted Pig
   Philippe
22 Da Silvano
21 Leopard at des Artistes∇
20 Darby∇
   Lion
⎯ Crown

CHILD-FRIENDLY

23 Otto
22 Shake Shack
21 Carmine's
   Landmarc
20 Bubby's
19 Serendipity 3
18 Two Boots
⎯ PSbklyn

DINING AT THE BAR

28 Gotham Bar & Grill
27 Gramercy Tavern
24 Hearth
   Lincoln
   Colicchio & Sons
23 Freemans
22 Oyster Bar
   Plaza Food Hall

DRINKS DOWNTOWN

26 SHO Shaun Hergatt
25 Bond Street
23 Minetta Tavern
   Spice Market
   Stanton Social
   Harry's Cafe/Steak

   Freemans
21 Standard Grill

DRINKS MIDTOWN

27 Four Seasons
26 Modern
25 Le Cirque
23 Casa Lever
22 21 Club
   Zengo
19 Bar Basque
18 Monkey Bar

DRINKS UPTOWN

29 Daniel
24 Ouest
   Bar Boulud
23 Atlantic Grill
22 Mark
21 Cafe Luxembourg
   Red Rooster
⎯ Crown

FOOD TRUCKS

(see ZAGAT.com for reviews)
27 Nauti
26 Taïm Mobile
25 Wafels & Dinges
   Van Leeuwen Ice Cream Truck
   Korilla Food Truck
   Big Gay Ice Cream Truck
   Kelvin Natural
   Yvonne's Jamaican

GROUP DINING

25 Ilili
24 Buddakan
23 Stanton Social
   Otto
   Churrascaria
22 Rosa Mexicano
   Tao
21 Carmine's

HIPSTER HANGOUTS

26 Roberta's (Bklyn)
25 Meatball Shop
24 Marlow & Sons (Bklyn)
23 Hecho en Dumbo
22 Fedora
   Breslin
21 Fatty 'Cue
⎯ Nights and Weekends (Bklyn)

HISTORIC PLACES

28 Peter Luger (Bklyn)
27 Four Seasons

25 Keens
   Palm
22 21 Club
   Oyster Bar
17 P.J. Clarke's (Third Ave.)
15 Pete's Tavern

HOT SERVERS

25 Del Frisco's
23 Spice Market
22 Indochine
   Abe & Arthur's
21 44 & X/44½
17 Brother Jimmy's
- Miss Lily's
- Nights & Weekends

HOT SPOTS

25 Rubirosa
24 Dutch
22 Beauty & Essex
21 Lavo
20 Peels
19 Bar Basque
- Miss Lily's
- Nights & Weekends

HUSH-HUSH

27 Bohemian∇
26 Zenkichi
25 Hudson Clearwater∇
   Sakagura
24 Burger Joint
23 Kashkaval
   La Esquina
   Freemans

LATE DININIG

29 Soto
27 Mas
   Momofuku Ko
   Milos
   Gari/Sushi
   Traif (Bklyn)
   Babbo
   Sugiyama

LOCAVORE

27 Blue Hill
   Mas
26 Telepan
   Craft
   Roberta's (Bklyn)
25 ABC Kitchen
   Riverpark
23 Bell Book & Candle

MILESTONES

75th Carnegie Deli
50th La Grenouille
     Sylvia's
25th Aquavit
     Bice
     China Grill
     Docks Oyster Bar
     La Lunchonette

POWER LUNCH

28 Marea
27 Four Seasons
24 Smith & Wollensky
23 Casa Lever
   Patroon
22 21 Club
   China Grill
   Michael's

PRIVATE PARTIES

28 Eleven Madison Park
   Marea
27 Four Seasons
26 River Café
   Il Buco
25 Maialino
   Keens
22 Breslin

QUICK BITES

26 Azuri Cafe
23 Eataly
22 Empanada Mama
   Crif Dogs
   Hummus Place
21 Kati Roll Co.
   Baoguette
18 FoodParc

SENIOR APPEAL

28 La Grenouille
27 Del Posto
26 Felidia
   River Café (Bklyn)
   Aureole
   Piccola Venezia (Qns)
25 Triomphe
24 Arabelle

SINGLES SCENES

24 Buddakan
23 Spice Market
22 Beauty & Essex
   STK
   Tao
21 Lavo

20 Hurricane Club	28 Per Se
17 Brother Jimmy's BBQ	Bouley
	Jean Georges
SOCIETY WATCH	Eleven Madison Park
25 David Burke Townhouse	Sushi Yasuda
24 Elio's	La Grenouille
22 Desmond's∇	
Ze Café	**WINE BARS**
21 Sant Ambroeus	27 Danny Brown (Qns)
Leopard at des Artistes∇	25 Casellula
20 Le Caprice	24 SD26
18 Swifty's	Peasant
	Felice
24-HOUR	Bocca Lupo (Bklyn)
23 Kang Suh	Bar Boulud
22 Empanada Mama	23 Kashkaval
Kum Gang San	
Gahm Mi Oak	**WINNING WINE LISTS**
21 WonJo	29 Daniel
Sarge's Deli	28 Bouley
20 Gray's Papaya	Eleven Madison Park
Coppelia	27 Del Posto
	26 Adour
VISITORS ON EXPENSE	Veritas
ACCOUNT	23 Tribeca Grill
29 Le Bernardin	Otto
Daniel	

BY LOCATION

CHELSEA	Sakagura
27 Del Posto	Il Postino
26 Morimoto	Palm
Scarpetta	
25 Txikito	**EAST 50s**
Ilili	28 La Grenouille
24 Buddakan	27 L'Atelier/Joël Robuchon
Da Umberto	Four Seasons
La Bergamote	26 Felidia
	Adour
CHINATOWN	Gilt
23 Great NY Noodle	Wolfgang's
Xi'an Famous Foods	San Pietro
Oriental Garden	
Big Wong	**EAST 60s**
Peking Duck	29 Daniel
Nice Green Bo	27 Sushi Seki
22 Ping's Seafood	26 Scalinatella
Bo-Ky	25 David Burke Townhouse
	JoJo
EAST 40s	Park Avenue . . .
28 Sushi Yasuda	24 Fishtail
26 Num Pang	Arabelle
Sparks Steak	
25 Aburiya Kinnosuke	**EAST 70s**
Avra	29 Sasabune
	27 Café Boulud

Gari/Sushi
25 Alloro
24 Lusardi's
Candle 79
Carlyle
23 Caravaggio

EAST 80s

27 Donguri
26 Sistina
25 Sandro's
Spigolo
Erminia
Poke
24 Elio's
Wa Jeal

EAST 90s & 100s

24 Nick's
23 Square Meal
Sfoglia
Paola's
El Paso Taqueria
Pinocchio
22 Pio Pio

EAST VILLAGE

27 Degustation
Momofuku Ko
26 Jewel Bako
Dirt Candy
Kanoyama
Kyo Ya
Jack's Lux. Oyster
Pylos

FINANCIAL DISTRICT

26 SHO Shaun Hergatt
24 Delmonico's
Capital Grille
23 Luke's Lobster
Toloache
Adrienne's Pizza
MarkJoseph Steak
Cipriani Wall St.

FLATIRON/UNION SQ.

28 Eleven Madison Park
27 Gramercy Tavern
Union Square Cafe
26 15 East
Veritas
Craft
25 Aldea
Tocqueville

GARMENT DISTRICT

27 Ai Fiori
25 Keens
23 Frankie & Johnnie's
Kang Suh
Szechuan Gourmet
Uncle Jack's
Lazzara's
22 Cho Dang Gol

GRAMERCY

26 BLT Prime
25 Casa Mono
Maialino
Novitá
24 Posto
Defonte's
Yama
23 Ponty Bistro

GREENWICH VILLAGE

28 Gotham Bar & Grill
27 Blue Hill
Il Mulino
Babbo
26 Tomoe Sushi
Num Pang
25 Lupa
Strip House

HARLEM

23 Rao's
El Paso Taqueria
22 Dinosaur BBQ
22 Covo
21 Red Rooster
Hudson River Café
Amy Ruth's
5 & Diamond

LITTLE ITALY

23 Pellegrino's
Angelo's/Mulberry St.
Il Fornaio
Ferrara
La Esquina
22 Il Cortile
Bo-Ky
Wild Ginger

LOWER EAST SIDE

25 WD-50
Frankies Spuntino
Clinton St. Baking Co.
Meatball Shop
24 Falai
Ápizz

Katz's Deli
Café Katja

MEATPACKING

26 Valbella
24 Old Homestead
23 Spice Market
22 Macelleria
Paradou
STK
Abe & Arthur's
21 Standard Grill

MURRAY HILL

27 Sushi Sen-nin
26 Wolfgang's
25 HanGawi
Riverpark
Marcony
24 Dhaba
Saravanaa Bhavan
SD26

NOHO

26 Il Buco
25 Bond Street
24 Bianca
23 Aroma
Hecho en Dumbo
22 Five Points
Chinatown Brasserie
21 Great Jones Cafe

NOLITA

27 Torrisi Italian
25 Lombardi's
Rubirosa
24 Peasant
Public
23 Balaboosta
Socarrat Paella
Ed's Lobster Bar

SOHO

26 Aquagrill
Blue Ribbon Sushi
25 No. 28
Blue Ribbon
L'Ecole
24 Caffe Falai
Osteria Morini
Aurora

TRIBECA

28 Bouley
27 Scalini Fedeli
26 Nobu

Il Giglio
Pepolino
Marc Forgione
Wolfgang's
25 Corton

WEST 40s

27 Gari/Sushi
26 Aureole
Sushi Zen
25 Del Frisco's
Esca
Triomphe
DB Bistro Moderne
Print

WEST 50s

29 Le Bernardin
28 Marea
27 Milos
Sugiyama
26 Modern
Nobu 57
Azuri Cafe
La Silhouette

WEST 60s

28 Per Se
Jean Georges
27 Picholine
Masa/Bar Masa
26 Telepan
25 Asiate
24 Lincoln
Bouchon Bakery

WEST 70s

27 Gari/Sushi
26 Dovetail
25 Salumeria Rosi
24 Saravanaa Bhavan
Tolani
Ocean Grill
23 'Cesca
22 FishTag

WEST 80s

24 Spiga
Celeste
Recipe
Ouest
Barney Greengrass
23 Luke's Lobster
Momoya
Prime KO

WEST 90s & UP

24 Thai Market
   Gennaro
   Pisticci
23 Max SoHa/Caffe
   Awash
   Sookk
   Community Food
   Noche Mexicana

WEST VILLAGE

29 Soto
28 Annisa
27 Mas
26 Pearl Oyster Bar
   Taïm
   Wallsé
   Perry St.
   Perilla

BROOKLYN

BAY RIDGE

26 Tanoreen
24 Areo
   Fushimi
23 Agnanti
   Tuscany Grill
   Pearl Room
22 Chadwick's
21 Cebu

BKLYN HTS/DUMBO

26 River Café
24 Henry's End
   Noodle Pudding
   Grimaldi's
   Queen
23 Jack the Horse
21 Rice
   Chip Shop

CARROLL GARDENS/ BOERUM & COBBLE HILLS

27 Saul
   Grocery
26 Lucali
   Hibino
25 Ki Sushi
   Chocolate Room
   Frankies Spuntino
   Fragole

FORT GREENE/ PROSPECT HEIGHTS

25 Franny's
23 Amorina
   James
   Vanderbilt

   No. 7
22 Ici
   Smoke Joint
   Habana Outpost

PARK SLOPE

27 Al Di La
26 Blue Ribbon Sushi
   Rose Water
25 Convivium Osteria
   Stone Park Café
   Blue Ribbon
   Applewood
   Chocolate Room

WILLIAMSBURG

28 Peter Luger
27 Traif
26 Zenkichi
   Fette Sau
25 Dressler
24 1 or 8
   Caracas
   Aurora

OTHER AREAS

29 Brooklyn Fare Kitchen
   (Downtown)
27 Locanda Vini/Olii
   (Clinton Hill)
26 Di Fara (Midwood)
   Roberta's (Bushwick)
25 Taci's Beyti (Midwood)
   Pacificana (Sunset Park)
   Vinegar Hill House
   (Vinegar Hill)
   Good Fork (Red Hook)

OTHER BOROUGHS

BRONX

27 Roberto
25 Zero Otto Nove
24 Dominick's
Jake's
Patricia's
23 Enzo's
Artie's
Beccofino

QUEENS: ASTORIA/L.I.C.

27 Tratt. L'incontro
26 Taverna Kyclades
Piccola Venezia
25 Tournesol
23 Elias Corner
BareBurger
Agnanti
Christos Steak

QUEENS: OTHER AREAS

27 Danny Brown (Forest Hills)
26 Sripraphai (Woodside)
25 Don Peppe (Ozone Park)
24 Park Side (Corona)
Erawan (Bayside)
Grimaldi's (Douglaston)
Sapori D'Ischia (Woodside)
Zum Stammtisch (Glendale)

STATEN ISLAND

26 Denino's
Trattoria Romana
25 Bocelli
24 Carol's Cafe
Fushimi
Joe & Pat's
23 Da Noi
Bayou

Top Decor

28	Asiate
	Per Se
	Four Seasons
	Daniel
	River Café (Bklyn)
	Eleven Madison Park
	La Grenouille
	Gilt

27	Le Bernardin
	Bouley
	Adour
	Beauty & Essex
	Carlyle
	Buddakan
	Del Posto
	Jean Georges
	One if by Land
	SHO Shaun Hergatt
	Riverpark

26	Hurricane Club
	Modern

Kittichai
Marea
Megu
Spice Market
EN Japanese
Le Cirque
Palm Court
Grand Tier
FireBird
Water Club
Park Avenue . . .
Gramercy Tavern
Morimoto
Boathouse
Lincoln
Robert
Tao

25	Gotham Bar & Grill
	Russian Tea Room

PATIOS/GARDENS

Aurora
Barbetta
Barolo
Battery Gardens
Boathouse
Brasserie Ruhlmann
Bryant Park
Cávo

I Coppi
I Trulli
Morgane (Bklyn)
New Leaf
Pure Food & Wine
Raoul's
Salinas
ViceVersa

ROMANCE

Barmarché
Erminia
Flor de Sol
Gascogne
House
Il Buco
Kings' Carriage
Lambs Club

Mas
One if by Land
Peasant
Place
River Café (Bklyn)
Valentino's (Qns)
Wallsé
Zenkichi (Bklyn)

VIEWS

Asiate
A Voce (W 60s)
Battery Gardens
Boathouse
Gigino Wagner Park
Hotel Chantelle
Lincoln
Michael Jordan's

Modern
River Café (Bklyn)
Riverpark
Robert
Terrace in the Sky
View
Water Club
Water's Edge (Qns)

Top Service

29	Per Se

28	Le Bernardin
	Daniel
	Eleven Madison Park
	La Grenouille
	Jean Georges

27	Bouley
	Four Seasons
	Gramercy Tavern
	Annisa
	Mas
	Del Posto
	Adour
	Gotham Bar & Grill
	Blue Hill

26	Marea
	Picholine
	Scalini Fedeli
	L'Atelier/Joël Robuchon
	Gilt

Union Square Cafe
Café Boulud
Il Tinello
Asiate
Carlyle
Tocqueville
River Café (Bklyn)
Modern
Veritas

25	Jean Georges' Nougatine
	Ai Fiori
	Aureole
	Valbella
	Telepan
	Corton
	One if by Land
	Tratt. L'incontro (Qns)
	Saul (Bklyn)
	Grocery (Bklyn)
	Degustation

Best Buys

Everyone loves a bargain, and NYC offers plenty of them. Bear in mind: (1) lunch typically costs 25 to 30% less than dinner, (2) outer-borough dining is far less costly than in Manhattan, (3) most Indian restaurants offer incredibly inexpensive prix fixe lunch buffets and (4) biannual Restaurant Weeks (in January and July) are big bargains.

ALL YOU CAN EAT

- [24] Chola
- [23] Churrascaria
- Becco
- Yuka
- Yuva
- [22] Indus Valley
- Salaam Bombay
- [21] Sapphire Indian
- Chennai Garden
- Darbar

BYO

- [26] Lucali (Bklyn)
- Di Fara (Bklyn)
- [25] Taci's Beyti (Bklyn)
- Poke
- [23] Phoenix Garden
- Peking Duck (C-town)
- [22] Tartine
- Angelica Kit.
- Nook
- [21] Amy Ruth's

CHEAP DATES

- [25] Keste Pizza e Vino
- Meatball Shop
- [24] Caracas
- Soba-ya
- [23] Social Eatz
- Kashkaval
- [22] Cafe Mogador
- Holy Basil
- [20] La Lanterna Vittorio

EARLY-BIRD

- [26] La Silhouette
- [25] JoJo
- [24] Ouest
- Queen (Bklyn)
- Ocean Grill
- [23] Italianissimo
- [22] Sueños
- Maze
- Kefi
- [21] Pascalou

FAMILY-STYLE

- [26] Piccolo Angolo
- [25] Don Peppe (Qns)
- [24] Pisticci
- Dominick's (Bronx)
- Nick's
- [23] Spice Market
- Rao's
- Manducatis (Qns)
- [21] Carmine's
- Tony's Di Napoli

PRE-THEATER

- [27] Jean Georges' Nougatine
- Milos
- Sugiyama
- [25] DB Bistro Moderne
- [24] Oceana
- South Gate
- [23] Molyvos
- Kellari Taverna
- [22] China Grill
- [21] Abboccato

PRIX FIXE LUNCH

- [28] Jean Georges ($32)
- Sushi Yasuda ($23)
- Gotham Bar & Grill ($25)
- [27] Milos ($24)
- Café Boulud ($32)
- Jean Georges' Nougatine ($28)
- Four Seasons ($35)
- [26] Telepan ($22)
- Felidia ($30)
- [23] Má Pêche ($25)

PRIX FIXE DINNER

- [28] Sushi Yasuda ($23)
- [27] Danny Brown (Qns) ($28)
- [26] Marc Forgione ($39)
- Rose Water (Bklyn) ($26)
- [25] Tournesol (Qns) ($25)
- Stone Park Café (Bklyn) ($32)
- JoJo ($38)
- Aki ($30)
- HanGawi ($40)
- Poke ($38)

BEST BUYS: FULL MENU

Azuri Cafe | *Israeli*
Bereket | *Turkish*
Big Wong | *Chinese*
Bo-Ky | *Noodle Shop*
Brennan & Carr (Bklyn) | *Sandwiches*
Calexico | *Mexican*
Chickpea | *Mideastern*
Dos Toros | *Mexican*
Egg (Bklyn) | *Southern*
Eisenberg's | *Sandwiches*
Excellent Dumpling | *Chinese*
Hide-Chan | *Noodle Shop*
Hummus Place | *Israeli/Veg.*
Ippudo | *Noodle Shop*
Joe & Pat's (S.I.) | *Italian/Pizza*
Joya (Bklyn) | *Thai*
La Bergamote | *Bakery/French*
Liebman's | *Deli/Kosher*
Mandoo Bar | *Korean*
Maoz | *Mideastern/Veg.*
Mill Basin Deli (Bklyn) | *Deli/Kosher*
Mimi's Hummus (Bklyn) | *Mideastern*
Molly's | *Pub Food*
Nanoosh | *Mediterranean*
Nha Trang | *Vietnamese*

Noche | *Mexican*
Num Pang | *Cambodian*
Oaxaca | *Mexican*
Omonia Café (Qns) | *Greek*
Peacefood Café | *Vegan/Veg.*
Pho Bang | *Vietnamese*
Pho Viet Huong | *Vietnamese*
Pies-n-Thighs (Bklyn) | *Soul Food*
Quantum Leap | *Health/Veg.*
Rai Rai Ken | *Noodle Shop*
Ramen Setagaya | *Noodle Shop*
Rice | *Eclectic*
Saravanaa Bhavan | *Indian/Veg.*
Schnipper's | *American*
Shanghai Café | *Chinese*
Song (Bklyn) | *Thai*
Sookk | *Thai*
Taïm | *Israeli/Veg.*
Thai Market | *Thai*
Tiffin Wallah | *Indian/Veg.*
Tom's (Bklyn) | *Diner*
Totto Ramen | *Noodle Shop*
Xi'an | *Chinese*
Zaytoons (Bklyn) | *Mideastern*
Zuzu Ramen | *Noodle Shop*

BEST BUYS: SPECIALTY SHOPS

Artichoke Basille's | *Pizza*
Baoguette | *Sandwiches/Viet.*
BaoHaus | *Sandwiches*
BareBurger | *Burgers*
Bark (Bklyn) | *Hot Dogs*
Black Iron | *Burgers*
Brgr | *Burgers*
Burger Joint | *Burgers*
Caracas | *Arepas*
Carl's | *Cheesesteaks*
ChikaLicious | *Dessert*
Chocolate Room (Bklyn) | *Dessert*
Cosi | *Sandwiches*
Crif Dogs | *Hot Dogs*
Defonte's | *Sandwiches*
Denino's (S.I.) | *Pizza*
Dumpling Man | *Dumplings*
Elevation | *Burgers*
Empanada Mama | *Empanadas*
Ferrara | *Dessert*
Five Guys | *Burgers*
FoodParc | *Eclectic*
Goodburger | *Burgers*
Gray's Papaya | *Hot Dogs*
Hale & Hearty | *Soup*

Hampton Chutney | *Dosas*
Hanco's (Bklyn) | *Sandwiches*
Joe's Pizza | *Pizza*
Kati Roll Co. | *Kati Wraps*
Momofuku Milk Bar | *Dessert*
Nicky's Viet. | *Sandwiches*
99 Miles to Philly | *Cheesesteaks*
Once Upon a Tart | *Baked Goods*
Papaya King | *Hot Dogs*
Peanut Butter | *Sandwiches*
Porchetta | *Sandwiches*
Press 195 (Bklyn/Qns) | *Sandwiches*
Pret a Manger | *Sandwiches*
Rickshaw | *Dumplings*
Roll-n-Roaster (Bklyn) | *Sandwiches*
Shake Shack | *Burgers*
Shorty's | *Cheesesteaks*
67 Burger | *Burgers*
S'MAC | *Mac 'n' Cheese*
SNice | *Sandwiches*
Sweet Melissa (Bklyn) | *Dessert*
Two Boots | *Pizza*
Vanessa's | *Dumplings*
Veniero's | *Dessert*
'Wichcraft | *Sandwiches*

BEST BUYS: PRIX FIXE MENUS

LUNCH: $35 OR LESS

A.J. Maxwell's	$30	La Rivista	20
Al Bustan	19	L'Ecole	30
Almond	21	Le Perigord	32
Ammos	33	Le Pescadeux	15
Armani Ristorante	34	Le Singe Vert	20
Asiate	34	Le Veau d'Or	22
Atlantic Grill	24	Má Pêche	25
Aureole	34	Maria Pia	15
Avra	30	Marseille	24
Bar Boulud	29	Maze	24
Beacon	28	Mercer Kitchen	28
Becco	18	Milos	24
Benoit	24	Molyvos	24
Bistro Vendôme	20	Momofuku Ssäm Bar	25
Bobby Van's (W. 50s)	30	Mr. K's	24
Braai	15	Ocean Grill	24
Brasserie Cognac	27	Orsay	25
Brasserie 8½	25	Padre Figlio	23
Café Boulud	32	Pampano	28
Cafe Un Deux Trois	21	Parlor Steakhouse	25
Ça Va	24	Patroon	27
Caviar Russe	25	Periyali	26
Chez Napoléon	32	Persephone	20
Chin Chin	24	Petrossian	28
Cibo	25	Pó	35
David Burke Townhouse	24	Remi	24
Dawat	15	Riverpark	28
DBGB	24	Robert	29
Del Frisco's	33	Rouge Tomate	29
Docks Oyster Bar	28	Sardi's	30
Duane Park	24	Sazon	25
Felidia	30	SD26	26
15 East	29	Seäsonal	27
Fishtail	24	Serge	30
Five Points	26	Shalezeh	25
Four Seasons	35	SHO Shaun Hergatt	27
Gallagher's Steak	32	South Gate	24
Gascogne	21	Spice Market	24
Gigino	23	Sushi Yasuda	23
Giorgio's/Gramercy	24	Table d'Hôte	24
Gotham Bar & Grill	25	Tamarind	25
HanGawi	20	Tao	27
Jean Georges/Noug.	32/28	Telepan	22
JoJo	28	Terrace in the Sky	35
Josephina	24	Thalia	17
Kellari Taverna	27	Tía Pol	18
Kings' Carriage	19	Tocqueville	29
La Boîte en Bois	27	Tse Yang	31
L'Absinthe	28	Turkish Kitchen	10
La Mangeoire	20	ViceVersa	22
La Petite Auberge	20	Water Club	24

DINNER: $40 OR LESS

PT = pre-theater only; where two prices are listed, the first is pre-theater and the second for normal dinner hours.

Abboccato/PT	$35	Maria Pia	25
Akdeniz	24	Marseille	35
Aki	30	Maze/PT	35
Alouette/PT	25	McCormick & Schmick/PT	30
Ammos/PT	33	Miranda	28
Apiary	35	Molyvos/PT	35
Atlantic Grill/PT	35	Nice Matin	35
Bacchus (Bklyn)	25	Ninja	38
Becco	23	North Square	38
Benoit	38	Ocean Grill/PT	30
Bobby Van's (W. 50s)	40	Orsay/PT	35
Bombay Palace	30	Ouest/PT	34
Brasserie Cognac/PT	27	Padre Figlio	39
Brasserie 8½	35	Park Avenue Bistro/PT	29
B. Smith's/PT	35	Parlor Steakhouse	35
Cafe Cluny/PT	33	Pascalou/PT	23
Cafe Loup	30	Pasha/PT	27
Cafe Un Deux Trois	28	Patroon	39
Ça Va	35	Periyali	35
Cebu (Bklyn)/PT	25	Persephone/PT	35
Centro Vinoteca/PT	25	Petrossian	38
Chez Napoléon	32	Poke	38
China Grill/PT	38	Pomaire	25
Cibo	35	Quercy (Bklyn)	30
Circo/PT	38	Remi	35
Cole's Dock Side (SI)/PT	22	Re Sette	35
Cornelia St. Café	25	Rose Water (Bklyn)	26
Dawat	24	Saju Bistro/PT	28
Dervish/PT	28	Salute!	35
Docks Oyster Bar/	32	Scarlatto	30
Etcetera Etcetera	35	Serge	30
Gascogne/PT	27	Shalezeh/PT	25
Gigino	28	South Gate/PT	35
Giorgio's/Gramercy	35	Stone Park (Bklyn)	32
HanGawi	40	Sueños/PT	30
Indochine/PT	35	Sugiyama/PT	32
Jean Georges' Nougatine/PT	38	Sushi Yasuda	23
Jewel of India/PT	30	Table d'Hôte	24/33
JoJo/PT	38	Thalia/PT	35
Josephina	35	Tommaso (Bklyn)	27
Kefi/PT	17	Tournesol (Qns)	25
Kellari Taverna/PT	33	Turkish Cuisine	27
Kittichai/PT	35	Turkish Kitchen/PT	22
La Bonne Soupe	26	Ushiwakamaru	33
La Mangeoire	29	Utsav/PT	32
La Petite Auberge	30	Vatan	30
La Sirène/PT	30	ViceVersa	35
Le Pescadeux/PT	26	Villa Berulia	35
Le Relais de Venise	25	Water Club	35
Le Rivage	39/25	Water's Edge	35
Madison Bistro	36	West Bank Cafe	30

RESTAURANT
DIRECTORY

	FOOD	DECOR	SERVICE	COST

Abboccato *Italian* | 21 | 18 | 20 | $58

W 50s | Blakely Hotel | 136 W. 55th St. (bet. 6th & 7th Aves.) | 212-265-4000 | www.abboccato.com

"Tasty", "artfully plated" Italian fare, "attentive" staffers and "pleasant" digs draw showgoers aplenty to this "reliable" Midtowner "near Carnegie Hall" and "across from City Center"; to avoid "spendy" tabs, go for the "terrific" $35 pre-theater prix fixe.

Z ABC Kitchen *American* | 25 | 24 | 22 | $58

Flatiron | ABC Carpet & Home | 35 E. 18th St. (bet. B'way & Park Ave. S.) | 212-475-5829 | www.abckitchennyc.com

"Jean-Georges Vongerichten does it again" with this "modern-rustic" "stunner" inside the Flatiron's ABC Carpet, where chef Dan Kluger's "farm-to-table" New Americana is "divine in its freshness and simplicity", and delivered by a "courteous", "plaid"-clad crew; just know it costs plenty of "green", and "reservations are tough" given its large "locavoracious" fan base.

Abe & Arthur's *American* | 22 | 23 | 20 | $68

Meatpacking | 409 W. 14th St. (bet. 9th Ave. & Washington St.) | 646-289-3930 | www.abeandarthursrestaurant.com

The vibe is "classic Meatpacking" at this "flashy" bi-level "scene" "buzzing" with more "beautiful people" than a "model casting call", not to mention "the occasional celeb"; the New American eats are "surprisingly good" ("go for steak"), but just make sure "your expense account" is in shape.

Abigael's *Eclectic/Kosher* | 20 | 16 | 18 | $51

Garment District | 1407 Broadway (bet. 38th & 39th Sts.) | 212-575-1407 | www.abigaels.com

Chef Jeff Nathan unlocks the "varied" potential of "upscale kosher" cuisine at this Garment District "staple", where the "high quality" extends to sushi and Pan-Asian fare upstairs; still, nitpicking noshers slam the "catering hall" decor and service that's "fine – if you're not in a hurry."

Aburiya Kinnosuke *Japanese* | 25 | 20 | 22 | $56

E 40s | 213 E. 45th St. (bet. 2nd & 3rd Aves.) | 212-867-5454 | www.aburiyakinnosuke.com

"As authentic as non-sushi Japanese gets in NYC", this "intimate" Midtown izakaya wows with "delicious" robata-grill dishes and "housemade tofu" that go down well with "top-notch sake"; the "transported"-to-"Tokyo" experience is "pricey", except for the "fantastic-bargain" lunch (seven courses for $35).

Acappella *Italian* | 24 | 21 | 24 | $71

TriBeCa | 1 Hudson St. (Chambers St.) | 212-240-0163 | www.acappella-restaurant.com

"*Bravissimo!*" sing supporters of this "over-the-top" "old-fashioned" TriBeCa Northern Italian, where "superb" eats arrive via tuxedoed waiters who'll "pamper" you "like a don" (they even filmed a *Sopranos* scene here); post-meal the "gratis grappa" eases the pain of paying the check.

Accademia di Vino *Italian* | 18 | 19 | 19 | $50

E 60s | 1081 Third Ave. (bet. 63rd & 64th Sts.) | 212-888-6333

(continued)

Accademia di Vino

W 80s | 2427 Broadway (bet. 89th & 90th Sts.) | 212-787-3070
www.accademiadivino.com

Whether for a "light bite", "full-on grazing" (hello "truffle pizza") or just a selection from the "extensive wine list", these "upbeat" crosstown Italians do a "decent" job; some knock the "corporate" feel, but the fact that they're "always crowded" speaks for itself.

Acqua *Italian*

20 | 18 | 20 | $46

W 90s | 718 Amsterdam Ave. (95th St.) | 212-222-2752 | www.acquanyc.com

Slinging "delicious" pizzas and trattoria basics, this "reliable neighborhood Italian" hits the spot for Upper Westsiders when "value" and "nothing fancy" are prime prereqs; the "friendly", "low-key" atmosphere and Symphony Space proximity further endear it to locals.

☑ Adour ⬛Ⓜ *French*

26 | 27 | 27 | $114

E 50s | St. Regis Hotel | 2 E. 55th St. (bet. 5th & Madison Aves.) | 212-710-2277 | www.adour-stregis.com

"For those truly special occasions" there's Alain Ducasse's "*magnifique*" Midtowner, where "exquisite" French "haute cuisine" is matched with an "amazing wine list", "impeccable" service and one "beauty" of a "luxurious" space designed by David Rockwell; yes, "it may be cheaper to fly to Paris", but to most it's "well worth" the occasional "splurge."

Adrienne's Pizzabar ◑ *Pizza*

23 | 16 | 17 | $26

Financial District | 87 Pearl St. (bet. Coenties Slip & Hanover Sq.) | 212-248-3838 | www.adriennespizzabar.com

"Corporate" types collect at this "casual" Financial District "lunch favorite" that commands "long waits" for its "awesome thin-crust pies" at prime times; regulars say sitting out on "delightful", "historic" Stone Street "on a sunny day" makes "uneven" service easy to overlook.

Aegean Cove *Greek*

22 | 18 | 21 | $41

Astoria | 20-01 Steinway St. (20th Ave.) | Queens | 718-274-9800 | www.aegeancove.com

A "change from the usual taverna", this "fancier" ("yet homey") Astoria entry offers "old-world" Greek cuisine with an "upscale" gloss delivered by "friendly" staffers; it's "off the beaten track", but "parking nearby" helps ease the odyssey.

🆕 Affaire ◑Ⓜ *French*

- | - | - | M

E Village | 50 Ave. B (bet. 3rd & 4th Sts.) | 212-375-0665 | www.affairenyc.com

Modern burlesque meets old-world château at this sultry East Village French bistro where petite plates and midpriced entrees are served in an upstairs den, while DJs draw partyers to two lower-level lounges; plush banquettes, chandeliers and lots of candles complete the look.

Afghan Kebab House *Afghan*

20 | 11 | 18 | $27

E 70s | 1345 Second Ave. (bet. 70th & 71st Sts.) | 212-517-2776
W 50s | 764 Ninth Ave. (bet. 51st & 52nd Sts.) | 212-307-1612
Astoria | 25-89 Steinway St. (28th Ave.) | Queens | 718-777-7758 |
www.afghankebabs.com ◑

(continued)

(continued)

Afghan Kebab House

Jackson Heights | 74-16 37th Ave. (bet. 74th & 75th Sts.) | Queens | 718-565-0471

When a "kebab craving" calls, this "no-frills" Afghan quartet "does the trick" with its "deftly seasoned" skewers and "sauces that shine"; some may "wish they'd redecorate", but "friendly" service and "cheap" prices abetted by a BYO policy keep even aesthetes coming back.

Agave *Southwestern*   19 | 19 | 18 | $39

W Village | 140 Seventh Ave. S. (bet. Charles & W. 10th Sts.) | 212-989-2100 | www.agaveny.com

"Twentysomethings" plus "lots of tequila" add up to a "loud", "fun" "buzz" at this "rowdy" Village Southwesterner with a whitewashed "adobe-inspired" look; the moderately priced fare is "solid", if "nothing special", while the service is what you'd expect at a "mob scene."

Agnanti *Greek*   23 | 16 | 19 | $36

Bay Ridge | 7802 Fifth Ave. (78th St.) | Brooklyn | 718-833-7033
Astoria | 19-06 Ditmars Blvd. (19th St.) | Queens | 718-545-4554
www.agnantimeze.com

"You'll never again think Greek food is just gyros" after sampling the "wide array" of "fresh, flavorful" dishes at these "nothing-fancy", "well-priced" Astoria–Bay Ridge tavernas; at the "crowded" Queens original, sitting "outside facing the park in summer" alone is "worth the trip."

Z NEW Ai Fiori ◐ *Italian*   27 | 24 | 25 | $93

Garment District | Setai Fifth Avenue Hotel | 400 Fifth Ave. (37th St.) | 212-613-8660 | www.aifiorinyc.com

"Another hit" from Michael White (Marea, Osteria Morini), this "sleek", "spacious" arrival to the Garment District's Setai Fifth Avenue Hotel delivers "heavenly" dishes inspired by the French-Italian Riviera, matched with "fantastic" wines and "top-notch" service; it draws "expense-account" wielders and others who hail it as a "much-needed" "upscale" addition to a "challenged" zone.

Aja ◐ *Asian*   21 | 20 | 20 | $43

E 50s | 1068 First Ave. (58th St.) | 212-888-8008 | www.ajaasiancuisine.com

As "exotic" as it gets in Sutton Place, this standby "caters to younger palates" with its "something-for-everyone" Pan-Asian "fusion standards" (including "tasty sushi") and "giant Buddha"-"koi pond" decor; "big drinks" keep "dates" on track at the "busy" bar.

Aji Sushi *Japanese*   21 | 15 | 20 | $31

Murray Hill | 519 Third Ave. (bet. 34th & 35th Sts.) | 212-686-2055 | www.ajisushinyc.com

"Tasty", "fresh" rolls conveyed by "proficient" servers for an "inexpensive" sum make for steady business at this "dependable" Murray Hill "neighborhood sushi staple"; just "don't expect any ambiance" – it's strictly a "no-frills" scene.

A.J. Maxwell's Steakhouse *Steak*   22 | 20 | 22 | $66

W 40s | 57 W. 48th St. (bet. 5th & 6th Aves.) | 212-262-6200 | www.ajmaxwells.com

For "massive" slabs served in "classic" chophouse digs, "loosen your belt and dig in" at this "no-gimmicks" Rock Center cow palace, where a

	FOOD	DECOR	SERVICE	COST

"friendly" staff caters to "men in suits"; prices are "high", but "you're paying for" the "can't-be-beat" location "near the Theater District."

Akdeniz ⌧ *Turkish* · 21 · 12 · 19 · $32

W 40s | 19 W. 46th St. (bet. 5th & 6th Aves.) | 212-575-2307 | www.akdenizturkishusa.com
Amounting to a "pleasant" "Bosphorus" layover "en route to the theater", this Midtown Turk proffers "well-prepared" plates via "fast" staffers; it boasts "not much in the way of decor", but "value"-seekers suggest focusing on the "excellent" $24 dinner prix fixe instead.

Aki *Japanese* · 25 · 14 · 21 · $47

W Village | 181 W. Fourth St. (bet. Barrow & Jones Sts.) | 212-989-5440
Ya mon, "top-grade" sushi with a "Caribbean twist" is the "original" and "tasty" concept behind this Village Japanese "favorite"; despite "matchbox-size" digs, "friendly" service and "reasonable" rates, everything's gonna be alright here.

A La Turka *Turkish* · 19 · 14 · 18 · $38

E 70s | 1417 Second Ave. (74th St.) | 212-744-2424 | www.alaturkarestaurant.com
Folks "from the neighborhood" favor this UES Turk for "well-executed" "classics" offered for a "reasonable price"; "the sultan's palace it's not" and service can be "slow" – but no matter so long as you "go with people you like and concentrate on them."

Alberto *Italian* · 24 · 21 · 23 · $48

Forest Hills | 98-31 Metropolitan Ave. (bet. 69th & 70th Aves.) | Queens | 718-268-7860 | www.albertorestaurant.com
An "oldie but goodie", this Forest Hills "favorite" holds its "neighborhood institution" status firm with "good-all-the-time" Northern Italiana and "treat-you-like-family" service; kinda "pricey" tabs don't deter "loyal fans" who've been "returning again and again for the past 30 years."

Al Bustan *Lebanese* · 20 · 19 · 21 · $48

E 50s | 319 E. 53rd St. (bet. 1st & 2nd Aves.) | 212-759-5933 | www.albustanny.com
The "underrepresented" cuisine of Lebanon gets its due at this "appealing", "upscale" East Side duplex turning out "lovely" "classic" dishes; despite "friendly" service, it "looks empty" at times – maybe there's just "too much space" in its "elegant", "chandeliered" room.

Aldea ⌧ *Portuguese* · 25 · 22 · 24 · $66

Flatiron | 31 W. 17th St. (bet. 5th & 6th Aves.) | 212-675-7223 | www.aldearestaurant.com
"Haute Portuguese" is "not an oxymoron" at "talented" chef George Mendes' "refined" Flatironer, where the "creative" turns on traditional dishes make for "a real experience", especially if you "sit by the open kitchen" and "watch the chefs make their magic"; "smart" service, "modern" decor and relatively "sensible" prices round out the endorsement.

⌧ Al Di La *Italian* · 27 · 18 · 23 · $49

Park Slope | 248 Fifth Ave. (Carroll St.) | Brooklyn | 718-783-4565 | www.aldilatrattoria.com
"Go early or wait late" is the only way to "snag a coveted seat" for dinner at this "unpretentious", no-rez Park Slope Italian, where "every

bite" of the "simple, rustic" Venetian cooking is an "OMG moment"; "caring" service and "should-be-more-expensive" prices are other reasons for its enduring "popularity"; P.S. to "beat the line", eat at its "around-the-corner wine bar", or go at "relaxing" lunchtime.

NEW Alfama *Portuguese*
- - - M

E 50s | 214 E. 52nd St. (bet. 2nd & 3rd Aves.) | 212-759-5552 | www.alfamanyc.com

Originally in the West Village, this Portuguese eatery is back – now in the East 50s – with a new menu and a contemporary vibe; longtime loyalists needn't worry: favorites like *bife na pedra* (stone-grilled filet mignon) survived the move, as did a couple of the old tile murals.

Al Forno Pizzeria *Pizza*
20 | 13 | 18 | $26

E 70s | 1484 Second Ave. (bet. 77th & 78th Sts.) | 212-249-5103 | www.alfornopizzeria77.com

When a "local, casual meal" is in order, UESers swing by this "family-friendly" Italian "staple" for "tasty thin-crust pizzas" from a brick oven or "fairly good" pastas and salads; "inexpensive" tabs trump "not much" ambiance, which can include "noisy children" in earlier hours.

Alfredo of Rome *Italian*
21 | 20 | 20 | $49

W 40s | 4 W. 49th St. (bet. 5th & 6th Aves.) | 212-397-0100 | www.alfredos.com

The namesake fettuccine is "made the way it's supposed to be" at this "busy" Rock Center Italian that's "surprisingly good" given its perennial pigeonholing as a "tourist trap"; a "welcoming" staff and "Hirschfeld drawings" on the walls balance "pricey-for-the-quality" tabs.

Algonquin Hotel Round Table *American*
18 | 24 | 21 | $59

W 40s | Algonquin Hotel | 59 W. 44th St. (bet. 5th & 6th Aves.) | 212-840-6800 | www.algonquinhotel.com

"Atmosphere is everything" at this circa-1902 Theater Districter, a slice of "literary history" where "the walls still echo with the witty comments" of "Dorothy Parker" and her circle; as the "overpriced" American eats are "so-so", many just go to toast the "ghosts of NY past" with drinks in the handsome wood-paneled lobby.

Alias ⓂAmerican
21 | 15 | 21 | $41

LES | 76 Clinton St. (Rivington St.) | 212-505-5011 | www.aliasrestaurant.com

"They aim to please – and succeed" at this "tiny" Lower East Side American favored by "neighborhood" folk for its "fresh", "flavorful", "stick-to-your-ribs" fare in "unassuming" environs; its "no-sticker-shock" pricing reaches its "value" apex with the $20 'blue-plate special' (Tuesday–Thursday).

Ali Baba *Turkish*
20 | 15 | 19 | $34

E 40s | 862 Second Ave. (46th St.) | 212-888-8622 | www.alibabasterrace.com

Murray Hill | 212 E. 34th St. (bet. 2nd & 3rd Aves.) | 212-683-9206 | www.alibabaturkishcuisine.com

"Istanbul beckons" at these "friendly" East Side Turks dishing up "the real thing" at "easy-on-the-wallet" rates; saying "open sesame" won't ease their "cramped" interiors, but the "wonderful rooftop terrace" at the Second Avenue outpost offers elbow room aplenty.

	FOOD	DECOR	SERVICE	COST

Alloro *Italian* — 25 | 18 | 24 | $54

E 70s | 307 E. 77th St. (bet. 1st & 2nd Aves.) | 212-535-2866 | www.alloronyc.com

"Not your typical" UES Italian, this "little gem" run by a "charming" husband-and-wife team injects a bit of "adventure" into the local scene with its "upscale", "innovative" (even "strange") "riffs on traditional" dishes; attention, critics of the "ghastly green" color scheme: "they got rid of it."

Alma *Mexican* — 19 | 21 | 18 | $37

Carroll Gardens | 187 Columbia St., 2nd fl. (Degraw St.) | Brooklyn | 718-643-5400 | www.almarestaurant.com

To take in a "sunset to remember" – along with a "knock-your-socks-off" margarita – hit this "festive" West Carroll Gardens Mexican boasting a "million-dollar rooftop view"; the midpriced food "isn't half bad" either, but that ain't the reason it's "so busy" here.

Almond *French* — 20 | 19 | 20 | $46

Flatiron | 12 E. 22nd St. (bet. B'way & Park Ave. S.) | 212-228-7557 | www.almondnyc.com

"Just as good" as the Bridgehampton original, this "lively" Flatironer offers "solid" "midpriced" French bistro fare (including a "delicious brunch") in "cavernous" "countrified" digs; the "big bar scene" and "pool room" kick up some "noise", but its "young crowd" doesn't seem to mind.

Alouette Ⓜ *French* — 20 | 17 | 19 | $46

W 90s | 2588 Broadway (bet. 97th & 98th Sts.) | 212-222-6808 | www.alouettenyc.com

"Consistently well-prepared" French bistro "standards" for not too many francs spell *le succès* at this "charming" UWS "fixture"; its "affable" staff, Symphony Space–convenient location and "bargain" $25 early-bird prix fixe compensate for "somewhat cramped" split-level digs.

Alta *Mediterranean* — 25 | 23 | 20 | $49

G Village | 64 W. 10th St. (bet. 5th & 6th Aves.) | 212-505-7777 | www.altarestaurant.com

Tapas get a "fine-dining upgrade" at this Village duplex where "unbelievable" Med flavors and a "wine list better than it has to be" translate to "tremendous fun"; "cozy" and fireplace-equipped, it appeals to "dates and groups" alike, but just know an alta bill can "add up quickly."

Amaranth ❶ *Mediterranean* — 19 | 18 | 19 | $59

E 60s | 21 E. 62nd St. (bet. 5th & Madison Aves.) | 212-980-6700 | www.amaranthrestaurant.com

"Food is secondary" for the "nipped, tucked and tanned" types who "air-kiss" and "show off their new Chanel everything" at this "tiny" UES "see-and-be-seen" bistro; the "pricey" Med eats are actually "ok", and might even come via a "friendly" staffer – "if you're a regular."

Amarone ❶ *Italian* — 20 | 16 | 19 | $43

W 40s | 686 Ninth Ave. (bet. 47th & 48th Sts.) | 212-245-6060 | www.lunapienanyc.com

"Delicious fresh pastas" and other "dependable" Italian basics come to table "quick" at this "homey" Hell's Kitchen trattoria that's a "pre-theater favorite"; factor in "reasonable" rates, and no surprise it's so "cramped" at prime times you could almost "eat your neighbor's meal."

Amazing 66 *Chinese* 21 | 10 | 14 | $27

Chinatown | 66 Mott St. (bet. Bayard & Canal Sts.) | 212-334-0099

A "solid choice" in C-town, this Cantonese staple plies a "tasty" array from standards to more "unusual" specialties (e.g. short ribs with pumpkin); "bargain prices" – especially the $5.95 lunch "steal" – trump the "cafeteria" ambiance and "rushed" service.

Amber ● *Asian* 19 | 18 | 18 | $36

E 80s | 1406 Third Ave. (80th St.) | 212-249-5020 | www.orderamberuppereast.com
G Village | 432 Sixth Ave. (bet. 9th & 10th Sts.) | 212-477-5880 | www.ambernyc.com
Murray Hill | 381 Third Ave. (bet. 27th & 28th Sts.) | 212-686-6388 | www.ambergramercy.com
W 70s | 221 Columbus Ave. (70th St.) | 212-799-8100 | www.amberwestside.com

Picture a cheaper, "tamer version of Tao" and you've got this Pan-Asian quartet rolling out a "scary-big" lineup of "fresh sushi" and "satisfying" entrees in ersatz-"trendy" environs; service "can be an issue", but "with the Buddha's blessing" you'll find it "decent" overall.

Amma *Indian* 24 | 18 | 22 | $48

E 50s | 246 E. 51st St. (bet. 2nd & 3rd Aves.) | 212-644-8330 | www.ammanyc.com

Who needs "curry in a hurry" when there's this "high-end" Midtowner offering "beautiful" Northern Indian specialties conveyed by a "solicitous" staff; maybe the decor "isn't the sexiest", but there's "hot stuff" aplenty on the plate – especially the "real-treat" $50 tasting menu.

Ammos ⊠ *Greek/Seafood* 21 | 21 | 20 | $53

E 40s | 52 Vanderbilt Ave. (bet. 44th & 45th Sts.) | 212-922-9999 | www.ammosnewyork.com

It's Mykonos in Midtown at this "bright, airy" Grand Central–area Greek, a "buzzy" "business-lunch" terminus for "outstanding" seafood dishes and other "elegant" classics; while the $33 prix fixe (lunch and pre-theater) is a "deal", the "by-the-pound" fish prices can be "steep."

Amorina *Italian/Pizza* 23 | 15 | 20 | $26

Prospect Heights | 624 Vanderbilt Ave. (Prospect Pl.) | Brooklyn | 718-230-3030 | www.amorinapizza.com

Doing itself proud in Prospect Heights, this "friendly" Italian "favorite" puts forth "excellent Roman-style" pizzas with "crispy" crusts and "innovative toppings", plus "delicious pastas"; "informal" ambiance and "great prices" seal its standing as a "family-dining hot spot."

Amy Ruth's *Soul Food* 21 | 12 | 17 | $24

Harlem | 113 W. 116th St. (bet. Lenox & 7th Aves.) | 212-280-8779 | www.amyruthsharlem.com

"Soul foodies" make pilgrimages to this Harlem "mecca" of "Southern home cooking", where the "rich, delicious", low-priced chicken 'n' waffles, collards and such come in "almost obscene" portions; it's "not for the diet-conscious" or decor-focused, but the "long lines" at "Sunday brunch" speak for themselves.

| | FOOD | DECOR | SERVICE | COST |

An Choi *Vietnamese*
▽ 21 | 17 | 18 | $20

LES | 85 Orchard St. (Broome St.) | 212-226-3700 | www.anchoinyc.com
"Creative takes" on "the classic Vietnamese" banh mi (adding a "fried egg is a must") is the thing at this "hip" Lower Eastsider that also ladles a "nice bowl of pho"; given that "your wallet isn't much lighter" post-meal, the "bare" setting is barely an issue.

Andre's Café *Hungarian*
20 | 12 | 17 | $27

E 80s | 1631 Second Ave. (bet. 84th & 85th Sts.) | 212-327-1105 | www.andrescafeny.com
Yorkville's "vanishing" Hungarian enclave lives on at this "tiny" restaurant/bakery where "hearty" "home cooking" and "phenomenal pastries" put a little "Budapest" in your belly; the "old-world charm" extends to the "inexpensive" prices, if not the "basic" service and decor.

Anella Ⓜ⇄ *American/Mediterranean*
▽ 24 | 21 | 20 | $42

Greenpoint | 222 Franklin St. (bet. Green & Huron Sts.) | Brooklyn | 718-389-8100 | www.anellabrooklyn.com
At this "down-to-earth", wood-paneled Greenpointer, the "fresh, interesting" Med–New American meals start off with crowd-pleasing bread baked and served "in a flowerpot"; the "charming back garden", "superb brunch" and cash-only policy cement its "typical Brooklyn" standing.

Angelica Kitchen ⇄ *Vegan/Vegetarian*
22 | 17 | 19 | $27

E Village | 300 E. 12th St. (bet. 1st & 2nd Aves.) | 212-228-2909 | www.angelicakitchen.com
You'll "feel your arteries *un*clogging" at this "landmark" circa-'76 East Village vegan, where the "healthy" edibles are "rather tasty" and "low-priced" to boot; the "minimal furnishings" and BYOB/cash-only policies stay true to its "earthy" ethos, while service trends toward "spacey."

Angelina's Ⓜ *Italian*
22 | 21 | 20 | $58

Tottenville | 399 Ellis St. (off Arthur Kill Rd.) | Staten Island | 718-227-2900 | www.angelinasristorante.com
Given its "stunning" tri-level space on the Tottenville waterfront, live music and "over-the-top" fare, this "upscale" Italian is the "perfect spot to impress"; "Manhattan prices" aside, the colorful "scene" is unmistakably Staten Island.

Angelo & Maxie's *Steak*
21 | 19 | 21 | $55

Flatiron | 233 Park Ave. S. (19th St.) | 212-220-9200 | www.angelo-maxies.com
From the "gigantic" slabs to the "stiff" cocktails, "they don't skimp" at this "boisterous" Flatiron steakhouse whose "high-testosterone" client base appreciates its "courteous" service and relative "value"; P.S. it was bought by the Landry's chain post-Survey.

Angelo's of Mulberry Street Ⓜ *Italian*
23 | 16 | 20 | $46

Little Italy | 146 Mulberry St. (bet. Grand & Hester Sts.) | 212-966-1277 | www.angelomulberry.com
The "touristy allure" of this Little Italy "mainstay" is well earned – it's been dispensing "soul-satisfying" "red-gravy" Neapolitan staples since 1902, seemingly via the "same waiters"; decor that "could use a makeover" rates as another mark of "authenticity", as do the "lines" on weekends.

	FOOD	DECOR	SERVICE	COST

Angelo's Pizzeria *Pizza* — 20 | 13 | 16 | $26

E 50s | 1043 Second Ave. (55th St.) | 212-521-3600
W 50s | 117 W. 57th St. (bet. 6th & 7th Aves.) | 212-333-4333
W 50s | 1697 Broadway (bet. 53rd & 54th Sts.) | 212-245-8811
www.angelospizzany.com

For a "casual meal in Midtown", these "family-friendly" pizzerias "get
the job done" with "tasty" brick-oven pies and "basic" pastas and salads; "nondescript" "chainlike" decor and sometimes "below-par" service are "worth putting up with" given the "affordable" bill.

Angus McIndoe ◑ *American* — 16 | 16 | 19 | $43

W 40s | 258 W. 44th St. (bet. B'way & 8th Ave.) | 212-221-9222 |
www.angusmcindoe.com

Join "the Broadway community" at this Times Square triplex located
"steps from your show" and known as a "magnet" for "theater folk"
pre- and post-curtain; just plan on American eats that are merely
"ok" – and know that "the stars hide upstairs."

Ann & Tony's Ⓜ *Italian* — 20 | 15 | 19 | $35

Fordham | 2407 Arthur Ave. (bet. 187th & 188th Sts.) | Bronx |
718-933-1469 | www.annandtonysonline.com

"Family-owned for generations", this "classic Arthur Avenue" fixture
is still in the game as a "casual", "no-nonsense" supplier of "tasty"
"red-sauce" standards; hey, you'll pay a "reasonable price" and "leave
full", so whatsa matta with the just-"passable" decor?

❷ Annisa *American* — 28 | 24 | 27 | $81

W Village | 13 Barrow St. (bet. 7th Ave. S. & W. 4th St.) | 212-741-6699 |
www.annisarestaurant.com

"A real grown-up's restaurant", Anita Lo's "quiet powerhouse" in the
West Village delivers "superb", "upscale" New American cuisine with
"elegant Asian inflections", "interesting wines" from "female vint-
ners" and "impeccable" "pro" service; it all comes in "refreshingly
minimalist" environs that "put the focus on the food", but are also
"perfect for a special occasion."

Antica Venezia *Italian* — 23 | 21 | 24 | $56

W Village | 396 West St. (W. 10th St.) | 212-229-0606 |
www.avnyc.com

Sited as "way far West" as it gets, this Village Italian "find" rewards
the "trek" with "top-notch" "old-world" fare, "highly attentive" waiters and "unstoppably romantic" "candlelit" surroundings "overlooking
the Hudson"; "complimentary appetizers and cordials" take the sting
out of the "pricey" bill.

Antonucci *Italian* — 23 | 17 | 21 | $57

E 80s | 170 E. 81st St. (bet. Lexington & 3rd Aves.) | 212-570-5100

As a "neighborhood Italian place", this "happy" Upper Eastsider is an
"absolute favorite" given its "superb pastas" and other "splendid"
dishes delivered by a "lovely" crew; unsurprisingly it's "full every night"
despite "Prada prices" and "small" digs that get "hectic and noisy."

A.O.C. ◑ *French* — 20 | 18 | 17 | $40

W Village | 314 Bleecker St. (Grove St.) | 212-675-9463 |
www.aocnyc.com

(continued)

A.O.C. Bistro ❶ *French*

Park Slope | 259 Fifth Ave. (Garfield Pl.) | Brooklyn | 718-788-1515 | www.aocbistro.com

Francophiles favor these "homey", "laid-back" Village–Park Slope French bistros for "satisfying" classics via a staff that exudes "the right attitude" (i.e. "indifference"); "reasonable" pricing, "especially good brunch" and a "lovely garden" at the Bleecker original help keep 'em "busy."

Apiary *American*

25 | 20 | 23 | $56

E Village | 60 Third Ave. (bet. 10th & 11th Sts.) | 212-254-0888 | www.apiarynyc.com

Cross-pollinate a "high-end", "pro"-staffed venue with "groovy" "East Village vibes" and you get this "stylish", "vibrant" showcase for Scott Bryan's "inventive" New American cooking; it's "noise city", but those "chattering" "crowds" pack in "with good reason"; P.S. "wine connoisseurs" collect on "corkage-free" Monday BYO nights.

Ápizz *Italian*

24 | 21 | 22 | $50

LES | 217 Eldridge St. (bet. Rivington & Stanton Sts.) | 212-253-9199 | www.apizz.com

"Homey" and "intimate" as can be, this "hidden" Lower Eastsider delivers "amazingly delish pizzas" and other "seductive" wood-oven dishes via a "friendly" staff; maybe it's "somehow still slightly under the radar", but "plan ahead" 'cause it can be "hard to get in."

NEW APL *American*

- | - | - | M

LES | 146 Orchard St. (bet. Rivington & Stanton Sts.) | 212-777-8600 | www.aplnewyork.com

Offering candy-garnished cocktails and clever New American dishes within funky digs, this LES playground sports Day-Glo paint and bronze sneakers hanging from fake telephone wires; it's open till 4 AM on weekends, so look out for guest DJs and late-night specials.

Applewood Ⓜ *American*

25 | 21 | 23 | $51

Park Slope | 501 11th St. (bet. 7th & 8th Aves.) | Brooklyn | 718-788-1810 | www.applewoodny.com

"Among the best on Brooklyn's local-seasonal scene", this Park Sloper offers "sustainably satisfying" Americana within "farmhouse-in-the-borough" digs manned by a "committed" crew; that slice of "upstate on your plate" is "not inexpensive", however, and the "fine brunch" often requires a "wait."

Ⓩ Aquagrill *Seafood*

26 | 20 | 23 | $61

SoHo | 210 Spring St. (6th Ave.) | 212-274-0505 | www.aquagrill.com

Downing *"bellissimo* bivalves" from an "unbeatable raw bar" is "the way to start" a meal at this "longtime favorite" SoHo seafooder creating "phenomenal" fare from "super-fresh" catch; it's known as one of the "best for the money" in town, so "crowds" are as sure as the tide.

Aquamarine ❶ *Asian*

21 | 21 | 19 | $36

Murray Hill | 713 Second Ave. (bet. 38th & 39th Sts.) | 212-297-1880 | www.orderaquamarine.com

"Quality", "value"-priced Pan-Asian fare and sushi in "sleek", "soothing water wall"–equipped digs set this "Murray Hill standby" apart in

| | FOOD | DECOR | SERVICE | COST |

a zone known as a "restaurant wasteland"; its "young crowd" kicks up "a bit of a scene" at the bar most nights.

❷ Aquavit *Scandinavian* `25` `23` `24` `$109`

E 50s | 65 E. 55th St. (bet. Madison & Park Aves.) | 212-307-7311 | www.aquavit.org

Surveyors say "*skol!*" to this Midtowner's "splendid" Scandinavian eats and flights of the namesake spirit dispensed by "informed" staffers in "minimalist-elegant" environs; true, its prix fixe–only menus are "not for the light of wallet", but the à la carte "front cafe is less costly."

Arabelle *American/French* `24` `26` `26` `$85`

E 60s | Plaza Athénée Hotel | 37 E. 64th St. (bet. Madison & Park Aves.) | 212-606-4647 | www.arabellerestaurant.com

A "first-class" staff facilitates "refined", "leisurely" dining on "fabulous" seasonal French-American fare at this "exquisite" "throwback" in the Plaza Athénée Hotel; what may be "a bit sedate" for upstarts is a "rare" treat for mature connoisseurs of "privacy" and "quiet conversation" – but expect to pay for the privilege.

Areo ●Ⓜ *Italian* `24` `19` `20` `$52`

Bay Ridge | 8424 Third Ave. (bet. 84th & 85th Sts.) | Brooklyn | 718-238-0079

"How you doin'?" – at this Bay Ridge Italian "hot spot", the "pasta is perfectly cooked" and as "plentiful" as the "muscle shirts" and other "real Brooklyn" "characters" in attendance; "high prices" and staffers with "egos" are part of the deal, as is the *Saturday Night Fever*–era decor in need of "sprucing up."

Arepas Café *Venezuelan* ▽ `25` `14` `20` `$20`

Astoria | 33-07 36th Ave. (34th St.) | Queens | 718-937-3835 | www.arepascafe.com

The "excellent" arepas at this "friendly" "little" Astoria Venezuelan "cause addiction", so just plan on having "more than one" of the low-cost stuffed corn cakes; "midnight cravings", "hangover" hankerings and willingness to "make the trip to Queens" are other common side effects.

Arirang Hibachi Steakhouse *Japanese* `20` `19` `22` `$38`

Bay Ridge | 8814 Fourth Ave. (bet. 88th & 89th Sts.) | Brooklyn | 718-238-9880
Great Kills | 23A Nelson Ave. (Locust Pl.) | Staten Island | 718-966-9600
www.partyonthegrill.com

"Look out for flying shrimp" at these "boisterous" Bay Ridge–Staten Island "Benihana clones" where "food-tossing" hibachi chefs "put on a show" that's "fun for the family"; it's an "Americanized" spin on the Japanese steakhouse, but the "knife-flipping" is the genuine article – "don't try it at home."

Armani Ristorante *Italian* `21` `23` `20` `$66`

E 50s | Armani/5th Ave. | 717 Fifth Ave., 3rd fl. (56th St.) | 212-207-1902 | www.armanilifestyle.com

The "Armani aesthetic" goes gastro at this "chic" Italian eatery atop the designer's Midtown flagship, where "size-zero" sorts toy with "delicious", "pricey" fare delivered by "capable" (if "bored") would-be "models"; "better for lunch", it's "rarely crowded" after midday.

	FOOD	DECOR	SERVICE	COST

Arno ⊠ *Italian*
20 | **18** | **22** | **$52**

Garment District | 141 W. 38th St. (bet. B'way & 7th Ave.) | 212-944-7420 | www.arnoristorante.com

A favorite fallback for "fashion industry" types, this "spacious" Garment District vet is a "reliable choice" for "well-prepared" Italian "basics" brought by "pro" staffers; with "not much competition" nearby, most take the "tired decor" and "pricey" tabs in stride.

Aroma Kitchen & Winebar ● *Italian*
23 | **17** | **21** | **$44**

NoHo | 36 E. Fourth St. (bet. Bowery & Lafayette St.) | 212-375-0100 | www.aromanyc.com

With its "creative" Italian pastas, wines and "personal" service, this NoHo "charmer" certainly smells like a "find"; regulars only "wish the walls could be stretched" – it's "snug" and fills up fast, so "go early."

Arté Café *Italian*
18 | **17** | **18** | **$38**

W 70s | 106 W. 73rd St. (bet. Amsterdam & Columbus Aves.) | 212-501-7014 | www.artecafenyc.com

This UWS "staple" is a "casual", "dependable" bet for "decent", "fair-priced" Italiana; despite "spotty" service, its local "crowd-pleaser" status is secure thanks to the "unlimited-drinks brunch" and "bargain" $15 pre-theater prix fixe.

Artichoke Basille's Pizza ● *Pizza*
22 | **8** | **14** | **$13**

NEW **Chelsea** | 114 10th Ave. (17th St.) | 212-792-9200
E Village | 328 E. 14th St. (bet. 1st & 2nd Aves.) | 212-228-2004 ⇥
NEW **G Village** | 111 MacDougal St. (bet. Bleecker & W. 3rd Sts.) | 646-278-6100
www.artichokepizza.com

"Rapidly expanded" to three locales – including a "sit-down" site in West Chelsea – this "no-frills" pizza outfit generates "horrendous lines" even in the "wee hours" for its signature slice, a "gooey-delish mess" that's basically "artichoke dip on crust"; service is "inept" but when it's "2 AM and you're drunk", who notices?

Artie's *Seafood/Steak*
23 | **17** | **22** | **$42**

City Island | 394 City Island Ave. (Ditmars St.) | Bronx | 718-885-9885 | www.artiesofcityisland.com

"Verified by the locals", this City Island "staple" has been inspiring "repeat visits" since 1967 with its "tasty", prodigious Italian surf 'n' turf offerings and "friendly" vibe; the decor's on the "bland" side and "you can't see the water", but "that's ok" – it's "not full of tourists."

Artie's Deli *Deli*
18 | **10** | **15** | **$26**

W 80s | 2290 Broadway (bet. 82nd & 83rd Sts.) | 212-579-5959 | www.arties83rd.com

"Medicinal chicken soup", piled-high sandwiches and other "typical" Jewish deli staples "satisfy longings" at this "feed-an-army" UWS deli; maybe it "lacks the charm" of its better-known brethren, but the "diner"-like decor and "abrupt" servers are a "close approximation."

Artisanal *French*
23 | **21** | **20** | **$53**

Murray Hill | 2 Park Ave. (enter on 32nd St., bet. Madison & Park Aves.) | 212-725-8585 | www.artisanalbistro.com

"It's all about the cheese" at Terry Brennan's "hustly-bustly" Murray Hill brasserie that's beloved for its "spectacular" fromage selection, though the "well-crafted" Gallic cooking (including "fab fondue") also hits the spot; while you may feel "you're in Paris", "airport runway-level" noise interferes with the illusion.

Arturo's Pizzeria ● *Pizza* | 21 | 14 | 17 | $27

G Village | 106 W. Houston St. (Thompson St.) | 212-677-3820
"Divey" "speakeasy"-like digs, "live jazz" and "darn good brick-oven pizzas" keep the "1960s-bohemian" Greenwich Village spirit "funky" fresh at this beloved "old soldier"; "kitsch appeal" aside, its "inexpensive" tabs and "late-night" hours fill a useful niche.

NEW Asellina ● *Italian* | 19 | 23 | 17 | $63

Murray Hill | Gansevoort Park Avenue Hotel | 420 Park Ave. S. (29th St.) | 212-317-2908 | www.togrp.com
The owners of STK bring their Meatpacking magic to Murray Hill with this "cool" arrival at the Gansevoort Park Avenue Hotel, a high-ceilinged "sexy-rustic" stage for "simple" Italian fare and "sophisti-cated" cocktails; critics say it's a "more-about-the-scene" kind of place, and "should be better" for the price.

Z Asiate *American/Asian* | 25 | 28 | 26 | $111

W 60s | Mandarin Oriental Hotel | 80 Columbus Circle, 35th fl. (60th St. at B'way) | 212-805-8881 | www.mandarinoriental.com
With "stunning" views of Central Park and the UWS "cityscape", "fantabulous" Asian–New American fusion fare and near-"flawless" service, this "jewel box" in the Mandarin Oriental (once again voted No. 1 for Decor) is "stratospheric" all around; it's "like eating on a cloud" – and though "expensive" prix fixe–only dinner tabs rain on some parades, the $34 lunch is a "deal."

NEW Astor Room Ⓜ *American/Continental* | ▽ 22 | 22 | 19 | $43

Astoria | Kaufman Astoria Studios | 34-12 36th St. (bet. 35th & 36th Aves.) | Queens | 718-255-1947 | www.astorroom.com
A subterranean cafeteria for silent film folk in the 1920s, this "throwback" in the Kaufman Astoria Studios has been remade as a supper club, with period cocktails and a "retro" American-Continental menu (e.g. prime rib, lobster Thermidor); a piano player and a speakeasy-esque entrance complete the vibe.

Atlantic Grill *Seafood* | 23 | 20 | 21 | $56

E 70s | 1341 Third Ave. (bet. 76th & 77th Sts.) | 212-988-9200
W 60s | 49 W. 64th St. (bet. B'way & CPW) | 212-787-4663
www.atlanticgrill.com
"Delicious, fresh" catch and a "wonderful brunch" have both sides of Central Park "hooked" on Steve Hanson's "lively" seafooders, despite "packed-to-the-gills" digs and "raucous" noise; the UES original still reels 'em in "after all these years", while its "stylish" Lincoln Center-area offshoot is a new "UWS favorite."

August *European* | 22 | 21 | 20 | $50

W Village | 359 Bleecker St. (bet. Charles & W. 10th Sts.) | 212-929-8727 | www.augustny.com
Romantics "never tire" of this "intimate" West Village European's "flavorful" wood-oven fare and its "charming, rustic" vibe; the "back garden room" is "pretty year-round" and the staff is "smart and cool" (if occasionally "slow"), leaving most marveling "what's not to like?"

	FOOD	DECOR	SERVICE	COST

Au Mandarin *Chinese*

Financial District | World Financial Ctr. | 200-250 Vesey St. (West St.) | 212-385-0313 | www.aumandarin.com

FOOD 19 | DECOR 15 | SERVICE 18 | COST $33

Wall Streeters get their "dressed-up Chinese" staples from this "fast-paced" WFC go-to, where "quick", "easy" takeout comes at "pricey"-"for-what-you-get" rates; with almost "nothing else nearby", its Battery Park "monopoly" holds firm, "food court" decor notwithstanding.

❷ Aureole ❶ *American*

W 40s | Bank of America Tower | 135 W. 42nd St. (bet. B'way & 6th Ave.) | 212-319-1660 | www.charliepalmer.com

FOOD 26 | DECOR 24 | SERVICE 25 | COST $116

Charlie Palmer's "flagship" near Bryant Park "wows" with New American "culinary delights" – now from a "new chef", Marcus Gleadow-Ware – ferried by a "gracious" staff; opinions diverge on the "modern" Adam Tihany–designed space ("cool", "airy" vs. "too corporate") and its prix fixe-only tabs are steep – but there's always the "less-formal", "more lively" front bar area, whose cheaper à la carte menu is a "treat" too.

Aurora *Italian*

SoHo | 510 Broome St. (bet. Thompson St. & W. B'way) | 212-334-9020
Williamsburg | 70 Grand St. (Wythe Ave.) | Brooklyn | 718-388-5100 ⊅
www.auroraristorante.com

FOOD 24 | DECOR 21 | SERVICE 21 | COST $51

"Rustic-farmhouse" "charmers", these "romantic" SoHo-Williamsburg Italians deliver "simple, fresh" fare via a "welcoming" staff; the original is "full of hipsters and their parents" but "still one of the best date places in the 'Burg", with a *magnifico* patio making up for the cash-only policy.

A Voce *Italian*

Flatiron | 41 Madison Ave. (26th St.) | 212-545-8555 🖾
W 60s | Time Warner Ctr. | 10 Columbus Circle, 3rd fl. (60th St. at B'way) | 212-823-2523
www.avocerestaurant.com

FOOD 23 | DECOR 23 | SERVICE 22 | COST $66

"Talented" chef Missy Robbins' "wonderful pastas" and other "imaginative, seasonal" Italiana are delivered by a "cordial" crew at this "pricey", "informally elegant" duo; the "sleek", "spacious" TWC outlet offers "spectacular views over Central Park", while Madison Park boasts a "cool bijou" patio.

Avra ❶ *Greek/Seafood*

E 40s | 141 E. 48th St. (bet. Lexington & 3rd Aves.) | 212-759-8550 | www.avrany.com

FOOD 25 | DECOR 22 | SERVICE 22 | COST $60

The "Mediterranean meets Manhattan" at this "fabulous upscale" East Side Greek seafooder that's "always jammed" with seekers of "meticulously prepared meze" and "perfectly grilled" fish; look past the "noise" and "Olympian" per-pound pricing – just focus on the "fresh" catch.

Awash *Ethiopian*

E Village | 338 E. Sixth St. (bet. 1st & 2nd Aves.) | 212-982-9589
W 100s | 947 Amsterdam Ave. (bet. 106th & 107th Sts.) | 212-961-1416
www.awashny.com

FOOD 23 | DECOR 12 | SERVICE 18 | COST $25

Stews "full of flavor" scooped up with "spongy" injera flatbread make for a "filling", "finger-licking" adventure at these "laid-back" Ethiopians; "dingy decor" and "slow service" are drawbacks, but rarely is a belly made "happy" for such "amazing prices."

Ayza Wine & Chocolate Bar *French/Mediterranean*

20 | 18 | 19 | $38

Garment District | 11 W. 31st St. (bet. B'way & 5th Ave.) | 212-714-2992 | www.ayzanyc.com

A "can't-go-wrong" pick for "a date or girls' night out", this "cute" Garment Districter plies "tasty" French-Med tapas and Jacques Torres chocolates alongside "affordable" wines; claustrophobes cite "tiny", "squished" digs, but it's a "popular" area "go-to" nonetheless.

Azuri Cafe ⊅ *Israeli/Kosher*

26 | 5 | 11 | $15

W 50s | 465 W. 51st St. (bet. 9th & 10th Aves.) | 212-262-2920

"Biblically delicious" falafel and other "heavenly" Israeli staples lure fans to this "complete dump" in remote Hell's Kitchen; the "cheap" eats are "sublime" enough to overshadow the "depressing decor" and "abuse" from the "famously" "cantankerous" proprietor.

☒ Babbo ● *Italian*

27 | 22 | 24 | $80

G Village | 110 Waverly Pl. (bet. MacDougal St. & 6th Ave.) | 212-777-0303 | www.babbonyc.com

Still the "stuff of legends" after "more than a decade", this "magical" Batali-Bastianich "class act" in the Village presents "mind-blowing" Italian feasts with "perfect" "wine pairings" and "unpretentious" pro service; yes, the "charming" carriage house quarters can be "crowded and noisy" and it's a "reservation nightmare" with "upscale" tabs, but the "transcendent" experience will "make you happy you're alive."

Bacchus *French*

19 | 18 | 19 | $38

Boerum Hill | 409 Atlantic Ave. (bet. Bond & Nevins Sts.) | Brooklyn | 718-852-1572 | www.bacchusbistro.com

"Expats" and other fans of "real" French "comfort food" collect at this "welcoming" Boerum Hill bistro seemingly "transplanted from Paris"; "gracious" service, "tasty" wines and "gentle prices" are other pluses, while the back garden is "perfect for a quiet respite."

Baci & Abbracci ● *Italian*

▽ 21 | 19 | 21 | $38

Williamsburg | 204 Grand St. (bet. Bedford & Driggs Aves.) | Brooklyn | 718-599-6599 | www.baciny.com

"Amazing" wood-oven pizzas and "fresh pastas" come via a "warm", seemingly "straight-from-Italy" staff at this "cozy" Williamsburg Italian; factor in "moderate" prices and a "lovely garden", and it's no wonder "neighborhood" admirers send it Xs and Os.

Back Forty *American*

21 | 18 | 19 | $39

E Village | 190 Ave. B (bet. 11th & 12th Sts.) | 212-388-1990 | www.backfortynyc.com

Peter Hoffman's "affordable", "rustic" East Village New American is a "locavore paradise" whose "consistent" (if "limited") "seasonal" menu includes a "grass-fed burger" rated "one of the best around"; it "does get crowded" and "loud", but the "garden is surprisingly peaceful."

Balaboosta *Mediterranean/Mideastern*

23 | 18 | 21 | $49

NoLita | 214 Mulberry St. (bet. Prince & Spring Sts.) | 212-966-7366 | www.balaboostanyc.com

This balaboosta ('perfect housewife') must've been "made in heaven" rave reviewers of this NoLita Med-Mideastern "crowd-pleaser" from the Taïm folks, whose "superb", midpriced, "modern takes" on traditional dishes come via an "attentive" staff; the only rub is tables "packed" "cheek by jowl" in its "homey" space.

Ɀ Balthazar ❶ *French* 24 | 23 | 21 | $57

SoHo | 80 Spring St. (bet. B'way & Crosby Sts.) | 212-965-1414 | www.balthazarny.com

A "perpetual" SoHo "star", Keith McNally's "gorgeous" "Left Bank" brasserie facsimile is "buzzing" "morning, noon and night" with everyone from "celebs and power brokers" to "wide-eyed tourists"; "preposterous waits", "crowds" and "noise" are the price for "delectable" French classics, "congenial" service and "people-watching" – all in all it's like a "ticket to Paris."

Baluchi's *Indian* 19 | 15 | 17 | $29

E 80s | 1724 Second Ave. (bet. 89th & 90th Sts.) | 212-996-2600 | www.baluchis.com
Murray Hill | 329 Third Ave. (bet. 24th & 25th Sts.) | 212-679-3434 | www.baluchis.com
TriBeCa | 275 Greenwich St. (Warren St.) | 212-571-5343 | www.baluchis.com
W 50s | 240 W. 56th St. (bet. B'way & 8th Ave.) | 212-397-0707 | www.baluchis.com
Park Slope | 310 Fifth Ave. (bet. 2nd & 3rd Sts.) | Brooklyn | 718-832-5555 | www.parkslopebaluchis.com
Forest Hills | 113-30 Queens Blvd. (bet. 76th Ave. & 76th Rd.) | Queens | 718-520-8600 | www.baluchis.com

"You get what you expect" from this local "franchise": "competent", "inexpensive" Indian staples rated darn "tasty for a chain"; variable decor and just-"ok" service have many opting for "quick delivery" – though you have to eat in to get the "famous 50%-off" lunch deal.

Bamonte's *Italian* 24 | 17 | 22 | $46

Williamsburg | 32 Withers St. (bet. Lorimer St. & Union Ave.) | Brooklyn | 718-384-8831

Open since 1900 and still owned by the "great" Bamonte family, this beloved Williamsburg Italian delivers "tasty" "red-sauce" standards via "cordial", "tuxedo-clad" waiters; if a few whisper the "old-fashioned" decor "could use an update", loyalists plead "don't change a thing", not even the prices.

NEW B&B ❶ *American* 24 | 21 | 21 | $37
(fka Burger & Barrel)

SoHo | 25 W. Houston St. (bet. Greene & Mercer Sts.) | 212-334-7320 | www.burgerandbarrel.com

From the Lure Fishbar folks, this "upscale" new SoHo American draws a "cool crowd" for "mouthwatering burgers" and other pub fare paired with "barrel wines" and brews; "efficient" service and sexy, retro-California decor wrap up "a good package at a reasonable price."

Banjara ❶ *Indian* 22 | 16 | 18 | $34

E Village | 97 First Ave. (6th St.) | 212-477-5956 | www.banjaranyc.com

With "fabulous" Nothern Indian fare that "packs a nice punch", this East Villager "outshines" most of its "Curry Row" competition; sure, service is "lackluster" and its "dim", kinda-"cheesy" quarters "could use a makeover", but "the price is right."

Bann *Korean*

22 | 20 | 21 | $46

W 50s | Worldwide Plaza | 350 W. 50th St. (bet. 8th & 9th Aves.) |
212-582-4446 | www.bannrestaurant.com

The younger sibling of the erstwhile Woo Lae Oak brings the same
"upscale" "DIY Korean barbecue" and "friendly" service to Midtown's
Worldwide Plaza; the "stylish" setup's a far cry from "K-town" and "you
pay for it", but for a "flavorful" "fix" most consider it "worth the splurge."

Bann Thai *Thai*

21 | 18 | 19 | $31

Forest Hills | 69-12 Austin St. (bet. 69th Rd. & Yellowstone Blvd.) |
Queens | 718-544-9999 | www.bannthairestaurant.com

"Everything's fresh" and bursting with "authentic flavors" at this affordable Forest Hills Thai "hideaway" rated "a cut above" nearby contenders;
"courteous" service, "pleasant", "brightly colored" digs and a "menu that
goes on for pages" compensate for the "out-of-the-way" locale.

Baoguette *Vietnamese*

21 | 7 | 15 | $13

Financial District | 9 Maiden Ln. (B'way) | 212-233-3400
Murray Hill | 61 Lexington Ave. (bet. 25th & 26th Sts.) |
212-532-1133
W Village | 120 Christopher St. (Bedford St.) | 212-929-0877

Baoguette Cafe *Vietnamese*

E Village | 37 St. Marks Pl. (bet. 2nd & 3rd Aves.) | 212-380-1487
www.baoguette.com

"Tasty" "modern takes" on banh mi sandwiches are the "stars" at
Michael 'Bao' Huynh's "simple, accessible" Vietnamese mini-chain;
"tiny", "dumpy" setups and "long lines at lunch" are part of the deal,
but when you want "cheap, fast" and "spicy", they "can't be beat."

BaoHaus *Chinese*

20 | 8 | 14 | $14

NEW E Village | 238 E. 14th St. (bet. 2nd & 3rd Aves.) |
646-669-8889
LES | 137 Rivington St. (bet. Norfolk & Suffolk Sts.) |
646-684-3835
www.baohausnyc.com

"It's just about" the "innovative", "cheap", "crave-tastic" Taiwanese
bao (steamed buns) at this Lower Eastsider from "notorious" chef
Eddie Huang – not the "Ikea stool"-lined "sub-basement" space and
so-so service; P.S. the East Village offshoot opened post-Survey.

Bao Noodles *Vietnamese*

19 | 14 | 17 | $26

Gramercy | 391 Second Ave. (bet. 22nd & 23rd Sts.) | 212-725-7770 |
www.baonoodles.com

"Solid" Vietnamese pho and noodles come without the "Chinatown
bustle" at this "low-key", low-cost Gramercy "hangout" for "young"
locals; with "efficient service", it's a "find" for the neighborhood,
"nothing-to-look-at" decor notwithstanding.

Bar Americain *American*

23 | 23 | 22 | $65

W 50s | 152 W. 52nd St. (bet. 6th & 7th Aves.) | 212-265-9700 |
www.baramericain.com

"Flayistas" abound at this "buzzy" Midtowner from "celeb chef" Bobby
Flay, an "expense-account staple" whose "bold" New American brasserie dishes come in "roomy", "inviting" (if "kinda corporate") digs; an
"energetic" staff and "high-end clientele" bolster the "wow" factor.

	FOOD	DECOR	SERVICE	COST

Baraonda ● *Italian* | 18 | 18 | 17 | $52

E 70s | 1439 Second Ave. (75th St.) | 212-288-8555 | www.baraondany.com

"There's never a dull moment" at this "loud as hell" UES Italian where the "wine pours freely" and a "Euro" "dance party" kicks up "after midnight"; there's a "solid meal" to be had if you're "impervious to price" and so-so service, but as a "place to be seen", it's hard to beat.

NEW Bar Basque *French* | 19 | 19 | 19 | $61

Chelsea | Eventi Hotel | 839 Sixth Ave., 2nd fl. (bet. 29th & 30th Sts.) | 646-600-7150 | www.chinagrillmgt.com

At Jeffrey Chodorow's pricey arrival to Chelsea's Eventi Hotel, the "deep-red", "futuristic" look by *Tron* designer Syd Mead gets mixed reviews ("weird" vs. "very cool"), but most like the Basque menu; a "trendy" bar scene, wines via "vending machine" and an atrium roof "that opens in summer" keep it humming.

Barbès ● *French/Moroccan* | 20 | 18 | 20 | $45

Murray Hill | 21 E. 36th St. (bet. 5th & Madison Aves.) | 212-684-0215 | www.barbesrestaurantnyc.com

Coming as a "pleasant surprise" "near the Morgan Library", this "tiny" French-Moroccan "oasis" in a zone "not known for great food" delivers "adventures" with its "tasty tagines", "transporting" "Marrakesh" vibe and "sexy staff"; it can be "crowded and noisy", but that comes with the territory.

Barbetta ● M *Italian* | 21 | 23 | 22 | $64

W 40s | 321 W. 46th St. (bet. 8th & 9th Aves.) | 212-246-9171 | www.barbettarestaurant.com

"There are reasons" this "classy" Theater District "fixture" has "been around" since 1906: first-class Northern Italian cooking, "solicitous" service, a "magical garden" and a "stunning" "villalike" interior; it's deemed "worth every cent" since it'll make you "forget you're in the busy city."

Barbone *Italian* | 25 | 18 | 23 | $45

E Village | 186 Ave. B (bet. 11th & 12th Sts.) | 212-254-6047 | www.barbonenyc.com

Between the "terrific" "rustic" Italian dishes and "gracious" owner making "spot-on wine recommendations", it's amazing this East Villager remains "relatively unknown"; factor in "value" prices and a "pretty garden", and it's no wonder those who know it "can't wait to go back."

Z Bar Boulud ● *French* | 24 | 20 | 22 | $62

W 60s | 1900 Broadway (bet. 63rd & 64th Sts.) | 212-595-0303 | www.danielnyc.com

A "first-rate" wine bar and a slice of "charcuterie heaven", this French bistro "gift to Lincoln Center" is counted "among Daniel Boulud's more inspired creations"; it's "definitely pricey", and you have to "snake your way" through "crowds" in its "narrow", "tunnel-ish" room – but the "alfresco" summer seating is "delightful."

Barbounia *Mediterranean* | 21 | 22 | 18 | $49

Flatiron | 250 Park Ave. S. (20th St.) | 212-995-0242 | www.barbounia.com

Sure, this "entertaining" Flatironer proffers "tasty" Med fare, but what's "exciting" here is watching "beautiful people" dine in "stunning", vaulted-ceilinged surrounds; "steep prices", uneven service and "deafening" acoustics can annoy, but an "artisanal cocktail" or two helps.

Bar Breton *French*   18 | 14 | 18 | $43

Chelsea | 254 Fifth Ave. (bet. 28th & 29th Sts.) | 212-213-4999 | www.barbreton.com

Chef Cyril Renaud brings "tasty", well-priced Bretagne classics ("galletes, cider") to Chelsea with this "neighborhood" "nook"; critics cite "hit-or-miss" cooking, a "narrow layout" and "disappointing" service, but to "Francophiles" it's *un gagnant*.

Barbuto *Italian*   25 | 20 | 22 | $55

W Village | 775 Washington St. (bet. Jane & W. 12th Sts.) | 212-924-9700 | www.barbutonyc.com

Using "market-fresh ingredients", "master chef" Jonathan Waxman turns out "simple", "scrumptious" Italian "pleasures" at this "welcoming", "industrial-chic" West Villager; it gets "noisy" in its "former-garage" space, but acoustics improve in summer when they "roll up the doors."

Bar Carrera ● *Spanish*   ▽ 21 | 19 | 21 | $34

G Village | 146 W. Houston St. (MacDougal St.) | 212-253-9500 | www.barcarrera.com

Tapas "a cut above average" and "wines by the glass" are delivered by a "knowledgeable" crew at this well-priced Village Basque; "simple" and "welcoming", it's also host to a "surprisingly good bar scene."

BareBurger *Burgers*   23 | 17 | 20 | $22

NEW **G Village** | 535 La Guardia Pl. (bet. Bleecker & W. 3rd Sts.) | 212-477-8125
NEW **Murray Hill** | 514 Third Ave. (bet. 34th & 35th Sts.) | 212-679-2273
NEW **Park Slope** | 170 Seventh Ave. (1st St.) | Brooklyn | 718-768-2273
Astoria | 33-21 31st Ave. (34th St.) | Queens | 718-777-7011
www.bareburger.com

"Sustainable"-minded sorts seek out "scrumptious burgers" made from "humanely-raised" beef (and "elk, bison and ostrich") at this "pleasant" mini-chain, where the decor "rocks recycled" materials; prices are "a little high" for the genre, but who knew "healthy living" "could be this good"?; P.S. branches are on the way in Chelsea and Astoria.

Bar Henry ● ⓩ *American*   21 | 18 | 22 | $47

G Village | 90 W. Houston St., downstairs (bet. La Guardia Pl. & Thompson St.) | 646-448-4559 | www.barhenry.com

Given its location in Village "college bar" territory, this "cute" cellar dweller "surprises" with both its "ample wine list" boasting "many half-bottle options" and its "knowledgeable" staff; the American bistro fare is "solid" too, if on the "expensive" side for the zip code.

Bar Italia ● *Italian*   21 | 19 | 19 | $52

NEW **E 60s** | 768 Madison Ave. (66th St.) | 917-546-6676
E 70s | 1477 Second Ave. (77th St.) | 212-249-5300
www.baritalianyc.com

"Euros" and "well-heeled" locals gravitate to these Eastsiders for "enjoyable" Italian basics in stylishly "stark, white" environs; they're a "refreshing" change from the usual "cookie-cutter" options, so long as you don't mind "high decibels" from the "happening bar scene."

	FOOD	DECOR	SERVICE	COST

Bar Jamon ◐ *Spanish* — 23 | 18 | 18 | $42

Gramercy | 125 E. 17th St. (Irving Pl.) | 212-253-2773

"You're in Barcelona" at Mario Batali's "teeny" Gramercy tapas bar, which matches "delectable" Spanish snacks with "excellent" wines, and serves as the unofficial "waiting room" for around-the-corner sib Casa Mono; it's a "fun, bustling" scene, but "prepare to throw some elbows" to get a stool at one of its "packed" communal tables.

Bark Hot Dogs *Hot Dogs* — 21 | 15 | 18 | $16

Park Slope | 474 Bergen St. (bet. 5th & Flatbush Aves.) | Brooklyn | 718-789-1939 | www.barkhotdogs.com

"Arf!" – "totally-off-the-chain" hot dogs and other "haute fast food" with a "farm-to-table"/"sustainable" spin make for "less-guilty" pig-outs at this Park Slope "stroller destination" rated "worth the extra few dollars"; locals are rejoicing that it "now delivers" – plus in summertime there's an outlet in Brooklyn Bridge Park.

Barmarché ◐ *American* — ▽ 21 | 21 | 20 | $41

NoLita | 14 Spring St. (Elizabeth St.) | 212-219-2399 | www.barmarche.com

"Don't let the casual atmosphere fool you" – there's "lots of romance" at this "charming" NoLita "nook" manned by a "friendly, attractive" staff; better still, its "no-fuss" New American fare and "well-crafted" cocktails come at "reasonable" rates, especially given the "prime" locale.

⚡ Barney Greengrass Ⓜ⇄ *Deli* — 24 | 8 | 15 | $30

W 80s | 541 Amsterdam Ave. (bet. 86th & 87th Sts.) | 212-724-4707 | www.barneygreengrass.com

Beloved as a "landmark in appetizing" since 1908, this UWS "must" is "still going strong" with "phenomenal" smoked fish and other "kosher-style goodies" "par excellence"; the "quintessential" "NY Jewish deli", it features "gruff service", "dingy" digs, "kvetch"-worthy "lines", a "cash-only" policy and fierce "devotees."

Barolo *Italian* — 19 | 21 | 18 | $57

SoHo | 398 W. Broadway (bet. Broome & Spring Sts.) | 212-226-1102 | www.nybarolo.com

A "bit-of-paradiso" garden amid SoHo's "hustle and bustle" is this Italian's "biggest plus", followed closely by its "broad" wine list and "unsurpassed people-watching"; however, critics who cite just-"decent", "overpriced" fare and "offhand service" say "stick to drinks."

Barosa *Italian* — 21 | 17 | 21 | $38

Rego Park | 62-29 Woodhaven Blvd. (62nd Rd.) | Queens | 718-424-1455 | www.barosas.com

"Consistency counts" say "neighborhood" admirers of this "old-fashioned" Rego Park Italian's reliably "fresh" "red-sauce" basics; "waits can be long", but Sinatra's always on, the "huge" portions make for "one of the best deals in town" and the "pro" staff "won't rush you."

Bar Pitti ◐⇄ *Italian* — 22 | 14 | 18 | $42

G Village | 268 Sixth Ave. (bet. Bleecker & Houston Sts.) | 212-982-3300

"Cosmopolitan" types collect at this "unpretentious", "cash-only" Village Italian, as much for the "celeb spottings" as the "alfresco" dining and "affordable", "to-die-for" pastas; "absent" decor and "no reservations" are a pitti, but "the meatballs alone are worth it."

			FOOD	DECOR	SERVICE	COST

Basilica ◗ *Italian* — **20** | **14** | **20** | **$34**

W 40s | 676 Ninth Ave. (bet. 46th & 47th Sts.) | 212-489-0051 | www.basilicarestaurant.net

Broadway "gypsies" and "chorus kids" "squeeze" into this "tiny" Hell's Kitchen standby for "damn good" Italian standards; the $28 pre-theater prix fixe with a bottle of wine included "can't be beat", while the "friendly" staff gets you out with "plenty of time" to make "the show."

Basso56 *Italian* — **23** | **18** | **24** | **$52**

W 50s | 234 W. 56th St. (bet. B'way & 8th Ave.) | 212-265-2610 | www.basso56.com

"Close to Carnegie Hall", this "thriving" Italian gives no "treble", just a "dynamite menu" and "baritone" $19 prix fixe lunch; a "quiet" vibe and "*molto bene servicio*" elicit "bravos", but "narrow", "not-much-to-mention" digs have surveyors going *sotto voce*.

Basta Pasta *Italian* — **23** | **17** | **21** | **$45**

Flatiron | 37 W. 17th St. (bet. 5th & 6th Aves.) | 212-366-0888 | www.bastapastanyc.com

"Nonna would never get it", but the seemingly "odd" "Japanese-influenced Italian" fare at this Flatironer "totally works", especially the pasta "tossed in a Parmesan wheel"; the "sparse" room's a little "dated", but a "sweet staff" and "reasonable pricing" keep things simpatico.

Battery Gardens *American/Continental* — **19** | **24** | **20** | **$52**

Financial District | SW corner of Battery Park (State St.) | 212-809-5508 | www.batterygardens.com

"Unbeatable views" of "Lady Liberty" and "NY Harbor sunsets" from a "beautiful terrace" are the lure at this Battery Park American-Continental; "friendly" service is a plus, but it can seem like the pricey "food's an afterthought"; P.S. there's a beer garden in summer.

Bayou *Cajun* — **23** | **21** | **21** | **$41**

Rosebank | 1072 Bay St. (bet. Chestnut & St. Mary's Aves.) | Staten Island | 718-273-4383 | www.bayounyc.com

"If you can't get to Mardi Gras", there's always this affordable SI "joint" catering to those "ragin' for Cajun" with its "authentic" cooking and Big Easy drinks; a "caring staff" and "wonderfully redecorated" small space further "bring to life" the French Quarter vibe.

B. Café *Belgian* — **21** | **16** | **19** | **$40**

E 70s | 240 E. 75th St. (bet. 2nd & 3rd Aves.) | 212-249-3300
W 80s | 566 Amsterdam Ave. (bet. 87th & 88th Sts.) | 212-873-1800
www.bcafe.com

These "convivial" crosstown bistros showcase the "three great Belgian contributions to Western civilization: mussels, frites and beer"; both "hideaway" spaces can get "noisy" and "cramped", but the "staff tries hard" and in summer you can "eat outside."

Beacon *American* — **23** | **21** | **22** | **$59**

W 50s | 25 W. 56th St. (bet. 5th & 6th Aves.) | 212-332-0500 | www.beaconnyc.com

Waldy Malouf "still does it right" at his Midtown vet whose "luscious" "wood-grilled" New Americana is a "shining light", brightened by a "warm", "spacious" setting and "welcoming" staff; "be sure your credit line's stocked" before "power-lunching" here – otherwise, stick to the "bargain" prix fixes.

NEW Beagle ● *American*

FOOD	DECOR	SERVICE	COST
-	-	-	M

E Village | 162 Ave. A (bet. 10th & 11th Sts.) | 212-228-6900 | thebeaglenyc.com

With owners from Portland, OR, this rustic East Village American gastro-pub brings touches like 'pairing boards' – appetizers served with small cocktails – to complement its meat-heavy offerings; the pre-Prohibition Era drinks list may be the most ornate thing about this no-frills place.

Beast *Mediterranean*

FOOD	DECOR	SERVICE	COST
21	15	18	$34

Prospect Heights | 638 Bergen St. (Vanderbilt Ave.) | Brooklyn | 718-399-6855 | www.brooklynbeast.com

"Grazing with friends" on "reasonable, tasty" Mediterranean tapas makes for good "fun" at this "quaint" Prospect Heights standby; the "impressive" weekend brunch and outdoor seating are other pluses, but locals say ultimately "you go for camaraderie."

NEW Beaumarchais ● *French*

FOOD	DECOR	SERVICE	COST
-	-	-	E

Meatpacking | 409 W. 13th St. (bet. 9th Ave. & Washington St.) | 212-675-2400 | www.brasseriebeaumarchais.com

Formerly Bagatelle, this Meatpacking French brasserie held on to its whitewashed Med decor, attractive Euro staff and kissy clientele that nibbles pricey classics to a DJ's epically "loud" soundtrack; true scenesters hit the weekend 'Le Grand Brunch' for champagne-fueled "fun."

☑NEW Beauty & Essex ● *American*

FOOD	DECOR	SERVICE	COST
22	27	21	$63

LES | 146 Essex St. (bet. Rivington & Stanton Sts.) | 212-614-0146 | www.beautyandessex.com

Behind a LES "fake pawn shop", this "gorgeous" New American "sister to Stanton Social" is done up like a "modern-day speakeasy" with Vegas-worthy "draping chandeliers, recessed rooms" and even a "champagne bar in the ladies' room"; given all that, the *Gossip Girl* crowd doesn't mind much that the "clever", eclectic small plates "get expensive."

Becco ● *Italian*

FOOD	DECOR	SERVICE	COST
23	18	21	$47

W 40s | 355 W. 46th St. (bet. 8th & 9th Aves.) | 212-397-7597 | www.becco-nyc.com

At Joe and Lidia Bastianich's Restaurant Row Italian, "bargain-hunters" with "big appetites" "gorge" on "fantastic" "unlimited" pasta for $23, washed down with "can't-miss" $25-a-bottle wines; it's "crazy busy", but the "attentive" staff gets you "out in time for your curtain."

Beccofino *Italian*

FOOD	DECOR	SERVICE	COST
23	18	21	$37

Riverdale | 5704 Mosholu Ave. (bet. Fieldston Rd. & Spencer Ave.) | Bronx | 718-432-2604

This "quaint" Riverdale "staple" plies "surprisingly good" Italiana via an "efficient" staff; it's "small" and "doesn't take reservations", but for "super-size" portions at "reasonable" tabs, locals brave the "long waits."

NEW Beecher's Handmade Cheese *American*

FOOD	DECOR	SERVICE	COST
-	-	-	I

Flatiron | 900 Broadway (20th St.) | 212-466-3340 | www.beechershandmadecheese.com

Seattle's fromage favorite comes East with this big Flatironer, where a cheese factory behind glass windows steals the show; the housemade goods go into mac 'n' cheese and sandwiches at the counter-service cafe, and get paired with wines in the cellar bar/aging cave.

Belcourt *European*   20 | 17 | 17 | $38
E Village | 84 E. Fourth St. (2nd Ave.) | 212-979-2034 | www.belcourtnyc.com
Courting favor with "solid" Pan-European plates and "amazing" cocktails, this "low-key" East Villager works the "faux" "French-bistro" look ("hexagonal-tile floor, mirrored walls"); service can be "slow" and acoustics "noisy", but "fair prices" and "outdoor seating" keep most "content."

Bella Blu ◑ *Italian*   21 | 18 | 20 | $54
E 70s | 967 Lexington Ave. (bet. 70th & 71st Sts.) | 212-988-4624 | www.baraondany.com
A "very East Side clientele" crowds into this "local" "go-to" for "pricey", "rock-solid" Italian basics like "fresh pastas" and "wonderful" "wood-oven pizzas" ferried by an "attentive" staff; "colorful murals" lend a "lively" look, but oh, "the noise and cramped tables."

Bella Via *Italian*   22 | 17 | 20 | $35
LIC | 47-46 Vernon Blvd. (48th Ave.) | Queens | 718-361-7510 | www.bellaviarestaurant.com
"Manhattan quality without the cost" is what regulars expect from this "unpretentious" LIC Italian, an "airy" trattoria known for "knockout pastas and wood-grilled pizzas"; throw in "nice-size portions" and a "friendly", "family-run" feel, and "what more can you ask for"?

NEW Bell Book & Candle *American*   23 | 23 | 23 | $48
W Village | 141 W. 10th St. (bet. Greenwich Ave. & Waverly Pl.) | 212-414-2355 | www.bbandcnyc.com
Talk about "farm-to-table" – in season, a "rooftop garden provides most of the produce" at this "charming" West Villager plying "fresh", "fantastic" New Americana and "creative cocktails"; sealing its "keeper" status are "warm" service and "casual, cozy" downstairs digs.

Belleville *French*   19 | 21 | 19 | $39
Park Slope | 330-332 Fifth St. (5th Ave.) | Brooklyn | 718-832-9777 | www.bellevillebistro.com
This Park Slope "neighborhood drop-in" pairs "lovely" "Parisian bistro" atmosphere with "simple" Gallic "comfort" fare at "friendly prices"; the less-impressed shrug "nothing spectacular", but even they concede it's a local "best bet" for brunch.

Bello *Italian*   22 | 19 | 23 | $49
W 50s | 863 Ninth Ave. (56th St.) | 212-246-6773 | www.bellorestaurant.com
At this "old-fashioned-in-a-good-way" Hell's Kitchen Italian, "delicious" "red-sauce" standards are "well served" by a "gracious" "pro" staff; a recent "sprucing up" has taken the "subdued" decor up a notch, and "free parking next door" after 5 PM "doesn't hurt either."

Ben & Jack's Steak House *Steak*   23 | 19 | 22 | $68
E 40s | 219 E. 44th St. (bet. 2nd & 3rd Aves.) | 212-682-5678
Murray Hill | 255 Fifth Ave. (bet. 28th & 29th Sts.) | 212-532-7600
www.benandjackssteakhouse.com
These "civilized" East Side Luger "mimics" "carry on" the "beef emporium" tradition, supplying "high-quality" steaks, the "usual sides" and

"plentiful booze pours" in "clubby" quarters; an "expense account" helps – "at least they take credit cards."

Ben Benson's *Steak*

| 24 | 19 | 23 | $71 |

W 50s | 123 W. 52nd St. (bet. 6th & 7th Aves.) | 212-581-8888 | www.benbensons.com

It's "carnivore paradise" at this "classic" Midtown "meatery" where "fabulous beef" and "top-notch" sides come in a "stark" space "laced with testosterone"; "heck yeah, it's expensive", but the "pro" staffers have "a sense of humor" – and "boy can they mix a cocktail."

Benjamin ● *American*

| 18 | 14 | 18 | $36 |

Murray Hill | 603 Second Ave. (33rd St.) | 212-889-0750 | www.benjaminny.com

"Every neighborhood should have" a "handy" fallback like this Murray Hill American dispensing "simple" classics rated a "step up" from bar grub; as bonuses, it won't set you back "too many Benjamins", and the "unexciting" ambiance gets a boost "when they light the fireplace."

Benjamin Steak House *Steak*

| 24 | 22 | 23 | $76 |

E 40s | Dylan Hotel | 52 E. 41st St. (bet. Madison & Park Aves.) | 212-297-9177 | www.benjaminsteakhouse.com

"Hidden" just south of Grand Central, this "palace" for "steak connoisseurs" delivers "cooked-to-perfection" cuts in a "double-height" "art deco" space manned by "gracious" waiters; it's a "refreshing" change from the "usual steakhouse" – though it's "best" on "someone else's expense account."

Benoit ⊠ *French*

| 21 | 21 | 20 | $63 |

W 50s | 60 W. 55th St. (bet. 5th & 6th Aves.) | 646-943-7373 | www.benoitny.com

Since the arrival of a new chef, Alain Ducasse's "elegant" Midtowner is "on an uptick" according to admirers of its "redone" (but still "classic") bistro menu; others say the cuisine and service remain "uneven", while prices are "not inexpensive" – though all agree the $22 prix fixe lunch is a "steal."

Ben's Best *Deli/Kosher*

| 23 | 9 | 17 | $24 |

Rego Park | 96-40 Queens Blvd. (bet. 63rd Rd. & 64th Ave.) | Queens | 718-897-1700 | www.bensbest.com

Rego Park noshers kvell over this "outstanding" Jewish deli, a circa-1945 "staple" for "outrageous" "overstuffed sandwiches" and other "real kosher" classics; "time-warp" decor and "spotty" service are beside the point – this "Queens institution" deserves "landmark protection."

Ben's Kosher Deli *Deli/Kosher*

| 19 | 12 | 16 | $27 |

Garment District | 209 W. 38th St. (bet. 7th & 8th Aves.) | 212-398-2367
Bayside | Bay Terrace | 211-37 26th Ave. (Bell Blvd.) | Queens | 718-229-2367
www.bensdeli.net

Members of a "vanishing breed", these Garment District–Bayside Jewish delis dispense "mile-high" sandwiches and other "artery-hardening" kosher "staples" like "your grandpa enjoyed"; never mind "tired" decor and "rushed" service – eat, "enjoy" and leave "as fat and happy as a knockwurst."

	FOOD	DECOR	SERVICE	COST

Bereket ●⇝ *Turkish* | 21 | 5 | 14 | $14

LES | 187 E. Houston St. (Orchard St.) | 212-475-7700

"Hang with the taxi drivers" and "bar-hoppers" at this 24/7 LES Turk; its "super-cheap", "filling" kebabs and other "hearty", alcohol-absorbing basics are "fab" at any hour, so the "tipsy", "late-night" clientele happily overlooks its decidedly "no-frills" setting.

NEW Berlyn *German* | ▽ 19 | 16 | 19 | $42

Fort Greene | 25 Lafayette Ave. (Ashland Pl.) | Brooklyn | 718-222-5800 | www.berlynrestaurant.com

Boasting an "extremely handy location" across from BAM, this "pleasant" arrival slings "solid" schnitzel, strudel and other German standards in the old Thomas Beisl space; "fancy cocktails" suit the "fancy patrons", and "whimsical decor" (gnomes, deer heads) gives 'em plenty to look at.

Betel *SE Asian* | 22 | 20 | 20 | $51

W Village | 51 Grove St. (bet. Bleecker St. & 7th Ave. S.) | 212-352-0460 | www.betelnyc.com

This "upscale" Villager gets accolades for "innovative" (and "pricey") SE Asian–inspired fare, "wonderful cocktails" and "lovely" service; the "scene" rife with "pretty people" at communal tables can get "loud", but those who look past the "chatter" may find a culinary "delight."

NEW Betto ● *Italian* | - | - | - | M

Williamsburg | 138 N. Eighth St. (bet. Bedford Ave. & Berry St.) | Brooklyn | 718-384-1904 | www.bettonyc.com

Jason Denton ('Ino, 'Inoteca) takes his brand of casual Italian dining across the bridge with this Williamsburg newcomer offering wellpriced small plates and lots of wines by the glass; the casual, airy room features communal seating and a garage door that opens to the street.

Bettola ● *Italian* | 21 | 16 | 20 | $38

W 70s | 412 Amsterdam Ave. (bet. 79th & 80th Sts.) | 212-787-1660 | www.bettolanyc.com

"Unpretentious" it may be, but "excellent" thin-crust pizzas and other affordable "basics" have made this "convivial" UWS Italian a "neighborhood stalwart"; many prefer its "sidewalk seating" to the "simple", "narrow" interior, but service is "quick and accommodating" throughout.

Beyoglu *Turkish* | 22 | 17 | 18 | $37

E 80s | 1431 Third Ave. (81st St.) | 212-650-0850

"Amazing meze" ranks high among the "cheap eats" at this "on-themark" UES Turk that's also touted for its "delectable" kebabs, veggie fare and bread you "can't stop eating"; it's so "worthwhile", most put up with "noise" and "dicey" service – or "eat upstairs", where it's "less harried."

Bianca ⇝ *Italian* | 24 | 18 | 21 | $34

NoHo | 5 Bleecker St. (bet. Bowery & Elizabeth St.) | 212-260-4666 | www.biancanyc.com

"Rich" Emilia-Romagna dishes dominate the "superb" offerings at this "cute little" NoHo Italian whose "warm" service boosts the "purely pleasurable" experience; the "only downsides": it takes "no reservations" (there's "usually a wait") and is "cash only" – though "you don't need a lot" thanks to the "un-NYC pricing."

	FOOD	DECOR	SERVICE	COST

Bice ● *Italian* | 20 | 19 | 19 | $67

E 50s | 7 E. 54th St. (bet. 5th & Madison Aves.) | 212-688-1999 |
www.bicenewyork.com

You'd better "brush up on your air-kissing" and "go with a regular" for
best results at this "chic" Midtown Italian where "Europeans", "suits"
and "tourists" collect for "reliable, classic" fare; "aloof" service can
rankle – especially given the "Bulgari bauble"–worthy prices.

Big Nick's Burger Joint *Burgers* | 18 | 7 | 15 | $18

W 70s | 2175 Broadway (77th St.) | 212-362-9238 ●
W 70s | 70 W. 71st St. (bet. Columbus Ave. & CPW) | 212-799-4444
www.bignicksny.com

"Funky is the word" for these separately owned "classic" "greasy
spoons", where Upper Westsiders "grab some grub" from a "menu as
long as the Bible" (go for the "gigundo burgers" or "killer pizza"); both
offer "cheap tabs" and "fast" service, and the Broadway original's
open 'round the clock.

Big Wong ⊄ *Chinese* | 23 | 6 | 12 | $15

Chinatown | 67 Mott St. (bet. Bayard & Canal Sts.) | 212-964-0540

"Old-school Chinatown" lives on at this "showcase of Cantonese fast
food" known for its "unforgettable name" and "mouthwatering" con-
gee and roast meats; ok, "it's a dump" and the service is "gruff" at
best, but you can "go famished and leave full" for "ridiculously cheap."

Bill's Bar & Burger *Burgers* | 19 | 14 | 17 | $24

Meatpacking | 22 Ninth Ave. (13th St.) | 212-414-3003 ●
NEW **W 50s** | 16 W. 51st St. (bet. 5th & 6th Aves.) | 212-705-8510
www.billsbarandburger.com

Steve Hanson shows how to "make a burger-and-beer joint hip" with
this dynamic duo dispensing "solid" patties, brews and "boozy milkshakes"; in the Meatpacking it's "no-frills" and at Rock Center "filled
with tourists", but the grub comes "fast and cheap" at both.

NEW **Bi Lokma** ⊠ *Turkish* | – | – | – | I

E 40s | 212 E. 45th St. (bet. 2nd & 3rd Aves.) | 212-687-3842 |
www.bi-lokma.com

The latest from chef Orhan Yegen (Sip Sak), this tiny Turk near Grand
Central focuses on takeout and delivery; late-night, it morphs into an
iskembeci, an informal spot where folks can drop by for a nibble – the
name translates as 'one bite.'

Bino *Italian* | 24 | 21 | 24 | $44

Carroll Gardens | 276 Smith St. (bet. Degraw & Sackett Sts.) | Brooklyn |
718-875-1980 | www.binobrooklyn.com

"Everything's the same as when it was Po" at this "grown-up" "little"
Carroll Gardens Italian, from the "sophisticated" fare "with a dash of
locavore" to the "welcoming" vibe and "lovely" staff; that leaves just
"three words" of advice: "reserve, reserve, reserve!"

Biricchino ⊠ *Italian* | 21 | 14 | 19 | $40

Chelsea | 260 W. 29th St. (8th Ave.) | 212-695-6690 | www.biricchino.com

"Fabulous housemade sausages" star at this "under-the-radar"
Chelsea Northern Italian, but "whatever they make goes down
easy"; a "sweet" staff tends the "casual" room, and tabs "won't

break the bank", but its biggest blessing is the location "near Madison Square Garden."

NEW Birreria ● *Italian* ▽ 21 | 20 | 20 | $45

Flatiron | Eataly | 200 Fifth Ave., 15th fl. (bet. 23rd & 24th Sts.) | 212-937-8910 | www.eataly.com

Requiring "extremely long waits" from day one, Eataly's crowning-touch rooftop beer garden provides "first-rate" suds and a "limited menu" of Italian cheeses, salumi and such; 15 stories up, with Flatiron views from some seats, it has heat lamps and a retractable roof for all-weather accessibility.

Bistango *Italian* 22 | 18 | 23 | $40

Murray Hill | 415 Third Ave. (29th St.) | 212-725-8484 | www.bistangonyc.com

This "pleasant", "casual" Murray Hill Italian offers "delicious gluten-free" pasta options (perfect for "celiac" sufferers) on its menu of "comforting" fare; a "hospitable" owner leads the "bend-over-backwards" service, and "reasonable" tabs are another "pleasant surprise."

Bistro Cassis *French* 21 | 18 | 19 | $47

W 70s | 225 Columbus Ave. (bet. 70th & 71st Sts.) | 212-579-3966 | www.bistrocassisnyc.com

For "French food in the 'hood", Upper Westsiders hasten to this "dependable standby" slinging "satisfying" bistro fare that won't "bankrupt you"; its "mahogany-and-mirrors" digs "evoke France" and the "warm" service doesn't – no wonder it's "always hopping."

Bistro Chat Noir *French* 19 | 18 | 20 | $55

E 60s | 22 E. 66th St. (bet. 5th & Madison Aves.) | 212-794-2428 | www.bistrochatnoir.com

"Very UES", this "tiny", "unsung" French bistro turns out "traditional" fare that suits "blonde-streaked natives", "ladies who lunch" and seekers of "quiet business" meals; cheap it's not, but "charming" service makes it a local "oasis" despite "rather ordinary" townhouse digs.

Bistro Citron *French* 19 | 18 | 19 | $46

W 80s | 473 Columbus Ave. (bet. 82nd & 83rd Sts.) | 212-400-9401 | www.bistrocitronnyc.com

"Like a mini-vacation to Paris", this "pleasant" UWS bistro offers "simple, satisfying" Gallic "standards" that are "well prepared and cheerfully served" with a "touch of French swagger"; "authentic" environs and tolerance for "well-behaved tykes" ensure it's "an asset" to the area.

Bistro Les Amis ● *French* 20 | 19 | 23 | $45

SoHo | 180 Spring St. (Thompson St.) | 212-226-8645 | www.bistrolesamis.com

From the "warm greeting" to the pleasing, "priced-right" French fare, this "cheerful" bistro provides a "respite from the SoHo scene"; "comfy" environs and sidewalk seating for watching the "passing mob" help make it a "sentimental favorite" that lives up to its name.

Bistro Le Steak *French* 18 | 15 | 18 | $48

E 70s | 1309 Third Ave. (75th St.) | 212-517-3800 | www.bistrolesteak.com

UES "carnivores" collect at this "old-time" French bistro where "steak pommes frites" star on the "something-for-everyone" menu of standards; service is mostly "pleasant" and prices "moderate", so most overlook "dreary" decor in need of "a refresher."

Bistro Milano *Italian* ▽ 21 | 19 | 20 | $51

W 50s | 1350 Sixth Ave. (enter on 55th St., bet. 5th & 6th Aves.) | 212-757-2600 | www.bistromilanonyc.com

"Bright" and "modern", this "busy" Midtown Italian from the Bice people serves up "tasty" pastas and such in the shadow of City Center and Carnegie Hall; "accommodating" service, patio seating and a "nice bar" make it good for a "business" meetup à la expense account.

Bistro 61 *French* 20 | 15 | 19 | $42

E 60s | 1113 First Ave. (61st St.) | 212-223-6220 | www.bistro61.com

A "welcome surprise" nestled by the Queensboro Bridge, this "little-piece-of-Paris" bistro turns out "tasty" French standards "with Moroccan overtones" via a staff with "panache"; it's looking a "bit tired", but the "cool, jazzy vibe" and "moderate prices" keep it a local "favorite."

Bistro Vendôme *French* 22 | 19 | 20 | $55

E 50s | 405 E. 58th St. (bet. 1st Ave. & Sutton Pl.) | 212-935-9100 | www.bistrovendomenyc.com

"Booked solid every day", this Sutton Place "neighborhood gem" pleases necessarily well-heeled "Chanel-Prada" types with its French bistro classics, "gracious" (if "noisy") tri-level space and "helpful" staffers; try for a table on the "beautiful tree-lined terrace" in summer.

Black Duck *American/Seafood* 21 | 18 | 21 | $51

Murray Hill | Park South Hotel | 122 E. 28th St. (bet. Lexington Ave. & Park Ave. S.) | 212-448-0888 | www.blackduckny.com

Appreciated as a "hospitable" "hideaway" in a Murray Hill "boutique hotel", this slightly "pricey" New American standby offers "well-presented" seafood-centric eats; weekend jazz and a "sweet fire-place" in its "cozy" "publike" space make it a "good call for a date."

Black Iron Burger Shop ●⌀ *Burgers* 23 | 14 | 19 | $18

E Village | 540 E. Fifth St. (bet. Aves. A & B) | 212-677-6067 | www.blackironburger.com

"Charred, juicy burgers" matched with "killer fries" and "lovely tap beers" have turned this "casual", cash-only East Village "joint" into a "neighborhood favorite"; the frills-free setting is trumped by late hours and "cheap tabs" – "what else could one want?"

Black Whale *American* 22 | 20 | 22 | $31

City Island | 279 City Island Ave. (Hawkins St.) | Bronx | 718-885-3657 | www.dineatblackwhale.com

"Manhattanites" and others "join City Island locals" at this "comfy" and "affordable" "oldie" offering "well-prepared" New American faves plus particularly "scrumptious desserts"; the "nautical-kitsch" interior has some opting for the "back patio", especially for the "terrific brunch."

Blaue Gans *Austrian/German* 22 | 18 | 19 | $47

TriBeCa | 139 Duane St. (bet. Church St. & W. B'way) | 212-571-8880 | www.kg-ny.com

From "divine spaetzle" to "amazing strudel", the Austro-German fare at Kurt Gutenbrunner's "convivial" TriBeCan is "lighter and more mod-

| | FOOD | DECOR | SERVICE | COST |

ern than you'd think"; "poster-covered walls add character" to the "pleasantly plain" room, while a laid-back staff boosts the "relaxed" mood – *alles "wunderbar."*

Blockheads Burritos *Mexican*   17 | 11 | 15 | $20

E 50s | 954 Second Ave. (bet. 50th & 51st Sts.) | 212-750-2020
E 80s | 1563 Second Ave. (bet. 81st & 82nd Sts.) | 212-879-1999
Financial District | Courtyard at 4 World Financial Ctr. (North & Vesey Sts.) | 212-619-8226
Murray Hill | 499 Third Ave. (bet. 33rd & 34th Sts.) | 212-213-3332
W 50s | Worldwide Plaza | 322 W. 50th St. (bet. 8th & 9th Aves.) | 212-307-7029
W 100s | 951 Amsterdam Ave. (bet. 106th & 107th Sts.) | 212-662-8226
www.blockheads.com

"Ginormous burritos" and other "super-cheap", "kinda Mexican" grub is the draw at these "mobbed" cantinas where a "rowdy" crowd downing $4 "hi-octane" margaritas makes for a "festive" scene; it "works best if you're in your 20s", otherwise opt for "quick grab 'n' go" or "delivery."

Blossom *Vegan/Vegetarian*   22 | 18 | 20 | $37

Chelsea | 187 Ninth Ave. (bet. 21st & 22nd Sts.) | 212-627-1144
W 80s | 466 Columbus Ave. (bet. 82nd & 83rd Sts.) | 212-875-2600
www.blossomnyc.com

"Who knew" vegan food could be "lick-your-plate" "scrumptious"? marvel "meat-and-potato" converts at this "deluxe" duo that also produces "swoon-worthy" desserts; the "charming" Chelsea "townhouse" is a step up from the UWS' "bare-bones" digs, but both feature "helpful" service and relatively "haute" prices.

BLT Bar & Grill *American*   22 | 20 | 20 | $53

Financial District | W Hotel Downtown | 123 Washington St. (bet. Albany & Carlisle Sts.) | 646-826-8666 | www.bltrestaurants.com

In a Financial District corner "where there aren't many choices", this "hip" eatery inside the W Downtown is "welcome" for its "pricey" but "better-than-average" American "staples"; the "vaulted-ceilinged", bi-level space fills up at lunch with "business" types and "Trade Center site" visitors alike.

BLT Burger *Burgers*   21 | 15 | 18 | $29

G Village | 470 Sixth Ave. (bet. 11th & 12th Sts.) | 212-243-8226 | www.bltburger.com

"Luscious burgers, mind-altering" milkshakes (some "with alcohol") and "superior sides" add up to "solid" meals at this "easygoing" Village "BLT offshoot"; "kids love it" and don't sweat "spotty service" or "noisy", "not-so-chic" digs, but their parents may find the tab "pricey for what it is."

BLT Fish ⧉ *Seafood*   24 | 21 | 22 | $63

Flatiron | 21 W. 17th St. (bet. 5th & 6th Aves.) | 212-691-8888 | www.bltfish.com

A "responsive" crew tends to diners at this "sumptuous" Flatiron seafooder while its kitchen "performs magic" with the "freshest fish"; the "elegant", "glass-ceilinged" upstairs affords "spectacular" sky-gazing, but those not into "paying top dollar" stick with the "casual", relative-"bargain" Fish Shack downstairs.

	FOOD	DECOR	SERVICE	COST

BLT Market *American*   **24** | **22** | **22** | **$68**

W 50s | Ritz-Carlton Central Park | 1430 Sixth Ave. (CPS) | 212-521-6125 |
www.bltmarket.com

Laurent Tourondel's "garden"-fresh New American fare comes via an
"on-point" staff at this "sophisticated" hotel dining room that feels
far more "country" than you'd expect at the Ritz-Carlton; it's "a treat
if you can afford it" – "sit outside" and gaze at Central Park.

☑ BLT Prime *Steak*   **26** | **23** | **24** | **$75**

Gramercy | 111 E. 22nd St. (bet. Lexington Ave. & Park Ave. S.) |
212-995-8500 | www.bltprime.com

"Not your run-of-the-mill steakhouse", this "high-energy" Gramercy
chop shop dispenses "deliciously charred" meats in "modern" digs;
add "a superb wine list" and "expert" service and you can imagine the "oy
vey!" bill, but the "sensational popovers" alone are "worth" the outlay.

☑ BLT Steak *Steak*   **25** | **22** | **23** | **$76**

E 50s | 106 E. 57th St. (bet. Lexington & Park Aves.) | 212-752-7470 |
www.bltsteak.com

"Cougars and tigers play" alongside "macho" "corporate types" at this
"glam" Midtown BLT progenitor proffering "perfect" slabs, "decadent
sides" and "hard-to-get wines"; service that "hits the mark" and serious tabs complete the "wow"-worthy experience.

Blue Fin ❶ *Seafood*   **22** | **21** | **21** | **$57**

W 40s | W Hotel Times Sq. | 1567 Broadway (47th St.) | 212-918-1400 |
www.bluefinnyc.com

"Quite the scene", Steve Hanson's "big", "glitzy" seafooder is a "classy
escape" from Times Square, drawing theatergoers and tourists for "artfully prepared" fin fare; the bill can be "painful", likewise the "din" –
though atop the "Busby Berkeley–esque staircase" it's "more sedate."

Blue Ginger *Asian*   **21** | **16** | **20** | **$38**

Chelsea | 106 Eighth Ave. (bet. 15th & 16th Sts.) | 212-352-0911

"Tasty" sushi and "creative" cooked dishes "without the high price"
lure locals to this "under-the-radar" Chelsea Pan-Asian; the "simple
storefront" look "won't win awards", but it's "pleasant" enough and
hard to beat as a "Joyce Theater"-convenient "standby."

☑ Blue Hill *American*   **27** | **23** | **27** | **$83**

G Village | 75 Washington Pl. (bet. MacDougal St. & 6th Ave.) |
212-539-1776 | www.bluehillfarm.com

"King of the locavore movement", "genius" chef Dan Barber produces
"tantalizing", "brilliant meals" that "epitomize farm-to-table" at his
"serene", "well-run" Village American; it "ain't cheap" but it's "utterly
worth it" – especially given the "first-rate" service – but it's even more
"frustrating" getting a reservation ever since "the Obamas stopped by."

☑ Blue Ribbon ❶ *American*   **25** | **19** | **23** | **$55**

SoHo | 97 Sullivan St. (bet. Prince & Spring Sts.) | 212-274-0404
Park Slope | 280 Fifth Ave. (bet. 1st St. & Garfield Pl.) | Brooklyn |
718-840-0404
www.blueribbonrestaurants.com

"Tried 'n' true" and "terrific", these "energetic" SoHo–Park Slope
New Americans from the Bromberg brothers feature "all-over-the-

map" menus of "splendid" eats from "oysters to omelets", "cheerfully" served into the wee hours; they're "pricey", no-rez and "packed", but always "fun."

Blue Ribbon Bakery ● *American* | 25 | 19 | 22 | $44 |

W Village | 35 Downing St. (Bedford St.) | 212-337-0404 | www.blueribbonrestaurants.com

"Heavenly breads" baking on-site lend "intoxicating" aromas to the Brombergs' "welcoming" bistro, a West Village "icon" thanks to its "fantastic", "something-for-everyone" New American fare, "cool vibe" and "patient" service; "hipsters mix with families" at "wonderful brunch", while "claustrophobes" skip the "cramped" main room and "eat downstairs."

☑ Blue Ribbon Sushi ● *Japanese* | 26 | 20 | 23 | $59 |

SoHo | 119 Sullivan St. (bet. Prince & Spring Sts.) | 212-343-0404
Park Slope | 278 Fifth Ave. (bet. 1st St. & Garfield Pl.) | Brooklyn | 718-840-0408
www.blueribbonrestaurants.com

"The Bromberg brothers show how it's done, Kyoto-style" at this "understated" SoHo–Park Slope pair where "chopstick gurus" gush over the "out-of-sight" sushi and "impeccable" cooked dishes; sure, the bill hurts, but the fact that there's usually a "tough wait" shows that most think it's "all worth it."

Blue Ribbon Sushi
Bar & Grill ● *Japanese* | 25 | 20 | 22 | $61 |

W 50s | 6 Columbus Hotel | 308 W. 58th St. (bet. 8th & 9th Aves.) | 212-397-0404 | www.blueribbonrestaurants.com

A "spot of downtown" in Midtown (minus "Village funk"), this "cool", "classy" Columbus Circle Japanese offers "sublime" sushi and "excellent" grill dishes in "chic hotel" environs; "helpful" service and "open-late" hours help justify "expense account"-worthy tabs.

Blue Smoke *BBQ* | 22 | 17 | 20 | $42 |

Murray Hill | 116 E. 27th St. (bet. Lexington Ave. & Park Ave. S.) | 212-447-7733
Flushing | Citi Field | 126th St. & Roosevelt Ave. (behind the scoreboard) | Queens | no phone
www.bluesmoke.com

"Another Danny Meyer smash", this Murray Hill "pseudo-roadhouse" dishes up "boffo BBQ" and a "prodigious range" of beers and bourbons, all "comfortably priced"; it's a "scene", so "bring earplugs", unless headed downstairs to the "terrific" "built-in jazz venue"; P.S. the Citi Field outpost is a "home run" too, despite "waits measured in innings."

☑ Blue Water Grill *Seafood* | 24 | 22 | 22 | $57 |

Union Sq | 31 Union Sq. W. (16th St.) | 212-675-9500 | www.bluewatergrillnyc.com

At Steve Hanson's "upbeat" Union Square piscatorium, "superb", "steep-priced" seafood is ported by a "personable" crew adept at "navigating the perpetual throngs"; the "lavish" "old-bank" setup affords "people-watching" aplenty (especially "on the terrace"), while the Jazz Room downstairs is more "romantic."

	FOOD	DECOR	SERVICE	COST

Boathouse *American* — 18 | 26 | 18 | $56

E 70s | Central Park | Central Park Lake, enter on E. 72nd St. (Park Dr. N.) | 212-517-2233 | www.thecentralparkboathouse.com

Given its "magical setting" on the "Central Park lake", this NYC "icon"-cum-party venue is an "ideal" spot to take "an out-of-town guest" for a "relaxing" interlude; despite "costly", "routine" American eats and "perfunctory" service, it's "not to be missed" – even if you "just have drinks"; P.S. labor issues at press time threaten to burst the "tranquil" mood.

Bobby Van's Steakhouse *Steak* — 22 | 20 | 22 | $66

E 40s | 230 Park Ave. (46th St.) | 212-867-5490 🗷
E 50s | 131 E. 54th St. (bet. Lexington & Park Aves.) | 212-207-8050
Financial District | 25 Broad St. (Exchange Pl.) | 212-344-8463 🗷
Jamaica | JFK Airport | American Airlines Terminal 8 | Queens | 718-553-2100

Bobby Van's Grill *Steak*

NEW W 40s | 120 W. 45th St. (bet. 6th & 7th Aves.) | 212-575-5623
W 50s | 135 W. 50th St. (bet. 6th & 7th Aves.) | 212-957-5050
www.bobbyvans.com

For a "power lunch" or "boys' night out", this steakhouse mini-chain "comes through" with "mammoth hunks of beef" delivered by staffers who "know how to serve" in a "guy's-place" setting that suits the "suits"; the FiDi branch's "cool bank vault" is fitting since you'll need "wads of cash" at checktime.

Bobo *American* — 22 | 24 | 22 | $60

W Village | 181 W. 10th St. (7th Ave. S.) | 212-488-2626 | www.bobonyc.com

"Euros" and "beautiful" types nibble on "original" New American bites at this "gorgeous" West Village "boho-chic" brownstone, whose antiques-filled dining room is adjoined by a "wonderful patio"; drinks in the "clubby" downstairs bar complete the "cool" (if "pricey") "night out."

Boca Chica *Pan-Latin* — 22 | 16 | 19 | $32

E Village | 13 First Ave. (1st St.) | 212-473-0108

"Utterly delicious" Pan-Latin eats offered in "huge portions" at "bargain" rates have lured "festive" "young" crowds to this East Villager since 1989; margaritas that "come by the pint" fuel the "loud", "party" vibe, and make just-"ok" service and "elbow-to-elbow" seating easy to take.

Bocca *Italian* — 22 | 19 | 21 | $47

Flatiron | 39 E. 19th St. (bet. B'way & Park Ave. S.) | 212-387-1200 | www.boccanyc.com

"Wonderful" Roman specialties "soar" at this Flatiron offshoot of Cacio e Pepe, where the showstopper is the "decadent" pasta dish "tossed tableside in a huge cheese wheel"; "helpful" staffers, "more-than-fairly-priced" wines and a "cozy" vibe mean all's "*molto bene.*"

Bocca ◑ *Italian* — 22 | 20 | 19 | $47

NEW E 70s | 1496 Second Ave. (78th St.) | 212-249-1010 | www.boccadibaccoeast.com

Bocca di Bacco ◑ *Italian*

W 50s | 828 Ninth Ave. (bet. 54th & 55th Sts.) | 212-265-8828 | www.boccadibacconyc.com

"Low lights", "savory, plentiful" Italian fare and "affordable wines by the glass" make this "snazzy" Hell's Kitchen "staple" a "busy" "scene";

service "can be iffy", but it's a "local haven" all the same; P.S. the new UES outpost follows the same formula.

Bocca Lupo Italian — 24 | 21 | 21 | $33

Cobble Hill | 391 Henry St. (Warren St.) | Brooklyn | 718-243-2522 | www.boccalupo391.com

A "wonderful" "parade" of "affordable" Italian small plates and "fantastic" vinos comes via a "capable" crew at this "chill" Cobble Hill wine bar; the "stroller-friendly" vibe makes it "fun" for families, while night owls appreciate that it's "open late."

Bocelli Italian/Seafood — 25 | 22 | 23 | $54

Grasmere | 1250 Hylan Blvd. (bet. Old Town Rd. & Parkinson Ave.) | Staten Island | 718-420-6150 | www.bocellirest.com

"Delicious", "carefully crafted", seafood-centric cooking places this Staten Island Italian "a cut above" the pack, as does its "elegant, over-the-top" decor and "exceptional" service with owners "working the room"; it's "expensive" by local standards, but valet parking and live music add value.

Bodrum Mediterranean/Turkish — 20 | 16 | 20 | $38

W 80s | 584 Amsterdam Ave. (bet. 88th & 89th Sts.) | 212-799-2806 | www.bodrumnyc.com

"Addictive, warm-from-the-oven" bread and "tasty thin-crust pizzas" are among the "modestly priced" Turkish-Med dishes that await at this "cozy" Upper Westsider; a "sweet staff" makes sure you're "never rushed", but considering the "cramped quarters", patio dining is a "bonus."

Bogota Latin Bistro Pan-Latin — 21 | 17 | 19 | $31

Park Slope | 141 Fifth Ave. (bet. Lincoln & St. Johns Pls.) | Brooklyn | 718-230-3805 | www.bogotabistro.com

"Exuberant and spiced-up" describes both the "fantastic", "inexpensive" Pan-Latin *comida* and the "happening", "cacophonic" vibe at this Park Slope "instant party"; the "funky" interior and "lively music" "suit the crowd" downing "margaritas and mojitos", but for quieter moments the "back garden's a treat."

Bohemian Japanese — ▽ 27 | 25 | 28 | $80

NoHo | Japanese Premium Beef | 57 Great Jones St. (bet. Bowery & Lafayette St.) | no phone

"Hidden behind a butcher shop" in NoHo, this "tiny" Japanese "find" keeps a low profile via a "referral concept" (an unlisted phone number and mandatory reservations), but those who "stumble" upon it find "fantastic", "original" comfort fare and "fanciful drinks" served in "sexy" rec-room-like digs; insiders willing to pay its rarefied prices plead "please don't tell."

Bo-Ky Noodle Shop — 22 | 5 | 10 | $15

Chinatown | 80 Bayard St. (bet. Mott & Mulberry Sts.) | 212-406-2292
Little Italy | 216 Grand St. (Elizabeth St.) | 212-219-9228

"Fast, cheap and delicious", this Chinatown–Little Italy duo slings "superb" Chinese and Vietnamese noodle dishes (plus "perfectly made duck") as the "reward" for putting up with "dive" decor and "rush-rush" service; the slurps are so "satisfying", you may celebrate your next notice for "jury duty."

| | FOOD | DECOR | SERVICE | COST |

Bombay Palace *Indian*   19 | 18 | 19 | $40

W 50s | 30 W. 52nd St. (bet. 5th & 6th Aves.) | 212-541-7777 |
www.bombay-palace.com

An "oldie but a goodie", this "dependable" Midtown Indian turns out
"well-seasoned" classics via a "solicitous" staff"; the "quiet" digs are
"pleasant", if "dated", and rates are "fair", though the "fantastic" $16
lunch buffet "remains the best deal."

Bombay Talkie *Indian*   20 | 17 | 16 | $40

Chelsea | 189 Ninth Ave. (bet. 21st & 22nd Sts.) | 212-242-1900 |
www.bombaytalkie.com

"Bollywood memorabilia" makes a "playful" backdrop for "sophisticated" Indian "street food" and "funky cocktails" at this Chelsea
"change of pace"; despite gripes about "pricey" tabs for "smallish
servings" (excepting the $10 lunch buffet), the "main hurdle" is ser-
vice via "friendly amateurs."

Bon Chon Chicken *Chicken*   20 | 11 | 13 | $19

NEW **E 50s** | 957 Second Ave. (51st St.) | 212-308-8810 ●
E Village | 9 St. Marks Pl. (bet. 2nd & 3rd Aves.) | 212-228-2887 ●
Financial District | 104 John St. (Cliff St.) | 646-682-7747
Garment District | 207 W. 38th St. (bet. 7th & 8th Aves.) | 212-221-3339 ●
Murray Hill | 325 Fifth Ave. (bet. 32nd & 33rd Sts.) | 212-686-8282 ●
Bayside | 45-37B Bell Blvd. (bet. 45th Dr. & 45th Rd.) | Queens |
718-225-1010
www.bonchon.com

This chain's "delectably crispy", "crazy-good" Korean-style fried
chicken "gives Southern-fried a run for its money"; the cooked-to-
order goods are "cheap" and "addictive" enough for the hungry hordes
to endure "killer waits", "diner"-style setups and "haphazard"
service – though insiders "call ahead" and "take it home."

Bond 45 *Italian*   20 | 18 | 20 | $53

W 40s | 154 W. 45th St. (bet. 6th & 7th Aves.) | 212-869-4545 |
www.bond45.com

Set in Times Square's former Bond clothing store, Shelly Fireman's
"brassy" Italian operates on a "grand scale" with its "vast menu" (try the
"enticing antipasti") served in "cavernous" digs so "spirited" it gets "ear-
piercing"; "time-sensitive" staffers make it "a safe bet" for showgoers.

Bond Street ● *Japanese*   25 | 22 | 21 | $65

NoHo | 6 Bond St. (bet. B'way & Lafayette St.) | 212-777-2500 |
www.bondstrestaurant.com

It's an "eye-candy wonderland" at this "sexy" NoHo Japanese, where
"supermodels" and "the glitterati" nibble on "far-out", "revelatory"
sushi in the "chic", "dark" downstairs lounge or the "quieter upstairs";
even the servers are "good-looking", so though it's "a splurge", you'll
"feel like one of the cool kids."

Boqueria *Spanish*   22 | 19 | 19 | $45

Flatiron | 53 W. 19th St. (bet. 5th & 6th Aves.) | 212-255-4160
SoHo | 171 Spring St. (bet. Thompson St. & W. B'way) | 212-343-4255 ●
www.boquerianyc.com

"Takes you back to Barcelona" say surveyors of this "high-energy"
Flatiron-SoHo duo turning out "stellar", "rather pricey" tapas; "no

rez" makes it "impossible to get in without a wait" and it's "cheek-by-jowl" when you do, but the Spanish wines help "soften the experience."

Bottega del Vino *Italian*

E 50s | 7 E. 59th St. (bet. 5th & Madison Aves.) | 212-223-2724 | www.bottegadelvinonyc.com

"Italian visitors" help make it "feel like Europe" at this "busy" Midtown Verona outpost where "attentive" waiters serve "good-all-around" eats matched by an "endless wine list"; granted, it's "costly", but being "an easy shot" from Bergdorf's and the Apple Store, "what do you expect?"

Bottino *Italian*

19 18 18 $47

Chelsea | 246 10th Ave. (bet. 24th & 25th Sts.) | 212-206-6766 | www.bottinonyc.com

It's "big with the art-gallery crowd", so "wear black" if you want to blend in at this "buzzy" West Chelsea Italian dispensing "simple", "tasty" Tuscan fare; "spotty service" comes with the "laid-back" vibe, while the "delightful garden" provides a "real escape."

Bouchon Bakery *American/French*

24 15 18 $28

NEW **W 40s** | 1 Rockefeller Plaza (48th St., bet. 5th & 6th Aves.) | 212-782-3890

W 60s | Time Warner Ctr. | 10 Columbus Circle, 3rd fl. (60th St. at B'way) | 212-823-9366
www.bouchonbakery.com

"Thomas Keller meets food court" at this "tempting" TWC cafe/patisserie, where "quick stops for refueling" are rewarded with "scrumptious light fare" and "eye-popping pastries"; "zilch" decor and "hustle-bustle" are easily eclipsed by "breathtaking bird's-eye views" over Columbus Circle; P.S. the new Rock Center sib is mainly takeout.

☑ Bouley ● *French*

28 27 27 $104

TriBeCa | 163 Duane St. (bet. Greenwich & Hudson Sts.) | 212-964-2525 | www.davidbouley.com

"Sublime from start to finish", David Bouley's "stunning" TriBeCa mother ship conjures "magic" with "nuanced", "flawless" French cuisine, a "glorious" setting and pro service that "borders on mind-reading"; it all makes for an "unforgettable" experience that's "worth" the steep cost - though the "greatest gift to Gotham gourmets" is its "leisurely" $55 five-course prix fixe lunch.

NEW Boulud Sud ● *Mediterranean*

W 60s | 20 W. 64th St. (bet. B'way & CPW) | 212-595-1313 | www.danielnyc.com

Daniel Boulud completes a triple play across from Lincoln Center with this "welcome" Med arrival around the corner from Bar Boulud and his new Epicerie Boulud; the "pricey" menu features small plates and a handful of mains that roam from the South of France and Spain to Turkey and North Africa, while the "airy", "gracious" space is enlivened by an open kitchen and a front bar/lounge.

Bourbon Street Café *Cajun/Southern*

18 17 18 $33

Bayside | 40-12 Bell Blvd. (bet. 40th & 41st Aves.) | Queens | 718-224-2200 | www.bourbonstreetny.com

"It's always Mardi Gras" at Bayside's "lively" Cajun, where you can "getcha gumbo", "share a po' boy" or dig into other Southern-accented, "bargain"-priced "grub"; lots of "action at the bar" and "massive TVs" for "watching the game" add up to a "noisy", "fun" "night out."

Bourgeois Pig ◐ *French*

20 | 24 | 20 | $37

E Village | 111 E. Seventh St. (bet. Ave. A & 1st Ave.) | 212-475-2246
"Dark, sultry and romantic", this East Village French wine bar plies "scrumptious" fondues and small plates plus "excellent", "affordable" wines and cocktails; what with "enticing", "red-walled" Victorian decor and "flea market" couches "perfect for nuzzling", it's great "for a date."

Braai *South African*

20 | 18 | 18 | $45

W 50s | 329 W. 51st St. (bet. 8th & 9th Aves.) | 212-315-3315 | www.braainyc.com
A "world of new flavors" awaits at this "unusual" South African "barbecue bistro" in Hell's Kitchen, where ostrich, venison and "less-exotic" specialties come with "interesting sauces" via "helpful servers"; the "charming", "on-safari" setting helps make it a sure shot pre-theater.

Brasserie *French*

21 | 21 | 21 | $54

E 50s | Seagram Bldg. | 100 E. 53rd St. (bet. Lexington & Park Aves.) | 212-751-4840 | www.patinagroup.com
"Power suits galore" pervade this "sleek" Midtown "dealmaker's paradise" whose three-meal-a-day French brasserie "classics" show "enough flair to keep it interesting"; "friendly servers" help you "rack up a big bill" from breakfast till late, while "scenesters" kick up an "incredible din" in the "fashionable bar."

Brasserie Cognac ◐ *French*

19 | 19 | 19 | $50

W 50s | 1740 Broadway (55th St.) | 212-757-3600 | www.cognacrestaurant.com
All "dark wood and mirrors", this "charming" Midtown "Francophile haunt" doles out "dependable" brasserie eats and wines in "comfortable" digs just "steps from" Carnegie Hall and City Center; sidewalk seating "is a plus", as is the adjacent boulangerie.

Brasserie 8½ *French*

21 | 23 | 22 | $59

W 50s | 9 W. 57th St. (bet. 5th & 6th Aves.) | 212-829-0812 | www.patinagroup.com
After making a "movie-star" entrance via the "sweeping staircase", patrons of this "stunning", "underground" Midtown French brasserie are "pampered" in a "hushed" room – while livelier sorts join the "bar scene"; it's "expensive", but the $25 prix fixe lunch is a "deal."

Brasserie Ruhlmann *French*

20 | 21 | 19 | $54

W 50s | 45 Rockefeller Plaza (enter on 50th St., bet. 5th & 6th Aves.) | 212-974-2020 | www.brasserieruhlmann.com
"Dine in art deco splendor" or "watch the world go by" from the patio while savoring Laurent Tourondel's "classic" French brasserie fare at this Rock Center standout; steep tariffs make it an "expense-account citadel" for area "business-lunchers."

NEW Bread & Tulips ⧄ *Italian*

- | - | - | M

Murray Hill | Hotel Giraffe | 365 Park Ave. S. (26th St.) | 212-532-9100 | www.breadandtulipsnyc.com
Rustic greenery and elegant lighting lend a terrarium-chic vibe at this subterranean Italian arrival in the Hotel Giraffe; its affordable small

plates and mains are heavy on the greenmarket ingredients, and there are also pizzas fired in an oven imported from Italy.

Bread Tribeca *Italian* 21 | 15 | 17 | $34
TriBeCa | 301 Church St. (Walker St.) | 212-334-8282 | www.breadtribeca.com
Bread ● *Sandwiches*
NoLita | 20 Spring St. (bet. Elizabeth & Mott Sts.) | 212-334-1015 | www.orderbreadsoho.com
"Terrific" panini, "tomato soup from heaven" and all-around "solid Italian cuisine" mean these "laid-back" NoLita-TriBeCa vets continue "keepin' it real" for their "good-looking" clientele; "service is dicey" and the settings "dull", but "low tabs" and "hip" atmosphere trump all.

Breeze *French/Thai* 20 | 14 | 19 | $32
W 40s | 661 Ninth Ave. (bet. 45th & 46th Sts.) | 212-262-7777 | www.breezenyc.com
It "looks like a diner" done up in "bright colors" but this "sliver" of a Hell's Kitchener actually turns out "sophisticated" Thai-French fusion cuisine, and "fast" enough to make it "fine for pre-theater"; "pretty" tropical drinks and almost "alarmingly low" prices "add to the appeal."

Brennan & Carr ●⇕ *Sandwiches* 22 | 10 | 17 | $19
Sheepshead Bay | 3432 Nostrand Ave. (Ave. U) | Brooklyn | 718-646-9559
"Unchanged" through the decades, this Sheepshead Bay standby keeps turning out its "famous" specialty: "drippy, messy, delicious" "double-dipped roast beef sandwiches"; "hokey decor" and "spotty service" don't dent its "neighborhood staple" status for those "nostalgic" for "classic Brooklyn."

☑ Breslin, The ● *British* 22 | 21 | 18 | $51
Chelsea | Ace Hotel | 16 W. 29th St. (bet. B'way & 5th Ave.) | 212-679-1939 | www.thebreslin.com
Set in Chelsea's "hot" Ace Hotel (aka "hipster-ville"), this "way-cool" destination from Ken Friedman and April Bloomfield dispenses a "carnivorous feast" of "high-priced" "nouveau Brit grub" in "dark, oaky" "publike" digs; "distracted servers", "noise" and no-rez-induced "hellish waits" aside, you'll likely "waddle away" raving "smashing, guv'nor"; P.S. order the "whole roast pig" for a "sublime" chef's table party.

Brgr *Burgers* 19 | 12 | 14 | $16
Chelsea | 287 Seventh Ave. (bet. 26th & 27th Sts.) | 212-488-7500
E 60s | 1026 Third Ave. (bet. 60th & 61st Sts.) | 212-588-0080
www.brgr.us
"Darn good", "organic" beef, turkey or veggie burgers are made "custom" with "tasty toppings" at this "cafeteria-style" duo also dispensing "delicious" shakes; the "smpl decor" is ok, but some balk at "slow service" and prices kinda "high" for patties that are "a few letters short of great."

Bricco *Italian* 20 | 18 | 21 | $48
W 50s | 304 W. 56th St. (bet. 8th & 9th Aves.) | 212-245-7160 | www.bricconyc.com
Those who "love pasta or pizza" pre–Carnegie Hall find "reliably good" renditions at this "comfy" Hell's Kitchen Italian; a wood-burning oven

adds to the "welcoming" vibe in digs where "lipstick-laden kisses on the ceiling" attest to just how "enjoyable" it is.

Brick Cafe *French/Italian*

22 | 21 | 20 | $31

Astoria | 30-95 33rd St. (31st Ave.) | Queens | 718-267-2735 | www.brickcafe.com

"Are we really in Astoria?" marvel first-timers to this "quaint" "European"-style cafe serving inexpensive French-Italian fare; a "sweet staff" oversees the scene, and though it's "a tight squeeze" within, the "crowd spills" out to "sidewalk seating" when it's warm.

Brick Lane Curry House *Indian*

22 | 14 | 17 | $30

E 50s | 235 E. 53rd St. (bet. 2nd & 3rd Aves.) | 212-339-8353 | www.bricklanetoo.com

E Village | 306-308 E. Sixth St. (bet. 1st & 2nd Aves.) | 212-979-2900 | www.bricklanecurryhouse.com

"Delicious" "British-Indian" curries "span the spice-o-meter" from "mild" to the "scorchingly hot" "double-dare-you" phaal at this East Side duo; the Midtowner's a "hole-in-the-wall" with "one long table", while the East Village original's a touch "nicer than the usual Sixth Street" suspects.

Bridge Cafe *American*

21 | 20 | 21 | $48

Financial District | 279 Water St. (Dover St.) | 212-227-3344 | www.bridgecafenyc.com

A "treasure" in the "shadow of the Brooklyn Bridge", this "charming" 1794 tavern eatery offers "satisfying" American fare, "warm service" and an ample "sense of history" ("you can't manufacture this ambiance"); a "stellar bar" and "terrific brunch" are other endearments.

Brio *Italian*

19 | 16 | 18 | $45

E 60s | 137 E. 61st St. (Lexington Ave.) | 212-980-2300

NEW **Flatiron** | 920 Broadway (21st St.) | 212-673-2121

www.brionyc.com

"Personal pizzas" and other "simple" Italian staples "a stone's throw" from Bloomie's make this "busy" Midtown vet a go-to for "refueling shoppers"; midrange rates and "lovely outside seating" balance so-so service and decor; the jury's still out on the "quiet" new Flatiron offshoot.

Brioso *Italian*

23 | 18 | 21 | $50

New Dorp | 174 New Dorp Ln. (9th St.) | Staten Island | 718-667-1700 | www.briosoristorante.com

"One of the best" on SI, this New Dorp "treat" turns out "wonderful", "homestyle" Italian fare and "specials in a league of their own"; "groups of friends looking for a good time" keep the "rustic" room "loud" at prime times, but it's so much "fun", "you hardly notice."

Brooklyn Diner USA *◑ Diner*

18 | 15 | 17 | $34

W 40s | 155 W. 43rd St. (bet. B'way & 6th Ave.) | 212-265-5400

W 50s | 212 W. 57th St. (bet. B'way & 7th Ave.) | 212-977-2280

www.brooklyndiner.com

A "plethora of tourists" and theatergoers tuck into "finer diner" grub at Shelly Fireman's "retro"-style Midtown duo dishing up "old-fashioned" American faves all day; "outlandish portions" appease those who "flinch at the prices", because a "large doggy bag" makes it a "bargain."

	FOOD	DECOR	SERVICE	COST

☑ Brooklyn Fare Kitchen ⌧ Ⓜ *French* `29` `19` `25` `$241`
Downtown Bklyn | 200 Schermerhorn St. (Hoyt St.) | Brooklyn | 718-243-0050 | www.brooklynfare.com

In an unlikely location – the glassed-in kitchen of a Downtown Brooklyn gourmet grocery – this "holy grail for foodies" features "fast-paced", 18- to 20-course prix fixe "feasts" comprising "daring", "exquisite" Japanese-inflected French small plates made by "genius" chef Cesar Ramirez; it's "on the silly end of expensive", with seating limited to 18 stools at a stainless-steel prep counter, but "good luck getting a rez."

Brooklyn Fish Camp ⌧ *Seafood* `23` `15` `19` `$40`
Park Slope | 162 Fifth Ave (bet. Degraw & Douglass Sts.) | Brooklyn | 718-783-3264 | www.brooklynfishcamp.com

"Super-fresh" fish and a "premier lobster roll" are the lures at this "casual" Park Slope spawn of Mary's Fish Camp; "noisy" and "crowded", in summer it's "peaceful" if you "score a garden table", leaving only "Manhattan prices" to "feel crabby" about.

Brooklyn Star ● *Southern* ▽ `25` `22` `23` `$31`
Williamsburg | 593 Lorimer St. (Conselyea St.) | Brooklyn | 718-599-9899 | www.thebrooklynstar.com

Risen again after a fire and now in a slightly "larger" space, this Williamsburg Southerner ("by way of Texas") is once again "rife with hipsters" hunting "delicious", "off-the-beaten-path" specimens like "fried pig tails", or kicking back with "down-home" staples; cocktails and carefully curated tap beers round out the "priced-right" package.

Brother Jimmy's BBQ *BBQ* `17` `12` `15` `$28`
E 70s | 1485 Second Ave. (bet. 77th & 78th Sts.) | 212-288-0999
E 90s | 1644 Third Ave. (92nd St.) | 212-426-2020
Garment District | 416 Eighth Ave. (31st St.) | 212-967-7603
Gramercy | 116 E. 16th St. (bet. Irving Pl. & Union Sq. E.) | 212-673-6465
Murray Hill | 181 Lexington Ave. (31st St.) | 212-779-7427 ●
W 80s | 428 Amsterdam Ave. (bet. 80th & 81st Sts.) | 212-501-7515 ●
www.brotherjimmys.com

"Belly-busting BBQ", "deep-fried cheap eats", "giant fishbowl drinks" and "the game" on TV is the "formula" that draws "youthful" "mobs" to these pseudo-Southern "dives"; "*Texas Chainsaw* decor", an "invisible" staff and a "frat-tastic" vibe lead gentler souls to go "takeout."

☑ NEW Brushstroke ⌧ *Japanese* ▽ `28` `27` `27` `$150`
TriBeCa | 30 Hudson St. (Duane St.) | 212-791-3771 | www.davidbouley.com

David Bouley's long-awaited "melding of minds with Osaka's Tsuji Culinary Institute", this TriBeCa arrival showcases near-"flawless" modern Japanese kaiseki cookery, "pure art" rendered by chefs in an open kitchen that forms the centerpiece of the "beautifully designed", "all-wood" room; its seasonal prix fixe–only menus start at $85 per person, but it's possible to order à la carte in the lounge; P.S. try for a seat at the bar by the kitchen.

Bryant Park Grill/Cafe *American* `18` `22` `19` `$49`
W 40s | behind NY Public Library | 25 W. 40th St. (bet. 5th & 6th Aves.) | 212-840-6500 | www.arkrestaurants.com

A "picturesque" Bryant Park "oasis", this two-in-one American draws "out-of-towners" and others who "forgive" its "forgettable food" and "iffy" service given the "gorgeous setting"; the "refined" Grill is a "business lunch" fallback and the Cafe offers "delightful" "open-air" repasts, but prices aren't cheap at either.

B. Smith's Restaurant Row *Southern* | 19 | 18 | 20 | $48 |

W 40s | 320 W. 46th St. (bet. 8th & 9th Aves.) | 212-315-1100 | www.bsmith.com

It's easy to B. "full and happy" given the "sophisticated" spins on soul cooking and "Southern-style hospitality" at this "classy" Restaurant Row "stalwart" owned by the eponymous TV personality; the "convenient location" means it's especially popular pre-theater.

Bubby's *American* | 20 | 16 | 17 | $33 |

TriBeCa | 120 Hudson St. (N. Moore St.) | 212-219-0666
Dumbo | 1 Main St. (bet. Plymouth & Water Sts.) | Brooklyn | 718-222-0666 ⊟
www.bubbys.com

"Stick-to-your-ribs" breakfast "at all hours" is "the star" at this "step-up-from-a-diner" American "comfort" duo in TriBeCa and Dumbo; the "hearty" weekend brunch is "legendary", but it "tests patience" with "long lines", "uneven" service, "kiddie mayhem" and "oy vey" noise levels.

⊠ Buddakan ◑ *Asian* | 24 | 27 | 22 | $66 |

Chelsea | 75 Ninth Ave. (bet. 15th & 16th Sts.) | 212-989-6699 | www.buddakannyc.com

Stephen Starr's "ultrachic" Chelsea "palace" "delights" its "glamorous" patrons, blending a "spectacular", "sprawling" space with "memorable", "pricey" Asian cuisine and "hip music"; despite the "caring" service, some find it too "circus"-y and "tilted toward the young" – which is just what keeps it "packed."

Buenos Aires ◑ *Argentinean/Steak* | 23 | 15 | 20 | $46 |

E Village | 513 E. Sixth St. (bet. Aves. A & B) | 212-228-2775 | www.buenosairesnyc.com

"Awesome steaks" bathed in "chimichurri sauce" and accompanied by "rivers of Malbec" make for a "meat lover's" dream at this "small, no-frills" Argentine beefery in the East Village; it's a "deal" too, but growing "popularity" makes it "hard to get a table" at prime times.

Bukhara Grill *Indian* | 22 | 16 | 19 | $41 |

E 40s | 217 E. 49th St. (bet. 2nd & 3rd Aves.) | 212-888-2839 | www.bukharany.com

The "authentically spiced", "upscale" North Indian cuisine is "served with pride" at this multilevel U.N.-area eatery; most easily "get over" the slightly "threadbare" decor, and those who find the menu's prices a tad "expensive" tout the "excellent" $17 lunch buffet.

Bull & Bear *Steak* | 21 | 22 | 21 | $71 |

E 40s | Waldorf-Astoria | 301 Park Ave. (enter on Lexington Ave. & 49th St.) | 212-872-1275 | www.bullandbearsteakhouse.com

Brimming with "classic old-New York" "elegance", this "gorgeous" circa-1960 steakhouse in the Waldorf-Astoria plies "standout" fare and "stout drinks" to the "banker-lawyer set" by way of "ultra-attentive" servers; "bull"-ish tariffs are a given, but it's fun "hobnobbing" at the bar.

	FOOD	DECOR	SERVICE	COST

Burger Heaven *Burgers*　　　17 | 11 | 16 | $20

E 40s | 20 E. 49th St. (bet. 5th & Madison Aves.) | 212-755-2166
E 40s | 291 Madison Ave. (41st St.) | 212-685-6250
E 50s | 9 E. 53rd St. (bet. 5th & Madison Aves.) | 212-752-0340
E 60s | 804 Lexington Ave. (62nd St.) | 212-838-3580
www.burgerheaven.com

These "affordable, easygoing" Eastsiders dispense "decent" burgers via "efficient, if less-than-charming" staffers; the "coffee-shop" decor has "no personality", and overall expect "nothing heavenly", but loyalists lean on them "like a reliable old shoe."

Z Burger Joint at　　　24 | 11 | 13 | $17
Le Parker Meridien ●⊄ *Burgers*

W 50s | Le Parker Meridien | 119 W. 56th St. (bet. 6th & 7th Aves.) | 212-708-7414 | www.parkermeridien.com

"Lines out the door" give away the "hidden entrance" to this "intentionally divey" burger mecca "behind the velvet curtain" in the Parker Meridien's "posh" lobby; though the "juicy" patties are "among the best in town", obstacles include "rude" service and "nightmares" trying to "score a table."

Butter 𝌍 *American*　　　22 | 23 | 20 | $64

E Village | 415 Lafayette St. (bet. Astor Pl. & 4th St.) | 212-253-2828 | www.butterrestaurant.com

"Woodsy-chic" is the mood at this East Village New American showcase for chef Alex Guarnaschelli's "intriguing", "seriously good food"; it's "serene" upstairs but a "scene" in the "dark", "sexy", "loungelike" space below, with a sprinkling of "celebs" adding cachet – no surprise, there's a "high price tag."

Buttermilk Channel *American*　　　24 | 21 | 22 | $42

Carroll Gardens | 524 Court St. (Huntington St.) | Brooklyn | 718-852-8490 | www.buttermilkchannelnyc.com

"Delectable", "rock-solid" "remakes of classic" New American dishes and a "fab" brunch keep this "down-home-but-classy" Carroll Gardens "storefront" a "hip-yet-family-friendly" "hot spot"; add "stylish" (if "squished") digs staffed by "nice people", and the only "pain" is "no rez", causing waits that are "a drag."

NEW Buvette ● *French*　　　24 | 22 | 22 | $48

W Village | 42 Grove St. (bet. Bedford & Bleecker Sts.) | 212-255-3590 | www.ilovebuvette.com

Chef Jody Williams (ex Gottino, Morandi) "does it again, with a French accent" at this "outstanding" new West Village 'gastroteque' supplying "wonderful" small plates plus "interesting" wines; the only "kink" is "harried" service when the "cute" little room gets "crowded."

BXL Café ● *Belgian*　　　18 | 14 | 18 | $33

W 40s | 125 W. 43rd St. (bet. B'way & 6th Ave.) | 212-768-0200
BXL East ● *Belgian*

E 50s | 210 E. 51st St. (bet. 2nd & 3rd Aves.) | 212-888-7782 | www.bxlcafe.com

"Marvelous" moules frites "rule" the menu of "Belgian classics" at these "jam-packed" Midtown "pubs" pouring "superior" suds; "sports on TV" help put the "'din' in dinner", but tabs are "cheap"

	FOOD	DECOR	SERVICE	COST

and "you can't beat" the "all-you-can-eat mussel feasts" on Sunday and Monday nights.

Cabana *Nuevo Latino* | 21 | 18 | 18 | $39 |

E 60s | 1022 Third Ave. (bet. 60th & 61st Sts.) | 212-980-5678 ◐
Seaport | Pier 17 | 89 South St. (Fulton St.) | 212-406-1155
Forest Hills | 107-10 70th Rd. (bet. Austin St. & Queens Blvd.) | Queens | 718-263-3600
www.cabanarestaurant.com

"Just the right amount of caliente" animates both the "tasty" cuisine and "lively" scene at this "hopping" Nuevo Latino trio; "service could be better", but "everyone's having a good time" – especially with the bonus of an "amazing" water view at the Seaport branch.

Cacio e Pepe *Italian* | 21 | 16 | 19 | $42 |

E Village | 182 Second Ave. (bet. 11th & 12th Sts.) | 212-505-5931 | www.cacioepepe.com

The atmosphere is "mellow" at this "rustic" little Italian "refuge" in the East Village whose "limited" roster of "solid", "affordable" Roman cooking is highlighted by the "sight-to-see" "namesake pasta dish" tossed tableside in a wheel of "goopy pecorino"; a "sweet" garden seals the deal.

Cacio e Vino ◐ *Italian* | 21 | 16 | 20 | $41 |

E Village | 80 Second Ave. (bet. 4th & 5th Sts.) | 212-228-3269 | www.cacioevino.com

"Small tables, big plates and medium-size bills" suit most at this "no-hype" East Village Italian; among its "honest Sicilian" specialties are "fabulous thin-crust pizzas" from a wood-burning oven – which, along with "friendly" service, warms an otherwise "no-frills" space.

Cafe Asean ⊅ *SE Asian* | 22 | 15 | 20 | $30 |

W Village | 117 W. 10th St. (bet. Greenwich & 6th Aves.) | 212-633-0348 | www.cafeasean.com

For "cheap eats" of the "tasty" Southeast Asian variety, Villagers tout this "mellow" "favorite" near the Jefferson Market Library; it's "cash only" and "postage stamp"–size, but service is "sweet", the mood "happy" and a "pretty" garden eases the crush.

⧉ Café Boulud *French* | 27 | 24 | 26 | $81 |

E 70s | Surrey Hotel | 20 E. 76th St. (bet. 5th & Madison Aves.) | 212-772-2600 | www.danielnyc.com

UES "socialites" and "old-money" types collect at Daniel Boulud's "grown-up" standby where "everything's fab", from the "deluxe" French fare "expertly prepared" by chef Gavin Kaysen to the "pampering" service and "swank" setting; you'll "shell out" for such "luxury", but the "heavenly" $35 lunch prix fixe is a "bargain"; P.S. "go early and enjoy a drink" in the adjacent Bar Pleiades.

Cafe Centro ⊠ *Mediterranean* | 21 | 19 | 21 | $49 |

E 40s | MetLife Bldg. | 200 Park Ave. (45th St.) | 212-818-1222 | www.patinagroup.com

"Perfect for a biz lunch", this "congenial" contender near Grand Central serves "surprisingly good" Med fare in a spacious setting that's "jumping" midday but "calmer" come evening; "prompt" service, a "terrific" $37 dinner prix fixe and "lovely" outdoor seating are other pluses.

| | FOOD | DECOR | SERVICE | COST |

Cafe Cluny ❶ *American/French* | 20 | 19 | 19 | $50 |

W Village | 284 W. 12th St. (4th St.) | 212-255-6900 | www.cafecluny.com
"Comfy", "chichi" and "Page Six"-oriented all at once, this "vibrant" West Village Franco-American bistro dispenses "delightful" food to a "cosmopolitan" clientele via a "responsive" staff; its "cute" digs can be a "squeeze", and generally you have to "wait" for the "delicious brunch", but it's "always fun."

Café d'Alsace ❶ *French* | 21 | 17 | 18 | $48 |

E 80s | 1695 Second Ave. (88th St.) | 212-722-5133 | www.cafedalsace.com
Yorkville's "replication" of a "Strasbourg brasserie" packs 'em in for "robust" Alsace classics backed by a "knockout" brew list (guided by a "beer sommelier"); the "happy vibe" spells "high decibels", but it's a "much needed" area staple – and the "sidewalk cafe" is quieter.

Café du Soleil *French/Mediterranean* | 19 | 17 | 17 | $40 |

W 100s | 2723 Broadway (104th St.) | 212-316-5000 | www.cafedusoleilny.com
A vaguely "Left Bank feel" and French-Med bistro standards highlight this "cheerful" "UWS-Columbia standby"; service is "nonchalant" at best, but "bargain" rates compensate, and "there's always takeout" for those who find "packed and noisy" problematic.

Cafe Español ❶ *Spanish* | 20 | 15 | 19 | $38 |

G Village | 172 Bleecker St. (bet. MacDougal & Sullivan Sts.) | 212-505-0657
W Village | 78 Carmine St. (bet. Bedford St. & 7th Ave. S.) | 212-675-3312
www.cafeespanol.com
"You get your money's worth" at these separately owned Village "landmarks" dishing up "well-done Spanish classics" in "abundant" supply; "old-fashioned" with "old-time service" to match, they're so "crowded" there's "barely room for decor" – but "oh, that sangria!"

Café Evergreen *Chinese* | 18 | 12 | 18 | $34 |

E 60s | 1288 First Ave. (bet. 69th & 70th Sts.) | 212-744-3266 | www.cafeevergreenchinese.com
Upper Eastsiders who "don't want to schlep to Chinatown" depend on this "reliable" vet for "terrific" dim sum and other "quality" Chinese classics dished up by "pleasant" servers; if "frozen-in-the-'80s" digs don't suit, "speedy delivery" lets you munch at home.

Café Fiorello ❶ *Italian* | 20 | 18 | 19 | $52 |

W 60s | 1900 Broadway (bet. 63rd & 64th Sts.) | 212-595-5330 | www.cafefiorello.com
A "convenient", if "costly", "curtain-raiser" pre-Lincoln Center, this "fast-paced" Italian "perennial" proffers "fabulous thin-crust pizzas" and other "savory" selections led by a "fantastico" antipasto bar; to avoid "crazy-crowded" conditions and "harried" service, go "post-performance" and "sit outside" for prime "people-watching."

Café Frida *Mexican* | 19 | 16 | 18 | $39 |

W 70s | 368 Columbus Ave. (bet. 77th & 78th Sts.) | 212-712-2929
W 90s | 768 Amsterdam Ave (bet. 97th & 98th Sts.) | 212-749-2929
www.cafefrida.com
"Straightforward", "satisfying" *comida*, "fair prices" and "serious margaritas" make these "popular" UWS Mexicans a "decent bet" for "lively,

satisfying" repasts; the West 70s original hosts a "hopping bar scene", while the "delightful" garden makes the West 90s outpost feel "special."

Cafe Gitane ● *French/Moroccan* | 20 | 19 | 16 | $32 |

NoLita | 242 Mott St. (Prince St.) | 212-334-9552 ✂
W Village | Jane Hotel | 113 Jane St. (bet. Washington & West Sts.) | 212-255-4113

The "good-looking" collect at these "cool" French-Moroccans whose "delicious" couscous, merguez and such come "cheap" but with "an extra helping of attitude"; the "tiny, cramped" NoLita original offers prime Mott Street "people-watching", while the Jane Hotel outpost is just as "happening" but "more comfortable."

Café Habana ● *Cuban/Mexican* | 22 | 15 | 15 | $23 |

NoLita | 17 Prince St. (Elizabeth St.) | 212-625-2001 | www.cafehabana.com
Habana Outpost ●✂ *Cuban/Mexican*
Fort Greene | 755-757 Fulton St. (S. Portland Ave.) | Brooklyn | 718-858-9500 | www.ecoeatery.com

If you "survive the line of hungry hipsters" you're in for some "huge" Mexican-Cuban flavors on the "cheap" at this "funky, fun" NoLita stalwart famed for "life-changing" grilled corn; the Fort Greene outpost's "feel-good, eco-friendly" ethos and "stellar patio" make it a "summer hot spot."

Café Henri ● *French* | 20 | 16 | 18 | $26 |

W Village | 27 Bedford St. (Downing St.) | 212-243-2846
LIC | 10-10 50th Ave. (bet. Jackson Ave. & Vernon Blvd.) | Queens | 718-383-9315

An "authentic French vibe" permeates this "pint-size" LIC–West Village duo, where "huge cups of café au lait" and "showstopper crêpes" start the day, and "informal meals" are on tap till midnight; "low prices" and "unpretentious" service outweigh "cramped" digs.

Cafe Joul ● *French* | 19 | 13 | 18 | $45 |

E 50s | 1070 First Ave. (bet. 58th & 59th Sts.) | 212-759-3131

A "welcome presence" in Sutton Place, this "sweet" bistro "has staying power" thanks to its "quality" French "basics" and location in a zone "lacking in good casual restaurants"; "pleasant" service warms "drab" decor, while relatively "reasonable" rates assure return visits.

Café Katja ● *Austrian* | 24 | 17 | 24 | $37 |

LES | 79 Orchard St. (bet. Broome & Grand Sts.) | 212-219-9545 | www.cafe-katja.com

When a "spaetzle jones" hits, this "out-of-the-way" LES Austrian provides "fabulous" fixes in "portions almost bigger" than its "tiny" space; equally *wunderbar* are "fantastic, friendly" staffers, "large steins" of "amazing beer" and "great prices."

NEW Café Kristall ● *Austrian* | ▽ 23 | 22 | 23 | $42 |

SoHo | Swarovski | 70 Mercer St. (bet. Broome & Spring Sts.) | 212-274-1500 | www.kg-ny.com

White, "ultramodern" and "sparkling" all over, this "gem" in the back of SoHo's Swarovski Crystallized Boutique features a "chic" cafe and lounge made for ladies who shop and work up an appetite; chef Kurt Gutenbrunner is behind the "wonderful" Austrian dishes and "delicious pastries."

| | FOOD | DECOR | SERVICE | COST |

Cafe Lalo ●⊄ *Coffeehouse/Dessert*   19 | 19 | 15 | $25

W 80s | 201 W. 83rd St. (bet. Amsterdam Ave. & B'way) | 212-496-6031 |
www.cafelalo.com

Still riding on its *You've Got Mail* fame, this "cute", "cash-only" UWS
vet vends an "astonishing roster" of "sinful desserts", plus light savor-
ies; it can be a "madhouse" with "loud music", "scrunched-together"
tables and barely "adequate" service, but the "throngs" keep coming.

Cafe Loup ● *French*   20 | 18 | 20 | $44

W Village | 105 W. 13th St. (bet. 6th Ave. & 7th Ave. S.) | 212-255-4746 |
www.cafeloupnyc.com

"Soul-warming" French bistro classics, "personable" service and "ok
prices" – not to mention "good Sunday jazz" – keep West Villagers
counting on this longtime "neighborhood favorite"; the "quaint" decor's
"a bit worn", but "loyal patrons" liken it to a "comfortable old sweater."

Cafe Luluc ⊄ *French*   20 | 16 | 18 | $31

Cobble Hill | 214 Smith St. (Baltic St.) | Brooklyn | 718-625-3815

A "Cobble Hill favorite", this cash-only "Paris-in-Brooklyn" bistro is
beloved for its "terrific brunch" starring "pillows-of-wonderfulness"
pancakes; "cheerful" servers man its "classic" quarters boasting a
"lovely garden", and best of all it "won't dent your wallet."

Cafe Luxembourg *French*   21 | 19 | 20 | $54

W 70s | 200 W. 70th St. (bet. Amsterdam & West End Aves.) |
212-873-7411 | www.cafeluxembourg.com

"Fashionable and arty" types mix with "media" people and the occasional "celeb" at this perennially "buzzy" French stalwart near Lincoln
Center; thanks to the "wonderful" bistro eats and cream-colored digs
aglow in "glam lighting", "everyone's here" – naturally it can be
"elbow-to-elbow" and "noisy."

Cafe Mogador ● *Moroccan*   22 | 16 | 19 | $29

E Village | 101 St. Marks Pl. (bet. Ave. A & 1st Ave.) | 212-677-2226 |
www.cafemogador.com

"Crazy-good" Moroccan staples get "a big thumbs-up" at this "offbeat" East Village vet whose "cavelike" digs are done up with "vintage
flair"; being "cheap" and "open late" help make it a "hot spot" – "odds
are you'll wait for a table", but it's "worth it"; P.S. a Williamsburg outpost is in the works.

Cafe Ronda *Mediterranean/S American*   20 | 16 | 18 | $39

W 70s | 249-251 Columbus Ave. (bet. 71st & 72nd Sts.) | 212-579-9929 |
www.caferonda.com

"Terrific tapas" and "hard-to-find Argentinean dishes" share menu
space at this "easygoing" UWS Med–South American "mainstay";
sidewalk seating eases the "tight", "loud" crush, and a "cheerful" crew,
"reasonable" rates and "killer sangria" bolster the "happy" mood.

Café Sabarsky/Café Fledermaus *Austrian*   22 | 24 | 20 | $44

E 80s | Neue Galerie | 1048 Fifth Ave. (86th St.) | 212-288-0665 |
www.kg-ny.com

The "closest NYC" gets to a "classic Viennese" coffeehouse, Kurt
Gutenbrunner's "civilized" cafe in the Neue Galerie delivers "savory"
bites and "delectable pastries" ("*mit schlag, naturlich*") in a "gorgeous

room", or downstairs at the "less-posh" Fledermaus; the only rub is "schtiff prices" for "ladylike portions."

Café Select *Swiss*
▽ 19 | 16 | 16 | $36

SoHo | 212 Lafayette St. (bet. Broome & Spring Sts.) | 212-925-9322 | www.cafeselectnyc.com

"Genre-busting, tasty" Swiss cooking comes in "tiny, retro-chic" digs done up like a Euro rail-station cafe at this SoHo "hipster" hangout; it's priced for "value", and the answer for iffy service is to "people-watch" until they "get around to you."

Cafe Steinhof *Austrian*
19 | 16 | 19 | $28

Park Slope | 422 Seventh Ave. (14th St.) | Brooklyn | 718-369-7776 | www.cafesteinhof.com

"Austrian comfort food" comes "cheap" at this "kitschy" Park Slope "joint" – and on $6 "goulash Mondays" it's "practically free"; factor in the "solid" suds selection, "casual, kid-friendly" vibe and live music on Wednesdays, and it's "so homey you don't want to go home."

Cafeteria ● *American*
19 | 16 | 16 | $35

Chelsea | 119 Seventh Ave. (17th St.) | 212-414-1717 | www.cafeteriagroup.com

Long a lure for "nocturnal" snackers, this "raucous", 24/7 Chelsea "scene" dispenses "affordable", "updated" American "comfort food" via a "couldn't-care-less" crew; if it's "past its prime", it "still hums along" with a "loud", "lively" show "worth the price of admission" alone.

Cafe Un Deux Trois ● *French*
17 | 16 | 17 | $44

W 40s | 123 W. 44th St. (bet. B'way & 6th Ave.) | 212-354-4148 | www.cafeundeuxtrois.biz

"A little worn around the edges" it may be, but Times Square's "grande dame" of "pre-theater dining" is a still-"serviceable" source for French bistro eats in a sprawling, "pretend-Paris" milieu; the unimpressed yawn "un deux blah", but all can appreciate the "affordable" tabs.

Caffe Cielo *Italian*
21 | 17 | 21 | $43

W 50s | 881 Eighth Ave. (bet. 52nd & 53rd Sts.) | 212-246-9555 | www.caffecielonyc.com

Both a "quiet neighborhood" fallback and a "dependable" choice "pre- or après-theater", this West 50s stalwart slings "satisfying", "moderately priced" Italiana via an "efficient" team; the "homey" decor's "aging a bit", but a "warm" vibe compensates, as does the "not-to-miss" brunch.

Caffe e Vino *Italian*
▽ 24 | 18 | 23 | $38

Fort Greene | 112 DeKalb Ave. (bet. Ashland Pl. & St. Felix St.) | Brooklyn | 718-855-6222 | www.caffeevino.com

Given the "simple, excellent" Italian fare, you'd think "nonna's in the kitchen" at this "rustic" trattoria "right near BAM"; "hospitable", "cheerful" staffers keep the feel "warm" even when its "small" setting gets "jammed" "pre-theater."

Caffe Grazie *Italian*
20 | 18 | 21 | $50

E 80s | 26 E. 84th St. (bet. 5th & Madison Aves.) | 212-717-4407 | www.caffegrazie.com

"Familiar" Italian "favorites", "gracious" service and a "we're-all-friends" vibe make this UES "haunt" just the place "after visiting the

| | FOOD | DECOR | SERVICE | COST |

Met"; wallet-conscious diners "relaxing" in its "townhouse" setting say *"molto grazie"* for the $16 prix fixe lunch.

☑ Calexico *Mexican*
24 | **12** | **16** | **$17**

Carroll Gardens | 122 Union St. (bet. Columbia & Hicks Sts.) | Brooklyn | 718-488-8226 ⊘
NEW **Greenpoint** | 645 Manhattan Ave. (Bedford Ave.) | Brooklyn | 347-763-2129
www.calexicocart.com
Having "graduated from street cart to sit-down", these "tiny", no-frills West Carroll Gardens–Greenpoint "joints" nab "best Mexican in the city" honors with their tacos, burritos and tortas (try the "justly famous pulled-pork" filling); "in-a-jiffy" service and "complete-steal" prices seal the "super-laid-back" deal.

Calle Ocho *Nuevo Latino*
21 | **21** | **19** | **$47**

W 80s | Excelsior Hotel | 45 W. 81st St. (bet. Columbus Ave. & CPW) | 212-873-5025 | www.calleochonyc.com
"Still simpatico" since settling into "dramatic new Excelsior Hotel digs, this "brash, happening" UWS vet continues to supply "bold", "fantastic" Nuevo Latino fare paired with "sublime mojitos"; regulars are relieved that the "wild" "party" vibe and Sunday brunch's "unlimited sangria deal" made the move intact.

CamaJe ◐ *American/French*
22 | **15** | **22** | **$36**

G Village | 85 MacDougal St. (bet. Bleecker & Houston Sts.) | 212-673-8184 | www.camaje.com
Very "Village-y", this "cozy" French-American "nook" showcases chef Abigail Hitchcock's "tasty", "original" cooking at "excellent value" prices in a "funky", "thrift-shop" setting; "regular cooking classes" show how it's done, while "dark-dining" nights when you eat blindfolded are "highly entertaining."

Campagnola ◐ *Italian*
23 | **18** | **21** | **$72**

E 70s | 1382 First Ave. (bet. 73rd & 74th Sts.) | 212-861-1102
"Cougars", "beauties with their 'fathers'" and "loyal", "Mario Puzo"–worthy "regulars" rub shoulders at this "higher-end" Upper East Side Italian offering "outstanding" cooking plus a "stunning antipasto bar"; "it helps if they know you" and if you have a "broker to negotiate the bill", but the "celebrated" "people-watching" scene's "worth the money."

Canaletto *Italian*
20 | **16** | **22** | **$57**

E 60s | 208 E. 60th St. (bet. 2nd & 3rd Aves.) | 212-317-9192
A "find" in the "swank" zone "near Bloomie's", this "old-guard" Northern Italian combines "tried-and-true" cuisine with "observant" service and a room "quiet" enough for "conversation"; no surprise, it "attracts a slew of regulars" despite up-there prices.

Candle Cafe *Vegan/Vegetarian*
23 | **14** | **20** | **$33**

E 70s | 1307 Third Ave. (bet. 74th & 75th Sts.) | 212-472-0970 | www.candlecafe.com
This "wholesome, delicious" UES vegan is the "cheaper", "plainer older sis of Candle 79"; the "casual" setting's a little "shabby" with "sardine" seating (expect "a wait"), but to devotees its food is "uplifting" and "worth any inconvenience."

	FOOD	DECOR	SERVICE	COST

Candle 79 *Vegan/Vegetarian* — 24 | 20 | 23 | $48

E 70s | 154 E. 79th St. (bet. Lexington & 3rd Aves.) | 212-537-7179 |
www.candle79.com

"Nirvana" for "herbivores", this UES "upscale vegan" offers "complex", "well-thought-out" preparations that'll make even a "meateater's mouth water"; some wish "prices were less", but "lovely" digs, "hot" patrons and "congenial" staffers compensate.

Canyon Road *Southwestern* — 19 | 16 | 18 | $38

E 70s | 1470 First Ave. (bet. 76th & 77th Sts.) | 212-734-1600 |
www.arkrestaurants.com

Relied upon as an UES "old faithful", this "upbeat" cantina caters to "fun-lovers" with "generous helpings" of "good" Southwestern victuals at "fair" prices; service can be "slow" and the "decibel level" high, but after a couple of "sprightly margaritas" no one notices.

Capital Grille *Steak* — 24 | 23 | 24 | $69

E 40s | Chrysler Ctr. | 155 E. 42nd St. (bet. Lexington & 3rd Aves.) |
212-953-2000
Financial District | 120 Broadway (Nassau & Pine Sts.) | 212-374-1811 🛇
W 50s | Time-Life Building | 120 W. 51st St. (bet. 6th & 7th Aves.) |
212-246-0154
www.thecapitalgrille.com

The "formula works" at these "class-act" steakhouses that "deliver every time" with "superbly aged", "perfectly cooked" beef served in "plush" settings (especially at the Chrysler Building) where you're "pampered" by a "pro" staff; "for a chain", the "high quality" is a "pleasant surprise" – the predictably "high prices" less so.

Capsouto Frères *French* — 24 | 23 | 25 | $59

TriBeCa | 451 Washington St. (Watts St.) | 212-966-4900 |
www.capsoutofreres.com

An "almost textbook French bistro", this "lovely" TriBeCa "landmark" is a "sentimental favorite" for "scrumptious" "upscale" classics and "gracious" service in "airy", "brick-walled" surrounds; it's a "challenge" to find but "worth the effort", especially considering the "easy parking."

Caracas Arepa Bar *Venezuelan* — 24 | 14 | 17 | $20

E Village | 93½ E. Seventh St. (bet. Ave. A & 1st Ave.) | 212-529-2314
Caracas Brooklyn *Venezuelan*
Williamsburg | 291 Grand St. (bet. Havemeyer & Roebling Sts.) |
Brooklyn | 718-218-6050
Caracas to Go *Venezuelan*
E Village | 91 E. Seventh St. (1st Ave.) | 212-228-5062
www.caracasarepabar.com

"Addictive", "low-cost" arepas are the mainstay of these "funky", "high-energy" Venezuelans whose fans "willingly withstand long lines" and "tiny, dingy" digs at the East Village original and its take-out neighbor; the "larger" Williamsburg outpost with a bar and garden is an "improvement."

Cara Mia *Italian* — 21 | 16 | 20 | $39

W 40s | 654 Ninth Ave. (bet. 45th & 46th Sts.) | 212-262-6767 |
www.caramiany.com

The "traditional" Italian cooking at this "cute" Hell's Kitchen fallback is about "as homemade as it gets" for pre-theater dining; "speedy" staffers will "get you out in time for your show", but it's "better after the crowd thins" because the "intimate" digs make for a "tight squeeze."

Caravaggio *Italian* | 23 | 23 | 24 | $87 |

E 70s | 23 E. 74th St. (bet. 5th & Madison Aves.) | 212-288-1004
Combining a "beautiful", "discreet" setting with "serious", "complex" Italian cuisine and "impeccable" service, this "elegant" Upper Eastsider guarantees its upper-crust clientele "leisurely", "luxurious" dining; yes, tabs get "awfully expensive", but the $28 prix fixe lunch is "a deal" by comparison.

Caravan of | 22 | 13 | 17 | $28 |
Dreams ⊅ *Kosher/Vegan/Vegetarian*

E Village | 405 E. Sixth St. (1st Ave.) | 212-254-1613 |
www.caravanofdreams.net
"Chanting and crystals are optional", but "zesty", "inventive" kosher vegan fare is standard-issue for the "healthy types" at this "lived-in" East Village "diner"; it's "belly-filling without being budget-busting", but "be patient" with the "sweet", "slow" staff and "bring cash."

NEW Cardinal, The ● *Southern* | - | - | - | I |

E Village | 234 E. Fourth St. (bet. Aves. A & B) | 212-995-8600 |
www.thecardinalnyc.com
A flown Bubby's chef re-nests in Alphabet City at this cheap, casual Southern arrival cooking up carnivorous classics like smothered and fried pork chops, fried chicken and BBQ; bistro tables and a bar occupy the raw, bi-level space, where taxidermy meets whitewashed brick.

Carl's Steaks *Cheesesteaks* | 21 | 6 | 13 | $13 |

Murray Hill | 507 Third Ave. (34th St.) | 212-696-5336 ●
TriBeCa | 79 Chambers St. (bet. B'way & Church St.) |
212-566-2828
www.carlssteaks.com
"Spot-on" Philly cheesesteaks in all their "authentic" "greasy goodness" are the thing at these Murray Hill–TriBeCa "holes-in-the-wall"; they're "dingy" and service seems to have "exited on the turnpike", but they're the "next best" to the "real deal" – especially "when you're hungover."

☑ Carlyle Restaurant *French* | 24 | 27 | 26 | $91 |

E 70s | Carlyle Hotel | 35 E. 76th St. (Madison Ave.) | 212-570-7192 |
www.thecarlyle.com
From breakfast till bedtime, it's "luxe all the way" at this UES "throwback to a more civilized era", where "exquisite" New French cuisine, "gracious" service and "gorgeous" quarters draw the upper crust; no surprise, such "swank" is "fearfully expensive", but "well worth" getting "dressed up" for (jackets required at dinner).

Carmine's *Italian* | 21 | 16 | 19 | $43 |

W 40s | 200 W. 44th St. (bet. B'way & 8th Ave.) |
212-221-3800 ●
W 90s | 2450 Broadway (bet. 90th & 91st Sts.) | 212-362-2200
www.carminesnyc.com
Embodying *"abbondanza"*, these "big", "boisterous" Theater District–UWS Italians supply "over-the-top" family-style platters of "garlicky" "red-sauce staples" to "hordes" of customers ("tourists" on 44th Street,

| | FOOD | DECOR | SERVICE | COST |

locals on Broadway); "sketchy" service, "routine waits" and even the "din" are "part of the experience" – "get a gang together" and "share."

☑ Carnegie Deli ●✏ Deli
22 | 10 | 14 | $30

W 50s | 854 Seventh Ave. (55th St.) | 212-757-2245 | www.carnegiedeli.com

The "real deal", this Midtown deli is "legendary" for its "sky-high sandwiches" and mega-cheesecake served by "bossy waiters" in an "elbow-to-elbow" space with the charm of a "bus terminal"; it's "not cheap", but for the "quintessential" "New Yawk" experience, it's "priceless."

Carol's Cafe ☒ Ⓜ Eclectic
24 | 19 | 22 | $57

Dongan Hills | 1571 Richmond Rd. (bet. Four Corners Rd. & Seaview Ave.) | Staten Island | 718-979-5600 | www.carolscafe.com

At SI "food star" Carol Frazzetta's "quaint" Dongan Hills "oasis", she struts her stuff with "marvelous" Eclectic fare followed by "desserts to die for"; it's "a tad expensive" for the location, but romeos rate it "great for a date", and Carol shows how she does it at weekly cooking classes.

NEW Carpe Diem Italian
22 | 19 | 21 | $56

E 70s | 181 E. 78th St. (bet. Lexington & 3rd Aves.) | 212-772-3436

An UES "local hang", this "welcoming" arrival turns out "terrific pastas" and other "surprisingly good" Italiana via a "cheerful" crew; upscale tabs, "tight tables" and "noise" when the L-shaped room fills up are "negatives", but "overall it's enjoyable."

Casa Lever ☒ Italian
23 | 25 | 23 | $74

E 50s | 390 Park Ave. (enter on 53rd St., bet. Madison & Park Aves.) | 212-888-2700 | www.casalever.com

"*Mad Men*" types looking for an "un-stuffy" Midtown "power spot" hit this "stunning" Milanese member of the "Sant Ambroeus empire" ensconced in landmark Lever House digs with "Warhols on the walls"; "fabulous" fare, "cool" service and a "classy bar scene" complete the picture – natch, it's "best with someone else's money"; P.S. check out the new terrace.

☑ Casa Mono ● Spanish
25 | 18 | 20 | $59

Gramercy | 52 Irving Pl. (17th St.) | 212-253-2773 | www.casamononyc.com

"Chic-sters" at Mario Batali's "on-fire" Gramercy Spaniard are so "blown away" by the "glorious" tapas and "brilliant wines", they willingly "squeeze" into its "miniature space" and "rack up a tab"; "sit at the bar" if you can – "half the fun is watching the chefs" concoct those "interesting little plates."

NEW Casa Nonna Italian
- | - | - | E

Garment District | 310 W. 38th St. (bet. 8th & 9th Aves.) | 212-736-3000 | www.casanonna.com

New from the BLT group, this Garment District behomoth offers a wide menu of kinda pricey Italian eats served in a space that includes two dining rooms, a bar and a separate pizza counter; it manages to feel homey thanks to banquette seating, warm lighting and kitschy decorations.

Cascabel ● Mexican
23 | 16 | 17 | $29

E 80s | 1538 Second Ave. (80th St.) | 212-717-8226

(continued)

(continued)

NEW Cantina by Cascabel ● *Mexican*

E 80s | 1542 Second Ave. (bet. 80th & 81st Sts.) | 212-717-7800
www.nyctacos.com

"Muy sabroso" tacos are "irresistible" at this "lively", "ultracasual" UES taqueria where "memorable" flavors and "economy" tabs "seal the deal"; the new "bigger" space is also a "plus", but "overwhelming buzz" means they still "pack 'em in"; P.S. the Cantina opened post-Survey.

Casellula ● *American*   25 | 20 | 22 | $43

W 50s | 401 W. 52nd St. (bet. 9th & 10th Aves.) | 212-247-8137 |
www.casellula.com

A "wine and cheese–lover's dream", this "enoteca-ish" Hell's Kitchen "nibble" niche provides "impressive" pairings with "incredible" from-ages, plus "scrumptious" New American small plates; its "cozy" con-fines are "popular", meaning you "have to be willing to wait."

Ça Va *French*   22 | 21 | 22 | $60

W 40s | InterContinental NY Times Sq. | 310 W. 44th St. (8th Ave.) |
212-803-4545 | www.cavatoddenglish.com

Proving "Todd English knows French", this West 40s brasserie "hit" plies "pricey", "enjoyable" eats from breakfast on; its "understated" setting gets some yawns, but factor in the lounge's "inviting fireplace" and a handy "take-out" market, and to most it's "way better than alright."

Caviar Russe ⓩ *American*   24 | 23 | 24 | $97

E 50s | 538 Madison Ave., 2nd fl. (bet. 54th & 55th Sts.) | 212-980-5908 |
www.caviarrusse.com

If "it's caviar you crave", indulge "in style" at this "luxurious" East Side New American "rendezvous", where "sublime" roe and sushi are "ex-pertly served" amid "Russian fantasy" decor; prices run "all the way up to impossible", but the $20 prix fixe weekday lunch is a "bargain."

Cávo ●Ⓜ *Greek*   21 | 25 | 19 | $49

Astoria | 42-18 31st Ave. (bet. 42nd & 43rd Sts.) | Queens | 718-721-1001 |
www.cavoastoria.com

You "feel like you're on vacation" at this Hellenic Astorian, whose "sur-prisingly" "large" size, "energetic" vibe and "wonderful", waterfall-lined garden boost the "wow factor"; its "enjoyable" Greek fare is "a bit expensive", though, and as the night goes on "it turns into a club."

Cebu ● *Continental*   21 | 19 | 20 | $38

Bay Ridge | 8801 Third Ave. (88th St.) | Brooklyn | 718-492-5095 |
www.cebubrooklyn.com

"Relax and enjoy" urge "neighborhood" boosters who report this Bay Ridge Continental is "never a letdown" for "impromptu" meals, "week-end brunch" or "late-night" bites (served till 3 AM); it's also "popular" with the "younger set", so expect a "jumping" "bar scene."

Celeste ⌀ *Italian*   24 | 12 | 17 | $36

W 80s | 502 Amsterdam Ave. (bet. 84th & 85th Sts.) | 212-874-4559

UWS *amici* deem this "local fave" a "steal and a half" for "honest" Neapolitan dishes and "amazing cheese plates" served in a "sparse", "cheek-by-jowl" setting; though it's "too bad they don't take reserva-tions" or credit cards, it still "fills up early" so "count on a wait."

	FOOD	DECOR	SERVICE	COST

Cellini *Italian*
23 | 19 | 23 | $58

E 50s | 65 E. 54th St. (bet. Madison & Park Aves.) | 212-751-1555 |
www.cellinirestaurant.com

They "aim to please" at this East Midtown Italian "standby", a "tried-and-true" choice for "genuine" classics from a "top" staff that'll "welcome you with open arms"; widely favored as a "business-lunch" hub, it's equally "reliable" for a "quiet dinner."

Centolire *Italian*
22 | 20 | 21 | $61

E 80s | 1167 Madison Ave. (bet. 85th & 86th Sts.) | 212-734-7711 |
www.pinoluongo.com

Comfortably "upmarket", Pino Luongo's bi-level Carnegie Hill "winner" is a "solid performer" where "locals" let loose lotsa lire for "fine" Tuscan fare and "spot-on" service; for the "money-conscious", the "casual first-floor" cafe features "well-conceived panini."

Centrico *Mexican*
20 | 19 | 20 | $49

TriBeCa | 211 W. Broadway (Franklin St.) | 212-431-0700 |
www.myriadrestaurantgroup.com

"Not your average taco", the "updated" offerings from TV chef Aarón Sanchez mark this "spacious" TriBeCa Mexican as a "flavorful", "fairly priced" "change of pace"; "inventive" cocktails, "accommodating" service and a "festive" feel signal "good times to be had."

Centro Vinoteca ● *Italian*
20 | 18 | 19 | $50

W Village | 74 Seventh Ave. S. (Barrow St.) | 212-367-7470 |
www.centrovinoteca.com

This "modern" West Village Italian's appeal centers on "tasty" *piccolini* (small plates) and "marvelous" wines "earnestly" served in a "loud lower-level bar and "quieter upstairs"; while it's still "inviting", a few rue chef changes that cost it "some of its spark."

'Cesca Ⓜ *Italian*
23 | 22 | 22 | $63

W 70s | 164 W. 75th St. (Amsterdam Ave.) | 212-787-6300 |
www.cescanyc.com

"A rarity on the UWS", this "higher-end" Southern Italian delivers "dazzling" food and wine in "rustic yet elegant" surroundings manned by a "pro" staff; it's typically "humming" with "convivial" devotees who declare "sophistication" makes the "steep" price tag "bearable."

Chadwick's *American*
22 | 19 | 22 | $48

Bay Ridge | 8822 Third Ave. (89th St.) | Brooklyn | 718-833-9855 |
www.chadwicksny.com

"Old Bay Ridge" endures at this '80s-era American "staple" for "consistently good" food and "competent service" that "won't cost you an arm and a leg" (especially the Monday–Thursday "early-bird"); despite decor that "needs updating", "hometown" fans "continue to return."

Chai Home Kitchen ● *Thai*
∇ 22 | 15 | 18 | $26

W 50s | 930 Eighth Ave. (55th St.) | 212-707-8778
Williamsburg | 124 N. Sixth St. (Berry St.) | Brooklyn |
718-599-5889
www.chai-restaurants.com

"Reliably fresh" renditions of typical Thai dishes make this "informal" Hell's Kitchen–Williamsburg pair a pleasing "low-key" "alternative" to myriad rivals; the digs are "a little tight" for "anyone to linger", but the prices "can't be beat."

Char No. 4 ● Southern
23 | 19 | 21 | $41

Cobble Hill | 196 Smith St. (bet. Baltic & Warren Sts.) | Brooklyn | 718-643-2106 | www.charno4.com

This Cobble Hill Southerner supplies a "perfect combination" of "baconlicious" eats with a "smoky" "edge" and a "killer bourbon list"; the "dark-wood interior" encourages "easy nights out" that run "reasonable – if you can control" your sipping.

Chef Ho's Peking Duck Grill Chinese
22 | 14 | 20 | $35

E 80s | 1720 Second Ave. (bet. 89th & 90th Sts.) | 212-348-9444 | www.chefho.com

"Fantastic" Peking duck gives "local followers" "something to quack about" at this ho-spitable longtime Chinese "favorite" in Yorkville; it "never fails to deliver" the "quality of Chinatown" for "about the same price" and atmosphere, hence it's "deservedly crowded."

Chelsea Ristorante Italian
20 | 16 | 22 | $42

Chelsea | 108 Eighth Ave. (bet. 15th & 16th Sts.) | 212-924-7786 | www.chrnyc.com

"The opposite of trendy", this "homey" Chelsea Italian attracts "traditionalists" with a "dependable" lineup of pizzas and other wood-oven eats served "without attitude"; maybe the decor's "uninspired", but never mind – it's "fairly priced" and "you can get in."

Chennai Garden Indian/Kosher/Vegetarian
21 | 11 | 15 | $24

Murray Hill | 129 E. 27th St. (Park Ave. S.) | 212-689-1999

A "vegetarian's delight" and "kosher too", this Curry Hill Indian's "wonderful" dosas and such make it a "standout", as does the "ridiculous-bargain" $7 lunch buffet; given the food quality and low prices, most find the "uneven service" and "very simple" setting easily "tolerable."

Chestnut Ⓜ American
23 | 19 | 21 | $45

Carroll Gardens | 271 Smith St. (bet. Degraw & Sackett Sts.) | Brooklyn | 718-243-0049 | www.chestnutonsmith.com

The "combination of refined and earthy" "comes across beautifully" at this Smith Street New American "mainstay"; add "responsive service", a "Brooklyn-chic" space and a "garden in back", and no wonder it's a longtime "neighborhood" "favorite."

Chez Jacqueline ● French
20 | 18 | 20 | $50

G Village | 72 MacDougal St. (bet. Bleecker & Houston Sts.) | 212-505-0727 | www.chezjacquelinerestaurant.com

"Year in, year out", this "sweet little" Village bistro plies "comforting French" fare served without "any pretensions whatsoever"; even though "Jacqueline's gone" and there are "never big crowds", it's a "formula" that has "stood the test of time."

Chez Josephine ●Ⓜ French
20 | 22 | 22 | $54

W 40s | 414 W. 42nd St. (bet. 9th & 10th Aves.) | 212-594-1925 | www.chezjosephine.com

"Ooh-la-la", this enduring Theater District "homage to Josephine Baker" remains "a show unto itself" with her "*charmant*" son Jean-Claude serving as the "textbook host"; between the "old-fashioned

French" menu, "piano player" and "Parisian" "bordello" decor, it's a "pre- and after-"curtain" "staple."

Chez Lucienne *French*

FOOD	DECOR	SERVICE	COST
20	17	18	$41

Harlem | 308 Lenox Ave. (bet. 125th & 126th Sts.) | 212-289-5555 | www.chezlucienne.com

It "could've been a bistro in Paris" attest *amis* of this "welcome" Harlem "asset", where the "well-executed" "traditional French" cooking comes *pas cher*; with a "cute" staff and "comfortable" milieu, it's "cementing its presence" for a "lively" local crowd.

Chez Napoléon 🗷 *French*

FOOD	DECOR	SERVICE	COST
22	16	22	$48

W 50s | 365 W. 50th St. (bet. 8th & 9th Aves.) | 212-265-6980 | www.cheznapoleon.com

"*Grand-mère*" cooks up "favorites of yesteryear" at this "warm" Theater District bistro, a family-owned "mainstay" since 1960; the "dinky" digs are "a little worn", but "senior Francophiles" and others "bitten by the nostalgia bug" say it "still stands up" for "homestyle" French fare at "fair prices."

Chickpea *Mideastern*

FOOD	DECOR	SERVICE	COST
18	10	15	$12

E Village | 210 E. 14th St. (bet. 2nd & 3rd Aves.) | 212-228-3445 ❶
NEW **Financial District** | 110 William St. (John St.) | 212-566-5666 🗷
Flatiron | 688 Sixth Ave. (bet. 21st & 22nd Sts.) | 212-243-6275 ❶
www.getchickpea.com

In a "virtuous" but "tasty" twist on "fast food", this Mideastern trio turns out "baked (not fried) falafel" in "basic" quarters where "take-out's best"; even skeptics who see "nothing exceptional" concede "the price is right."

ChikaLicious *Dessert*

FOOD	DECOR	SERVICE	COST
24	14	17	$19

E Village | 203 E. 10th St. (bet. 1st & 2nd Aves.) | 212-995-9511 | www.chikalicious.com Ⓜ
E Village | 204 E. 10th St. (bet. 1st & 2nd Aves.) | 212-475-0929 ❶

"Incredible desserts" are the thing at this "nifty" East Village nook that inspires "sweet bliss" with three-course prix fixes of "creative" "delights" paired with wines; critics who cite "claustrophobic" digs and "indifferent" service head to the even-side-of-the-street satellite for "decadence" to go.

Chimichurri Grill ❶ *Argentinean/Steak*

FOOD	DECOR	SERVICE	COST
23	16	22	$52

W 40s | 609 Ninth Ave. (bet. 43rd & 44th Sts.) | 212-586-8655

"For beef before the theater", this Hell's Kitchen "hideaway" is a "reliable" source of "awesome" Argentine-style steaks – slathered in the namesake sauce – "without the overhead" of the major meateries; as for the "small" digs, regulars report "no frills, but no disappointments."

China Chalet *Chinese*

FOOD	DECOR	SERVICE	COST
19	13	18	$29

Financial District | 47 Broadway (bet. Exchange Pl. & Morris St.) | 212-943-4380
Eltingville | Eltingville Shopping Ctr. | 4326 Amboy Rd. (bet. Armstrong & Richmond Aves.) | Staten Island | 718-984-8044
www.chinachalet.com

FiDi and Staten Island folks keep this "decent" if "unimaginative" duo on "standby" for a "quick" fix of "your average Chinese fare"; nattier sorts smirk they work best "for takeout" "unless your decor's as poor as theirs."

China Grill *Asian* | 22 | 21 | 20 | $58

W 50s | 60 W. 53rd St. (bet. 5th & 6th Aves.) | 212-333-7788 | www.chinagrillmgt.com

"Still going strong", this "time-tested" Midtown "icon" remains a "tony" "showcase" for "jazzed-up" Asian fare and a "happening" "corporate" scene with "runway-at-JFK" decibel levels; the tabs are "on the high side", but hey, with all those cuties at the bar, "they must be doing something right."

Chinatown Brasserie *Chinese* | 22 | 22 | 18 | $47

NoHo | 380 Lafayette St. (Great Jones St.) | 212-533-7000 | www.chinatownbrasserie.com

A "gorgeous, sprawling space" and "sophisticated dishes" from "high-class dim sum" to "not-to-be-missed" Peking duck keep this NoHo Chinese "lively"; just know that its "glam" "1930s Shanghai" atmosphere comes at "a premium" – it's way "more spendy than the real Chinatown."

Chin Chin ● *Chinese* | 23 | 19 | 23 | $54

E 40s | 216 E. 49th St. (bet. 2nd & 3rd Aves.) | 212-888-4555 | www.chinchinny.com

Appreciated as a Midtown "cut above" since the '80s, this Chinese standby keeps "buzzing" "during the lunch hour" and beyond thanks to its "gourmet" cooking (including "can't-resist" off-menu Grand Marnier shrimp) and "spot-on" service; it's "pricey" and "a little dated", but there are few complaints.

ChipShop *British* | 21 | 16 | 20 | $23

Brooklyn Heights | 129 Atlantic Ave. (bet. Clinton & Henry Sts.) | Brooklyn | 718-855-7775 ●
Park Slope | 383 Fifth Ave. (bet. 6th & 7th Sts.) | Brooklyn | 718-832-7701
www.chipshopnyc.com

"Never mind the bollocks" – these "laid-back" Brooklyn Brits render "real English pub" favorites like "tip-top" fish 'n' chips and "coronary-inducing" "deep-fried Twinkies and candy bars"; the "inexpensive" grub "hits the spot" when you're stuck on "this side of the pond."

Chocolate Room, The *Dessert* | 25 | 19 | 21 | $20

Cobble Hill | 269 Court St. (bet. Butler & Douglass Sts.) | Brooklyn | 718-246-2600
Park Slope | 86 Fifth Ave. (bet. Prospect Pl. & St. Marks Ave.) | Brooklyn | 718-783-2900
www.thechocolateroombrooklyn.com

"Your sweet tooth will tingle" from the "exciting array" of "house-made" desserts at these Brooklyn "chocolate wizards" also known for their "smart wine pairings"; the Park Slope original's more "intimate", but both are "irresistible" – provided "you can handle the sugar high."

Cho Dang Gol *Korean* | 22 | 15 | 17 | $32

Garment District | 55 W. 35th St. (bet. 5th & 6th Aves.) | 212-695-8222 | www.chodanggolny.com

Specializing in "silky" "handmade" tofu, this "affordably priced" Garment District Korean is a dang "authentic" outfit proffering "hearty, healthful" dishes of a "high caliber"; while "not at all glitzy", it's frequently "jammed with expats" and other lovers of "highly flavored" fare.

Chola *Indian*

FOOD	DECOR	SERVICE	COST
24	16	20	$40

E 50s | 232 E. 58th St. (bet. 2nd & 3rd Aves.) | 212-688-4619

With its "flavor-packed" mix of "common and uncommon" dishes, the "huge menu" elevates this Indian "favorite" to the "upper echelon" of its East 58th Street block, aka "Uptown Sixth Street"; the prices are likewise "palatable", and the "roll-me-home" $14 lunch buffet is a "steal."

Christos Steak House ● *Steak*

FOOD	DECOR	SERVICE	COST
23	18	22	$61

Astoria | 41-08 23rd Ave. (41st St.) | Queens | 718-777-8400 |
www.christossteakhouse.com

"Thankful" Astorians salute this "consistent" cow palace for "classic" steaks done "to perfection" and preceded by starters with "terrific" Greek "twists"; maybe it's "expensive" for Queens, but "service is attentive" and with "easy valet parking" you "can't go wrong."

Churrascaria Plataforma ● *Brazilian/Steak*

FOOD	DECOR	SERVICE	COST
23	19	22	$75

W 40s | 316 W. 49th St. (bet. 8th & 9th Aves.) | 212-245-0505 |
www.churrascariaplataforma.com

Churrascaria TriBeCa ● *Brazilian/Steak*

TriBeCa | 221 W. Broadway (bet. Franklin & White Sts.) | 212-925-6969 |
www.churrascariatribeca.com

Carnivores can "seriously" "binge" at this Midtown-TriBeCa "bacchanalian" Brazilian rodizio duo, where the waiters "just keep coming" with "mouthwatering" "meat on skewers" ("I'm still stuffed from eating there two years ago"); the "vast" salad bar's a "feast in itself", but "save room for the real meal" to "get your money's worth."

Z NEW Ciano *Italian*

FOOD	DECOR	SERVICE	COST
25	23	22	$74

Flatiron | 45 E. 22nd St. (bet. B'way & Park Ave. S.) | 212-982-8422 |
www.cianonyc.com

This "hot new" Flatiron Italian is rated "top-notch" "all around", thanks to ex-Cru chef Shea Gallante's "artfully delicious" cuisine served by a "suave" team in "beautiful" "rustic Tuscan" environs focused on a "roaring" fireplace; even with "sky-high" tabs, it's been "jam-packed from the get-go" ("plan ahead"); P.S. oenophiles say "grazie" for the "astounding wine-by-the-half-bottle" selection.

Cibo *American/Italian*

FOOD	DECOR	SERVICE	COST
21	19	22	$48

E 40s | 767 Second Ave. (41st St.) | 212-681-1616 |
www.cibonyc.com

A "surprising find" near the U.N., this "inviting" Tuscan–New American furnishes a "solid" "seasonal menu" and "oh-so-accommodating" service in an area that "suffers from a dearth" of choices; it's "fairly priced" to boot, with a $35 dinner prix fixe that's a "real bargain."

Cilantro *Southwestern*

FOOD	DECOR	SERVICE	COST
18	15	18	$32

E 70s | 1321 First Ave. (71st St.) | 212-537-4040 ●
E 80s | 1712 Second Ave. (bet. 88th & 89th Sts.) |
212-722-4242 ●
W 80s | 485 Columbus Ave. (bet. 83rd & 84th Sts.) | 212-712-9090
www.cilantronyc.com

Perpetually "poppin'" with "noisy young" posses, this "casual-dress" trio slings "low-cost" Southwestern "standards" with "no surprises";

though the decor is "fake" and the eating "average at best", after a couple of "super-strong margaritas" that's all "incidental."

Cipriani Dolci ● *Italian*

21 | 19 | 19 | $58

E 40s | Grand Central | 89 E. 42nd St. (Vanderbilt Ave.) | 212-973-0999 | www.cipriani.com

"Sip a perfect Bellini" and "watch the hustle-bustle" from this "prime" "balcony" overlooking the Grand Central Concourse, which combines vivacious Venetian fare with an "energy" level you "can't beat"; while admittedly "high-priced", it's "convenient" for an "assignation" – and you'll "still get your train."

Cipriani Downtown ● *Italian*

22 | 21 | 21 | $76

SoHo | 376 W. Broadway (bet. Broome & Spring Sts.) | 212-343-0999 | www.cipriani.com

"Put yourself together" before joining this "total scene" in SoHo, where "slick Euro" types "flock" for "simple yet scrumptious" Italian bites, "a Bellini or two" and a "fabulous time"; abundant "attitude" is "expected" since "it's all about being seen, darling" – "if you can afford it" (when you see the price of the burger, you may think "the cow was fed gold and lived in an Upper East Side penthouse prior to its demise").

Cipriani Wall Street ⌷ *Italian*
(aka Cipriani Club 55)

23 | 22 | 22 | $64

Financial District | 55 Wall St., 2nd fl. (bet. Hanover & William Sts.) | 212-699-4096 | www.cipriani.com

"The expense account has found a home" at this Financial District member of the chichi Italian clan, where Wall Streeters "bank on" "outstanding preparations" for a "power breakfast", biz lunch or after-the-bell wind-down; a "civilized" setting with a columned terrace helps justify "the splurge."

Circo ● *Italian*
(fka Osteria del Circo)

23 | 24 | 23 | $64

W 50s | 120 W. 55th St. (bet. 6th & 7th Aves.) | 212-265-3636 | www.osteriadelcirco.com

The "Maccioni touch" is evident at this "classy circus" of a Le Cirque offshoot, a "bright", "energetic" Midtowner where "top-notch" Tuscan fare comes in "hospitable" environs "close to City Center"; it's "not cheap", but "affordable" prix fixes put a swing in the show.

Circus *Brazilian/Steak*

20 | 19 | 20 | $53

E 60s | 132 E. 61st St. (bet. Lexington & Park Aves.) | 212-223-2965 | www.circusrestaurante.com

"Low-key and not pretentious", this "quiet" East Side "alternative" brings on "serious Brazilian" dishes with an "emphasis on meats" amid "charming" big-top decor; add "caring service" and "super caipirin-has", and it's an act those "in the know" "never tire of."

Citrus Bar & Grill *Asian/Nuevo Latino*

20 | 18 | 18 | $40

W 70s | 320 Amsterdam Ave. (75th St.) | 212-595-0500 | www.citrusnyc.com

Get "ready to party" at this "UWS standby" where the "young set" touts "easygoing" atmospherics together with "tasty" Latin-Asian fusion fare; since this "joint jumps" with groups "hanging out" over "sugary drinks", bring "earplugs" or "check your hearing at the door."

		FOOD	DECOR	SERVICE	COST

City Bakery *Bakery* — 22 | 13 | 15 | $20

Flatiron | 3 W. 18th St. (bet. 5th & 6th Aves.) | 212-366-1414 | www.thecitybakery.com

A "handy" "pit stop", this Flatiron bakery boasts "wicked good" hot chocolate and other "sweets and treats", as well as a "tempting" salad bar with a "locavore bent"; it's "def expensive" given the "cafeteria-like" setup, but "high standards" keep it "humming."

City Crab & Seafood Co. *Seafood* — 19 | 17 | 19 | $47

Flatiron | 235 Park Ave. S. (19th St.) | 212-529-3800 | www.citycrabnyc.com

"Roll up your sleeves" for "no-fuss seafood" at this Flatiron "standby" whose whale-size lineup "from the deep" comes in "huge" digs with a "lively bar"; some crab about "slapdash" service and a "commercial" feel, but it "gets the job done" "without breaking the bank."

City Hall ⓩ *Seafood/Steak* — 21 | 22 | 21 | $58

TriBeCa | 131 Duane St. (bet. Church St. & W. B'way) | 212-227-7777 | www.cityhallnyc.com

The "movers and shakers" get "clubby" at Henry Meer's TriBeCa "class" act, which "still delivers" "first-rate" surf 'n' turf with a side of "pol-watching" in "classic NY" quarters "well run" by a "gracious" staff; regulars respect its "chops", even if they need a "municipal loan" to settle the check.

City Island Lobster House ◑ *Seafood* — 19 | 15 | 18 | $48

City Island | 691 Bridge St. (City Island Ave.) | Bronx | 718-885-1459 | www.cilobsterhouse.com

A City Island "fixture", this "nothing-fancy" seafooder remains a "solid" source of "messy" shore staples ("try the lobster special") proffered at "good prices" considering "all you get"; crustier customers contend it's "past its prime", but the open-air "view of the Sound" never gets old.

City Lobster & Steak *Seafood* — 19 | 17 | 18 | $52

W 40s | 121 W. 49th St. (6th Ave.) | 212-354-1717 | www.citylobster.com

Join the "tourists" and "pre-theater" types "diving in" to "basic" surf 'n' turf at this Rock Center–area "oasis"; despite "competent" cooking, "courteous" service and "reasonable" prix fixe "deals", critics call it "run-of-the-mill" "for the money."

Clinton St. Baking Co. *American* — 25 | 15 | 18 | $27

LES | 4 Clinton St. (bet. Houston & Stanton Sts.) | 646-602-6263 | www.clintonstreetbaking.com

"Brunchers" wait an "eternity" for entrée into this "postage stamp-size" Lower East Side bakery/cafe, whose "mouthwatering" roster is led by "the best", "fluffiest" pancakes "on the planet"; note that the American "comfort" fare is also "delish" during "off times", when the "brutal" lines subside.

Club A Steak House ⓩ *Steak* — 24 | 21 | 23 | $73

E 50s | 240 E. 58th St. (bet. 2nd & 3rd Aves.) | 212-688-4190 | www.clubasteak.com

Despite steep tabs and a "random location" near the Queensboro Bridge, this "warm, clubby" duplex meatery "holds its own" with "superb" steaks, "gracious service" and a "handsome" "red" setting; "re-

| | FOOD | DECOR | SERVICE | COST |

laxed" enough for either "romancing or bromancing", most rate it "really worth the money."

Co. *Pizza*
23 | 16 | 18 | $33

Chelsea | 230 Ninth Ave. (24th St.) | 212-243-1105 | www.co-pane.com
Its "dough rises to the top" say fans of "master baker" Jim Lahey's "cool" Chelsea pizza place, where the "artisanal" pies with "fancy" toppings are particularly prized for their "airy", "charred" crusts; it's "wildly popular" with "hip" types keeping company at "tight" "communal" tables.

Coco Roco *Peruvian*
19 | 13 | 17 | $28

Cobble Hill | 139 Smith St. (bet. Bergen & Dean Sts.) | Brooklyn | 718-254-9933
Park Slope | 392 Fifth Ave. (bet. 6th & 7th Sts.) | Brooklyn | 718-965-3376
www.cocorocorestaurant.com
"The spices they use should be a controlled substance" say addicts of this Brooklyn duo's "exemplary" rotisserie chicken and other "traditional Peruvian dishes" that satisfy "hearty eaters" at a "fair price"; those less than loco about the ambiance go "mainly for takeout."

Coffee Shop ● *American/Brazilian*
16 | 13 | 13 | $32

Union Sq | 29 Union Sq. W. (16th St.) | 212-243-7969 | www.thecoffeeshopnyc.com
A "very known quantity" on Union Square, this Brazilian-American "mainstay" is forever "hopping" despite its "hit-or-miss" menu, "worn" setting and "not so hot" service from an "eye-candy" staff; however, as the "colorful crowd" can attest, "no one goes here for the food."

Colbeh *Kosher/Persian*
21 | 16 | 19 | $44

Garment District | 43 W. 39th St. (bet. 5th & 6th Aves.) | 212-354-8181
You won't need a "flying carpet" to find "high-quality Persian cuisine" thanks to this recently relocated Garment District specialist – and "the fact that it's kosher is a plus" too; first-timers may be "thrown by" the "sushi menu", but aficionados advise "stick to" the Iranian side.

Cole's Dock Side *Seafood*
∇ 21 | 17 | 20 | $38

Great Kills | 369 Cleveland Ave. (Hylan Blvd.) | Staten Island | 718-948-5588 | www.colesdockside.com
"Hometown" types "meet and eat" at this "casual" Staten Island seafooder with a "warm-weather" porch and "peaceful water views" over Great Kills Harbor; "tasty" fin fare served with a "smile" at "good prices" have most "wishing to return."

Colicchio & Sons *American*
24 | 24 | 23 | $72

Chelsea | 85 10th Ave. (bet. 15th & 16th Sts.) | 212-400-6699 | www.colicchioandsons.com
Top Chef's Tom Colicchio "does it again" with this West Chelsea "destination" whose "innovative" American fare, "personable" service and "lofty" space "deserve the buzz"; the "high price tag" also "wows", but for lunch and "everyday" dining, the "inviting" Tap Room is a "bargain."

NEW Colonie *American*
∇ 26 | 28 | 24 | $47

Brooklyn Heights | 127 Atlantic Ave. (bet. Clinton & Henry Sts.) | Brooklyn | 718-855-7500 | www.colonienyc.com
"Much needed" in "restaurant-barren" Brooklyn Heights, this "exciting" arrival debuts with "delicious" New American "farm-to-table"

| | FOOD | DECOR | SERVICE | COST |

fare and "interesting wines" served by "charming" staffers; factor in "super-warm" digs with an "open kitchen" and vertical "herb garden", and no wonder it's "already a total hit."

Commerce American
23 | 20 | 20 | $58

W Village | 50 Commerce St. (Barrow St.) | 212-524-2301 | www.commercerestaurant.com

From the "phenomenal" bread basket on, this "tucked-away" West Villager is a "charmer" for "first-rate" New American fare served with "no airs" in "sexy" quarters; get past the "deafening decibel level" and "annoying no-cash policy" and you'll know why it's so "buzzy."

Commodore, The ◑ Southern
▽ 25 | 15 | 11 | $19

Williamsburg | 366 Metropolitan Ave. (Havemeyer St.) | Brooklyn | 718-218-7632

It's a "blast" washing down "outstanding fried chicken" and other "re-visited" Southern fare with "super" cocktails at this Williamsburg "dive", a "'70s rec-room look-alike from a Pies-n-Thighs vet; ordering from "surly" bartenders and "dog-eat-dog seating" can be a pain unless you "beat the rush."

Community Food & Juice American
23 | 18 | 18 | $34

W 100s | 2893 Broadway (bet. 112th & 113th Sts.) | 212-665-2800 | www.communityrestaurant.com

"Health-conscious" hordes head for this "informal" New American "asset" in "underserved Morningside Heights", where "Ivy Leaguers" commune over "high-quality" "local and organic" eats; it's also a "vibrant brunch spot" – if you can stomach "lines out the door."

Congee Bowery ◑ Chinese
20 | 12 | 13 | $25

LES | 207 Bowery (bet. Rivington & Spring Sts.) | 212-766-2828
Congee Village ◑ Chinese
LES | 100 Allen St. (bet. Broome & Delancey Sts.) | 212-941-1818
www.congeevillagerestaurants.com

With "spot-on" "traditional" dishes led by the eponymous rice porridge ("a must"), this LES Cantonese couple furnishes "satisfying", "best-buy" meals; they're typically "bustling" with converts who "grin and bear" the "corny" decor and "nonexistent" service.

Convivium Osteria Mediterranean
25 | 24 | 22 | $55

Park Slope | 68 Fifth Ave. (bet. Bergen St. & St. Marks Ave.) | Brooklyn | 718-857-1833 | www.convivium-osteria.com

You'll "be transported" at this Park Slope "local gem" thanks to an "attentive staff", "delectable", "soul-warming" Mediterranean cooking and "terrific" wines; the "enchanting" "rustic farmhouse" surroundings rate "A-1" "for date night", especially in the garden or "intimate" wine cellar.

Cookshop ◑ American
22 | 19 | 20 | $52

Chelsea | 156 10th Ave. (20th St.) | 212-924-4440 | www.cookshopny.com

"Greenmarket meets comfort food" at this "upbeat" Chelsea American "right off the High Line", whose "innovative dishes" tailored to the "vida locavore" really "hit the mark"; the "pleasant" room is manned by a crew that's "hospitable" even when things get "crazy busy" at its "fabulous brunch."

NEW Co-op Food & Drink M _American_

— | — | — | E

LES | The Hotel on Rivington | 107 Rivington St. (bet. Essex & Ludlow Sts.) | 212-796-8040 | www.co-oprestaurant.com

Blown-up Polaroids of iconic NYers line the walls at the latest eatery inside the Hotel on Rivington; pricey New American small plates and sushi are shared at a communal table or on banquettes within gritty-but-glamorous confines, which also feature a mirror-tiled bar.

NEW Copacabana ● ⊠ M _Nuevo Latino_

— | — | — | E

W 40s | 264 W. 47th St., 2nd fl. (8th Ave.) | 212-221-2672 | www.thecopacabana.com

Now in its fourth incarnation, this storied supper club has opened in Times Square, serving Latin food via Alex Garcia (ex Calle Ocho); the room includes luminescent palm trees and live music from an eight-piece band, and after dinner there's a massive dance floor one flight up.

NEW Coppelia ● _Diner/Nuevo Latino_

▽ 20 | 18 | 22 | $31

Chelsea | 207 W. 14th St. (bet. 7th & 8th Aves.) | 212-858-5001

Julian Medina (Yerba Buena, Toloache) pays homage to the classic Cuban luncheonette with this well-priced Chelsea arrival dishing up Pan-Latin comfort fare – sandwiches, burgers, nachos, breakfast faves – 24/7; palm trees, wall-mounted steel fans and a marble counter with swivel stools boost the Havana vibe.

Coppola's ● _Italian_

19 | 16 | 19 | $43

Murray Hill | 378 Third Ave. (bet. 27th & 28th Sts.) | 212-679-0070
W 70s | 206 W. 79th St. (bet. Amsterdam Ave. & B'way) | 212-877-3840
www.coppolas-nyc.com

"Reliable" is the "operative word" at these "decently priced", "old-fashioned" Murray Hill–UWS Southern Italians that are local "survivors"; while the "predictable red-sauce" eating can be "surprisingly good", aesthetes say the "time-warp" decor "could use revamping."

Cornelia Street Cafe ● _American/French_

19 | 17 | 19 | $39

W Village | 29 Cornelia St. (bet. Bleecker & W. 4th Sts.) | 212-989-9319 | www.corneliastreetcafe.com

A "homey" "reminder of the old" West Village, this "convivial" neighborhood "fixture" "still beckons" with "quite decent" French-American bites and "fair prices"; it hosts a "popular" brunch, and "culture-seekers" head downstairs for "live jazz" and poetry.

Corner Bistro ● ⊟ _Burgers_

22 | 10 | 14 | $19

W Village | 331 W. Fourth St. (Jane St.) | 212-242-9502 | www.cornerbistrony.com

You have to "elbow in" for the "awesome", "two-handed" burgers served on "disposable plates" and chased with "McSorley's on tap" at this "dumpy" West Village "haunt"; if you can abide the "lines" and "overcrowded" "college bar" milieu, one bite will explain its "popularity"; P.S. an LIC branch is in the works.

Corsino ● _Italian_

21 | 18 | 18 | $46

W Village | 637 Hudson St. (Horatio St.) | 212-242-3093 | www.corsinocantina.com

"Another fine" notion from Jason Denton ('Ino, 'Inoteca), this "friendly" West Villager "gets simplicity right" with "_delizioso_" Italian small

| | FOOD | DECOR | SERVICE | COST |

plates, including "fantastic crostini"; the "rustic quarters are "tight", but the "unhurried" pace allows for "lingering", as do the "tables outside."

☑ Corton ☒ *French* | 25 | 23 | 25 | $117 |

TriBeCa | 239 W. Broadway (bet. Walker & White Sts.) | 212-219-2777 | www.cortonnyc.com

"Wow!" is the consensus at this "elegant" TriBeCan from Drew Nieporent and "culinary rock star" Paul Liebrandt, whose near-"flawless", prix fixe-only New French dinners amount to a "modernist" "journey"; "impeccable" service and a "minimalist"-"chic" interior almost allow you to "forget" you're paying "top dollar."

Così *Sandwiches* | 16 | 11 | 13 | $15 |

E 40s | 38 E. 45th St. (bet. Madison & Vanderbilt Aves.) | 212-370-0705
E 50s | 60 E. 56th St. (bet. Madison & Park Aves.) | 212-588-1225
Financial District | World Financial Ctr. | 200 Vesey St. (West St.) | 212-571-2001
Financial District | 55 Broad St. (bet. Beaver St. & Exchange Pl.) | 212-344-5000 ☒
Flatiron | 700 Sixth Ave. (bet. 22nd & 23rd Sts.) | 212-645-0223
G Village | 53 E. Eighth St. (bet. B'way & Mercer St.) | 212-260-1507
G Village | 841 Broadway (bet. 13th & 14th Sts.) | 212-614-8544 ◗
Murray Hill | 461 Park Ave. S. (31st St.) | 212-634-3467
W 40s | 11 W. 42nd St. (bet. 5th & 6th Aves.) | 212-398-6662
W 50s | Paramount Plaza | 1633 Broadway (50th St.) | 212-397-9838
www.getcosi.com
Additional locations throughout the NY area

"When you're out and about", this handy sandwich chain is a "fast and easy" "fallback" for a "lunch fix", where flatbread "right out of the oven" is the "saving grace"; although "generic" and occasionally "chaotic", it's "perfectly adequate in a pinch", especially a penny pinch.

NEW Counter, The *Burgers* | 17 | 12 | 15 | $20 |

W 40s | 1451 Broadway (41st St.) | 212-997-6801 | www.thecounterburger.com

"Have it your way" at this new Times Square link of a national "build-your-own-burger" chain, where umpteen "creative choices" – patties, toppings, buns, sides – ensure a combo that "suits you"; the unimpressed counter that it's all "unremarkable."

Covo ◗ *Italian* | 22 | 19 | 20 | $35 |

Harlem | 701 W. 135th St. (12th Ave.) | 212-234-9573 | www.covony.com
An "out-of-the-way" "neighborhood favorite", this "welcoming" Harlem Italian does a "first-rate" job "for the money", serving pasta and brick-oven pizza in an "old-world" setting that "just needs a little sound-proofing"; P.S. night owls can adjourn to the art-lined upstairs lounge.

Cowgirl *Southwestern* | 17 | 19 | 18 | $30 |

W Village | 519 Hudson St. (W. 10th St.) | 212-633-1133 | www.cowgirlnyc.com

Cowgirl Sea-Horse *Southwestern*

Seaport | 259 Front St. (Dover St.) | 212-608-7873 | www.cowgirlseahorse.com

"Giddy up" and "get your Southwestern grub on" at this "busy" West Villager, where the "fried goodness" "widens waistlines" amid "themey" "saloon" decor best enjoyed by the "stroller set" at lunch and by margarita-sipping "singles" come evening; the Seaport "hide-away" adds seafood to the mix.

☑ Craft *American*   26 | 24 | 25 | $82

Flatiron | 43 E. 19th St. (bet. B'way & Park Ave. S.) | 212-780-0880 | www.craftrestaurant.com

Ever a "knockout", this Flatiron flagship of *Top Chef*'s Tom Colicchio is still "hard to top" for "exceptional" ingredients "crafted with care" but "without fuss" into "impressive" New American cuisine; "paying per item" raises the à la carte bill "sky high", but given the food quality, "anticipatory" service and "seductive" setting, there are few complaints.

Craftbar *American*   23 | 20 | 22 | $54

Flatiron | 900 Broadway (bet. 19th & 20th Sts.) | 212-461-4300 | www.craftrestaurant.com

"Hipper" habitués of Craft's "more affordable and accessible" Flatiron New American follow-up cheer its "spot-on" food, "well-versed" service and "big, airy" setting; it's "a bit loud", but that only bolsters the "buzzing" "scene."

Crema *Mexican*   23 | 18 | 20 | $45

Chelsea | 111 W. 17th St. (bet. 6th & 7th Aves.) | 212-691-4477 | www.cremarestaurante.com

"Imaginative" chef Julieta Ballesteros "obliterates any clichés" as she lends her Nuevo Mexicano menu an "haute" French "spin" that lifts this "unobtrusive" Chelsea haven "several cuts above the norm"; compadres equally "thrilled by" the "reasonable prices" and solid service call it a "keeper."

Crif Dogs ● *Hot Dogs*   22 | 12 | 16 | $12

E Village | 113 St. Marks Pl. (bet. Ave. A & 1st. Ave.) | 212-614-2728
NEW **Williamsburg** | 555 Driggs Ave. (N. 7th St.) | Brooklyn | 718-302-3200
www.crifdogs.com

"You'll never go back to the cart" thanks to this East Village "dive" and its Billyburg outpost, where "specialty" hot dogs (like the "bacon-wrapped") are "deep-fried" and "slathered" with "toppings galore"; no wonder they're "popular" with the "late-night" "drunks"; P.S. "shh, PDT" about St. Marks' "secret connecting bar."

Crispo ● *Italian*   24 | 19 | 20 | $49

W Village | 240 W. 14th St. (bet. 7th & 8th Aves.) | 212-229-1818 | www.crisporestaurant.com

"Outstanding spaghetti carbonara" coaxes "pasta lovers" to this "rock-steady" West Villager, an "unpretentious" "favorite" for "full-flavored", fair-"value" Northern Italian fare; the "secret is out" about the "close" seating and "noise level", so the cognoscenti try for its "year-round courtyard."

NEW CrossBar *American*   - | - | - | M

Flatiron | Limelight Marketplace | 47 W. 20th St. (6th Ave.) | 212-359-5550 | www.crossbarny.com

Todd English celebrates the swine at this affordable gastropub where whole roast suckling pig can be ordered daily from the fire-pit rotisserie, along with other Americana; its sexy bi-level Limelight Marketplace space reflects its church roots with rich details like onyx crosses and reclaimed pews.

NEW Crown *Continental*

FOOD	DECOR	SERVICE	COST
–	–	–	E

E 80s | 24 E. 81st St. (Madison Ave.) | 646-559-4880

Aiming to bring The Lion's exclusivity to the UES, this arrival from chef-to-the-stars John DeLucie rolls out Continental fare in a 1920s NY townhouse adorned with wood paneling and leather upholstery, complete with a greenhouselike rear dining room; steep tabs don't faze its high-flying crowd.

Cuba *Cuban*

FOOD	DECOR	SERVICE	COST
23	19	21	$41

G Village | 222 Thompson St. (bet. Bleecker & W. 3rd Sts.) | 212-420-7878 | www.cubanyc.com

"Awesome" food, "amazing mojitos" and "upbeat" staffers kindle "merry-making" the "Cuban way" at this "cute little" Village *cucina*; with extras like live Latin combos and an on-site "cigar roller", it's "like being back in Havana" at a pocket-pleasing price.

Cubana Café ⊄ *Cuban*

FOOD	DECOR	SERVICE	COST
20	15	18	$26

G Village | 110 Thompson St. (bet. Prince & Spring Sts.) | 212-966-5366
Carroll Gardens | 272 Smith St. (bet. Degraw & Sackett Sts.) | Brooklyn | 718-858-3980
Park Slope | 80 Sixth Ave. (St. Marks Pl.) | Brooklyn | 718-398-9818

Sí, they're "tiny" and "cramped", but this frill-free threesome serves up "authentic Cuban eats" and "strong" drinks at "totally affordable" rates; supporters swear the "slow" pace and "side-by-side seating" are "part of the vibe."

Cucina di Pesce *Italian/Seafood*

FOOD	DECOR	SERVICE	COST
19	15	19	$32

E Village | 87 E. Fourth St. (bet. Bowery & 2nd Ave.) | 212-260-6800 | www.cucinadipesce.com

An East Village "old standby" for a "boisterous" "core of regulars", this Italian seafooder delivers "decent fish" in "plain" digs with a "quaint" rear "garden"; even those who maintain it's merely "middling" "can't argue" with the cost, especially the $14 early-bird.

Curry Leaf *Indian*

FOOD	DECOR	SERVICE	COST
19	12	16	$29

Murray Hill | 99 Lexington Ave. (27th St.) | 212-725-5558 | www.curryleafnyc.com

"Satisfying" cooking with "just the right kick" "tickles your taste buds" at this Curry Hill Indian from the Kalustyan's crew; otherwise "service is spotty" and the room's "nothing much to look at", but most are happy to focus on the "unbeatable price."

Da Andrea *Italian*

FOOD	DECOR	SERVICE	COST
22	17	21	$40

G Village | 35 W. 13th St. (bet. 5th & 6th Aves.) | 212-367-1979 | www.daandreanyc.com

"Come hungry and leave satisfied" at this "welcoming" Village "neighborhood trattoria", where the "home-cooked" Emilia-Romagna dishes are a "steal" considering the "quality"; ergo, its "simple" space is bound to be "packed" and "unbelievably noisy" with a "devoted clientele."

Da Ciro *Italian/Pizza*

FOOD	DECOR	SERVICE	COST
23	19	22	$48

Murray Hill | 229 Lexington Ave. (bet. 33rd & 34th Sts.) | 212-532-1636 | www.daciro.com

The house-specialty focaccia Robiola "melts in your mouth" at this Murray Hill "local Italian", a "friendly", bi-level outfit that's also "convenient" for "old-fashioned" staples and "super wood-oven pizza"; it's a "popular hangout" albeit "a bit pricey" for the neighborhood.

| | FOOD | DECOR | SERVICE | COST |

Dafni Greek Taverna *Greek* | 20 | 15 | 20 | $36

W 40s | 325 W. 42nd St. (bet. 8th & 9th Aves.) | 212-315-1010 | www.dafnitaverna.com

Settled into a "surprising" location "opposite the Port Authority", this casual "Greek island" provides "generous" helpings of "tasty" basics at "economical" rates; despite decor that "isn't elegant", it's an "overall decent" pick for "quick", "lively" pre-theater meals.

Daisy May's BBQ USA *BBQ* | 23 | 7 | 14 | $26

W 40s | 623 11th Ave. (46th St.) | 212-977-1500 | www.daisymaysbbq.com

It's "worth traveling" to West Hell's Kitchen for "sticky ribs" and other "kick-ass BBQ" with "all the fixin's" at Adam Perry Lang's "meat cafeteria"; the "humble surroundings" are "as basic as it gets", but "serious" 'cue hounds just "focus on the food" and how well it travels.

Dallas BBQ ● *BBQ* | 16 | 11 | 15 | $25

Chelsea | 261 Eighth Ave. (23rd St.) | 212-462-0001
E 70s | 1265 Third Ave. (bet. 72nd & 73rd Sts.) | 212-772-9393
E Village | 132 Second Ave. (St. Marks Pl.) | 212-777-5574
Washington Heights | 3956 Broadway (bet. 165th & 166th Sts.) | 212-568-3700
W 40s | 241 W. 42nd St. (bet. 7th & 8th Aves.) | 212-221-9000
W 70s | 27 W. 72nd St. (bet. Columbus Ave. & CPW) | 212-873-2004
University Heights | 281 W. Fordham Rd. (Major Deegan Expwy.) | Bronx | 718-220-2822
Downtown Bklyn | 180 Livingston St. (bet. Hoyt & Smith Sts.) | Brooklyn | 718-643-5700
NEW **Rego Park** | 61-35 Junction Blvd. (I-495) | Queens | 718-592-9000
www.dallasbbq.com

"Pig out" with "the masses" at this citywide chain, whose "monster" helpings of "good", "sloppy" BBQ, "big ol'" "slushy drinks" and "bargain" prices "really pack 'em in"; "tacky" setups and "mass-produced" quality remind you that this definitely "ain't Dallas."

Da Nico *Italian* | 20 | 17 | 20 | $44

Little Italy | 164 Mulberry St. (bet. Broome & Grand Sts.) | 212-343-1212 | www.danicoristorante.com

"Among lots of competition", this Little Italy "joint" is a "favorite" for "hearty" "old-school Italian" in "plentiful" portions that ensure "you get your money's worth"; best of all, the "cute back garden" offers a "respite from the hustle and bustle of Mulberry Street."

☑ Daniel *French* | 29 | 28 | 28 | $137

E 60s | 60 E. 65th St. (bet. Madison & Park Aves.) | 212-288-0033 | www.danielnyc.com

"When you want the best of everything", Daniel Boulud's "stately" East Side namesake delivers the goods, "perennially" inspiring "superlatives" for its "breathtaking" New French prix fixes, "stellar wine list" and "world-class service"; at the "zenith of formal" dining ("jackets required") with prices to match, it's "worth every centime" to "celebrate in style"; P.S. the slightly less "lavish" lounge menu is à la carte.

	FOOD	DECOR	SERVICE	COST

NEW Danji ●Ⓩ *Korean* ▽ 24 | 20 | 21 | $44

W 50s | 346 W. 52nd St. (bet. 8th & 9th Aves.) | 212-586-2880 | www.danjinyc.com

Getting "brilliant" early notices, this midpriced Hell's Kitchen Korean small-plates specialist offers two menus: Traditional, featuring "flavorful" classics like seared tofu with ginger dressing, and Modern, with "inventive" fusion takes like bulgogi sliders; shelves full of *danji* (clay kimchi pots) add a rustic touch to the sparse-but-"cute" room.

Ⓩ Danny Brown 27 | 21 | 25 | $52
Wine Bar & Kitchen Ⓜ *European*

Forest Hills | 104-02 Metropolitan Ave. (71st Dr.) | Queens | 718-261-2144 | www.dannybrownwinekitchen.com

Forest Hills locals boast this "off-the-beaten-path" find "rivals many in Manhattan" for "flair and flavor" with its "delectable" European cuisine, "simpatico service" and "classy" "bistro" quarters; devotees drawn to "first-rate" wining and dining at relatively "reasonable" prices are "so happy it exists."

Da Noi *Italian* 23 | 19 | 23 | $49

Shore Acres | 138 Fingerboard Rd. (Tompkins Ave.) | Staten Island | 718-720-1650
Travis | 4358 Victory Blvd. (Service Rd.) | Staten Island | 718-982-5040
www.danoirestaurant.com

They "treat ya and feed ya" "like family" at this "welcoming" Staten Island twosome, where the "delicious" "old-time" Italian dishes and "top-notch" service add up to "excellent value"; despite locations "you may need your GPS to find", they're often "crowded" and (yes) "noisy."

Darbar *Indian* 21 | 16 | 18 | $36

E 40s | 152 E. 46th St. (bet. Lexington & 3rd Aves.) | 212-681-4500 | www.darbarny.com
Darbar Grill *Indian*
E 50s | 157 E. 55th St. (bet. Lexington & 3rd Aves.) | 212-751-4600 | www.darbargrill.com

Midtowners who "don't feel like trekking to Indian Row" count on this East Side twosome for "solid" subcontinental standards and "civil" service in "understated" but "pleasant" enough digs; for seekers of "lunchtime value", the "bountiful" $13 buffet is "addicting."

NEW Darby, The *American* ▽ 20 | 25 | 19 | $84

W Village | 246 W. 14th St. (bet. 7th & 8th Aves.) | 212-242-4411 | www.thedarbynyc.com

A West Village "hot spot", this retro "supper club" draws "models and the guys who drool over them", plus a sprinkling of celebs ("saw LeBron"), to its "gorgeous" "throwback" interior; add "ok" New American nibbles from Alex Guarnaschelli (Butter) and a "talented" house band, and it's "pretty darn cool" – if you "don't mind paying."

Da Silvana Ⓜ *Italian* ▽ 22 | 18 | 22 | $39

Forest Hills | 71-51 Yellowstone Blvd. (bet. Clyde & Dartmouth Sts.) | Queens | 718-268-7871 | www.dasilvana.com

Long a "favorite" in Forest Hills, this "homey" "little" Italian is a "father-and-son" operation where the "wonderful" "old-school" cooking "brings back a lot of regulars"; first-timers can expect a cool reception, but all in all they're apt to be "pleasantly surprised."

☑ Da Silvano *Italian* | 22 | 17 | 18 | $67 |

G Village | 260 Sixth Ave. (Bleecker St.) | 212-982-2343 | www.dasilvano.com

"Grazing and stargazing" compete at this "scene-driven" Village "celeb city", a "legend" for supplying "reliably good" Tuscan fare to the "kiss-kiss" "glitterati" ("put away that camera!"); just "cash in your 401(k)" first – and count on a "haughty" reception "if they don't know you."

Da Tommaso ❶ *Italian* | 20 | 14 | 20 | $48 |

W 50s | 903 Eighth Ave. (bet. 53rd & 54th Sts.) | 212-265-1890 | www.datommasony.com

As a "pre- or post-theater" fallback, this "longtime" Hell's Kitchen Italian "consistently" comes through with "traditional" dishes "done right"; maybe the decor's starting to look "over the hill", but the "accommodating" staff and "affordable" prices remain "good reasons" for its enduring "popularity."

Da Umberto ☒ *Italian* | 24 | 19 | 24 | $69 |

Chelsea | 107 W. 17th St. (bet. 6th & 7th Aves.) | 212-989-0303 | www.daumbertonyc.com

It "doesn't get much better" for "classic" Northern Italian dining than this "quiet" Chelsea "institution" that dependably "delights" with "fabulous" cuisine from waiters who "can't do enough for you"; sure, the cost is "steep", but "after all these years" they "know what they're doing" here.

David Burke at Bloomingdale's *American* | 19 | 13 | 15 | $34 |

E 50s | Bloomingdale's | 150 E. 59th St. (bet. Lexington & 3rd Aves.) | 212-705-3800 | www.burkeinthebox.com

Bloomie's browsers "regroup" over "a quickie" at this "in-store" cafe and its "fast food–esque" annex, where the "casual" New American chow profits from David Burke's "panache"; service is "haphazard" and the setup "not very comfortable", but for a "department store", it's "not a bad option."

NEW David Burke Kitchen ❶ *American* | 24 | 22 | 21 | $63 |

SoHo | James Hotel | 23 Grand St., downstairs (6th Ave.) | 212-201-9119 | www.davidburkekitchen.com

"In true David Burke tradition", this "new 'it' spot" in SoHo's James Hotel delivers "whimsically wonderful" New American dishes via an "attentive" crew in "inspired" urban-rustic digs; there's a patio/bar one level up, and a jaw-droppingly "great view" at Jimmy, the "cool rooftop bar."

☑ David Burke Townhouse *American* | 25 | 25 | 24 | $72 |

E 60s | 133 E. 61st St. (bet. Lexington & Park Aves.) | 212-813-2121 | www.davidburketownhouse.com

Frequented by "UES society", David Burke's New American "delight" elicits "oohs and aahs" for its "lovely" lunch and "epicurean event" dinner; the "bright, elegant" townhouse setting and "pro" staff are also "special", but tables are "tightly packed" and you may want to "take out a mortgage first."

	FOOD	DECOR	SERVICE	COST

Dawat *Indian*   23 | 19 | 21 | $50

E 50s | 210 E. 58th St. (bet. 2nd & 3rd Aves.) | 212-355-7555 |
www.dawatrestaurant.com

A "winner" in Midtown since 1986, this "high-end" Indian "palate-
pleaser" presents chef/cookbook doyenne Madhur Jaffrey's "refined"
cuisine in a "civilized room" staffed by an "informed" team; despite "a bit
of sticker shock", the bottom line is "you get what you pay for."

🗹 DB Bistro Moderne *French*   25 | 22 | 24 | $67

W 40s | City Club Hotel | 55 W. 44th St. (bet. 5th & 6th Aves.) |
212-391-2400 | www.danielnyc.com

Thanks to Daniel Boulud's "magic touch", this "smart" French bistro is
among "D Best" in the Theater District with "fab food" delivered by a
"skillful staff"; the "moderne" digs are on the "tight" side and tabs tilt
"high", but the $45 pre-theater prix fixe is a "bargain."

DBGB ◐ *French*   23 | 22 | 21 | $52

E Village | 299 Bowery (bet. 1st & Houston Sts.) | 212-933-5300 |
www.danielnyc.com

"Daniel Boulud takes a trip Downtown" and "scores again" with this
"energetic" Bowery "meat mecca", a "sleekly" "stylish" Gallic showcase
for "fancy burgers" and "succulent sausages" chased with "interesting
craft beers"; the "hopping" scene means you'll need to "shout to be
heard", but it's an "exhilarating" place "if you're cool – or want to be."

Dee's 🅼 *Mediterranean/Pizza*   22 | 18 | 20 | $32

Forest Hills | 107-23 Metropolitan Ave. (74th Ave.) | Queens |
718-793-7553 | www.deesnyc.com

A "real Forest Hills gem", this "cheerful", "family-oriented" pizzeria
"satisfies" dee-votees "in the neighborhood" with "brick-oven" pies
and a "varied menu" of dishes with "Med flair"; it's also "well priced" –
no wonder it's "always busy."

Defonte's Sandwich Shop *Sandwiches*   24 | 8 | 19 | $15

Gramercy | 261 Third Ave. (21st St.) | 212-614-1500
Red Hook | 379 Columbia St. (Luquer St.) | Brooklyn | 718-625-8052
www.defontesofbrooklyn.com

"Are these sandwiches or battering rams?" marvel patrons of these
"old-time" grinder vendors, whose "humongous" heros are a "top-of-
the-line" fix for "man-size appetites"; the circa-1922 Red Hook "original"
is a "classic", but "you get the real deal" at the Gramercy offshoot too.

DeGrezia 🅂 *Italian*   23 | 22 | 24 | $64

E 50s | 231 E. 50th St. (bet. 2nd & 3rd Aves.) | 212-750-5353 |
www.degreziaristorante.com

If "it feels like you should be celebrating something" at this East Side
"hideaway", credit the "superb" Italian fare, "gracious" service and
"beautiful" "underground" setting where "people can actually converse";
though costs can mount, a "loyal following" deems it "worth every dime."

🗹 Degustation *French/Spanish*   27 | 20 | 25 | $79

E Village | 239 E. Fifth St. (bet. 2nd & 3rd Aves.) | 212-979-1012 |
www.degustationnyc.com

"Sit at the counter and prepare to be wowed" at this "teeny" East
Villager from Jack and Grace Lamb, where a tasting bar affords "ring-

side" seats as seemingly "choreographed" chefs create a "masterful" Franco-Spanish "small plates medley"; it's "pricey", but after the "blow-your-mind" performance, epicures have "absolutely no regrets."

Del Frisco's ● Steak
25 | 23 | 23 | $78

W 40s | 1221 Sixth Ave. (bet. 48th & 49th Sts.) | 212-575-5129 | www.delfriscos.com

NEW Del Frisco's Grille Steak
W 50s | 50 Rockefeller Plaza (51st St., bet. 5th & 6th Aves.) | 212-767-0371 | www.delfriscosgrille.com

"Corporate" carnivores sharpen their teeth for "superior steaks" from a "pro staff" at this "big, bustling" Midtowner, a "power scene" with "lots of razzmatazz" and "action at the bar"; it's "not for the faint of wallet", unless you go for the "little-known" prix fixe deals ($32 lunch, $50 pre-theater); P.S. the roomy, more casual Rock Center offshoot opened post-Survey.

Delicatessen ● American
18 | 19 | 16 | $39

NoLita | 54 Prince St. (Lafayette St.) | 212-226-0211 | www.delicatessennyc.com

You wouldn't know it from the humble moniker, but this "semi-sceney" NoLita hangout plies "inventive" Americana in a "cool" space with a basement bar and retractable walls that "open to the street"; whether "for a snack, brunch or late-night", it's generally "hopping."

☑ Dell'anima ● Italian
25 | 19 | 21 | $56

W Village | 38 Eighth Ave. (Jane St.) | 212-366-6633 | www.dellanima.com

As "small" as it is "trendy", this "pulsating" West Villager is an "up-scale" source of "exceptional" Italian fare where the "chef's counter" by the open kitchen adds "an element of theater"; it's a "tough reservation" and you may "need a shoehorn" to wedge in, but the payoff is "well worth advance planning"; P.S. there's also a next-door wine bar, Anfora.

Delmonico's ☒ Steak
24 | 23 | 23 | $67

Financial District | 56 Beaver St. (S. William St.) | 212-509-1144 | www.delmonicosny.com

"In the same spot since 1837", this "landmark" FiDi chop shop "takes you back" with "old-timey elegance" and "outstanding steaks" that are still sure to "impress a client"; you'll feel like a "robber baron back in the day" – so long as you pack a "fat wallet."

☑ Del Posto Italian
27 | 27 | 27 | $102

Chelsea | 85 10th Ave. (bet. 15th & 16th Sts.) | 212-497-8090 | www.delposto.com

Like being "transported" to "Roma", this Chelsea "Italian masterpiece" from the Batali-Bastianich bunch is "in a class unto itself" with "rarefied" cuisine, "spectacular wines" and "psychic" "white-glove" service; it comes in an "opulent" "palazzo"-like space complete with "velvet curtains, marble floors", "dramatic stairs" and "even a piano player"; *certo*, "you pay dearly for the privilege", but you'll "relish every minute."

Delta Grill ● Cajun/Creole
19 | 15 | 19 | $34

W 40s | 700 Ninth Ave. (48th St.) | 212-956-0934 | www.thedeltagrill.com

"If you're cravin'" a taste of "authentic Nola", this low-budget Hell's Kitchen roadhouse replica obliges with "fine renderings" of "rib-sticking"

Cajun-Creole "comfort cooking" and "Abita on tap"; it's especially "exuberant" on weekends when "*les bon temps*" roll with live bands.

☑ Denino's Pizzeria ⊅ *Pizza*

| 26 | 11 | 19 | $22 |

Port Richmond | 524 Port Richmond Ave. (bet. Hooker Pl. & Walker St.) | Staten Island | 718-442-9401 | www.deninos.com

A "top" local pizzeria "since the dinosaurs" (1937, that is), this "family-run" Staten Islander continues to ply Port Richmond partisans with its "renowned" pies and "no-nonsense" service; it "draws huge crowds" of folks who know "you don't go for the ambiance."

Dervish ◐ *Mediterranean*

| 19 | 16 | 19 | $40 |

W 40s | 146 W. 47th St. (bet. 6th & 7th Aves.) | 212-997-0070 | www.dervishrestaurant.com

A "real boon" for "office workers" and showgoers, this Theater District "standby" is worth a "whirl" for "palatable" Med plates from a "solicitous" staff; maybe the room "needs a refurb", but the tabs (including a $28 pre-theater prix fixe) "won't break the bank."

NEW Desmond's ◐☒ *American*

| ▽ 22 | 24 | 21 | $62 |

E 60s | 153 E. 60th St. (bet. Lexington & 3rd Aves.) | 212-207-4949 | www.desmondsny.com

A former bank opposite Bloomingdale's is home to this "stylish" arrival serving British-accented Americana in a "gorgeous", high-ceilinged, Dorothy Draper–esque room; it's already a hit with a smart local set that includes designer types from the nearby D&D Building.

Deux Amis *French*

| 19 | 16 | 20 | $51 |

E 50s | 356 E. 51st St. (bet. 1st & 2nd Aves.) | 212-230-1117

This East Midtown "haunt" is a longtime "neighborhood favorite" for "authentic" French bistro fare and "welcoming" service led by a "real charmer" of an owner; the "homey" space is "a little tight", so regulars go for the "outdoor tables" in summer.

Dévi *Indian*

| 24 | 20 | 22 | $55 |

Flatiron | 8 E. 18th St. (bet. B'way & 5th Ave.) | 212-691-1300 | www.devinyc.com

"Leaps and bounds above" the usual, this "sophisticated", "pricey" Flatiron Indian furnishes "delectably seasoned" dishes dévised by "gourmet" chef Suvir Saran; with "lovely" "adult" surroundings manned by a "very attentive" team, it works "magic" for those who can't jump a flight to Delhi.

Dhaba ◐ *Indian*

| 24 | 17 | 19 | $30 |

Murray Hill | 108 Lexington Ave. (bet. 27th & 28th Sts.) | 212-679-1284 | www.dhabanyc.com

With the "vibrant flavors" of its "delectable" ("read: hot") cooking, this "lively" "modern" Indian "stands out" even on Curry Hill; the "tight, narrow" space is "deservedly crowded" and "noisy" too, but given the "astonishingly" "modest cost", "who cares?"

☑ Di Fara ☒⊅ *Pizza*

| 26 | 5 | 9 | $18 |

Midwood | 1424 Ave. J (15th St.) | Brooklyn | 718-258-1367 | www.difara.com

Pizzaphiles insist "nothing tops" the pies "lovingly" "handmade" by "master craftsman" Dom DeMarco at this '60s-era Midwood "legend"; it's a "dump" with "limited seating" and "endless waits", but the output is "definitive."

Dim Sum Go Go *Chinese* | 21 | 11 | 14 | $25 |

Chinatown | 5 E. Broadway (Chatham Sq.) | 212-732-0797
Selecting "A-ok" dim sum "from a menu" removes the "agita" of the usual rolling trolleys at this "no-frills" Chinatown joint; sticklers for "authenticity" scoff there's "no substitute" for the "carts experience", but the go-go atmosphere proves it's "popular" enough.

Diner ● *American* | 23 | 17 | 19 | $36 |

Williamsburg | 85 Broadway (Berry St.) | Brooklyn | 718-486-3077 | www.dinernyc.com
"Retro cool" snares the "skinny jeans" set at this South Williamsburg "faux dive" in an "old-fashioned dining car"; thanks to its "creative", "seasonal" New American "comfort" fare, it's a perpetual "go-to" for brunch, even if some wish the staff would "drop the attitude."

Dinosaur Bar-B-Que *BBQ* | 22 | 17 | 18 | $32 |

Harlem | 700 W. 125th St. (12th Ave.) | 212-694-1777 | www.dinosaurbarbque.com
Even in "bigger" new digs, this "rollicking" West Harlem "road-house" is "mobbed" with pilgrims who "strap on the feedbag" for "mammoth portions" of "serious", "shiver-up-your-spine" BBQ, "scrumptious sides" and "brewskis"; the "crazy waits" are a "has-sle", but for a "well-priced" chowdown with weekend "live music", it's the "real deal."

☑ Dirt Candy 🅂🅼 *Vegetarian* | 26 | 17 | 24 | $49 |

E Village | 430 E. Ninth St. (bet. Ave. A & 1st Ave.) | 212-228-7732 | www.dirtcandynyc.com
"Charming" chef-owner Amanda Cohen's "ingenuity" elevates vegetar-ian cooking to "inspiring" "heights" at this East Village "treasure", where the specialties are "revelatory" even "for carnivores"; the "teeny" space and sizable following make it a "difficult rez", so "plan ahead."

Dishes *Sandwiches* | 21 | 12 | 13 | $19 |

E 40s | 6 E. 45th St. (bet. 5th & Madison Aves.) | 212-687-5511 🅂
E 40s | Grand Central | lower level (42nd St. & Vanderbilt Ave.) | 212-808-5511
E 50s | Citigroup Ctr. | 399 Park Ave. (54th St.) | 212-421-5511 🅂
www.dishestogo.com
"Midday" "meccas" for "Midtown professionals", this "lunch-on-the-go" triad is a "superior" source of "fancified" soups, salads and sand-wiches; "the variety and quality" are "worth the extra few bucks", but "everybody knows it" so "brace yourself" for the "scrum."

Ditch Plains ● *Seafood* | 18 | 16 | 18 | $39 |

NEW **W 80s** | 100 W. 82nd St. (bet. Amsterdam & Columbus Aves.) | 212-362-4815
W Village | 29 Bedford St. (Downing St.) | 212-633-0202
www.ditch-plains.com
"For the surfer dude in you", Marc Murphy's "informal" West Village seafooder salutes its namesake (a Montauk beach) with a "simple" seafaring menu that's "swell", if somewhat "ordinary"; its "kid-friendly" UWS sib is "airier" but way less "mellow."

	FOOD	DECOR	SERVICE	COST

Divino *Italian* — 20 | 17 | 21 | $45

E 80s | 1556 Second Ave. (bet. 80th & 81st Sts.) | 212-861-1096
"Reasonably priced" and "never pretentious", this UES staple "aims to please" its "neighborhood" clientele with "traditional Italian" cooking and an "engaging" staff; the usually "quiet" quarters perk up with "live music" on weekends.

Docks Oyster Bar *Seafood* — 21 | 18 | 20 | $52

E 40s | 633 Third Ave. (40th St.) | 212-986-8080 | www.docksoysterbar.com
It's "steady as she goes" at this "spacious", "high-volume" Grand Central–area "fish house" with "well-prepared" seafood and "hopping bar" action; "fancy it's not", but the "predictable" execution and "moderate prices" keep its "bustling", "noisy" "business crowd" happy.

Do Hwa *Korean* — 21 | 18 | 19 | $40

W Village | 55 Carmine St. (Bedford St.) | 212-414-1224 | www.dohwanyc.com
Korean goes "Downtown" at this "happening", relatively "upscale" West Villager, where "trendy" twentysomethings sample "fun cocktails" and get "participatory" at grill-equipped "barbecue tables"; it's typically "crowded" despite tabs "pricier than Koreatown."

Dominick's 🍴 *Italian* — 24 | 11 | 19 | $39

Fordham | 2335 Arthur Ave. (bet. Crescent Ave. & E. 187th St.) | Bronx | 718-733-2807
"Mangia" on "lusty" "homemade Italian" classics at this circa-1966 "Arthur Avenue fave", where patrons "rub elbows" at "communal tables" and "rely on the fast-talking waiters" when ordering ("there's no menu") and paying ("they just tell you the amount"); it's "cash only" and the no-rez policy spells "waits", but most exit "satisfied" all the same.

NEW Donatella *Pizza* — 21 | 20 | 20 | $42

Chelsea | 184 Eighth Ave. (bet. 19th & 20th Sts.) | 212-493-5150 | www.donatellanyc.com
Donatella Arpaia's latest, a "groovy" Chelsea pizza parlor, produces "high-end" Neapolitan pies and other "quality" Italiana rated a "treat" despite prices a bit "steep for a neighborhood" place; the setup balances "casual and upscale", with a "blingy" "gilded oven" that just may "become a tourist attraction."

Ⓩ Donguri Ⓜ *Japanese* — 27 | 17 | 25 | $68

E 80s | 309 E. 83rd St. (bet. 1st & 2nd Aves.) | 212-737-5656 | www.dongurinyc.com
Though "unassuming" and "smaller than small", this UES "authentic" Japanese impresses with "attentive-but-not-intrusive" service and "lovely", "distinctive" specialties from the Kansai region – notably udon, soba and "super-fresh sashimi" ("no sushi"); connoisseurs "marvel" at the "complexity of flavors", but warn "you pay for it."

Donovan's ●🍴 *Pub Food* — 20 | 15 | 18 | $28

Woodside | 57-24 Roosevelt Ave. (58th St.) | Queens | 718-429-9339
"Tons of regulars" tout this Woodside "oldie" as a "real Irish watering hole" known for "wonderful burgers" washed down with "a pint or three"; it "only accepts cash", but with prices so "reasonable", no one's complaining too loudly.

	FOOD	DECOR	SERVICE	COST

Don Pedro's *Caribbean/European*   **21** | **16** | **21** | **$43**

E 90s | 1865 Second Ave. (96th St.) | 212-996-3274 | www.donpedros.net
"Quite a surprise" on a wanting UES stretch, this "small" Euro-Caribbean "really delivers" with its "hearty" cooking, "playful tropical drinks" and service with a "personal touch"; "hidden" amid the "Second Avenue subway construction" chaos, it's a "transporting" "change of pace."

Don Peppe Ⓜ⇗ *Italian*   **25** | **12** | **19** | **$49**

Ozone Park | 135-58 Lefferts Blvd. (bet. 135th & 149th Aves.) | Queens | 718-845-7587
"Come hungry" and feast "with the locals" at this "old-line" "red-sauce nirvana" in Ozone Park, where waiters "out of central casting" deliver "mountains" of "awesome" "family-style" Italian classics; it's "low on decor" and "they don't take plastic", but never mind – "you won't want to stop eating."

Dos Caminos *Mexican*   **19** | **19** | **18** | **$44**

E 50s | 825 Third Ave. (bet. 50th & 51st Sts.) | 212-336-5400
Meatpacking | 675 Hudson St. (14th St.) | 212-699-2400
Murray Hill | 373 Park Ave. S. (bet. 26th & 27th Sts.) | 212-294-1000
SoHo | 475 W. Broadway (bet. Houston & Prince Sts.) | 212-277-4300
www.doscaminos.com
"Twentysomethings" down "fab" "tableside guac" and "banging" margs at Steve Hanson's "high-energy" Mexican crowd-pleasers known both for their "raucous" scenes and their *"muy bueno"* eats; despite a "commercial vibe" and service sometimes "on siesta", they "do the trick."

Dos Toros *Mexican*   **23** | **8** | **16** | **$12**

NEW **E 70s** | 1111 Lexington Ave. (bet. 77th & 78th Sts.) | 212-535-4658
E Village | 137 Fourth Ave. (13th St.) | 212-677-7300
NEW **W Village** | 11 Carmine St. (bet. Bleecker St. & 6th Ave.) | 212-627-2051
www.dostorosnyc.com
Delivering "quality" with no bull, this "low-cost" East Village taqueria earns Mexican mavens' "stamp of approval" for its "fantastic" "San Fran–style tacos and burritos"; a "mobbed" "NYU" magnet, it was joined post-Survey by UES and West Village outposts.

Ⓩ Dovetail *American*   **26** | **23** | **25** | **$74**

W 70s | 103 W. 77th St. (Columbus Ave.) | 212-362-3800 | www.dovetailnyc.com
A "beacon" among the "classy spots on the UWS", John Fraser's "civilized" split-level provides "the complete package" with its "impeccably executed" New American fare, "stellar service" and "contemporary" setting; the tab is "high-end", but the $46 Sunday 'suppa' is an "amazing deal."

Dressler *American*   **25** | **23** | **23** | **$60**

Williamsburg | 149 Broadway (bet. Bedford & Driggs Aves.) | Brooklyn | 718-384-6343 | www.dresslernyc.com
Further evidence that "Brooklyn can compete with Manhattan" for "sophistication", this "warm" Billyburg New American presents "superb" seasonal fare delivered by a "pro" crew in "beautiful" digs

adorned with "original ironwork"; the prices are "more upscale than most" in the area, but "for that special night out" it's a "destination."

Duane Park ⌧Ⓜ American | 22 | 20 | 21 | $56 |

TriBeCa | 157 Duane St. (bet. Hudson St. & W. B'way) | 212-732-5555 | www.duaneparknyc.com

Still somewhat "unknown", this "genteel" TriBeCan adds a "Southern touch" to "reliably" "tasty" New American fare served amid "plantation-redux" decor; earning extra "kudos" with nightly "jazz and burlesque shows", it's a "well-kept secret" that can be "a real treat."

Due Ⓞ Italian | 22 | 17 | 21 | $49 |

E 70s | 1396 Third Ave. (bet. 79th & 80th Sts.) | 212-772-3331 | www.duenyc.com

"Dependable" since 1988, this "straightforward" Upper East Side Northern Italian "fits the bill" for the "locals" who appreciate its "friendly" service and "solid" menu; while "unadventurous", the "accommodating" style keeps it duly "busy."

DuMont American | 23 | 17 | 19 | $29 |

Williamsburg | 432 Union Ave. (bet. Devoe St. & Metropolitan Ave.) | Brooklyn | 718-486-7717

DuMont Burger Ⓞ American

Williamsburg | 314 Bedford Ave. (bet. S. 1st & 2nd Sts.) | Brooklyn | 718-384-6127
www.dumontnyc.com

In the "heart of hipsterhood", this Williamsburg New American is a "go-to" for "crowd-pleasing" "homestyle" fare best enjoyed in the "year-round garden"; its more humble sib on Bedford dispenses "amazing burgers" in a "tight space" that's "popular" into the "late hours."

Dumpling Man Chinese | 21 | 8 | 14 | $13 |

E Village | 100 St. Marks Pl. (bet. Ave. A & 1st Ave.) | 212-505-2121 | www.dumplingman.com

"Go get 'em" – "fabulous fat dumplings" are "stuffed and rolled" "in front of you" at this "budget" East Village Chinese that's the "perfect place to satisfy your craving"; its "minute" space is decidedly "no-frills", so even enthusiasts "do takeout."

ɴᴇᴡ Duo American | - | - | - | E |

Murray Hill | 72 Madison Ave. (bet. 27th & 28th Sts.) | 212-686-7272 | www.duonewyork.com

A humming corner of Murray Hill is home to this new seafood-focused American where the main course seems to be the nightclub-ish mood; the blinged-out space flaunts backlit menus, golden bathroom sinks, lots of Swarovski crystal and enormous, Pre-Raphaelite-style portraits of the owners, two Russian sisters.

⨀ɴᴇᴡ Dutch, The Ⓞ American | 24 | 22 | 21 | $69 |

SoHo | 131 Sullivan St. (Prince St.) | 212-677-6200 | www.thedutchnyc.com
Andrew Carmellini (Locanda Verde) "doesn't disappoint" with this "high-flying" SoHo "hipster" scene, whose "amazing" regional American cooking is "hard to define, but easy to like"; make a rez if you don't want to "wait", and opt for the back room over the "noisy" tiled front – or "forgo conversation and just text your dining partners"; P.S. a "late-night menu keeps the party going into the wee hours."

	FOOD	DECOR	SERVICE	COST

Dylan Prime *Steak*
| | 24 | 23 | 23 | $70 |

TriBeCa | 62 Laight St. (Greenwich St.) | 212-334-4783 |
www.dylanprime.com

For "steak and a date", this TriBeCa meatery "distinguishes itself"
serving beef "like buttah" and martinis "without peer" in "sultry" digs
that offer an "alternative to the clubby men's steakhouse scene"; sure,
it's "pricey", but the "romantic" potential is "nice for a change."

NEW E&E Grill House *Steak*
| | - | - | - | M |

W 40s | Pearl Hotel | 233 W. 49th St. (bet. B'way & 8th Ave.) |
212-505-9909 | www.eegrillhouse.com

In Times Square's Pearl Hotel, this cozy new steakhouse boasts colorful decor featuring retro-patterned banquettes and a sleek bar; the
midpriced lunch and dinner menus are traditional and accessible,
while breakfast service is in the works.

East Buffet *Asian/Eclectic*
| | 19 | 14 | 13 | $29 |

Flushing | 42-07 Main St. (bet. Franklin & Maple Aves.) | Queens |
718-353-6333 | www.eastusa.com

"Big eaters" leave "blissfully satisfied" from this Flushing Asian-
Eclectic's unlimited dinner buffet, a "real bargain" given its "impressive" "variety and taste"; a "huge", tri-level complex with an "à la carte
dining room", it's a "popular" destination – "go early" on weekends.

NEW East End Kitchen *American*
| | - | - | - | M |

E 80s | 539 E. 81st St. (bet. East End & York Aves.) | 212-879-0450 |
www.eastendkitchennyc.com

In the former Boeuf à la Mode space, this Yorkville American serves up
dishes with a major emphasis on seasonal fruits and vegetables; distressed wood panels and white beadboard lend a rustic-beachy vibe
that'll take Upper Eastsiders straight to the Hamptons, sans Jitney.

East Manor *Chinese*
| | 19 | 13 | 14 | $26 |

Flushing | 46-45 Kissena Blvd. (bet. Kalmia & Laburnum Aves.) |
Queens | 718-888-8998

"Rolling carts" facilitate "Hong Kong-style" dim sum feasts at this
"huge" Flushing Chinese – and "if you have a big appetite, the buffet is
a bargain" too; the food's "tasty", but the service is "just ok" and the
"crowded" space "could be better."

E.A.T. *American*
| | 20 | 12 | 15 | $40 |

E 80s | 1064 Madison Ave. (bet. 80th & 81st Sts.) | 212-772-0022 |
www.elizabar.com

A neighborly "place to meet" since 1973, Eli Zabar's UES American
"still rocks" as a "Met Museum"-area "drop-in" that "provides comfort" with its "appealing" sandwiches and deli fare; less appetizing are
the "hurried" service and "steep" prices ("if you have to ask, you
can't afford it").

Ⓩ Eataly *Italian*
| | 23 | 18 | 17 | $42 |

Flatiron | 200 Fifth Ave. (bet. 23rd & 24th Sts.) | 212-229-2560 |
www.eataly.com

The "Batali-Bastianich juggernaut" has another "mega-hit" with this
"cavernous" Flatiron "food hall" (modeled on the "original in Turin"),
where "the masses" "shop and snack" at "endless" stations supplying

| | FOOD | DECOR | SERVICE | COST |

a "mind-altering" "array" of "everything Italian"; the "touristy" "hordes", "unwieldy" layout and "costly" goods can be "off-putting", but "wowed" aficionados "want to move in" all the same; P.S. the steakhouse Manzo and roof-topper Birreria are also on-site.

Eatery ◐ *American*   19 | 15 | 17 | $35

W 50s | 798 Ninth Ave. (53rd St.) | 212-765-7080 | www.eaterynyc.com

"Happening" but "unpretentious", this Hell's Kitchen New American is "more than serviceable" for "creative" comfort fare (like mac 'n' jack "to lust for") that "satisfies" "without emptying your wallet"; the "hip" clientele "feels like Chelsea", as does "the decibel level."

Ecco ⊠ *Italian*   24 | 19 | 23 | $56

TriBeCa | 124 Chambers St. (bet. Church St. & W. B'way) | 212-227-7074 | www.eccorestaurantny.com

"Years and years" in TriBeCa lend a "special charm" to this Italian vet, where "dependable" traditional dishes come in "old-time" digs that ecco yesteryear and get "a lift" from a pianist on weekends; tabs run "a bit high", but its followers plead "don't change a thing."

NEW Edi & the Wolf ◐ *Austrian*   22 | 22 | 20 | $72

E Village | 102 Ave. C (bet. 6th & 7th Sts.) | 212-598-1040 | www.ediandthewolf.com

"Rewarding" treks to Alphabet City, this rookie from the Seäsonal folks presents the chance to wolf down "delicious" Austrian specialties (e.g. "can't-be-beat schnitzel") with wines from the old country; both "offbeat" and "inviting", the wood-lined space "gets pretty busy", but a back garden lends elbow room.

Ed's Chowder House ◐ *Seafood*   20 | 20 | 19 | $57

W 60s | Empire Hotel | 44 W. 63rd St., mezzanine (bet. B'way & Columbus Ave.) | 212-956-1288 | www.chinagrillmgt.com

A "stone's throw" from Lincoln Center, this "upbeat" eatery's "upscale seafood", "earnest" service, "sleek" setting and "high" prices all "belie the down-home name"; even those who discern "no wow factor" grant it's "extremely handy" "before or after a performance."

Ed's Lobster Bar *Seafood*   23 | 15 | 19 | $45

NEW LES | 25 Clinton St. (bet. Houston & Stanton Sts.) | 212-777-7370

NoLita | 222 Lafayette St. (bet. Kenmare & Spring Sts.) | 212-343-3236 www.lobsterbarnyc.com

The "succulent" signature lobster roll is "what they do best" at this "friendly" New England–style seafooder in NoLita, a "casual" (but "not inexpensive") "trip to the shore"; given the "functional" setup's "tight" tables, a berth at the "excellent bar" may be a "better bet"; P.S. the LES offshoot opened post-Survey.

Egg ⊅ *Southern*   23 | 15 | 17 | $23

Williamsburg | 135A N. Fifth St. (bet. Bedford Ave. & Berry St.) | Brooklyn | 718-302-5151 | www.pigandegg.com

Williamsburg's early-risers are "egg-static" over this "tiny" Southerner, where the "spectacular" farmhouse fare is chock-full of "local and super-green" "goodness"; "if you can stand waiting" and paying cash, it's "well worth" a crack at "any time of day."

	FOOD	DECOR	SERVICE	COST

Eisenberg's Sandwich Shop *Sandwiches* | 18 | 11 | 16 | $17 |

Flatiron | 174 Fifth Ave. (bet. 22nd & 23rd Sts.) | 212-675-5096 |
www.eisenbergsnyc.com

"Talk about a throwback" – this circa-1929 Flatiron lunch counter is a
"cheap", "quick" source of "simple" sandwiches and deli classics
with "Depression-era" "authenticity" and "grunge" intact; some say
the nosh "ain't that great", but "nostalgia is the draw" for "tourists
and locals" alike.

EJ's Luncheonette ⊭ *Diner* | 16 | 10 | 15 | $25 |

E 70s | 1271 Third Ave. (73rd St.) | 212-472-0600

Long a "local fave", this "busy, busy" UES "family central" is "ever reliable" for "filling" American "favorites" that sate the "stroller set" at
"bargain" prices; just "bring cash" and prepare to "weather l-o-n-g
lines" on weekends.

El Centro ◗ *Mexican* | 22 | 18 | 20 | $35 |

W 50s | 824 Ninth Ave. (54th St.) | 646-763-6585 | www.elcentro-nyc.com

"*Olé!*" cheer compadres of this Hell's Kitchen cantina where "laid-
back" staffers ferry "addictive" chilaquiles and other "*fabuloso*" Mexican
plates; the decor is on the "cheesy" side, but "the price is right" and
when the margaritas flow its "young clientele" has "a blast."

El Charro Español *Spanish* | ▽ 23 | 15 | 23 | $49 |

W Village | 4 Charles St. (bet. Greenwich & 7th Aves.) | 212-242-9547 |
www.el-charro-espanol.com

"The old times" endure at this circa-1925 West Village Spaniard that's
still "on the money" with its "traditional" dishes and "polite" service;
the subterranean space "needs refurbishing", but there's "nothing
faux" about it – and "that works just fine" for longtime loyalists.

Elephant & Castle ◗ *Pub Food* | 19 | 16 | 19 | $29 |

W Village | 68 Greenwich Ave. (bet. Perry St. & 7th Ave. S.) | 212-243-1400 |
www.elephantandcastle.com

"Oh-so-reliable" for "everyday", this "fairly priced" West Village "favorite" proffers "pub" basics "with a smile" in "casual" '70s-vintage
digs; it's "the definition of cramped", but there's "a reason" it's "always humming" and "way packed" at weekend brunch.

NEW Elevation Burger *Burgers* | 20 | 12 | 18 | $12 |

Chelsea | 103 W. 14th St. (bet. 6th & 7th Aves.) | 212-924-4448 |
www.elevationburger.com

"Fast food" gets an "ecology-oriented" lift at this "affordable" Chelsea
outlet of a VA franchise, where "grass-fed", "sustainable beef" burgers
(and veggie versions) deliver "quality" with "none of the guilt"; the
"design-your-own" options and "upbeat" vibe are likewise a "step up."

⧉ Eleven Madison Park ⧉ *French* | 28 | 28 | 28 | $117 |

Flatiron | 11 Madison Ave. (24th St.) | 212-889-0905 |
www.elevenmadisonpark.com

"Top of the line" even for Danny Meyer, this New French "experience"
on Madison Square Park is "exquisite from beginning to end", match-
ing chef Daniel Humm's "exhilarating" tasting menu–only cuisine with
"world-class" service ("even the busboys have Cornell degrees") in a
"majestic" "art deco" space; surveyors split on the "cryptic new

	FOOD	DECOR	SERVICE	COST

"sudoku"-card menu format ("an engaging adventure" vs. "precious"), and, of course, tabs are "in the stratosphere."

El Faro ● Ⓜ *Spanish*   22 | 11 | 19 | $42

W Village | 823 Greenwich St. (bet. Horatio & Jane Sts.) | 212-929-8210 | www.elfaronyc.com

Dating to 1927, this "small" West Villager remains "as good as ever" for "hearty", "garlic-infused" tapas and Spanish standards ("paella is the big draw") at "recession" rates; the "vintage" space is due for "a makeover", but regulars recommend "close your eyes and just eat."

Eliá Ⓜ *Greek*   ▽ 27 | 21 | 24 | $55

Bay Ridge | 8611 Third Ave. (bet. 86th & 87th Sts.) | Brooklyn | 718-748-9891 | www.eliarestaurant.com

"You'll think you're in Santorini" given the "excellent", "authentic Greek" dishes and "warm" service at this "fine" Bay Ridge Hellene; factor in its "cozy" and "unpretentious" space with a garden deck, and it's a "definite winner" – albeit one that's "pricey" for the area.

Elias Corner ● ⊄ *Greek/Seafood*   23 | 9 | 15 | $40

Astoria | 24-02 31st St. (24th Ave.) | Queens | 718-932-1510

Expect "no nonsense" from this "simple" Astoria Greek "mainstay", an '80s survivor that's "still cranking out" affordable, "super-fresh" seafood grilled "to perfection"; there's "no decor, no menu" and "no credit cards accepted" – but it also makes do "without the attitude."

☑ Elio's ● *Italian*   24 | 17 | 21 | $68

E 80s | 1621 Second Ave. (bet. 84th & 85th Sts.) | 212-772-2242

Witness the "UES fashion show" at this "cliquish", circa-1981 standby, an "energizing" "society" magnet "crammed" with "sexy" "locals and celebs"; just know the "top-notch" Italian bites are priced for "moneyed folks", and "disenchanted" outsiders add "it helps if they know you."

NEW Ellabess *American*   - | - | - | E

NoLita | Nolitan Hotel | 153 Elizabeth St. (Kenmare St.) | 212-925-5559 | www.ellabessnyc.com

The folks behind Dell'anima and L'Artusi go New American with this Nolitan Hotel newcomer pairing seasonal fare with a deep wine list and old-school cocktails; black tables offset gray-concrete pillars in its sleek room, whose hip crowd likes dodging the epic waits at its West Village cousins.

El Malecon ● *Dominican*   20 | 9 | 15 | $22

Washington Heights | 4141 Broadway (175th St.) | 212-927-3812
W 90s | 764 Amsterdam Ave. (bet. 97th & 98th Sts.) | 212-864-5648
Kingsbridge | 5592 Broadway (231st St.) | Bronx | 718-432-5155

Specializing in "luscious" rotisserie chicken "seasoned to perfection" with "lotsa garlic", this "rough-and-ready" trio is also favored for "stick-to-your-ribs" Dominican "home cooking"; maybe its outlets are "not pretty", but they dish out "ample" rations *para poco dinero.*

El Parador Cafe *Mexican*   23 | 17 | 21 | $46

Murray Hill | 325 E. 34th St. (bet. 1st & 2nd Aves.) | 212-679-6812 | www.elparadorcafe.com

"Homey" and "semi-hidden", this Murray Hill "oldie but goodie" (since 1959) is "much appreciated" for its "carefully prepared", "traditional"

Mexican dishes, "smooth" margaritas and "polished" staff; it's a "decent value" too – no wonder customers "keep coming back."

El Paso Taqueria *Mexican*

23 | 15 | 19 | $28

E 100s | 1643 Lexington Ave. (104th St.) | 212-831-9831
E 90s | 64 E. 97th St. (bet. Madison & Park Aves.) | 212-996-1739
Harlem | 237 E. 116th St. (3rd Ave.) | 212-860-4875
www.elpasotaqueria.com

Uptowners say this "cheerful" trio "easily rivals" some better-known outfits with its "beautifully spiced" Mexicana; the setups are "cheek-to-jowl" (with a "hidden patio" on Lex), but if you can do "without the frills" it's an "authentic experience" that "won't break your wallet."

El Porrón *Spanish*

23 | 21 | 21 | $46

E 60s | 1123 First Ave. (bet. 61st & 62nd Sts.) | 212-207-8349 |
www.elporronnyc.com

"If you can't go to Spain", this "welcoming" East Side tapas bar "will certainly do" with its "wide-ranging" lineup of "delightful" tidbits and "well-priced" vinos siphoned from *porróns* (spouted glass pitchers); lately "discovered", the "warm but cool" space can get "crowded."

El Pote 🗷 *Spanish*

22 | 15 | 22 | $43

Murray Hill | 718 Second Ave. (bet. 38th & 39th Sts.) | 212-889-6680 |
www.elpote.com

For a "true taste" of Spain, try this Murray Hill vet, where "large portions" of "excellent paella" and other "traditional" faves are prepared "with love" and served by "been-there-forever" staffers; sure, the '70s-era space is "a bit worn", but the "value" is "worth returning for."

El Quijote ◗ *Spanish*

21 | 15 | 20 | $45

Chelsea | 226 W. 23rd St. (bet. 7th & 8th Aves.) | 212-929-1855

At this Chelsea Spanish "fixture" (since 1930), you can "count on" "garlicky fun times" with "best-buy" lobster and paella plus "delicious sangria" served by a "sweet", "efficient" staff; its "loyal following" urges "get past" the "cheesy" interior and "feel the party vibe."

El Quinto Pino ◗ *Spanish*

▽ 21 | 15 | 20 | $39

Chelsea | 401 W. 24th St. (bet. 9th & 10th Aves.) | 212-206-6900 |
www.elquintopinonyc.com

The lucky few who "squeeze in" to this "micro" Cheslea wine-and-tapas bar (and Txikito sib) "snag" barstool seats and sample "high-quality" "regional Spanish" bites, including an "orgasmic" uni panini; it may be "pricey" "for a snack", but it stays "busy" all the same.

El Rio Grande *Tex-Mex*

18 | 15 | 16 | $38

Murray Hill | 160 E. 38th St. (bet. Lexington & 3rd Aves.) | 212-867-0922 |
www.arkrestaurants.com

It's "your choice of Texas or Mexico" at this "Murray Hill staple" serving "decent, if typical, Tex-Mex" for "moderate" moola; many maintain the "lethal margaritas" that fuel the "crowded" scene are its "best feature."

Embers Ⓜ *Steak*

20 | 14 | 18 | $47

Bay Ridge | 9519 Third Ave. (bet. 95th & 96th Sts.) | Brooklyn |
718-745-3700

Maybe it looks like a "relic", but this "long-running" Bay Ridge steakhouse still sparks "neighborhood" loyalty with its "good cuts" offered

| | FOOD | DECOR | SERVICE | COST |

at prices "well below the competition"; even so, the "crammed" seating inspires cries of "fuhgeddaboudit – they need to expand!"

Emilio's Ballato *Italian*   ▽ 25 | 18 | 22 | $52

NoLita | 55 E. Houston St. (Mott St.) | 212-274-8881

A "credit to the neighborhood" since 1956, this "old-style" NoLita Italian remains a "treat" for "fantastic" traditional cooking delivered by a "pro" crew; the space straight out of "historic Little Italy" has been "newly expanded", causing regulars to "hope it isn't discovered."

Empanada Mama ● *S. American*   22 | 12 | 15 | $19

W 50s | 763 Ninth Ave. (bet. 51st & 52nd Sts.) | 212-698-9008 |
www.empmamanyc.com

"Out-of-this-world" empanadas with "inventive" flavors and "24/7 availability" are the temptation at this Hell's Kitchen South American; though "hole-in-the-wall" digs can cause "discomfort", to most the "cheap" goods are "worth bumping elbows for"; P.S. a Village branch is in the works.

NEW Empellón ● *Mexican*   21 | 17 | 20 | $49

W Village | 230 W. Fourth St. (W. 10th St.) | 212-367-0999 |
www.empellon.com

Alex Stupak (WD-50) veers "upscale Mexican" at this "fun" new West Villager whose "terrific" dishes include some offbeat flourishes like tacos with head cheese, accompanied by "high-octane mezcal and cocktails"; it's "crowded and noisy" most nights, but the "back room is quieter"; P.S. an East Village branch is in the works at 105 First Avenue.

NEW Empire Steakhouse *Steak*   ▽ 20 | 18 | 22 | $78

E 50s | 36 W. 52nd St. (bet. 5th & 6th Aves.) | 212-582-6900 |
www.empiresteakhousenyc.com

In the former Anthos digs, this new Midtown moo house from alums of Ben & Jack's and Peter Luger rolls out "typical steakhouse fare" at recession-be-damned rates; service is "attentive", and upstairs there's a handsome room for private parties.

Empire Szechuan ● *Chinese*   17 | 10 | 15 | $25

Washington Heights | 4041 Broadway (bet. 170th & 171st Sts.) |
212-568-1600
W 60s | 193 Columbus Ave. (bet. 68th & 69th Sts.) | 212-496-8778
W 100s | 2642 Broadway (bet. 100th & 101st Sts.) | 212-662-9404
W Village | 173 Seventh Ave. S. (bet. Perry & W. 11th Sts.) |
212-243-6046
www.empiretogo.com

It "may not set off culinary fireworks", but this "convenient", "fair"-priced Chinese chainlet "competently" cooks up "standards" ("varied" with sushi) that have "fit the bill" for "many years" now; given the "drab" decor and "perfunctory" service, many "indulge via phone."

Emporio *Italian*   23 | 20 | 19 | $46

NoLita | 231 Mott St. (bet. Prince & Spring Sts.) | 212-966-1234 |
www.auroraristorante.com

"Hipsters and locals" alike find this NoLita Italian from the Aurora folks "accessible" for "soul-satisfying" pastas and pizzas in "congenial" "rustic"-meets-industrial digs; the "skylit back room" works "for a chilled-out date", but get closer since it "can be noisy."

| | FOOD | DECOR | SERVICE | COST |

EN Japanese Brasserie *Japanese* `25` `26` `24` `$65`

W Village | 435 Hudson St. (Leroy St.) | 212-647-9196 |
www.enjb.com

Bound to make a "big first impression", this West Village Japanese
en-spires raves with its "gorgeous", "graciously quiet" space where
"pro" staffers offer a "pristine" menu highlighting "freshly made tofu"
(a "revelation") and "top-notch" "izakaya-style" plates paired with
"superb" sakes; the "somewhat pricey" tabs are predictable given that
it "sets the bar so high."

Enoteca Maria ⍇⌿ *Italian* ▽ `25` `19` `23` `$48`

St. George | 27 Hyatt St. (Central Ave.) | Staten Island | 718-447-2777 |
www.enotecamaria.com

"Talk about homemade" – this "cash-only" Staten Island wine bar near
"the St. George ferry" has "real nonnas" cooking "flavorful", small
plate–centric fare "from different regions of Italy" on alternating nights;
"it's no gimmick", so naturally the "small" space is often "bustling."

Enzo's *Italian* `23` `17` `21` `$41`

Fordham | 2339 Arthur Ave. (bet. Crescent Ave. & E. 186th St.) | Bronx |
718-733-4455
Morris Park | 1998 Williamsbridge Rd. (Neill Ave.) | Bronx | 718-409-3828
www.enzosofthebronx.com

They're "not breaking new ground", but these "real-deal" Arthur
Avenue–Williamsbridge Italians divert "da Bronx" with heaping helpings
of "gravy"-laden "standards" from a "friendly" team; the setups are
nothing fancy, but who cares – you'll have "cash left" over afterwards.

NEW Eolo *Italian* ▽ `24` `17` `21` `$52`

Chelsea | 190 Seventh Ave. (bet. 21st & 22nd Sts.) | 646-225-6606 |
www.eolonyc.com

"Originality" and "flair" mark this new Chelsea Italian serving a "well-
conceived" menu of "housemade pastas" and other "lovingly prepared" Sicilian specialties in an ambiance of "friendly" rusticana; just
"don't be fooled by" the modest decor – it's a "real find" and "not cheap."

Epices du Traiteur *Mediterranean/Tunisian* `21` `15` `19` `$42`

W 70s | 103 W. 70th St. (Columbus Ave.) | 212-579-5904

A "break from the ordinary", this Upper Westsider's Med-Tunisian
"mix" is "offbeat", "appealing" and "well priced"; those who find the
"skinny" digs "claustrophobic" can "opt for the garden" or arrive after
8 when the "Lincoln Center" crowd has left.

Erawan *Thai* `24` `20` `20` `$38`

Bayside | 42-31 Bell Blvd. (bet. 42nd & 43rd Aves.) | Queens | 718-428-2112 |
www.erawan-nyc.com

For a "local place", this Bayside Thai can "surprise" given its "glorious
dishes" with "interesting touches" delivered by servers ready "to edu-
cate you" on the nuances; no wonder it's "busy" and "packed."

Erminia ⍈ *Italian* `25` `23` `24` `$69`

E 80s | 250 E. 83rd St. (bet. 2nd & 3rd Aves.) | 212-879-4284 |
www.erminiaristorante.com

With its "dimly lit" "farmhouse" setting, "luscious" Roman cuisine and
"impeccable" service, this "intimate" UES "hideaway" remains "wor-

thy of its reputation" as a "sentimental favorite" for "romance"; paramours primed "to woo" hardly mind if it's "pricey" and quite "compact."

⏹ Esca ● Italian/Seafood
25 | 20 | 23 | $72

W 40s | 402 W. 43rd St. (9th Ave.) | 212-564-7272 | www.esca-nyc.com
An established "top draw" "pre-Broadway", the Batali-Bastianich-Pasternack crew's Hell's Kitchen standout "continues to amaze" with "heavenly" Italian seafood, including "fantastic" crudo and pasta dishes, "seamlessly" served in "rustic yet elegant" surrounds; it'll set you back "a few fins", but the "quality justifies" the "splurge."

Etcetera Etcetera Italian
22 | 19 | 22 | $51

W 40s | 352 W. 44th St. (bet. 8th & 9th Aves.) | 212-399-4141 | www.etcrestaurant.com
This "little sister of ViceVersa" puts a "flavorful twist" on Italian classics in "hip, modern" Hell's Kitchen environs with a choice of "convivial" first-floor "din" or upstairs "quiet"; "congenial, efficient" service makes for an "easy in and out" before "curtain" time.

Ethos Greek
21 | 16 | 19 | $43

E 50s | 905 First Ave. (51st St.) | 212-888-4060
Murray Hill | 495 Third Ave. (bet. 33rd & 34th Sts.) | 212-252-1972
www.ethosrestaurants.com
Known for its "flair for fish", this "lively" taverna twosome "never fails to deliver" for fans of "abundant" "Greek staples" served with "no attitude"; the Murray Hill site's "not as upscale" as its Sutton Place offshoot, but they're both "worth the money."

Euzkadi Spanish
20 | 17 | 18 | $40

E Village | 108 E. Fourth St. (bet. 1st & 2nd Aves.) | 212-982-9788 | www.euzkadirestaurant.com
Something of a "local secret", this East Villager is "sure to seduce" with its "real Basque" roster featuring "awesome" tapas and "wines to match" at a "reasonable price"; "small" and "sultry" with live flamenco on Tuesdays, it makes for a "fun date."

Excellent Dumpling House ⊅ Chinese
21 | 4 | 13 | $17

Chinatown | 111 Lafayette St. (bet. Canal & Walker Sts.) | 212-219-0212
The "name doesn't lie", but "don't stop with the dumplings" at this Chinatown "dive", a "mainstay" for "tasty" Shanghainese fare proffered "so fast you're not late back to jury duty"; "bargain" tabs redress the "brusque" service and decor that "could use serious help."

Extra Virgin Mediterranean
23 | 19 | 18 | $44

W Village | 259 W. Fourth St. (Perry St.) | 212-691-9359 | www.extravirginrestaurant.com
With its "appealing" Med menu and "hopping" milieu, this "cute" West Villager is a "favorite" "gathering spot" for "trendy" "young" things; hospitality "depends on the server" and the interior's extra "crammed", but "if you can sit outside" it provides "perfect people-watching."

Fabio Piccolo Fiore Italian
23 | 20 | 23 | $54

E 40s | 230 E. 44th St. (bet. 2nd & 3rd Aves.) | 212-922-0581 | www.fabiopiccolofiore.com
"Worth finding" near Grand Central, this "somewhat upscale" Italian offers "wonderful" "classic" dishes from an "accommodating" crew,

led by the "sweetest chef" (he'll take requests to "cook anything to order"); an "unrushed", "normal-decibel" vibe boosts the fab factor.

Fairway Cafe   American

| | 18 | 9 | 12 | $26 |

NEW E 80s | 240 E. 86th St. (2nd Ave.) | 212-327-2008
W 70s | 2127 Broadway, 2nd fl. (74th St.) | 212-595-1888
Red Hook | 480-500 Van Brunt St. (Reed St.) | Brooklyn | 718-694-6868
www.fairwaymarket.com

"If you have to eat in a grocery store", these "fairly priced" cafes furnish "adequate" American eats for a "quick nosh", plus steaks on the UWS; downsides include "erratic service" and "no decor" – aside from Red Hook's view of "Ms. Liberty"; P.S. the UES branch opened post-Survey.

Falai   Italian

| | 24 | 18 | 20 | $54 |

LES | 68 Clinton St. (bet. Rivington & Stanton Sts.) | 212-253-1960

Falai Panetteria   Italian

LES | 79 Clinton St. (Rivington St.) | 212-777-8956

Caffe Falai   Italian

SoHo | 265 Lafayette St. (Prince St.) | 212-274-8615
www.falainyc.com

So long as you "don't expect any red sauce", chef Iacopo Falai's "artful" Italiana will "impress every time", making this "cool" LES "surprise" "worth the excursion"; meanwhile, the "simple"Panetteria and SoHo's "now not-so-tiny" Caffe provide breakfast and lunch at lower prices.

F & J Pine Restaurant   Italian

| | 21 | 18 | 20 | $37 |

Morris Park | 1913 Bronxdale Ave. (bet. Matthews & Muliner Aves.) | Bronx | 718-792-5956 | www.fjpine.com

"Famous" for its "super-size" portions of "solid" red-gravy basics, this "old-style" Italian stalwart appeals to "real Bronxites" plus "Yankee players from time to time"; maybe the "service and ambiance are ordinary", but "you'll leave stuffed to the gills" for a fair price.

Farm on Adderley   American

| | 24 | 20 | 21 | $37 |

Ditmas Park | 1108 Cortelyou Rd. (bet. Stratford & Westminster Rds.) | Brooklyn | 718-287-3101 | www.thefarmonadderley.com

"Grateful" Ditmas Park denizens "salute" this "top-of-the-line" neighborhood "treat" for its "inventive" New American fare made with "fresh", "locally grown" ingredients; in "comfortable" bistro digs with a "wonderful garden", it's a "winner" that won't cost a bushel.

NEW Fat Goose   American

| | - | - | - | E |

Williamsburg | 125 Wythe Ave. (N. 8th St.) | Brooklyn | 718-963-2200 | www.fatgoosewilliamsburg.com

In West Williamsburg, this New American gastropub offers a rotating menu of pricey, sophisticated plates meant for sharing; the slick setting seems designed for the nearby luxe-condo set with its high-gloss wood floors, ornate chandelier and marble bar dispensing creative cocktails.

NEW Fat Radish ● Ⓜ British

| | 20 | 22 | 19 | $48 |

LES | 17 Orchard St. (bet. Canal & Hester Sts.) | 212-300-4053 | www.thefatradishnyc.com

"Anglophiles rejoice" in this "hip" LES arrival proving its "chops" with "creative", "veggie"-centric Modern British fare served in "relaxed", "airy", brick-walled digs; the staff's "charming" but "a bit slow" – no surprise since it's "always packed" with *Gossip Girl* types.

	FOOD	DECOR	SERVICE	COST

Fatty Crab ● *Malaysian* — 20 | 13 | 16 | $44

W 70s | 2170 Broadway (77th St.) | 212-496-2722
W Village | 643 Hudson St. (bet. Gansevoort & Horatio Sts.) | 212-352-3590
www.fattycrab.com

At Zak Pelaccio's "happening" pair, you "get down and dirty" with "mouth-awakening" Malaysian "street food" served by "über-hip" staffers; those crabby over the Village original's "cramped" digs should know the UWS outlet has "more space" but is equally "edgy" and "ear-ringing."

Fatty 'Cue *BBQ/SE Asian* — 21 | 14 | 18 | $40

NEW **W Village** | 50 Carmine St. (bet. Bedford & Bleecker Sts.) | 212-929-5050
Williamsburg | 91 S. Sixth St. (Berry St.) | Brooklyn | 718-599-3090 ●
www.fattycue.com

For a "new kind of 'cue", hit this Williamsburg "bohemian" "hot spot", where Zak Pelaccio's union of "meatalicious" American BBQ and "zippy" Southeast Asian accents "works miracles"; expect an "airy, industrial" space "buzzing" with "hipsters to ogle"; P.S. the West Village offshoot opened post-Survey.

Fatty Fish *Asian* — 21 | 16 | 20 | $39

E 60s | 406 E. 64th St. (bet. 1st & York Aves.) | 212-813-9338 | www.fattyfishnyc.com

"Solid" sushi and Asian fusion fare with "many surprising combinations" is the lure at this UES "haven"; "caring" servers oversee the "spare" interior and "beautiful patio", while BYO with "no corkage on your first bottle" boosts the "affordability" factor.

NEW **Fedora** ● *American/French* — 22 | 20 | 22 | $58

W Village | 239 W. Fourth St., downstairs (bet. Charles & W. 10th Sts.) | 646-449-9336 | www.fedoranyc.com

"Grow a beard and wear flannel" to fit in at this "hip" "remake" of a West Village basement "icon" from Gabe Stulman (Joseph Leonard, Jeffrey's Grocery), where "delicious" French-American fare is served by a "cheerful" staff; the "refurbished" space "mixing new with old" completes the "cool" "scene."

Felice *Italian* — 24 | 22 | 22 | $47

E 60s | 1166 First Ave. (64th St.) | 212-593-2223
NEW **E 80s** | 1593 First Ave. (83rd St.) | 212-249-4080 ●
www.felicewinebar.com

"Anything but stuffy", this UES wine bar's a "fave" of "young" types who mingle over "well-priced" vintages and a "limited" list of "appetizing" Italiana; manned by a "down-to-earth" staff, the "compact" space mixes "easy vibes" with "major noise"; P.S. the Uptown offshoot opened post-Survey.

☑ Felidia *Italian* — 26 | 22 | 24 | $80

E 50s | 243 E. 58th St. (bet. 2nd & 3rd Aves.) | 212-758-1479 | www.felidia-nyc.com

Still "setting the bar high" after three decades, Lidia Bastianich's East Side Italian "flagship" exhibits her "masterful" cooking "graciously served" in "coddling" "townhouse" environs; despite "showing its age" and affording limited "elbow room", it's "worth" those tabs that'll "unpad your wallet."

Ferdinando's Focacceria 🄑⊐ *Italian* ▽ 25 | 13 | 18 | $26

Carroll Gardens | 151 Union St. (bet. Columbia & Hicks Sts.) | Brooklyn | 718-855-1545

It seemingly "hasn't changed" since 1904, and that pleases fans of this cash-only Carroll Gardens Italian possessing an "endearing" way with "Sicilian soul food" like the panelle sandwich ("fuhgeddaboudit"); the digs are "dated" but perfect for "kicking it old school."

Ferrara ◑ *Bakery* 23 | 17 | 17 | $20

Little Italy | 195 Grand St. (bet. Mott & Mulberry Sts.) | 212-226-6150 | www.ferraracafe.com

A taste of "la dolce vita" awaits at this "landmark" Little Italy bakery, the "real deal" since 1892 for "sinful" Italian desserts ("cannoli are a must") and "a jolt of espresso"; it attracts "zoolike crowds" of "tourists", but "your sweet tooth" will be "appeased."

⊠ Fette Sau *BBQ* 26 | 15 | 14 | $29

Williamsburg | 354 Metropolitan Ave. (bet. Havemeyer & Roebling Sts.) | Brooklyn | 718-963-3404 | www.fettesaubbq.com

It's "worth fighting through the hipsters" for "incredible BBQ" rated the "best in NYC" at this Williamsburg "hawg heaven" in a "converted auto garage"; the "ethereal" meat is "priced by the pound" and chased with "brown liquors" and "quality suds", but you have to endure "long waits" in "cafeteria-style" lines and "picniclike" "communal" seating.

⊠ 15 East 🄑 *Japanese* 26 | 22 | 24 | $89

Union Sq | 15 E. 15th St. (bet. 5th Ave. & Union Sq. W.) | 212-647-0015 | www.15eastrestaurant.com

For "artistry, service and ambiance", this "Zen"-like Union Square sushi "temple" from the Tocqueville team is "one of the standard-bearers"; its "ridiculously fresh", "simple" yet "magical" preparations and "high-level" hospitality are sure to be a "rewarding" experience, but if you "go omakase", bring plenty of yen.

Fig & Olive *Mediterranean* 20 | 20 | 18 | $48

E 50s | 10 E. 52nd St. (bet. 5th & Madison Aves.) | 212-319-2002
E 60s | 808 Lexington Ave. (bet. 62nd & 63rd Sts.) | 212-207-4555
Meatpacking | 420 W. 13th St. (bet. 9th Ave. & Washington St.) | 212-924-1200
www.figandolive.com

"Delightful" small plates and mains "focused around different, high-quality olive oils" are the draw at these "chic", midpriced Mediterraneans; the Eastsiders are "solid choices" for "refueling after shopping", while the "busy, noisy" Meatpacking venue's just the place to "kick off a night of bar-hopping."

Filippo's Ⓜ *Italian* ▽ 25 | 21 | 23 | $53

Dongan Hills | 1727 Richmond Rd. (bet. Buel & Seaver Aves.) | Staten Island | 718-668-9091 | www.filipposrestaurant.com

"Spectacular" specials "outnumber" the regular menu items at this family-run, "energy-filled" SI Italian, a once-"sleepy" eatery that's now "a real hot spot" despite being "tucked" away in a Dongan Hills "strip mall"; "personable" service helps make up-there tabs "worth it."

	FOOD	DECOR	SERVICE	COST

Fiorentino's ☑ *Italian* | 21 | 15 | 20 | $37 |

Gravesend | 311 Ave. U (bet. McDonald Ave. & West St.) | Brooklyn | 718-372-1445

"Plentiful", "garlicky" Neapolitan "red-sauce" classics like "when you were growing up" can be found at this Gravesend "oldie but goodie"; it's loved by "a cast of neighborhood characters" for its "welcoming" vibe and "economically sound" prices, if not its "noise" and "face-lift"-ready decor.

Fiorini ☒ *Italian* | 21 | 19 | 21 | $54 |

E 50s | 209 E. 56th St. (bet. 2nd & 3rd Aves.) | 212-308-0830 | www.fiorinirestaurant.com

Lello Arpaia's "hospitable" East Midtown Italian refuge presents a "peaceful", "quiet" (some say "stodgy") setting that lets the "traditional" Neapolitan fare "speak for itself"; it's "on the short list" for "adult" locals who don't mind that checks are "a bit steep."

FireBird ☑ *Russian* | 20 | 26 | 22 | $67 |

W 40s | 365 W. 46th St. (bet. 8th & 9th Aves.) | 212-586-0244 | www.firebirdrestaurant.com

Like a slice of old "St. Petersburg", this "regal" Restaurant Row Russian "harks back" to pre-revolutionary times with "delicacies à la Russe", a vodka selection to "make your head spin", "opulent" digs and an "old-style" staff; of course, "dining like a czar doesn't come cheap."

Firenze ◐ *Italian* | 22 | 20 | 23 | $53 |

E 80s | 1594 Second Ave. (bet. 82nd & 83rd Sts.) | 212-861-9368 | www.firenzeny.com

Somwhat "unsung", this Upper East Side Tuscan "aims to please" with "delicious" "traditional Florentine" cuisine via an "old-world-gracious" crew; that its "homey" "candlelit" quarters conjure your "vacation in Italy" is another reason it's a "winning" "little place."

Fish *Seafood* | 23 | 15 | 19 | $41 |

W Village | 280 Bleecker St. (Jones St.) | 212-727-2879 | fishrestaurantnyc.com

It's "Cape Cod" on Bleecker Street at this "laid-back" Villager presenting "fresh", "delish" catch in "tiny" "retro-fish-shack" digs complete with a "small raw bar"; "dockside prices" get even better when you go for the $8 bivalve-and-booze combo (maybe the "best deal in NY").

NEW FishTag *Greek/Seafood* | 22 | 17 | 20 | $52 |

W 70s | 222 W. 79th St. (bet. Amsterdam Ave. & B'way) | 212-362-7470 | www.fishtagrestaurant.com

Navigating the "complex menu" of "interchanging" appetizers and mains, plus wine pairings, you'll reel in some "un-flipping-believable" Greek seafood at Michael Psilakis' latest on the UWS; despite "engaging" service, the "boxed-in", "earplug"-worthy dining room leads some to "chow at the bar" instead.

Fishtail *Seafood* | 24 | 24 | 23 | $66 |

E 60s | 135 E. 62nd St. (bet. Lexington & Park Aves.) | 212-754-1300 | www.fishtaildb.com

Pescephiles take the bait at David Burke's "top-notch" Upper Eastsider, where "congenial" staffers deliver "whimsical" renditions of "serious"

American seafood in "gorgeous" townhouse quarters; factor in a "busy bar scene" and you've got a "fun" night out – "if you can afford it."

5 & Diamond ⓜ *American*

21 | 18 | 18 | $44

Harlem | 2072 Frederick Douglass Blvd. (112th St.) | 646-684-4662 | www.5anddiamondrestaurant.com

This "tiny" Harlem yearling draws a "young" crowd for its "upscale" New American cooking served in "casual" digs on a prime stretch of Frederick Douglass Boulevard; maybe it has "some wrinkles to iron out", but to most it's a "welcome" player in the area's "budding" dining scene.

Five Guys *Burgers*

20 | 9 | 15 | $14

E 40s | 690 Third Ave. (bet. 43rd & 44th Sts.) | 646-783-5060
G Village | 496 La Guardia Pl. (bet. Bleecker & Houston Sts.) | 212-228-6008
W 40s | 36 W. 48th St. (bet. 5th & 6th Aves.) | 212-997-1270
W 50s | 43 W. 55th St. (bet. 5th & 6th Aves.) | 212-459-9600
W Village | 296 Bleecker St. (7th Ave. S.) | 212-367-9200 ◗
Bay Ridge | 8510 Fifth Ave. (bet. 85th & 86th Sts.) | Brooklyn | 718-921-9380
Brooklyn Heights | 138 Montague St. (bet. Clinton & Henry Sts.) | Brooklyn | 718-797-9380
NEW Downtown Bklyn | 2 Metrotech Ctr. (bet. Bridge & Lawrence Sts.) | Brooklyn | 718-852-9380
Park Slope | 284 Seventh Ave. (bet. 6th & 7th Sts.) | Brooklyn | 718-499-9380
Glendale | 73-25 Woodhaven Blvd. (bet. 74th & Rutledge Aves.) | Queens | 718-943-3483
www.fiveguys.com
Additional locations throughout the NY area

"Fast food at its finest" – i.e. "quality" burgers "made to order" with "unlimited" fixin's and "even better fries" – places this chain "light years ahead of the golden arches"; "value" prices and "free peanuts" make up for deliberately "plain" decor – but "keep the diet coach on speed dial."

Five Leaves ◗ *American*

▽ 25 | 19 | 19 | $32

Greenpoint | 18 Bedford Ave. (bet. Lorimer St. & Manhattan Ave.) | Brooklyn | 718-383-5345 | www.fiveleavesny.com

Gain "entry into cooldom" at this "bustling" Greenpoint boîte, whose "well-sourced" Australian-accented American "comfort" faves draw "scenesters aplenty"; "insane waits" (especially at "amazing brunch") and "rushed" service from "super-hip" staffers come with the territory.

5 Napkin Burger ◗ *Burgers*

21 | 17 | 18 | $29

W 40s | 630 Ninth Ave. (bet. 44th & 45th Sts.) | 212-757-2277
W 80s | 2315 Broadway (84th St.) | 212-333-4488
Astoria | 35-01 36th Ave. (35th Ave.) | Queens | 718-433-2727
www.5napkinburger.com

"Sloppy eating" gets a "gourmet" bump at this "upscale" burger trio whose namesake patty is "big", "yummy" and bound to "drip down your arm"; its "butcher shop–inspired" settings are generally "mobbed", so expect "overwhelmed" staff and "scream-to-be-heard" acoustics; P.S. an East Village branch is in the works at 150 East 14th Street.

5 Ninth *American*

19 | 22 | 18 | $48

Meatpacking | 5 Ninth Ave. (bet. Gansevoort & Little W. 12th Sts.) | 212-929-9460 | www.5ninth.com

The "coziest of rooms" and a garden that "rocks" mean this "charming", tri-level Meatpacking townhouse is tailor-made for "date night"; the less-enthused cite so-so service and New American fare that's "interesting" yet "not worth the price", still the "hip bar" gets no complaints.

Five Points *American/Mediterranean*   22 | 21 | 21 | $49

NoHo | 31 Great Jones St. (bet. Bowery & Lafayette St.) | 212-253-5700 |
www.fivepointsrestaurant.com

It merits "at least 10 Points" rave reviewers of this longtime NoHo "charmer" that "still delivers" with its "fantastic", "fairly priced" New American cooking in a "casual-but-sophisticated" setting with a "little river running through"; it's generally "jammed", especially at "perfect brunch."

Fives *American/French*   ▽ 22 | 23 | 25 | $73

W 50s | Peninsula Hotel | 700 Fifth Ave. (55th St.) | 212-903-3918 |
www.peninsula.com

A "posh" "getaway", this "classy" hotel haven presents "upscale" New American–French cuisine via "pampering", "stiff-upper-lip" servers in an "elegant" room; prices are predictably "way" up there, but it fills the bill for "power breakfasts" (there's Rudy G), "quiet lunches" and "special-occasion" dinners.

Flatbush Farm *American*   21 | 19 | 17 | $40

Park Slope | 76 St. Marks Ave. (Flatbush Ave.) | Brooklyn | 718-622-3276 |
www.flatbushfarm.com

"Local ingredients done simply" with "spot-on" results have made this "pleasant" Park Slope American a "neighborhood staple"; a "tranquil back garden" and "doesn't-break-the-bank" pricing balance sometimes-"lacking" service; P.S. the adjacent Bar(n) is just right "for a burger and beer."

Flex Mussels *Seafood*   23 | 18 | 20 | $46

E 80s | 174 E. 82nd St. (bet. Lexington & 3rd Aves.) | 212-717-7772
NEW W Village | 154 W. 13th St. (bet. 6th & 7th Aves.) |
212-229-0222
www.flexmusselsny.com

Bivalve buffs binge on a "dazzling array" of "mussels in every imaginable" iteration, backed by an "interesting beer list", at these "cheery", "nothing-fancy" UES–West Village "tastes of Prince Edward Island"; they're generally "noisy madhouses" with reservations "a must."

Flor de Mayo ⚫ *Chinese/Peruvian*   20 | 10 | 16 | $23

W 80s | 484 Amsterdam Ave. (bet. 83rd & 84th Sts.) | 212-787-3388
W 100s | 2651 Broadway (bet. 100th & 101st Sts.) | 212-663-5520
www.flordemayo.com

"Succulent" rotisserie chicken is the star at these "get-'em-in, get-'em-out" UWS Peruvian-Chinese "joints" satisfying "beans, rice and *pollo* cravings" "cheap"; they're "frequently mobbed" despite "pit"-like setups – no wonder they "do a major business" in takeout and delivery.

Flor de Sol *Spanish*   21 | 20 | 19 | $48

TriBeCa | 361 Greenwich St. (bet. Franklin & Harrison Sts.) | 212-366-1640 |
www.flordesolnyc.com

This TriBeCa Spaniard's tapas "leave your taste buds dancing"; the "dimly lit", "rustic" digs tailor-made for "groups", "live flamenco" and "kick-ass sangria" are also easy to swallow, but come at slightly "pricey" rates.

Fonda ⓜ *Mexican* `23` `19` `21` `$38`

Park Slope | 434 Seventh Ave. (bet. 14th & 15th Sts.) | Brooklyn |
718-369-3144 | www.fondarestaurant.com

"Upscale Mexican" cooking with "rich layers of flavor" goes "way beyond" the "usual" at this "sexy" South Sloper, likewise the bar's "creative drink list"; "small" dimensions lead to "legendary" table waits,
but the back garden provides some "lovely" elbow room.

ⓃⒺⓌ FoodParc *Eclectic* `18` `15` `14` `$19`

Chelsea | Eventi Hotel | 845 Sixth Ave. (bet. 29th & 30th Sts.) |
646-600-7140 | www.foodparc.com

Jeffrey Chodorow's Chelsea "food court" boasts a "futuristic" look
(think "JFK's JetBlue terminal") and a "high-tech" "touch-screen"/
"texting" ordering system for its vendors' offerings, from "custom
burgers" to "Asian and Italian specialties"; some deem it a "cool concept" and others "gimmicky", but the ratings speak for themselves.

ⓃⒺⓌ Forcella *Pizza* `-` `-` `-` `I`

Williamsburg | 485 Lorimer St. (bet. Grand & Powers Sts.) | Brooklyn |
718-388-8820 | www.forcellaeatery.com

Naples-born pizzaiolo Giulio Adriani's Williamsburg parlor takes the
unusual step of flash-frying the dough before its pies are crowned with
housemade mozz and quality toppings; in its folksy room, the center
of attention is the open kitchen's brightly tiled oven; P.S. a NoHo
branch is in the works at 334 Bowery.

Forlini's ⓞ *Italian* `19` `14` `19` `$43`

Chinatown | 93 Baxter St. (Walker St.) | 212-349-6779

To dine near "the judge who just" presided over your trial, try this
circa-1945 "red-sauce Italian" "standby" sited "near the courts
and City Hall"; maybe the cooking's "plain" and the red-Naugahyde
decor "tired", but to its gallery of "pols", "lawyers and litigants",
it's a "treasure."

Fornino *Pizza* `22` `18` `20` `$35`

Park Slope | 256 Fifth Ave. (bet. Carroll St. & Garfield Pl.) | Brooklyn |
718-399-8600 | www.forninoparkslope.com
Williamsburg | 187 Bedford Ave. (bet. 6th & 7th Sts.) | Brooklyn |
718-384-6004 | www.forninopizza.com

"Serious" "artisanal" wood-oven pizzas made with "super-fresh ingredients" (e.g. "herbs from their garden") are "the reason to go" to this
Williamsburg standout; the more "upscale" Park Slope offshoot is now
separately owned and garnering slightly less-rapturous notices for its
"grilled" "flatbread"-style pies.

Fort Defiance *American* ▽ `21` `17` `21` `$30`

Red Hook | 365 Van Brunt St. (bet. Coffey & Dikeman Sts.) | Brooklyn |
347-453-6672 | www.fortdefiancebrooklyn.com

This "chill" Red Hook hang from an ex-Pegu Club bartender turns out
"fantastic cocktails" and "delicious", "value"-priced pub eats; "small,
charming" and "unpretentious", it's a "reliable" bet for breakfast and
lunch too – no wonder it's a "neighborhood favorite."

44 & X ⓞ *American* `21` `19` `21` `$46`

W 40s | 622 10th Ave. (44th St.) | 212-977-1170

(continued)

44½ ◗ *American*

W 40s | 626 10th Ave. (bet. 44th & 45th Sts.) | 212-399-4450
www.heaveninhellskitchen.com

At this "gay-friendly" Hell's Kitchen twosome, the "kicked-up-a-notch" "comfort" fare is "delicious", but it's the "fabulous" waiters who are "the main show" (is there a "modeling school nearby"?); it's a "favorite" "pre-and post-theater" and for "yummy brunch", "noisy" acoustics notwithstanding.

⊠ Four Seasons ⊠ *American* 27 | 28 | 27 | $101

E 50s | 99 E. 52nd St. (bet. Lexington & Park Aves.) | 212-754-9494 |
www.fourseasonsrestaurant.com

A "timeless classic", this "stunning" Midtown modernist "landmark" designed by Philip Johnson and stewarded by Alex von Bidder and Julian Niccolini "continues to shine" with "top-level" New American food delivered by super-"pro" servers; whether dining in the "buzzing" Grill Room with its "quintessential NY power" scene or in the "elegant", more ladylike Pool Room, you're "splurging on perfection" – likewise they have fine party spaces; P.S. jackets (with deep pockets) required.

Fragole *Italian* 25 | 17 | 22 | $34

Carroll Gardens | 394 Court St. (bet. Carroll St. & 1st Pl.) | Brooklyn |
718-522-7133 | www.fragoleny.com

"No wonder locals flock" to this rustic Carroll Gardens Italian "given how delicious" and "affordable" its housemade pastas and other "simple" classics can be; the "not-too-fancy" room is "small" but "cute", and a "gracious" staff keeps things "comfortable."

Francisco's Centro Vasco *Seafood/Spanish* 22 | 13 | 19 | $51

Chelsea | 159 W. 23rd St. (bet. 6th & 7th Aves.) | 212-645-6224 |
www.centrovasco.ypguides.net

Those looking to "cure a lobster jones" claw their way to this Chelsea Spaniard, a seafood "paradise" whose "ginormous", "value"-priced crustaceans may be the "best buy in town"; "rushed" service and "close" quarters in need of a "makeover" are part of the "messy fun."

Frank ◗⊄ *Italian* 24 | 14 | 17 | $36

E Village | 88 Second Ave. (bet. 5th & 6th Sts.) | 212-420-0202 |
www.frankrestaurant.com

Still "hitting the mark" "after all these years", this "boisterous" East Village nook supplies "first-rate" pastas and other "homey Italian" fare served "family-style" for "crazy cheap"; despite "no-rez, cash-only" policies and "worn" "sardine-can" digs, there's "always a wait."

Frankie & Johnnie's Steakhouse ⊠ *Steak* 23 | 16 | 21 | $66

Garment District | 32 W. 37th St. (bet. 5th & 6th Aves.) |
212-947-8940

W 40s | 269 W. 45th St., 2nd fl. (bet. B'way & 8th Ave.) |
212-997-9494 ◗

www.frankieandjohnnies.com

This onetime "speakeasy"-turned-"vintage" "steak joint" is a Theater District "institution" that's been luring "carnivores" up its "narrow stairway" for "thick, juicy" chops since the 1920s; its sleeker Garment

| | FOOD | DECOR | SERVICE | COST |

District offspring in "John Barrymore's former townhouse" features equally "crusty" service and "pricey" tabs.

☑ Frankies Spuntino *Italian* `25` `19` `21` `$40`
LES | 17 Clinton St. (bet. Houston & Stanton Sts.) | 212-253-2303 ●
NEW **W Village** | 570 Hudson St. (11th St.) | 212-924-0818
Carroll Gardens | 457 Court St. (bet. 4th Pl. & Luquer St.) | Brooklyn | 718-403-0033
www.frankiesspuntino.com
"Simple", "soul-satisfying" Italiana dished up in "friendly", "unfussy" style for "reasonable" rates has made a "phenom" of this "hopping" twosome; the Carroll Gardens original's "beautiful garden" gives it an edge over the "tiny" Lower East Sider, but no-rez policies make "waits" inevitable at both – at least there's now a new (post-Survey) West Village outlet.

☑ Franny's *Pizza* `25` `17` `20` `$39`
Prospect Heights | 295 Flatbush Ave. (bet. Prospect Pl. & St. Marks Ave.) | Brooklyn | 718-230-0221 | www.frannysbrooklyn.com
As "outstanding" as "they're cracked up to be", this Prospect Heights Italian's "locavore pizzas" are made with "the freshest" ingredients, ditto its "irresistible appetizers and cocktails"; the only gripes are about "pricey"-for-the-genre tabs and "crowded" conditions.

Fratelli *Italian* `21` `17` `22` `$38`
Pelham Gardens | 2507 Eastchester Rd. (Mace Ave.) | Bronx | 718-547-2489
A "make-you-feel-like-family" "favorite" in Pelham Gardens, this "lively", "comfortable" Italian is a "popular" fallback for "simple" red-sauce fare in "huge portions"; "neighborhood" admirers suspect its "value" prices would be "much higher" if it were sited "south of da Bronx."

Fraunces Tavern ● *American* `17` `21` `19` `$47`
(aka The Porterhouse Brewing Co. at Fraunces Tavern)
Financial District | 54 Pearl St. (Broad St.) | 212-968-1776 | www.frauncestavern.com
Where "George Washington bade farewell to the boys" in 1783, this FiDi "landmark" has reopened again with an "excellent" beer list and "ok" Irish-American grub; purists grumble "after the renovations, it's just another brewpub" – ironically, now owned by a U.K. chain.

Fred's at Barneys NY *American/Italian* `20` `19` `19` `$50`
E 60s | Barneys NY | 660 Madison Ave., 9th fl. (60th St.) | 212-833-2200 | www.barneys.com
"Fashionistas" "pick at" posh salads and other "above-average" Italian-American nibbles at this "modern" department store "ladies-who-lunch" hub, where the "see-and-be-seen crowd" is the real "attraction"; dinner is less of a "scene", and, yes, it's "expensive" – "duh, it's Barneys."

Freemans ● *American* `23` `23` `20` `$49`
LES | Freeman Alley (off Rivington St., bet. Bowery & Chrystie St.) | 212-420-0012 | www.freemansrestaurant.com
"Present your hipster ID at the door" at this LES "trendsetter" in a "dark alley", whose "smart" cocktails and New American bites are "delicious"

but almost beside the point; "cool" "hunting lodge"-esque digs and "cute" staffers are a "feast for the eyes", but figure on "killer waits."

Fresco by Scotto 🗷 *Italian* | 23 | 19 | 21 | $54 |

E 50s | 34 E. 52nd St. (bet. Madison & Park Aves.) | 212-935-3434

Fresco on the Go 🗷 *Italian*

E 50s | 40 E. 52nd St. (bet. Madison & Park Aves.) | 212-754-2700
Financial District | 114 Pearl St. (Hanover Sq.) | 212-635-5000
www.frescobyscotto.com

"Fresh" Tuscan fare and "gracious" service led by the Scotto family draw *"Today Show"* folks to this Eastsider ("now I know where in the world Matt Lauer is"); it's a "madhouse at lunch" and best on the "company tab", but those looking for speed and extra value hit the "on the Go" offshoots.

Friedman's Lunch *American* | 21 | 12 | 18 | $24 |

Chelsea | Chelsea Mkt. | 75 Ninth Ave. (bet. 15th & 16th Sts.) | 212-929-7100 | www.friedmanslunch.com

Not just for lunch, this affordable Chelsea Market New American slings sandwiches, salads and soups starring "fresh ingredients" three meals a day; it's a "pleasant surprise" where enlightened "vegetarians and carnivores can dine together" – and the "gluten-intolerant" too – no wonder "weekend waits" are the norm.

Friend of a Farmer *American* | 18 | 18 | 17 | $35 |

Gramercy | 77 Irving Pl. (bet. 18th & 19th Sts.) | 212-477-2188 | www.friendofafarmerny.com

The "only thing missing is a rooster crowing" at this "faux-rural" Gramercy Park veteran where "dependable" Americana comes in "cute" "country farmhouse" quarters; however, "weekend brunch madness" and "spotty" service may dispel the pastoral mood.

Fuleen Seafood ❶ *Chinese/Seafood* | 22 | 8 | 16 | $30 |

Chinatown | 11 Division St. (Bowery) | 212-941-6888 | www.fuleenrestaurant.com

"If it lives in the sea, you can eat it" at this "noisy, frantic" Hong Kong–style eatery where "crazy-tasty" fish "right out of the tank" at "cheap" prices "dare you to be adventure-ish"; jury duty convenience and late hours (till 2:30 AM) balance "no atmosphere whatsoever."

Fulton *Seafood* | 23 | 20 | 20 | $57 |

E 70s | 205 E. 75th St. (bet. 2nd & 3rd Aves.) | 212-288-6600 | www.fultonnyc.com

"It's all about the fish" at this UES "around-the-corner" offshoot of Citarella, an "urbane" oasis for oh-so-"fresh" seafood in "uncontrived preparations"; "sleek" but "low-key" quarters and "civilized" service ensure that its "uptown" clientele doesn't blink at "steep pricing."

Fushimi *Japanese* | 24 | 24 | 20 | $45 |

Bay Ridge | 9316 Fourth Ave. (bet. 93rd & 94th Sts.) | Brooklyn | 718-833-7788
Grant City | 2110 Richmond Rd. (Lincoln Ave.) | Staten Island | 718-980-5300
www.fushimi-us.com

These "sexy, sleek" sushi siblings in Staten Island and Bay Ridge serve "high-end Japanese fare" with "dance music" and a happening "bar scene" on the side; "beautiful" "Buddha"-enhanced digs draw "young" types who happily overlook "loud" acoustics, uneven service and "Manhattan prices."

Gabriela's *Mexican*

| 19 | 17 | 18 | $36 |

W 90s | 688 Columbus Ave. (bet. 93rd & 94th Sts.) | 212-961-9600 | www.gabrielas.com

"Totally satisfying" Mexican standards with a few "creative twists", plus "damn-good" margaritas, keep Upper Westsiders coming to this "friendly" vet that's also touted for its "big outdoor space"; it's "noisy", but that's part of the "festive", "family-friendly" vibe.

Gabriel's 🖾 *Italian*

| 23 | 19 | 23 | $62 |

W 60s | 11 W. 60th St. (bet. B'way & Columbus Ave.) | 212-956-4600 | www.gabrielsnyc.com

A "favorite" for "pre-opera pastas" and "off-the-charts risotto", this "bustling" Columbus Circle Northern Italian "never loses its charm" thanks to "well-prepared" fare, a "fine wine list" and "media bigwig sightings"; service that "shines" under owner Gabriel Aiello "covers small flaws", like "touchup"-ready decor and spendy checks.

Gahm Mi Oak ◑ *Korean*

| 22 | 15 | 15 | $25 |

Garment District | 43 W. 32nd St. (bet. B'way & 5th Ave.) | 212-695-4113

The signature *sollongtang* beef soup at this 24/7 Garment District Korean will "warm your soul" after a "long night out", and the "house-made kimchi" is "some of the best" going; tabs are modest – as is decor – but "be prepared to wave your server down."

Gallagher's Steak House ◑ *Steak*

| 21 | 18 | 20 | $67 |

W 50s | 228 W. 52nd St. (bet. B'way & 8th Ave.) | 212-245-5336 | www.gallaghersnysteakhouse.com

After 85 years in the Theater District, this "quintessential" "checkered-tablecloth" New York City carnivore's club still supplies "steaks like buttah" in a "time-warp" space packed with sports memorabilia that's "a spectacle in itself"; equally "traditional" are the "pro service with a hint of gruff" and "high prices" – though the $32 prix fixe lunch is a "bargain."

Garden Café *American*

| ▽ 22 | 19 | 21 | $33 |

Inwood | 4961 Broadway (bet. Isham & 207th Sts.) | 212-544-9480 | www.gardencafenyc.com

"One of the better options in 'Upstate Manhattan'", this "friendly", "informal" Inwood cafe makes a "strong showing" with its diverse range of "surprisingly fresh, well-made" New American dishes; a "lovely" garden, "bargain" prices and regular "jazz evenings" are other perks that keep locals coming.

Gargiulo's *Italian*

| 22 | 19 | 22 | $49 |

Coney Island | 2911 W. 15th St. (bet. Mermaid & Surf Aves.) | Brooklyn | 718-266-4891 | www.gargiulos.com

"Nostalgia" central, this circa-1907 "wedding-hall"-like Coney Island "favorite" features "tuxedoed waiters" distributing "plentiful", "saucy, cheesy" Southern Italian "soul food" "straight outta Brooklyn's heyday"; "pick the right number" from "*la tombola*" and you'll win a "free dinner."

	FOOD	DECOR	SERVICE	COST

☑ Gari ● *Japanese* — 27 | 15 | 21 | $82

W 70s | 370 Columbus Ave. (bet. 77th & 78th Sts.) | 212-362-4816

☑ Sushi of Gari 46 ● *Japanese* —

W 40s | 347 W. 46th St. (bet. 8th & 9th Aves.) | 212-957-0046 | www.sushiofgari.com

"The omakase is a religious experience" at this Japanese sushi trio from "genius" chef Gari Sugio, whose "incomparable" style shines through with every "fresh, innovative", "exquisitely prepared" morsel; open a "line of credit" first and prepare for "plain" surroundings, and you'll "love every minute."

Gascogne *French* — 21 | 19 | 20 | $53

Chelsea | 158 Eighth Ave. (bet. 17th & 18th Sts.) | 212-675-6564 | www.gascognenyc.com

"Extremely French – in a good way", this "romantic" Chelsea bistro serves up "solid Gascogne" classics via "charming" servers in "pleasant" (if "cramped") "rustic" quarters; "interesting" wines "from Southwest France" add appeal, but for many the "charming garden" is the "best part."

NEW GastroArte ● *Spanish* — 22 | 22 | 23 | $60
(fka Graffit)

W 60s | 141 W. 69th St. (bet. B'way & Columbus Ave.) | 646-692-8762 | www.graffitrestaurant.com

New Yorkers "finally" sample Spanish "molecular gastronomy" at this "chic" Lincoln Center–area newcomer showcasing chef Jesús Núñez's "whimsical", "surprising", "*delicioso*" cuisine, including "over-the-top tapas"; Núñez himself painted the "graffiti" that lends the *muy* "friendly" scene a dash of "downtown" – the word is you "can't go wrong."

Gazala Place *Mideastern* — 21 | 11 | 18 | $29

W 40s | 709 Ninth Ave. (bet. 48th & 49th Sts.) | 212-245-0709
W 70s | 380 Columbus Ave., upstairs (78th St.) | 212-873-8880 | www.gazalaplace.com

If "you're not flying to Daliyat" anytime soon, this "friendly" BYO duo can hook you up with "tasty", "low-priced" Druze Middle Eastern fare in "huge helpings"; the Hell's Kitchen original is "tiny" and "dingy", but the digs at the new UWS offshoot are "more compelling."

Geido ☒ *Japanese* — ∇ 25 | 15 | 23 | $31

Prospect Heights | 331 Flatbush Ave. (7th Ave.) | Brooklyn | 718-624-8866

"Retro '80s"-"punk" drawings on the walls hint at the "quirky" soul of this "beloved" Prospect Heights "institution", where the "terrific" sushi and Japanese cooking come at "value" prices; "full of local color", its "lively" scene is boosted by "warm staffers and regulars."

Gemma ● *Italian* — 20 | 23 | 19 | $48

E Village | Bowery Hotel | 335 Bowery (bet. 2nd & 3rd Sts.) | 212-505-7300 | www.theboweryhotel.com

"Candelabras with half-melted candles" set the "stylish scene" at this "rustic"-chic Bowery Hotel dining room serving "solid" Italiana to "hipsters, wannabe hipsters and tourists"; there's "amusing people-watching" aplenty – but given "long lines", scenesters just "wish they took rezzies."

Gennaro ⊭ *Italian*

FOOD	DECOR	SERVICE	COST
24	15	18	$42

W 90s | 665 Amsterdam Ave. (bet. 92nd & 93rd Sts.) | 212-665-5348

"Discovered by too many", this "homey" Upper West Side trattoria at least has gotten "roomier" since its "umpteenth" expansion, which also helped ease "waits"; its "fantastic" Italian fare remains a *delizioso* "value", but those high "decibels" and that "cash-only thing" still need work.

Ghenet *Ethiopian*

FOOD	DECOR	SERVICE	COST
▽ 24	18	19	$26

Park Slope | 348 Douglass St. (bet. 4th & 5th Aves.) | Brooklyn | 718-230-4475 | www.ghenet.com

"Spicy, crave-worthy" meat and vegetable stews "lovingly served" with "tangy" injera bread have "global foodies flocking" to this Ethiopian on the Park Slope–Gowanus border; "value" checks and "interesting, minimalist" decor make it a "hands-down" winner.

Gigino Trattoria *Italian*

FOOD	DECOR	SERVICE	COST
20	20	19	$46

TriBeCa | 323 Greenwich St. (bet. Duane & Reade Sts.) | 212-431-1112 | www.gigino-trattoria.com

Gigino at Wagner Park *Italian*

Financial District | 20 Battery Pl. (West St.) | 212-528-2228 | www.gigino-wagnerpark.com

You'd "think you were sitting in Tuscany" given the "country farmhouse" vibe at this "lovely" TriBeCa Italian appreciated for its "designer pizzas" and pastas; the Wagner Park spin-off is all about "spectacular views" of "Lady Liberty" and river "sunsets", redeeming slightly pricey checks.

❷ Gilt *American*

FOOD	DECOR	SERVICE	COST
26	28	26	$112

E 50s | NY Palace Hotel | 455 Madison Ave. (bet. 50th & 51st Sts.) | 212-891-8100 | www.giltnewyork.com

"Really, the name says it all" about this Palace Hotel "stunner" geared to the "splurging foodie" with its "sensational" prix fixe–only New American cuisine and "fantasy wine list", not to mention the "exquisite" "mansion" setting and service "fit for a king and queen"; no surprise, the prices are "equally fantastic", but one way or another it's sure to put a shine on your day.

Giorgione *Italian*

FOOD	DECOR	SERVICE	COST
23	21	21	$55

Hudson Square | 307 Spring St. (bet. Greenwich & Hudson Sts.) | 212-352-2269 | www.giorgionenyc.com

The "'in' crowd" collects at this "cozy", kinda pricey Hudson Square Italian known for its wood-oven pizzas and pastas "prepared with élan and passion"; despite the "trendy" rep, service is "friendly" – and it's "the icing on the cake when" owner Giorgio DeLuca (of Dean & you-know-who) is in the house.

Giorgio's of Gramercy *American*

FOOD	DECOR	SERVICE	COST
21	18	22	$48

Flatiron | 27 E. 21st St. (bet. B'way & Park Ave. S.) | 212-477-0007 | www.giorgiosofgramercy.com

"Attentive, earnest" service and "quality" New American fare account for the fact that this Flatiron District "neighborhood staple"

	FOOD	DECOR	SERVICE	COST

is "still going strong" after nearly 20 years; "comfortable" "bordello decor that works" and tabs requiring only "moderate outlay" are other keys to its longevity.

Giovanni Venticinque *Italian*

| 24 | 21 | 24 | $68 |

E 80s | 25 E. 83rd St. (bet. 5th & Madison Aves.) | 212-988-7300 | www.giovanniventicinque.com

"Wonderful after the Met", this "refined" Italian has a "loyal" "old-line" UES fan base for its "truly fine" Tuscan dishes and "gracious" (if sometimes "snooty") service; that it's "quiet" enough for "conversation" makes it "worth every penny" of the serious tab.

Girasole *Italian*

| 22 | 17 | 20 | $62 |

E 80s | 151 E. 82nd St. (bet. Lexington & 3rd Aves.) | 212-772-6690

Most agree that this UES "fixture" is a "better-than-usual neighborhood" "standby" serving "very good" Italian fare to a "loyal regular" "Park Avenue" crowd; however, there's a "split view" when it comes to service ("competent", "attentive" vs. "arrogant") and decor ("pleasant" vs. "tired") – you decide.

NEW Giuseppina's ⊘ *Pizza*

| - | - | - | I |

Greenwood Heights | 691 Sixth Ave. (20th St.) | Brooklyn | 718-499-5052

This cousin of Lucali lures Greenwood Heights and Park Slope pie-sanis into its low-key digs; it follows a familiar, cash-only format: pizzas and calzones only, cooked to crispy, charred perfection in a wood-fired oven that casts a glow over the dimly lit room – but here there's wine and beer to boot.

Glass House Tavern ● *American*

| 20 | 19 | 21 | $45 |

W 40s | 252 W. 47th St. (bet. B'way & 8th Ave.) | 212-730-4800 | www.glasshousetavern.com

Picture a Theater Districter that "doesn't feel like an assembly-line" eatery and you've got this "welcoming" duplex ("with a fireplace in back") serving "just-right" New Americana; "fair prices", an "active bar scene" and "late" hours earn standing ovations.

Gnocco ● *Italian*

| 23 | 17 | 20 | $39 |

E Village | 337 E. 10th St. (bet. Aves. A & B) | 212-677-1913 | www.gnocco.com

"Simple" and "substantial" Emilian cuisine that borders on "amazing", especially "considering the prices", is the deal at this "friendly", "vibrant" East Village Italian "off Tompkins Square Park"; a "cute back garden" supplements its interior barely bigger than a *gnocco*.

Gobo *Vegan/Vegetarian*

| 22 | 18 | 20 | $36 |

E 80s | 1426 Third Ave. (81st St.) | 212-288-5099
W Village | 401 Sixth Ave. (bet. 8th St. & Waverly Pl.) | 212-255-3242
www.goborestaurant.com

"You don't have to be" an herbivore to appreciate the "highly inventive" "faux meats" and other vegan eats at this "serene" Upper East Side-Village twosome, where even carnivores get "a run for their taste buds"; "well-intentioned" service and "reasonable" prices clinch the deal.

	FOOD	DECOR	SERVICE	COST

🆕 Go Burger ◑ *Burgers* <u>22</u> <u>18</u> <u>19</u> <u>$27</u>

E 70s | 1450 Second Ave. (bet. 75th & 76th Sts.) | 212-988-9822
Garment District | 310 W. 38th St. (bet. 8th & 9th Aves) |
212-290-8000
www.goburger.com

At this new national chain from the BLT Burger people, "surprisingly upscale" patties (try the "ultimelt"), along with "amazing Kobe hot dogs" and "spiked shakes", spell "fun"; still, "glorified-sports-bar" setups and uneven service have some questioning tabs a "tad pricey" for just "a burger joint."

Golden Unicorn *Chinese* <u>21</u> <u>13</u> <u>15</u> <u>$27</u>

Chinatown | 18 E. Broadway, 2nd fl. (Catherine St.) | 212-941-0911 |
www.goldenunicornrestaurant.com

An "endless" "parade of carts" loaded with "inventive" tidbits "weaves through" this "cavernous" Chinatown "dim sum palace" that's as heavily trafficked as "the LIE" at rush hour; "great prices" and "high quality" balance "loud", "circuslike" conditions and "lengthy waits" on weekends.

Good *American* <u>20</u> <u>16</u> <u>20</u> <u>$40</u>

W Village | 89 Greenwich Ave. (bet. Bank & W. 12th Sts.) | 212-691-8080 |
www.goodrestaurantnyc.com

The "name pretty much says it all" about this "reasonably priced" West Village "crowd-pleaser" plying "fresh", "well-prepared" New American "comfort" fare; brunch "is far and away" the "star" attraction, so be "prepared to wait."

Goodburger *Burgers* <u>17</u> <u>9</u> <u>13</u> <u>$15</u>

E 40s | 800 Second Ave. (42nd St.) | 212-922-1700
E 50s | 636 Lexington Ave. (54th St.) | 212-838-6000
Financial District | 101 Maiden Ln. (Pearl St.) | 212-797-1700
Flatiron | 870 Broadway (bet. 17th & 18th Sts.) | 212-529-9100
W 40s | 23 W. 45th St. (bet. 5th & 6th Aves.) | 212-354-0900
W 50s | 977 Eighth Ave. (bet. 57th & 58th Sts.) | 212-245-2200 ◑
www.goodburgerny.com

Supporters call this the "better-for-you" burger joint chain because it supplies the usual patties, fries and milkshake options "minus the unnatural McIngredients"; still, "dingy" setups and "slow" service have some saying "more like okayburger."

Good Enough to Eat *American* <u>21</u> <u>16</u> <u>18</u> <u>$29</u>

W 80s | 483 Amsterdam Ave. (bet. 83rd & 84th Sts.) | 212-496-0163 |
www.goodenoughtoeat.com

Aka "Good Enough to Wait", this "definitive UWS brunch spot" inspires "painful" weekend lines for its "delicious", "decent-priced" American "home cooking" in "faux-Vermont" digs; even when you clear the "white picket fence", expect "wedged-in" conditions; P.S. dinner's "less crowded."

🄳 Good Fork 🅼 *Eclectic* <u>25</u> <u>18</u> <u>22</u> <u>$44</u>

Red Hook | 391 Van Brunt St. (bet. Coffey & Van Dyke Sts.) | Brooklyn |
718-643-6636 | www.goodfork.com

"Well worth the venture" to Red Hook, this "quirky" "hideaway" turns out "clever", "delicious" Asian-accented Eclectic fare via a "charming", "low-

	FOOD	DECOR	SERVICE	COST

key" crew; its "intimate" digs reminiscent of "the inside of a ship" are augmented by a "delightful backyard" and "incredibly reasonable" tabs.

Gordon Ramsay ⌧ Ⓜ *French* **23 | 24 | 23 | $105**

W 50s | London NYC Hotel | 151 W. 54th St. (bet. 6th & 7th Aves.) | 212-468-8888 | www.gordonramsay.com

Though "celebrity chef" Gordon Ramsay is now just a consultant at this "high-end" Midtown French hotel dining room, "splendid" prix fixe-only meals come via a "solicitous" staff in "chic", "modern" environs; however, naysayers citing "outrageous" prices ("two words: expense account") and "inconsistent" quality claim it "doesn't live up to the hype."

⌧ Gotham Bar & Grill *American* **28 | 25 | 27 | $81**

G Village | 12 E. 12th St. (bet. 5th Ave. & University Pl.) | 212-620-4020 | www.gothambarandgrill.com

"Years of practice make perfect" at Alfred Portale's circa-1984 Village "landmark in fine dining" that remains "at the top of its game" with "magical" "skyscraping" New American cuisine, "marvelously orchestrated" service and a "spacious", casually "sophisticated" setting; the "unforgettable experience" is "well worth the final bill" – but if "money's tight" try the $25 "greenmarket lunch" (possibly "NYC's best deal").

Gottino ◗ *Italian* **20 | 19 | 18 | $42**

W Village | 52 Greenwich Ave. (bet. Charles & Perry Sts.) | 212-633-2590 | www.ilmiogottino.com

"Delicious tidbits" and "terrific wines" are the thing at this Italian small-plates specialist, a diminutive, "rustic" West Village enoteca "staffed by happy foodies"; the "adorable backyard" and "fair" pricing provide "date-spot" appeal, and locals say it's also "delightful for breakfast."

Grace's Trattoria *Italian* **19 | 16 | 19 | $47**

E 70s | 201 E. 71st St. (bet. 2nd & 3rd Aves.) | 212-452-2323 | www.gracestrattoria.net

"Clubby and comfortable", this UES "neighborhood haunt" next to Grace's Marketplace is an "easy place to go" for an "informal" Italian "pasta repast"; the decor's "tired", and "no one would call it trendy", but at least it's there when you need it with "fresh ingredients" and "moderate prices."

Gradisca *Italian* **23 | 19 | 22 | $56**

W Village | 126 W. 13th St. (bet. 6th Ave. & 7th Ave. S.) | 212-691-4886 | www.gradiscanyc.com

Barring a flight to The Boot, this West Villager is "the closest you'll get to Italy" given its "fresh", "terrific" pastas handmade "up front" by the owner's "mama"; "genuine, caring service" and an all-around "enjoyable atmosphere" take the edge off the upscale prices.

Graffiti Ⓜ *Eclectic* **25 | 15 | 23 | $48**

E Village | 224 E. 10th St. (bet. 1st & 2nd Aves.) | 212-677-0695 | www.graffitinyc.com

"Big", "amazing" flavors come in an "absurdly small" space at "gracious" chef Jehangir Mehta's midpriced East Village Eclectic; diners "squeeze into shared tables" but "all is quickly forgiven" when the "thought-provoking", Indian-accented fare arrives via "wonderful" staffers.

	FOOD	DECOR	SERVICE	COST

⊠ Gramercy Tavern *American*   **27** | **26** | **27** | **$114**

Flatiron | 42 E. 20th St. (bet. B'way & Park Ave. S.) | 212-477-0777 |
www.gramercytavern.com

"Still a model" of New American dining "at its finest", Danny Meyer's
"forever fabulous" Flatiron "destination" offers "inspired" "farm-
fresh" cuisine from chef Michael Anthony via an "exemplary" staff
that "glides you through the evening" in a "gorgeous", "refined"-
"rustic" space designed to recall a 19th century New England tavern;
yes, you "pay dearly" but it's resoundingly declared "worth it", so "beg
for a reservation" in the prix fixe–only main room, or opt for the
"lower-priced", à la carte, non-reserving front tavern room; P.S. the
22-seat private room is equally appealing.

Grand Sichuan *Chinese*   **21** | **9** | **14** | **$28**

NEW **Chelsea** | 172 Eighth Ave. (bet. 18th & 19th Sts.) | 212-243-1688
Chelsea | 229 Ninth Ave. (24th St.) | 212-620-5200 ●
Chinatown | 125 Canal St. (Chrystie St.) | 212-625-9212
E 50s | 1049 Second Ave. (bet. 55th & 56th Sts.) | 212-355-5855
E Village | 19-23 St. Marks Pl. (bet. 2nd & 3rd Aves.) | 212-529-4800
Murray Hill | 227 Lexington Ave. (bet. 33rd & 34th Sts.) | 212-679-9770
W 40s | 368 W. 46th St. (bet. 8th & 9th Aves.) | 212-969-9001
NEW **W 70s** | 307 Amsterdam Ave. (bet. 74th & 75th Sts.) | 212-580-0277
W Village | 15 Seventh Ave. S. (bet. Carmine & Leroy Sts.) | 212-645-0222
Rego Park | 98-108 Queens Blvd. (bet. 66th Rd. & 67th Ave.) | Queens |
718-268-8833
www.thegrandsichuan.com
Additional locations throughout the NY area

"Tonsil-tingling"-"fiery" Sichuan dishes are the specialty of this "fast,
loud" Chinese chain that fans tout as "the place" to "get your super-spicy
fix" at "cheap" prices; just "don't sweat" the "shabby" "red-tassels-and-
pandas" decor and "brusque" staff eager to "swipe your plate."

Grand Tier ⊠ *Italian*   **21** | **26** | **25** | **$86**

W 60s | Metropolitan Opera House, 2nd fl. | Lincoln Center Plaza
(bet. 63rd & 65th Sts.) | 212-799-3400 | www.patinagroup.com

Lincoln Center–goers can't beat the "convenience" of this "elegant"
Italian within the Met, which lets you "stroll to your seat" after eating,
then "pop back for dessert at intermission"; it's a "luxurious", well-
orchestrated affair, with accordingly "extravagant" tabs, but hey, if
you can "afford opera tickets", you can swing dinner here – though
some say "the food should be so much better."

Grano Trattoria *Italian*   **23** | **18** | **22** | **$45**

W Village | 21 Greenwich Ave. (W. 10th St.) | 212-645-2121 |
www.granonyc.com

"Everyone feels welcome" at this "family-owned" West Village Italian
"standby" thanks to "hearty" "well-priced" dishes that are "served
with gusto" in "warm, pleasant" environs; all told, it's a "reliable",
"low-key" choice.

NEW **Gravy** *Southern*   **-** | **-** | **-** | **M**

Flatiron | 32 E. 21st St. (bet. B'way & Park Ave. S.) | 212-600-2105 |
www.gravyny.com

The Flatiron gets a heaping helping of down-home cooking at this midpriced Southerner putting modern, upscale twists on classics like fried

chicken and grits; flashy teal-and-mustard geometric prints, hanging orb lights and low-slung loungers in the front bar exude a vibe more groovy than gravy.

Gray's Papaya ●✝ *Hot Dogs*

FOOD	DECOR	SERVICE	COST
20	5	14	$7

G Village | 402 Sixth Ave. (8th St.) | 212-260-3532
W 70s | 2090 Broadway (72nd St.) | 212-799-0243

"Inhaling" a couple of "snappy, satisfying" franks and a tropical juice "chaser" at these 24/7 "bargain" dog dealers is part of the "quintessential NYC" experience (the 72nd Street original just turned 30); nosh "standing up" or – given the "glaring lights" and "interesting" patrons – "walk and eat."

Great Jones Cafe ● *Cajun*

FOOD	DECOR	SERVICE	COST
21	15	18	$31

NoHo | 54 Great Jones St. (bet. Bowery & Lafayette St.) | 212-674-9304 | www.greatjones.com

"Down-home" Cajun cooking "done right" and offered "cheap" in "ramshackle" digs is the deal at this "no-pretensions" NoHo "classic that's still vibrant"; it's most popular for its "killer brunch", "strong drinks" and "best-in-town jukebox", "typical waits" notwithstanding.

Great NY Noodle Town ●✝ *Noodle Shop*

FOOD	DECOR	SERVICE	COST
23	5	12	$19

Chinatown | 28½ Bowery (Bayard St.) | 212-349-0923

"Delicious" and "cheap as hell" is the lowdown on the "noodles galore" and "salt-baked seafood" served till the wee hours at this "closet-size", "steamy-window" C-town "cult classic"; just know it's "cash-only" and seriously "no-frills", with service that's "slam-bam-thank-you-ma'am – without the thank-you."

Greek Kitchen *Greek*

FOOD	DECOR	SERVICE	COST
21	14	20	$31

W 50s | 889 10th Ave. (58th St.) | 212-581-4300 | www.greekkitchennyc.com

"Solid" Greek "staples" come via "cheerful" servers at this "casual" West 50s taverna "not far from Lincoln Center"; there's "nothing flashy here", just "good value" – plus, it's "not in Astoria"; P.S. a post-Survey redo and expansion isn't reflected in the above Decor score.

Greenhouse Café *American*

FOOD	DECOR	SERVICE	COST
21	20	21	$37

Bay Ridge | 7717 Third Ave. (bet. 77th & 78th Sts.) | Brooklyn | 718-833-8200 | www.greenhousecafe.com

Starring a "lovely" "greenhouse" room, this Bay Ridge "staple" is a place for "family and friends" to tuck into New Americana that "doesn't disappoint", but also perhaps "rarely inspires"; "live music on weekends" adds to the appeal, as do "reasonable" rates and "value" prix fixe deals.

Greenwich Grill/ Sushi Azabu *Italian/Japanese*

FOOD	DECOR	SERVICE	COST
25	21	22	$64

TriBeCa | 428 Greenwich St. (bet. Laight & Vestry Sts.) | 212-274-0428 | www.greenwichgrill.com

Something of a "sleeper", this two-in-one TriBeCan features "clever" Italian-Japanese fusion fare on the "inviting" ground level and "fantastic sushi" in a basement "hideaway"; "attentive" service and an all-around "serene" vibe complete the "refined experience" – at least until bill-paying time.

	FOOD	DECOR	SERVICE	COST

Grifone 🗷 *Italian* — 24 | 18 | 24 | $72

E 40s | 244 E. 46th St. (bet. 2nd & 3rd Aves.) | 212-490-7275 |
www.grifonenyc.com

"Outstanding" Northern Italian cooking and "attentive service" from
"real professionals" distinguish this U.N.-area "old-school ristorante";
money is apparently "no object" for its crowd of mature "regulars", but
all agree the "dated" digs could use "a little fluffing up."

Grimaldi's ⊅ *Pizza* — 24 | 12 | 15 | $23

NEW Flatiron | Limelight Marketplace | 47 W. 20th St. (6th Ave.) |
212-359-5523
Dumbo | 19 Old Fulton St. (bet. Front & Water Sts.) | Brooklyn |
718-858-4300
Douglaston | Douglaston Plaza | 242-02 61st Ave. (bet. Douglaston Pkwy. &
244th St.) | Queens | 718-819-2133
www.grimaldis.com

"Transcendent" "charred-crust" pies require "infernal, eternal" waits
to get in and "cranky" service once inside at this "Dumbo mainstay"
(hint: "order ahead for pickup", then eat at the "new Brooklyn Bridge
Park"); the Douglaston and Flatiron outposts "haven't been overrun"
yet, but all three are "cash only."

🗷 Grocery, The 🗷🅼 *American* — 27 | 18 | 25 | $62

Carroll Gardens | 288 Smith St. (bet. Sackett & Union Sts.) | Brooklyn |
718-596-3335 | www.thegroceryrestaurant.com

An emphasis on "the freshest" "local" ingredients dispatched with
"simple", "superb" technique makes for "inspiring" results at this
"pricey" Carroll Gardens New American, a Smith Street "standout"
also known for its "super-friendly" yet "professional" service; its
"tiny", "tight" interior "brings a new definition to the term 'understated'", but the back garden is "lovely."

Gruppo *Pizza* — ▽ 26 | 13 | 22 | $24

E Village | 186 Ave. B (bet. 11th & 12th Sts.) | 212-995-2100 |
www.gruppothincrust.com

"Delicious" "wafer-thin" pizzas with "unique" toppings endear this
"no-frills" East Village "haunt" to locals, who squeeze into the "tiniest
tables outside of Lilliput" and call it a solid "casual night out";
"friendly" service and price-is-right tabs keep the regulars regular.

Guantanamera ◑ *Cuban* — 20 | 16 | 20 | $40

W 50s | 939 Eighth Ave. (bet. 55th & 56th Sts.) | 212-262-5354 |
www.guantanameranyc.com

"You'll feel you've been transported" to Havana at this "kitschy"
Midtown Cuban, a "TGIF destination" where "hopping" live music and
"fun" libations "set the mood"; the "reasonably priced" food's "fine" too,
but prepare for "supersonic" decibels to match the "vibrant" scene.

Gusto *Italian* — 21 | 18 | 19 | $51

W Village | 60 Greenwich Ave. (Perry St.) | 212-924-8000 |
www.gustonyc.com

The "atmosphere's very alive" at this "modern" West Village Italian, an
"underappreciated" "local favorite" plying "creative takes" on pastas and
such; its "diverse" crowd digs in with gusto despite semi-"pricey"
checks, attended to by an "amiable" (if slightly "taken-with-itself") staff.

| | | FOOD | DECOR | SERVICE | COST |

Gyu-Kaku *Japanese* | 21 | 19 | 20 | $44

E 40s | 805 Third Ave., 2nd fl. (bet. 49th & 50th Sts.) | 212-702-8816
E Village | 34 Cooper Sq. (bet. Astor Pl. & 4th St.) | 212-475-2989
www.gyu-kaku.com

"Cook-it-yourself" Japanese BBQ "beats grilling on the fire escape" at these "friendly" East Side yakiniku specialists with a "heated" brazier at each table – a "fun" setup conducive to "big group dinners"; the "costs can add up", so "those on a budget" go for the "happy-hour deals."

Hale & Hearty Soups *Sandwiches/Soup* | 19 | 8 | 14 | $13

NEW Chelsea | 655 Sixth Ave. (bet. 20th & 21st Sts.) | 212-792-9922
Chelsea | Chelsea Mkt. | 75 Ninth Ave. (bet. 15th & 16th Sts.) | 212-255-2400
E 40s | 685 Third Ave. (bet. 43rd & 44th Sts.) | 212-681-6460 ⓢ
E 60s | 849 Lexington Ave. (bet. 64th & 65th Sts.) | 212-517-7600
Financial District | 55 Broad St. (bet. Beaver St. & Exchange Pl.) | 212-509-4100 ⓢ
Garment District | 462 Seventh Ave. (35th St.) | 212-971-0605 ⓢ
W 40s | 30 Rockefeller Plaza (49th St.) | 212-265-2117 ⓢ
W 40s | 49 W. 42nd St. (bet. 5th & 6th Aves.) | 212-575-9090 ⓢ
W 50s | 55 W. 56th St. (bet. 5th & 6th Aves.) | 212-245-9200 ⓢ
Brooklyn Heights | 32 Court St. (Remsen St.) | Brooklyn | 718-596-5600 ⓢ
www.haleandhearty.com
Additional locations throughout the NY area

They've got the "quick-and-filling" "formula" down pat at these "soup-lovers'" stop-ins with umpteen flavors "changing daily", plus sandwiches and salads; they're "cattle-call cafeterias" with "tight" quarters and "long lines" at "peak lunch hours", but there's always "takeout or delivery."

Hampton Chutney Co. *Indian* | 20 | 10 | 15 | $17

SoHo | 68 Prince St. (bet. Crosby & Lafayette Sts.) | 212-226-9996
W 80s | 464 Amsterdam Ave. (bet. 82nd & 83rd Sts.) | 212-362-5050
www.hamptonchutney.com

"Healthy, fresh" dosas with novel fillings and lotsa "chutney options" keep these "relaxed" SoHo–West 80s "counter-service" twins "bustling"; "finding a perch" can "be tricky", especially at lunch (when the UWS branch is "overparked with strollers").

Hanci Turkish Cuisine *Turkish* | 22 | 13 | 21 | $34

W 50s | 854 10th Ave. (bet. 56th & 57th Sts.) | 212-707-8144 | www.hanciturkishnyc.com

A "real find" on a "deserted" sweep of 10th Avenue, this "casual" "family-run" Turk scores points for "fresh" chow prepared "with careful attention" at "super-reasonable" prices; what the "small" space "lacks in flash" it makes up for in "prompt, helpful" service.

Hanco's *Vietnamese* | 21 | 7 | 14 | $11

Boerum Hill | 85 Bergen St. (bet. Hoyt & Smith Sts.) | Brooklyn | 718-858-6818 ⌷
Park Slope | 350 Seventh Ave. (10th St.) | Brooklyn | 718-499-8081
www.hancosny.com

Working the Vietnamese banh mi-and-bubble tea "combo" in Brooklyn, these "no-frills" sibs remain "on their game" with ultra-"fresh" sandwiches and a delightful "deliciousness-to-dollar" ratio; the Boerum

Hill original is cash-only, while Park Slope adds pho to the formula; P.S. a Brooklyn Heights branch is in the works.

❷ HanGawi *Korean/Vegetarian* | 25 | 24 | 23 | $49 |

Murray Hill | 12 E. 32nd St. (bet. 5th & Madison Aves.) | 212-213-0077 | www.hangawirestaurant.com

Like a "magical" "Zen refuge", this "serenely beautiful", "upscale" Murray Hill Korean vegetarian has followers rhapsodizing over its "heavenly" "healthy" cuisine and "exceedingly polite" service; the "transcendental journey" begins by "leaving shoes at the door", so "wear clean socks."

NEW Ha Noi *Vietnamese* | - | - | - | I |

Park Slope | 448 Ninth St. (7th Ave.) | Brooklyn | 718-788-7755

To an area already brimming with banh mi joints comes this Park Slope Vietnamese that proffers the popular sandwich, but goes beyond with inexpensive appetizers, pho variations and homestyle entrees; nothing-fancy digs get a boost when the front opens up in summer.

Harrison, The *American* | 24 | 21 | 23 | $63 |

TriBeCa | 355 Greenwich St. (Harrison St.) | 212-274-9310 | www.theharrison.com

"Going on 10 years", Jimmy Bradley's TriBeCa New American "hasn't missed a beat" as a "simple yet special" kind of place "every neighborhood should have"; its "wonderful" "seasonal cooking", "inviting" digs and "warm" "pro" staff ensure its "classy but casual clientele" doesn't blink at slightly "pricey" tabs.

Harry Cipriani ● *Italian* | 22 | 22 | 21 | $94 |

E 50s | Sherry-Netherland Hotel | 781 Fifth Ave. (bet. 59th & 60th Sts.) | 212-753-5566 | www.cipriani.com

The "chichi crowd" at this "buzzy" Sherry-Netherland Italian comes as much for the "fabulous people-watching" as for the Venetian vittles and "must-have" Bellinis; "waiters who know how to please" neutralize "outrageous price tags", but skeptics suggest "sell your Chopard" and "donate to charity instead."

Harry's Cafe ●🗷 *Steak* | 23 | 21 | 21 | $55 |

Financial District | 1 Hanover Sq. (bet. Pearl & Stone Sts.) | 212-785-9200

Harry's Steak 🗷 *Steak*

Financial District | 97 Pearl St. (bet. Broad St. & Hanover Sq.) | 212-785-9200
www.harrysnyc.com

In the FiDi's landmark India House, this "quintessential power" place caters to "Wall Street" types with its "old-school" steakhouse downstairs and modestly priced Eclectic cafe next door, both serving fare that's laudably "steady – unlike the markets"; still, the "phenomenal wine list" may be its strongest asset – especially on the day you receive your bonus.

Harry's Italian *Italian* | 21 | 17 | 18 | $32 |

Financial District | 2 Gold St. (bet. Maiden Ln. & Platt St.) | 212-747-0797
NEW W 40s | 30 Rockefeller Plaza, Concourse Level (on 6th Ave., bet. 49th & 50th Sts.) | 212-218-1450
www.harrysitalian.com

Thin-crust pizzas with "fabulous toppings" and Italian basics in "huuuge portions" make this "unpretentious" member of the Harry's dy-

| | FOOD | DECOR | SERVICE | COST |

nasty an "all-around solid" FiDi choice; when "crowded" it's "acoustically challenged", so sit outside; P.S. the new Rockefeller Plaza offshoot opened post-Survey.

Haru *Japanese* 　　　21 | 17 | 18 | $42

E 40s | 280 Park Ave. (enter on 48th St., bet. Madison & Park Aves.) | 212-490-9680
E 70s | 1327 Third Ave. (76th St.) | 212-452-1028 ◑
E 70s | 1329 Third Ave. (76th St.) | 212-452-2230 ◑
Financial District | 1 Wall Street Ct. (bet. Beaver & Pearl Sts.) | 212-785-6850
Flatiron | 220 Park Ave. S. (18th St.) | 646-428-0989 ◑
W 40s | 205 W. 43rd St. (bet. B'way & 8th Ave.) | 212-398-9810 ◑
W 80s | 433 Amsterdam Ave. (bet. 80th & 81st Sts.) | 212-579-5655 ◑
www.harusushi.com

"Consistently fresh" sushi and "creative" (read: "Americanized") combos make this "trendy" "Benihana-owned" Japanese chain a "reliable" choice for a "casual", if "rushed", meal at "reasonable" cost; just know that "deafening" decibels may have you saying "can't hearu."

Hasaki ◑ *Japanese* 　　　23 | 14 | 19 | $45

E Village | 210 E. Ninth St. (bet. 2nd & 3rd Aves.) | 212-473-3327 | www.hasakinyc.com

This "homestyle sushi den" in the East Village "stands out" with super-"fresh" fish and "interesting" takes on Japanese cooking; "tiny" digs and a "steady clientele" mean it's "always crowded", even if it's a tad "pricey" for the area and there's "no atmosphere" to speak of.

Hatsuhana ⬚ *Japanese* 　　　24 | 17 | 22 | $55

E 40s | 17 E. 48th St. (bet. 5th & Madison Aves.) | 212-355-3345
E 40s | 237 Park Ave. (46th St.) | 212-661-3400
www.hatsuhana.com

Having "maintained its standards for years" – the 48th Street original opened in 1976 – this "classic" Midtown Japanese duo offers "perfectly fresh" sushi (no "hokey combos" here) and "respectful" service; it draws both "suits and tourists", yet given the "not-inexpensive" tabs, the settings are due for an "update."

Havana Alma de Cuba *Cuban* 　　　22 | 18 | 21 | $38

W Village | 94 Christopher St. (bet. Bedford & Bleecker Sts.) | 212-242-3800 | www.havananyc.com

"It really feels like Havana" at this West Village Cuban whose "hearty" classics are served "with a touch of style" at ok prices; tables are "close" but it doesn't matter after "a few mojitos" or "when the music starts" – and there's always the "outdoor area" in summer.

Havana Central *Cuban* 　　　18 | 18 | 17 | $35

W 40s | 151 W. 46th St. (bet. 6th & 7th Aves.) | 212-398-7440
W 100s | 2911 Broadway (bet. 113th & 114th Sts.) | 212-662-8830
www.havanacentral.com

Offering a taste of "romanticized" Havana to a "boisterous" crowd, this high-decibel duo delivers low-cost Cuban chow varying from "*sabroso*" to "so-so", with "potent potables" and "live music" taking the edge off "slow service"; the Columbia-area outpost is "less touristy" than the Midtowner.

	FOOD	DECOR	SERVICE	COST

Haveli ● *Indian* | 22 | 17 | 20 | $33

E Village | 100 Second Ave. (bet. 5th & 6th Sts.) | 212-982-0533 |
www.havelinyc.com

It's just a "few steps" away from the "Curry Row" "competition", but
this East Village Indian vet is a "big step up" thanks to its "fabulous"
fare; it also curries favor with "comfortable" (if "not fancy") environs
and "gracious service", all at the "right price point."

▨▧▨ Heartbreak ●▧ *German/Swiss* | 24 | 22 | 21 | $49

E Village | 29 E. Second St. (2nd Ave.) | 212-777-2502 |
www.heartbreakrestaurant.com

An "über-cool" showcase for chef Ingrid Roettele, this new East Villager
produces "fondue of the gods" and other "wonderful" Swiss-German
classics; "classy" "Zurich nightclub" decor, "attentive" service and fair
tabs also get the nod, so surveyors simply "can't explain the name."

Hearth *American/Italian* | 24 | 20 | 23 | $66

E Village | 403 E. 12th St. (1st Ave.) | 646-602-1300 |
www.restauranthearth.com

"Almost–Iron Chef" Marco Canora "brings the love" to "every morsel" at
this "top-notch", "expensive" East Village Tuscan–New American, a
"marriage of refined and hearty" with "polished service" and "interesting" wines; insiders say the "best seats" are at the "kitchen counter."

Heartland Brewery *Pub Food* | 15 | 14 | 16 | $30

Garment District | Empire State Bldg. | 350 Fifth Ave. (34th St.) |
212-563-3433
Seaport | 93 South St. (Fulton St.) | 646-572-2337
Union Sq | 35 Union Sq. W. (bet. 16th & 17th Sts.) | 212-645-3400
W 40s | 127 W. 43rd St. (bet. B'way & 6th Ave.) | 646-366-0235
W 40s | Port Authority | 625 Eighth Ave. (41st St.) | 646-214-1000
W 50s | 1285 Sixth Ave. (51st St.) | 212-582-8244
www.heartlandbrewery.com

HB Burger *Burgers*

W 40s | 127 W. 43rd St. (bet. B'way & 6th Ave.) | 212-575-5848 |
www.hbburger.com

"Tasty craft beers" are the highlight at this microbrew chain dispensing "belly-filler" pub basics to a crowd heavy on out-of-towners and
"loud groups"; its "cavernous" outposts can feel "generic" ("could be
in Peoria"), but "affordability" and "convenience" keep 'em "packed."

Hecho en Dumbo ● *Mexican* | 23 | 17 | 19 | $39

NoHo | 354 Bowery (bet. 4th & Great Jones Sts.) | 212-937-4245 |
www.hechoendumbo.com

"Ridiculously small portions" pack "huge" flavor at this "nouveau"
Mexican street-food specialist, now in NoHo, whose "cramped",
"funky-rustic" digs are ever-"jammed" with "hipsters"; "fair prices"
trump "weak" service and "long waits" – though it's possible to reserve the tasting menu-only chef's table.

Heidelberg *German* | 19 | 17 | 18 | $40

E 80s | 1648 Second Ave. (bet. 85th & 86th Sts.) | 212-628-2332 |
www.heidelbergrestaurant.com

It's "gemütlichkeit central" at this "unapologetically old-school"
Yorkville German, where "dirndl and lederhosen"-clad staffers dish out

"sehr gut" wursts and schnitzel plus "beer in a boot!"; the sometimes-"gruff" service clashes with "Disney-esque Bavarian" decor, but "you get a lot for your money."

Hell's Kitchen *Mexican*

22 | 16 | 19 | $44

W 40s | 679 Ninth Ave. (bet. 46th & 47th Sts.) | 212-977-1588 | www.hellskitchen-nyc.com

The "creatively done" chow is *"muy bueno"* and the margaritas "powerful" at this "always-crowded", often-"noisy" Clinton Nuevo Mexican; it's particularly popular "pre-theater" despite "cheek-by-jowl" seating and "nondescript" surrounds.

Henry Public ●🏳 *Pub Food*

20 | 20 | 19 | $32

Cobble Hill | 329 Henry St. (bet. Atlantic & Pacific Sts.) | Brooklyn | 718-852-8630 | www.henrypublic.com

A "friendly feel" pervades this Cobble Hill "hipster hang", a "Prohibition-style pub" starring cocktails "thoughtfully" mixed by "mustache-wielding, suspender-wearing" bartenders and a "mini-menu" led by an "OMG" turkey-leg sandwich; it garners "bonus points" for late-night hours, demerits for "cash only."

Henry's *American*

19 | 19 | 20 | $41

W 100s | 2745 Broadway (105th St.) | 212-866-0600 | www.henrysnyc.com

There's "something for everyone" at this "calm" "Columbia-area" New American bistro appealing to "young families" and local "blue hairs" with affable service and tables "spaced for conversation"; the "faux Arts and Crafts interior" gets mixed reviews, but all appreciate the "sensible" tabs for such "good food."

Henry's End *American*

24 | 16 | 23 | $50

Brooklyn Heights | 44 Henry St. (bet. Cranberry & Middagh Sts.) | Brooklyn | 718-834-1776 | www.henrysend.com

When you're jonesing for "elk chops", hit this circa-1973 Brooklyn Heights "landmark" famed for its "seasonal" "wild game festival" and year-round "first-rate" New American fare delivered by "sweet" long-time staffers; yes, the "simple" space is "cramped and crowded" – but in a "warm, welcoming" way.

Hibino *Japanese*

26 | 19 | 23 | $35

Cobble Hill | 333 Henry St. (Pacific St.) | Brooklyn | 718-260-8052 | www.hibino-brooklyn.com

"Not your typical" sushi seller, this Cobble Hill Japanese "radiates authenticity" with "delectable" *obanzai* (small plates), "swoon-worthy" housemade tofu and "fantastic fresh" fish – there's "nothing else like it in brownstone Brooklyn"; "super" service, "relaxed decor" and modest checks "don't hurt either."

Hide-Chan ● *Noodle Shop*

21 | 13 | 14 | $21

E 50s | 248 E. 52nd St., 2nd fl. (bet. 2nd & 3rd Aves.) | 212-813-1800

"Heaping bowls" of "belly-warming" soup with "slurpy" noodles and "the richest broth" never fail to hit the spot at this East Midtown Japanese ramen bar, which makes you rue "the cheap stuff" you guzzled "in college"; though the decor and service "could be more appealing", "the price is right."

| | FOOD | DECOR | SERVICE | COST |

NEW Highliner, The ● *American* — — — I

Chelsea | 210 10th Ave. (22nd St.) | 212-206-6206 |
www.thehighlinernyc.com

Though this circa-1929 Chelsea classic's sign still reads 'Empire
Diner', it's got a new name, new owners and a refreshed interior; still,
it's kept the focus on diner standards with a few upscale twists, served
three meals a day, enjoyed either on a stool at the counter, in a booth
or out in the sidewalk seats that lure gallery-goers.

Highpoint Bistro *American* ▽ 22 16 22 $42

Chelsea | 216 Seventh Ave. (bet. 22nd & 23rd Sts.) | 646-410-0120 |
www.highpointnyc.com

"Trying hard and mostly succeeding", this "simple, modern" Chelsea
yearling features Hudson Valley ingredients in its "flavorful" New
American dishes, some served in "toy grocery carts (seriously)"; service
is "sweet" and tabs "moderate" – all in all, it's an "enjoyable" "find."

Hill Country *BBQ* 22 16 15 $33

Flatiron | 30 W. 26th St. (bet. B'way & 6th Ave.) | 212-255-4544 |
www.hillcountryny.com

Straight outta "Texas Hill Country", this "cafeteria-style" Flatironer
dishes up "perfectly smoked" BBQ meats on "butcher paper" with a
"plethora of sides" to a crowd heavy on "fratty carnivores"; "come
with your stretchy pants on", prepare to "stand in line" at the counter
and know that the "by-the-pound" prices can "add up."

NEW Hill Country Chicken *Southern* 19 13 14 $21

Flatiron | 1123 Broadway (25th St.) | 212-257-6446 |
www.hillcountrychicken.com

"Succulent" "diet-busting birds" will make you "forget the Colonel" at
this "cafeteria-style" Flatiron poultry palace from the Hill Country BBQ
folks, where even the "unimpressed" admit the "divine" mini-pies are
"worth the trip alone"; as for the "ironically tacky" bi-level space, "who
gives a cluck?"

Hillstone *American* 22 20 21 $42
(fka Houston's)

E 50s | Citicorp Bldg. | 153 E. 53rd St. (enter on 3rd Ave. & 54th St.) |
212-888-3828
Murray Hill | NY Life Bldg. | 378 Park Ave. S. (27th St.) |
212-689-1090
www.hillstone.com

The "winning" "formula" behind this "casual" upmarket "chain": "solid"
"popularly priced" Americana (including "amazing" signature spinach-
artichoke dip) and "spot-on" service that fill the bill when "you need a
non-NY fix"; "long waits" and lively "happy-hour" legions are part
of the package.

Holy Basil ● *Thai* 22 17 19 $33

E Village | 149 Second Ave., 2nd fl. (bet. 9th & 10th Sts.) | 212-460-5557 |
www.holybasilrestaurant.com

"Piquant" Thai fare and "potent" cocktails make this East Villager
"better than typical", while "cheap prices" offer solid "bang for your
buck"; the staff "gets it done", and the "romantic" dimly lit "upstairs"
is just the place to "take your yoga date."

	FOOD	DECOR	SERVICE	COST

Home *American* — 22 | 17 | 20 | $46

W Village | 20 Cornelia St. (bet. Bleecker & W. 4th Sts.) | 212-243-9579 | www.homerestaurantnyc.com

"Perfectly named" given its "homey setting", this West Villager packs 'em into "narrow" "country-charming" confines for "simple but generous" American classics, especially at its "quaint brunch"; "friendly" service and a "lovely" back garden are additional perks.

Hop Kee ●⇄ *Chinese* — 22 | 8 | 15 | $23

Chinatown | 21 Mott St., downstairs (bet. Chatham Sq. & Mosco St.) | 212-964-8365

With all the earmarks of the "stereotypical" "old-school" C-towner – "big", "cheap" Cantonese platters, "lightning speed" and "basement" "dive" environs – this "hidden" contender can also "surprise" with its "wonderful dishes" and "accommodating" service; "late-night" hours are the crowning touch.

NEW Hospoda ⑧ *Czech* — - | - | - | M

E 70s | Bohemian National Hall | 321 E. 73rd St. (bet. 1st & 2nd Aves.) | 212-861-1038 | www.hospodanyc.com

This upscale arrival to the UES' newly restored Bohemian National Hall presents modern spins on classic Czech dishes, like Prague-style ham with horseradish foam; the name translates as 'beer hall', and suds are a focus here – there's even a draft-master presiding over the pours.

NEW Hotel Chantelle Ⓜ *American* — - | - | - | M

LES | 92 Ludlow St. (bet. Broome & Delancey Sts.) | 212-254-9100 | www.hotelchantelle.com

One of Manhattan's rare rooftop eateries, this new LESer flaunts 360-degree Downtown panoramas paired with midpriced New American eats; a retractable glass roof makes it an all-seasons affair, and two lounges downstairs are just the thing for after-dinner cocktailing.

Hotel Griffou ● *American* — 19 | 25 | 21 | $58

G Village | 21 W. Ninth St., downstairs (bet. 5th & 6th Aves.) | 212-358-0228 | www.griffou.com

The "exclusive feel" of this "underground" Villager lures an "über-chic" clientele for "imaginative cocktails" and "tasty"-enough New American nibbles; the "dark", "romantic" townhouse space has five uniquely appointed rooms, so you can pick one "to suit your mood", but it's "pricey" throughout.

House, The ● *American* — 21 | 24 | 22 | $51

Gramercy | 121 E. 17th St. (bet. Irving Pl. & Park Ave. S.) | 212-353-2121 | www.thehousenyc.com

The "romantic", "charming" air of this "beautiful" tri-level Gramercy "getaway" ensconced in a carriage house dating to 1854 almost "eclipses" its "tasty" New American fare and "knowledgeable" service; kinda "costly" checks help keep it a "well-kept secret."

NEW Hudson Clearwater ●⑧Ⓜ *American* ▽ 25 | 23 | 22 | $48

W Village | 447 Hudson St. (enter on Morton St., bet. Greenwich & Hudson Sts.) | 212-989-3255 | www.hudsonclearwater.com

Although this "secret" ("sshh!") West Village arrival makes you go through the rigmarole of locating an unmarked door that leads you into the space's back entry, the pretension ends there; once inside, you'll find a local crowd drawn to the seasonal American cuisine and convivial vibe; P.S. try to snag a seat at the chef's counter.

Hudson Place *American* | 19 | 19 | 19 | $39 |

Murray Hill | 538 Third Ave. (36th St.) | 212-686-6660 |
www.hudsonplacenyc.com

"Reliable" for "basic" American chow, this Murray Hill "hangout" offers a no-pretense menu that fills the bill "when you don't want to be surprised"; a "relaxed", "pleasant" atmosphere and tabs that "won't break the bank" help keep it a "neighborhood" mainstay.

Hudson River Café *American/Seafood* | 21 | 22 | 20 | $50 |

Harlem | 697 W. 133rd St. (12th Ave.) | 212-491-9111 |
www.hudsonrivercafe.com

"Breathtaking views" of the Hudson steal the spotlight at this "fun" New American seafooder in West Harlem, where the cuisine "works" and the "loungelike" quarters host live jazz and R&B; "attentive" service and "rooftop space" help justify "upscale" price tags.

Hummus Place ❍ *Israeli/Kosher/Vegetarian* | 22 | 12 | 17 | $19 |

E Village | 109 St. Marks Pl. (bet. Ave. A & 1st Ave.) | 212-529-9198
W 70s | 305 Amsterdam Ave. (bet. 74th & 75th Sts.) | 212-799-3335
W 90s | 2608 Broadway (bet. 98th & 99th Sts.) | 212-222-1554
W Village | 71 Seventh Ave. S. (bet. Barrow & Bleecker Sts.) | 212-924-2022
www.hummusplace.com

These "niche" Israelis "do justice" to their namesake with "creamy", "addictive" hummus joined by "fluffy pita", "tasty falafel" and other "fresh", "cheap" kosher-vegetarian noshes; so-so service and "basic" setups are in keeping with the "fast food–type" milieu.

Hunan Kitchen of Grand Sichuan ❍ *Chinese* | ∇ 24 | 13 | 19 | $29 |

Flushing | 42-47 Main St. (Franklin Ave.) | Queens | 718-888-0553

It's related to the Grand Sichuan chain, but this "friendly", "bargain"-priced Flushing Chinese is devoted to "spicy", "wonderful" Hunan specialties, like cumin lamb and "must-try" whole barbecued fish; orange backlit walls modernize its small space, while gratis bites like star anise-fried peanuts keep things traditional.

Hundred Acres *American* | 20 | 21 | 20 | $45 |

SoHo | 38 MacDougal St. (Prince St.) | 212-475-7500 |
www.hundredacresnyc.com

The pleasing "farmhouse" vibe whisks diners "out of NYC for a bit" at this midpriced SoHo New American, a sibling to Five Points and Cookshop that's touted for "fantastic" (and "crowded") brunch; a "friendly" staff ferries its "solid", "local ingredients-focused" fare.

NEW Hung Ry ❍ *Chinese/Noodle Shop* | 20 | 17 | 19 | $31 |

NoHo | 55 Bond St. (bet. Bowery & Lafayette Sts.) | 212-677-4864 |
www.hung-ry.com

A "cute name" belies the "serious" food at this "trendy" Chinese slurp shop in NoHo, home to "hand-pulled noodles" in "steamy soups" complete with "organic" ingredients and "nourishing broths"; a "hip location" and "expensive-for-what-it-is" tariffs explain the "Manolo-clad" crowd.

	FOOD	DECOR	SERVICE	COST

Hurricane Club ❂ *Polynesian* — 20 | 26 | 22 | $62

Flatiron | 360 Park Ave. S. (26th St.) | 212-951-7111 |
www.thehurricaneclub.com

A "beautiful crowd" gets its "tasty" "mai tai" and "pupu platters" on
this Flatiron "mega"-Polynesian, a "theme park" for "adults" with a
"gorgeous", AvroKO-designed "Vegas"-meets-"South Pacific" interior and waiters "dressed in dinner jackets"; "group" cocktails served
in "fishbowls" are a "total blast", but don't be surprised if you "leave
wasted with an empty wallet."

Ici *American/French* — 22 | 20 | 21 | $44

Fort Greene | 246 DeKalb Ave. (bet. Clermont & Vanderbilt Aves.) |
Brooklyn | 718-789-2778 | www.icirestaurant.com

"Market-fresh" "local" ingredients and a "welcoming" vibe make this
"grown-up" Fort Greene French-American "perfect for pre-BAM" dining or a "friendly neighborhood" repast; "pleasant" service and
"calm", "spare" digs with a "lovely garden" raise the question of why
it's "not more discovered."

I Coppi *Italian* — 22 | 21 | 22 | $46

E Village | 432 E. Ninth St. (bet. Ave. A & 1st Ave.) | 212-254-2263 |
www.icoppinyc.com

As if you "turned left and landed in Tuscany", this "date-night" "escape"
in the East Village offers a "beautiful" "year-round" garden as a backdrop
for its "quite good" "rustic" Northern Italiana; "make-you-feel-at-
home" service and "reasonable" rates keep it on the "go-back" list.

Il Bagatto ❂ Ⓜ *Italian* — 23 | 17 | 19 | $44

E Village | 192 E. Second St. (bet. Aves. A & B) | 212-228-0977 |
www.ilbagattonyc.com

Cultivating an "ever-expanding family of regulars", this "happening"
East Villager puts forth "first-class pastas" and other "homespun" Italian
fare at a fair price; no wonder there's generally a "wait" to "crowd" into
either its "lively" upstairs or "charming" downstairs "hideaway."

Il Bambino *Italian* — ▽ 26 | 19 | 23 | $23

Astoria | 34-08 31st Ave. (bet. 34th & 35th Sts.) | Queens | 718-626-0087 |
www.ilbambinonyc.com

Panini worthy of "Florence and Rome" layering "high-quality meats
and cheeses" in "perfect flavor combinations" are the draw at this
Astoria Italian that augments its no-frills interior with a pleasant garden; "warm" service and "inexpensive" checks cinch the "bravo!"

⊠ Il Buco ❂ *Italian/Mediterranean* — 26 | 24 | 23 | $64

NoHo | 47 Bond St. (bet. Bowery & Lafayette St.) | 212-533-1932
Il Buco Alimentari/Vineria *Italian/Mediterranean*
🆕 **NoHo** | 52 Great Jones St. (bet. Bowery & Lafayette St.) |
212-837-2622
www.ilbuco.com

"Tops all-around", this perennial NoHo "favorite" sends out "perfectly
sourced, stunningly executed" Med-Italian dishes ("oh, baby, the pastas!") in "transporting" "farmhouse"-"chic" digs; "stellar" service
helps justify the "expensive" check – you "owe it" to "your taste buds",
especially "if you can book" the "romantic wine cellar"; P.S. the nearby
market/wine bar offshoot opened post-Survey.

	FOOD	DECOR	SERVICE	COST

Il Cantinori *Italian*

24 | 22 | 23 | $64

G Village | 32 E. 10th St. (bet. B'way & University Pl.) | 212-673-6044 | www.ilcantinori.com

"Beautiful flower arrangements" set the tone at this "long-running" yet "still chic" Greenwich Village Northern Italian that "struts" its culinary stuff with "pricey", "terrific" Tuscan cooking; it's a favorite of the "limo"-driven set, but "doting" waiters "make everyone feel like a rock star."

Il Corallo Trattoria *Italian*

∇ 23 | 13 | 17 | $27

SoHo | 176 Prince St. (bet. Sullivan & Thompson Sts.) | 212-941-7119

"More pasta varieties" than you can twirl a fork at offered "cheap" keep this SoHo Italian "cramped" with "regulars"; "spotty service" and "blah" decor are part of the package – "don't go if you want to be pampered."

Il Cortile *Italian*

22 | 21 | 21 | $54

Little Italy | 125 Mulberry St. (bet. Canal & Hester Sts.) | 212-226-6060 | www.ilcortile.com

"Locals mix with tourists" at this "surviving" piece of Little Italy, a "Mulberry institution" rated *molto buono* for its "satisfying", "more upscale" fare dispensed by "old-world" staffers; a "lovely", airy space with an "interior garden" takes the sting out of prices that are "a bit high."

Il Fornaio *Italian*

23 | 16 | 21 | $40

Little Italy | 132A Mulberry St. (bet. Grand & Hester Sts.) | 212-226-8306 | www.ilfornaionyc.com

You get "your money's worth" and then some at this "comfortable" Italian vet considered "one of the better" Little Italy options given its "terrific" pizzas and pastas and "reliable" service; the "ultracasual" interior isn't much, but sit outside and you can "watch the people go by."

Il Gattopardo ● *Italian*

23 | 19 | 23 | $68

W 50s | 33 W. 54th St. (bet. 5th & 6th Aves.) | 212-246-0412 | www.ilgattopardonyc.com

"Even new customers get the love" at this Italian "across from MoMA" that supplies "fabulous", "fresh" Neapolitan fare and "wines that match"; its tony townhouse digs "bustle during peak times" with "expense-account" wielders and deep-pocketed museum-goers.

Il Giglio ☒ *Italian*

26 | 20 | 24 | $70

TriBeCa | 81 Warren St. (bet. Greenwich St. & W. B'way) | 212-571-5555 | www.ilgigliorestaurant.com

"Classics are treated with respect" at this "elegant" TriBeCa Italian, a "serene" vet providing "impressive old-school" meals that begin with "terrific" "free" antipasti; regulars consider it like "Il Mulino without the hype", where "prices are high – but so's the level of service."

Ilili *Lebanese*

25 | 23 | 22 | $55

Chelsea | 236 Fifth Ave. (bet. 27th & 28th Sts.) | 212-683-2929 | www.ililinyc.com

Seriously "upmarket", this Chelsea Lebanese "scene" is ideal for "groups" of "adventurous eaters" looking to share "richly satisfying" small plates ("two words: Brussels sprouts!") in a "gorgeous", "glowing-wood" setting; "soaring prices" and "high-decibel" "techno" are the only downsides, but "brunch is a sleeper."

	FOOD	DECOR	SERVICE	COST

☑ Il Mulino ⧅ *Italian*   27 | 20 | 24 | $88

G Village | 86 W. Third St. (bet. Sullivan & Thompson Sts.) | 212-673-3783 | www.ilmulino.com

"For those who are starting the diet 'tomorrow'", there's this "old-world" Village Italian "must" where "almost-impossible-to-get" rezzies are rewarded with "amazing", "super-rich" Abruzzi-style dishes that just "keep rolling out" via "cheerful" "tuxedoed waiters" who try "to stuff you like a cannelloni"; a "big, hearty bill" and "really packed", "celeb"-studded room come with the territory, though "lunch is less hectic."

Il Palazzo *Italian*   ∇ 24 | 19 | 21 | $49

Little Italy | 151 Mulberry St. (bet. Grand & Hester Sts.) | 212-343-7000

One of the "better" options in Little Italy, this "pleasant" vet plies "solid" Italian staples in "huge portions"; the service is so "attentive" it's almost "intrusive", but the "less-touristy" back garden room is just right.

Il Postino ◐ *Italian*   25 | 21 | 22 | $72

E 40s | 337 E. 49th St. (bet. 1st & 2nd Aves.) | 212-688-0033 | www.ilpostinony.com

Waiters recite the lengthy specials list at "breakneck speed", *"Rain Man"*-style, at this "upscale" Italian near the U.N.; its "diplomatic crowd" appreciates the "delicious" "classic" cuisine and "old-world" (some say "stuffy") milieu, and doesn't flinch at "high" prices.

Il Riccio ◐ *Italian*   21 | 16 | 20 | $58

E 70s | 152 E. 79th St. (bet. Lexington & 3rd Aves.) | 212-639-9111

A "hideaway in plain sight", this "cozy", "expensive" Southern Italian is a "go-to" for "UES matrons and patriarchs" (is that "Mayor Bloomberg"?) seeking an "adult dining experience" with "well-prepared", "traditional" fare and "genial" service; it gets "tight", but in summer the crowd can spread into the "lovely" "courtyard."

☑ Il Tinello ⧅ *Italian*   26 | 21 | 26 | $76

W 50s | 16 W. 56th St. (bet. 5th & 6th Aves.) | 212-245-4388

"Premium" Northern Italian fare in "refined" environs is the draw at this staid Midtown "mainstay" where a "well-dressed" crowd gets the "VIP" treatment from a "stellar" "tuxedoed" staff; it's "wonderfully calm" and "quiet", but "prepare for a hefty tab" and "don't bother if you're in a hurry" since this is a place to dine, not just filler-up.

NEW Imperial No. Nine ◐ *Seafood*   ∇ 25 | 28 | 23 | $62

SoHo | Mondrian SoHo Hotel | 9 Crosby St. (bet. Grand & Howard Sts.) | 212-389-0000 | www.mondriannewyork.com

"Wow" – this Mondrian SoHo Hotel arrival's "glitzy" "greenhouse" of a space is nearly as "sexy" as its chef, "creative" "celeb" toque Sam Talbot; factor in an equally "beautiful" crowd, and it's hard to focus on the "fabulous" "sustainable" fin fare and "helpful" service, which shore up its standing as a "winner" worth the hit to your "credit card."

Inakaya *Japanese*   23 | 21 | 23 | $60

W 40s | NY Times Bldg. | 231 W. 40th St. (bet. 7th & 8th Aves.) | 212-354-2195 | www.inakayany.com

The "entertaining" formula at this Midtown Japanese robata has staffers presenting "totally delicious" grill dishes on "long paddles"; some say it's a "great time" and others "gimmicky", but all agree it's "pricey."

	FOOD	DECOR	SERVICE	COST

Inatteso Pizzabar Casano *Italian/Pizza* ▽ 24 | 20 | 22 | $36

Financial District | 28 West St. (1st Pl.) | 212-267-8000 | www.inattesopizzabar.com

An "oasis" in a restaurant-challenged zone, this "casual" Battery Park City Italian fills a neighborhood need with its "fresh" pizzas and pastas offered up in "modern", "classy" environs; equitable pricing and "charming" service cement its standing as a "local gem."

Indochine ◐ *French/Vietnamese* 22 | 21 | 20 | $55

E Village | 430 Lafayette St. (bet. Astor Pl. & 4th St.) | 212-505-5111 | www.indochinenyc.com

"Age and beauty" happily coalesce at this "soigné" Vietnamese-French "'80s throwback" across from the Public Theater that still "draws trendy crowds"; to a few it's "not what it used to be", but most say "dress well" because the "model"-esque servers are "gorgeous" as ever.

Indus Valley *Indian* 22 | 16 | 20 | $34

W 100s | 2636 Broadway (100th St.) | 212-222-9222 | www.indusvalleyus.com

Upper Westsiders find this "friendly" standby a "refreshing change from run-of-the-mill Indian" thanks to its "well-spiced, delicate" dishes in a "pleasant"-enough space; the "great-value" $14 weekend lunch buffet is another reason it's much-appreciated in the area.

'Ino ◐ *Italian* 24 | 16 | 21 | $30

W Village | 21 Bedford St. (bet. Downing St. & 6th Ave.) | 212-989-5769 | www.cafeino.com

"Panini pressed to pefection" and brunch favorites like truffled egg toast "hit all the pleasure centers" at this "teeny", ever-"popular" West Village wine bar; "late" hours, low prices and "knowledgeable" service are pluses, but it's not for "claustrophobes" or "big groups."

'Inoteca ◐ *Italian* 22 | 18 | 19 | $42

LES | 98 Rivington St. (Ludlow St.) | 212-614-0473
Murray Hill | 323 Third Ave. (24th St.) | 212-683-3035
www.inotecanyc.com

"Brilliant" "little plates" and "unusual" wines and cocktails attract an "enthusiastic young crowd" to these "sexy", "modern" LES-Murray Hill Italians; though "helpful" staffers and a "handy glossary" help, some suggest "it'd be easier if the menu were in English."

Ippudo ◐ *Noodle Shop* 25 | 19 | 19 | $29

E Village | 65 Fourth Ave. (bet. 9th & 10th Sts.) | 212-388-0088 | www.ippudo.com

"Get your slurp on" at this "funky", "affordable" East Village Japanese delivering "bliss in a bowl" with its "full-bodied", "deeply flavored" ramen soups, plus "must-try" pork buns; a "group shout-out" greets every arrival, but "punishing" waits are also part of the drill; P.S. a Midtown branch is in the works at 321 W. 51st Street.

NEW Isa ⊄ *Mediterranean* - | - | - | M

Williamsburg | 348 Wythe Ave. (S. 2nd St.) | Brooklyn | 347-689-3594 | www.isa.gg

The latest from Taavo Somer (Freemans, Peels), this new Williamsburg nook is focused on an open kitchen that's a showcase for the Med stylings of chef Ignacio Mattos (ex Il Buco); the industrial-rustic decor is a woodworker's dream with custom-made furniture, salvaged beams on the ceiling and stacks of firewood, while a roll-up front door and big sash windows lend an open-to-the-elements feel.

	FOOD	DECOR	SERVICE	COST

Isabella's *American/Mediterranean*   `20` `19` `19` `$45`
W 70s | 359 Columbus Ave. (77th St.) | 212-724-2100 | www.isabellas.com
"Locals" mingle with "Museum of Natural History"–goers at this "UWS staple" doling out "delicious" Med-American fare in "comfortable" digs augmented with "sidewalk" tables "ideal for people-watching"; it's "not haute", but it's a "dependable" bet, especially at the "terrific brunch."

Ise *Japanese*   `21` `12` `17` `$40`
E 40s | 151 E. 49th St. (bet. Lexington & 3rd Aves.) | 212-319-6876
Financial District | 56 Pine St. (bet. Pearl & William Sts.) | 212-785-1600 🗷
W 50s | 58 W. 56th St. (bet. 5th & 6th Aves.) | 212-707-8702
www.iserestaurant.com
"Reliable" sushi and "homestyle" Japanese cooking, plus lunch specials that pack serious "bang for the buck", ensure this "honest" izakaya trio is "crazy busy" with suits at midday; maybe it works "best if you read Japanese", but all appreciate that it's "nothing flashy", "just really good."

Island Burgers & Shakes *Burgers*   `21` `9` `17` `$19`
W 50s | 766 Ninth Ave. (bet. 51st & 52nd Sts.) | 212-307-7934
NEW **W 80s** | 422 Amsterdam Ave. (80th St.) Ⓜ
www.islandburgersny.com
"Now that they serve fries they have everything" cheer fans of this Hell's Kitchen "dive" known for its "thick shakes" and "incredible selection" of "big, juicy" burgers with "outlandish" toppings; it's "fast" and "priced right", so never mind the lack of decor; P.S. the new UWS offshoot opened post-Survey.

I Sodi ⏺ *Italian*   `24` `18` `23` `$54`
W Village | 105 Christopher St. (bet. Bleecker & Hudson Sts.) | 212-414-5774 | www.isodinyc.com
This "tiny" West Villager is a "favorite" of "in-the-know" types thanks to its "simple" *"perfetto"* Italian dishes made with "fresh ingredients" and "lots of love"; "gracious", "knowledgeable" service is another reason it's "worth every euro" despite "cute" but sorta "cramped" quarters.

Italianissimo *Italian*   `23` `17` `23` `$53`
E 80s | 307 E. 84th St. (bet. 1st & 2nd Aves.) | 212-628-8603 | www.italianissimonyc.net
A "terrific East 80s find", this Italian "gem" turns out a "focused menu of classics" via a "warm" crew in "snug", "understated" environs; it may not be worth venturing outside your "walking radius" – except possibly for the "value" $27 early-bird deal including wine.

Ithaka *Greek/Seafood*   `20` `16` `21` `$48`
E 80s | 308 E. 86th St. (bet. 1st & 2nd Aves.) | 212-628-9100 | www.ithakarestaurant.com
"Taverna simplicity" meets "upmarket quality" at this Yorkville Greek where the "fresh grilled fish" and "accommodating" service create an "authentic" "Santorini" feel; "liberal portions" and a "talk-friendly" milieu are two more reasons folks leave "completely satisfied."

	FOOD	DECOR	SERVICE	COST

I Trulli *Italian* | 23 | 21 | 22 | $60

Murray Hill | 122 E. 27th St. (bet. Lexington Ave. & Park Ave. S.) | 212-481-7372 | www.itrulli.com

"Superb" pastas and other "*authentico*" Pugliese plates make a "people-pleaser" of this "lovely" Murray Hill Southern Italian, ditto "fabulous wines" from the next-door enoteca; an "excellent" staff, "enchanting fireplace" and "blissful" garden are other reasons it's trulli worth the "high prices."

Itzocan ◐⊄ *Mexican* | 24 | 10 | 19 | $34

E Village | 438 E. Ninth St. (bet. Ave. A & 1st Ave.) | 212-677-5856 | www.itzocanrestaurant.com

"Adventurous gourmet Mex" is "*muy sabroso*" at this "miniature" East Villager; on the downside, it's a "tight" squeeze and cash-only, not to mention the fact that it "lacks margaritas."

Jack's Luxury Oyster Bar ☒ *Continental/French* | 26 | 16 | 23 | $71

E Village | 101 Second Ave. (bet. 5th & 6th Sts.) | 212-979-1012

Owner Jack Lamb provides an "exquisite" (aka "expensive") experience with "surprises in every meticulous small course" at this "under-the-radar" East Village French-Continental with a focus on "sublime" seafood; the "nicely decorated" but "minuscule" room can feel "tight", but "swift", "balletic" service keeps things simpatico.

Jackson Diner *Indian* | 21 | 11 | 16 | $24

NEW G Village | 72 University Pl. (bet. 10th & 11th Sts.) | 212-466-0820
Jackson Heights | 37-47 74th St. (bet. Roosevelt & 37th Aves.) | Queens | 718-672-1232
www.jacksondiner.com

"Don't expect burgers and fries at this diner" - just "tasty", "homespun" Indian "staples" and a "sumptuous" lunch buffet; the new Village outpost's food doesn't measure up to the "beloved" Jackson Heights original's, but both balance a "lack of ambiance" and "spotty" service with "amazing value."

Jackson Hole *Burgers* | 18 | 11 | 16 | $23

E 60s | 232 E. 64th St. (bet. 2nd & 3rd Aves.) | 212-371-7187 ◐
E 80s | 1611 Second Ave. (bet. 83rd & 84th Sts.) | 212-737-8788 ◐
E 90s | 1270 Madison Ave. (91st St.) | 212-427-2820
Murray Hill | 521 Third Ave. (35th St.) | 212-679-3264 ◐
W 80s | 517 Columbus Ave. (85th St.) | 212-362-5177
Bayside | 35-01 Bell Blvd. (35th Ave.) | Queens | 718-281-0330 ◐
Jackson Heights | 69-35 Astoria Blvd. (70th St.) | Queens | 718-204-7070 ◐
www.jacksonholeburgers.com

Decades old, this mini-chain remains a "favorite" of "teens" and others seeking diner "basics" (notably "huge", "loaded" burgers) offered "fast" and "cheap"; the "old-malt-shop" look is "tired", and critics warn "never confuse quantity with quality", but still they're "always jumping."

Jack the Horse Tavern *American* | 23 | 19 | 21 | $46

Brooklyn Heights | 66 Hicks St. (Cranberry St.) | Brooklyn | 718-852-5084 | www.jackthehorse.com

Brooklyn Heights' "relaxed but elegant" pub offers "innovative" American comfort faves (e.g. "off-the-charts" mac 'n' cheese) paired with "impressive" cocktails; maybe it's "pricey for a neighborhood joint", but most tout it as a "grown-up" option that's "perfect" for brunch.

Jacques *French* — 18 | 16 | 18 | $45

E 80s | 206 E. 85th St. (bet. 2nd & 3rd Aves.) | 212-327-2272
NoLita | 20 Prince St. (bet. Elizabeth & Mott Sts.) | 212-966-8886
www.jacquesnyc.com

"Crave-worthy" moules frites and textbook "Parisienne" ambiance keep these "low-key", "traditional" Upper East Side–NoLita French brasseries "noisy and crowded"; service varies, but relatively "reasonable" tabs ensure their popularity.

Jaiya Thai *Thai* — 23 | 15 | 17 | $33

Murray Hill | 396 Third Ave. (28th St.) | 212-889-1330 | www.jaiya.com
"Spicy really means spicy" at this Murray Hill "destination" deemed "one of the best Thais" in town thanks to its "superbly prepared" yet "reasonably priced" fare; the recently redone decor's "over the top" but the service is not so hot.

Jake's Steakhouse *Steak* — 24 | 20 | 22 | $56

Riverdale | 6031 Broadway (242nd St.) | Bronx | 718-581-0182 | www.jakessteakhouse.com
The "Bronx's premier steakhouse" is this "gem" across from Van Cortlandt Park, where the "fabulous" beef comes at rates "reasonable" for the genre (if "pricey for the neighborhood"); a "huge" beer list and "welcoming" service have locals cheering it as a "find."

James *American* — 23 | 21 | 23 | $47

Prospect Heights | 605 Carlton Ave. (St. Marks Ave.) | Brooklyn | 718-942-4255 | www.jamesrestaurantny.com
This "upscale" Prospect Heights American "bridges seamlessly between a casual burger to something much more special" with its "robust" seasonal menu; set in a brownstone "with modern details", it's "hip", "lovely" and "lives up to the buzz."

Jane *American* — 21 | 17 | 19 | $39

G Village | 100 W. Houston St. (bet. La Guardia Pl. & Thompson St.) | 212-254-7000 | www.janerestaurant.com
"Over a decade" and "she's still got it" say fans of this "friendly" Village American dishing up "delicious", "moderately priced" fare; if somewhat "plain", it gets "thronged" at "don't-miss" brunch, though, so "count on waiting if you don't have a reservation."

Japonica *Japanese* — 23 | 16 | 21 | $49

G Village | 100 University Pl. (12th St.) | 212-243-7752 | www.japonicanyc.com
It's "easy to go wild" and order an "endless procession" of "big", "beautifully prepared" rolls at this "crowd-pleasing" Village sushi "stalwart"; some find it "overpriced", especially given kinda "tired" decor, but regulars laud the "amiable" service and "untrendy" vibe.

Jean Claude ⊅ *French* — ∇ 22 | 16 | 21 | $45

SoHo | 137 Sullivan St. (bet. Houston & Prince Sts.) | 212-475-9232 | www.jeanclauderestaurant.com
Scoring "excellent" marks in "what the French call the *rapport qualité-prix*", this "adorable" SoHo Gallic plies "superior" bistro fare at "eco-

nomical" rates; it's an "enjoyable" "winner" that works for a "first date", so most forgive its vexing "cash-only" policy.

⛦ Jean Georges ⌧ French
28 | 27 | 28 | $127

W 60s | Trump Int'l Hotel | 1 Central Park W. (bet. 60th & 61st Sts.) | 212-299-3900 | www.jean-georges.com

Expect "brilliant everything" at Jean-Georges Vongerichten's "standard setter" in Columbus Circle, where the "transcendent" New French "works of culinary art" and "superior wines" are "exciting every time"; a "gorgeous", "soothing" modern space and "choreographed" pro service fully justify the "steep" bill, while the $32 prix fixe lunch remains one of the city's "best bargains."

⛦ Jean Georges' Nougatine French
27 | 24 | 25 | $66

W 60s | Trump Int'l Hotel | 1 Central Park W. (bet. 60th & 61st Sts.) | 212-299-3900 | www.jean-georges.com

"Less formal than Jean Georges but just as tantalizing", this "relaxed" front room provides "extraordinary" New French cooking and "personal" service, not to mention "floor-to-ceiling views of Central Park"; its $28 three-course prix fixe lunch may be the "deal of the century", but "business" types say it's "even better" for "not-crowded" breakfast or after-work drinks and snacks.

NEW Jeffrey's Grocery ● American
▽ 21 | 22 | 20 | $44

W Village | 172 Waverly Pl. (Christopher St.) | 646-398-7630 | www.jeffreysgrocery.com

"No longer a grocery", this tiny, "relaxed" West Village sibling of Joseph Leonard offers oysters, sandwiches and other "foodie-friendly" American fare packing flavor "bigger than the space"; it's a local "hot spot" where you may get "bumped into by servers", but never mind – you'll be "part of the scene."

⛦ Jewel Bako ⌧ Japanese
26 | 22 | 23 | $79

E Village | 239 E. Fifth St. (bet. 2nd & 3rd Aves.) | 212-979-1012

"Perfect", "deliciously fresh" fish is the key to the "stellar sushi" at this "phenomenal" East Village Japanese that's a magnet for "cool types"; "refined" sakes, "jewel box" decor (natch) and "excellent" service overseen by owners Jack and Grace Lamb help justify the "expensive" tab.

Jewel of India Indian
20 | 19 | 19 | $42

W 40s | 15 W. 44th St. (bet. 5th & 6th Aves.) | 212-869-5544 | www.jewelofindianyc.com

"Wonderfully spiced" Indian fare is "served with panache" at this "upscale" Midtowner whose "quiet", "spacious" digs allow for actual "conversation"; tabs are on the "pricey" side, but the "excellent" $17 lunch buffet (served upstairs) and $30 pre-theater prix fixe are "bargains."

J.G. Melon ●⊅ Pub Food
21 | 12 | 16 | $29

E 70s | 1291 Third Ave. (74th St.) | 212-744-0585

You'll see "many a popped collar" at this "classic", cash-only UES pub crammed with "preps of all ages" downing "juicy, flavorful" burgers and "oh, those cottage fries"; the decor's "worn" and service "grumpy", but it "won't bust your wallet."

	FOOD	DECOR	SERVICE	COST

Jimmy's No. 43 ◑⌕ *American* ▽ 21 | 18 | 19 | $33

E Village | 43 E. Seventh St., downstairs (bet. 2nd & 3rd Aves.) | 212-982-3006 | www.jimmysno43.com

"Fanatically local, religiously good" American small plates and a "killer beer list" come in a no-frills East Village basement at this "hipster" magnet; a "friendly" bastion of "underground cool", it plays host to lots of "creative foodie gatherings."

Jing Fong *Chinese* 20 | 12 | 12 | $22

Chinatown | 20 Elizabeth St., 2nd fl. (bet. Bayard & Canal Sts.) | 212-964-5256

"Ride up the escalator to dim sum heaven" at this "cavernous" C-town Cantonese "spectacle" where "whizzing carts" dispense a "dizzying" array of "wonderful" dumplings for "cheap"; weekends are "madness", but the "frenzy" only bolsters the "authentic" "Hong Kong" feel.

Joe Allen ◑ *American* 18 | 17 | 20 | $46

W 40s | 326 W. 46th St. (bet. 8th & 9th Aves.) | 212-581-6464 | www.joeallenrestaurant.com

"Running longer than *Phantom* and *Wicked* combined", this circa-'63 Theater District "Broadway clubhouse" has "character" aplenty to "elevate" its "ordinary" American eats ("go for the burger"); "stage luminaries" often appear "after the show", while the "flops posters" have their own way of "uplifting the spirit."

Joe & Pat's *Italian/Pizza* 24 | 13 | 18 | $23

Castleton Corners | 1758 Victory Blvd. (Manor Rd.) | Staten Island | 718-981-0887

Whether the "secret's in the cheese", the "amazing sauce" or "cracker-thin crust", this "busy, noisy", "family-owned" SI "oldie but goodie" makes one "awesome pizza"; there's a "wonderful variety" of other Italiana too, but it best rewards those on a pie "quest."

JoeDoe *American* 24 | 18 | 22 | $49

E Village | 45 E. First St. (bet. 1st & 2nd Aves.) | 212-780-0262 | www.chefjoedoe.com

"Joe and Jill are the Waltucks of the East Village" enthuse fans of this "tiny", "quirky" sleeper that plays with "American flavors in a big way" ("fried matzo is genius"); most agree it's "hard to find food this good at this price", not to mention such "terrific" service.

Joe's Ginger ⌕ *Chinese* 21 | 9 | 13 | $24

Chinatown | 25 Pell St. (Doyers St.) | 212-285-0999 | www.joeginger.com

Savvy C-town soup-dumpling seekers beat the lines at Joe's Shanghai and head "a few doors down" for the "same freaking *xiao long bao*" at this "excellent" sib; "grouchy" greetings and "bare-bones" decor are part of the "bargain", but at least "you get your own table."

Joe's Pizza *Pizza* 23 | 7 | 15 | $10

W Village | 7 Carmine St. (bet. Bleecker St. & 6th Ave.) | 212-255-3946 | www.joespizzanyc.com ◑⌕
Park Slope | 137 Seventh Ave. (bet. Carroll St. & Garfield Pl.) | Brooklyn | 718-398-9198 | www.joespizza.com

"Classic NYC" slices at their "crispy-crusted" "finest" fly out "fast" at this West Village pizzeria open for "stand-up or take-out" till the wee hours; the separately owned Park Slope standby does a "solid" job too, but just "ain't the same."

Joe's Shanghai *Chinese*
22 | 9 | 14 | $27

Chinatown | 9 Pell St. (bet. Bowery & Mott St.) | 212-233-8888 ✄
W 50s | 24 W. 56th St. (bet. 5th & 6th Aves.) | 212-333-3868
Flushing | 136-21 37th Ave. (bet. Main & Union Sts.) | Queens | 718-539-3838 ✄
www.joeshanghairestaurants.com

"Absolutely lip-smacking, soup-slurping dumplings" are the "rightfully famous" star attraction at this "favorite" Shanghainese trio that's an "out-of-towners'" "must-try"; expect "painful" waits, "abrupt" service and "communal seating at noncommunal tables" (at the C-town branch), but "low prices" compensate.

NEW John Dory Oyster Bar ◖ *Seafood*
23 | 21 | 19 | $57

Chelsea | Ace Hotel | 1196 Broadway (W. 29th St.) | 212-792-9000 |
www.thejohndory.com

"Reincarnated" in the Ace Hotel, this "cool" seafooder from April Bloomfield and Ken Friedman (Spotted Pig, The Breslin) offers a "fantastic raw bar" and "stunning" small plates in "fun" nautical-kitsch digs; the catches are "impossible waits" and "high cost" for "bite-size" nibbles.

John's of 12th Street ✄ *Italian/Vegetarian*
22 | 15 | 20 | $33

E Village | 302 E. 12th St. (2nd Ave.) | 212-475-9531 |
www.johnsof12thstreet.com

"One of the last of a dying breed", this century-old East Villager delivers "down-to-earth" "red-sauce" Italian fare in "dark", "homey" digs evoking "bygone days"; with "cheerful" service and "reasonable" tabs, no wonder it "never loses its appeal"; P.S. "props for the vegan menu!"

John's Pizzeria *Pizza*
23 | 14 | 16 | $25

E 60s | 408 E. 64th St. (bet. 1st & York Aves.) | 212-935-2895
W 40s | 260 W. 44th St. (bet. B'way & 8th Ave.) | 212-391-7560 ◖
W Village | 278 Bleecker St. (bet. 6th Ave. & 7th Ave. S.) |
212-243-1680 ◖✄
www.johnspizzerianyc.com

"Praise be" for this "venerable", booth-lined Village pizzeria, the "brick house of brick-oven" pies ("no slices") baking up "thin, crispy" crust "the way it should be"; the "dramatic" Times Square offshoot offers "casual meals" in a converted church, while the UES outlet draws area "families."

JoJo *French*
25 | 23 | 24 | $70

E 60s | 160 E. 64th St. (bet. Lexington & 3rd Aves.) | 212-223-5656 |
www.jean-georges.com

In a "gracious" UES townhouse, this "Jean-Georges gem" supplies "superb" French bistro fare, "top-notch" service and a "welcome respite from high-decibel dining"; take "that someone special for a celebratory evening" – or go for the "fab" lunch and early-bird "deals."

NEW Jones Wood Foundry *British*
∇ 23 | 23 | 22 | $47

E 70s | 401 E. 76th St. (bet. 1st & York Aves.) | 212-249-2700 |
www.joneswoodfoundry.com

"Like a posh little London pub", this "wonderful UES addition" dishes up "fish 'n' chips done right" and other British staples washed down

| | FOOD | DECOR | SERVICE | COST |

with Euro beers in casual wood-paneled quarters; the "warm" vibe already has locals treating it as a "neighborhood haunt" despite "pricey"-for-the-genre tabs.

Joseph Leonard ● American

| 22 | 20 | 22 | $49 |

W Village | 170 Waverly Pl. (Grove St.) | 646-429-8383 | www.josephleonard.com

Gabe Stulman's "tiny", "happening" West Villager "hits the mark" with a "small" but "well-chosen" menu of "beautifully prepared", "fairly priced" New American dishes; a "genial" staff and "cool" zinc bar make it the "ultimate neighborhood" standby – "if you can handle a wait."

Josie's Eclectic

| 19 | 15 | 18 | $36 |

Murray Hill | 565 Third Ave. (37th St.) | 212-490-1558
W 70s | 300 Amsterdam Ave. (74th St.) | 212-769-1212
www.josiesnyc.com

Food that "tastes indulgent" but is "healthy" and "affordable" lures the "younger set" and "stroller"-pushers alike to these "crowded", "loud" Murray Hill–UWS Eclectics; despite fairly "bland" looks, the vibe's "pleasant", with "brisk" service keeping "the tables turning."

Joya ⊄ Thai

| 23 | 17 | 18 | $23 |

Cobble Hill | 215 Court St. (bet. Warren & Wyckoff Sts.) | Brooklyn | 718-222-3484 | www.joyanyc.com

Thai cooking "at its best" – "simple, fresh and tasty" – offered "cheap" keeps this "cash-only" Cobble Hill vet "very crowded" ("be prepared to wait"); "cool" and "live DJ"-equipped, it can get "unbearably noisy", but the back garden is a "pleasant" refuge.

Jubilee French

| 22 | 16 | 19 | $52 |

E 50s | 347 E. 54th St. (bet. 1st & 2nd Aves.) | 212-888-3569 | www.jubileeny.net

"Quietly holding its own", this "classy" "throwback" of an East Side bistro attracts "local Sutton Place" swells and the "U.N. French crowd" with "reliable", if "*cher*", Gallic standards ("love those moules"); just know "tight quarters" mean "you'd better like your neighbor."

Junior's Diner

| 19 | 13 | 17 | $28 |

E 40s | Grand Central | lower level (42nd St. & Vanderbilt Ave.) | 212-983-5257
W 40s | Shubert Alley | 1515 Broadway (enter on 45th St., bet. B'way & 8th Ave.) | 212-302-2000 ●
Downtown Bklyn | 386 Flatbush Ave. Ext. (DeKalb Ave.) | Brooklyn | 718-852-5257 ●
www.juniorscheesecake.com

"Nostalgia" – not to mention the "best cheesecake in the universe" – "erases all imperfections" at this "kitschy" trio slinging "classic" diner grub via "crusty" staffers; if you can't schlep to the "landmark" Brooklyn "original", you'll have to "play the tourist" at one of the Midtown offshoots.

NEW Junoon Indian

| 23 | 26 | 23 | $71 |

Flatiron | 27 W. 24th St. (bet. 5th & 6th Aves.) | 212-490-2100 | www.junoonnyc.com

"Hot chef" Vikas Khanna and his "tantalizing" takes on Indian cooking induce "swoons" at this "opulent" new Flatironer, while the "pricey" tab may too; the "gorgeous" space centered on an open kitchen is "suitable for business" dining – and the $25 lunch "steal" works "if you're footing the tab."

Kabab Café Ⓜ⇟ _Egyptian_
▽ 24 | 14 | 20 | $35

Astoria | 25-12 Steinway St. (25th Ave.) | Queens | 718-728-9858
A "place like no other", "national treasure" Ali El Sayed's "wonderfully friendly" Astoria "hole-in-the-wall" is an Egyptian "stronghold" with "magic in the kitchen" and a BYO policy to boost the "value"; come with "a sense of humor" and "let the chef cook for you" – "you won't be disappointed", even when you get the bill.

Kajitsu Ⓜ _Japanese/Vegetarian_
▽ 28 | 23 | 26 | $88

E Village | 414 E. Ninth St. (bet. Ave. A & 1st Ave.) | 212-228-4873 | www.kajitsunyc.com
"Step into an alternate universe of beauty" at this East Village Japanese "oasis of calm" whose "exquisite" kaiseki-style vegetarian "feasts" comprise "edible works of art" showcasing the "ancient Buddhist" _shojin_ cuisine; "considerate" service further justifies the "pricey" tab.

Kang Suh ◑ _Korean_
23 | 13 | 18 | $36

Garment District | 1250 Broadway (32nd St.) | 212-564-6845
For "delicious" Korean BBQ that'll have you "smelling of garlic for hours", "count on" this "24-hour" Garment District "standby" that also supplies "spicy soups" and sushi; unfortunately, "long lines", "diner" decor and "rushed" service come with the low tabs.

🆉 Kanoyama ◑ _Japanese_
26 | 16 | 20 | $56

E Village | 175 Second Ave. (bet. 11th & 12th Sts.) | 212-777-5266 | www.kanoyama.com
"The secret" is long out about this "small", "tightly packed" East Villager slicing "wonderfully fresh", "beautifully presented" sushi at prices "lower than its better-known peers"; for a "first-class experience", try the "omakase-only" next-door sake/oyster bar and watch the chefs "go to work."

Kashkaval _Mediterranean_
23 | 17 | 18 | $28

W 50s | 856 Ninth Ave. (56th St.) | 212-581-8282 | www.kashkavalfoods.com
"Hidden behind" a Hell's Kitchen "deli", this wine bar dispenses "delicious", "well-priced" Mediterranean meze, cheese plates and fondue in a "cozy" back room; it's "perfect for a date" or a "meet-up with friends", but the no-rez policy spells "long waits."

Kati Roll Co. _Indian_
21 | 7 | 12 | $12

Garment District | 49 W. 39th St. (bet. 5th & 6th Aves.) | 212-730-4280
G Village | 99 MacDougal St. (bet. Bleecker & W. 3rd Sts.) | 212-420-6517 ◑
www.thekatirollcompany.com
"Less-than-nothing decor" and so-so service at this Village–Garment District Indian duo is a "fair trade-off" for its "spicy little" kati wraps brimming with flavor; it fills the bill for a "quick, cheap" and "satisfying" meal or nosh "after the bars" – "when you need it, you need it."

Katsu-Hama _Japanese_
20 | 12 | 17 | $30

E 40s | 11 E. 47th St. (bet. 5th & Madison Aves.) | 212-758-5909

(continued)

Katsu-Hama

W 50s | 45 W. 55th St., 2nd fl. (bet. 5th & 6th Aves.) | 212-541-7145 ◐
www.katsuhama.com

"Japanese office workers" and other "Midtown lunchers" descend on these "temples to deep-frying" specializing in "quality katsu" (i.e. pork cutlets), plus "soba and udon specials", at a "fair price"; most are in "pig heaven" despite basic decor and "rushed" service.

☑ Katz's Delicatessen *Deli*

24 | 10 | 13 | $25

LES | 205 E. Houston St. (Ludlow St.) | 212-254-2246 |
www.katzdeli.com

The "gold standard for Jewish delis in NYC", famed for that "orgasmic" scene in *When Harry Met Sally*, this circa-1888 "LES landmark" appeals to "locals, tourists and the world in general" with "the best" pastrami sandwiches, hot dogs and "oh, those pickles!"; it all comes in sprawling "cafeteria-style" digs where "nothing changes" – "except the prices"; P.S. "don't lose your ticket" and remember it doesn't hurt to "tip the slicer."

☑ Keens Steakhouse *Steak*

25 | 24 | 24 | $72

Garment District | 72 W. 36th St. (bet. 5th & 6th Aves.) | 212-947-3636 |
www.keens.com

"The soul of old Gotham", this circa-1885 Garment District meatery-cum–party site–cum–museum of Americana remains a "dark, manly" haven for "perfectly done" steaks and "fabled mutton chops"; "accommodating" waiters and some 88,000 "antique clay pipes on the ceiling" enhance the "19th-century" feel, and though prices are "Donald Trump" modern, the "cozy pub room" is cheaper.

Kefi *Greek*

22 | 16 | 18 | $39

W 80s | 505 Columbus Ave. (bet. 84th & 85th Sts.) | 212-873-0200 |
www.kefirestaurant.com

"Brilliant" chef Michael Psilakis' UWS Greek is "always bustling" thanks to "superior", "low-priced" Hellenic "home cooking" that tastes "more authentic than what they serve you in the Plaka"; "rushed" service and "deafening noise" are part of the "bargain", ditto the $17 early-bird dinner.

Kellari Taverna ◐ *Greek*

23 | 22 | 21 | $53

W 40s | 19 W. 44th St. (bet. 5th & 6th Aves.) | 212-221-0144 |
www.kellari.us

Clearly the "Greek gods are smiling" upon this "upscale" Midtown Hellenic where "fresh, well-prepared" seafood comes amid "pleasant" "Athens atmosphere"; it's a "business-lunch" "go-to" that's also appreciated for its "bargain" $33 pre-theater prix fixe and "lively bar scene."

Kenmare ◐ *American*

19 | 20 | 17 | $59

Little Italy | 98 Kenmare St. (bet. Lafayette & Mulberry Sts.) | 212-274-9898 |
www.kenmarenyc.com

"Scene" trumps cuisine at this Little Italy "hot spot" where "beautiful" things pose under "sexy lighting" ("I saw Sienna Miller in sparkly hot pants!") and toy with "decent", "expensive" New American bites; the real "buzz" is in the exclusive downstairs lounge – but good luck getting past the "attitude" force field at the "hostess desk."

	FOOD	DECOR	SERVICE	COST

Keste Pizza e Vino *Pizza* | 25 | 13 | 19 | $28 |

W Village | 271 Bleecker St. (Morton St.) | 212-243-1500 |
www.kestepizzeria.com

"Chewy, thin" "mmm" pizzas like on Naples' "Spaccanapoli" "pack 'em
in" to this "tiny", "nothing-fancy" Village pie place where "ultrarapid"
service balances "painful" table waits ("beste get on line before 5"); it's
"not cheap" for the genre, but at least you get "real-deal" tastes of Italy.

Kings' Carriage House Ⓜ *American* | 22 | 24 | 24 | $63 |

E 80s | 251 E. 82nd St. (bet. 2nd & 3rd Aves.) | 212-734-5490 |
www.kingscarriagehouse.com

"One of the great romantic nooks of NYC", this "charming" UES "carriage house" is "so elegant, so English, so afternoon-tea-and-
crumpets" – with a "precious" prix fixe-only New American menu "to
match"; a find "for the ladies", it's "delightful" for "parties and showers."

King Yum *Chinese/Polynesian* | 19 | 17 | 21 | $29 |

Fresh Meadows | 181-08 Union Tpke. (181st St.) | Queens | 718-380-1918 |
www.kingyumrestaurant.com

"Step back" to the 1950s at this "Trader Vic's-style" Fresh Meadows "institution" that mixes Chinese-Polynesian "classics" with "dated" "tiki
hut" decor, "umbrella" drinks and "karaoke"; it's a "select from columns
A and B" experience – "if you're looking for daring, keep on walking."

Kin Shop *Thai* | 24 | 17 | 21 | $50 |

W Village | 469 Sixth Ave. (bet. 11th & 12th Sts.) | 212-675-4295 |
www.kinshopnyc.com

Top Chef champ Harold Dieterle "hits the target" again with this West
Village "take on modern Thai" turning out "subtle, surprising", "OMG-
delicious" dishes with "fresh" ingredients; its "terrific" service and
"nice open space" help justify slightly "pricey" tabs.

Ki Sushi *Japanese* | 25 | 20 | 22 | $37 |

Boerum Hill | 122 Smith St. (bet. Dean & Pacific Sts.) | Brooklyn |
718-935-0575 | www.ki-sushi.com

"Excellent sushi" at realistic rates is the "ki to the success" of this "elegant" Boerum Hill Japanese where the "gorgeous fish" tastes "right from
the sea"; some shrug it off as simply a "solid neighborhood joint" but
"nothing to go out of your way" for, but even they laud its "lunch deals."

Kitchenette *Southern* | 19 | 14 | 16 | $25 |

TriBeCa | 156 Chambers St. (bet. Greenwich St. & W. B'way) |
212-267-6740
W 100s | 1272 Amsterdam Ave. (bet. 122nd & 123rd Sts.) | 212-531-7600
www.kitchenetterestaurant.com

Like "dropping in at your grandmother's", this "down-home" TriBeCa-
UWS duo "makes you feel all warm and fuzzy" with its "righteous,
retro" Southern "comfort standards" and "y'all-come-back-soon" service; no wonder the "cute setting" turns "cramped on weekends."

Kittichai *Thai* | 23 | 26 | 21 | $62 |

SoHo | 60 Thompson Hotel | 60 Thompson St. (bet. Broome & Spring Sts.) |
212-219-2000 | www.kittichairestaurant.com

An "LA-like scene" complete with "sexy ambiance", "amazing people-
watching" and a "floating orchid pool" awaits at this "high-end" Thai

in SoHo's Thompson Hotel; yes, the "delicious" dishes "with a twist" are "pricey", but it makes a "fun chichi night out."

Knickerbocker Bar & Grill ☉ *American*

FOOD	DECOR	SERVICE	COST
20	18	19	$51

G Village | 33 University Pl. (9th St.) | 212-228-8490 | www.knickerbockerbarandgrill.com

A Village "secret" since 1977, this "relaxing" New American "tavern" draws "neighborhood" types averaging "at least twice the age of the NYU students in the area"; service is "prompt", the "excellent" steaks "more affordable" than elsewhere and there's weekend jazz as a "bonus."

Koi *Japanese*

FOOD	DECOR	SERVICE	COST
23	23	21	$65

W 40s | Bryant Park Hotel | 40 W. 40th St. (bet. 5th & 6th Aves.) | 212-921-3330 | www.koirestaurant.com

"Hang with the fashionistas" at this "trendy" Los Angeles import in the Bryant Park Hotel, where "creative" sushi and Japanese cooked dishes come in "electric" environs (including maybe "a celebrity or two"); it gets "loud" and "you pay" for the "cool vibe" – but the "elite" clientele doesn't notice.

Ko Sushi *Japanese*

FOOD	DECOR	SERVICE	COST
20	13	20	$36

E 70s | 1329 Second Ave. (70th St.) | 212-439-1678
E 80s | 1619 York Ave. (85th St.) | 212-772-8838
www.newkosushi.com

"Satisfying" "fresh sushi and cold sake" hit the spot at these separately owned, "reliable" UES Japanese "joints"; maybe the settings are "not anything spectacular", but modest tabs and "happy-to-help" staffers make them a "regular" stop.

Kouzan ☉ *Japanese*

FOOD	DECOR	SERVICE	COST
21	19	21	$35

W 90s | 685 Amsterdam Ave. (93rd St.) | 212-280-8099 | www.kouzanny.com

"Lucky Upper Westsiders" have this Japanese "gem" as a "neighborhood go-to" for "high-quality" sushi, "scrumptious" cooked dishes and a "Zen" waterfall–abetted atmosphere; factor in "very reasonable" prices and "neighborly", "aim-to-please" service, and it's a "keeper."

Kuma Inn ⊅ *Filipino/Thai*

FOOD	DECOR	SERVICE	COST
23	11	19	$36

LES | 113 Ludlow St., 2nd fl. (bet. Delancey & Rivington Sts.) | 212-353-8866 | www.kumainn.com

There's a "sure hand in the kitchen" at this LES Filipino-Thai, where the "delectable" small plates come "cheap" in "tiny" digs atop a "steep" flight of stairs; never mind "nonexistent" decor – it's "hip", "lively" and "fun for groups", and BYO to boot.

Kum Gang San ☉ *Korean*

FOOD	DECOR	SERVICE	COST
22	17	17	$34

Garment District | 49 W. 32nd St. (bet. B'way & 5th Ave.) | 212-967-0909
Flushing | 138-28 Northern Blvd. (bet. Bowne & Union Sts.) | Queens | 718-461-0909
www.kumgangsan.net

"You can grill your own kalbi 24 hours a day" at these "steady", "affordable" Korean BBQ "joints"; a few find the Flushing branch "more authentic", but others thrill to K-town's "waterfall with musicians perched atop it."

| | FOOD | DECOR | SERVICE | COST |

☑ Kuruma Zushi *Japanese* ▽ 28 | 17 | 25 | $127

E 40s | 7 E. 47th St., 2nd fl. (bet. 5th & Madison Aves.) | 212-317-2802 | www.kurumazushi.com

For the "definitive sushi experience", try this "hidden" yet "firmly established" Midtowner from "master" chef Toshihiro Uezu; despite the "nondescript" mezzanine space, it's worth the "Ginza prices" – just be sure your credit card has an "unlimited ceiling."

Kyochon Chicken ● *Chicken* 19 | 14 | 14 | $20

Murray Hill | 319 Fifth Ave. (bet. 32nd & 33rd Sts.) | 212-725-9292
Flushing | 156-50 Northern Blvd. (bet. 156th & 157th Sts.) | Queens | 718-939-9292
www.kyochon.com

"Ultracrispy, incendiary wings" will "blow your taste buds off" – and the soy-garlic variety is "just as flavorful" – at these Murray Hill-Flushing links of a global Korean chain; "modern" and "quick", they "outclass" most other "chicken joints", even if some find 'em "pricey" for poultry.

Kyotofu ●Ⓜ *Dessert/Japanese* 21 | 18 | 18 | $30

W 40s | 705 Ninth Ave. (bet. 48th & 49th Sts.) | 212-974-6012 | www.kyotofu-nyc.com

The "artistry is half the fun" at this Hell's Kitchen Japanese confectioner-cum-eatery concocting "light" "small bites" (both vegetarian and not) and soy-based desserts in a "cute", "capsule"-like space; "sweet" service rounds out the "enjoyable", "something-different" experience.

Kyo Ya ● *Japanese* 26 | 22 | 26 | $99

E Village | 94 E. Seventh St., downstairs (1st Ave.) | 212-982-4140

"Sublime" "Kyoto-style" kaiseki dinners "wow" at this East Village "secret" providing "delicate", "meticulously prepared" multicourse extravaganzas at a "leisurely pace"; "serene", "unique" and "not for the unadventurous", it's "minimalist in everything but price."

La Baraka *French* 22 | 18 | 25 | $45

Little Neck | 255-09 Northern Blvd. (2 blocks east of Little Neck Pkwy.) | Queens | 718-428-1461 | www.labarakarest.com

Thanks to "charmer hostess Lucette", "you always feel welcome" – and well fed – at this "been-around-forever" Little Neck "institution" known for "delicious" Moroccan-accented French fare; "consistency" is the key to its longevity, hence the "time-warp" decor.

La Bergamote *Bakery/French* 24 | 16 | 16 | $19

Chelsea | 177 Ninth Ave. (20th St.) | 212-627-9010
W 50s | 515 W. 52nd St. (bet. 10th & 11th Aves.) | 212-586-2429
www.labergamotenyc.com

"*Très délicieux*" is the word on these Paris-*sur*-Hudson patisserie/cafes specializing in "worth-the-calories" baked treats that evoke the "good life"; recent upgrades include a "new, larger" home for the Chelsea original and full-menu dining at the "little-known" Hell's Kitchen spin-off.

La Boîte en Bois *French* 22 | 16 | 20 | $53

W 60s | 75 W. 68th St. (bet. Columbus Ave. & CPW) | 212-874-2705 | www.laboitenyc.com

A "trusted standby" close to Lincoln Center, this longtime "pre-theater" magnet offers "solid", "no-surprises" French cooking for "sensi-

	FOOD	DECOR	SERVICE	COST

ble" sums backed up by service "geared to curtain time"; the single drawback is "beyond-cramped", "shoulder-to-shoulder" dimensions.

La Bonne Soupe *French*
| | 19 | 13 | 16 | $33 |

W 50s | 48 W. 55th St. (bet. 5th & 6th Aves.) | 212-586-7650 | www.labonnesoupe.com

For a "dependable" French fix near City Center, try this Midtown "oldie but goodie" whose "typical" bistro lineup includes "one of the best onion soups anywhere"; given the "thrifty" pricing, few mind the "so-so" service and somewhat "shabby" digs.

L'Absinthe *French*
| | 22 | 23 | 22 | $68 |

E 60s | 227 E. 67th St. (bet. 2nd & 3rd Aves.) | 212-794-4950 | www.labsinthe.com

The "Seine can't be far away" from this "classy" UES brasserie exuding an *authentique* "night-in-Paris" air, from its "fine" French cooking to its "belle époque" setting; true, it can be "pricey", but "they aim to please" and provide "old-world" dining the "way it used to be."

La Carbonara *Italian*
| | 20 | 16 | 18 | $36 |

W Village | 202 W. 14th St. (bet. 7th & 8th Aves.) | 212-255-2060 | www.lacarbonaranyc.com

"Solid" Southern Italiana arrives in "sensible portions" with price tags to match at this "no-frills" West Village refuge where the "happy", "la dolce vita" mood can make for "pretty noisy" dining; insiders call the pastas the "best choice" here.

Lady Mendl's *Tearoom*
| | 21 | 26 | 24 | $45 |

Gramercy | Inn at Irving Pl. | 56 Irving Pl. (bet. 17th & 18th Sts.) | 212-533-4466 | www.ladymendls.com

"White kid gloves" come in handy at this "delightfully feminine", "old-fashioned" Gramercy tearoom where "oversize dollhouse" decor and "expert" service will thrill "your favorite auntie"; the "delicious" finger sandwiches and scones on offer add to the "back-in-time" feeling, though the tabs are strictly current-day.

La Esquina ● *Mexican*
| | 23 | 21 | 18 | $47 |

Little Italy | 114 Kenmare St. (bet. Cleveland Pl. & Lafayette St.) | 646-613-7100 | www.esquinanyc.com

NEW Cafe de la Esquina ● *Mexican*

Williamsburg | 225 Wythe Ave. (N. 3rd St.) | Brooklyn | 718-393-5500 | www.esquinabk.com

A "no-frills" taqueria and sit-down cafe are preludes to the main event at this "hip" Little Italy Mexican: a "bouncer"-guarded basement "speakeasy", accessed "down the stairs and via the kitchen"; reservations for the latter are "hard to get", but the payoffs are "tasty" vittles and a "sexy", "candlelit" scene that "doesn't get any cooler"; P.S. the new Williamsburg satellite features a diner setting and easier access.

La Flor ⊄ *Bakery/Mexican*
| | ▽ 25 | 15 | 20 | $28 |

Woodside | 53-02 Roosevelt Ave. (53rd St.) | Queens | 718-426-8023 | www.laflorrestaurant.com

"Interesting" Mexican "home cooking" with Eclectic flourishes is the "inspired" hook at this "tiny" Woodside bakery/cafe "hidden under the 7 line"; "inexpensive" tabs compensate for the "nongrand" decor, "out-of-the-way" site and cash-only rule.

NEW La Follia *Italian*

▽ 23 | 20 | 22 | $38

Gramercy | 226 Third Ave. (19th St.) | 212-477-4100 | www.lafollianyc.com

Part osteria, part wine bar, this "cozy" new Gramercy Italian from the "seasoned" Irving Mill team is already a "neighborhood favorite" thanks to the surefire recipe of "tasty" cooking and "friendly" service; "good-value" – nothing over $20 – seals the deal.

La Fonda del Sol ⊠ *Spanish*

21 | 21 | 21 | $57

E 40s | MetLife Bldg. | 200 Park Ave. (enter on 44th St. & Vanderbilt Ave.) | 212-867-6767 | www.patinagroup.com

Above Grand Central, this double-duty Spaniard presents "top-quality tapas" in its "vibrant bar" area and more "formal dining" in its "quieter" rear dining room; overall, it does a good job of resurrecting the namesake "'60s original" and brings "something different" to Midtown.

La Gioconda *Italian*

21 | 16 | 22 | $47

E 50s | 226 E. 53rd St. (bet. 2nd & 3rd Aves.) | 212-371-3536 | www.lagiocondany.com

Ok, it may be "nothing exciting" to look at, but this "teeny tiny" Turtle Bay Italian is a "good bet" for "freshly prepared" food, "welcoming" service and "quiet"-as-a-museum acoustics; prices are "reasonable" too.

Z La Grenouille ⊠ *French*

28 | 28 | 28 | $108

E 50s | 3 E. 52nd St. (bet. 5th & Madison Aves.) | 212-752-1495 | www.la-grenouille.com

Just about "every superlative" applies to Charles Masson's "luxuriant" Midtown standard-bearer – the last (and best) of NYC's great classic French restaurants – from the "sublime" haute cuisine and "seamless service" to the "gorgeous floral displays" and overall sense of *"ancien régime* splendor"; now in its 50th year, this "time-tested" indulger of "expensive tastes" can be experienced at a "bargain" $36 lunch in the upstairs room; P.S. jackets required.

Lake Club *Continental/Eclectic*

21 | 24 | 24 | $51

St. George | 1150 Clove Rd. (Victory Blvd.) | Staten Island | 718-442-3600 | www.lake-club.com

"Picturesque dining" on the shores of "tranquil" Clove Lake is the draw at this "romantic" SI destination in St. George; the "lovely" room's on par with the "white-glove service", but ultimately the debatable Continental/Eclectic cooking ("good" vs. "could be better") plays second fiddle to the "beautiful" view.

La Lanterna di Vittorio ● *Italian*

20 | 23 | 19 | $30

G Village | 129 MacDougal St. (bet. W. 3rd & 4th Sts.) | 212-529-5945 | www.lalanternacaffe.com

"Hidden away on MacDougal Street", this longtime Village "date spot" exudes a "relaxed", off-the-radar ambiance via "flattering lighting", a "nice fireplace" and Italian bites like pizzas and panini; late hours and live jazz in the adjoining bar add to its "romantic" appeal.

La Lunchonette *French*

22 | 15 | 20 | $45

Chelsea | 130 10th Ave. (18th St.) | 212-675-0342

Now celebrating its 25th birthday, this "bohemian" West Chelsea bistro brings "Montmartre to the High Line" area with an "honest", "affordable" French menu that "far exceeds its modest name"; on

	FOOD	DECOR	SERVICE	COST

Sundays, the "funky" "old barroom" setting comes alive when an accordion-wielding "chanteuse" entertains.

La Mangeoire *French*

| 21 | 20 | 20 | $52 |

E 50s | 1008 Second Ave. (bet. 53rd & 54th Sts.) | 212-759-7086 | www.lamangeoire.com

The arrival of "exceptional" chef Christian Delouvrier should "revitalize" this "been-around-forever" Midtown French known for its "warm welcome", "beautiful flowers" and "cozy" "countryside" ambiance; its "moderate prices" for a virtual "transport to Provence" explain its "staying power."

La Masseria ◐ *Italian*
| 23 | 19 | 22 | $56 |

W 40s | 235 W. 48th St. (bet. B'way & 8th Ave.) | 212-582-2111 | www.lamasserianyc.com

A "find amid the marquees", this Theater District Southern Italian proffers a "delicious" taste of "Puglia" ferried by a staff "well rehearsed" in the art of "quick" pre-show turnaround; while the "rustic" setting channels a "country farmhouse", the "pricey" tabs and "hustle and bustle" scream big city.

Lambs Club *American*
| 21 | 25 | 21 | $69 |

W 40s | Chatwal Hotel | 132 W. 44th St. (bet. 6th & 7th Aves.) | 212-997-5262 | www.thelambsclub.com

"Stunning deco" decor (including a *Citizen Kane*–worthy fireplace) is the glamorously "retro" backdrop for chef Geoffrey Zakarian's "wonderful" New American food at this "inner sanctum" in the Theater District's Chatwal Hotel; though you may have to sacrifice a "lion's share of your wallet" for the privilege, there's always the liquid alternative in the "gorgeous upstairs bar."

La Mirabelle *French*
| 22 | 18 | 23 | $55 |

W 80s | 102 W. 86th St. (bet. Amsterdam & Columbus Aves.) | 212-496-0458 | www.lamirabelle-ny.com

"Mature" Upper Westsiders "feel appreciated" in the "civilized" confines of this "hasn't-changed-in-years" bistro, a "family-run haven" favored for its "well-done" French classics and *très amiable* hospitality; adding "charm" are prices that "won't break the bank" and waitresses who occasionally break into song.

Land *Thai*
| 22 | 15 | 19 | $30 |

E 80s | 1565 Second Ave. (bet. 81st & 82nd Sts.) | 212-439-1847
W 80s | 450 Amsterdam Ave. (bet. 81st & 82nd Sts.) | 212-501-8121
www.landthaikitchen.com

If you like it "spicy", "inexpensive" and "in a hurry", you're on "solid" ground at these "unassuming", "consistently good" crosstown Thais; just "bring a shoehorn" to squeeze into the "closet"-size settings – or opt for "quick delivery" to sidestep the "crowds" altogether.

L & B Spumoni Gardens *Dessert/Pizza*
| 24 | 12 | 17 | $24 |

Bensonhurst | 2725 86th St. (bet. W. 10th & 11th Sts.) | Brooklyn | 718-449-6921 | www.spumonigardens.com

"Awesome" square pizza followed by "luscious" spumoni is the plan of action at this "been-there-forever" Bensonhurst "icon"; "people-watching" regulars snag an "outdoor picnic table" during the peak "summertime" season and soak in the "true Brooklyn flavor."

Landmarc *French*

21 | 20 | 20 | $49

TriBeCa | 179 W. Broadway (bet. Leonard & Worth Sts.) | 212-343-3883
W 60s | Time Warner Ctr. | 10 Columbus Circle, 3rd fl. (60th St. at B'way) | 212-823-6123
www.landmarc-restaurant.com

Chef Marc Murphy offers "something for everyone" at this "popular" French duo known for "affordable" grub and "wine bargains" galore; "no rezzies" is the rule at both the "rustic" TriBeCa original and the "cavernous" Time Warner Center satellite, though "late-night" hours ensure that everyone eats.

Landmark Tavern *Pub Food*

17 | 19 | 19 | $39

W 40s | 626 11th Ave. (46th St.) | 212-247-2562 | www.thelandmarktavern.org

"Historic ambiance" is the specialty of the house at this circa-1868 tavern slinging a "basic" pub grub lineup in an "isolated" West Hell's Kitchen locale; it's an "after-work" clubhouse for nearby "Ogilvy execs" in the mood for something "inexpensive" and "down to earth."

Lantern Thai Kitchen *Thai*

18 | 17 | 18 | $26

Gramercy | 311 Second Ave. (18th St.) | 212-777-2770
Brooklyn Heights | 101 Montague St. (bet. Henry & Hicks Sts.) | Brooklyn | 718-237-2594
www.lanternthai.com

"Dependable" if "nothing spectacular", these Siamese twins in Gramercy and Brooklyn Heights offer a "quick and easy" Thai fix in "chill" environs for "affordable" sums; the "neighborhood" folks who frequent them tout the "solid lunch special."

La Palapa *Mexican*

22 | 18 | 19 | $36

E Village | 77 St. Marks Pl. (bet. 1st & 2nd Aves.) | 212-777-2537 | www.lapalapa.com

A "taste of Mexico City except without the crime" comes to the East Village via this "friendly" furnisher of "authentic" south-of-the-border grub, where first-timers order a "potent margarita" to blend in with the "festive" atmosphere; P.S. the West Village spin-off has shuttered.

La Petite Auberge *French*

22 | 17 | 22 | $49

Murray Hill | 116 Lexington Ave. (bet. 27th & 28th Sts.) | 212-689-5003 | www.lapetiteaubergeny.com

It may be "old-fashioned", but "year after year" this 1977-vintage Murray Hill bistro demonstrates its "staying power" with "rock-steady" French cooking ferried by a "cordial" crew; in exchange for "no surprises" on the plate or the bill, its graying crowd excuses the "lack of decor."

NEW La Petite Maison *French*

19 | 19 | 18 | $70

W 50s | 13-15 W. 54th St. (bet. 5th & 6th Aves.) | 212-616-9931 | www.lapetitemaisonnyc.com

Part of the Bagatelle empire, this "raucous" new spin-off of a popular spot in Nice brings a "party" vibe to Midtown, where a "gorgeous stick-figure" staff delivers "seasonal" niçoise dishes courtesy of chef Alain Allegretti; its "fancy" following turns up "more for the scene than the cuisine", and takes the "ridiculously" expensive tabs in stride.

	FOOD	DECOR	SERVICE	COST

La Pizza Fresca Ristorante *Italian* | 24 | 18 | 20 | $42 |

Flatiron | 31 E. 20th St. (bet. B'way & Park Ave. S.) | 212-598-0141 | www.lapizzafrescaristorante.com

A "dependable" performer that somehow flies "under the radar", this "white-tablecloth" Flatiron trattoria boasts "fabulous" Neapolitan pizza and pastas, paired with an "amazing" Italian wine list; staffers are "friendly", but "can slow to a crawl" when the going gets busy.

La Ripaille *French* | 22 | 20 | 23 | $51 |

W Village | 605 Hudson St. (bet. Bethune & W. 12th Sts.) | 212-255-4406 | www.laripailleny.com

"Oh-so-French" West Village bistro where the "high-quality" cooking arrives in a "feels-like-Paris" setting warmed by a working fireplace; the "quirky" owner is "quite the character", but then again his "attention to detail" explains why this "standby" has been thriving since 1980.

La Rivista ● *Italian* | 21 | 19 | 22 | $48 |

W 40s | 313 W. 46th St. (bet. 8th & 9th Aves.) | 212-245-1707 | www.larivistanyc.com

Whether you drop in "before, during or instead of a show", it's "steady" as she goes at this 25-year-old Restaurant Row "standby", a "pleasant" pick for "tasty", "reasonably priced" Italian basics and "efficient" service.

L'Artusi *Italian* | 26 | 23 | 23 | $59 |

W Village | 228 W. 10th St. (bet. Bleecker & Hudson Sts.) | 212-255-5757 | www.lartusi.com

"Damn delicious" is the consensus on the "fun-to-share" small plates on offer at this "highly recommended" West Village Italian from the Dell'anima folks; equally delicious is the "pro service", "beautiful bi-level space" and "chic, energetic" scene, leaving the "hard-to-get" reservations and "hard-to-hear" acoustics as the only off-notes.

Lasagna *Italian* | 18 | 14 | 18 | $33 |

Chelsea | 196 Eighth Ave. (20th St.) | 212-242-4551
E 50s | 941 Second Ave. (50th St.) | 212-308-5353 ●
www.lasagnarestaurant.com

Sure enough, lasagna is "what they do well" at these "basic" Italians where the "ooey-gooey" signature dish is available in "every variety imaginable"; though "dreary" settings detract, the Chelsea satellite compensates with a Chelsea boy staff that's as "piping hot" as the food.

☑ NEW La Silhouette *French* | 26 | 21 | 25 | $70 |

W 50s | 362 W. 53rd St. (bet. 8th & 9th Aves.) | 212-581-2400 | www.la-silhouettenyc.com

An instant "hit", this "chic" Hell's Kitchen newcomer run by Le Bernardin alums ("it shows") already boasts a "loyal following" thanks to "first-rate" French cuisine and "thoroughly professional" service; granted, it's "expensive" and some suggest the "stark", meandering setting "needs more warmth", but so far, "so good."

La Sirène ⊄ *French* | ▽ 25 | 14 | 23 | $47 |

Hudson Square | 558½ Broome St. (Varick St.) | 212-925-3061 | www.lasirenenyc.com

This "outstanding" Hudson Square French bistro seduces locals with "superb" meals cooked to "buttery perfection", "cheerful" hospitality and a money-saving, "no-corkage-fee" BYO policy; despite "cramped" dimensions, "hole-in-the-wall" decor and that cash-only rule, "it's a pleasure to eat here."

Las Ramblas ● *Spanish* | 23 | 15 | 18 | $41 |

W Village | 170 W. Fourth St. (bet. Cornelia & Jones Sts.) | 646-415-7924 | www.lasramblasnyc.com

Behold the "best of Spain squeezed into a thimble" at this ultra-"tiny" Village tapas joint where the "delightful" small plates and "dangerous" sangria trump the appropriately "tapas-size" setting; regulars say it has a "big heart" courtesy of "energetic owner" Natalie Sanz, who "makes everyone feel like family."

La Superior ●⊅ *Mexican* | ▽ 24 | 13 | 17 | $23 |

Williamsburg | 295 Berry St. (bet. S. 2nd & 3rd Sts.) | Brooklyn | 718-388-5988 | www.lasuperiornyc.com

The "tiny tacos" are "to kill for" at this wee Williamsburg taqueria slinging a "unique" lineup of "top-quality", "refreshingly cheap" Mexican street eats; wash it all down with a "great margarita" to blot out the unsuperior service, no-plastic policy and "long wait" to get in.

La Taza de Oro ⊠⊅ *Puerto Rican* | ▽ 21 | 7 | 18 | $16 |

Chelsea | 96 Eighth Ave. (bet. 14th & 15th Sts.) | 212-243-9946

Little has changed at this Eisenhower-era "greasy spoon" in Chelsea, from the "filling" Puerto Rican comfort chow to the cafe con leche that still "packs a punch"; it's "serious eating" and "cheap" to boot, so ignore the "divey" decor and just dig in.

☑ L'Atelier de Joël Robuchon *French* | 27 | 25 | 26 | $136 |

E 50s | Four Seasons Hotel | 57 E. 57th St. (bet. Madison & Park Aves.) | 212-829-3844 | www.fourseasons.com

Super-toque Joël Robuchon's "artfully composed" Japanese-inflected French creations make for "world-class" dining at this very "refined" Midtowner in the Four Seasons whose seating chart includes a much-coveted counter offering a "fascinating" view of the "incredible talent" in the open kitchen; though a few cite "smaller-than-small" portions, "uneven" performance and "through-the-roof" pricing, most "feel like a king" here.

Lattanzi ● *Italian* | 22 | 19 | 21 | $56 |

W 40s | 361 W. 46th St. (bet. 8th & 9th Aves.) | 212-315-0980 | www.lattanzinyc.com

After the "curtain-catchers" leave for the theater, the "real show" begins at this "unique" Restaurant Row Italian renowned for its "delicious" Roman-Jewish menu available after 8 PM; at all hours, "attentive" service and "pleasant" atmospherics are part of the somewhat "pricey" package.

Laut *Malaysian/Thai* | 22 | 14 | 18 | $30 |

Union Sq | 15 E. 17th St. (bet. B'way & 5th Ave.) | 212-206-8989 | www.lautnyc.com

Taking Asian food "to the next level", this "genuine article" off Union Square offers an "incredibly varied menu" with "tasty" stops in Malaysia and Thailand; it's a "fast", "budget-friendly" affair, giving those who "can't get enough" every excuse to return "soon and often."

	FOOD	DECOR	SERVICE	COST

Lavagna *Italian* — 24 | 18 | 21 | $49

E Village | 545 E. Fifth St. (bet. Aves. A & B) | 212-979-1005 | www.lavagnanyc.com

At this "laid-back" Alphabet City "neighborhood staple", "terrific" Tuscan cooking and a "serious" wine list combine for a "frequently crowded" scene; "smooth" service and "reasonable-for-the-quality" tariffs compensate for the "small" setting and "bare-bones" look.

La Vela *Italian* — 20 | 16 | 20 | $38

W 70s | 373 Amsterdam Ave. (bet. 77th & 78th Sts.) | 212-877-7818

UWS "locals" tout the "dependable" performance of this 20-year-old Tuscan "mainstay", an "always satisfying" supplier of "simple, delicious" meals that "won't break the bank"; it's definitely "not fancy", but when you've got the "family" in tow, those "checkered tablecloths" can be a beautiful sight.

La Vigna *Italian* — ∇ 24 | 19 | 23 | $41

Forest Hills | 100-11 Metropolitan Ave. (70th Ave.) | Queens | 718-268-4264 | www.lavignany.com

With a Lidia Bastianich protégé in the kitchen preparing "excellent" "homestyle" food, this "aromatic" Italian is like a "breath of fresh air" on the Forest Hills dining scene; though it tilts "more upscale" than the area norm, prix fixe menus "keep costs down."

La Villa Pizzeria *Pizza* — 21 | 16 | 19 | $29

Mill Basin | Key Food Shopping Ctr. | 6610 Ave. U (bet. 66th & 67th Sts.) | Brooklyn | 718-251-8030

Park Slope | 261 Fifth Ave. (bet. 1st St. & Garfield Pl.) | Brooklyn | 718-499-9888 | www.lavillaparkslope.com

Howard Bch | Lindenwood Shopping Ctr. | 82-07 153rd Ave. (82nd St.) | Queens | 718-641-8259

"Wood-fired pizza" and "satisfying Italian" entrees do the job "just fine" at these "family-friendly" places that are "more than just pizzerias"; even though decor and service are fairly "standard", they're "frequently packed", a testimony to the "cut-above" Neapolitan pies.

NEW Lavo ☽ *Italian/Steak* — 21 | 21 | 19 | $64

E 50s | 39 E. 58th St. (bet. Madison & Park Aves.) | 212-750-5588 | www.lavony.com

"Pretty people", "posers" and "cougars" flock to this "trendy" new Midtown eatery-cum-"zoo", an import from Vegas and a sibling of Tao across the street; the "wide" Italian steakhouse menu is "better than you'd expect", but incidental to the "noisy", "total scene" in progress; P.S. a "Eurotrashy" nightclub downstairs keeps the party going till the wee hours.

Lazzara's *Pizza* — 23 | 12 | 17 | $23

Garment District | 221 W. 38th St., 2nd fl. (bet. 7th & 8th Aves.) | 212-944-7792 🖪

W 40s | 617 Ninth Ave. (bet. 43rd & 44th Sts.) | 212-245-4440 ☽ www.lazzaraspizza.com

"Crispy" thin-crust square pizza for "small tabs" "takes you back in time" to "old NY" at these Midtown pie palaces; the "hidden", second-floor Garment District original may be roomier, but the "hole-in-the-wall" Hell's Kitchen satellite serves by the slice.

	FOOD	DECOR	SERVICE	COST

Ⓩ Le Bernardin Ⓧ *French/Seafood* — **29** | **27** | **28** | **$146**

W 50s | 155 W. 51st St. (bet. 6th & 7th Aves.) | 212-554-1515 | www.le-bernardin.com

"*Formidable*" is the consensus on this newly renovated, drop-dead "gorgeous" Midtown French seafooder via Maguy LeCoze and chef Eric Ripert, where the nuanced cooking is so "dazzling" that it's taken Top Food and Most Popular honors in this Survey; "starchy" service, a "reverential" crowd and a "civilized" milieu combine for an "unforgettable" dining experience, and though the prix fixe–only menus come dear, the $70 lunch is a relative bargain; P.S. there's party space upstairs.

Le Bilboquet *French* — **21** | **16** | **16** | **$62**

E 60s | 25 E. 63rd St. (bet. Madison & Park Aves.) | 212-751-3036

Brace yourself for a "chic-de-la-chic" scene at this "Euro"-centric UES French bistro that's a "tight squeeze" what with all the "lookers" and "Wall Street princes" packed in; the food's "very good" and the music "loud", but don't expect much service "unless you're someone special."

Le Caprice ● *European* — **20** | **23** | **22** | **$78**

E 60s | Pierre Hotel | 2 E. 61st St. (5th Ave.) | 212-940-8195 | www.lecapriceny.com

"Trendy" and "old-fashioned" sensibilities collide at this "adult" U.K. import in the Pierre Hotel done up in "black-and-white art deco" decor; the Modern European cooking shows a ratings uptick from last time out, but the "overly Botoxed" crowd and "ridiculous" prices lead many to say it's just "not as good as the London original."

Le Charlot *French* — ▽ **21** | **16** | **17** | **$59**

E 60s | 19 E. 69th St. (bet. Madison & Park Aves.) | 212-794-1628

This "little piece of Paris" off Madison Avenue is a "nice escape" thanks to "delicious" "upscale" bistro food and an "energetic", "charmingly Gallic" vibe; given the "tight" space populated by a "jet-set clientele", you "can't hear yourself chew."

Ⓩ Le Cirque Ⓧ *French* — **25** | **26** | **25** | **$97**

E 50s | One Beacon Court | 151 E. 58th St. (bet. Lexington & 3rd Aves.) | 212-644-0202 | www.lecirque.com

Sirio Maccioni's "iconic" Midtown nexus of "over-the-top" fine dining continues its "crowd-pleasing" run with "fabulous" French cooking, "superb" service and a "showy", "sophisticated" setting; while it's dressy ("jacket required") and top dollar, there's also an informal, less expensive cafe with a $35 prix fixe dinner.

L'Ecole *French* — **25** | **20** | **24** | **$55**

SoHo | Intl. Culinary Ctr. | 462 Broadway (Grand St.) | 212-219-3300 | www.frenchculinary.com

"Budding star chefs" "give the best they've got" at this "student-run" affair in SoHo's French Culinary Institute; there may be "a misstep or two", but its "aim-to-please" mien and "value" prix fixes keep it "memorable."

Le Colonial *French/Vietnamese* — **21** | **23** | **20** | **$59**

E 50s | 149 E. 57th St. (bet. Lexington & 3rd Aves.) | 212-752-0808 | www.lecolonialnyc.com

"Palm fronds and ceiling fans" right out of a "spy movie" enhance the "sultry" "old Indochina" mood at this "high-end" Midtown French-

| | FOOD | DECOR | SERVICE | COST |

Vietnamese; the "beautifully presented" fusion fare lives up to the "exotic" ambiance, and that "inviting lounge" upstairs is "great for dating and hanging out."

NEW Left Bank ▯ American

| | - | - | - | M |

W Village | 117 Perry St. (Greenwich St.) | 212-727-1170 | www.leftbankmanhattan.com

Quiet and low-key, this West Village newcomer offers a limited, mid-priced American menu made from local, sustainable ingredients; the spare – verging on plain – setting puts the focus on the hip local crowd that's beginning to discover it.

Le Gigot ▯ French

| | 24 | 19 | 24 | $58 |

W Village | 18 Cornelia St. (bet. Bleecker & W. 4th Sts.) | 212-627-3737 | www.legigotrestaurant.com

"Tiny but terrific", this Village French bistro is a "quietly confident" supplier of "top-notch" Provençal food, "warm hospitality" and "romantic" airs; in short, it's the "real thing", save for the "cramped" tables and rather "expensive" tabs.

Le Grainne Cafe ● French

| | ▽ 23 | 18 | 17 | $27 |

Chelsea | 183 Ninth Ave. (21st St.) | 646-486-3000 | www.legrainnecafe.com

Follow up a "High Line stroll" with a "really good" crêpe and a cup of café au lait "large enough to swim laps in" at this "charming" Chelsea French cafe; an "unrushed meal" at "any time of day" is the essence of its appeal, rendering the "slow" service moot.

Le Magnifique ● French

| | 18 | 17 | 18 | $52 |

E 70s | 1022A Lexington Ave. (73rd St.) | 212-879-6190 | www.lemagnifiquerestaurant.com

Hints of "hip Euro flair" liven up this midpriced UES French bistro where the "cute" setup includes sidewalk seats, a "pleasant" upstairs dining room and a DJ-equipped ground-floor bar; if critics yawn "nothing special", supporters insist it's "trying hard" to live up to its name.

Le Marais French/Kosher/Steak

| | 22 | 16 | 17 | $57 |

W 40s | 150 W. 46th St. (bet. 6th & 7th Aves.) | 212-869-0900 | www.lemarais.net

"First-rate" kosher steaks are the specialty of this "always buzzing" Theater District French meatery where prayers for "better service" and a "makeover" of the "dreary" setting remain unanswered; luckily, the "attached butcher shop" supplies plenty of consolation.

Le Monde French

| | 18 | 18 | 16 | $37 |

W 100s | 2885 Broadway (bet. 112th & 113th Sts.) | 212-531-3939 | www.lemondenyc.com

"Proximity to Columbia" and "reasonable" prices keep this "reliable" bistro populated with "academic" sorts who tout its "consistent" French cuisine from the Loire Valley; sidewalk seating, a "convivial" mood and an "impressive beer lineup" make the "slow" service easier to shrug off.

Lemongrass Grill Thai

| | 17 | 12 | 16 | $26 |

Financial District | 84 William St. (Maiden Ln.) | 212-809-8038 | www.lemongrassgrillnyc.com

(continued)

(continued)

Lemongrass Grill

Murray Hill | 138 E. 34th St. (bet. Lexington & 3rd Aves.) | 212-213-3317 | www.lemongrassgrill34thst.com

Cobble Hill | 156 Court St. (bet. Dean & Pacific Sts.) | Brooklyn | 718-522-9728

When "cheap and filling" are priorities, these "basic" Thais are a "reliable" source of "satisfying" if "unspectacular" eating; since there's "nothing to write home about" on the decor and service fronts, regulars opt for "super-fast delivery."

NEW Leopard at des Artistes ● *Italian*   ▽ 21 | 25 | 23 | $84

W 60s | 1 W. 67th St. (bet. Columbus Ave. & CPW) | 212-787-8767 | www.theleopardnyc.com

"Cleaning out the cobwebs" from the former Café des Artistes space, this "refreshed" reinterpretation of the UWS landmark comes via the Il Gattopardo team, and serves "tasty" Southern Italiana in a brighter, more "inviting" setting (Howard Chandler Christy's "spectacular" murals remain); its "adult", clubby following is heavy on media celebs and local power brokers.

Leo's Latticini ⊠Ⓜ *Deli/Italian*   ▽ 27 | 10 | 23 | $17
(aka Mama's of Corona)

Corona | 46-02 104th St. (46th Ave.) | Queens | 718-898-6069

Flushing | Citi Field | 126th St. & Roosevelt Ave. | Queens | no phone

Run by "three fantastic sisters" who "know their stuff", this no-frills, third-generation Corona deli is "without rival" when it comes to "well-stuffed" Italian subs and "homemade mozzarella"; it also brings "good food to the ballpark" via its Citi Field stand.

Le Pain Quotidien *Bakery/Belgian*   19 | 15 | 15 | $24

E 60s | 833 Lexington Ave. (bet. 63rd & 64th Sts.) | 212-755-5810

E 70s | 252 E. 77th St. (bet. 2nd & 3rd Aves.) | 212-249-8600

E 80s | 1131 Madison Ave. (bet. 84th & 85th Sts.) | 212-327-4900

Flatiron | ABC Carpet & Home | 38 E. 19th St. (bet. B'way & Park Ave. S.) | 212-673-7900

G Village | 10 Fifth Ave. (8th St.) | 212-253-2324

G Village | 801 Broadway (11th St.) | 212-677-5277

SoHo | 100 Grand St. (bet. Greene & Mercer Sts.) | 212-625-9009

W 50s | 922 Seventh Ave. (58th St.) | 212-757-0775

W 60s | 60 W. 65th St. (bet. B'way & CPW) | 212-721-4001

W 70s | 50 W. 72nd St. (bet. Columbus Ave. & CPW) | 212-712-9700
www.lepainquotidien.com

Additional locations throughout the NY area

"Irresistible carbs" fill out the menu of this "ubiquotidien" Belgian bakery/cafe chain that's well regarded for its "strong coffee", "crusty breads" and "mostly organic" menus; "good eavesdropping" at the "get-to-know-your-neighbor" communal tables distracts from the sometimes "slow service."

Le Parisien *French*   22 | 17 | 22 | $42

Murray Hill | 163 E. 33rd St. (bet. Lexington & 3rd Aves.) | 212-889-5489 | www.leparisiennyc.com

Murray Hill denizens experience "Paris without the airfare" at this "cozy neighborhood" bistro whose "authentic" Gallic menu focuses on the "basics" to "*très bon*" effect; "attentive service" and "reasonable prices" offset the ultra-"small" setting.

	FOOD	DECOR	SERVICE	COST

Le Perigord *French*
24 | 22 | 25 | $79

E 50s | 405 E. 52nd St. (bet. FDR Dr. & 1st Ave.) | 212-755-6244 | www.leperigord.com

Owner Georges Briguet "runs a class operation" at this "old-line", circa-1964 Sutton Place exemplar of "elegant-everything" French dining; classic cuisine and tuxedoed service are de rigueur here, and if what's "civilized" to some seems "antiquated" to others, its "grown-up" admirers like "being well looked after" – and have the means to pay for it.

Le Pescadeux ● M *French/Seafood*
∇ 23 | 21 | 24 | $51

SoHo | 90 Thompson St. (bet. Prince & Spring Sts.) | 212-966-0021 | www.lepescadeux.com

For something "different", check out this "cozy" SoHo French-Canadian seafooder whose "tasty" menu – which allows two half-portions to be ordered as one main – enables diners to "try a lot"; a "welcoming host" and "live jazz" make the experience extra "worthwhile."

Le Relais de Venise L'Entrecôte *Steak*
20 | 17 | 19 | $42

E 50s | 590 Lexington Ave. (52nd St.) | 212-758-3989 | www.relaisdevenise.com

With its "one-choice menu" of steak frites with a green salad, ordering at this Midtown French import is easier than pronouncing its name; "priced right" at $25 and served "quick", it takes no reservations but is usually easy to access.

Le Rivage *French*
21 | 17 | 21 | $47

W 40s | 340 W. 46th St. (bet. 8th & 9th Aves.) | 212-765-7374 | www.lerivagenyc.com

As "pre-theater" routines go, "they've got it down" at this vintage-1958 Restaurant Row "mainstay" where ticket-holders take a "quick, reliable" tour of "old-time French cuisine" in "unapologetically retro" digs; insiders drop in after 8 when it rolls out a "great" $25 prix fixe.

Les Halles ● *French*
20 | 17 | 17 | $46

Financial District | 15 John St. (bet. B'way & Nassau St.) | 212-285-8585
Murray Hill | 411 Park Ave. S. (bet. 28th & 29th Sts.) | 212-679-4111
www.leshalles.net

Steak frites aficionados report that these "no-nonsense" French bistros do an "affordable", "quality" job, including "reliable" renderings of the genre's other "usual suspects"; "jammed" settings and *beaucoup de* "noise" are the norm, but for a glimpse of "chef-at-large" Anthony Bourdain, "watch TV."

Le Singe Vert ● *French*
18 | 16 | 17 | $44

Chelsea | 160 Seventh Ave. (bet. 19th & 20th Sts.) | 212-366-4100 | www.lesingevert.com

"Easy" does it at this Chelsea "neighborhood" bistro with a no-monkeying-around menu of "reasonably priced" French "standards" served in "simple" digs; regulars sit outside for the "Left-Bank-on-Seventh-Avenue" effect – and to duck the "noisy" acoustics indoors.

Le Veau d'Or ⊠ *French*
20 | 17 | 20 | $56

E 60s | 129 E. 60th St. (bet. Lexington & Park Aves.) | 212-838-8133

A "time capsule" of "authentic Paris", this 75-year-old East Side survivor stays in the game with *"comme il faut"* French bistro classics served by a "friendly" crew; if price-sensitive old-timers grumble it ain't "what it used to be", nostalgia lovers delight in its "shabby" sheen.

L'Express ● *French* | 18 | 16 | 15 | $36 |

Flatiron | 249 Park Ave. S. (20th St.) | 212-254-5858 | www.lexpressnyc.com

Whether "after the clubs" or when the sun's still up, this "basic" 24/7 Flatiron bistro delivers a "decent" French fix for a "fair price"; "spotty" service and noise levels "rivaling the subway" detract, but all is forgiven "because it's there when you need it" at 3 AM.

Le Zie 2000 ● *Italian* | 21 | 14 | 19 | $44 |

Chelsea | 172 Seventh Ave. (bet. 20th & 21st Sts.) | 212-206-8686 | www.lezie.com

"Seriously good" Venetian cooking at seriously "reasonable" rates makes this Chelsea Italian a "reliable go-to"; just know the "specials are much more expensive than the regular menu" – "ask beforehand" – and the "loud" decibels can be avoided in the "quieter back room."

NEW Lido Ⓜ *Italian* | ▽ 26 | 18 | 23 | $42 |

Harlem | 2168 Frederick Douglass Blvd. (117th St.) | 646-490-8575 | www.lidoharlem.com

On a "rapidly changing" stretch of Harlem, this Italian newcomer makes a play for local foodies and Apollo Theater ticket-holders with an "amazingly fine", midpriced menu served in an "airy", brick-walled setting; early reports indicate that it's "off to a great start."

Liebman's *Deli/Kosher* | 22 | 12 | 18 | $22 |

Riverdale | 552 W. 235th St. (Johnson Ave.) | Bronx | 718-548-4534 | www.liebmansdeli.com

As "authentic" as "Cel-Ray soda", this circa-1953 Bronx kosher deli keeps it real with a "can't-go-wrong" roster of "overstuffed sandwiches" and "terrific matzo ball soup"; "unappealing" decor and "crotchety" staffers are "the way it's supposed to be."

Lil' Frankie's Pizza ●⊟ *Pizza* | 23 | 17 | 18 | $29 |

E Village | 19 First Ave. (bet. 1st & 2nd Sts.) | 212-420-4900 | www.lilfrankies.com

"Fantastic" wood-fired pizza and other "super-fresh" Italiana "hit the spot" at this "funky", easy-on-the-wallet East Village spin-off of Frank; the "cramped" seating and cash-only policy are a lil' unpopular, but late hours ensure the "legit" eats are available "whenever."

🅉 Lincoln *Italian* | 24 | 26 | 23 | $88 |

W 60s | Lincoln Ctr. | 142 W. 65th St. (bet. Amsterdam Ave. & B'way) | 212-359-6500 | www.lincolnristorante.com

No stranger to lavish productions, Lincoln Center is home to this "dazzlingly modern" "glass palace" on its plaza, where Per Se alum Jonathan Benno plies "stylish" Italian fare in an "open kitchen"; despite early lumps for "service kinks", a "cold" ambiance and four-score-and-more pricing, a year on the intended "vision has come to fruition."

Lion, The ● *American* | 20 | 23 | 19 | $76 |

G Village | 62 W. Ninth St. (bet. 5th & 6th Aves.) | 212-353-8400 | www.thelionnyc.com

Chef-owner John DeLucie plays "ringmaster" to "celebs", "power players" and other "hip" cats at this "roaring" Village American set in a "gorgeous" evocation of "old NY" fitted out with a skylight, eclectic artworks and photographs; the "expensive" eats are "pretty good" but you're "paying for the scene" – "it's a jungle in there."

Lisca *Italian*
20 | 15 | 20 | $40

W 90s | 660 Amsterdam Ave. (bet. 92nd & 93rd Sts.) | 212-799-3987 | www.liscanyc.com

This "reliable" UWS neighborhood trattoria keeps it *molto* simple with "adept" Tuscan cooking delivered by an "accommodating" staff; "family-run and it shows", it's the sort of "unpretentious" place "regulars love" and anyone seeking "reasonable prices" can easily appreciate.

Little Giant *American*
22 | 18 | 20 | $41

LES | 85 Orchard St. (Broome St.) | 212-226-5047 | www.littlegiantnyc.com

Proof that "good things come in little packages", this "petite" LES 35-seater fills "foodie" tummies with "creative" American comfort chow made from seasonal, organic ingredients; for an incentive to go loca-vore on weekends, the "great brunch" is a natural.

Little Owl *American/Mediterranean*
25 | 18 | 22 | $56

W Village | 90 Bedford St. (Grove St.) | 212-741-4695 | www.thelittleowlnyc.com

A "small place that makes a big impression", this West Villager earns kudos for chef Joey Campanaro's "inventive" Med–New American plates and the "caring staff" that ferries them; too bad it's "so hard to snag a reservation", but this "fabulous find" didn't stay a secret for long.

NEW Little Town NYC ❷ *American*
- | - | - | M

Gramercy | 118A E. 15th St. (Irving Pl.) | 212-677-6300 | www.littletown.com

Saluting the Empire State, this new Gramercy brewhouse purveys an American menu drawn from statewide specialties (think Buffalo wings, Hudson Valley cheese) washed down with suds from local craft breweries; it's a strictly informal scene, with wood- and brick-lined walls, high-top butcher-block tables and stools.

Lobster Box ❷ *Seafood*
20 | 16 | 19 | $46

City Island | 34 City Island Ave. (bet. Belden & Rochelle Sts.) | Bronx | 718-885-1952 | www.lobsterboxrestaurant.com

"Seafood with a waterfront view" nets a "tourist"-laden crowd at this City Island lobster specialist that's been overlooking Long Island Sound since 1946; too bad critics contend the "old-hat" eats are no match for the panorama and advise a "redo."

Locale *Italian*
∇ 23 | 23 | 22 | $36

Astoria | 33-02 34th Ave. (33rd St.) | Queens | 718-729-9080 | www.localeastoria.com

For a dose of "Downtown Manhattan" minus the cab ride, Astorians turn to this "lovely corner" Italian promoting "well-presented" dishes, "friendly" service and a tolerably "trendy" air; whether for a "romantic" night or "nice brunch", it's an appreciated asset on the "local" scene.

⊠ Locanda Verde *Italian*
25 | 23 | 21 | $62

TriBeCa | Greenwich Hotel | 377 Greenwich St. (N. Moore St.) | 212-925-3797 | www.locandaverdenyc.com

Andrew Carmellini's TriBeCa "mainstay", this "energetic" tavern turns out "smart" takes on "rustic Italian" eats for an "'in' crowd" tended by an "attentive" team; "expensive" tabs and "intense" decibels come with the "happening" scene, but good luck getting a reservation.

☒ Locanda Vini & Olii Ⓜ *Italian* 27 | 26 | 25 | $53

Clinton Hill | 129 Gates Ave. (bet. Cambridge Pl. & Grand Ave.) | Brooklyn | 718-622-9202 | www.locandany.com

"Still super after 10 years", this Clinton Hill "gem" housed in an old pharmacy wows locals and folks from "across the river" alike with a "fantastic", "ever-changing" Tuscan menu that "seamlessly combines contemporary and traditional" dishes; "knowledgeable" staffers and moderate tabs make the overall package "hard to top."

Lombardi's ⇔ *Pizza* 25 | 14 | 17 | $25

NoLita | 32 Spring St. (bet. Mott & Mulberry Sts.) | 212-941-7994 | www.firstpizza.com

"Wonderful" "thin-crust" pizza emerges from the coal-fired ovens at this cash-only NoLita "landmark"; granted, "long lines are the norm" – "tourists" know about it too – but sometimes a "century-old" operation speaks for itself: "just go" already!

London Lennie's *Seafood* 23 | 18 | 20 | $44

Rego Park | 63-88 Woodhaven Blvd. (bet. Fleet Ct. & Penelope Ave.) | Queens | 718-894-8084 | www.londonlennies.com

"Great fish, period" is the credo of this "family-owned" Rego Park seafooder that's been serving "fresh", "simply cooked" catch since 1959; right-o, it's kinda "drab" and often "crowded", but "if you can't trek to Maine", hook a reservation and sail over.

Loreley *German* 19 | 17 | 18 | $30

LES | 7 Rivington St. (bet. Bowery & Chrystie Sts.) | 212-253-7077
Williamsburg | 64 Frost St. (bet. Leonard & Lorimer Sts.) | Brooklyn | 718-599-0025
www.loreleynyc.com

For an "authentic German biergarten" experience without the lederhosen, these basic brauhauses are "just the ticket"; though the "great beer selection" and "lovely outdoor patios" are the main draws, the "stick-to-your-ribs" brats and schnitzels are "surprisingly good" at soaking up the suds.

Lorenzo's *Italian* 21 | 24 | 23 | $46

Bloomfield | Hilton Garden Inn | 1100 South Ave. (Lois Ln.) | Staten Island | 718-477-2400 | www.lorenzosdining.com

"Omnipresent owners" and their "attentive staff" ensure "you're always taken care of" at this "classy" Italian in Bloomfield's Hilton Garden Inn; if a few say the cuisine is "hit-or-miss", a "great Sunday brunch" and live cabaret acts solidify its status as "one of Staten Island's better spots."

🆕 Lotus of Siam ☒ *Thai* 20 | 17 | 18 | $53

G Village | 24 Fifth Ave. (9th St.) | 212-529-1700 | www.lotusofsiamny.com

"High-end" Thai cuisine showcasing "authentic", "off-the-beaten-path" dishes is the lotus operandi of this Village newcomer; however, "erratic" service, "boring" decor and "steep" prices lead some to sense too much "hype", especially now that the chef-owner of the beloved "Vegas original" is no longer affiliated.

	FOOD	DECOR	SERVICE	COST

NEW Lowcountry ● Southern
20 | 17 | 19 | $43

W Village | 142 W. 10th St. (bet. Greenwich Ave. & Waverly Pl.) |
212-255-2330 | www.lowcountrynewyork.com

This Bar Blanc replacement brings a slice of "Charleston" to the West
Village via "contemporary" Southern-comfort cooking, bourbon-
boosted drinks and "laid-back" vibes; so long as you're ok with a little
fried-green "noise" and "not dieting" ("is Paula Deen in the kitchen?"),
"fun" times await.

Z Lucali ⊭ Pizza
26 | 18 | 19 | $26

Carroll Gardens | 575 Henry St. (bet. Carroll St. & 1st Pl.) | Brooklyn |
718-858-4086

With a rep for "one of the best pies" around, this Carroll Gardens
pizza/calzone purveyor's "inhalable" eats lead to "long lines", but
boosters say it's "worth the wait" and the "trek"; one "big plus" compensates for its no-rez, no-plastic and "no-salad" policies: it's BYO;
P.S. a Kenmare Street spin-off is in the works.

Lucien ● French
22 | 18 | 21 | $48

E Village | 14 First Ave. (1st St.) | 212-260-6481 |
www.luciennyc.com

"As warm as its namesake owner", this "jolly" East Villager "brings
Paris to mind" with "well-executed" Gallic staples and an "unpretentious" vibe that skews "lively" late-night; granted, you'll be "on
top of the people next to you", but there's more "breathing room" if
you go "early."

Lucky Strike ● French
17 | 17 | 16 | $33

SoHo | 59 Grand St. (bet. W. B'way & Wooster St.) | 212-941-0772 |
www.luckystrikeny.com

A SoHo "throwback" with a "loyal local following", Keith McNally's
"cool and easy" French bistro is always ready when a "late-night"
burger craving strikes; most forgive the "average" eats and "indifferent" service given the "untrendy", come-as-you-are ambiance.

Luke's Lobster Seafood
23 | 10 | 17 | $23

E 80s | 242 E. 81st St. (bet. 2nd & 3rd Aves.) | 212-249-4241
E Village | 93 E. Seventh St. (bet. Ave. A & 1st Ave.) | 212-387-8487
NEW Financial District | 26 S. William St. (Stone St.) | 212-747-1700
NEW W 80s | 426 Amsterdam Ave. (bet. 80th & 81st Sts.) |
212-877-8800
www.lukeslobster.com

These "no-frills" crustacean stations bring an affordable "slice of
Maine" to Manhattan with "superb" lobster rolls, packed with "fresh"
catch "not dripping in mayo and filler"; while surely "more convenient"
than going to "Kennebunkport", they've got "really limited seating", so
it may be "better to take out."

Lumi ● Italian
20 | 19 | 21 | $61

E 70s | 963 Lexington Ave. (70th St.) | 212-570-2335 |
www.lumirestaurant.com

Operating out of a "homey", fireplace-equipped townhouse, this longtime UES Italian features "well-prepared" Tuscan cuisine (including
"excellent gluten-free" options) brought by a "pro staff"; although on
the "pricey" side, it's a "charming" choice for "low-key" interludes.

	FOOD	DECOR	SERVICE	COST

Luna Piena *Italian*   21 | 17 | 19 | $45

E 50s | 243 E. 53rd St. (bet. 2nd & 3rd Aves.) | 212-308-8882 |
www.lunapienanyc.com

Often "overlooked", this Midtown Italian proffers a variety of "tasty",
"authentic" eats for moderate sums, and is "convenient" for the area
"work crowd"; "friendly" staffers "with accents" and a "lovely" year-
round garden enhance the "casual" atmosphere.

Lunetta Ⓜ *Italian*   22 | 17 | 20 | $42

Boerum Hill | 116 Smith St. (bet. Dean & Pacific Sts.) | Brooklyn |
718-488-6269 | www.lunetta-ny.com

"Inventive" Italian small plates with a "seasonal" bent are a "reliable"
source of Smith Street fun at this "charming" Boerum Hiller; while largely
a "low-key" venue (complete with a garden), it's most enjoyable in a seat
at the "kitchen bar" with a view of the chef's "dinnertime show."

Lupa ◑ *Italian*   25 | 18 | 21 | $55

G Village | 170 Thompson St. (bet. Bleecker & Houston Sts.) |
212-982-5089 | www.luparestaurant.com

Entrée to Mario Batali's "restaurant fiefdom" is feasible for the "hungry masses" at this moderately priced Village "perennial favorite" that
offers "excellent", "down-to-earth" Roman cooking and a "superb
wine list"; loyalists wish it weren't so "small", "crowded" and "hard to
get into" – otherwise, they'd be by "any day, any time."

Lure Fishbar *Seafood*   23 | 22 | 20 | $57

SoHo | 142 Mercer St., downstairs (Prince St.) | 212-431-7676 |
www.lurefishbar.com

Fin fans are on board with the "excellent seafood" and "quality sushi"
served at this ever-"trendy" SoHo fishfest, where the "attractive"
"yacht"-like setting is "packed to the gills" with cute "young" things;
bring "earplugs" to muffle the din and plan on parting with a few ducats.

Lusardi's ◑ *Italian*   24 | 19 | 23 | $65

E 70s | 1494 Second Ave. (bet. 77th & 78th Sts.) | 212-249-2020 |
www.lusardis.com

Where UES "grown-ups" head for "old-school" dining, this "clubby"
neighborhood trattoria is a "much appreciated" provider of "touch-of-
class" Tuscan cooking and "hands-on" hospitality led by owner Mauro
Lusardi; given its "nicely attired" habitués, it's no surprise that the "expensive" tabs arouse little protest.

Luz *Nuevo Latino*   ▽ 22 | 17 | 20 | $36

Fort Greene | 177 Vanderbilt Ave. (bet. Myrtle Ave. & Willoughby St.) |
Brooklyn | 718-246-4000 | www.luzrestaurant.com

"Off the beaten track" in Fort Greene, this "solid" Nuevo Latino supplies "innovative cuisine" and "potent cocktails" in a "spare", brick-
walled setting; despite a "great vibe" and "bargain" tabs, somehow it's
"not as mobbed" as others in the neighborhood.

Luzzo's *Pizza*   25 | 14 | 18 | $29

E Village | 211 First Ave. (bet. 12th & 13th Sts.) | 212-473-7447 |
www.lzny.us

Even in the "pizza-heavy" East Village, this joint stands out due to
century-old coal ovens that produce its "divine" thin-crust pies;

| | FOOD | DECOR | SERVICE | COST |

though the decor's as "casual" as the "laid-back" service, fans say this is the "real thing", just "don't waste your calories on the pasta."

Ⓩ Lychee House *Chinese*   23 | 16 | 22 | $40

E 50s | 141 E. 55th St. (bet. Lexington & 3rd Aves) | 212-753-3900 | www.lycheehouse.com

With an "exhaustive menu" that "shows more originality" than the norm, this "must-try" Midtown yearling puts a "modern" spin on Chinese chow with "interesting" Shanghainese items and "refined" dim sum; "adroit" service and "value" pricing trump the bland decor.

NEW Lyon *French*   20 | 21 | 21 | $52

W Village | 118 Greenwich Ave. (13th St.) | 212-242-5966 | www.lyonnyc.com

"Rising from the ashes of Café de Bruxelles", this instantly "lively" West Village newcomer takes its inspiration from Lyon's traditional bouchons, serving a "hearty", meat-centric French menu of "unaffected classics" in an oak-paneled space; a "few kinks" need to be ironed out – i.e. "Parisian prices" and "not much wiggle room" – but overall this one's a "real comer."

NEW Mable's Smoke House *BBQ*   - | - | - | I

Williamsburg | 44 Berry St. (enter on N. 11th St. bet. Berry St. & Wythe Ave.) | Brooklyn | 718-218-6655 | www.mablessmokehouse.com

Located near West Williamsburg's new high-rise developments, this cavernous BBQ vendor offers "great" St. Louis–style ribs, beef brisket and pulled pork in a funky, honky-tonk setting equipped with mismatched chairs and a wagon-wheel chandelier; diners order at a counter, then chow down at communal tables or at the central bar.

Macao Trading Co. ❍ *Chinese/Portuguese*   19 | 22 | 17 | $52

TriBeCa | 311 Church St. (bet. Lispenard & Walker Sts.) | 212-431-8750 | www.macaonyc.com

West meets East at this "exotic" TriBeCa homage to Macao's melting-pot cuisine, offering a "hit-or-miss" mix of Chinese and Portuguese small plates; some say it's "more of a nightlife destination", what with the "kitschy", high-seas decor, "dangerously fab" drinks and "loud" "eye-candy" crowd.

Macelleria ❍ *Italian/Steak*   22 | 19 | 21 | $57

Meatpacking | 48 Gansevoort St. (bet. Greenwich & Washington Sts.) | 212-741-2555 | www.macelleria.com

Given the name (which translates as 'butcher shop'), it's no surprise that this Italian steakhouse supplies "top-notch" chops in digs outfitted with original meat hooks; though regulars suggest a "table in the wine cellar", it also offers "alfresco" seats with a "full view" of the rollicking Meatpacking scene.

Madangsui *Korean*   22 | 12 | 17 | $36

Garment District | 35 W. 35th St. (bet. 5th & 6th Aves.) | 212-564-9333 | www.madangsui.com

A "cut above" the Garment District norm, this Korean BBQ "value" grills "succulent" meats – with plenty of "doggy-bag" potential – preceded by an array of "surprisingly nice" free appetizers; the grub's "cooked at your table" by a "speedy" crew, injecting some "entertainment" into an otherwise "basic" setting.

	FOOD	DECOR	SERVICE	COST

Madiba ● *African* ▽ 20 | 20 | 18 | $35

Fort Greene | 195 DeKalb Ave. (Carlton Ave.) | Brooklyn | 718-855-9190 |
www.madibarestaurant.com

"Unique" decor (e.g. a "Coke-bottle chandelier") mirrors the "exotic"
South African cooking plied at this "very Brooklyn", "completely Fort
Greene" scene; folks like its "leisurely pace" and "reasonable" pricing,
but warn the live music and "happening" vibe can be "too loud."

Madison Bistro *French* 21 | 16 | 20 | $48

Murray Hill | 238 Madison Ave. (bet. 37th & 38th Sts.) | 212-447-1919 |
www.madisonbistro.com

Locals laud this "unassuming" Murray Hill bistro, a "delightfully average"
neighborhood joint with "dependable" French chow and a side of
"cheery" service; it's "like stepping into a Parisian cafe" – only
"friendlier" – and a recent redo may not be reflected in the Decor score.

Madison's *Italian* 20 | 17 | 20 | $39

Riverdale | 5686 Riverdale Ave. (259th St.) | Bronx | 718-543-3850
"Something upscale" for Riverdale, this "popular" Italian offers "consistently good" cooking and "feel-at-home" service in a "casual"
(verging on "bland") setting; a few protest "pricey" tariffs, but its
"loyal following" insists "you get what you pay for" here.

☑ Maialino *Italian* 25 | 23 | 25 | $68

Gramercy | Gramercy Park Hotel | 2 Lexington Ave. (21st St.) |
212-777-2410 | www.maialinonyc.com

"Everything clicks" at Danny Meyer's latest "showstopper", this "ebul-
lient" take on a Roman trattoria in the Gramercy Park Hotel that "hits the
trifecta" via its "trademark" "perfect service", "relaxed country" setting and "wonderful" Italian food (notably the "melt-in-your-mouth"
namesake suckling pig); it's a bona fide "hot ticket", so prepare to "use
all your connections" for a table, or wing it at the walk-up wine bar.

Maison ● *French* 19 | 18 | 18 | $41

W 50s | 1700 Broadway (53rd St.) | 212-757-2233 | www.maisonnyc.com
Proximity to "City Center", a "24/7" open-door policy and a vast outdoor
seating area are the key selling points of this serviceable Theater District
French brasserie; although the "standard" menu items are "reliable"
enough, too many "tourists" and not enough service draw brickbats.

Malagueta Ⓜ *Brazilian* ▽ 24 | 15 | 20 | $36

Astoria | 25-35 36th Ave. (28th St.) | Queens | 718-937-4821 |
www.malaguetany.com

"Not easy to find", this Astoria "change of pace" is "worth the search"
for its "authentic", "old-fashioned" Brazilian cooking and modest tabs;
the "small" corner setting is strictly "low-key", but service is "gracious" and there's a "surprisingly good wine list" to boot.

NEW Malaparte ●≠ *Italian* - | - | - | M

W Village | 753 Washington St. (Bethune St.) | 212-255-2122 |
www.malapartenyc.com

Pizza and seafood are the specialties of this "calm", cash-only new West
Village Northern Italian spun off from neighborhood favorite Malatesta;
"rustic countryside" decor, a small bar and homey knickknacks lend a
"cozy" vibe, while "inexpensive" prices reinforce the welcoming mood.

	FOOD	DECOR	SERVICE	COST

Malatesta Trattoria ●🥢 *Italian* — 24 | 18 | 21 | $35

W Village | 649 Washington St. (Christopher St.) | 212-741-1207 |
www.malatestatrattoria.com

"Flavorful" Northern Italian "basics" wow West Villagers at this "no-frills" trattoria where the "homemade pasta" and other "simple" dishes come "cheap"; "sexy" waiters and sidewalk seats overlooking the Christopher Street parade make the "cash-only" policy easier to swallow.

Maloney & Porcelli *Steak* — 23 | 20 | 22 | $70

E 50s | 37 E. 50th St. (bet. Madison & Park Aves.) | 212-750-2233 |
www.maloneyandporcelli.com

For best results, "bring a huge appetite" to Alan Stillman's "bustling" Midtown steakhouse where "man-size" chops and "giant martinis" keep its "deal-closing" "power-broker" crowd content; regulars tout the signature pork shank, while bargain-hunters call the weekend wine dinner one of the "best deals in town."

Mamá Mexico *Mexican* — 19 | 16 | 18 | $36

E 40s | 214 E. 49th St. (bet. 2nd & 3rd Aves.) | 212-935-1316
W 100s | 2672 Broadway (102nd St.) | 212-864-2323 ●
www.mamamexico.com

"Every day is Cinco de Mayo" at this "party"-hearty pair where the "gringo Mexican" grub may be "nothing inventive" but the portions are "hefty" enough to "soak up multiple margaritas"; "fun" (or "annoying") mariachi bands ratchet up the decibels to "louder than loud."

Mama's Food Shop Ⓜ🥢 *American* — ▽ 22 | 12 | 17 | $18

E Village | 200 E. Third St. (bet. Aves. A & B) | 212-777-4425 |
www.mamasfoodshop.com

"Good, old-fashioned" dishes "like mama used to make" are slung at this "hippie" Alphabet City American that's a natural for "homesick" types; no one minds the "minimal service" and "cash-only" policy when tabs are this "cheap" and the portions so "generous."

Mandarin Court *Chinese* — ▽ 22 | 11 | 15 | $24

Chinatown | 61 Mott St. (bet. Bayard & Canal Sts.) | 212-608-3838
Do-it-yourself types "create their own meal" at this "classic" C-town dim sum parlor where you "pick and choose" "consistently good" items without fear of a hefty bill; even though it's gotten a "new paint job", "don't expect ambiance" (or service), and prepare for weekend lines.

Mandoo Bar *Korean* — 22 | 12 | 18 | $22

Garment District | 2 W. 32nd St. (bet. B'way & 5th Ave.) | 212-279-3075
"Cheap eats" are "done right" at this Garment District Korean famed for "hit-the-spot" dumplings "made fresh" in the window; since the "hole-in-the-wall" setting is "cramped", "good luck getting a table."

Manducatis *Italian* — 23 | 15 | 21 | $46

LIC | 13-27 Jackson Ave. (47th Ave.) | Queens | 718-729-4602 |
www.manducatis.com
Manducatis Rustica *Italian*
LIC | 46-33 Vernon Blvd. (bet. 46th & 47th Sts.) | Queens | 718-937-1312 |
www.manducatisrustica.com

Like something "out of your childhood", this "old-school" LIC Italian "mainstay" offers "red-sauce" dishes crafted with a "deft hand";

maybe the "old *Sopranos* set" decor could stand a "makeover", but the "family welcome" is fine as is; P.S. the Vernon Boulevard spin-off is best for pizzas and calzones.

Manetta's ☒ *Italian*   22 | 17 | 22 | $42

LIC | 10-76 Jackson Ave. (49th Ave.) | Queens | 718-786-6171
Fans of this family-owned LIC "standby" show up for its "extensive" Southern Italian menu that's "chock-full of favorites" including a "fab" thin-crust pizza; a "working fireplace" and service that "goes the extra mile" complete the picture.

Mangia ☒ *Mediterranean*   20 | 12 | 14 | $24

E 40s | 16 E. 48th St. (bet. 5th & Madison Aves.) | 212-754-7600
Flatiron | 22 W. 23rd St. (bet. 5th & 6th Aves.) | 212-647-0200
W 50s | 50 W. 57th St. (bet. 5th & 6th Aves.) | 212-582-5882

Mangia Organics ☒ *Mediterranean*
Garment District | 45 W. 39th St. (bet. 5th & 6th Aves.) |
212-921-9100
www.mangiatogo.com
"Mobs" of office workers and "on-the-go" lunchers salute the "vast array" of "fresh salads and sandwiches" offered at this "convenient" Mediterranean mini-chain; the new Garment District offshoot specializes in locally grown organic items, but shares the "self-service" and pay-"by-the-pound" policies of its brethren.

Manzo *Italian/Steak*   24 | 14 | 22 | $75

Flatiron | Eataly | 200 Fifth Ave. (bet. 23rd & 24th Sts.) | 212-229-2180 |
www.eataly.com
From the Batali-Bastianich team, this Eataly eatery brings "sophisticated dining" to the Flatiron food-hall phenom via a "terrific" beef-centric, Italian-accented menu; granted, it "doesn't come cheap" and the "middle-of-a-grocery-store" setting is "odd" (and "noisy"), but "adventurous" cooking and "personable" service make it a tough ticket.

Maoz Vegetarian *Mideastern/Vegetarian*   21 | 9 | 15 | $12

G Village | 59 E. Eighth St. (bet. B'way & University Pl.) |
212-420-5999
Union Sq | 38 Union Sq. E. (bet. 16th & 17th Sts.) | 212-260-1988
W 40s | 558 Seventh Ave. (40th St.) | 212-777-0820 ◐
NEW **W 40s** | 683 Eighth Ave. (bet. 43rd & 44th Sts.) | 212-265-2315 ◐
W 70s | 2047 Broadway (enter on Amsterdam Ave., bet. 70th & 71st Sts.) |
212-362-2622 ◐
W 100s | 2857 Broadway (bet. 110th & 111th Sts.) | 212-222-6464
www.maozusa.com
Fast food gets a "guilt-free" spin at this Mideastern-vegetarian franchise supplying "nutritious" falafels and salads customized at a "never-ending" toppings bar; "long lines", "minimal" seating and "bare-bones" decor are disregarded given the "student-budget" price tags.

Má Pêche *French/Vietnamese*   23 | 18 | 21 | $60

W 50s | Chambers Hotel | 15 W. 56th St. (bet. 5th & 6th Aves.) |
212-757-5878 | www.momofuku.com
David Chang brings "Momoland" to Midtown with this "peachy" French-Vietnamese offering dishes with "vibrant flavors" including a "must-try" Beef Seven Ways group feast; the "clumsy", "sparsely furnished" basement setting leaves many "cold", but at least get-

ting in is "no hassle"; P.S. check out the "real treat" sweets at the Milk Bar adjunct.

𝗡𝗘𝗪 Marble Lane ◑ *Steak* — | — | — | E

Chelsea | Dream Downtown Hotel | 355 W. 16th St. (bet. 8th & 9th Aves.) | 212-229-2559 | www.dreamdowntown.com

Top Chef alum Manuel Treviño is behind the burners at this new steakhouse in Chelsea's Dream Downtown Hotel, where the menu includes lots of globe-trotting side dishes; the dark setting has nightclub aspirations, with black leather banquettes, white marble tables and a flashy chandelier made of hand-blown glass orbs.

𝟮 Marc Forgione *American* 26 | 23 | 23 | $69

TriBeCa | 134 Reade St. (bet. Greenwich & Hudson Sts.) | 212-941-9401 | www.marcforgione.com

Next Iron Chef Marc Forgione "hits it out of the park" with "ingenious" farm-to-table New Americana at this TriBeCa "wonder" that "just gets better and better"; guests are "served with élan" in a "romantic", "candlelit" room, and though prices are "big", that signature Chicken Under a Brick sure is "memorable."

Marcony *Italian* 25 | 22 | 26 | $62

Murray Hill | 184 Lexington Ave. (bet. 31st & 32nd Sts.) | 646-837-6020 | www.marconyusa.com

A "shot in the arm for Murray Hill", this "upscale" duplex is "worth tuning into" owing to "wonderful" Italian cooking, "personable" service and a "modern", whitewashed space that suggests a villa in "Capri"; be aware that a bit of "sticker shock" comes with the territory.

Marco Polo Ristorante 🄼 *Italian* 21 | 18 | 22 | $46

Carroll Gardens | 345 Court St. (Union St.) | Brooklyn | 718-852-5015 | www.marcopoloristorante.com

"Old-world" Italian meals arrive in an "old Brooklyn" setting at this 1983-vintage Carroll Gardens "standby", where the "homey" vibe matches the "warm" service; it's a "red-sauce" joint and "proud of it", made for a "family get-together."

𝟮 Marea *Italian/Seafood* 28 | 26 | 26 | $101

W 50s | 240 Central Park S. (bet. B'way & 7th Ave.) | 212-582-5100 | www.marea-nyc.com

Chef Michael White demonstrates "how a kitchen should be run" at this "sophisticated" CPS "stunner", voted NYC's No. 1 Italian thanks to a "scrumptious" seafood-slanted menu backed up with first-rate pasta and "flawless" service; the "glamorous", "celeb"-studded room burnishes the overall experience, but for best results, go on "someone else's dime" – this exercise in "sheer perfection" comes at a "titanic price", at least for dinner.

Maria Pia *Italian* 19 | 17 | 20 | $40

W 50s | 319 W. 51st St. (bet. 8th & 9th Aves.) | 212-765-6463 | www.mariapianyc.com

"Convenience to the theaters" is the calling card of this "pleasant" if "predictable" Hell's Kitchen Italian that draws pre-curtain crowds with "inexpensive" red-gravy standards; prime-time "noise" makes familiarity with "sign language" a must, but the decibels are "more tolerable" after 8 and in the "delightful back garden."

	FOOD	DECOR	SERVICE	COST

Marina Cafe *Seafood*
22 | 23 | 21 | $44

Great Kills | 154 Mansion Ave. (Hillside Terr.) | Staten Island | 718-967-3077 | www.marinacafegrand.com

Staten Islanders drop anchor for the "fresh" catch at this Great Kills Harbor seafood standby where the weekday "prix fixe rocks"; its "young crowd" is also hooked on the "tiki bar" and "outstanding" nightly entertainment, while the "wonderful view" is an extra lure.

Marinella *Italian*
∇ 22 | 17 | 23 | $43

W Village | 49 Carmine St. (Bedford St.) | 212-807-7472

"Been there forever", this West Village "throwback" exudes "old-fashioned" charm with Italian eats "like grandma made" and a "hasn't-changed-in-years" staff; a "rolling" chalkboard menu lists the ever-changing specials, while the feeling of "coming home" is a constant.

Mario's Ⓜ *Italian*
21 | 16 | 21 | $42

Fordham | 2342 Arthur Ave. (bet. 184th & 186th Sts.) | Bronx | 718-584-1188 | www.mariosrestarthurave.com

The "pride of Arthur Avenue" since 1919, this Bronx "classic" is "always a pleasure" for "traditional" Southern Italian "comfort food" including a "fabulous pizza"; whether you're there for the memories or the meatballs, the "friendly" staff will take you on a "trip back through time", including the moment you get your bill.

Mari Vanna ❶ *Russian*
∇ 20 | 22 | 20 | $65

Flatiron | 41 E. 20th St. (bet. B'way & Park Ave. S.) | 212-777-1955 | www.marivanna.ru

A "boisterous" crowd lubricated by "flowing vodka" says "*da*" to this Flatiron "change of pace" serving "surprisingly good" Russian food; the "kitschy" setting looks like your Soviet "grandma's dacha" and makes for a "lovely respite" – at least until you pay.

Ⓩ Mark, The ❶ *American*
22 | 24 | 22 | $82

E 70s | Mark Hotel | 25 E. 77th St. (bet. 5th & Madison Aves.) | 212-606-3030 | www.jeangeorges.com

The Upper East Side's latest "'it' spot", this "fine-dining" New American via Jean-Georges Vongerichten "hits the mark" with a wide-ranging menu and "spacious", "*Architectural Digest*-worthy" setting; "fresh flowers", "space between tables" and "attentive" service keep its "silk-stocking" crowd content, while the "lively bar scene" makes you wish you were younger and richer.

Market Table *American*
24 | 20 | 22 | $54

W Village | 54 Carmine St. (Bedford St.) | 212-255-2100 | www.markettablenyc.com

"Proof that the freshest ingredients make the finest food", this "very West Villagey" New American lures a mix of "hipsters" and "neighborhood" types with its first-rate "green" menu; "large windows" and "warm service" add to the "country feel", broken only by "very loud" acoustics.

MarkJoseph Steakhouse Ⓩ *Steak*
23 | 18 | 21 | $74

Financial District | 261 Water St. (bet. Dover St. & Peck Slip) | 212-277-0020 | www.markjosephsteakhouse.com

FiDi "expense account"–wielders tout this "secret" chop shop near the Seaport for its "tender juicy steaks" and "sizzling bacon" appetizer;

the dinner hour "isn't as bustling" as lunchtime, but whenever you show up you can expect a "men's club" mood and challenging price tags.

Markt *Belgian*   18 | 16 | 17 | $42

Flatiron | 676 Sixth Ave. (21st St.) | 212-727-3314 |
www.marktrestaurant.com

Moules frites "galore", a "huge beer selection" and "straightforward" Flemish fare keep this "bustling" Flatiron Belgian bistro "boisterous"; ok, it's as "crammed" as a mussel pot and "conversing can be a problem", but no one minds given the "reasonable" pricing.

Marlow & Sons ● *American*   24 | 20 | 18 | $43

Williamsburg | 81 Broadway (bet. Berry St. & Wythe Ave.) | Brooklyn |
718-384-1441 | www.marlowandsons.com

"Adventurous" small plates crafted from farm-fresh "seasonal" items distinguish this "real-deal" Williamsburg New American; set in a "funky" storefront with a small market up front, it can be "noisy" going, with "hipster"-heavy, "can-of-sardines" conditions.

Marseille *French/Mediterranean*   20 | 19 | 20 | $48

W 40s | 630 Ninth Ave. (bet. 44th & 45th Sts.) | 212-333-2323 |
www.marseillenyc.com

"Always reliable", this Hell's Kitchen brasserie "does the job" with "hearty" French-Med fare served in a "dimly lit", "tarnished-mirror" setting; it's good for a pre-theater "quickie" since its staff "knows the drill", however, what's "high energy" to some is "too loud" for others.

Maruzzella ● *Italian*   22 | 15 | 21 | $44

E 70s | 1483 First Ave. (bet. 77th & 78th Sts.) | 212-988-8877 |
www.maruzzellanyc.com

Affordably feeding a "neighborhood gang", this UES Italian serves the "freshest pasta" dressed in "sauces that sing"; "attentive", "feel-like-part-of-the-family" service compensates for the "drab" interior.

Mary Ann's *Tex-Mex*   16 | 11 | 15 | $29

Chelsea | 116 Eighth Ave. (16th St.) | 212-633-0877
E Village | 80 Second Ave. (bet. 4th & 5th Sts.) | 212-475-5939
TriBeCa | 353 Greenwich St. (Harrison St.) | 212-766-0911

"Relics of the Tex-Mex craze", these "longtime rice-and-beans destinations" sling "just decent", "gringo" grub to a crowd doing "more drinking than eating"; ultra-"cheap" tabs make the "lack of decor" and "overworked" staff less noticeable.

NEW Mary Queen of Scots *Scottish*   ▽ 21 | 24 | 21 | $52

LES | 115 Allen St. (Delancey St.) | 212-460-0915 |
www.maryqueenofscotsnyc.com

Annexing the LES digs abdicated by Allen & Delancey, this new Scottish gastropub puts forth an "interesting" menu paired with "whiskey-themed cocktails"; maybe it's "still getting the kinks out", but the "stellar atmosphere" – a blend of brick and "tartan" upholstery – is fine as is.

Mary's Fish Camp ⊠ *Seafood*   25 | 14 | 19 | $45

W Village | 64 Charles St. (W. 4th St.) | 646-486-2185 |
www.marysfishcamp.com

Bringing the "salt air" of Maine to the West Village, this "funky little hole-in-the-wall" offers a "simple" "clam-shack" menu led by the "mother of all lobster rolls"; trade-offs include "no reservations", "long lines" and seating akin to "steerage on the Titanic", but ultimately this "compact marvel" is more than "worth it."

Z Mas ● *American* | 27 | 24 | 27 | $88 |

W Village | 39 Downing St. (bet. Bedford & Varick Sts.) | 212-255-1790 | www.masfarmhouse.com

Achieving the "perfect harmony" of "comfort and cool", this West Village "sea of tranquility" showcases chef Galen Zamarra's "creative" yet "approachable" New American menu that's catnip for "Greenmarket food fanatics"; though "expensive", the "sophisticated", low-key setting emits enough "romance" to work for a "big date", while the "gracious" service and "excellent" food "encourage repeat visits."

Z Masa ⊠ *Japanese* | 27 | 22 | 24 | $585 |

W 60s | Time Warner Ctr. | 10 Columbus Circle, 4th fl. (60th St. at B'way) | 212-823-9800

Bar Masa ⊠ *Japanese*

W 60s | Time Warner Ctr. | 10 Columbus Circle, 4th fl. (60th St. at B'way) | 212-823-9800

www.masanyc.com

There's no question that "mighty" Masayoshi Takayama's Time Warner Center "temple of sushi" is "brutally expensive" (prix fixes start at $450), but the "heavenly" Japanese fare, "personalized service" and "serene" Zen setting "make a lifetime impression"; for still "exorbitant" but "more affordable" tabs, the "casual" next-door bar's à la carte menu reflects "the master's touch" too.

NEW Masten Lake *American* | - | - | - | M |

Williamsburg | 285 Bedford Ave. (bet. Grand & S. 1st Sts.) | Brooklyn | 718-599-5565

The de-grungefication of Williamsburg's Bedford Avenue continues with this slick small-plater that breaks up its midpriced American menu into four sections: 'cheese', 'cold', 'pasta' and 'protein'; the simply elegant digs, done up with wood-slat benches, cork ceilings and a long bar, leave the flash to its clientele.

Matsuri ● *Japanese* | 23 | 26 | 23 | $59 |

Chelsea | Maritime Hotel | 369 W. 16th St., downstairs (9th Ave.) | 212-243-6400 | www.matsurinyc.com

"Hip" types hype this "dazzling" underground Japanese beneath Chelsea's Maritime Hotel, citing chef Tadashi Ono's "superb" sushi paired with an "outstanding sake list"; "attentive" service and a "vast", "stylish" setting festooned with "huge paper lanterns" make patrons "feel good", the "expense-account" pricing notwithstanding.

Max *Italian* | 22 | 16 | 17 | $33 |

E Village | 51 Ave. B (bet. 3rd & 4th Sts.) | 212-539-0111
TriBeCa | 181 Duane St. (bet. Greenwich & Hudson Sts.) | 212-966-5939
www.max-ny.com

"Low on atmosphere" but "great on taste", this Southern Italian Downtown duo plates "homemade" pastas in "big portions" that make "perfect leftovers" the next day; alright, it's "not much of a scene", but the prices won't max out anyone's credit card.

	FOOD	DECOR	SERVICE	COST

Max Brenner ● *Dessert*
20 | 19 | 16 | $30

G Village | 841 Broadway (bet. 13th & 14th Sts.) | 212-388-0030 |
www.maxbrenner.com

"Douse your sorrows in chocolate" at this Village "treatery" where
"teeth-achingly good" desserts draw "tourists", "kids" and "chocoholics
of all ages"; sourpusses find this "novelty act" "gimmicky", with
"spotty" service and a "chainlike" mood, but "throngs" still show up
for "the smell" alone.

Max SoHa ●⇄ *Italian*
23 | 17 | 19 | $26

W 100s | 1274 Amsterdam Ave. (123rd St.) | 212-531-2221
Max Caffe ● *Italian*
W 100s | 1262 Amsterdam Ave. (bet. 122nd & 123rd Sts.) | 212-531-1210
www.maxsoha.com

Popular "neighborhood joints" for the Columbia student body, these
"cozy" Upper Westsiders earn kudos for "basic", "hearty" Italian cooking
and most "reasonable" rates; the "eclectically furnished" settings are
comfortable enough to "sit all day", especially at SoHa's outdoor tables.

Maya *Mexican*
23 | 19 | 20 | $53

E 60s | 1191 First Ave. (bet. 64th & 65th Sts.) | 212-585-1818 |
www.richardsandoval.com

A "different kind" of Mexican, this "first-rate" Upper Eastsider features
"haute" cooking with "sensitive" spicing, served in an "under-lit" room
that's more "refined" than the norm; the electric mood is "like walking
into a party", but one that requires "*mucho dinero*" for admittance.

Maze *French*
22 | 20 | 20 | $65

W 50s | London NYC Hotel | 151 W. 54th St. (bet. 6th & 7th Aves.) |
212-468-8889 | www.gordonramsay.com

Parked in the London Hotel, this "casual" French alternative serves
"beautifully presented" small plates in a room that feels "like an airport lounge"; while it does a good job, some say "nothing distinguishes
it" from the pack except possibly its steep prices.

Maz Mezcal *Mexican*
21 | 18 | 20 | $40

E 80s | 316 E. 86th St. (bet. 1st & 2nd Aves.) | 212-472-1599 |
www.mazmezcal.com

Yorkville locals applaud this "old-style" Mexican vet for "hearty",
"tasty" cooking that's "better than it needs to be"; besides a "festive",
"keep-the-margaritas-coming" mood, it also boasts "affordable" tariffs and an "always on-site" owner.

McCormick & Schmick's *Seafood*
20 | 18 | 20 | $53

W 50s | 1285 Sixth Ave. (enter on 52nd St., bet. 6th & 7th Aves.) |
212-459-1222 | www.mccormickandschmicks.com

As a "perfectly ok" if "generic" alternative to pricier seafood palaces,
this "steady" chain link near Rock Center dispenses "surprisingly
good" fish delivered by a "knowledgeable" crew; too bad about the
"bland" decor and "buttoned-up" vibe, but there's nothing wrong with
its "insane happy-hour deals."

Meatball Shop ● *Sandwiches*
25 | 17 | 18 | $24

LES | 84 Stanton St. (bet. Allen & Orchard Sts.) | 212-982-8895

(continued)

(continued)

Meatball Shop

NEW Williamsburg | 170 Bedford Ave. (bet. N. 7th & 8th Sts.) | Brooklyn | 718-551-0520
www.themeatballshop.com

The "single-item restaurant trend" is "well executed" at this LES "hipster" sandwich shop vending "low-cost", high-"quality" meatballs slathered with "spicy" sauces; "super-duper long waits" are a drag, but the overall "cool concept" is "so appealing"; P.S. "L train riders" are psyched that a new Williamsburg outlet has opened, and a West Village branch is in the works.

Mediterraneo ● *Italian*   19 | 16 | 17 | $42

E 60s | 1260 Second Ave. (66th St.) | 212-734-7407 | www.mediterraneonyc.com

"Successful-looking" folks with "interesting accents" patronize this "popular" UES Italian that garnishes its "moderately priced" pizzas and pastas with throbbing "techno music"; in fact, it's enough of a "scene" that "service depends on how young and cute you are."

Mee Noodle Shop *Noodle Shop*   17 | 4 | 12 | $18

E 40s | 922 Second Ave. (49th St.) | 212-888-0027
Murray Hill | 547 Second Ave. (bet. 30th & 31st Sts.) | 212-779-1596
W 50s | 795 Ninth Ave. (53rd St.) | 212-765-2929 | www.meenoodleshopnyc.com

For a "quick slurp on a cold day", it's hard to beat this Chinese noodle shop trio where the "filling" fare arrives at "blink-of-an-eye" speed for "yesteryear prices"; "shoddy" looks and "charmless" service explain its "extensive delivery business."

Megu *Japanese*   24 | 26 | 23 | $84

TriBeCa | 62 Thomas St. (bet. Church St. & W. B'way) | 212-964-7777
Megu Midtown *Japanese*

E 40s | Trump World Tower | 845 United Nations Plaza (1st Ave. & 47th St.) | 212-964-7777
www.megurestaurants.com

Everything's "artfully prepared" at this "dazzling" Japanese duo, from the "beyond-fresh" fish to the "fancy-schmancy" setting built around an "impressive" Buddha ice sculpture; the service is "well rehearsed" and the layout's "spacious", but regulars usually "have some sake before getting the bill" to cushion the sticker shock.

NEW **Mehtaphor** ⊠ *Eclectic*   25 | 19 | 23 | $52

TriBeCa | Duane Street Hotel | 130 Duane St. (Church St.) | 212-542-9440 | www.mehtaphornyc.com

Graffiti chef Jehangir Mehta brings "bold flavors" to TriBeCa's Duane Street Hotel via this new Eclectic purveying "adventurous" small plates in a setting so "tiny" that it could "fit inside a subway car"; "fair prices" and a "feel-at-home" mood complete the "excellent" picture.

Melba's *American*   ∇ 20 | 18 | 19 | $32

Harlem | 300 W. 114th St. (Frederick Douglass Blvd.) | 212-864-7777 | www.melbasrestaurant.com

Part of Harlem's renaissance, this "decent little" place slings "home-cooked" American comfort food that's priced to please; the "simple" space comes alive due to the "infectious charm" of owner Melba Wilson, though some say the staff "could be more efficient."

Melt ☒ *American*   20 | 16 | 19 | $31

Park Slope | 440 Bergen St. (bet. 5th & Flatbush Aves.) | Brooklyn | 718-230-5925 | www.meltnyc.com

One of Park Slope's few "best-kept secrets", this "casual" New American is "worth a try" for its "terrific burgers" and "fun brunch"; "polite" servers work hard to warm up the "clinical", "minimalist" setting, but the "excellent" pricing is fine as is.

NEW Mémé *Mediterranean*   ▽ 24 | 18 | 22 | $37

W Village | 581 Hudson St. (Bank St.) | 646-692-8450 | www.memeonhudson.com

"Covering all areas of the Mediterranean" (with a long stop in Morocco), this new West Village "keeper" serves a "delicious" menu that's "skillfully spiced" and "well priced"; "attentive" service compensates for "small dimensions" and a "no-rez" policy.

Menchanko-tei *Noodle Shop*   21 | 12 | 16 | $24

E 40s | 131 E. 45th St. (bet. Lexington & 3rd Aves.) | 212-986-6805

W 50s | 43-45 W. 55th St. (bet. 5th & 6th Aves.) | 212-247-1585 ◑

www.menchankotei.com

"Oodles of noodles" are dispensed at these "fulfilling" Midtown "slurp" shops where "cheap", "piping hot" bowls of ramen and udon "soothe the soul"; "chaotic" midday crowds, "elbow-to-elbow" dining and "rush-you-out" service are the trade-offs.

Mercadito *Mexican*   23 | 16 | 18 | $37

E Village | 179 Ave. B (bet. 11th & 12th Sts.) | 212-529-6490

Mercadito Grove ◑ *Mexican*

W Village | 100 Seventh Ave. S. (bet. Bleecker & Grove Sts.) | 212-647-0830

www.mercaditorestaurants.com

"Tacos are the way to go" at these Mexican storefronts that earn "*olés*" for "amazing" small plates, "super guacamole" and "potent" pops; cynics nix "forgetful" service and "little breathing room", but applaud the "affordable" tabs and the West Villager's "terrace" seating.

Mercat *Spanish*   20 | 20 | 20 | $51

NoHo | 45 Bond St. (bet. Bowery & Lafayette St.) | 212-529-8600 | www.mercatnyc.com

"Quality ingredients" and "solid" Catalan cuisine make for "delicious" dining at this NoHo Spaniard; alright, the small-plates format can make for an "inflated" bill, but the service is "fine" and the "dark", tile-lined setting exudes "romance."

Mercato ◑ *Italian*   ▽ 23 | 19 | 22 | $41

Garment District | 352 W. 39th St. (bet. 8th & 9th Aves.) | 212-643-2000 | www.mercatonyc.com

Set in the "emerging raw area" around Port Authority, this "inviting" yearling serves "simple", "rustic" Italiana to a mix of "locals", theater-goers and "expats"; the "exposed-brick"-and-weathered-wood decor makes for a "cozy" feel, as does the "pleasant" staff and "modest" tabs.

| | FOOD | DECOR | SERVICE | COST |

Mercer Kitchen ⚫ *American/French*   22 | 22 | 19 | $55

SoHo | Mercer Hotel | 99 Prince St. (Mercer St.) | 212-966-5454 |
www.jean-georges.com

"Still going strong" in its "dimly lit underground" digs, this "hip" SoHo
"hideaway" from Jean-Georges Vongerichten rolls out an "excellent"
French-American menu to a "chic" clutch of "beautiful" folk including
the "inevitable celebs"; yup, it's a tad "pricey" and service can be "underwhelming", but ultimately it's "worthy of repeat visits."

Mermaid Inn *Seafood*   22 | 18 | 20 | $45

E Village | 96 Second Ave. (bet. 5th & 6th Sts.) | 212-674-5870
W 80s | 568 Amsterdam Ave. (bet. 87th & 88th Sts.) |
212-799-7400

Mermaid Oyster Bar *Seafood*

G Village | 79 MacDougal St. (bet. Bleecker & Houston Sts.) |
212-260-0100
www.themermaidnyc.com

"Martha's Vineyard" comes to Manhattan via this "Cape Cod"-
style trio that "gets the formula right" with "delish" fish (including a
"fab lobster roll"), "cheery" servers and "nautical" settings; it's
"well priced", and at meal's end, the gratis chocolate pudding is
a "sweet closer."

Mesa Coyoacan ⚫ *Mexican*   ▽ 25 | 21 | 23 | $36

Williamsburg | 372 Graham Ave. (bet. Conselyea St. & Skillman Ave.) |
Brooklyn | 718-782-8171 | www.mesacoyoacan.com

"Real Mexico City dishes" fill out the "artful" menu of this "worthwhile" Williamsburg cantina where the tabs are as "cheap" as the food
is "flavorful"; "communal tables" and "mean cocktails" fuel the "happening", "Cinco de Mayo" mood, while "knowledgeable" staffers seal
the good deal.

Z Mesa Grill *Southwestern*   24 | 20 | 22 | $59

Flatiron | 102 Fifth Ave. (bet. 15th & 16th Sts.) | 212-807-7400 |
www.mesagrill.com

Food Networker Bobby Flay supplies "just the right amount of kick" at
his Southwestern "cash cow" in the Flatiron known for its "vivid" flavors and "vibrant" feel; aesthetes citing "tarnished" decor say it's
"time for a tune-up", but the "sunny" service and "darn good" grub are
fine as is.

Meskerem *Ethiopian*   21 | 11 | 17 | $27

G Village | 124 MacDougal St. (bet. Bleecker & W. 3rd Sts.) | 212-777-8111
W 40s | 468 W. 47th St. (bet. 9th & 10th Aves.) | 212-664-0520

These "dependable", "low-priced" Ethiopians give diners the chance
to "eat with their hands", scooping up the "unique" stews with injera
bread; purists turn up for the "make-you-sweat" spicing, but aesthetes are turned off by "dingy" settings and "slooow" service.

Mexicana Mama Ⓜ *Mexican*   24 | 14 | 19 | $34

G Village | 47 E. 12th St. (bet. B'way & University Pl.) |
212-253-7594
W Village | 525 Hudson St. (bet. Charles & W. 10th Sts.) | 212-924-4119

"Serious eaters" tout the "serious Mexican" food served at these
"first-rate" Villagers known for their "tiny" dimensions and tiny tabs;

waits "measured in geologic time" and space issues make many "wish they'd expand."

Mexican Radio ◐ *Mexican*

| 19 | 12 | 17 | $32 |

NoLita | 19 Cleveland Pl. (bet. Kenmare & Spring Sts.) | 212-343-0140 | www.mexrad.com

Mole mavens tune into this "long-standing" NoLita cantina for its "good renditions of Mexican standards" served for a "cheap" price in "loud, rowdy" digs; maybe the "kitschy" decor is as "cheesy" as the quesadillas, but "it doesn't really matter" after a couple of "perfect margaritas."

NEW Mexicue *BBQ/Mexican*

| - | - | - | I |

Chelsea | 345 Seventh Ave. (bet. 29th & 30th Sts.) | 212-244-0002 🗷
LES | 106 Forsyth St. (bet. Broome & Grand Sts.) | 646-559-4100 ◐
www.mexicue.com

These brick-and-mortar offshoots of the popular food truck offer the same Mexican-meets-BBQ menu (think smoked short rib tacos, beef brisket sliders) dispensed in colorful, compact settings; low price tags have made them instant hits.

Mezzaluna ◐ *Italian*

| 22 | 16 | 19 | $48 |

E 70s | 1295 Third Ave. (bet. 74th & 75th Sts.) | 212-535-9600 | www.mezzalunany.com

Pizza Mezzaluna *Pizza*

G Village | 146 W. Houston St. (MacDougal St.) | 212-533-1242 | www.pizzamezzalunanyc.com

On the UES scene since 1984, this "teeny-tiny" trattoria serves "simple" Italian standards plus "excellent" wood-fired pizza; the setup's so "tight" that regulars "hope their neighbors' conversation is interesting", while the smaller Village spin-off is primarily a take-out outlet.

Mezzogiorno *Italian*

| 21 | 17 | 20 | $47 |

SoHo | 195 Spring St. (Sullivan St.) | 212-334-2112 | www.mezzogiorno.com

Ever "popular" after 25 years in SoHo, this midpriced Italian "standby" is a "convenient" nexus for "consistently good" pasta and thin-crust pizza; since the "decor needs updating", it's most "charming" outdoors from a "watch-the-world-go-by" sidewalk seat.

Mia Dona 🗷 *Italian*

| 19 | 18 | 18 | $50 |

E 50s | 206 E. 58th St. (bet. 2nd & 3rd Aves.) | 212-750-8170 | www.miadona.com

"Solid" regional Italian dishes starring some "serious meatballs" turn up at this "satisfying" boîte near Bloomie's; while a few find the proceedings "workmanlike, no better", admirers applaud the "modernist" setting, moderate prices and "fine" service led by hostess with the mostest Donatella Arpaia.

Michael Jordan's
The Steak House NYC *Steak*

| 20 | 20 | 19 | $66 |

E 40s | Grand Central | Northwest Balcony (43rd St. & Vanderbilt Ave.) | 212-655-2300 | www.michaeljordansnyc.com

Set on Grand Central's mezzanine beneath a "magnificent" ceiling, this chophouse offers "slam-dunk" steaks along with "stunning" views of the teeming masses; it's a natural for "business" lunching and quieter dinners, but whenever you go, expect way-above-the-rim pricing.

	FOOD	DECOR	SERVICE	COST

⬛ **Michael's** ⓢ *Californian*   `22` `22` `23` `$71`

W 50s | 24 W. 55th St. (bet. 5th & 6th Aves.) | 212-767-0555 | www.michaelsnewyork.com

"A-list" media types of the "Brokaw-Couric variety" frequent this stylish Midtowner better known for its "power" breakfasts and lunches than its "refined" Californian grub; service is "top-notch" for regulars and "not so friendly" to irregulars, though the "expensive" pricing extends to all.

Mike's Bistro *American/Kosher*   ▽ `23` `18` `21` `$69`

W 70s | 228 W. 72nd St. (bet. B'way & West End Ave.) | 212-799-3911 | www.mikesbistro.com

"Haute kosher" cooking is no oxymoron at this UWS American where the "sumptuous" menu is both "imaginative" and "well presented"; though you'll pay "top dollar" for the privilege, the observant say the food and service deserve a "bigger reputation" beyond its "limited" following.

Mile End *Deli*   `24` `13` `18` `$24`

Boerum Hill | 97A Hoyt St. (bet. Atlantic & Pacific Sts.) | Brooklyn | 718-852-7510 | www.mileendbrooklyn.com

Something "different" for Boerum Hill, this Montreal-style "hipster" Jewish deli is celebrated for "quality" meats cured and smoked in-house; though the menu is as "limited" as the seats in this "minuscule" "hole-in-the-wall", it's worth the "hour-long" wait for a taste of "paradise" on rye.

🆕 **Milk Street Café** ⓢ *Eclectic/Kosher*   `-` `-` `-` `I`

Financial District | Trump Bldg. | 40 Wall St. (William St.) | 212-542-3663 | www.milkstreetcafe.com

A smorgasbord of Eclectic eats hits Wall Street via this sprawling food court with hot and cold self-serve stations whose offerings range from rotisserie items to salads, pastas and sushi; with a whimsical mural and granite-topped tables, the spacious seating area is a step up from the typical grab-and-go milieu, but so are prices, since everything's kosher.

Mill Basin Kosher Deli *Deli/Kosher*   `23` `16` `20` `$25`

Mill Basin | 5823 Ave. T (59th St.) | Brooklyn | 718-241-4910 | www.millbasindeli.com

"Pastrami rules" at this 40-year-old Brooklyn "keeper" where "traditional" kosher deli eats are served alongside artwork that's for sale; it's "unpretentious" and "old-fashioned", save for "Manhattan pricing."

🆕 **Millesime** *Seafood*   `21` `23` `20` `$70`

Murray Hill | Carlton Hotel | 92 Madison Ave., 2nd fl. (29th St.) | 212-889-7100 | www.millesimerestaurant.com

Hidden in Murray Hill, this new brasserie features "wonderful" seafood prepared with a French accent in an open kitchen or plucked from its raw bar; "excellent" service and a "quite lovely" mezzanine setting make the "expensive" tabs more palatable.

⬛ **Milos, Estiatorio** ◗ *Greek/Seafood*   `27` `24` `24` `$84`

W 50s | 125 W. 55th St. (bet. 6th & 7th Aves.) | 212-245-7400 | www.estiatoriomilos.com

A "calm" atmosphere and "airy", whitewashed setting bring "Santorini" to Midtown via this "glorious" Greek serving "picture-perfect" seafood "displayed on ice"; by-the-pound pricing makes for "second mortgage"–worthy tabs, so bargain-hunters stick to the appetizers.

	FOOD	DECOR	SERVICE	COST

Mimi's Hummus *Mideastern*   24 | 14 | 22 | $22

Ditmas Park | 1209 Cortelyou Rd. (Westminster Rd.) | Brooklyn |
718-284-4444 | www.mimishummus.com

Bringing a "change of pace" to Ditmas Park, this low-cost Middle
Easterner specializes in "fresh" hummus scooped up with the "softest
pita" around; since the "limited menu" is a match for the "tiny" space,
regulars go the take-out route, adding items from the next-door market.

Minca ●⑤ *Noodle Shop*   ▽ 24 | 11 | 18 | $20

E Village | 536 E. Fifth St. (bet. Aves. A & B) | 212-505-8001 |
www.newyorkramen.com

"Just like Tokyo – including the lines" – this "out-of-the-way" Alphabet
City noodle shop serves "delicious" ramen awash in a "perfectly bal-
anced broth"; ok, it "ain't fine dining" what with the "no-frills" decor and
service, yet the combo of "rich" flavors and "cheap" tabs is hard to beat.

⨎ Minetta Tavern ● *French*   23 | 21 | 20 | $66

G Village | 113 MacDougal St. (bet. Bleecker & W. 3rd Sts.) | 212-475-3850 |
www.minettatavernny.com

Keith McNally's "remodel" of a 1937-vintage Villager offers "excellent" French bistro cooking in an "old NY" setting, and is famed for its
"epic" burger and "major celebrity" scene with nonstop bar action; it's
no surprise that reservations are "tough", but definitely "worth the
struggle"; "ask for the back room" – the "elbow-bumping" front bar is
"so crowded even Yogi doesn't go there anymore."

Mint *Indian*   ▽ 22 | 19 | 19 | $43

E 50s | San Carlos Hotel | 150 E. 50th St. (bet. Lexington & 3rd Aves.) |
212-644-8888 | www.mintny.com

Curry gets a "chic" spin at this "pleasant" Midtown Indian where the
"cool", "understated" decor and "quiet" acoustics add up to "soothing" dining; a "creatively spiced", "wide-ranging" menu explains why
the tabs are a bit high for the genre.

Miranda *Italian/Pan-Latin*   ▽ 25 | 22 | 27 | $40

Williamsburg | 80 Berry St. (N. 9th St.) | Brooklyn | 718-387-0711 |
www.mirandarestaurant.com

An "interesting" mix of Italian and Pan-Latin dishes fills out the menu
of this "undiscovered" Williamsburger, one of the few "grown-up restaurants in hipsterland"; "rustic" environs, really "warm" service and
fair pricing make it the "kind of place you want to see succeed."

Miriam *Israeli/Mediterranean*   22 | 19 | 20 | $33

Park Slope | 79 Fifth Ave. (Prospect Pl.) | Brooklyn | 718-622-2250 |
www.miriamrestaurant.com

Park Slope meets the Middle East at this "inventive" Israeli-Med, a
"satisfying" nexus for "unique" dishes that bring you "back to Tel
Aviv"; it's "super-busy" for brunch (they "know how to scramble an
egg"), and both the service and pricing are "fine."

Mishima *Japanese*   24 | 13 | 19 | $38

Murray Hill | 164 Lexington Ave. (bet. 30th & 31st Sts.) | 212-532-9596 |
www.mishimany.com

Although "around for years", this Murray Hill Japanese remains firmly
"under the radar" despite "high-quality" sushi at tabs that "don't

break the bank"; even though the decor's pretty "basic" and there "aren't many seats", fans feel it "should be better known."

NEW Miss Lily's ◑ *Jamaican*   - | - | - | M

G Village | 132 W. Houston St. (Sullivan St.) | 646-588-5375 | www.misslilysnyc.com

Runway-ready types are all over this happening new Village Jamaican via scenemaker Serge Becker (La Esquina), where midpriced Caribbean eats are dispatched by staffers as comely as the customers; the downscale setting recalls a Kingston luncheonette (Formica tabletops, dish towel napkins), while an egalitarian door policy leads to long waits.

Miss Mamie's *Soul Food/Southern*   ∇ 18 | 10 | 15 | $27

Harlem | 366 W. 110th St. (bet. Columbus & Manhattan Aves.) | 212-865-6744

Miss Maude's *Soul Food/Southern*

Harlem | 547 Lenox Ave. (bet. 137th & 138th Sts.) | 212-690-3100 www.spoonbreadinc.com

"From catfish to cornbread", "solid" soul food is the draw at these Harlem siblings where the secret to traditional Southern cooking is "in the spices"; ok, service is "slooow" and there's "nothing fancy" going on decorwise, but they really feel like rural North Carolina, right down to the backcountry prices.

☒ Modern, The ⊠ *American/French*   26 | 26 | 26 | $127

W 50s | Museum of Modern Art | 9 W. 53rd St. (bet. 5th & 6th Aves.) | 212-333-1220 | www.themodernnyc.com

"Haute" museum dining turns up at this Danny Meyer "winner" in MoMA, where chef Gabriel Kreuther's "artfully presented" French-New American menu approaches "perfection"; the "sleek" space is split in two: a "casual", "buzzy" barroom up front offering à la carte small plates and a "calming", prix fixe–only rear dining room looking out on the museum's "world-class" sculpture garden; no matter where you wind up, you can expect "impeccable" service, along with "memorable" tabs.

Moim Ⓜ *Korean*   23 | 22 | 19 | $40

Park Slope | 206 Garfield Pl. (bet. 7th & 8th Aves.) | Brooklyn | 718-499-8092 | www.moimrestaurant.com

Korean food gets a "chic" interpretation at this "nouveau" nook in Park Slope serving "unusual" Seoul food that's a lot "more than just kimchi"; "beautiful" "modern" decor and a "lovely garden" burnish the "sophisticated" mood.

Mojave *Southwestern*   ∇ 21 | 23 | 19 | $31

Astoria | 22-36 31st St. (bet. Ditmars Blvd. & 23rd Ave.) | Queens | 718-545-4100 | www.mojaveny.com

"Worthwhile" Southwestern standards are slung at this "friendly" Astorian, a magnet for "young 'uns" seduced by "fab drinks" and "not expensive" tabs; there's "plenty of space" in the "pleasant" dining room, plus a secret-weapon "great patio" out back.

Móle *Mexican*   23 | 15 | 18 | $38

LES | 205 Allen St. (Houston St.) | 212-777-3200 ⊅
W Village | 57 Jane St. (Hudson St.) | 212-206-7559

(continued)

Móle

NEW Williamsburg | 178 Kent Ave. (N. 4th St.) | Brooklyn | 347-384-2300 | www.molenyc.com

"Younger" folks looking for "something easy" like this "vibrant" Mexican mini-chain vending "flavorful" chow for "reasonable" dough; "wonderful" happy-hour deals make up for the "close quarters", "rushed" service and "noisy" decibels.

Molly's ● *Pub Food*

22 | 18 | 21 | $26

Gramercy | 287 Third Ave. (bet. 22nd & 23rd Sts.) | 212-889-3361 | www.mollysshebeen.com

"One heck of a burger" draws "crowds of all ages" to this Gramercy Irish pub where a "wood-burning fireplace" and "sawdust" under foot add to the "cozy" feel; throw in "perfect pints" served by a "staff from the auld sod" and it's easy to understand why it's been around since 1960.

Molyvos ● *Greek*

23 | 19 | 21 | $57

W 50s | 871 Seventh Ave. (bet. 55th & 56th Sts.) | 212-582-7500 | www.molyvos.com

"Expertly prepared fish" and other "first-rate" Hellenica are the hooks at this "favorite" Midtown Greek that's a "wonderful prelude" to Carnegie Hall or City Center; a "big floor plan", "considerate" service, "tolerable" acoustics and an "excellent" $37 prix fixe keep customers "satisfied."

☑ Momofuku Ko ● *American*

27 | 18 | 23 | $163

E Village | 163 First Ave. (bet. 10th & 11th Sts.) | 212-254-3500 | www.momofuku.com

"Exclusivity" is the thing at David Chang's 12-seat East Villager where "memorable" Asian-accented American food is served in a multicourse format for a "whopping" $125 charge; "backless stools" and the "byzantine" online-only reservations draw barbs, but "food nuts" say all is forgiven once the parade of "transcendent" plates begins.

Momofuku Milk Bar *Bakery*

23 | 14 | 17 | $17

E Village | 251 E. 13th St. (bet. 2nd & 3rd Aves.) | 212-254-3500 ●

W 50s | Chambers Hotel | 15 W. 56th St. (bet. 5th & 6th Aves.) | 212-777-7773

NEW Williamsburg | 382 Metropolitan Ave. (bet. Havemeyer St. & Marcy Ave.) | Brooklyn | 212-777-7773
www.momofuku.com

"Desserts like you've never seen" – think compost cookies and crack pies – turn up at this "hipster-chic", "insanely sweet" trio via übertoque David Chang; the "heavy-on-the-butter" treats are "dangerously addictive" (just thinking about them "can make your butt widen"), but the "no-seats" policy helps burn off a few calories; P.S. an UWS outlet is in the works.

Momofuku Noodle Bar *American*

24 | 16 | 18 | $38

E Village | 171 First Ave. (bet. 10th & 11th Sts.) | 212-777-7773 | www.momofuku.com

Where David Chang's empire began, this "visionary" East Villager rolls out Japanese-influenced Americana, highlighted by a "definitive pork bun" and "destination" ramen; trade-offs include "tight" quarters, "rushed" service and "half of Manhattan" lined up outside, but prices are "affordable" and the "serious" cooking "always tastes as good as the first time."

⑦ Momofuku Ssäm Bar ◐ *American* | 25 | 17 | 20 | $49 |

E Village | 207 Second Ave. (13th St.) | 212-254-3500 | www.momofuku.com

David Chang "does wonders with pig" at this "benchmark" East Villager where the "ever-changing", Asian-influenced American menu is celebrated for its "resistance-is-futile" pork bun and "decadent" *bo ssäm* feast; recently expanded, it may be a bit easier to access, though the "noise" and "uncomfortable" seats are constants.

Momo Sushi Shack Ⓜ↗ *Japanese* | - | - | - | I |

Bushwick | 43 Bogart St. (Moore St.) | Brooklyn | 718-418-6666 | www.momosushishack.com

Bushwick sushiphiles salute this cash-only Japanese serving affordable small plates and sushi bombs (i.e. rounded bites) that pair well with sake and Sapporo; the tiny setting outfitted with communal tables and a garage-style front door has that Brooklyn open-air feel.

Momoya *Japanese* | 23 | 19 | 20 | $44 |

Chelsea | 185 Seventh Ave. (21st St.) | 212-989-4466
W 80s | 427 Amsterdam Ave. (bet. 80th & 81st Sts.) | 212-580-0007
www.themomoya.com

"Attention to detail" makes this UWS/Chelsea Japanese duo a "popular" option, not to mention that its "splendid" sushi is "half the price of bigger names"; "cool, contempo" settings and "courtly" service round out the "always pleasant" dining experience.

Monkey Bar ◐Ⓩ *American* | 19 | 23 | 20 | $65 |

E 50s | Elysée Hotel | 60 E. 54th St. (bet. Madison & Park Aves.) | 212-308-2950 | www.monkeybarnewyork.com

Vanity Fair editor Graydon Carter's remake of a fabled Midtown dining room lures the "smart set" with "'30s supper club" looks and "stunning" Edward Sorel murals depicting Jazz Age movers and shakers; the "consistent" American chow is "good" and "expensive", but the "celebrity-watching" is even better and free of charge.

Mon Petit Cafe *French* | 20 | 16 | 20 | $41 |

E 60s | 801 Lexington Ave. (62nd St.) | 212-355-2233 | www.monpetitcafe.com

Perfect for refueling after some "heavy-duty shopping at Bloomingdale's", this "comfortable", tearoom-style Upper East Side cafe purveys "classic" if "predictable" Gallic fare that's "light on the wallet"; "unpretentious" service *avec* a "French accent" adds to its authenticity.

Mont Blanc ◐ *Austrian/Swiss* | 21 | 15 | 22 | $43 |

W 40s | 315 W. 48th St. (bet. 8th & 9th Aves.) | 212-582-9648 | www.montblancrestaurant.com

Since 1982, fondue fanatics have sworn by the "hearty" menu of this "reliable" Swiss-Austrian Theater District "relic"; "good value", a "charming" garden and "welcoming" service led by its "gracious hostess" trump the "dated" decor.

	FOOD	DECOR	SERVICE	COST

Montebello ⊠ *Italian*
23 | 19 | 23 | $60

E 50s | 120 E. 56th St. (bet. Lexington & Park Aves.) | 212-753-1447 |
www.montebellonyc.com

"Mature" types tout this "quiet", "old-world" Midtown Northern
Italian for its "wonderful" food served by a staff that's "attentive without being fussy"; some wonder why this place remains "largely
undiscovered" – perhaps it's due to the somewhat "expensive" tabs.

NEW Monument Lane ◑ *American*
- | - | - | M

W Village | 103 Greenwich Ave. (W. 12th St.) | 212-255-0155 |
www.monumentlane.com

Squab, fluke and oysters figure on the American menu at this new
West Villager that salutes the era when the city was a British colony;
the decor echoes the historic theme, with framed prints and maps of
olde NY, along with tables made from Colonial-era doors.

Morandi ◑ *Italian*
22 | 21 | 20 | $55

W Village | 211 Waverly Pl. (Charles St.) | 212-627-7575 |
www.morandiny.com

Simultaneously "homey" and "trendy", this "rocking" Village trattoria
via Keith McNally is like "Balthazar's Italian cousin", with "flavorful"
food, a "lively young crowd" and "lots of personality"; service is "well
informed", the "rustic", Chianti bottle–lined space has a "happy" hum
and there's "always at least one movie star" in attendance.

Morgan, The Ⓜ *American*
20 | 23 | 21 | $45

Murray Hill | The Morgan Library & Museum | 225 Madison Ave.
(bet. 36th & 37th Sts.) | 212-683-2130 | www.themorgan.org

Set inside Murray Hill's Morgan Library, this lunch-only American offers a "short but sophisticated" menu, served either in a "spacious"
atrium or in J. Pierpont's "elegant" former dining room; the "refined"
vibe is "classic NY", though the pricing's quite up to the minute.

NEW Morgane ◑ *French*
- | - | - | M

Williamsburg | 340 Bedford Ave. (bet. S. 2nd & 3rd Sts.) | Brooklyn |
347-599-0699 | www.morganerestaurant.com

A by-the-numbers take on a French bistro, this Williamsburg newcomer flaunts subway tile, globe lamps and open-to-the-sidewalk
doors, along with a big back garden; the midpriced menu sticks to the
Balthazar-on-Bedford formula with standards like steak au poivre.

⊉ Morimoto ⊠ *Japanese*
26 | 26 | 24 | $84

Chelsea | 88 10th Ave. (bet. 15th & 16th Sts.) | 212-989-4639 |
www.morimotonyc.com

"Culinary master" Masaharu Morimoto "lives up to his Iron Chef status" at this West Chelsea Japanese duplex where the "visually pleasing", "great tasting" dishes work well with the "futuristic", "all-white"
decor and "spot-on service"; since a "huge bill" is part of the experience, many "splurge" and spring for the "work-of-art omakase."

Morrell Wine Bar & Cafe *American*
19 | 16 | 18 | $49

W 40s | 1 Rockefeller Plaza (49th St., bet. 5th & 6th Aves.) | 212-262-7700 |
www.morrellwinebar.com

"Right in the heart of Rock Center", this New American wine bar-cum-
cafe offers a "serious by-the-glass selection" at a "wide range of

	FOOD	DECOR	SERVICE	COST

prices" paired with a "small, focused" menu; it's perfect "before bidding at Christie's" or "hitting the Nintendo store", with bonus "outdoor tables" supplying only-in-NY "people-watching."

Morton's The Steakhouse *Steak*

25	22	24	$76

E 40s | 551 Fifth Ave. (45th St.) | 212-972-3315
Downtown Bklyn | NY Marriott Brooklyn | 339 Adams St. (bet. Tillary & Willoughby Sts.) | Brooklyn | 718-596-2700
www.mortons.com

"They have it down to a science" at this utterly "consistent", wood-paneled chophouse chain, where everything's "huge", from the "Flintstone-size steaks" and "hearty" sides to the "you-only-live-once" prices; some could do without the "Saran-wrapped show-and-tell" prelude to the meal, but the food's "delicious" and everything else is upscale.

Motorino ● *Pizza*

24	14	18	$27

E Village | 349 E. 12th St. (bet. 1st & 2nd Aves.) | 212-777-2644 | www.motorinopizza.com

Refreshingly "low on attitude for a hipster haven", this low-budget East Village pizza joint turns out "sublime" pies with "paper-thin crusts" and "exotic toppings" (e.g. "Brussels sprouts"); purists ignore the "crowded" quarters, and show up for dinner "when the oven is hotter"; P.S. the Williamsburg original has closed.

Moustache ● *Mideastern*

22	13	16	$27

E 100s | 1621 Lexington Ave. (102nd St.) | 212-828-0030
E Village | 265 E. 10th St. (bet. Ave. A & 1st Ave.) | 212-228-2022
W Village | 90 Bedford St. (Grove St.) | 212-229-2220 ✍
www.moustachepitza.com

For a "cheap evening out", this "tasty" Middle Eastern trio "can't be beat" for its "heavenly pitzas" and "bargain" tabs; "cramped" digs and "barely passable" service to the contrary, there are always "clean plates" at meal's end.

NEW MPD ● *French*

▽ 20	22	21	$67

Meatpacking | 73 Gansevoort St. (Washington St.) | 212-541-6991 | www.mpdnyc.com

With the "location down pat" – across from a High Line staircase – this Meatpacking newcomer follows through with "tasty" French cooking and an airy setting; admirers say the place is "better than it has to be" given its neighborhood, but wish they'd make the prices more neighborly.

Mr. Chow ● *Chinese*

22	21	21	$76

E 50s | 324 E. 57th St. (bet. 1st & 2nd Aves.) | 212-751-9030
Mr. Chow Tribeca ● *Chinese*
TriBeCa | 121 Hudson St. (N. Moore St.) | 212-965-9500
www.mrchow.com

Either "still swinging after all these years" or "living on its past laurels", this elegant Midtown Chinese and its newer TriBeCa sibling offer "big-league" eats in "welcome-to-the-'80s" digs; surveyors split on the service – "friendly" vs. "pushy" – but agree it's way "too expensive" if you let the waiter "order for you"; P.S. check out the outdoor tables Downtown.

	FOOD	DECOR	SERVICE	COST

Mr. K's *Chinese*
24 | 24 | 23 | $60

E 50s | 570 Lexington Ave. (51st St.) | 212-583-1668 |
www.mrksny.com

An "over-the-top" pink deco interior sets the "ultrafancy" tone at this Midtown Chinese where the food is "splendid" and the bill "expensive"; the "tranquil" vibe extends to the "white-glove", "flowers-for-the-ladies" service, while the $28 prix fixe lunch lets common folk feel "like royalty."

NEW Mr. Robata ● *Japanese*
- | - | - | E

W 50s | 1674 Broadway (bet. 52nd & 53rd Sts.) | 212-757-1030 |
www.mrrobata.com

Like the name implies, this minuscule Theater District Japanese features a robata grill that produces a menu of French-influenced fare; since it's open late, it's an ideal choice for a post-show bite, even if the pricing's geared towards premium ticketholders rather than the TKTS crowd.

Mughlai *Indian*
20 | 13 | 16 | $38

W 70s | 320 Columbus Ave. (75th St.) | 212-724-6363 |
www.mughlainyc.com

"In business for many years for good reason", this UWS Indian maintains its "neighborhood-favorite" status thanks to "tasty", "well-prepared" dishes; the $10 lunch buffet "deal" makes the "typical" decor and "glum" service less noticeable.

NEW Mussel Pot ● *Seafood*
▽ 22 | 21 | 21 | $46

G Village | 174 Bleecker St. (bet. MacDougal & Sullivan Sts.) | 212-260-2700 |
www.themusselpot.com

"Plump" namesake bivalves offered in over two dozen "creative" preparations are the draw at this Village newcomer; "pleasant" service, "reasonable" tabs and a "lovely", "waterfall"-equipped back garden explain why this "Bleecker Street surprise" is off to such a "strong start."

Nam *Vietnamese*
▽ 22 | 19 | 20 | $41

TriBeCa | 110 Reade St. (W. B'way) | 212-267-1777 |
www.namnyc.com

"Serene and tranquil", this "no-pretense" TriBeCa Vietnamese offers "delicious", "delicate" dishes that are a "good value"; the "minimalist", white-tablecloth setting may be "too quiet" for outgoing types, but all praise the "pleasant" service.

Nanni ⚅ *Italian*
24 | 16 | 23 | $61

E 40s | 146 E. 46th St. (bet. Lexington & 3rd Aves.) | 212-697-4161
Circa-1968 Northern Italian near Grand Central that's a "favorite" for "simple, tasty" food (think "heavenly angel hair"), shuttled by "waiters who must have been there on opening day"; though loyalists call it a "reliable friend", the "tired" interior and wake-you-up prices detract.

Nanoosh *Mediterranean*
18 | 13 | 15 | $20

G Village | 111 University Pl. (bet. 12th & 13th Sts.) | 212-387-0744
Murray Hill | 173 Madison Ave. (bet. 33rd & 34th Sts.) | 212-447-4345 ⚅
W 60s | 2012 Broadway (bet. 68th & 69th Sts.) | 212-362-7922
www.nanoosh.com

"Hummus is king" at these Med "chickpea heavens" also known for "healthy", good "bang-for-the-buck" wraps and salads; "slow" service and decor that's "nothing to look at" lead many to opt for "takeout."

Naples 45 ⌷ *Italian*   18 | 15 | 17 | $37

E 40s | MetLife Bldg. | 200 Park Ave. (45th St.) | 212-972-7001 |
www.naples45.com

"Commuters" and the biz lunch bunch frequent this "vast" Southern
Italian for its "convenience" to Grand Central and "true Neapolitan
pizzas"; although it "needs sprucing up" and is "hugely noisy" midday,
at least "they move you in and out fast"; P.S. closed weekends.

NEW National, The ◑ *American*   20 | 19 | 16 | $52

E 50s | Benjamin Hotel | 557 Lexington Ave. (50th St.) | 212-715-2400 |
www.thenationalnyc.com

The latest from chef Geoffrey Zakarian (Lambs Club), this new dining
room in Midtown's Benjamin Hotel rolls out "simple" American bistro
items for breakfast, lunch and dinner; the "upscale", David Rockwell
setting recalls a European cafe, and though service skews "spotty",
prices are "reasonable" for the locale.

Natsumi ◑ *Japanese*   22 | 18 | 22 | $45

W 50s | Amsterdam Court Hotel | 226 W. 50th St. (bet. B'way & 8th Ave.) |
212-258-2988 | www.natsuminyc.com

A "pleasant" stop in the Theater District, this "modern" sushi specialist
earns "repeat visits" thanks to Japanese dishes with an "Italian twist";
ticket-holders tout the "quick, friendly" service and "reasonable" rates,
though aesthetes feel the furnishings "could use some help."

Naya *Lebanese*   22 | 20 | 21 | $43

E 50s | 1057 Second Ave. (bet. 55th & 56th Sts.) | 212-319-7777

Naya Express ⌷ *Lebanese*

E 40s | 688 Third Ave. (43rd St.) | 212-557-0007
www.nayarestaurants.com

"Ultramodern", "all-white" decor recalling the "space station in *2001*"
lends a "sophisticated" air to this East Midtown Lebanese where the
mezes are as "wonderful" as the service; the Grand Central-area spin-
off shares the same "narrow" dimensions, but is self-service only.

Neary's ◑ *Pub Food*   16 | 15 | 22 | $46

E 50s | 358 E. 57th St. (1st Ave.) | 212-751-1434 | www.nearys.com
"Terrific host" Jimmy Neary and his "supporting cast" of "senior
neighborhood regulars" make for a "jovial" atmosphere at this 45-
year-old Midtown "institution"; it's "as comfortable as an old shoe"
thanks to "reliably good" pub grub and "lifetime" staffers.

NEW Neely's Barbecue Parlor ◑ *BBQ*   - | - | - | M

E 60s | 1125 First Ave., 2nd fl. (62nd St.) | 212-832-1551 |
www.neelysbbqparlor.com

Food Network fixtures Pat and Gina Neely loan their name and signature
BBQ recipes to this UES 'cue parlor near the Queensboro Bridge; the
chandeliered, multiroom setting (meant to suggest a Southern manse) is
pretty swank for the genre, but the grub and pricing adhere to the norm.

Negril ◑ *Caribbean/Jamaican*   21 | 19 | 18 | $39

G Village | 70 W. Third St. (bet. La Guardia Pl. & Thompson St.) |
212-477-2804 | www.negrilvillage.com

For an "escape to the Caribbean" without leaving the city, try this "authentic" Village Jamaican where the "upscale" menu and rum punches

are "good substitutes" for a trip to the islands; a "fun", "party atmosphere" distracts from a staff that seems like it's "on vacation" too.

Nello ● *Italian* | 17 | 17 | 16 | $102 |

E 60s | 696 Madison Ave. (bet. 62nd & 63rd Sts.) | 212-980-9099

"Hermès bags are a dime a dozen" at this "limo"-friendly UES Italian that's a magnet for "Russian millionaires" and various "self-indulgent" types unfazed by "outrageously expensive" tabs; "so-so" food and "snooty" service come with the "supercilious" territory.

New Leaf Ⓜ *American* | 21 | 24 | 21 | $47 |

Washington Heights | Fort Tryon Park | 1 Margaret Corbin Dr. (190th St.) | 212-568-5323 | www.newleafrestaurant.com

"Beautiful Fort Tryon Park" is home to this "tranquil" American where a "delicious" menu is ferried by a "charming" crew; the rustic setting includes a "secluded" terrace perfect for "outdoor dining", and, better yet, the proceeds benefit Bette Midler's NY Restoration Project.

Nha Trang *Vietnamese* | 22 | 7 | 15 | $19 |

Chinatown | 148 Centre St. (bet. Walker & White Sts.) | 212-941-9292
Chinatown | 87 Baxter St. (bet. Bayard & Canal Sts.) | 212-233-5948

Perfect for "overhearing jurors discussing their cases", these C-town Vietnamese twins turn out "phantastic pho" and other "Mekong Delta treats" for "cheap" sums – "$10 goes a long way here"; service and decor is "not their strong point", but at least the food arrives "really fast."

Nice Green Bo ⊄ *Chinese* | 23 | 5 | 13 | $19 |

Chinatown | 66 Bayard St. (bet. Elizabeth & Mott Sts.) | 212-625-2359

Although far from gracious, this "in-and-out" C-town Chinese provides "excellent" Shanghai specialties and "wonderful soup dumplings"; trade-offs include "dumpy" digs, "no-frills" service and "elbow-to-elbow" communal tables, but with such "dirt-cheap" tabs, who's complaining?

Nice Matin *French/Mediterranean* | 20 | 18 | 18 | $48 |

W 70s | 201 W. 79th St. (Amsterdam Ave.) | 212-873-6423 | www.nicematinnyc.com

Good "morning, noon and night", this "all-purpose" UWS rendition of the "South of France" dispenses "reliable" French-Med bistro items in a "charming", "well-lit" setting; it's "really popular" (especially for brunch), so brace yourself for "noise" and "crowds", though "inviting alfresco" seats help ease the crush.

Nick & Toni's Cafe *Mediterranean* | 20 | 17 | 20 | $51 |

W 60s | 100 W. 67th St. (bet. B'way & Columbus Ave.) | 212-496-4000 | www.nickandtoniscafe.com

While not as trendy as the East Hampton original, this "unimposing" Lincoln Center Med maintains a "steady presence" with "better food than it gets credit for"; though the cost is debated, at least the "expeditious" staff will "feed you quickly pre-theater."

Nick's *Pizza* | 24 | 15 | 18 | $26 |

E 90s | 1814 Second Ave. (94th St.) | 212-987-5700 | www.nicksnyc.com
Forest Hills | 108-26 Ascan Ave. (bet. Austin & Burns Sts.) | Queens | 718-263-1126 ⊄

"Terrific thin-crust" pies keep the trade brisk at this cash-only Forest Hills pizzeria where the overall "attention to detail" doesn't apply to the "minimal" decor; its UES sibling ups the ante with basic Italian staples that win fans despite the Second Avenue subway "mess" outside.

Nicky's Vietnamese Sandwiches ⊅ *Sandwiches*

FOOD	DECOR	SERVICE	COST
22	7	16	$11

E Village | 150 E. Second St. (Ave. A) | 212-388-1088
NEW Financial District | 99-C Nassau St. (bet. Ann & Fulton Sts.) | 212-766-3388
Boerum Hill | 311 Atlantic Ave. (bet. Hoyt & Smith Sts.) | Brooklyn | 718-855-8838

Banh-vivants hype these cash-only Vietnamese "holes-in-the-wall" for their "out-of-this-world" banh mi sandwiches stuffed with "savory, spicy" ingredients; there's "no atmosphere" and not much service, but the "price is right" and portions quite "ample."

Nicola's ◐ *Italian*

FOOD	DECOR	SERVICE	COST
22	17	22	$66

E 80s | 146 E. 84th St. (bet. Lexington & 3rd Aves.) | 212-249-9850 | www.nicolasnyc.com

It "helps to be a familiar patron" at this "clubby" UES Italian "hangout" where "lots of regulars" tuck into "robust, reliable" cooking; sure, it's "on the pricey side", but at least the "service is suave . . . so long as the diner is too."

NEW Nights and Weekends ◐⊅ *Caribbean*

FOOD	DECOR	SERVICE	COST
–	–	–	I

Greenpoint | 1 Bedford Ave. (Manhattan Ave.) | Brooklyn | 718-383-5349 | www.nightsandweekendsny.com

Spun off from Five Leaves across the street, this new cash-only Greenpoint hipster haven pairs well-priced Caribbean eats with demon rum–centric cocktails; the funky triangular space conjures up Hemingway's Havana, while roll-up windows and garage doors allow the action to spill out onto the street.

NEW Niko ◐◗ *Japanese*

FOOD	DECOR	SERVICE	COST
▽ 22	20	19	$55

SoHo | 170 Mercer St., 2nd fl. (bet. Houston & Prince Sts.) | 212-991-5650 | www.helloniko.com

Very "of the moment", this new SoHo Japanese in the former Honmura An digs offers both "classical sushi" and "authentic" cooked items in a brick-walled, big-windowed space; its "young, good-looking" following reports that service is the sole shortcoming.

NEW 9 *American*

FOOD	DECOR	SERVICE	COST
20	19	20	$40

W 50s | 800 Ninth Ave. (53rd St.) | 212-956-3333 | www.9restaurantnyc.com

New to the "changing Ninth Avenue scene", this "clean-lined" Hell's Kitchen American features "faux-fiti"-painted walls and an "intimate yet fun" vibe; the kitchen's "creative", midpriced spins on comfort faves (e.g. brisket sliders, "heavenly" lobster hot dogs) keep it "packed" with a "young"-skewing crowd.

NEW 900 Degrees ◐ *Pizza*

FOOD	DECOR	SERVICE	COST
–	–	–	M

W Village | 29 Seventh Ave. S. (bet. Leroy & Morton Sts.) | 212-989-9880

From the owners of San Fran's highly rated Tony's Pizza Napoletana, this West Villager slings pies including a signature margherita that once won the World Pizza Cup in Naples; taking center stage in the loftlike space's open kitchen is a wood-fired oven that, yes, fires at 900 degrees.

	FOOD	DECOR	SERVICE	COST

99 Miles to Philly ●₱ *Cheesesteaks*

19 | 8 | 15 | $13

E Village | 94 Third Ave. (bet. 12th & 13th Sts.) | 212-253-2700 | www.99milestophilly.com

It's "gut bombs" away at this "cheap", cash-only East Village cheesesteak place whose "grease-a-licious", "authentic-Philly" signature sandwich "hits the spot", especially "late-night"; "hole-in-the-wall" digs with "not much seating" are trumped by "quick delivery."

Ninja *Japanese*

18 | 25 | 24 | $64

TriBeCa | 25 Hudson St. (bet. Duane & Reade Sts.) | 212-274-8500 | www.ninjanewyork.com

Small fry have "fun" at this "goofy" TriBeCa theme restaurant, set in a faux "medieval Ninja" village and attended by costumed staffers adept at "tableside magic"; it's admittedly "hokey" and "high-priced", with critics wishing the Japanese food was "as good as the show."

Nino's *Italian*

22 | 19 | 21 | $59

E 70s | 1354 First Ave. (bet. 72nd & 73rd Sts.) | 212-988-0002

Nino's Bellissima Pizza *Pizza*

E 40s | 890 Second Ave. (bet. 47th & 48th Sts.) | 212-355-5540

Nino's Positano ⧄ *Italian*

E 40s | 890 Second Ave. (bet. 47th & 48th Sts.) | 212-355-5540

Nino's Tuscany *Italian*

W 50s | 117 W. 58th St. (bet. 6th & 7th Aves.) | 212-757-8630 www.ninony.com

Led by "Nino himself", the "charming" staff "aims to please" at this "tried-and-true" Italian mini-chain praised for its *molto bene* cooking; all branches share "old-school" vibes and up-to-date tabs, though Positano's pizzeria adjunct is naturally more "casual."

Nirvana *Indian*

∇ 21 | 20 | 20 | $45

Murray Hill | 346 Lexington Ave. (bet. 39th & 40th Sts.) | 212-983-0000 | www.nirvanany.com

An "unexpected" find in an off-the-beaten-path Murray Hill address, this "modern Indian" plies "delicious", well-priced standards via an "attentive" team; the subdued upstairs dining room allows for "easy conversation" in contrast to the "happy-hour" scene in the street-level lounge.

Nizza ● *French/Italian*

19 | 16 | 19 | $38

W 40s | 630 Ninth Ave. (bet. 44th & 45th Sts.) | 212-956-1800 | www.nizzanyc.com

There's a "happy buzz" at this French-Italian "crowd-pleaser" in Hell's Kitchen whose "creative menu" includes "gluten-free" options and "authentic" socca pancakes; "gentle" pricing and "fast" service make it "perfect pre-theater", save for the "noise" and "crowds."

⊠ Nobu *Japanese*

26 | 23 | 23 | $83

TriBeCa | 105 Hudson St. (Franklin St.) | 212-219-0500

⊠ Nobu 57 ● *Japanese*

W 50s | 40 W. 57th St. (bet. 5th & 6th Aves.) | 212-757-3000

Nobu, Next Door *Japanese*

TriBeCa | 105 Hudson St. (bet. Franklin & N. Moore Sts.) | 212-334-4445 www.noburestaurants.com

Nobu Matsuhisa's 1994 TriBeCa "crowd-pleaser" "still has it", offering "memorable" Japanese-Peruvian dishes in a "minimalist" David

Rockwell-designed room, where the food tastes even better when "Denzel Washington" et al. are at the next table; the "fall-back option" next door is a bit cheaper and geared to walk-ins, while the Midtown satellite is a magnet for "tourists" and "hedge-fund" types; "sky-high" prices to the contrary, regulars "know the menu by heart."

Nocello *Italian*
22 | 19 | 22 | $50

W 50s | 257 W. 55th St. (bet. B'way & 8th Ave.) | 212-713-0224 | www.nocello.net

"Handy" to both Carnegie Hall and City Center, this "security-blanket" Tuscan draws "ticket-holders" and "retirees" with "excellent" food and a "pleasant" setting; "efficient service" and "reasonable" tabs ice the cake.

Noche Mexicana *Mexican*
23 | 13 | 19 | $22

W 100s | 852 Amsterdam Ave. (bet. 101st & 102nd Sts.) | 212-662-6900 | www.noche-mexicana.com

Ok, the decor's "nothing *bonito*", but "looks are deceiving" at this UWS Mexican whose cultlike following is crazy about its "unbeliev-able" tamales and burritos; though the staff "speaks little English", a "smile goes a long way" here – as does your dollar.

NoHo Star ● *American*
19 | 16 | 18 | $36

NoHo | 330 Lafayette St. (Bleecker St.) | 212-925-0070 | www.nohostar.com

It's all about "comfort" at this longtime NoHo New American with a "something-for-everyone" menu that includes some "surprisingly good" Chinese chow; "low prices" and a "chill", "coffee-shop" setting make it a "safe" (if somewhat "pedestrian") choice.

Noi Due *Italian/Kosher*
- | - | - | M

W 60s | 143 W. 69th St., downstairs (B'way) | 212-712-2222 | www.noiduecafe.com

Arched brick ceilings and a wood-burning oven lend a cozy air to this subterranean UWS kosher Italian serving midpriced pizzas and pas-tas, along with assorted dairy specialties; since the no-rez policy can lead to considerable dinnertime waits, insiders slip in for lunch.

Nomad *African/Spanish*
20 | 18 | 21 | $32

E Village | 78 Second Ave. (4th St.) | 212-253-5410 | www.nomadny.com

"Flavorful" North African eats including "delicious tagines" and ran-dom Spanish tapas lure East Village nomads into this "small", "souk-like" retreat with a "beautiful" back garden; "fast, friendly service" and a three-course $20 "deal" make it all the more "welcoming."

Nom Wah Tea Parlor *Chinese*
 ∇ 23 | 12 | 19 | $21

Chinatown | 13 Doyers St. (Bowery) | 212-962-6047 | www.nomwah.com

"Wonderful" dim sum is "ordered from the menu item from carts" at this "well-kept secret" on the Chinatown scene since 1920; though the authentically "retro" interior may be "a dive by any other name", it's "oh-so-cheap" and like a "visit to another world."

Noodle Bar ⊗ *Noodle Shop*
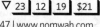 ∇ 20 | 12 | 17 | $23

LES | 172 Orchard St. (Stanton St.) | 212-228-9833

W Village | 26 Carmine St. (bet. Bedford & Bleecker Sts.) | 212-524-6800 www.noodlebarnyc.com

"Knockout noodle soups" and an "excellent variety" of wok-fired dishes come "fast and fresh" at these "cash-only" crosstown Asians;

"funky, dress-down" settings and only "serviceable" service are offset by "inexpensive" tabs.

Noodle Pudding Ⓜ ⊄ *Italian* 24 | 17 | 21 | $41

Brooklyn Heights | 38 Henry St. (bet. Cranberry & Middagh Sts.) | Brooklyn | 718-625-3737

"Not the secret it used to be", this "popular" Brooklyn Heights Italian is "always packed" owing to its "astonishingly good" cooking, "cheerful" service and "family-friendly" vibe; "incredible prices" make the "no-reservations" and "no-credit-card" rules more bearable.

Nook ⊄ *Eclectic* 22 | 11 | 16 | $33

W 50s | 746 Ninth Ave. (bet. 50th & 51st Sts.) | 212-247-5500

Like the "name implies", this Hell's Kitchen Eclectic with just 24 seats is a bona fide "micro-establishment" with a big local following due to its "keeper" cooking; regulars don't mind the "cash-only" rule and "could-be-better" service given the "bargain" rates and "fantastic" BYO policy.

Norma's *American* 25 | 18 | 20 | $44

W 50s | Le Parker Meridien | 119 W. 56th St. (bet. 6th & 7th Aves.) | 212-708-7460 | www.normasnyc.com

"Waffles and pancakes will never be the same" after a visit to this "tour de force" American in the Parker Meridien, renowned for its "superlative" breakfasts and brunches; despite serious tabs, "special-occasion" celebrants say this "gold-plated" experience is truly "worth the splurge" and a great way to start the day.

Northern Spy Food Company *American* 23 | 18 | 20 | $41

E Village | 511 E. 12th St. (bet. Aves. A & B) | 212-228-5100 | www.northernspyfoodco.com

It's all about "simplicity" at this "tiny" East Villager where "comforting", "straight-up" American dishes made from "farm-fresh" ingredients lure "bursting-at-the-seams crowds"; the rustic setting features "charming", "do-it-yourself" decor, while a rear shop sells "locavore" items.

North Square *American* 23 | 19 | 22 | $48

G Village | Washington Square Hotel | 103 Waverly Pl. (MacDougal St.) | 212-254-1200 | www.northsquareny.com

"Mostly known to locals" and "NYU professors", this "likable" New American on Washington Square offers "better food than you'd think" in a "blessedly quiet" corner space; its "grown-up" fan base eats up the "cordial" service and "civilized" pricing.

No. 7 ◐ Ⓜ *American* 23 | 16 | 19 | $31

Fort Greene | 7 Greene Ave. (bet. Cumberland & Fulton Sts.) | Brooklyn | 718-522-6370 | www.no7restaurant.com

No. 7 Sub Ⓢ *Sandwiches*

Chelsea | Ace Hotel | 1188 Broadway (bet. 28th & 29th Sts.) | 212-532-1680 | www.no7sub.com

"Before or after BAM", this "one-of-a-kind" Fort Greene New American features an "intriguing" menu served in "hipster-chic" digs; "knowledgeable" service, moderate tabs and a "busy bar scene" keep habitués "happy", while a counter-service sibling in Chelsea's Ace Hotel doles out "blow-your-mind" sandwiches.

	FOOD	DECOR	SERVICE	COST

No. 28 ⊅ *Pizza*
25 | 12 | 18 | $28

E Village | 176 Second Ave. (11th St.) | 212-777-1555 ◗
SoHo | 196 Spring St. (bet. Sullivan & Thompson Sts.) |
212-219-9020
W Village | 28 Carmine St. (bet. Bedford & Bleecker Sts.) |
212-463-9653
www.numero28.com

It's "unnecessary to ever travel to Brooklyn again" for pizza thanks to the "amazing" Neapolitan version plied at these crosstown Villagers (the takeout-focused SoHo outlet offers Roman-style pies); despite blah decor and "slow service", a great "quality-to-price ratio" keeps fans pie-eyed.

Nove Ⓜ *Italian*
∇ 24 | 22 | 24 | $57

Eltingville | 3900 Richmond Ave. (Amboy Rd.) | Staten Island |
718-227-3286 | www.noveitalianbistro.com

Staten Islanders starved for "sophistication" turn to this Eltingville Southern Italian for its "top-notch" cooking, "gracious" service and "elegant" surrounds; though "a little pricey" for these parts, it can be "tough" to access at prime times.

Novecento *Argentinean/Steak*
∇ 21 | 19 | 21 | $45

SoHo | 343 W. Broadway (bet. Broome & Grand Sts.) | 212-925-4706 |
www.novecento.com

Meat mavens mingle at this SoHo Argentine steakhouse for "casual" dining that features a "solid", beef-focused menu and "warm" service from a staff that's "hotter than the food"; still, what's "fun" to some is just plain "loud" to others.

Novitá *Italian*
25 | 19 | 22 | $58

Gramercy | 102 E. 22nd St. (bet. Lexington Ave. & Park Ave. S.) |
212-677-2222 | www.novitanyc.com

Habitués are "smitten" with this longtime Gramercy Parker whose "marvelous" Northern Italian food is almost "too pretty to eat"; sure, the "understated" room can be a "tight squeeze", but its "mature, well-heeled" following has no problem with the pricey tariffs given the "good quality."

Nuela *Pan-Latin*
22 | 23 | 21 | $59

Flatiron | 43 W. 24th St. (bet. B'way & 6th Ave.) | 212-929-1200 |
www.nuelany.com

"Inventive" Pan-Latin cooking, from small plates to a "fabulous suckling pig", is yours at this "huge", "sceney" Flatiron yearling that follows through with "upbeat" vibes; "expertly crafted cocktails" and "sexy" "*Miami Vice*" decor make for "festive" dining – and "hefty" prices.

Num Pang ⊅ *Cambodian*
26 | 6 | 16 | $12

NEW **E 40s** | 140 E. 41st St. (bet. Lexington & 3rd Aves.) |
212-867-8889
G Village | 21 E. 12th St. (bet. 5th Ave. & University Pl.) | 212-255-3271 |
www.numpangnyc.com

For "mouthwatering" Cambodian banh mi "sandwiches like no other", check out this "cash-only" Villager; service is functional but "fast", the digs "bare-bones" and the price "hard to beat", hence the "long waits" for entry; P.S. the Grand Central–area outlet arrived post-Survey.

	FOOD	DECOR	SERVICE	COST

Nurnberger Bierhaus *German*
∇ 21 | 17 | 22 | $35

New Brighton | 817 Castleton Ave. (bet. Davis & Pelton Aves.) | Staten Island | 718-816-7461 | www.nurnbergerbierhaus.com

"Traditional" German chow is slung at this Staten Island "meatfest" in New Brighton, where the "wursts are great", ditto the selection of Bavarian brews; dirndl-clad waitresses, a "lively" back garden and "inexpensive" tabs complete the overall gemütlich picture.

Nyonya ●⊭ *Malaysian*
22 | 14 | 15 | $24

Little Italy | 199 Grand St. (bet. Mott & Mulberry Sts.) | 212-334-3669
Bensonhurst | 2322 86th St. (bet. 23rd & 24th Aves.) | Brooklyn | 718-265-0888
Borough Park | 5323 Eighth Ave. (bet. 53rd & 54th Sts.) | Brooklyn | 718-633-0808
www.ilovenyonya.com

Adventurous sorts seeking a "change from the usual" recommend this "excellent" Malaysian trio where the food's as "flavorful" as the tabs are "affordable"; just overlook the "nonexistent" decor, "cash-only" policy and "pack-'em-in-get-'em-out" service.

NYY Steak *Steak*
20 | 21 | 18 | $70

Yankee Stadium | Yankee Stadium | 1 E. 161st St., Gate 6 (River Ave.) | Bronx | 646-977-8325 | www.nyysteak.com

"Whether you're going to a game or not", this year-round steakhouse in Yankee Stadium bats out "excellent" slabs of beef for out-of-the-park sums; team "memorabilia" serves as decor, the waiters "know their trivia" and there's no charge for the "testosterone on the side."

Oaxaca ⊭ *Mexican*
20 | 10 | 15 | $15

NEW E Village | 16 Extra Pl. (bet. Bowery & 2nd Ave.) | 212-677-3340 ●
Cobble Hill | 251 Smith St. (bet. Degraw & Douglass Sts.) | Brooklyn | 718-643-9630
Park Slope | 250 Fourth Ave. (bet. Carroll & President Sts.) | Brooklyn | 718-222-1122 | www.oaxacatacos.com ●

"Taco fixes" are supplied at this "real-deal" Mexican trio, "quick, easy" options for "delicious" eats at "inexpensive", "cash-only" prices; over-lit, undersize setups (and no liquor licenses) make the case for takeout.

Oceana *American/Seafood*
24 | 23 | 23 | $76

W 40s | McGraw Hill Bldg. | 120 W. 49th St. (bet. 6th & 7th Aves.) | 212-759-5941 | www.oceanarestaurant.com

"Quite fine indeed", this "big, open" Rock Center American seafooder offers "impeccable", "high-ticket" catch in a "corporate-canteen" setting with "lots of room between tables"; some find the space "cold" and "impersonal", but the "first-class" service and "top-notch" raw bar are more shipshape.

Ocean Grill *Seafood*
24 | 20 | 22 | $58

W 70s | 384 Columbus Ave. (bet. 78th & 79th Sts.) | 212-579-2300 | www.oceangrill.com

Still "on course" after 15 years, Steve Hanson's "bustling" UWS seafooder offers "pristine" fish and "excellent" raw items in a "breezy atmosphere"; service is "helpful" and the pricing "reasonable", but when it gets too "noisy", regulars opt for sidewalk seats and "watch the foot traffic" pass by.

			FOOD	DECOR	SERVICE	COST

Odeon, The ● *American/French* | 19 | 18 | 19 | $48

TriBeCa | 145 W. Broadway (bet. Duane & Thomas Sts.) | 212-233-0507 | www.theodeonrestaurant.com

It's all about "staying power" at this 1980-vintage TriBeCa bistro, a "still relevant" source of "winning" Franco-American eats and "competent" service; the *"Bright Lights, Big City"* crowd may be long gone, but it is "walking distance from jury duty" and gets rather "lively late-night."

Ofrenda *Mexican* | 20 | 17 | 22 | $41

W Village | 113 Seventh Ave. S. (bet. Christopher & W. 10th Sts.) | 212-924-2305 | www.ofrendanyc.com

"Innovative, nontraditional" Mexican dishes fill out the menu of this "refined" yearling with an "informal" mood that "charms" its "neighborhood" patrons; fair prices, "friendly" servers and margaritas "stronger than Superman" make it a "wonderful" West Village addition.

Old Homestead *Steak* | 24 | 19 | 22 | $76

Meatpacking | 56 Ninth Ave. (bet. 14th & 15th Sts.) | 212-242-9040 | www.theoldhomesteadsteakhouse.com

"Big-time carnivores" gnaw on "massive", "cooked-to-perfection" chops at this "vintage" steakhouse planted in the Meatpacking District since 1868; "venerable" waiters and "days of yore" decor supply the "nostalgic charm", but prices are decidedly more modern.

NEW Old Town Hot Pot *Chinese* | - | - | - | I

W Village | 70 Seventh Ave. S. (Commerce St.) | 212-929-2188

From the Grand Sichuan team comes this low-budget West Village Chinese specializing in make-it-yourself Beijing-style hot pots, assembled from a choice of soup bases, sauces, vegetables and proteins; the small digs boast big windows with primo Seventh Avenue South people-watching.

Olea *Mediterranean* | 22 | 19 | 20 | $37

Fort Greene | 171 Lafayette Ave. (Adelphi St.) | Brooklyn | 718-643-7003 | www.oleabrooklyn.com

There's "lots to like" at this "laid-back" Mediterranean, a "popular" pre– and post–Brooklyn Academy of Music nexus offering "wonderful tapas" and one of the "best brunches" in Fort Greene; further pluses include moderate costs, "live Spanish guitar" and a "high-ceilinged", stucco-walled setting.

Olio ● *Pizza* | ∇ 20 | 18 | 17 | $34

W Village | 3 Greenwich Ave. (bet. Christopher St. & 6th Ave.) | 212-243-6546 | www.olionyc.com

Both the "chef and the oven were imported from Naples" – and the "quality of the pizza shows it" at this West Village Neapolitan specialist (the "secret's in the crust"); the "mostly attentive" service is another matter, though costs are modest and the location "convenient."

Olives *Mediterranean* | 23 | 22 | 22 | $61

Union Sq | W Hotel Union Sq. | 201 Park Ave. S. (17th St.) | 212-353-8345 | www.toddenglish.com

"Tasty flatbreads" are a menu highlight at Todd English's "steady" modern Med in the W Union Square where the "quite good" food works well with its "chic" look and "considerate" service; too bad the

	FOOD	DECOR	SERVICE	COST

"pounding music" from the "bustling bar" next door makes it so darn "noisy" – and the prices may give you a pounding as well.

Ollie's *Chinese*
16 | 10 | 14 | $25

W 40s | 411 W. 42nd St. (bet. 9th & 10th Aves.) | 212-868-6588
W 60s | 1991 Broadway (bet. 67th & 68th Sts.) | 212-595-8181
W 80s | 2425 Broadway (bet. 89th & 90th Sts.) | 212-877-2298
W 100s | 2957 Broadway (116th St.) | 212-932-3300 ◐

"Utilitarian" Chinese chow arrives "quick" and "cheap" at this "assembly-line" West Side quartet, though the "drab" decor makes it best for "eat-and-run" types; many say they offer the "fastest delivery in town", swearing "they have a helicopter with a wok" on board.

Omai *Vietnamese*
23 | 15 | 19 | $43

Chelsea | 158 Ninth Ave. (bet. 19th & 20th Sts.) | 212-633-0550 |
www.omainyc.com

It's "hard to find" (there's "no sign") and equally "hard to get seats" (it's "small"), but this Chelsea Vietnamese remains a "popular" option thanks to "nuanced", "subtle" cooking backed up by "smiling service"; fortunately, the "minimalist" setting matches the minimalist pricing.

Omen ◐ *Japanese*
▽ 24 | 19 | 22 | $69

SoHo | 113 Thompson St. (bet. Prince & Spring Sts.) |
212-925-8923

Kyoto-style Japanese dishes are the specialty of this "old standby" in SoHo, where enthusiasts are enthralled by the "unusual" ("no sushi") country cooking; a "tranquil" ambiance and "attentive" staff make the way-"pricey" tabs easier to swallow.

Omonia Cafe ◐ *Greek*
19 | 15 | 17 | $21

Astoria | 32-20 Broadway (33rd St.) | Queens | 718-274-6650 |
www.omoniacafe.com

"Fantastic sweets" are the thing to order at this Astoria Greek coffee-house that draws "young" folks with "late-night" hours and "fun" vibrations; it's also good for "leisurely" conversation since "they serve you fast, then leave you alone"; P.S. its shuttered Bay Ridge sibling is undergoing an extensive renovation.

Once Upon a Tart ... *Coffeehouse*
22 | 14 | 15 | $15

SoHo | 135 Sullivan St. (bet. Houston & Prince Sts.) | 212-387-8869 |
www.onceuponatart.com

"Wonderful fragrances" waft out of this longtime SoHo coffeehouse where "terrific baked goods", sandwiches and the like make for "pleasant" repasts; since it's counter service–only and "limited" in size, "you may want to eat your tart outside."

☑ One if by Land, Two if by Sea *American*
24 | 27 | 25 | $111

W Village | 17 Barrow St. (bet. 7th Ave. S. & W. 4th St.) | 212-228-0822 |
www.oneifbyland.com

So "devastatingly romantic" that it's "even good with your wife", this 40-year-old West Villager seduces "fine-dining" fans with "outstand-ing" American food and a "serene" setting carved out of Aaron Burr's former carriage house; piano music and a roaring fireplace will "make you want to propose", even though the prix fixe–only tabs "aren't for the lighthearted."

	FOOD	DECOR	SERVICE	COST

101 *American/Italian* — 21 | 19 | 20 | $43
Bay Ridge | 10018 Fourth Ave. (101st St.) | Brooklyn | 718-833-1313
"So very Brooklyn" is the word on this "consistently decent" Italian-American's fare and even "better bar scene"; it's a "busy" Bay Ridge "neighborhood hangout" with a "view of the Verrazano", "valet parking" and plenty of loyalists who insist it "doesn't disappoint."

1 or 8 Ⓜ *Japanese* — 24 | 21 | 22 | $50
Williamsburg | 66 S. Second St. (bet. Kent & Wythe Aves.) | Brooklyn | 718-384-2152 | www.oneoreightbk.com
On the southern fringe of the "Williamsburg scene", this "chic" Japanese proffers "high-quality" sushi, "inventive" cooked dishes and "creative" cocktails; the "all-white" "mod" interior strikes some as "ultracool" and others as "antiseptic", but all agree the "gracious" service adds warmth.

☑ Oriental Garden *Chinese/Seafood* — 23 | 11 | 15 | $36
Chinatown | 14 Elizabeth St. (bet. Bayard & Canal Sts.) | 212-619-0085
"Seafood is the specialty" of this C-town Cantonese "oldie" but goodie where "sparkling fresh" catch is plucked from the tanks up front and "first-rate dim sum" is rolled out for lunch; "tacky" white Formica looks and "indifferent" service are drawbacks, but the "long lines" suggest its quality.

Original Soupman *Soup* — ∇ 23 | 6 | 13 | $15
W 50s | 259-A W. 55th St. (bet. B'way & 8th Ave.) | 212-956-0900 | www.originalsoupman.com
Made famous by the "*Seinfeld* spoof", this Hell's Kitchen soup stand slings "hearty" liquids that "hit the spot on a damp winter day"; there are "no seats" and strict "rules for the line", and what's more, the staff seems to have "inherited the founder's personality."

Orsay *French* — 18 | 20 | 17 | $60
E 70s | 1057 Lexington Ave. (75th St.) | 212-517-6400 | www.orsayrestaurant.com
This "faithful reproduction" of a French brasserie – right down to the Euro pricing – draws "au courant" UES locals with a yen for "classic" Gallic dining among "art nouveau" trappings; though the "decor shouts Paris", some say the "food and service don't keep up their end of the bargain."

☑ Orso ◐ *Italian* — 23 | 18 | 22 | $58
W 40s | 322 W. 46th St. (bet. 8th & 9th Aves.) | 212-489-7212 | www.orsorestaurant.com
"Always crowded" before the curtains rise, this "trustworthy" Restaurant Row perennial is applauded for its "top-notch" meals and "convenient" location; it's also known for the "famous faces" that wander in après-theater, though regulars "try not to gawk at the actors who eat (and work) there."

Osso Buco *Italian* — 19 | 16 | 19 | $42
E 90s | 1662 Third Ave. (93rd St.) | 212-426-5422 | www.ossobuco2010.com
"Reliable red-sauce" cooking arrives in "generous", family-style portions at this "steady" UES Italian near the 92nd Street Y; service may tend toward "forgetful", but given the "moderately priced" tabs, "you won't leave hungry *or* poor."

	FOOD	DECOR	SERVICE	COST

Osteria al Doge ● *Italian* — 20 | 18 | 20 | $51

W 40s | 142 W. 44th St. (bet. B'way & 6th Ave.) | 212-944-3643 |
www.osteria-doge.com

Near the theaters yet "off the tourist map", this "consistent" Italian offers "satisfying" Venetian fare in a "rustic" duplex setting; while the main floor is *molto festivo*, "upstairs is quieter", but either way you can expect "cheerful" service and tabs that are not inordinate.

Osteria Laguna ● *Italian* — 20 | 18 | 19 | $47

E 40s | 209 E. 42nd St. (bet. 2nd & 3rd Aves.) | 212-557-0001 |
www.osteria-laguna.com

"As Italian as 42nd Street will allow", this "solid" trattoria parked between Grand Central and the U.N. vends Venetian victuals in "pleasant" digs with French doors that open wide to the street; at lunchtime, it's a "Pfizer" canteen (it adjoins the company's corporate headquarters).

NEW Osteria Morini ● *Italian* — 24 | 19 | 20 | $61

SoHo | 218 Lafayette St. (bet. Broome & Spring Sts.) | 212-965-8777 |
www.osteriamorini.com

Michael White goes "casual" at this "happening" new SoHo Italian focusing on "luscious" rustic fare from the Emilia-Romagna region, including "melt-in-your-mouth" pastas; though "crowds", "noise" and "holier-than-thou" service are a drag, the faux-farmhouse setting is "cool" and it's a helluva lot "cheaper" than White's Marea.

Otto ● *Pizza* — 23 | 19 | 19 | $40

G Village | 1 Fifth Ave. (enter on 8th St., bet. 5th Ave. & University Pl.) |
212-995-9559 | www.ottopizzeria.com

"NYU students" and "family mobs" jam into this "too darn popular" Village enoteca/pizzeria from the Batali-Bastianich partnership, located in a mock "train-station" setting; the "standout" pizza and "overwhelming" wine list come at "affordable" tabs, though what's "high energy" to some is just "deafening" to others.

Z Ouest *American* — 24 | 21 | 23 | $67

W 80s | 2315 Broadway (84th St.) | 212-580-8700 |
www.ouestny.com

"Well-heeled" Upper Ouestsiders tout Tom Valenti's "stylish" New American offering "refined", "wonderfully prepared" comfort items in a "smart" setting fitted out with red leather banquettes; some fret it's "too pricey for every day", but an early-bird menu lures the "mature" set.

Our Place *Chinese* — 18 | 15 | 18 | $38

E 70s | 242 E. 79th St. (bet. 2nd & 3rd Aves.) | 212-288-4888 |
www.ourplace79.com

Now in a new locale, this longtime UES Chinese still offers the same "wide selection" of "middle-class" Cantonese dishes plus weekend dim sum; all agree it's "going through a transition", though detractors deem it "less attractive than before" – and "a bit more expensive."

Z Oyster Bar ⊠ *Seafood* — 22 | 18 | 17 | $50

E 40s | Grand Central | lower level (42nd St. & Vanderbilt Ave.) |
212-490-6650 | www.oysterbarny.com

For a "glimpse of NY's glamorous past", drop anchor at this "timeless", 99-year-old seafooder in the depths of Grand Central, where an

| | FOOD | DECOR | SERVICE | COST |

"incredible" bivalve selection and "classic oyster pan roasts" are served in a vast room crowned by a tiled "vaulted ceiling"; "minimal service" and "maximal noise" are "part of the experience", so insiders "head for the Saloon" for "more peaceful" dining.

☒ Pacificana *Chinese*   25 | 17 | 19 | $28

Sunset Park | 813 55th St., 2nd fl. (8th Ave.) | Brooklyn | 718-871-2880

The carts just "keep coming" at this Hong Kong–like 500-seater in Sunset Park known for its "divine dim sum" and "excellent" Cantonese food; it's "packed on weekends" (so "plan on shouting"), but no one cares when the service is this "friendly" and the tabs "so darn cheap."

Padre Figlio ☒ *Italian*   23 | 18 | 24 | $59

E 40s | 310 E. 44th St. (bet. 1st & 2nd Aves.) | 212-286-4310 | www.padrefiglio.com

"Personal attention" from father-and-son owners is the hallmark of this "secret" Italian chophouse near the U.N.; the "marvelous" Piedmontese steaks may skew "expensive", but a $39 dinner "deal" and weekend live jazz supply plenty of value.

☒ Palm, The *Steak*   25 | 19 | 23 | $74

E 40s | 837 Second Ave. (bet. 44th & 45th Sts.) | 212-687-2953 ☒
E 40s | 840 Second Ave. (bet. 44th & 45th Sts.) | 212-697-5198
TriBeCa | 206 West St. (bet. Chambers & Warren Sts.) | 646-395-6391
W 50s | 250 W. 50th St. (bet. B'way & 8th Ave.) | 212-333-7256
www.thepalm.com

"Don Draper would feel at home" at these "business lunch"-friendly chop shops known for "big fat steaks", "gigantic lobsters" and "manly" milieus decorated with "caricatures of famous folks"; all share "crusty" service and "expensive" tabs, but aficionados say the circa-1926 flagship (at 837 Second Avenue) is "the best" of the bunch.

Palma *Italian*   22 | 20 | 21 | $52

W Village | 28 Cornelia St. (bet. Bleecker & W. 4th Sts.) | 212-691-2223 | www.palmanyc.com

"Like eating at a friend's home", this "quaint" West Village "hideaway" offers "old-country" Sicilian cooking in "small", "rustic" digs that include a "charming" back garden; a carriage house adjunct serves as a "festive" private party option.

Palm Court *American*   20 | 26 | 23 | $66

W 50s | Plaza Hotel | 768 Fifth Ave. (59th St.) | 212-546-5300 | www.theplaza.com

"Old NY grandeur" soldiers on at this "plush", palm-lined American in the Plaza serving breakfast, lunch and brunch along with a "civilized" afternoon tea; yup, it's "expensive", but its "dressed-up" crowd laps up the same "top-notch" service and "Versailles"-like setting that your grandparents used to like.

Palo Santo *Pan-Latin*   ▽ 23 | 22 | 21 | $45

Park Slope | 652 Union St. (bet. 4th & 5th Aves.) | Brooklyn | 718-636-6311 | www.palosanto.us

They "aim to please and succeed" at this "special" Park Slope Pan-Latin where a "great chef-owner" prepares "creative" *comida* paired with a "carefully chosen" wine list; a "pleasant" brownstone location and "warm" service complete the overall "lovely" picture.

	FOOD	DECOR	SERVICE	COST

Pampano *Mexican/Seafood* — 24 | 22 | 22 | $57

E 40s | 209 E. 49th St. (bet. 2nd & 3rd Aves.) | 212-751-4545 |
www.modernmexican.com

The vibe's "upscale but low-key" at this "haute" Mexican seafooder
via chef Richard Sandoval and tenor Plácido Domingo, where the "cosmopolitan" chow comes at typical Midtown prices; insiders head for
the "crisp white" upstairs dining room (and its "delightful" outdoor
terrace), while bargain-hunters prefer its 'round-the-corner taqueria.

Pam Real Thai Food ⊅ *Thai* — 22 | 9 | 17 | $24

W 40s | 402 W. 47th St. (bet. 9th & 10th Aves.) | 212-315-4441
W 40s | 404 W. 49th St. (bet. 9th & 10th Aves.) | 212-333-7500
www.pamrealthaifood.com

"Spiced right" – and "priced right" – these "unassuming" Hell's
Kitchen Siamese dispense "authentic Thai" food in "modest", "no-
frills" settings; the "cash-only" policy is offset by "convenience to theaters", and though service can be "abrupt", it's also "super-fast."

Paola's *Italian* — 23 | 19 | 21 | $58

E 90s | Hotel Wales | 1295 Madison Ave. (92nd St.) | 212-794-1890 |
www.paolasrestaurant.com

Frequented by a "smartly dressed", "who's who" crowd, this Carnegie
Hill "asset" offers a "marvelous" Italian menu in civilized digs overseen by its "welcoming" namesake owner; too bad they can't "dull the
din", but the "upscale" pricing is no problem – "nobody's counting" in
this "fashionable" neck of the woods.

Papaya King ●⊅ *Hot Dogs* — 21 | 5 | 12 | $8

E 80s | 179 E. 86th St. (3rd Ave.) | 212-369-0648 | www.papayaking.com
A NYC "cult thing" (recently exported to LA), this UES "hot dog
heaven" is famed for "juicy" franks "with snap" and "addicting" papaya
drinks, priced for "tight budgets"; despite no seats, "sketchy" looks
and "counter service", its myriad fans cry out "long live the king!"

Pappardella ● *Italian* — 21 | 17 | 20 | $42

W 70s | 316 Columbus Ave. (75th St.) | 212-595-7996 |
www.pappardella.com

"Freshly made pasta" and other "surprisingly good" Italian dishes at
"won't-break-the-bank" tabs lend this "understated" Upper Westsider
neighborhood-"standby" status; "willing" staffers augment the
"happy" mood, ditto prime Columbus Avenue "people-watching."

Paradou *French* — 22 | 19 | 20 | $49

Meatpacking | 8 Little W. 12th St. (bet. Greenwich & Washington Sts.) |
212-463-8345 | www.paradounyc.com

Refreshingly "low-key" despite its trendy Meatpacking address, this
French bistro offers "enjoyable" meals in a "cozy" setting; it's the
"pretty" all-seasons garden and "boozy" brunch with "unlimited"
champagne cocktails – not the prices – that draw the crowds.

Park Avenue Bistro ☒ *French* — 21 | 19 | 21 | $57

Murray Hill | 377 Park Ave. S. (bet. 26th & 27th Sts.) | 212-689-1360 |
www.parkavenuebistronyc.com

Murray Hillers seeking "relaxing" dining "without a mob scene" cite this
"down-to-earth" Park Avenue bistro for its "interesting" French food

ferried by a "helpful" crew; "modern" decor and "white walls" brighten the "little sliver" of a space, even if the costs may darken the mood.

🚩 Park Avenue . . . American

FOOD	DECOR	SERVICE	COST
25	26	24	$76

E 60s | 100 E. 63rd St. (bet. Lexington & Park Aves.) | 212-644-1900 | www.parkavenyc.com

"Variety" is the name of the game at this "ingenious" Eastsider where the menu, decor and even the name "change with the season"; its "civilized" crowd commends the "beautifully presented" New American cuisine, "crisp" service and "knockout", AvroKO-designed settings, taking the "ritzy" price tags in stride.

Park Side ◗ Italian

FOOD	DECOR	SERVICE	COST
24	19	21	$49

Corona | 107-01 Corona Ave. (bet. 51st Ave. & 108th St.) | Queens | 718-271-9321 | www.parksiderestaurantny.com

"Big crowds" are a "testament" to this "tried-and-true" Corona red-sauce specialist famed for its "terrific" Italian food, "tuxedoed waiters" and "bada-bing" mood; the "old-school" digs are "comfortable", there's "valet parking" and the "price is right", but reserve "months ahead" – it's mighty "popular."

Parlor Steakhouse Steak

FOOD	DECOR	SERVICE	COST
21	20	20	$62

E 90s | 1600 Third Ave. (90th St.) | 212-423-5888 | www.parlorsteakhouse.com

"Desperately needed" in the "frontier land" of Carnegie Hill, this "good all-around" steakhouse lures "adults" with "choice" chops, "well-prepared" seafood and an "attractive" milieu; "beauty pageant"-worthy barkeeps keep the bar "perpetually jammed" and help distract from tabs that are "pricey for the 'hood."

Parma Italian

FOOD	DECOR	SERVICE	COST
22	14	21	$60

E 70s | 1404 Third Ave. (bet. 79th & 80th Sts.) | 212-535-3520

A "remnant of another time", this "clubby" UES Northern Italian vet dishes out "traditional" grub that's "not the most adventurous" yet "as consistent as can be"; ignore the "dated" decor and rather "expensive" pricing: the welcome is "warm" and the waiters' accents "charming."

Pascalou French

FOOD	DECOR	SERVICE	COST
21	15	19	$45

E 90s | 1308 Madison Ave. (bet. 92nd & 93rd Sts.) | 212-534-7522

"Cozy's an understatement" at this "tiny" UES duplex where "size-four" types savor "well-prepared" Gallic food and penny-pinchers marvel over the "reasonable" early-bird deals; it's "quieter" upstairs, but wherever you sit, service is "relaxed" and the mood *très charmant.*

Pasha Turkish

FOOD	DECOR	SERVICE	COST
21	19	21	$44

W 70s | 70 W. 71st St. (bet. Columbus Ave. & CPW) | 212-579-8751 | www.pashanewyork.com

Importing "Istanbul" to the UWS, this "complete Turkish experience" features a "flavorful" menu served in a "striking" skylit dining room; "well-meaning" staffers and good "bang for the buck" evoke "pashanate" responses, while proximity to Lincoln Center ices the cake.

Pasquale's Rigoletto Italian

FOOD	DECOR	SERVICE	COST
21	18	20	$45

Fordham | 2311 Arthur Ave. (Crescent Ave.) | Bronx | 718-365-6644

"Arthur Avenue charm abounds" at this "really old-world" Italian where "abundant" portions of "tasty" food is served by a "pleasant"

	FOOD	DECOR	SERVICE	COST

crew in a setting recalling a "wedding with the Sopranos"; it's particularly popular "post–Yankee games" and on Saturday nights when
there's "live music."

Pastis ● *French* · 21 · 21 · 18 · $51

Meatpacking | 9 Ninth Ave. (Little W. 12th St.) | 212-929-4844 |
www.pastisny.com

Keith McNally's "trailblazer" brings a "Left-Bank-on-the-Hudson experience" to Meatpacking land with "terrific" French bistro standards,
"postcard-perfect" old-Paris decor and a "well-heeled, high-heeled"
crowd; despite "harried" service, "long" waits to be seated and
"deafening" noise, the "teeming" crowds tell the story; P.S. breakfast
is "more subdued."

Pastrami Queen *Deli/Kosher* · 22 · 6 · 14 · $26

E 70s | 1125 Lexington Ave. (bet. 78th & 79th Sts.) | 212-734-1500 |
www.pastramiqueen.com

"Lean, perfectly salted" pastrami, "huge sandwiches" and matzo balls
"like bubbe used to make" beckon at this "old-fashioned" UES kosher
deli; just "don't look for decor" and "don't plan on lingering" – it's "es-
sentially for takeout" since there's barely "room to swing a cat" here.

Patricia's *Italian* · 24 · 17 · 22 · $35

Morris Park | 1082 Morris Park Ave. (bet. Haight & Lurting Aves.) |
Bronx | 718-409-9069 | www.patriciasnyc.com

This Bronx Italian in Morris Park earns kudos for its "out-of-this-world
pizza" (the "wood-burning oven makes a difference") and "hearty"
mains offered in "huge portions"; recently expanded and "newly decorated", it "looks good" though some report it's gotten "more expensive."

Patroon ⊠ *American* · 23 · 21 · 23 · $69

E 40s | 160 E. 46th St. (bet. Lexington & 3rd Aves.) | 212-883-7373 |
www.patroonrestaurant.com

"Geared to gentlemen", Ken Aretsky's "classy" East Side bastion of
"high-powered" business dining features "perfectly prepared" New
Americana served in a "clubby", "photograph"-lined space by staffers
who "know their stuff"; best on an "expense account", it also boasts a
"splendid rooftop bar" and "excellent" private dining rooms.

Patsy's *Italian* · 22 · 18 · 21 · $57

W 50s | 236 W. 56th St. (bet. B'way & 8th Ave.) | 212-247-3491 |
www.patsys.com

It's like "culinary time travel" at this Midtown Neapolitan "throwback", renowned as a "Sinatra" hangout back in the day and still dispensing the same "hearty" "red-sauce" dishes; the "old-time" waiters
and "decades-old" decor are "part of the mystique", and if "some of
the luster has been lost", its fan base hasn't noticed.

Patsy's Pizzeria *Pizza* · 20 · 13 · 16 · $27

Chelsea | 318 W. 23rd St. (bet. 8th & 9th Aves.) | 646-486-7400
NEW E 60s | 1279 First Ave. (69th St.) | 212-639-1000
E 60s | 206 E. 60th St. (bet. 2nd & 3rd Aves.) | 212-688-9707
G Village | 67 University Pl. (bet. 10th & 11th Sts.) | 212-533-3500
Harlem | 2287-91 First Ave. (bet. 117th & 118th Sts.) | 212-534-9783 🖘
Murray Hill | 509 Third Ave. (bet. 34th & 35th Sts.) | 212-689-7500 ●
(continued)

(continued)

Patsy's Pizzeria

W 70s | 61 W. 74th St. (bet. Columbus Ave. & CPW) |
212-579-3000
www.patsyspizzeriany.com

Those experiencing "pizza nostalgia" tout the circa-1933 East Harlem
flagship of this pizzeria chainlet known for its "old-school" mien, "generous salads" and some of the "best thin-crust" pies around; the "convenient", separately owned spin-offs are equally "real-deal", though
decor and service are strictly "low-fuss."

Paul & Jimmy's *Italian*

21 | 17 | 23 | $46

Gramercy | 123 E. 18th St. (bet. Irving Pl. & Park Ave. S.) | 212-475-9540 |
www.paulandjimmys.com

"Old-school fun" is in store at this circa-1950 Italian "fixture" in
Gramercy touted for its "real red-sauce" cooking, "expert" service and
"homey" ambiance suitable for "quiet conversation"; the "price is right"
too, notably the three-course prix fixes offered for lunch and dinner.

Peacefood Café *Kosher/Vegan/Vegetarian*

22 | 17 | 18 | $25

W 80s | 460 Amsterdam Ave. (82nd St.) | 212-362-2266 |
www.peacefoodcafe.com

"Nonmilitant vegans" patronize this "sunny" UWS joint where the
"happy" mood is reflected in the "wholesome" eats and "modest"
tabs; too bad about the "distracted" service, but its crunchy crowd
concurs it's a "fabulous everyday" option.

Peaches *Southern*

∇ 23 | 17 | 21 | $29

Bed-Stuy | 393 Lewis Ave. (bet. Decatur & MacDonough Sts.) | Brooklyn |
718-942-4162 | www.peachesbrooklyn.com

Peaches HotHouse Ⓜ *Southern*

Bed-Stuy | 415 Tompkins Ave. (Hancock St.) | Brooklyn | 718-483-9111 |
www.peacheshothouse.com

"Friendly waitresses" and "cozy" digs set the "down-home" mood at
this "off-the-beaten-path" Bed-Stuy twosome known for "consistently
good" Southern vittles and "great-value" tabs; regulars report "they
aren't kidding" about the spicy chicken's heat.

Peanut Butter & Co. *Sandwiches*

22 | 14 | 18 | $16

G Village | 240 Sullivan St. (bet. Bleecker & W. 3rd Sts.) | 212-677-3995 |
www.ilovepeanutbutter.com

Grown-ups "relive their childhood" at this "kid-friendly", wallet-
friendly Village "hole-in-the-wall" where the "sticky" "gimmick" is
"yummy" peanut butter, served in every kind of sandwich imaginable
("try the Elvis"); given the small setup, hard-core types get the "artisan" spreads to go and "mimic the experience" at home.

❑ Pearl Oyster Bar 🅢 *Seafood*

26 | 15 | 19 | $48

W Village | 18 Cornelia St. (bet. Bleecker & W. 4th Sts.) | 212-691-8211 |
www.pearloysterbar.com

Rebecca Charles' "real-deal New England" seafooder brings "Maine"
to the West Village with a "benchmark" lobster roll and fish so "pristine" that some think there's a "secret dock in the back"; ok, the "no-
rez" policy leads to "long lines", but there's consensus that this "fish
shack extraordinaire" is "still the champ."

	FOOD	DECOR	SERVICE	COST

Pearl Room *Seafood*

23 | **21** | **22** | **$52**

Bay Ridge | 8201 Third Ave. (82nd St.) | Brooklyn | 718-833-6666 | www.thepearlroom.com

"Fantastic fish", "pretty decor" and "wonderful service" – "everything comes together" at this "lovely" Bay Ridge seafooder that's just the ticket for "date night" or a "special event"; maybe you'll have to "spend that little extra", but then again it's considered to be "one of the best" in these parts.

Peasant Ⓜ *Italian*

24 | **22** | **20** | **$60**

NoLita | 194 Elizabeth St. (bet. Prince & Spring Sts.) | 212-965-9511 | www.peasantnyc.com

Perfumed by the "smell of burning wood" that fires its brick oven, this "romantic" NoLita Italian is known for "inventive, atypical" cooking that's catnip for "nonpretentious foodies"; the "understated", candlelit room (and its "grottolike" basement wine bar) oozes so much "rustic" charm that no one minds prices that "no peasant could afford."

Peels ⓿ *American*

20 | **22** | **18** | **$39**

E Village | 325 Bowery (2nd St.) | 646-602-7015 | www.peelsnyc.com

The "coolness factor" is the thing at this American "breath of fresh air on the Bowery" where the Freemans team dispenses a "dressed up", Southern-accented menu in a "bright white" bi-level setting; its "hipster" following finds the "shabby country chic" decor "aesthetically pleasing", though service and portion sizes get mixed marks.

Peking Duck House *Chinese*

23 | **14** | **18** | **$43**

Chinatown | 28 Mott St. (bet. Mosco & Pell Sts.) | 212-227-1810
E 50s | 236 E. 53rd St. (bet. 2nd & 3rd Aves.) | 212-759-8260
www.pekingduckhousenyc.com

"All it's quacked up to be", the eponymous signature dish at this "throwback" Chinese duo is "carved with surgical precision" tableside and overshadows the rest of the "so-so" menu; tabs are "reasonable" at both branches, though C-town's "BYO policy" makes for an especially "good deal."

Pellegrino's *Italian*

23 | **19** | **24** | **$48**

Little Italy | 138 Mulberry St. (bet. Grand & Hester Sts.) | 212-226-3177

Both "locals and tourists" feel like *paesani* at this "upscale" Little Italy "standout" that "exudes hospitality" and delivers "superb" "classic Italian" via an "accommodating", tuxedo-clad staff; tabs are "not cheap" but "enjoying the crowd" from a sidewalk perch is gratis.

Penelope *American*

21 | **18** | **18** | **$27**

Murray Hill | 159 Lexington Ave. (30th St.) | 212-481-3800 | www.penelopenyc.com

"Cute and girlie", this "popular" Murray Hill New American exudes the "quaint charm" of a "summer cottage" and offers an "updated" comfort-food menu ferried by a "sweet if flighty" crew; most folks "go for the buzz", which reaches its peak during the "fabulous" weekend brunch.

Pepe Giallo To Go *Italian*

19 | **11** | **17** | **$24**

Chelsea | 253 10th Ave. (bet. 24th & 25th Sts.) | 212-242-6055 | www.peperossotogo.com

(continued)

(continued)

Pepe Rosso Caffe *Italian*
E 40s | Grand Central | lower level (42nd St. & Vanderbilt Ave.) |
212-867-6054 | www.peperossotogo.com

Pepe Rosso To Go *Italian*
SoHo | 149 Sullivan St. (bet. Houston & Prince Sts.) | 212-677-4555 |
www.peperossotogo.com

Pepe Verde To Go *Italian*
W Village | 559 Hudson St. (bet. Perry & W. 11th Sts.) |
212-255-2221

Turning out "tasty" "home-cooked" Italian eats, this "casual" mini-chain is a "decent" fallback for panini- and pasta-philes "when funds are low"; "average service" and decor one "step above a cafeteria" make "takeout best" – unless you snag a table in the "delightful garden" at the Chelsea branch.

Z Pepolino *Italian*   26 | 19 | 24 | $55
TriBeCa | 281 W. Broadway (bet. Canal & Lispenard Sts.) | 212-966-9983 |
www.pepolino.com

One of TriBeCa's few "undiscovered treasures", this Northern Italian "standout" serves a "flawlessly executed" menu in an "out-of-the-way" location; indeed, fans say the cooking's so "brilliant" that the rather "old-fashioned" ambiance and "pricey" tariffs don't matter.

Pera *Mediterranean*   21 | 21 | 19 | $51
E 40s | 303 Madison Ave. (bet. 41st & 42nd Sts.) | 212-878-6301 |
www.peranyc.com

Convenience to Grand Central lures the "business" trade to this "steady" Midtown Med, a "pleasant" "change of pace" supplying "solid" Turkish-accented grub; an "upscale", "modern" mien and an after-work bar scene augment its "great vibe", while "prix fixe deals" help counteract the otherwise "high prices."

Perbacco ◗ *Italian*   25 | 17 | 21 | $50
E Village | 234 E. Fourth St. (bet. Aves. A & B) | 212-253-2038 |
www.perbacconyc.com

"Inventive without being crazy", this East Village Italian is known for its "imaginative" twists on traditional dishes; trade-offs include digs that are a "bit too cozy" and tabs a tad too "pricey", but most agree on its overall "unique" quality; P.S. a recent chef change puts its Food score in question.

Peri Ela *Turkish*   19 | 15 | 19 | $42
E 90s | 1361 Lexington Ave. (bet. 90th & 91st Sts.) | 212-410-4300 |
www.periela.com

"Authentic without being a parody" – i.e. no belly-dancing – this "tiny" Turk in Carnegie Hill rolls out a "simple" menu on which the "mezes outshine the entrees"; affordability and proximity to the 92nd Street Y make the "tight squeeze" more bearable.

Z Perilla *American*   26 | 20 | 24 | $59
W Village | 9 Jones St. (bet. Bleecker & W. 4th Sts.) | 212-929-6868 |
www.perillanyc.com

"*Top Chef* winner" Harold Dieterle prepares "unassuming haute cuisine" at this West Village American "triumph" where the "minimal" decor puts

| | FOOD | DECOR | SERVICE | COST |

the spotlight on the "delicious art on the plate"; service is "efficient", the mood "cozy" and the tabs "modest for the caliber" of cooking.

Periyali *Greek*

| 24 | 21 | 23 | $59 |

Flatiron | 35 W. 20th St. (bet. 5th & 6th Aves.) | 212-463-7890 | www.periyali.com

Now celebrating its 25th anniversary, this "chic Greek" in the Flatiron remains as "satisfying as ever" thanks to "superlative" seafood, "bend-over-backwards" service and a "serene" setting; sure, a "hefty" bill is part of the package, but this "adult" place also provides that rarest of Manhattan experiences, the ability to "talk with one's companions – and actually hear them."

Per Lei ◐ *Italian*

| 20 | 18 | 19 | $55 |

E 70s | 1347 Second Ave. (71st St.) | 212-439-9200 | www.perleinyc.com

"*La vita è bella*" at this "busy", "sceney" UES Italian where it's "always a party" thanks to an "attractive" "Euro crowd", "playful" staffers and "consistently good" food; party-poopers cite "killer noise", a "glorified singles bar" vibe and upscale prices.

☑ Perry St. *American*

| 26 | 25 | 24 | $69 |

W Village | 176 Perry St. (West St.) | 212-352-1900 | www.jean-georges.com

"Secluded" in the Way West Village, this "splendid" New American is a "serene oasis" showcasing the "complex" cooking of Jean-Georges Vongerichten (whose son, Cedric, runs the kitchen); the "quiet", "very adult" experience is a soigné mix of "smooth" service, "totally cool" customers and a "romantically minimalistic" Richard Meier–designed room; yes, it's "expensive", but the $28 prix fixe lunch is a bargain.

☑ Per Se *American/French*

| 28 | 28 | 29 | $325 |

W 60s | Time Warner Ctr. | 10 Columbus Circle, 4th fl. (60th St. at B'way) | 212-823-9335 | www.perseny.com

"Fine dining" is alive and well at Thomas Keller's "otherworldly" aerie in the Time Warner Center, a "destination restaurant if there ever was one", featuring "wonderfully orchestrated" French–New American meals; granted, the $295 prix fixe charge strikes some as "outlandish", but à la carte small plates are available in the salon, and there are the added perks of "classic" Central Park views and "second-to-none" service (fittingly rated No. 1 in this Survey); it's a "lengthy experience", but not that expensive on an hourly basis.

Persephone ⌧ *Greek*

| 22 | 20 | 22 | $55 |

E 60s | 115 E. 60th St. (bet. Lexington & Park Aves.) | 212-339-8363 | www.persephoneny.com

"High-end" "white-tablecloth" dining is yours at this "understated" Midtown Greek, a "best-kept secret" near the "craziness of Bloomingdale's"; "delicious" cooking, "kind" service and "sane" decibels all earn praise, but nitpickers shrug it's "not as good as its sister, Periyali", and almost as expensive.

Persepolis *Persian*

| 22 | 17 | 21 | $42 |

E 70s | 1407 Second Ave. (bet. 73rd & 74th Sts.) | 212-535-1100 | www.persepolisnyc.com

Its signature sour cherry rice is "reason enough to visit", but this "cut-above" UES Persian also lures "adventurous" types with "copious"

| | FOOD | DECOR | SERVICE | COST |

servings of "exotic" Iranian food; "friendly" service, a spare, "low-key" setting and "reasonable" tabs make it worth dodging the "Second Avenue subway construction" zone outside.

Petaluma *Italian*
19 | 17 | 20 | $48

E 70s | 1356 First Ave. (73rd St.) | 212-772-8800 | www.petalumarestaurant.com

An "updated menu" and "redone" digs (perhaps not yet reflected in the ratings) enliven this "been-in-the-neighborhood-forever" Italian that draws a cross-section of locals, "AARP" types and the "Sotheby's" crowd; though some yawn "not memorable", regulars retort it's "greatly improved" – "you could do a lot worse and you probably have."

☑ Peter Luger Steak House ☞ *Steak*
28 | 16 | 20 | $79

Williamsburg | 178 Broadway (Driggs Ave.) | Brooklyn | 718-387-7400 | www.peterluger.com

A charter member of the "Zagat Hall of Fame", this "essential" Williamsburg "beef bastion" – voted NYC's Top Steakhouse for the 28th year in a row – is renowned for its signature "gold-standard" porterhouse, "superlative" sides and "righteous" burgers; sure, the "steaks are as aged as the waiters" (but fortunately "not as tough") and the "too bright", German tavern–style room is "less than exciting", though nonetheless it's "packed shoulder-to-shoulder every night"; "bring wads of cash" – it doesn't accept plastic.

Pete's Tavern ● *Pub Food*
15 | 17 | 17 | $33

Gramercy | 129 E. 18th St. (Irving Pl.) | 212-473-7676 | www.petestavern.com

Not quite "as old as the Bible", this Gramercy Park "landmark" plies suds, "satisfying burgers" and "unremarkable" bar food in an "aged" tavern setting once haunted by O. Henry; "people-watching at the sidewalk tables" is a plus, ditto the "reasonable prices."

Petite Abeille *Belgian*
19 | 15 | 17 | $31

Flatiron | 44 W. 17th St. (bet. 5th & 6th Aves.) | 212-727-2989
Gramercy | 401 E. 20th St. (1st Ave.) | 212-727-1505
TriBeCa | 134 W. Broadway (bet. Duane & Thomas Sts.) | 212-791-1360
W Village | 466 Hudson St. (Barrow St.) | 212-741-6479 ☞
www.petiteabeille.com

"Terrific" moules frites collide with a "phenomenal" beer selection at this "economical" Belgian mini-chain where the "not-fancy" rooms are done up with "Tintin comic-book" decor; "haphazard" service comes with the petite territory.

Petite Crevette ☞ *Seafood*
▽ 24 | 16 | 20 | $41

Carroll Gardens | 144 Union St. (enter on Hicks St., bet. President & Union Sts.) | Brooklyn | 718-855-2632

Fish "cooked to perfection" is the lure at this "quirky" Carroll Gardens seafooder with a "rustic", "homey" mien; BYO and cash-only policies keep prices "low" while "friendly" staffers keep the energy level high, leaving a "small" setting and "close tables" as the only downsides.

Petrarca Vino e Cucina ● *Italian*
▽ 23 | 21 | 22 | $47

TriBeCa | 34 White St. (Church St.) | 212-625-2800 | www.petrarcatribeca.com

Despite "inventive" Italian cuisine matched by a "huge wine list", this "family-run" TriBeCa "sleeper" somehow remains "under the radar";

	FOOD	DECOR	SERVICE	COST

locals laud its "comfortable" setting and "hospitable" service – it would be a force to be reckoned with "in any other city."

Petrossian *Continental/French* | 24 | 25 | 24 | $77 |

W 50s | 182 W. 58th St. (7th Ave.) | 212-245-2214 | www.petrossian.com

"De-luxe" is the word on this "civilized" French-Continental near Carnegie Hall, where a "magnificent deco" setting, "soft-spoken" service and "luxurious" cuisine (think "caviar and all the trimmings") make patrons "feel like a million bucks"; however, if you're not "made of money", prix fixe "steals" and the next-door cafe are good options.

Philip Marie ●Ⓜ *American* | 20 | 18 | 20 | $44 |

W Village | 569 Hudson St. (W. 11th St.) | 212-242-6200 | www.philipmarie.com

A "typical Village place", this "popular" New American offers "not original but always delicious" dishes "of the comfort variety" in "comfortable" digs; critics say it has "pretensions of being something greater than it is", but ultimately "right-price" tariffs keep the trade brisk.

Philippe ● *Chinese* | 23 | 20 | 20 | $70 |

E 60s | 33 E. 60th St. (bet. Madison & Park Aves.) | 212-644-8885 | www.philippechow.com

"Celebrities", "gold diggers" and "need-to-be-seen" types mix with regular mortals at this "sexy" East Side "Mr. Chow clone" serving "surprisingly good" Chinese food in a "fancy", "jackhammer-loud" space; bargain-hunters sidestep the "extremely expensive" tabs by showing up for the $20 prix fixe lunch, but dissenters declare that neither the food or prices are Chinese – "only Barnum could explain why this place is a success."

Pho Bang ⊭ *Vietnamese* | 21 | 6 | 12 | $15 |

Little Italy | 157 Mott St. (bet. Broome & Grand Sts.) | 212-966-3797

Elmhurst | 82-90 Broadway (Elmhurst Ave.) | Queens | 718-205-1500

Flushing | 41-07 Kissena Blvd. (Main St.) | Queens | 718-939-5520

It's all about bang pho your buck at this "authentic" Vietnamese trio where the "super-tasty" signature soup is catnip for pho-natics; "grungy" looks and "gruff" waiters don't matter when prices that "defy the economic downturn" allow you to "order lots and share."

Phoenix Garden ⊭ *Chinese* | 23 | 9 | 15 | $32 |

Murray Hill | 242 E. 40th St. (bet. 2nd & 3rd Aves.) | 212-983-6666 | www.thephoenixgarden.com

Think "Chinatown uptown" to get the gist of this Murray Hill Cantonese BYO serving a "classic", "dream"-worthy menu touted for its "fantastic" salt and pepper shrimp; true, "it ain't much to look at", service is "curt" and the no-plastic policy perplexes, but you sure "can't beat the price."

Pho Viet Huong *Vietnamese* | 22 | 9 | 15 | $20 |

Chinatown | 73 Mulberry St. (bet. Bayard & Canal Sts.) | 212-233-8988 | www.phoviethuongnyc.com

The "only good part of jury duty", this Chinatown Vietnamese near the courts features "about 6,000 things on the menu", starting with some particularly "phenomenal pho"; regulars "overlook the service" and "cheesy" decor, mesmerized by the "miraculously small" tabs and big flavors.

	FOOD	DECOR	SERVICE	COST

Piccola Venezia *Italian* | 26 | 17 | 24 | $58 |

Astoria | 42-01 28th Ave. (42nd St.) | Queens | 718-721-8470 | www.piccola-venezia.com

"Just ask" and "they'll make any dish, any way you like it" at this "have-it-your-way" Astoria Italian where the cooking's "exceptional", the tuxedo-clad servers "professional" and the decor "so retro, it's fun"; alright, it's "costly" for Queens yet is "always full", because this "old classic never gets old."

Piccolo Angolo Ⓜ *Italian* | 26 | 13 | 21 | $45 |

W Village | 621 Hudson St. (Jane St.) | 212-229-9177 | www.piccoloangolo.com

"Colorful owner" Renato Migliorini oversees the "vibrant" scene at this Northern Italian "party" place that's the "worst best-kept secret" in the West Village; the "delectable" dishes are "served with pride" in "mamma mia!"–size portions, but the seating's "thisclose", so "reservations are a must" – "unless you like standing in line."

Ⓩ Picholine *French/Mediterranean* | 27 | 25 | 26 | $99 |

W 60s | 35 W. 64th St. (bet. B'way & CPW) | 212-724-8585 | www.picholinenyc.com

"Exquisite is the word" for Terrance Brennan's "elegantly restrained" "escape" near Lincoln Center, where "brilliant" French-Med cuisine capped by an "unparalleled" cheese course is enhanced by "perfect" service and "peaceful" surroundings; tabs that are "slightly cheaper than a trip to Paris" lend it "special-occasion" status, though "normal folk can live like kings" just sampling the "snacks at the bar"; P.S. check out the private rooms.

Picnic Market & Café *French* | 21 | 13 | 19 | $40 |

W 100s | 2665 Broadway (bet. 101st & 102nd Sts.) | 212-222-8222 | www.picnicmarket.com

Serving "swell" standards for breakfast and lunch, and Alsatian specialties at the dinner hour, this "unassuming" UWS French bistro attracts a "loyal local following" willing to overlook "tight" dimensions and "inconsistent" service; "reasonable" rates, sidewalk seats and "prepared foods to go" complete the "impressive" picture.

NEW Pier 9 *Seafood* ▽ | 23 | 24 | 22 | $45 |

W 50s | 802 Ninth Ave. (bet. 53rd & 54th Sts.) | 212-262-1299 | www.pier9nyc.com

Addressing the "dearth of good seafood in Hell's Kitchen", this "excellent" newcomer offers fish served "every imaginable way" (i.e. "lobster hot dogs") in a "cool", "cruise line"-ish setting; "personable" staffers and fair fares keep the experience "shipshape."

Pies-n-Thighs ◐⇪ *Soul Food* | 23 | 12 | 17 | $21 |

Williamsburg | 166 S. Fourth St. (Driggs Ave.) | Brooklyn | 347-529-6090 | www.piesnthighs.com

"Outstanding fried chicken" and "super-fluffy biscuits" are "washed down with pie" at this "casual" Williamsburg soul food "contender" that draws hordes of "hipsters" to its "kitschy", "rough-hewn" digs;

dirt-cheap tabs compensate for the "long lines", "unhappy" staffers and cash-only rule.

Pietro's 🗷 *Italian/Steak*

24 | 14 | 23 | $67

E 40s | 232 E. 43rd St. (bet. 2nd & 3rd Aves.) | 212-682-9760 | www.pietros.com

"Reassuringly traditional", this "turn-back-the-clock" perennial near Grand Central has been serving "unbeatable" steaks and "reliable" Italian standards since 1932; too bad about the "tired" decor, but the "old-style" service is "gallant" and regulars say it "fits like an old shoe."

Pigalle ● *French*

18 | 18 | 18 | $40

W 40s | Hilton Garden Inn | 790 Eighth Ave. (48th St.) | 212-489-2233 | www.pigallenyc.com

The setting's "thoroughly Paris" at this "handy" Theater District French brasserie providing "better-than-average" food and service designed to "get you in and out quickly"; *bien sûr*, it's "touristy", but tabs are "modest" and it offers "three meals a day."

Pig Heaven ● *Chinese*

20 | 14 | 19 | $39

E 80s | 1540 Second Ave. (bet. 80th & 81st Sts.) | 212-744-4333

Living up to its name, this longtime UES Chinese rolls out an "all-things-pig" menu highlighted by "to-die-for" spareribs; though the "kitschy" porcine decor is getting "worn", hostess Nancy Lee is as "charming" as ever and the "prices won't gouge you."

Ping's Seafood *Chinese/Seafood*

22 | 12 | 16 | $29

Chinatown | 22 Mott St. (bet. Chatham Sq. & Mosco St.) | 212-602-9988
Elmhurst | 83-02 Queens Blvd. (Goldsmith St.) | Queens | 718-396-1238 | www.pingsnyc.com

Hong Kong–style seafood "with zing" meets the "art of dim sum" at these "cheap", "packed-to-the-gills" Chinese seafooders that are particularly "wild scenes" for Sunday brunch; since "English is useless", fans order by "pointing."

Pink Tea Cup *Soul Food/Southern*

19 | 14 | 17 | $36

W Village | 88 Seventh Ave. S. (bet. Barrow & Grove Sts.) | 212-255-2124 | www.thepinkteacuprestaurant.com

"All the old favorites" are dished out at this "nostalgia"-inducing soul fooder, now in its third incarnation on Seventh Avenue South; it's more upscale these days, with "spiffed-up" digs, "higher prices" and occasional "live music", but it's just as "fattening" as ever.

Pinocchio 🅼 *Italian*

23 | 17 | 24 | $47

E 90s | 1748 First Ave. (bet. 90th & 91st Sts.) | 212-828-5810

A "neighborhood" joint that's "a cut above" the norm, this Upper East Side Italian delivers "delicious" dishes, "fair" tabs and "genial" staffers overseen by a "personable" owner; you may have to "take a deep breath" to wiggle into the "narrow little" setting, but regulars still "return again and again."

Pintaile's Pizza *Pizza*

20 | 6 | 14 | $16

E 80s | 1573 York Ave. (bet. 83rd & 84th Sts.) | 212-396-3479 | www.pintailespizza.com

Pizza partisans searching for a "healthy alternative" cite this "unique" Upper Eastsider dispensing pies with "wafer-thin" whole-wheat crusts topped with "clever" ingredients; what with the "sardine-can" dimensions and lack of decor, it's best for "takeout."

Pio Pio *Peruvian*
22 | 13 | 17 | $27

E 90s | 1746 First Ave. (bet. 90th & 91st Sts.) | 212-426-5800
Murray Hill | 210 E. 34th St. (bet. 2nd & 3rd Aves.) | 212-481-0034
W 40s | 604 10th Ave. (bet. 43rd & 44th Sts.) | 212-459-2929
W 90s | 702 Amsterdam Ave. (94th St.) | 212-665-3000
Mott Haven | 264 Cypress Ave. (bet. 138th & 139th Sts.) | Bronx | 718-401-3300
Jackson Heights | 84-02 Northern Blvd. (bet. 84th & 85th Sts.) | Queens | 718-426-4900
Rego Park | 62-30 Woodhaven Blvd. (62nd Rd.) | Queens | 718-458-0606
www.piopionyc.com

"Delish" rotisserie chicken slathered with "fiery green sauce" is the main event at these "popular" Peruvians supplying lots of grub for "little" dough; apart from the "spacious" Jackson Heights outlet, they're "noisy", "cheek-by-jowl" affairs, like a backstreet in Lima.

Pipa *Spanish*
21 | 24 | 18 | $44

Flatiron | ABC Carpet & Home | 38 E. 19th St. (bet. B'way & Park Ave. S.) | 212-677-2233

"Loads of fun", this "vibrant" Flatiron Spaniard is also a "sexy" option for "terrific tapas" lubricated with a "pitcher of sangria"; overhead "chandeliers with price tags" mesmerize "shoppers" in the crowd, and distract from the "indifferent" service.

Pisticci *Italian*
24 | 18 | 21 | $37

W 100s | 125 La Salle St. (B'way) | 212-932-3500 | www.pisticcinyc.com
"Nifty neighborhood noshing" thrills "Columbia" types at this brick-lined Italian near Grant's Tomb; praised as "inexpensive", "cheerful" and "cozy", it also offers "free Sunday night jazz" that makes the "no-reservations" policy easier to swallow.

NEW PizzArte *Pizza*
- | - | - | M

W 50s | 69 W. 55th St. (bet. 5th & 6th Aves.) | 212-247-3936 | www.pizzarteny.com
Considering that both the chef and the wood-fired oven hail from Naples, you can expect truly authentic pizzas at this midpriced Midtown duplex that ups the ante with other traditional Italian dishes; its sleek, white-on-white setting also doubles as a functioning art gallery.

☑ P.J. Clarke's *Pub Food*
17 | 16 | 17 | $38

E 50s | 915 Third Ave. (55th St.) | 212-317-1616
P.J. Clarke's at Lincoln Square ● *Pub Food*
W 60s | 44 W. 63rd St. (Columbus Ave.) | 212-957-9700
P.J. Clarke's on the Hudson *Pub Food*
Financial District | 4 World Financial Ctr. (Vesey St.) | 212-285-1500
www.pjclarkes.com

NY saloons don't get more "classic" than this 1884 Midtown pub famed for its "perfectly cooked" burgers, "convivial" crowd and a cameo in that "Ray Milland" movie; the spin-offs don't "ring as true" as the original, but the Lincoln Center outlet is "convenient" for culture vultures and the FiDi branch boasts "yacht basin" views.

	FOOD	DECOR	SERVICE	COST

Place, The *American/Mediterranean*   ▽ 25 | 25 | 23 | $49

W Village | 310 W. Fourth St. (bet. Bank & 12th Sts.) | 212-924-2711 |
www.theplaceny.com

Just the place for a "great date", this "well-established" West Villager
has the "comfort factor" down pat with "cozy", fireplace-equipped
digs, "wonderful" Med–New American food and "personable" service;
seating "thisclose" seems to be the sole hitch, but none of the "romantic" couples seem to mind.

Plaza Food Hall *Eclectic*   22 | 21 | 18 | $41

W 50s | Plaza Hotel | 1 W. 59th St., lower level (5th Ave.) | 212-986-9260 |
www.theplazafoodhall.com

"Dining at the bar" gets a new spin via Todd English's "upscale food
court" in the Plaza's lower level, where patrons grab counter seats and
order from a "quality" Eclectic menu running the gamut from grilled
and raw items to sushi, pasta and beyond; like "Eataly on a smaller
scale", one can "eat inexpensively or extravagantly" here.

Plein Sud *French*   20 | 20 | 18 | $53

TriBeCa | Smyth Hotel | 85 W. Broadway (bet. Chambers & Warren Sts.) |
212-204-5555 | www.pleinsudnyc.com

After a "rocky start", this wannabe-"trendy" brasserie in TriBeCa's
Smyth Hotel has found a "formula that works", dispensing "tasty"
French standards in a "cool" AvroKO-designed setting channeling
the South of France; despite a "not-so-sexy" corner address, it's
a "comfortable" option.

Pó *Italian*   25 | 18 | 22 | $52

W Village | 31 Cornelia St. (bet. Bleecker & W. 4th Sts.) | 212-645-2189 |
www.porestaurant.com

"So tiny yet so fine", this "high-energy" Italian has been "in the Village
for ages" yet still "packs a wallop" with "simply fab" food ferried by
"friendly" folk; despite the "snug" quarters, it's "easy to become a regular here" given the "fair" prices.

Poke ⊠⇗ *Japanese*   25 | 14 | 18 | $42

E 80s | 343 E. 85th St. (bet. 1st & 2nd Aves.) | 212-249-0569

"Damn good" sushi and "out-of-this-world" rolls keep this "no-frills"
UES Japanese "crowded" in spite of an "unassuming" setting and service that "could be better"; it takes neither reservations nor plastic,
but the BYO policy helps tabs stay "reasonable."

Pomaire *Chilean*   20 | 17 | 21 | $48

W 40s | 371 W. 46th St. (bet. 8th & 9th Aves.) | 212-956-3056 |
www.pomairenyc.com

"Something different" for Restaurant Row, this Chilean "surprise"
knocks out "unique", "flavorful" food paired with potent pisco sours;
an "intimate" vibe and "excellent" $25 prix fixe are additional pluses,
while "gracious" service seals the deal.

Pomodoro Rosso *Italian*   21 | 17 | 22 | $44

W 70s | 229 Columbus Ave. (bet. 70th & 71st Sts.) | 212-721-3009 |
www.pomodororossonyc.com

"Simple", "tasty" home cooking and "genial" atmospherics make this
"old-school" Italian near Lincoln Center a quintessential "neighbor-

hood staple"; the only catch is a no-reservations policy that "makes pre-theater dining a bit iffy."

Pongal *Indian/Kosher/Vegetarian* ∇ 22 14 18 $27

Murray Hill | 110 Lexington Ave. (bet. 27th & 28th Sts.) | 212-696-9458 | www.pongalnyc.com

Offering a menu with "many choices", this Curry Hill "dosa heaven" specializes in "authentically spiced" South Indian kosher-vegetarian eats that are "consistently" satisfying; "no-frills" service and "narrow" dimensions are offset by refreshingly "cheap" prices.

Pongsri Thai *Thai* 21 13 17 $29

Chelsea | 165 W. 23rd St. (bet. 6th & 7th Aves.) | 212-645-8808
Chinatown | 106 Bayard St. (Baxter St.) | 212-349-3132
W 40s | 244 W. 48th St. (bet. B'way & 8th Ave.) | 212-582-3392
www.pongsri.com

"Tangy" Thai dishes "prepared to order and fine-tuned for spiciness" are yours at this "reliable" trio that's "long on flavor and short on price"; given decor and service that "leaves a lot to be desired", many go the "take-out" route.

Ponte's *Italian* 25 22 23 $65
(fka F.illi Ponte)

TriBeCa | 39 Desbrosses St. (bet. Washington & West Sts.) | 212-226-4621 | www.filliponte.com

As far west as you can go without swimming in the Hudson, this circa-1967 TriBeCa Italian (fka F.illi Ponte) offers "old-fashioned goodness" extending to the "excellent" food, "attentive" service and "classic" decor; "high prices" lead some to reserve it for "special occasions", but "romantic" sunset views make any event special.

Ponticello *Italian* ∇ 24 20 23 $46

Astoria | 46-11 Broadway (bet. 46th & 47th Sts.) | Queens | 718-278-4514 | www.ponticelloristorante.com

"Way above average", this 30-year-old Astoria Northern Italian is known for its "delicious, time-honored" recipes and "semi-glitzy" digs tended by "career waiters"; it's "on the expensive side for where it is", but worth it, especially if you reserve the private wine-cellar room.

Ponty Bistro ● *African/French* 23 17 22 $44

Gramercy | 218 Third Ave. (bet. 18th & 19th Sts.) | 212-777-1616 | www.pontybistro.com

Something "different" for Gramercy Park, this "undiscovered" French-Senegalese features "original", "culturally diverse" cuisine jazzed up with "interesting" African spices; the "small" space "isn't so stylish", but service is "polite" and the tabs "approachable" – especially that "bargain" $19 prix fixe.

Pop Burger ● *Burgers* 17 13 13 $19

E 50s | 14 E. 58th St. (bet. 5th & Madison Aves.) | 212-991-6644
Meatpacking | 58-60 Ninth Ave. (bet. 14th & 15th Sts.) | 212-414-8686
Pop Pub ● *Burgers*
NEW G Village | 83 University Pl. (bet. 11th & 12th Sts.) | 212-477-7574
www.popburger.com

"Good but not outstanding" burgers turn up at this self-service mini-chain dispensing "slider-size" patties in "minimalist", Warholadorned settings where "inexpensive" tabs and "loud music" are constants; the new Village branch offers more extensive eats along with wine and beer.

Popover Cafe *American*

	19	13	17	$29

W 80s | 551 Amsterdam Ave. (bet. 86th & 87th Sts.) | 212-595-8555 | www.popovercafe.com

Big surprise, "popovers are the star" at this "been-around-forever", circa-1981 Upper West Side American; the "kitschy" decor is "a bit faded", service can be "hit-or-miss" and weekend "stroller" gridlock leads habitués to vow "never on Sunday", yet lots of locals label it "lovable."

Porchetta *Italian*

	24	9	17	$18

E Village | 110 E. Seventh St. (bet. Ave. A & 1st Ave.) | 212-777-2151 | www.porchettanyc.com

Chef Sara Jenkins "does one thing and does it well" at this East Village Italian, namely "crazy-good" pork, "roasted to perfection" and served as a sandwich or a platter accompanied by "tasty" sides; since the "cramped", "hole-in-the-wall" space has only six stools, most grab this "glorious" food deal to go.

NEW Porsena *Italian*

	22	16	20	$48

E Village | 21 E. Seventh St. (bet. 2nd & 3rd Aves.) | 212-228-4923 | www.porsena.com

"Simple tasty pastas" are the forte of this new East Village trattoria from Sara Jenkins, where the "lip-smacking-good", "reasonably priced" cooking is "worth blowing your Weight Watchers points"; a "very downtown" vibe draws a crowd of "hip young" things.

Porter House New York *Steak*

	24	24	24	$81

W 60s | Time Warner Ctr. | 10 Columbus Circle, 4th fl. (60th St. at B'way) | 212-823-9500 | www.porterhousenewyork.com

"Everything a steakhouse should be without the macho posing", chef Michael Lomonaco's "luxurious" TWC chop shop "has it down", from the "perfectly cooked" steaks and "courteous" staffers to the "handsome" setting with a Central Park view that's "worthy of the food"; sure, it'll cost you, but an experience this "civilized" is "worth every dime" and more.

Portofino *Italian/Seafood*

	▽ 21	20	20	$48

City Island | 555 City Island Ave. (Cross St.) | Bronx | 718-885-1220 | www.portofinocityisland.com

Whether for an "intimate celebration" or an "informal night out", this "popular" Italian fills the bill with "good" seafood-focused eats and "helpful" service; perhaps it's "a little pricey" for City Island, but the "romantic" open-air deck offers harbor views at no charge.

Post House *Steak*

	24	21	23	$75

E 60s | Lowell Hotel | 28 E. 63rd St. (bet. Madison & Park Aves.) | 212-935-2888 | www.theposthouse.com

"Brooks Brothers devotees" and "clubby" Upper Eastsiders populate this "old-school" steakhouse celebrated for its "high-quality" chops, "female-friendly" service and "classic" Americana-themed decor; it all adds up to "splendid" dining, and though expensive, you certainly "get what you pay for."

	FOOD	DECOR	SERVICE	COST

Posto *Pizza*

24 | 15 | 18 | $27

Gramercy | 310 Second Ave. (18th St.) | 212-716-1200 |
www.postothincrust.com

"Ultrathin" crusts with "delicate" toppings make for one "sexy" pizza
pie at this "hopping" Gramercy joint where insiders say the "must"-
have item is the "Shroomtown" version; "indifferent" service and "little elbow room" may make takeout the "best solution."

Press 195 *Sandwiches*

22 | 14 | 18 | $21

Park Slope | 195 Fifth Ave. (bet. Berkeley Pl. & Union St.) | Brooklyn |
718-857-1950
Bayside | 40-11 Bell Blvd. (bet. 40th & 41st Aves.) | Queens | 718-281-1950
www.press195.com

"Delicious things" are "pressed between delicious breads" at these
"tiny" panini purveyors in Bayside and Park Slope; "out-of-this-world"
fries, "inexpensive" costs and "great gardens" are compensation for
the "takes-forever" service.

Pret A Manger *Sandwiches*

18 | 11 | 16 | $14

E 40s | 205 E. 42nd St. (bet. 2nd & 3rd Aves.) | 212-867-1905
E 40s | 287 Madison Ave. (bet. 40th & 41st Sts.) | 212-867-0400 ⓢ
E 50s | 400 Park Ave. (bet. 54th & 55th Sts.) | 212-207-4101 ⓢ
E 50s | 630 Lexington Ave. (bet. 54th & 55th Sts.) | 646-497-0510 ⓢ
Financial District | 60 Broad St. (Beaver St.) | 212-825-8825 ⓢ
Garment District | 530 Seventh Ave. (bet. 38th & 39th Sts.) |
646-728-0750 ⓢ
W 40s | 11 W. 42nd St. (bet. 5th & 6th Aves.) | 212-997-5520
W 40s | 30 Rockefeller Plaza, concourse level (bet. 49th & 50th Sts.) |
212-246-6944 ⓢ
W 50s | 135 W. 50th St. (bet. 6th & 7th Aves.) | 212-489-6458 ⓢ
W 50s | 1350 Sixth Ave. (enter on 55th St., bet. 5th & 6th Aves.) |
212-307-6100 ⓢ
www.pret.com
Additional locations throughout the NY area

This "easy-breezy", London-bred chain offers "nicely packaged", "pre-
made" sandwiches and salads in the "tastiest combinations"; "chip-
per" staffers get you in and out "fast", and "bless their hearts", the
"leftovers are donated to charity" – in fact, when you pay the bill you
may think you're the charity.

Prime Grill *Kosher/Steak*

23 | 19 | 19 | $74

E 40s | 60 E. 49th St. (bet. Madison & Park Aves.) | 212-692-9292 |
www.theprimegrill.com

Prime KO *Kosher/Steak*

W 80s | 217 W. 85th St. (bet. Amsterdam Ave. & B'way) | 212-496-1888 |
www.primehospitalityny.com

"Impressive" cuts of meat and "surprisingly good sushi" are "blessed
by a higher authority" at these "top-notch" kosher steakhouses that
some call "the standard" of the genre; *oy vey*, the pricing's "astronomical", yet its observant clientele feels they're "worth every shekel."

Primehouse New York *Steak*

24 | 23 | 23 | $70

Murray Hill | 381 Park Ave. S. (27th St.) | 212-824-2600 |
www.primehousenyc.com

"Carnivores" commend the "cavernous" interior of this BR Guest steakhouse in Murray Hill, citing its "trendy", "not typical" design with "lots

of space between tables"; the "dry-aged" beef is "scrumptious" (ditto the "tableside" Caesar) and service is "on-point", making the premium pricing its prime deficit.

Prime Meats ◐ *American*   24 | 21 | 21 | $51

Carroll Gardens | 465 Court St. (Luquer St.) | Brooklyn | 718-254-0327 | www.frankspm.com

Another "quality" effort from the Frankies Spuntino folks, this Carroll Gardens exercise in "hipster chic" purveys "outstanding" New Americana with a "Teutonic" accent, served by a "suspender"-clad crew in a "speakeasy"-ish setting ("bring your fedora"); despite "no reservations" and "not-cheap" tabs, "there's always a crowd" waiting to get in.

Primola ◐ *Italian*   22 | 16 | 19 | $66

E 60s | 1226 Second Ave. (bet. 64th & 65th Sts.) | 212-758-1775

Everything's "better if they know you" at this UES Italian where "regulars", "limo passengers" and "Woody Allen" get the "royal treatment", while nobodies are relegated to "seats in the back"; still, the pasta is "tasty" ("despite the price") and it's always "fun to watch the show."

Print *American*   25 | 24 | 24 | $62

W 40s | Ink48 Hotel | 653 11th Ave. (bet. 47th & 48th Sts.) | 212-757-2224 | www.printrestaurant.com

Located so far west, "you could be in Cleveland", this Hell's Kitchen New American is "worth the expedition" for its "straightforward, locally sourced" cooking, "solid" service and "chic", David Rockwell-designed room; there's also applause for its "low noise levels" and "awesome rooftop bar", perfect for after-dinner drinks.

Provence en Boite *Bakery/French*   20 | 18 | 18 | $35

Carroll Gardens | 263 Smith St. (Degraw St.) | Brooklyn | 718-797-0707 | www.provenceenboite.com

A "touch of France" in Carroll Gardens, this "enjoyable" French bakery-cum-bistro "smells like the real thing" and puts out three squares a day, ranging from "just-like-Paris" croissants to "excellent" steak frites; "friendly" service from the husband-and-wife owners makes you feel like you're in Provence.

Prune *American*   25 | 16 | 20 | $54

E Village | 54 E. First St. (bet. 1st & 2nd Aves.) | 212-677-6221 | www.prunerestaurant.com

"Even harder to get into" now that chef "Gabrielle Hamilton's book is out", this East Village phenom draws crowds with "superbly simple" New Americana that's "as delicious as promised"; "exceptionally tight" digs and "long" waits don't stop folks from queuing up for its "legendary" weekend brunch.

NEW PSbklyn *American*   - | - | - | M

Park Slope | 833 Union St. (bet. 6th & 7th Aves.) | Brooklyn | 718-398-5474 | www.psbklyn.com

"Child-friendly" is putting it mildly at this Park Slope newcomer with "television screens everywhere" and a basement stocked with arcade games; the "affordable" American comfort-food menu could be "a little more adventurous", but then again the grub is secondary to the Chuck E. Cheese–like scene.

Public *Eclectic* | 24 | 24 | 22 | $61

NoLita | 210 Elizabeth St. (bet. Prince & Spring Sts.) | 212-343-7011 | www.public-nyc.com

Oozing "downtown chic", this "cool" NoLita Eclectic is designed by the AvroKO team to resemble a "retro library" and features an "adventurous", meat-centric menu with "Aussie-Kiwi" flair (think kangaroo, Tasmanian sea trout); a "hip crowd" and "attitude"-free service from "model-like" staffers round out the overall "impressive" experience.

Pukk ● *Thai/Vegetarian* | ▽ 23 | 17 | 20 | $22

E Village | 71 First Ave. (bet. 4th & 5th Sts.) | 212-253-2742 | www.pukknyc.com

"Memorable" Thai vegetarian cooking pleases "omnis and herbivores alike" at this "small" East Villager with "big ambitions"; while its futuristic, white-tiled setting divides voters, there's agreement on the "unbelievable bargain" tabs and that way "cool lavatory."

Pulino's ● *Pizza* | 19 | 18 | 18 | $39

NoLita | 282 Bowery (E. Houston St.) | 212-226-1966 | www.pulinosny.com
To get the gist of the "hopping" scene at Keith McNally's "crowd-pleasing" Bowery pizzeria, think "tasty" pizzas plus a "much-vaunted" breakfast pie served in the owner's "signature atmosphere" (i.e. subway tile, bottles galore); "pleasant" service is also in place, along with "louder-than-Times-Square" decibels.

Pure Food & Wine *Vegan/Vegetarian* | 23 | 21 | 21 | $54

Gramercy | 54 Irving Pl. (bet. 17th & 18th Sts.) | 212-477-1010 | www.purefoodandwine.com
"Totally unique" and "entirely satisfying", this "ingenious" Gramercy Parker serves "haute" vegan cuisine that's so "delectable" you'll "totally forget it's raw"; a "delightful garden" lends some "romantic" flair to the proceedings, though purists protest the "raw-deal" pricing and "precious" mindset.

NEW **Pure Thai Shophouse** *Thai* | ▽ 24 | 19 | 21 | $23

W 50s | 766 Ninth Ave. (bet. 51st & 52nd Sts.) | 212-581-0999 | www.purethaishophouse.com
"Handmade noodles" available in soup form or tossed with "delicate" ingredients are the specialty of this "authentic" new Hell's Kitchen Thai; you can also expect a "minuscule", canteen-esque setting, "friendly prices" and a "warm welcome and farewell."

Purple Yam *Asian* | 21 | 18 | 21 | $34

Ditmas Park | 1314 Cortelyou Rd. (bet. Argyle & Rugby Rds.) | Brooklyn | 718-940-8188 | www.purpleyamnyc.com
"Damn good" Pan-Asian cooking with a pronounced Filipino accent draws diners to this "popular" Ditmas Parker set on an "up-and-coming" food corridor; service is "efficient", the tabs as small as the setting.

Puttanesca *Italian* | 19 | 16 | 18 | $42

W 50s | 859 Ninth Ave. (56th St.) | 212-581-4177 | www.puttanesca.com
Dispensing "perfectly acceptable" red-gravy grub, this "straightforward" Hell's Kitchen Italian is just right for "rapid" pre-theater dining before Lincoln Center; though too "noisy" for some, it's "decently priced" with a "get-your-money's-worth", all-you-can-drink brunch.

	FOOD	DECOR	SERVICE	COST

☑ Pylos ● *Greek*
26 | 23 | 21 | $50

E Village | 128 E. Seventh St. (bet. Ave. A & 1st Ave.) | 212-473-0220 | www.pylosrestaurant.com

There's a "bumping" scene going on at this "lively", "lovely" East Village Hellenic where "clay pots adorn the ceiling" and "exceptional" Greek food fills the plates; the "narrow" setting makes for a "tight squeeze", but payoffs include "amiable service" and "reasonable prices for what they provide"; P.S. the "appetizers are a better bet than the entrees."

Qi *Asian*
∇ 20 | 21 | 17 | $26

Union Sq | 31 W. 14th St. (bet. 5th & 6th Aves.) | 212-929-9917

Qi Bangkok Eatery *Thai*
NEW **W 40s** | 675 Eighth Ave. (43rd St.) | 212-247-8991 | www.qirestaurant.com

The macrobiotic-leaning Thai, Indian and Vietnamese dishes "really work" (and are "incredibly affordable") at this Union Square Asian, where the "beautiful" decor is a match for the Taoist/Hindu philosophy of healthy dining; at the spacious new Times Square outlet, they offer an equally affordable Bangkok-inspired menu from chef Pichet Ong.

Quaint *American*
∇ 22 | 21 | 23 | $34

Sunnyside | 46-10 Skillman Ave. (bet. 46th & 47th Sts.) | Queens | 917-779-9220 | www.quaintnyc.com

"Satisfying", modestly priced New American entrees and "terrific seasonal specials" fill out the "limited menu" at this Sunnyside "neighborhood standby" where "friendly" service, a "pretty" back garden and a "homey", "name-says-it-all" setting add up to "dependable" dining.

Quality Meats *American/Steak*
24 | 23 | 22 | $76

W 50s | 57 W. 58th St. (bet. 5th & 6th Aves.) | 212-371-7777 | www.qualitymeatsnyc.com

Expect an appropriately "quality experience" at this "hip", Stillman family-run Midtown steakhouse famed for its "powerhouse" porterhouse and "standout" homemade ice cream; faux-butcher shop decor – a mix of "bricks and meat hooks" – lends a "trendy" air, though the "not-cheap" pricing is on par with the genre; P.S. a Bowery spin-off is in the works.

Quantum Leap *Health Food/Vegetarian*
21 | 12 | 17 | $22

E Village | 203 First Ave. (bet. 12th & 13th Sts.) | 212-673-9848 | www.quantumleapeastvillage.com
G Village | 226 Thompson St. (bet. Bleecker & W. 3rd Sts.) | 212-677-8050 | www.quantumleapwestvillage.com

"Quite the variety" of "tasty" vegetarian eats (along with "satisfying fish dishes") makes these crosstown Village health-fooders a "favorite" of the "crunchy" crowd; "cheap" costs compensate for the "ho-hum decor" and "lackadaisical service."

Quatorze Bis *French*
21 | 18 | 21 | $62

E 70s | 323 E. 79th St. (bet. 1st & 2nd Aves.) | 212-535-1414

Genuine "Gallic charm" pervades this "evening-in-Paris" boîte in the "UES arrondissement", where regulars of a certain age tuck into "uncomplicated" bistro classics delivered by a "personable staff"; *oui*, it's "costly", but steadfast followers say it's also *merveilleux.*"

Quattro Gastronomia Italiana ● *Italian* ▽ 23 | 24 | 24 | $67

FOOD | DECOR | SERVICE | COST

Hudson Square | Trump SoHo Hotel | 246 Spring St. (bet. 6th Ave. & Varick St.) | 212-842-4500 | www.quattronewyork.com

"Luxury dining in a luxury hotel" sums up the scene at this "outstanding" Hudson Square Northern Italian, an offshoot of a South Beach original; "delicious" food that's "true to its roots", "well-orchestrated" service and a "stylish", multilevel setting make the "pricey" tabs more palatable.

Quattro Gatti *Italian* 21 | 17 | 20 | $50

E 80s | 205 E. 81st St. (bet. 2nd & 3rd Aves.) | 212-570-1073

One of those "time-warp" restaurants that transport you to a "more civilized era", this "intimate" Upper East Side Italian dispenses "hearty" red-sauce dishes with "no fuss and no muss"; a "homelike" setting, "unaffected" service and fair enough rates explain why it's been in business since 1985.

Queen *Italian* 24 | 15 | 21 | $47

Brooklyn Heights | 84 Court St. (bet. Livingston & Schermerhorn Sts.) | Brooklyn | 718-596-5955 | www.queenrestaurant.com

After 50-plus years, this "much-loved" Brooklyn Heights "throwback" draws locals and the "Court Street lawyer crowd" with "traditional" Southern Italian food and "congenial" service; despite near "zero decor", it "still fulfills", starting with its "price-is-right" tabs.

Queen of Sheba ● *Ethiopian* ▽ 22 | 13 | 15 | $29

W 40s | 650 10th Ave. (bet. 45th & 46th Sts.) | 212-397-0610 | www.shebanyc.com

NY's "diverse ethnic restaurant scene" is embodied at this "singular" Hell's Kitchen Ethiopian featuring "no silverware" but plenty of "wonderful finger food" scooped up with spongy injera bread; "interesting" vegetarian options and "recession"-worthy rates distract from the "cramped" setting and "sluggish" service.

Quercy *French* 21 | 15 | 20 | $41

Cobble Hill | 242 Court St. (bet. Baltic & Kane Sts.) | Brooklyn | 718-243-2151

One of Cobble Hill's "best-kept secrets", this "comfortable" La Lunchonette sibling doles out "pleasant" country French cooking in "low-key" environs; despite "moderate" tabs and "personable" service, it's "surprisingly not busy" and easy to access sans reservations.

Rack & Soul *BBQ/Southern* 22 | 12 | 18 | $28

W 100s | 258 W. 109th St. (B'way) | 212-222-4800 | www.rackandsoul.com

"Huge portions" make "an appetite and a doggy bag" de rigueur at this "real-deal" Columbia-area Southerner where the BBQ is "falling-off-the-bone tender" and the sides "down-home good"; "scattershot" service and a "shacklike" setting make the case for "takeout."

Radegast Hall ● *European* 18 | 20 | 15 | $26

Williamsburg | 113 N. Third St. (Berry St.) | Brooklyn | 718-963-3973 | www.radegasthall.com

While "not quite Bavaria", this Williamsburg beer garden does a good impersonation with "fab" tap brews and European eats served in "industrial" digs outfitted with picnic tables and a retractable roof; despite "inconsistent" service and a "frat-party" vibe, it can be a "helluva lot of fun" for a cheap price.

Rai Rai Ken ●⇄ Noodle Shop

22 | 12 | 17 | $16

E Village | 214 E. 10th St. (bet. 1st & 2nd Aves.) | 212-477-7030

"Cheap", "comforting" ramen is served at the counter of this East Village "impersonation of a Tokyo noodle bar"; though it's a "hole-in-the-wall" with "uncomfortable" seating and a cash-only rule, fans say the "fast" service and "nourishing" chow "get the job done."

Ramen Setagaya Noodle Shop

18 | 10 | 16 | $17

E Village | 34A St. Marks Pl. (bet. 2nd & 3rd Aves.) | 212-387-7959

"Steaming bowls" of "hot, delicious" ramen are the lure at this "easygoing" East Village Japanese import; dirt-cheap pricing trumps the "small" setting and "no-frills" decor.

Rao's ☒⇄ Italian

23 | 16 | 22 | $77

Harlem | 455 E. 114th St. (Pleasant Ave.) | 212-722-6709 | www.raos.com

"Harder to get into than Skull and Bones", Frank Pellegrino's East Harlem "bucket-list" candidate is "worth whatever groveling you must do" to savor its "melt-in-your-mouth" Italian cooking and rub elbows with all those A-list celebs; since it's "impossible to get a reservation" before 3011, mere mortals "buy the cookbook" and their bottled red sauce, or check out the Vegas spin-off.

Raoul's ● French

24 | 21 | 22 | $62

SoHo | 180 Prince St. (bet. Sullivan & Thompson Sts.) | 212-966-3518 | www.raouls.com

"Quintessential" French bistro meets "SoHo chic" at this "timeless icon", a bastion of "hip" since 1975 thanks to "terrific food", "up-to-snuff" service and a "transporting" back garden accessed via the kitchen; ok, it's "loud" and a bit "pricey", but given the "very cool" vibe, who cares?

Rare Bar & Grill Burgers

21 | 17 | 18 | $32

Chelsea | Fashion 26 Hotel | 152 W. 26th St. (bet. 6th & 7th Aves.) | 212-807-7273

Murray Hill | Shelburne Murray Hill Hotel | 303 Lexington Ave. (37th St.) | 212-481-1999

www.rarebarandgrill.com

"Upscale burgers" and an "amazing french fry sampler" draw "young" folks to these "popular" patty palaces; the Chelsea outpost is more "stylish" (and spacious) than the Murray Hill original, but both share "hip" rooftop bars with "beautiful city views" that make waiting to be served seem pleasant.

Ravagh Persian

22 | 14 | 19 | $31

E 60s | 1237 First Ave. (bet. 66th & 67th Sts.) | 212-861-7900

Murray Hill | 11 E. 30th St. (bet. 5th & Madison Aves.) | 212-696-0300 | www.ravaghmidtown.com

"Multiculti" types frequent these "unpretentious" East Side Persians for "delicious" kebabs, cherry rice and other moderately "exotic" dishes; pluses include "accommodating" service and "fair prices", and if the "nondescript" settings are an issue, they're "good delivery options."

Rayuela *Pan-Latin*
23 | 24 | 21 | $60

LES | 165 Allen St. (bet. Rivington & Stanton Sts.) | 212-253-8840 | www.rayuelanyc.com

"Decidedly different", this "vibrant" Lower Eastsider dispenses "free-style" Pan-Latin dishes lubricated with "clever cocktails"; "helpful" service, "soft lighting" and a "conversation-piece" live olive tree enhance the "seductive" setting, but "costs can add up."

Real Madrid *Spanish*
▽ 24 | 16 | 22 | $42

Mariners Harbor | 2075 Forest Ave. (Union Ave.) | Staten Island | 718-447-7885 | www.realmadrid-restaurant.com

Staten Island's Mariners Harbor is home to this longtime Spaniard, named after the Spanish *fútbol* club and famed for "terrific" cooking, notably a "can't-beat-it-with-a-stick" two-for-one lobster deal; the decor may be "outdated", but it's "always packed" given the "huge portions", fair prices and a staff that "knows how to treat you."

Recette ● *American*
24 | 18 | 20 | $64

W Village | 328 W. 12th St. (Greenwich St.) | 212-414-3000 | www.recettenyc.com

"Inspired" New American plates are served at this "trendy" West Villager where the menu features "toothsome", "complex" dishes in "seriously small portions"; despite "expensive" tabs, "tight" dimensions and "deafening" decibels, surveyors say it's "what NY dining is all about."

Recipe *American*
24 | 17 | 21 | $43

W 80s | 452 Amsterdam Ave. (bet. 81st & 82nd Sts.) | 212-501-7755 | www.recipenyc.com

UWS "foodies in the know" flock to this New American "recipe for success" where the "fabulous", farm-to-table menu is "passionately prepared"; the "dinky", 26-seat setting makes "conversation with neighboring tables inevitable", but so what – the prices are "affordable."

Red Cat *American/Mediterranean*
24 | 19 | 22 | $57

Chelsea | 227 10th Ave. (bet. 23rd & 24th Sts.) | 212-242-1122 | www.theredcat.com

Simply the "cat's meow", this "bustling" Chelsea "institution" offers "exceptional" Med–New American dining that's catnip for "gallery gallivanters" and other smart types who like "eating well"; a "comfortable", "arty" atmosphere and "bend-over-backwards" service temper the slightly "expensive" tabs.

Red Egg *Chinese*
20 | 16 | 18 | $31

Little Italy | 202 Centre St. (Howard St.) | 212-966-1123 | www.redeggnyc.com

"Up a notch" from the typical dim sum experience, this "gentrified" Little Italy Chinese turns out "elevated" morsels that are "cooked to order" rather than "carted around"; "young, hip" staffers oversee the "modern", "nightclub"-esque room, without threatening your budget.

Redeye Grill ● *American/Seafood*
20 | 19 | 20 | $56

W 50s | 890 Seventh Ave. (56th St.) | 212-541-9000 | www.redeyegrill.com

An "exceptional variety" of New American fare, especially seafood, arrives in an "airy", "big-barn" setting at this "popular" nexus for "sightseers", Midtown "business-lunchers" and "Carnegie

Hall"–goers; despite the frequent "hubbub", service is "swift" and the pricing "reasonable."

NEW RedFarm ● Chinese | - | - | - | M |

W Village | 529 Hudson St. (bet. Charles & W. 10th Sts.) | 212-792-9700 | www.redfarmnyc.com

Restaurateur Ed Schoenfeld and chef Joe Ng (Chinatown Brasserie) reunite at this new West Villager that brings the locavore concept to Chinese cooking along with some particularly notable dim sum; the rustic barn of a room features exposed wooden beams, whitewashed walls, communal tables and a few booths; menus and utensils hang from exposed pipes.

Redhead, The ● American | 23 | 16 | 19 | $39 |

E Village | 349 E. 13th St. (bet. 1st & 2nd Aves.) | 212-533-6212 | www.theredheadnyc.com

East Village "cool" cats convene at this "unpretentious" New American for "fabulous fried chicken" and other "heartfelt", "Southern-flavored" eats; service is "friendly" (if "not polished"), and though the "tiny", "visually underwhelming" digs "fill up quickly", most agree it's "worth the squeeze."

Red Hook Lobster Pound Ⓜ Seafood | 24 | 9 | 17 | $23 |

Red Hook | 284 Van Brunt St. (bet. Verona St. & Visitation Pl.) | Brooklyn | 646-326-7650 | www.redhooklobsterpound.com

"Perfect" lobster rolls in both Maine (cold) and Connecticut (warm) versions are the draw at this way "out-of-the-way" Red Hook sea-fooder; the "less-than-basic" ambiance is "more picnic than dining", but the "prices are good" and the food's like "Kennebunkport without the driving."

Ⓩ NEW Red Rooster American/Southern | 21 | 23 | 21 | $53 |

Harlem | 310 Lenox Ave. (W. 125th St.) | 212-792-9001 | www.redroosterharlem.com

Marcus Samuelsson is the mind behind this "hip" Harlem "ground-breaker", an "inspired", "über-popular" New American that mixes Swedish meatballs with "down-home" Southern standards; the room's way "stylish", the crowd "diverse" and the service "well meaning", yet a few sigh it's "celeb chef hype" and warn that "unless your name is Obama", it may be tough getting a table.

Regency American | ∇ 19 | 23 | 21 | $69 |

E 60s | Loews Regency Hotel | 540 Park Ave. (61st St.) | 212-339-4050 | www.loewshotels.com

Breakfasting business and political bigwigs who "want to be seen" have come to this UES Tisch dining room in the Regency Hotel for so long that it has come to define the "power breakfast"; the New American food and service are "reliable", the ambiance comfortable and after dark, it morphs into Feinstein's cabaret, a supper club lubricated with bottles of "bubbly."

Regional Italian | 21 | 16 | 19 | $38 |

W 90s | 2607 Broadway (bet. 98th & 99th Sts.) | 212-666-1915 | www.regionalnyc.com

"Not your standard neighborhood joint", this "informal" Upper Westsider and its "cheerful" crew take you on a "Travel Channel-worthy" tour of regional Italian cuisine; "boring" decor to the contrary, "reasonable" rates win the day, especially the "bargain" specials on Monday and Tuesday.

Remi *Italian*

| 22 | 22 | 22 | $61 |

W 50s | 145 W. 53rd St. (bet. 6th & 7th Aves.) | 212-581-4242 | www.remi-ny.com

A "quiet" "class act", this Midtown Italian vet comes across "year after year" for "corporate" types and theatergoers with "elegant" Venetian fare; "pro service" and a "window-lined", "high-ceilinged" space with a "giant mural" of the Grand Canal help justify the "costly" tabs.

Republic *Asian*

| 19 | 14 | 16 | $24 |

Union Sq | 37 Union Sq. W. (bet. 16th & 17th Sts.) | 212-627-7172 | www.thinknoodles.com

"Nourishing" bowls of noodles keep this "longtime" Union Square "hub" mobbed with "twentysomethings" hungry for "low"-dough Asian staples; though the "soulless" decor, "community seating" and "ear-splitting din" can be "uncomfortable", service is "supersonic."

Re Sette *Italian*

| 21 | 17 | 19 | $58 |

W 40s | 7 W. 45th St. (bet. 5th & 6th Aves.) | 212-221-7530 | www.resette.com

Away from the "Times Square hubbub" yet just a "short walk" to the Theater District, this "dependable" Italian satisfies with "well-prepared" Barese regional specialties and "friendly" service; though far from cheap, it's a "favorite for business meals", as well as private parties in the King's Table upstairs.

Resto ◑ *Belgian*

| 20 | 17 | 19 | $45 |

Murray Hill | 111 E. 29th St. (bet. Lexington Ave. & Park Ave. S.) | 212-685-5585 | www.restonyc.com

"Effortlessly hitting all the right notes", this Murray Hill gastropub allows patrons to "eat big" with "killer burgers", moules frites and other "solid" Belgian items paired with "top-notch" Euro suds; it can get "loud" and "rambunctious", but "you can get a table easily."

Rice ⊄ *Eclectic*

| 21 | 16 | 18 | $24 |

NoHo | 292 Elizabeth St. (bet. Bleecker & Houston Sts.) | 212-226-5775 ◑
Dumbo | 81 Washington St. (bet. Front & York Sts.) | Brooklyn | 718-222-9880
www.riceny.com

Varieties of its namesake dish that "you never knew existed" make for "interesting" eating at these "economical", cash-only Eclectic "filling stations"; they're particularly "appetizing" alternatives for a "vegetarian-friendly" bite, with "hippie" service and decor that appeal to some but not to all.

Rice 'n' Beans ◑ *Brazilian*

| 21 | 10 | 19 | $26 |

W 50s | 744 Ninth Ave. (bet. 50th & 51st Sts.) | 212-265-4444 | www.riceandbeansmidtownwest.com

Although "tightly squeezed" into "smaller-than-small" digs, this Hell's Kitchen Brazilian supplies "quick" fixes of "tasty" chow and "lots of it" for "price-is-right" tabs; so long as you "don't care about atmosphere", it's "not half-bad" before a show.

	FOOD	DECOR	SERVICE	COST

Rickshaw Dumpling Bar *Chinese*　　18 | 9 | 15 | $15

NEW E 40s | 459 Lexington Ave. (45th St.) | 212-461-1750
Flatiron | 61 W. 23rd St. (bet. 5th & 6th Aves.) | 212-924-9220
www.rickshawdumplings.com

"Good-quality" dumplings make up the "simple" menu at this "fast-food" Chinese duo (plus a roaming food truck) that "hits the spot" for "utilitarian" dining; still, once the "novelty is gone", "meh"-sayers find the eats "only middling" now that Anita Lo is no longer involved.

Risotteria *Italian*　　21 | 11 | 18 | $29

W Village | 270 Bleecker St. (Morton St.) | 212-924-6664 |
www.risotteria.com

"Gluten-free everything" is the name of the game at this Village Italian "celiac heaven" known for "cooked-to-perfection" risottos and wheat-less pizza that even appeal to those with no "dietary restrictions"; prices are modest, so the "small", decor-free space usually has "every square inch accounted for."

☑ River Café *American*　　26 | 28 | 26 | $130

Dumbo | 1 Water St. (bet. Furman & Old Fulton Sts.) | Brooklyn |
718-522-5200 | www.rivercafe.com

"Million-dollar" views of Lower Manhattan, "lovingly prepared" New American food, "first-class service" and "fragrant flowers" are the draws at Buzzy O'Keeffe's "enchanting" Dumbo water's edge standby; even though the $100 prix fixe–only dinner may be a "splurge", most feel it's a fair price in exchange for experiencing the "essence of romance" or a perfect private party.

NEW Riverpark *American*　　25 | 27 | 24 | $66

Murray Hill | Alexandria Ctr. | 450 E. 29th St. (bet. FDR Dr. & 1st Ave.) |
212-729-9790 | www.riverparknyc.com

It's "so far east" you may need "water wings" to access it, but this "peaceful" newcomer in a Kips Bay "office park behind Bellevue" is a "beacon of civility", offering Tom Colicchio's "delectable" New American cooking and "gracious service" in a "handsome", "airy" room; free "validated parking", an on-site produce garden and "river views" from the outdoor terrace justify the expense.

Riverview ◗ *American*　　20 | 23 | 19 | $58

LIC | 2-01 50th Ave. (enter at Center Blvd. & 49th Ave.) | Queens |
718-392-5000 | www.riverviewny.com

"Out of the way" on the Long Island City waterfront, this roomy New American furnishes "fairly good food" and service in a loungey setting; after dinner, mashers bent on "romance" take a riverside ramble to admire the "picture-postcard view of Manhattan" and take their minds off the bill.

Rizzo's Pizza *Pizza*　　▽ 23 | 9 | 18 | $15

NEW E 90s | 1426 Lexington Ave. (93rd St.) | 212-289-0500
Astoria | 30-13 Steinway St. (bet. 30th & 31st Aves.) | Queens |
718-721-9862
www.rizzosfinepizza.com

Pizza completists in search of a "different kind" of pie opt for the "square" versions vended at this "local" Astoria "institution" known for its "thin crusts and super flavor"; a new Manhattan satellite brings the goods to the UES, but both outlets are low-budget when it comes to decor and cost.

Robataya *Japanese* 　　　　　　　　　　　　▽ 25 | 23 | 23 | $55

E Village | 231 E. Ninth St. (bet. 2nd & 3rd Aves.) | 212-979-9674 | www.robataya-ny.com

"Sitting at the robata counter is a must" at this "cool" East Village Japanese where you can "observe the chefs" preparing "perfectly grilled" specialties while "yelling loudly"; it's "difficult to leave without spending more than you intended", but the show is "worth the price of admission."

Robert ◑ *American* 　　　　　　　　　　　　20 | 26 | 21 | $59

W 50s | Museum of Arts and Design | 2 Columbus Circle, 9th fl. (bet. B'way & 8th Ave.) | 212-299-7730 | www.robertnyc.com

All about its "dazzling views" of Central Park and Columbus Circle, this museum aerie serves "just ok" American food that definitely "tastes better" from a "coveted window seat"; "glam" decor and "pleasant" service make the tabs more tolerable, though savvy sorts settle for sipping drinks in the "appealing" lounge.

☒ Roberta's ◑ *Pizza* 　　　　　　　　　　　26 | 17 | 19 | $34

Bushwick | 261 Moore St. (Bogart St.) | Brooklyn | 718-417-1118 | www.robertaspizza.com

Possibly the "best reason to go to Bushwick", this wood-oven pizza purveyor is celebrated for "gutsy" "artisanal" pies topped with "gorgeous seasonal veggies" plucked from its own roof garden; it's typically "overrun with hipsters", so beware if "you aren't cool enough" – and plan on a "wait" whether you are or aren't.

☒ Roberto ☒ *Italian* 　　　　　　　　　　　27 | 19 | 23 | $56

Fordham | 603 Crescent Ave. (Hughes Ave.) | Bronx | 718-733-9503 | www.roberto089.com

Chef Roberto Paciullo "regularly makes the rounds" at this Bronx "treasure" near Arthur Avenue, a "culinary trip to Salerno" that "stands with the best" for "exceptional" food plated in "generous portions"; "excellent" service and "dark", atmospheric digs make it a "real pleaser", but a "no-rez policy" and fervent "local following" may mean "long waits."

Roc ◑ *Italian* 　　　　　　　　　　　　　　21 | 20 | 21 | $53

TriBeCa | 190A Duane St. (Greenwich St.) | 212-625-3333 | www.rocrestaurant.com

There's "across-the-board quality" in play at this TriBeCa "staple" that rocks a "neighborhood" vibe as a "welcoming" owner and staff deliver "consistently delicious" Italiana in a "comfortable" interior or at "lovely alfresco" tables; granted, it's "not a cheap date", but most "feel totally at home" here.

Rocco *Italian* 　　　　　　　　　　　　　　22 | 16 | 22 | $41

G Village | 181 Thompson St. (bet. Bleecker & Houston Sts.) | 212-677-0590 | www.roccorestaurant.com

Now in its 90th year, this "quintessential" Village trattoria "keeps the quality up" via "affordable" Northern Italiana delivered in a "time-stands-still" setting; "friendly service is a given" – and you'll "still enjoy the dinner after the bill comes."

	FOOD	DECOR	SERVICE	COST

Rock Center Café *American* | 19 | 21 | 19 | $49 |

W 50s | Rockefeller Ctr. | 20 W. 50th St. (bet. 5th & 6th Aves.) |
212-332-7620 | www.patinagroup.com
Overlooking Rock Center's wintertime "skating rink" and "warmer-weather outdoor cafe", this well-situated American "appeals to tourists" and sentimental natives, especially during the "holidays"; the "pricey", "acceptable" chow plays a "secondary" role to the "prime location."

Rocking Horse Cafe *Mexican* | 21 | 17 | 18 | $37 |

Chelsea | 182 Eighth Ave. (bet. 19th & 20th Sts.) | 212-463-9511 |
www.rockinghorsecafe.com
A "favorite Chelsea hangout", this longtime Mexican is ever "reliable" for "solid" cooking, "big margaritas" and a "super" $15 prix fixe brunch; the mood's usually "manic" with folks having a "rocking great time."

Rolf's *German* | 13 | 21 | 15 | $42 |

Gramercy | 281 Third Ave. (22nd St.) | 212-477-4750 | www.rolfsnyc.com
Brace yourself for a "kitsch attack" at this "old-school" Gramercy German where the "dizzying" Oktoberfest and "Christmas wonderland" decorations "wow visitors"; given the "so-so" food and "mediocre service", cynics say this circa-1968 stalwart is simply "coasting."

Roll-n-Roaster ● *Sandwiches* | 21 | 10 | 15 | $16 |

Sheepshead Bay | 2901 Emmons Ave. (bet. Nostrand Ave. & 29th St.) |
Brooklyn | 718-769-5831 | www.rollnroaster.com
It doesn't get more "casual" than this Sheepshead Bay "fixture" that rolls out roast beef sandwiches and "gooey cheez fries" for not much dough; "elegant it ain't", but it's been "going strong" since 1970 "for a reason."

NEW Romera Ⓜ *Eclectic* | - | - | - | VE |

Chelsea | Dream Downtown Hotel | 355 W. 16th St. (bet. 8th & 9th Aves.) |
212-929-5800 | www.romeranewyork.com
Avant-garde, high-concept cooking comes to Chelsea's Dream Hotel via this holistic Eclectic from Barcelona chef-neurologist Miguel Sanchez Romera, which will offer an 11-course 'neurogastronomy' tasting menu eschewing fat and salt in favor of edible flowers and medicinal waters; the operating room–white subterranean setting includes a soothing hanging herb garden and spot-lit table settings, though the $245 prix fixe–only tab is rather heart-stopping.

Room Service ● *Thai* | 20 | 21 | 18 | $31 |

Chelsea | 166 Eighth Ave. (bet. 18th & 19th Sts.) | 212-691-0299
W 40s | 690 Ninth Ave. (bet. 47th & 48th Sts.) | 212-582-0099
"Flashy" decor incorporating "huge chandeliers" has a "young crowd" checking into this "snazzy" Thai twosome where the "flavorful" food arrives at "real-value" tabs; "disco-bar" atmospherics with "loud music layered on top" make them somewhat of a "scene."

Rosa Mexicano *Mexican* | 22 | 21 | 21 | $50 |

E 50s | 1063 First Ave. (58th St.) | 212-753-7407 ●
Flatiron | 9 E. 18th St. (bet. B'way & 5th Ave.) | 212-533-3350
W 60s | 61 Columbus Ave. (62nd St.) | 212-977-7700 ●
www.rosamexicano.com
"Jumping" is the word for this "flashy" Mexican trio that "gets it right" with "flavorful" food and "personable" service; the "mandatory" menu

item is the "sublime" guacamole, while the "atomic" pomegranate margaritas make the "ruckus" and rather "dear" pricing easier to digest.

Rosanjin 🛂 *Japanese*   ∇ 27 | 25 | 28 | $125

TriBeCa | 141 Duane St. (bet. Church St. & W. B'way) | 212-346-0664 | www.rosanjintribeca.com

"Japanese cuisine as ritual" comes to life at this "intimate" TriBeCan where the "unreal" kaiseki dinners are rendered with "architectural artistry"; a "minimalist" mien, "graceful servers in kimonos" and top-of-the-line pricing make for "special" dining you "won't soon forget."

Rose Water *American*   26 | 18 | 23 | $47

Park Slope | 787 Union St. (6th Ave.) | Brooklyn | 718-783-3800 | www.rosewaterrestaurant.com

"Locavore" longings are sated at this petite Park Slope New American whose "cultlike dedication" to "in-season ingredients" yields "superb" dishes served with "zero pretension"; space may be "at a premium", but the eating "always comes up roses", especially at its "must-go brunch."

Rossini's *Italian*   22 | 19 | 23 | $61

Murray Hill | 108 E. 38th St. (bet. Lexington & Park Aves.) | 212-683-0135 | www.rossinisrestaurant.com

The "old-line" style still "works like a charm" at this Murray Hill Northern Italian, a "white-tablecloth" holdover from 1978 with a weekday pianist and a "Saturday night opera singer"; it may be "expensive", but "first-rate" cuisine and "tuxedoed" service make it more than worthwhile.

Rothmann's *Steak*   23 | 20 | 23 | $70

E 50s | 3 E. 54th St. (bet. 5th & Madison Aves.) | 212-319-5500 | www.rothmannssteakhouse.com

Biz lunchers "impress clients" at this Midtown cow palace where "quality" beef, "smooth scotch" and "solicitous" service come with the territory, along with "expense-account" pricing; while it's "less celebrated" than some of its rivals, all those "suits" at the bar ensure "lots of activity."

Rouge Tomate 🛂 *American*   24 | 25 | 23 | $64

E 60s | 10 E. 60th St. (bet. 5th & Madison Aves.) | 646-237-8977 | www.rougetomatenyc.com

"Tony" East Side gals stay "svelte" at this "avant-garde" New American with a "green philosophy" that encourages "guilt-free indulgence"; "small portions at big prices" have some seeing rouge, but "sublime" cooking, "punctilious" service and a "chichi" setting are the rewards.

Rub BBQ *BBQ*   21 | 10 | 17 | $30

Chelsea | 208 W. 23rd St. (bet. 7th & 8th Aves.) | 212-524-4300 | www.rubbbq.net

"Slow-smoked", "super-tasty" Kansas City 'cue comes priced for "value" at this Chelsea BBQ shack where fans disregard the "truck-stop" feel and go early to "get the burnt ends" before they're "sold out"; P.S. the "fried Oreo is a thing of beauty and danger."

🆕 Rubirosa ● *Italian/Pizza*   25 | 18 | 21 | $34

NoLita | 235 Mulberry St. (bet. Prince & Spring Sts.) | 212-965-0500 | www.rubirosanyc.com

Named after '50s playboy Porfirio Rubirosa, this swinging NoLita Italian is touted for its "ambrosia"-like thin-crust pizzas and "delish" pastas, but its "cool" denizens dig its "decent" tabs and "loud music" too; "packed" digs and servers "too hip to be happy" are the main off-notes.

Ruby Foo's Asian
18 | 20 | 18 | $45

W 40s | 1626 Broadway (49th St.) | 212-489-5600 | www.rubyfoos.com
"Kitschy", "kid-friendly" and crammed with "tourists", this "high-energy" Times Square Asian is a "big", "campy" thing done up in "movie-set" Chinoiserie decor; the "mainstream" eats are "not half bad" (the "high-octane" drinks are better), yet sophistos still say "fooey!"

Rue 57 ◑ French
18 | 18 | 18 | $47

W 50s | 60 W. 57th St. (6th Ave.) | 212-307-5656 | www.rue57.com
It "may not be the Left Bank", but this "upbeat" Midtown brasserie is "popular" with "Euro tourists" in the mood for "decent, basic" French food, plus sushi (to meet women here, just "stand still and look straight"); some rue the "spotty" service and "rock-concert" decibels, but it "does the job" for a "moderate" price considering the locale.

Russian Samovar ◑ Continental
20 | 18 | 19 | $53

W 50s | 256 W. 52nd St. (bet. B'way & 8th Ave.) | 212-757-0168 | www.russiansamovar.com
Expats out of "central casting" let the "good times roll" at this Theater District Russian-Continental, an "authentic Muscovite experience" with "reliable" grub washed down with "splendid flavored vodkas"; a nightly pianist distracts from the "worn" decor and "unrefined clientele."

Russian Tea Room Continental
19 | 25 | 21 | $72

W 50s | 150 W. 57th St. (bet. 6th & 7th Aves.) | 212-581-7100 | www.russiantearoomnyc.com
Though nostalgic types miss its "former glory", this Russo-Continental party place to the left of Carnegie Hall is still a "feast for the eyes" with "glitzy" furnishings apropos for a "splurge" on caviar and blini; nyetniks contend the "overpriced", "so-so" eats are "less than revolutionary" and best left to the "tourist trade."

Ruth's Chris Steak House Steak
24 | 21 | 23 | $72

W 50s | 148 W. 51st St. (bet. 6th & 7th Aves.) | 212-245-9600 | www.ruthschris.com
"Sizzling" steaks "drenched in butter" are the signature of this Theater District "morale booster" that's part of the New Orleans–based chain; "uniform quality", "clubby" environs and "civil" service come with the territory, but bring a "wad of cash" or a friend with an expense account.

Rye American
24 | 23 | 22 | $42

Williamsburg | 247 S. First St. (bet. Havemeyer & Roebling Sts.) | Brooklyn | 718-218-8047 | www.ryerestaurant.com
"Bohemian" types travel "back in time" at this "atmospheric" Williamsburg American beloved for its "antique bar" and "old-school" cocktail shaking; the "sophisticated", "seasonal" menu is equally "comforting", so few mind "how easy it is to run up a tab" here.

Sac's Place Pizza
∇ 24 | 16 | 19 | $28

Astoria | 25-41 Broadway (29th St.) | Queens | 718-204-5002 | www.sacsplace.com
While "excellent" pies "straight from the brick oven" put this unassuming Astoria pizzeria on locals' "regular rotation", it also slings "basic

homestyle" Italian items for "decent" dough; though the "family atmo" is "relaxing" enough, the decor (and service) "could use an upgrade."

Sahara Turkish

FOOD	DECOR	SERVICE	COST
23	16	19	$31

Gravesend | 2337 Coney Island Ave. (bet. Aves. T & U) | Brooklyn | 718-376-8594 | www.saharapalace.com

"Well-established" in Gravesend since 1987, this "traditional" Turk "stokes the appetite" with "fine" cooking from an "open grill"; granted, the "large", "impersonal" setting is "hardly fashionable", but few care given "main courses big enough to share" and "excellent" prices.

Sahara's Turkish Cuisine Turkish

22	16	20	$34

Murray Hill | 513 Second Ave. (bet. 28th & 29th Sts.) | 212-532-7589 | www.saharasturkishrestaurant.com

Meze mavens dig into the "wonderful sharing options" at this seldom crowded Murray Hill Turk, a "local charmer" with a "reasonably priced" lineup that makes it "hard to stop eating"; the spare space is strictly "casual", but service is "polite" and "you're never rushed out the door."

Saigon Grill Vietnamese

21	11	16	$27

W 90s | 620 Amsterdam Ave. (90th St.) | 212-875-9072

"Dollar for dollar", this "hugely popular" UWS Vietnamese doles out eats with "major bang", served "faster than McDonald's" in a "hectic", "uncharacteristically spacious" setting; unfortunately, the "ongoing labor disputes" here remain unresolved.

Saju Bistro French

21	20	22	$46

W 40s | Mela Hotel | 120 W. 44th St. (bet. B'way & 6th Ave.) | 212-997-7258 | www.sajubistro.com

"Right in the middle of Times Square", this "real-thing" French bistro offers "well-prepared" Provençal standards along with "quaint" digs and a "welcoming" crew; "reasonable" tariffs and a $28 pre-theater deal have regulars returning for an "encore."

Sakagura Japanese

25	20	22	$54

E 40s | 211 E. 43rd St., downstairs (bet. 2nd & 3rd Aves.) | 212-953-7253 | www.sakagura.com

Like "stepping through a looking glass into Tokyo", this semi-"secret" Japanese izakaya hidden in an "office building basement" near Grand Central pairs "big-wow" small plates with an "encyclopedic sake selection", "minimalist" decor and "excellent" service; just plan to drop a "chunk of change" for all the "authenticity."

Sala Spanish

23	18	18	$41

Flatiron | 35 W. 19th St. (bet. 5th & 6th Aves.) | 212-229-2300 | www.salanyc.com

The tapas are "tasty" and the "sangria works" at this Flatiron Spanish "winner", a "dark", "lively" retreat where the "good times seem infectious"; insiders "go early" to sidestep the "loud crowd", but the "hit-or-miss" service is a constant.

Salaam Bombay Indian

22	17	19	$37

TriBeCa | 319 Greenwich St. (bet. Duane & Reade Sts.) | 212-226-9400 | www.salaambombay.com

Armed with a "solid" traditional menu and a $14 lunch buffet that's "quite lavish", this "veteran" TriBeCa Indian "soldiers on"; the rather "tired" setting is "easy to overlook" given the "well-meaning" service and the possibility of "quiet conversation."

Sala Thai ● *Thai*

| 20 | 14 | 18 | $34 |

E 80s | 1718 Second Ave. (bet. 89th & 90th Sts.) | 212-410-5557
UES denizens dub this 30-year-old Thai a "lasting standby" thanks to its "perfectly adequate" food and service; "not-expensive" tabs compensate for the downscale digs and "unpleasantness of the Second Avenue subway" construction outside.

NEW Salinas ● *Spanish*

| - | - | - | M |

Chelsea | 136 Ninth Ave. (bet. 18th & 19th Sts.) | 212-776-1990 | www.salinasnyc.com
The tapas experience gets a posh twist at this new Chelsea Spaniard where the midpriced, multiregional small plates arrive in swanky, supper club–like digs; an equally lush, all-seasons back garden equipped with a fireplace, water wall and retractable roof seals the deal.

Saltie ⊠⊄ *Sandwiches*

| ▽ 23 | 12 | 14 | $14 |

Williamsburg | 378 Metropolitan Ave. (bet. Havemeyer St. & Marcy Ave.) | Brooklyn | 718-387-4777 | www.saltieny.com
"Terrific sandwiches" and "fresh baked goods" are the come-ons at this Billyburg counter lauded for "creative" (mostly vegetarian) two-handers; it's strictly "grab-and-go" given zero decor and "unfriendly" service.

Salumeria Rosi Parmacotto *Italian*

| 25 | 18 | 20 | $48 |

W 70s | 283 Amsterdam Ave. (bet. 73rd & 74th Sts.) | 212-877-4800 | www.salumeriarosi.com
"Wildly popular and deservedly so", this *"buonissimo"* UWS enoteca/salumeria from chef Cesare Casella "transports you to Italy" with "superior" cured meats, "delightful" Tuscan small plates and "quality" vinos; "fancy" prices and a "tiny" "crammed" space are the trade-offs.

Salute! *Italian*

| 19 | 20 | 17 | $54 |

Murray Hill | 270 Madison Ave. (39th St.) | 212-213-3440 | www.salutenyc.com
"Full of suits at lunchtime", this Murray Hill Italian furnishes quite "good" food in a room that's "more upscale" (and "more pricey") than the neighborhood norm; "doing-you-a-favor" service doesn't keep the "stylish" set away from its "loud", "lively" bar after work.

Sambuca *Italian*

| 19 | 17 | 20 | $41 |

W 70s | 20 W. 72nd St. (bet. Columbus Ave. & CPW) | 212-787-5656 | www.sambucanyc.com
They're "not shy on portion size" at this UWS Italian where the family-style servings ("gluten-free options" included) are suited for "budget-minded" groups that don't mind "pedestrian" decor; like "Carmine's without the hype or the tourists", it has lasted 25 years for a reason.

Sammy's Fishbox ● *Seafood*

| 22 | 16 | 20 | $46 |

City Island | 41 City Island Ave. (Rochelle St.) | Bronx | 718-885-0920 | www.sammysfishbox.com
Ok, "there's nothing gourmet" about it, but "if you love seafood" – and "don't mind crowds" – this circa-1966 City Island "favorite" rolls out "supersize me"-size servings of the standards in "cheesy" environs; no surprise, it may be a "touristy zoo" come warm weather.

Sammy's Roumanian *Jewish*

20 | 9 | 18 | $59

LES | 157 Chrystie St. (Delancey St.) | 212-673-0330

A "sense of humor" and a "healthy liver" are musts before a visit to this "nutty" LES "instant party" where "schmaltzy", "belly-busting" Jewish cooking and "frozen vodka" are served in a "Borscht Belt" basement setting; *oy vey*, it's a "blast", but "don't have a blood test the next day."

Sandro's *Italian*

25 | 15 | 21 | $67

E 80s | 306 E. 81st St. (bet. 1st & 2nd Aves.) | 212-288-7374 | www.sandrosnyc.com

"Splendid" Roman food turns up at this "convivial" UES Italian overseen by "colorful" chef-owner Sandro Fioriti, who wanders the room in "pajama bottoms" and "talks to the customers"; despite "dreary" looks and "lofty" tariffs, fans consider it a "special neighborhood place."

Sanford's ● *American*

▽ 23 | 19 | 20 | $28

Astoria | 30-13 Broadway (bet. 30th & 31st Sts.) | Queens | 718-932-9569 | www.sanfordsnyc.com

This 1922-vintage diner has been "revamped" into a bona fide Astoria "hangout" offering "inspired" New American plates for "moderate" dough, 24/7; it's a "runaway success", particularly on weekends when the "unbeatable" $14 brunch deal is in effect.

ⓩ San Pietro ⑤ *Italian*

26 | 21 | 23 | $87

E 50s | 18 E. 54th St. (bet. 5th & Madison Aves.) | 212-753-9015 | www.sanpietro.net

"Power lunch" comes with a "power check" at this Midtown Southern Italian patronized by "name-brand investment bankers" and other assorted "heavy hitters"; the cuisine's "sublime" and the servers act like the "customer is king", though it may be "cheaper to fly to Italy."

Sant Ambroeus *Italian*

21 | 19 | 20 | $62

E 70s | 1000 Madison Ave. (bet. 77th & 78th Sts.) | 212-570-2211
W Village | 259 W. Fourth St. (Perry St.) | 212-604-9254
www.santambroeus.com

You can hobnob with the "international set" at these "smart" Milanese cafes where "fab" Italian bites arrive in surroundings as "suave" as the clientele; the Uptown outlet is a lunchtime scene for "older", "chichi" locals while the Village branch provides interesting people-watching, but both are "obscenely expensive."

Sapori D'Ischia Ⓜ *Italian*

24 | 17 | 19 | $51

Woodside | 55-15 37th Ave. (56th St.) | Queens | 718-446-1500

Stationed at the "intersection of nothing and nowhere" in "industrial" Woodside, this Italian "deli by day" morphs into a "top-shelf" Neapolitan bistro after dark; "so-so" service, "Manhattan prices" and "hobbyist opera singers" on Thursdays are part of the package.

Sapphire Indian *Indian*

21 | 19 | 20 | $46

W 60s | 1845 Broadway (bet. 60th & 61st Sts.) | 212-245-4444 | www.sapphireny.com

"Fine" Indian food "served with efficiency" in a "civilized" milieu distinguishes this Columbus Circle "alternative" that's a good "pre-Lincoln Center" choice; the "quality" may cost a few "extra bucks", but the "copious" $16 lunch buffet is a "steal."

	FOOD	DECOR	SERVICE	COST

Sarabeth's *American* | 20 | 17 | 18 | $38 |

Chelsea | Chelsea Mkt. | 75 Ninth Ave. (bet. 15th & 16th Sts.) | 212-989-2424 | www.sarabeth.com
E 90s | 1295 Madison Ave. (92nd St.) | 212-410-7335 | www.sarabeth.com
Garment District | Lord & Taylor | 424 Fifth Ave., 5th fl. (bet. 38th & 39th Sts.) | 212-827-5068 | www.sarabeth.com
NEW TriBeCa | 339 Greenwich St. (bet. Harrison & Jay Sts.) | 212-966-0421
W 50s | 40 Central Park S. (bet. 5th & 6th Aves.) | 212-826-5959 | www.sarabethscps.com
W 80s | 423 Amsterdam Ave. (bet. 80th & 81st Sts.) | 212-496-6280 | www.sarabeth.com

The "grande dame of brunch places", this "genteel" American comfort-food mini-chain is also known for its "substantial" breakfasts and "signature tomato soup"; sure, it "takes a while to get a table" at prime times, but at the dinner hour a "quieter", "retirement-home" sensibility prevails.

Saravanaa Bhavan *Indian/Vegetarian* | 24 | 14 | 14 | $22 |

Murray Hill | 81 Lexington Ave. (26th St.) | 212-679-0204
NEW W 70s | 413 Amsterdam Ave. (bet. 79th & 80th Sts.) | 212-721-7755
www.saravanabhavan.com

These "real-thing" Indian links of a national chain channel "Chennai" via "dosas to dream of" and other "outstanding" vegetarian dishes; "excellent" pricing makes up for "stiff" service and "sterile" settings.

Sardi's ⏺Ⓜ *Continental* | 18 | 21 | 20 | $56 |

W 40s | 234 W. 44th St. (bet. B'way & 8th Ave.) | 212-221-8440 | www.sardis.com

"Priceless" caricatures of B'way stars line the walls of this circa-1921 Theater District "warhorse", a magnet for "starstruck" tourists and random "celebs" who like "old-fashioned" Continental fare and vintage waiters; though "past its prime", it's tops for "theatrical history."

Sarge's Deli ⏺ *Deli* | 21 | 9 | 15 | $27 |

Murray Hill | 548 Third Ave. (bet. 36th & 37th Sts.) | 212-679-0442 | www.sargesdeli.com

A "cardiologist's nightmare" since 1964, this 24/7 Murray Hill deli is ever "reliable" for "fairly priced" Jewish "staples", notably "overflowing" corned beef and pastrami sandwiches; "surly" staffers and a "crummy" backdrop cement its "real-deal" rep.

⚡ Sasabune ⓈⓂ *Japanese* | 29 | 12 | 23 | $130 |

E 70s | 401 E. 73rd St. (bet. 1st & York Aves.) | 212-249-8583
Transporting diners "straight to Tokyo", this omakase-only UES sushi specialist offers a "food experience you'll never forget" thanks to chef-owner Kenji Takahashi's "phenomenal" creations; despite "bare-bones" decor and "super-expensive" tabs, it's so "on the money" that it's voted the Top Japanese in town.

⚡ Saul *American* | 27 | 20 | 25 | $69 |

Boerum Hill | 140 Smith St. (bet. Bergen & Dean Sts.) | Brooklyn | 718-935-9844 | www.saulrestaurant.com
Chef-owner Saul Bolton's "inimitable style" is on full display at this Boerum Hill storefront where "carefully crafted" New American dishes "go toe-to-toe" with Brooklyn's best; "spot-on" service and "minimalist" decor make the "Manhattan prices" more bearable.

	FOOD	DECOR	SERVICE	COST

Savoia ⊘ *Italian/Pizza* — 20 | 17 | 19 | $33

Carroll Gardens | 277 Smith St. (bet. Degraw & Sackett Sts.) | Brooklyn | 718-797-2727

"Neighborhood" types hype the "wonderful" Neapolitan-style pizza served at this Carroll Gardens Italian that's also an "easy" option for "solid" pastas and such; the homespun setting is "nothing fancy", but neither are the prices – or the new "cash-only" rule.

Sazon *Puerto Rican* — ▽ 21 | 20 | 20 | $43

TriBeCa | 105 Reade St. (bet. Church St. & W. B'way) | 212-406-1900 | www.sazonnyc.com

Expect "authentic *sabor*" at this TriBeCa home to "manly", "feed-a-family" portions of "distinctive" Puerto Rican food led by a "mouth-watering pernil"; fueled by a DJ and free-flowing sangria, the "festive scene" can be "super-noisy" or "great fun", your call.

Scaletta *Italian* — 21 | 20 | 23 | $54

W 70s | 50 W. 77th St. (bet. Columbus Ave. & CPW) | 212-769-9191 | www.scalettaristorante.com

"Grown-ups" eat up the "classic" Italian cooking, "courteous" service and "tasteful" setting at this "soothing" UWS standby where the prices are "fairly high" but "not over the moon"; "widely spaced tables" are a plus for those who "want to converse."

Z Scalinatella ● *Italian* — 26 | 18 | 23 | $87

E 60s | 201 E. 61st St., downstairs (3rd Ave.) | 212-207-8280

Nestled "below street level", this "upbeat" UES Italian is a "cozy" refuge where "well-heeled" folk tuck into "fabulous" Capri-style cuisine; be wary when the "cordial" staffers schooled in "upselling" recite the "countless", unpriced specials – you'll "pay for the privilege."

Z Scalini Fedeli ⧈ *Italian* — 27 | 25 | 26 | $90

TriBeCa | 165 Duane St. (bet. Greenwich & Hudson Sts.) | 212-528-0400 | www.scalinifedeli.com

Michael Cetrulo "scales the heights" at this TriBeCa Northern Italian "revelation" for "exceptional" cuisine and wines dispensed by a "gracious" team in a "civilized", "vaulted-salon" milieu; the $65 prix fixe-only dinner may seem a lot to some, but the deep-pocketed feel it "could charge more and get away with it."

Scarlatto *Italian* — 21 | 18 | 20 | $47

W 40s | 250 W. 47th St. (bet. B'way & 8th Ave.) | 212-730-4535 | www.scarlattonyc.com

"Perfect for pre-anything", this Theater District duplex features "above-average" Italian grub ferried by "efficient" servers; insiders sidestep the "over-the-top decibels" at prime times by dining upstairs.

Z Scarpetta *Italian* — 26 | 22 | 23 | $72

Chelsea | 355 W. 14th St. (bet. 8th & 9th Aves.) | 212-691-0555 | www.scarpettanyc.com

"Sexy, sassy" and "sophisticated", Scott Conant's "trendy" 14th Street "standout" is deemed "top-notch across the board" for its "superlative" Italian food, "capable" service and "sleek" setting; the "prices are steep" and reservations "tough", but it stays "hot" for "good reason" – the spaghetti is "life-altering" here.

	FOOD	DECOR	SERVICE	COST

Schiller's ● *Eclectic*
19 | 19 | 17 | $39

LES | 131 Rivington St. (Norfolk St.) | 212-260-4555 | www.schillersny.com
Dubbed "Pastis junior" for its "Parisian feel", Keith McNally's "happening" LES Eclectic is a "bright, busy" nexus for "on-par" chow and "unique cocktails" at a "low price point"; but when the "hipsters" and "yupsters" pile in for "late-night socializing", it's "impossible to talk" without "yelling."

Schnipper's Quality Kitchen *American*
19 | 13 | 15 | $17

W 40s | NY Times Bldg. | 620 Eighth Ave. (41st St.) | 212-921-2400 | www.schnippers.com
"Comfort-food lovers" commend this "cafeteria-style" American in the NY Times building for its "damn good burgers" and other "diet-destroying" grub at "utterly reasonable" prices; big windows supply "nice people-watching" of the teeming masses headed for Port Authority across the street; P.S. an outlet opposite Madison Square Park is in the works.

NEW Schnitzel & Things *Austrian*
▽ 20 | 10 | 16 | $16

E 40s | 723 Third Ave. (bet. 45th & 46th Sts.) | 212-905-0000
You can "get your schnitzel on" without "chasing their food truck" around town at this new Austrian niche near Grand Central that vends "super" fried cutlets (classic veal and other varieties) in a tiny, take-out-friendly setting; lunchtime loyalists "love the concept."

Scottadito Osteria Toscana Ⓜ *Italian*
▽ 23 | 21 | 22 | $36

Park Slope | 788A Union St. (bet. 6th & 7th Aves.) | Brooklyn | 718-636-4800 | www.scottadito.com
Park Slopers praise this "welcoming" Tuscan for its "on-point" Northern Italian cooking and "rustic" setting warmed by a working fireplace; always "affordable", it offers an "awesome" $18 weekend brunch.

SD26 *Italian*
24 | 24 | 23 | $73

Murray Hill | 19 E. 26th St. (bet. 5th & Madison Aves.) | 212-265-5959 | www.sd26ny.com
There's "electricity in the air" at this "high-style" follow-up to San Domenico opposite Madison Square Park, where "upscale" Italian dishes arrive in a "modernist" setting split between an "active" front wine bar and a "striking" rear dining room; overseen by "father-and-daughter" team Tony and Marisa May, it's first class all the way.

Sea *Thai*
21 | 22 | 17 | $30

Meatpacking | 835 Washington St. (Little W. 12th St.) | 212-243-3339
Williamsburg | 114 N. Sixth St. (Berry St.) | Brooklyn | 718-384-8850 ●
www.seathainyc.com
Favored by "young" Williamsburg and Meatpacking revelers, this "nightclub"-esque Thai twosome provides "flavorful", "price-is-right" chow in "awesome" digs outfitted with "ponds" and giant "Buddhas"; just brace yourself for "mob-scene" crowds and a "loud" soundtrack.

Sea Grill Ⓔ *Seafood*
24 | 25 | 23 | $72

W 40s | Rockefeller Ctr. | 19 W. 49th St. (bet. 5th & 6th Aves.) | 212-332-7610 | www.theseagrillnyc.com
Eyeballing the "ice skaters" and the "Christmas tree" from a "rinkside" window table is a "real treat" at this "handsome" Rock Center sea-

fooder, also applauded for its "scrumptious" catch and "outstanding" staff; it's admittedly "expensive" and "touristy", but a "quintessential NY experience" – "even for locals."

✓ Seäsonal *Austrian*   25 | 20 | 24 | $69

W 50s | 132 W. 58th St. (bet. 6th & 7th Aves.) | 212-957-5550 | www.seasonalnyc.com

"Austrian classics" get a "modern" spin at this "upscale" Midtowner where the "exceptional" cooking flaunts "seasonal flair" in a "fine-dining" setting overseen by "solicitous" staffers; it still seems "under the radar", but it's "worth the price" if you're bound for nearby Carnegie Hall.

2nd Ave Deli ◐ *Deli/Kosher*   23 | 13 | 17 | $29

NEW **E 70s** | 1442 First Ave. (75th St.) | 212-737-1700
Murray Hill | 162 E. 33rd St. (bet. Lexington & 3rd Aves.) | 212-689-9000
www.2ndavedeli.com

A "worthy successor" to the East Village "landmark deli", this Murray Hiller plies "almost the same" "gargantuan sandwiches" and other Jewish "heart-attack" staples that "grandpa always talks about"; service is "surly", decor "nonexistent" and "oy, is it expensive" "for what it is", but – "kvetching" aside – it's "always crowded"; P.S. the UES branch opened post-Survey.

Seersucker *Southern*   ∇ 21 | 20 | 22 | $34

Carroll Gardens | 329 Smith St. (bet. Carroll & President Sts.) | Brooklyn | 718-422-0444 | www.seersuckerbrooklyn.com

Suckers for "Southern comfort" chow salute this "small", "laid-back" Smith Street yearling for its "refined takes" on down-home favorites made from "fresh, local ingredients"; a "notch-above-the-usual" service and notch-below pricing complete the "cute concept."

Serafina ◐ *Italian*   19 | 16 | 17 | $44

E 50s | 38 E. 58th St. (bet. Madison & Park Aves.) | 212-832-8888 ⑤
E 60s | 29 E. 61st St. (bet. Madison & Park Aves.) | 212-702-9898
E 70s | 1022 Madison Ave., 2nd fl. (79th St.) | 212-734-2676
W 40s | Time Hotel | 224 W. 49th St. (bet. B'way & 8th Ave.) | 212-247-1000
W 50s | Dream Hotel | 210 W. 55th St. (B'way) | 212-315-1700
www.serafinarestaurant.com

"Dalton" kids, Euro "tourists" and the "ladies who lunch" pile into this "hustling, bustling" Italian mini-chain where the solid menu features a "can't-go-wrong" thin-crust pizza; sadly, service comes with "tons of attitude" and the noise can turn conversations into "shouting matches."

Serendipity 3 ◐ *Dessert*   19 | 20 | 16 | $31

E 60s | 225 E. 60th St. (bet. 2nd & 3rd Aves.) | 212-838-3531 | www.serendipity3.com

It's all about the "sugar buzz" at this "one-of-a-kind" East Side dessert parlor-cum-gift shop, famed for "foot-long" hot dogs and "bucket-list" frozen hot chocolate; "painfully slow" service and "brutal" waits detract, but it's always packed with "tourists" and "overstimulated" kids.

Serge ⑤ *French*   ∇ 22 | 16 | 20 | $46

Murray Hill | 165 Madison Ave. (bet. 32nd & 33rd Sts.) | 212-679-8077 | www.brasseriecafecreme.com

A "humorous", "hard-working" chef-owner "keeps it real" at this "little" Murray Hill brasserie offering "square French meals" in a tradi-

| | FOOD | DECOR | SERVICE | COST |

tional, "white-tablecloth" setting; middling costs and an "engaging" ambiance enhance its "reliable" rep.

Sette Mezzo 🚫 *Italian*

23 | 16 | 20 | $73

E 70s | 969 Lexington Ave. (bet. 70th & 71st Sts.) | 212-472-0400
UES "masters of the universe" frequent this "chic", "clubby" Italian known for its "air-kissing" and "table-hopping", not to mention some of the "most expensive pasta in NYC"; regulars enjoy "house charge accounts" and "impeccable" service, while unknowns "pay cash" and put up with "huge attitude."

Sevilla ◗ *Spanish*

24 | 15 | 21 | $42

W Village | 62 Charles St. (W. 4th St.) | 212-929-3189 |
www.sevillarestaurantandbar.com
"Garlic lovers rejoice" at this West Village "time warp", a modestly priced, 1941-vintage Spaniard plying *"muy bueno"* dishes dispatched by "gentlemanly servers"; the no-rez policy is a "drag", but the "tattered" surroundings somehow "add to the charm."

Sezz Medi' *Mediterranean/Pizza*

▽ 21 | 16 | 19 | $31

W 100s | 1260 Amsterdam Ave. (122nd St.) | 212-932-2901 |
www.sezzmedi.com
"Unassuming" yet "better than you'd think", this Morningside Heights Med draws the "Columbia" crowd with "excellent" brick-oven Neapolitan pizza and other "basic", "low-budget" items; "friendly" service lightens up the "dark", "pseudo-rustic" digs.

Sfoglia *Italian*

23 | 17 | 19 | $65

E 90s | 1402 Lexington Ave. (92nd St.) | 212-831-1402 |
www.sfogliarestaurant.com
The original proprietors are gone, but so far the transition seems "seamless" at this "truly fine" Carnegie Hill Northern Italian, purveying "authentic" cooking and "gracious" service in a "Tuscan" setting; while "fairly expensive", it's "popular" with "culture addicts" en route to the nearby 92nd Street Y.

Shabu-Shabu 70 *Japanese*

21 | 13 | 21 | $44

E 70s | 314 E. 70th St. (bet. 1st & 2nd Aves.) | 212-861-5635
You "cook it yourself" at this "humble" UES "swish-swish" standby where the eponymous tableside hot pots and "decent" sushi deliver an informal "taste of Japan" ("kids love it"); "no-pretense" service from a "wonderful staff" and moderate tabs compensate for its "long-in-the-tooth" look.

Shabu-Tatsu *Japanese*

▽ 22 | 14 | 19 | $36

E Village | 216 E. 10th St. (bet. 1st & 2nd Aves.) | 212-477-2972 |
www.tic-nyc.com
A "fun-filled dinner" awaits at this East Village shabu-shabu/sukiyaki joint offering an "authentic Japanese" experience via dip-your-own hot pots; the "tidy but spartan" digs are typically "crowded", given the good "value" and "welcoming" service.

Shake Shack *Burgers*

22 | 12 | 14 | $16

E 80s | 154 E. 86th St. (bet. Lexington & 3rd Aves.) | 646-237-5035
NEW Financial District | 215 Murray St. (bet. North End Ave. & West St.) |
646-545-4600

(continued)

(continued)

Shake Shack

Flatiron | Madison Square Park | 23rd St. (Madison Ave.) |
212-889-6600
W 40s | InterContinental NY Times Sq. | 300 W. 44th St. (8th Ave.) |
646-435-1035 ◗
W 70s | 366 Columbus Ave. (77th St.) | 646-747-8770
Flushing | Citi Field | 126th St. & Roosevelt Ave. (behind the scoreboard) |
Queens | no phone
www.shakeshack.com

Danny Meyer's "perpetually packed" patty franchise draws "fast foodies" with "killer burgers" and shakes that generate "killer waits" to get in; true, it's a "bit of a circus" with "not enough seating", but the "quality is great for the price" – and the experience is "better during off hours when there's no line"; P.S. a Downtown Brooklyn satellite in Fulton Mall is in the works.

Shalezeh *Persian*

22	18	21	$46

E 80s | 1420 Third Ave. (bet. 80th & 81st Sts.) | 212-288-0012 |
www.shalezeh.com

"Real-deal" Persian cooking is yours at this UES Persepolis sibling, where "excellent" dishes (with notably "wonderful rice choices") are ferried by "polite" folks; the "simple", "comfortable" setting keeps the focus on the "well-priced" plates.

Shang 🅂Ⓜ *Chinese*

∇ 20	21	18	$58

LES | Thompson LES Hotel | 187 Orchard St. (bet. Houston & Stanton Sts.) |
212-260-7900 | www.shangrestaurant.com

"Worth exploring", this "upscale" LES Chinese offers chef Susur Lee's "flavorful" creations in a "dramatic", modern room; however, those "expecting greatness" come away "disappointed", citing just "ok" edibles and "expense account"-worthy tabs; P.S. insiders sidestep a "climb up the stairs" and use the hotel's Allen Street entrance.

Shanghai Café ⊄ *Chinese*

22	10	12	$19

Little Italy | 100 Mott St. (bet. Canal & Hester Sts.) |
212-966-3988

This cash-only Little Italy Chinese shanghais bargain-hunters with "authentic" "slurpy soup dumplings" for ultra-"cheap" tabs; trade-offs include a "super-busy", "fluorescent-lit" setting and service that runs the gamut from "overly efficient" to "frantic."

Shanghai Cuisine ⊄ *Chinese*

∇ 23	11	17	$25

Chinatown | 89 Bayard St. (Mulberry St.) | 212-732-8988

Cognoscenti "swear by" the "ridiculously good" soup dumplings that headline the "excellent" Shanghai menu at this "accessible" Chinatown joint; "cheap" tabs trump the "worn" decor, so-so service and cash-only policy.

Shanghai Pavilion *Chinese*

21	17	20	$38

E 70s | 1378 Third Ave. (bet. 78th & 79th Sts.) | 212-585-3388 |
www.shanghaipavilionnyc.com

Though the "upscale" atmosphere is a "far cry from Chinatown", the Shanghai chow is just as "delicious" at this "traditional" UES Chinese haven helmed by a "responsive" team; the "white-tablecloth" "refinement" to the contrary, it's also a surprisingly "good value."

	FOOD	DECOR	SERVICE	COST

Shorty's ● *Cheesesteaks* | 21 | 12 | 18 | $20

W 40s | 576 Ninth Ave. (bet. 41st & 42nd Sts.) | 212-967-3055 | www.shortysnyc.com

"All Philly all the way", this "sports bar–ish" tribute to the City of Brotherly Love just north of Port Authority is a "legit" source of "gut-busting" cheesesteaks washed down with a variety of "craft beers"; predictably, the "loud", "scruffy" setting has "many TVs" tuned to "Phillies games"; P.S. a Murray Hill spin-off is in the works.

☑ SHO Shaun Hergatt 🖻 *French* | 26 | 27 | 24 | $92

Financial District | 40 Broad St., 2nd fl. (bet. Beaver St. & Exchange Pl.) | 212-809-3993 | www.shoshaunhergatt.com

FiDi diners are "blown away" by this "hidden treasure" helmed by Australian chef Shaun Hergatt, a "calm" showcase for "sumptuous", Asian-accented French cuisine, "perfectly served" in an "opulent", "take-your-breath-away" series of rooms; the $75 prix fixe–only dinner may be a "splurge" (unless you're a "Goldman Sachs employee"), but à la carte items are offered at lunch and in the Pearl Room bar.

Shula's Steak House ● *Steak* | 20 | 19 | 20 | $69

W 40s | Westin Times Sq. Hotel | 270 W. 43rd St. (bet. B'way & 8th Ave.) | 212-201-2776 | www.westinny.com

Gridiron great Don Shula's "steak chain" outlet in Times Square offers "one helluva hunk of meat" served amid pigskin paraphernalia aplenty; too bad some refs rule the "routine" playbook too "costly."

Shun Lee Cafe ● *Chinese* | 21 | 18 | 19 | $46

W 60s | 43 W. 65th St. (bet. Columbus Ave. & CPW) | 212-769-3888 | www.shunleewest.com

The carts of "tasty dim sum" are "oh-so-tempting" at this "busy" Lincoln Center Chinese that also boasts a dizzying, black-and-white checkerboard setting right out of an "Escher print"; while it's "less expensive and less formal" than its tony neighbor, tabs can still "add up."

☑ Shun Lee Palace ● *Chinese* | 25 | 22 | 23 | $59

E 50s | 155 E. 55th St. (bet. Lexington & 3rd Aves.) | 212-371-8844 | www.shunleepalace.com

Ever "on top of its game", Michael Tong's pioneering "high-class" East Side Chinese "never wavers" thanks to "fabulous food", "stately service" and "dignified" environs; it "ain't cheap", but then again this "sophisticated" spot is "in a class by itself."

Shun Lee West ● *Chinese* | 23 | 21 | 21 | $56

W 60s | 43 W. 65th St. (bet. Columbus Ave. & CPW) | 212-595-8895 | www.shunleewest.com

For "fancy Chinese" food handy to Lincoln Center, this "tried-and-true" Upper Westsider is the "gold standard" with top-notch food, "pro service" and "glitzy" (if "dated") digs; as a filler-upper before or after a performance, you can't do better.

Siam Square 🅜 *Thai* | ▽ 24 | 18 | 22 | $33

Riverdale | 564 Kappock St. (Henry Hudson Pkwy.) | Bronx | 718-432-8200 | www.siamsq.com

Although "a bit tricky to find", this "small" Riverdale Thai is worth seeking out for "first-rate standards" and spiced-up specialties dispatched by an "attentive" team; the "decor is not the best", but the square-deal pricing more than makes up for it.

Sinigual *Mexican*   21 | 21 | 21 | $41

E 40s | 640 Third Ave. (41st St.) | 212-286-0250 |
www.sinigualrestaurants.com

"Contemporary" Mexican grub and "unique" margaritas collide at this "fairly priced" Midtown cantina with "easy access" to Grand Central; the "dark", "spacious" setting is usually "festive" (i.e. "really loud") thanks to the "hot bar scene."

Sip Sak *Turkish*   21 | 14 | 17 | $36

E 40s | 928 Second Ave. (bet. 49th & 50th Sts.) | 212-583-1900 |
www.sip-sak.com

"Generous" portions of "tasty" Turkish cuisine are served at this "local standby" near the United Nations, where the mood is "unpretentious" and the prices "affordable"; a recent renovation has left the place looking like a "French bistro", but habitués say the cooking is "stronger than ever."

⌷ Sistina *Italian*   26 | 19 | 23 | $80

E 80s | 1555 Second Ave. (bet. 80th & 81st Sts.) | 212-861-7660

Serving "glorious" cuisine paired with a "superb" wine list, this enduring UES Northern Italian is "comparable to the finest" around; some protest the "aggressive pricing", but its well-heeled local following could care less given the quality of the food and service – "especially for regulars."

67 Burger *Burgers*   22 | 14 | 18 | $17

Fort Greene | 67 Lafayette Ave. (Fulton St.) | Brooklyn | 718-797-7150 |
www.67burger.com

"For a quick bite near BAM", you "can't beat" this "friendly" Fort Greene burger joint where "succulent" patties with "well-chosen complements" are "cooked-to-order" "fast" in "cafeteria-style" digs; a spin-off is in the works for Park Slope's burgeoning Bergen/Flatbush nexus.

S'MAC *American*   22 | 10 | 15 | $16

E Village | 345 E. 12th St. (bet. 1st & 2nd Aves.) | 212-358-7912 |
www.smacnyc.com

Mac 'n' cheese is an "art form" at this East Village one-off known for "really cool" varieties (including "gluten-free options") served in "little frying pans"; though the "carbo-loading" comes "cheap", the "indifferent" service and "little" storefront setting are "not so comforting."

Smith, The ◑ *American*   21 | 17 | 18 | $35

E Village | 55 Third Ave. (bet. 10th & 11th Sts.) | 212-420-9800 |
www.thesmithnyc.com

It's "all college kids" all the time at this "easy", "lively" East Villager featuring "satisfying" American cooking at a pleasing price point; it's perpetually "jammed", so be prepared to "shout across the table"; P.S. a Turtle Bay branch is in the works.

Smith & Wollensky *Steak*   24 | 19 | 22 | $74

E 40s | 797 Third Ave. (49th St.) | 212-753-1530 |
www.smithandwollenskynyc.com

You can almost "smell the testosterone" at this sprawling, 35-year-old Midtown "man's world" where "old boys' club" types assemble for "juicy" slabs of beef and a "kick-ass wine list" served by "old-pro" staffers; granted, the experience "doesn't come cheap", but given the high-rolling crowd you might come away thinking that there's "no recession here."

Smoke Joint *BBQ*

22 | 13 | 18 | $25

Fort Greene | 87 S. Elliott Pl. (Lafayette Ave.) | Brooklyn | 718-797-1011 | www.thesmokejoint.com

"Yee-haw", the "zippy" BBQ is "fall-off-the-bone" delicious at this "easygoing" Fort Greene pit stop that "makes up with quality what it lacks in elbow room"; the surroundings are "creaky" and the service "disorganized", but no one cares given the bargain rates and "excellent bourbon selection."

Smorgas Chef *Scandinavian*

19 | 16 | 18 | $39

Financial District | 53 Stone St. (William St.) | 212-422-3500 ◗
Murray Hill | Scandinavia Hse. | 58 Park Ave. (bet. 37th & 38th Sts.) | 212-847-9745
W Village | 283 W. 12th St. (4th St.) | 212-243-7073 ◗
www.smorgas.com

Those who "can't get to Ikea" get their "Swedish meatball fix" at this "reliable" trio of "solid" Scandinavians; most agree the "simple" surrounds and "cheerful" vibes are perfect for "unhurried" repasts, even if cynics yawn "uninspired."

Snack *Greek*

22 | 15 | 19 | $39

SoHo | 105 Thompson St. (bet. Prince & Spring Sts.) | 212-925-1040

Snack Taverna *Greek*

W Village | 63 Bedford St. (Morton St.) | 212-929-3499
www.snackny.com

While the SoHo original is "super-tiny" (just a dozen seats) and the West Village spin-off not much bigger (only 45 seats), at least these Downtown Greek eateries follow through with appropriately "small" checks; "creative" "modern" cooking and an overall "low-key" vibe keep locals loyal.

sNice *Sandwiches/Vegetarian*

20 | 16 | 17 | $16

SoHo | 150 Sullivan St. (bet. Houston & Prince Sts.) | 212-253-5405
W Village | 45 Eighth Ave. (bet. Horatio & Jane Sts.) | 212-645-0310
Park Slope | 315 Fifth Ave. (bet. 2nd & 3rd Sts.) | Brooklyn | 718-788-2121 ⊟

Just the ticket "after your yoga class", these "s'okay" cafes offer "all-veggie" selections of sandwiches and salads suitable for "quick", "casual" grazing; the "funky", "college-town" vibe draws equal numbers of "laptops" and "strollers."

Soba Nippon *Noodle Shop*

23 | 16 | 20 | $43

W 50s | 19 W. 52nd St. (bet. 5th & 6th Aves.) | 212-489-2525 | www.sobanippon.com

Noodle aficionados attest the "heavenly homemade soba" (grown on a house-owned farm) is "truly worth" the tabs at this Midtown Japanese "sleeper"; a "handy" lunchtime "favorite", it's "less hectic" at the dinner hour.

	FOOD	DECOR	SERVICE	COST

Soba Totto *Noodle Shop*
22 | 18 | 20 | $45

E 40s | 211 E. 43rd St. (bet. 2nd & 3rd Aves.) | 212-557-8200 |
www.sobatotto.com

"Genuine" Japanese dining sans sushi surfaces near Grand Central at this "authentic" Midtowner where "excellent soba" and a "wide choice of yakitori" lead the "intriguing" lineup; the "serene" service, "relaxed" atmosphere and good food will leave you feeling benign.

Soba-ya *Noodle Shop*
24 | 17 | 20 | $33

E Village | 229 E. Ninth St. (bet. 2nd & 3rd Aves.) | 212-533-6966 |
www.sobaya-nyc.com

"Full-flavored" bowls of "pristine" soba and udon "transport you to the Pacific" at this "popular" East Village Japanese noodle joint, lauded for its "Tokyo-like" service and decor (and "memorable toilets"); given "bargain" tabs and a "no-rez" rule, regulars advise ya to "show up early – or wait."

Socarrat Paella Bar *Spanish*
23 | 17 | 19 | $48

Chelsea | 259 W. 19th St. (bet. 7th & 8th Aves.) | 212-462-1000
NEW NoLita | 284 Mulberry St. (bet. Houston & Prince Sts.) |
212-219-0101
www.socarratpaellabar.com

"Exceptionally fine" paella, tapas and regional wines keep this "buzzy" Chelsea Spanish "shoebox" humming, though the single "communal table" leads to "shoulder-to-shoulder" dining and "contortionist" service; the new NoLita spin-off is thankfully "bigger", and now both locations take reservations; P.S. a third branch in Turtle Bay is in the works.

NEW Social Eatz *American/Sandwiches*
23 | 17 | 19 | $25

E 50s | 232 E. 53rd St. (bet. 2nd & 3rd Aves.) | 212-207-3339 |
www.socialeatz.com

"Surprising combinations" are the trademark of this East Midtown newcomer from *Top Chef* vet Angelo Sosa, who gives "traditional American" items a "zippy" Asian spin (e.g. the "incredible" bibimbop burger); the "affordable" tabs are in keeping with the "casual" setting, and after dark it gets "lively" with the "under-25" set.

Sofrito ● *Puerto Rican*
23 | 20 | 19 | $44

E 50s | 400 E. 57th St. (bet. 1st Ave. & Sutton Pl.) | 212-754-5999 |
www.sofritony.com

"San Juan" comes to Sutton Place via this "upscale" Puerto Rican known for "*delicioso*" grub served in "food coma–inducing portions" and a "jumping" Latino social scene; it's a "good time at a good price", but brace yourself for a "deafening" din and "'Happy Birthday' sung many times."

Sojourn ● *Eclectic*
23 | 18 | 20 | $47

E 70s | 244 E. 79th St. (bet. 2nd & 3rd Aves.) | 212-537-7745 |
www.sojournrestaurant.com

"Young" locals dig the "Downtown" mood of this "cool" UES Eclectic where "fun servers" ferry "appetite-whetting" small plates; the "dark" setting is "good for a date" (you "can't see all the imperfections"), but even the "rock concert" decibels can't disguise the fact that it's "expensive for what it is."

	FOOD	DECOR	SERVICE	COST

Solera ⌧ *Spanish*
22 | 19 | 22 | $58

E 50s | 216 E. 53rd St. (bet. 2nd & 3rd Aves.) | 212-644-1166 |
www.soleranym.com

Though it's "been around" a while, this "classy" Midtown duplex
demonstates its "staying power" with "excellent tapas" and other "authentic" Spanish dishes paired with "fine" Iberian wines; the "relaxed"
setting means "you can hear yourself chew", but the "overpriced" bills
can be conversation stoppers.

Solo *Kosher/Mediterranean*
∇ 24 | 23 | 23 | $83

E 50s | 550 Madison Ave. (bet. 55th & 56th Sts.) | 212-833-7800 |
www.solonyc.com

"Classy" kosher "fine dining" is alive and well at this Midtown
Mediterranean whose glatt kitchen produces "excellent" dishes
served by a "super" team; its observant "captive audience" soaks up
the "lovely" setting and seems to put up with the "sticker shock."

Song ⌗ *Thai*
22 | 18 | 17 | $22

Park Slope | 295 Fifth Ave. (bet. 1st & 2nd Sts.) | Brooklyn |
718-965-1108

"Super-fair prices" and "hefty portions" of "terrific" Thai standards
are the attraction at this "happening" Park Slope sibling of Joya; insiders avoid the "painfully noisy" acoustics by fleeing to the "backyard
seats", but there's no escaping the cash-only policy.

Sookk *Thai*
23 | 20 | 20 | $28

W 100s | 2686 Broadway (bet. 102nd & 103rd Sts.) | 212-870-0253 |
www.sookkrestaurant.com

"Different from the norm", this "tiny" UWS Thai vends "sophisticated"
takes on the kind of street food you'd find in Bangkok's Yaowarat
neighborhood; colorful "Silk Road" decor, "attentive" service and
"economical" rates are other reasons for its sookk-cess.

Sorella ◑ Ⓜ *Italian*
∇ 26 | 22 | 20 | $58

LES | 95 Allen St. (bet. Broome & Delancey Sts.) | 212-274-9595 |
www.sorellanyc.com

"Smart, stylish" types tout this "cool" LES Italian offering Piedmontese
small plates along with an old-country wine list; the "modern setting"
is overseen by a "crack team", though "small portions" at "full-portion
prices" may be keeping it "under the radar."

Sosa Borella ◑ *Argentinean/Italian*
20 | 16 | 19 | $44

W 50s | 832 Eighth Ave. (50th St.) | 212-262-7774 |
www.sosaborella.com

Italian-Argentinean cooking may "seem like a strange combination",
but this Hell's Kitchen hybrid is said to offer the "best of both worlds";
"affordable" rates and a "pleasantly restrained" duplex setting (with a
bonus outdoor deck) make it a "pre- and post-theater" natural.

ⓏSoto ◑⌧ *Japanese*
29 | 20 | 21 | $95

W Village | 357 Sixth Ave. (bet. 4th St. & Washington Pl.) |
212-414-3088

"Sushi connoisseurs" consider this West Village Japanese via
"master chef" Sotohiro Kosugi simply "sublime" thanks to "exquisite"
raw fish and "creative" cooked seafood dispatched in a "minimalistic"

(verging on "chilly") milieu; since prices are "astronomical", regulars "savor every bite."

South Gate *American*

24 | 26 | 21 | $70

W 50s | Jumeirah Essex Hse. | 154 Central Park S. (bet. 6th & 7th Aves.) | 212-484-5120 | www.154southgate.com

"Super on all fronts", this "sleek" New American in the Essex House is the "full package", starting with chef Kerry Heffernan's "memorable" cuisine and extending to the "fine" service and "stunning", "high-ceilinged" setting; all that "attention to detail" comes at an "upscale" price, perhaps why it's "surprisingly not packed."

☑ Sparks Steak House ☒ *Steak*

26 | 20 | 23 | $79

E 40s | 210 E. 46th St. (bet. 2nd & 3rd Aves.) | 212-687-4855 | www.sparkssteakhouse.com

"Testosterone" perfumes the air at this circa-1966 chop shop near Grand Central that's "still going strong" thanks to "big, serious" steaks, a "comprehensive wine list" and a "gent's-club" mood; sparks fly over "average" decor and "exorbitant" pricing, but it can't be beat for "old-school" service and serious "man-watching."

NEW Spasso Ⓜ *Italian*

24 | 20 | 23 | $54

W Village | 551 Hudson St. (Perry St.) | 212-858-3838 | www.spassonyc.com

"Exciting" eating "expands your comfort zone" at this new West Village "winner" where "high-level" rustic Italiana and a "concise wine list" are dispensed by an "on-point" staff; the "small", modern digs are often "packed (and rightly so)", though some wish for less "noise" and more spasso.

Spice *Thai*

19 | 16 | 17 | $28

Chelsea | 199 Eighth Ave. (bet. 19th & 20th Sts.) | 212-989-1116
Chelsea | 236 Eighth Ave. (22nd St.) | 212-620-4585
E 70s | 1411 Second Ave. (bet. 73rd & 74th Sts.) | 212-988-5348
NEW E 70s | 1479 First Ave. (77th St.) | 212-744-6374
E Village | 104 Second Ave. (6th St.) | 212-533-8900
E Village | 77 E. 10th St. (4th Ave.) | 212-388-9006
G Village | 39 E. 13th St. (bet. B'way & University Pl.) | 212-982-3758
NEW W 80s | 435 Amsterdam Ave. (81st St.) | 212-362-5861
NEW Park Slope | 61A Seventh Ave. (bet. Berkeley & Lincoln Pls.) | Brooklyn | 718-622-6353
www.spicethainyc.com

An "easy drop-in" for "ample" servings of "cookie-cutter" Thai chow, this burgeoning chainlet lures "college-aged" masses with "fast-food" tabs; still, "spartan" settings and "curt" service make them strictly "eat-and-run" propositions.

☑ Spice Market ◑ *Asian*

23 | 26 | 21 | $62

Meatpacking | 403 W. 13th St. (9th Ave.) | 212-675-2322 | www.jean-georges.com

"Wow" is the word on Jean-Georges Vongerichten's "swinging" Meatpacking "scene", combining a "dazzling", family-style menu of "upgraded" Southeast Asian street food with "fruity cocktails" and "hot", "polished" staffers; decorated in a "slinky" style reminiscent of a "Javanese Playboy mansion" (complete with "sexy" private rooms downstairs), it's "energizing" for both "New Yorkers and tourists" who report it will spice up your life.

	FOOD	DECOR	SERVICE	COST

Spicy & Tasty ♯ Chinese
23 | 10 | 13 | $25

Flushing | 39-07 Prince St. (39th Ave.) | Queens | 718-359-1601 | www.spicyandtasty.com

"Fiery and tasty is more like it" at this cash-only Flushing Chinese where "adventurous" types with "taste buds to burn" convene for "sensational" Sichuan cooking; "crummy decor" keeps the "focus on the food" and the "modest" cost.

Spiga Italian
24 | 19 | 21 | $53

W 80s | 200 W. 84th St. (bet. Amsterdam Ave. & B'way) | 212-362-5506 | www.spiganyc.com

"Charming" say fans of this UWS "secret" trattoria, a "total find" for "toothsome" Italian cooking, "discreet service" and a "tight" if "warm" setting; the cost hovers between "moderate" and "expensive", but you "get what you pay for" here, including a dose of "romance."

Spigolo Italian
25 | 15 | 21 | $61

E 80s | 1561 Second Ave. (81st St.) | 212-744-1100 | www.spigolonyc.com

"Small" is putting it mildly at this UES Italian where the "heavenly", "high-priced" fare arrives in "no-ambiance" digs overseen by "dedicated" owners Scott and Heather Fratangelo; it's "easy to become a regular" here but "tough to get a table", though alfresco seating "doubles its capacity" in warmer months.

Spina Italian
▽ 25 | 20 | 24 | $42

E Village | 175 Ave. B (11th St.) | 212-253-2250 | www.spinarestaurant.com

It's all about the "fantastic pasta (made "fresh" throughout the day) at this East Village Italian that also delivers "delicious", "seasonal" side dishes; "personable" service and manageable tabs leave "neighborhood" denizens "satisfied – and wanting more."

Spitzer's Corner ◑ American
19 | 17 | 16 | $33

LES | 101 Rivington St. (Ludlow St.) | 212-228-0027 | www.spitzerscorner.com

"Hipsters" scarf down "pretty good" American grub at this "busy" LES gastropub where the food plays second fiddle to the "phenomenal" suds selection; it's "overrun on weekends" despite "communal" picnic-table seating and service that "could be better."

☑ Spotted Pig ◑ European
23 | 19 | 18 | $48

W Village | 314 W. 11th St. (Greenwich St.) | 212-620-0393 | www.thespottedpig.com

Ever the "epicenter of cool", this perpetually "jammed" West Villager offers April Bloomfield's "inspired" Modern European "riffs on pub food" to a "sceney", "celeb"-sprinkled clientele ("hi Jay-Z"); "long-ass waits" are part of the package, though it's easier to access for lunch; P.S. the "burger is as good as advertised."

S.P.Q.R. Italian
19 | 19 | 19 | $50

Little Italy | 133 Mulberry St. (bet. Grand & Hester Sts.) | 212-925-3120 | www.spqrnyc.com

A "dependable" option in "Godfatherland", this Little Italy Italian matches "solid" standard dishes with "old-world" service and a "roomy", wood-paneled setting; the ample "space between tables" is good for parties and worth spending a "few extra bucks", but critics yawn "safe but not exciting."

Square Meal *American*

23 | 16 | 23 | $53

E 90s | 30 E. 92nd St. (bet. 5th & Madison Aves.) | 212-860-9872 | www.squaremealnyc.com

"Like home – only better" – this Carnegie Hill "local" caters to a "55-and-over" fan base with "marvelous" Americana served by an "accommodating" crew in "unpretentious" (verging on "plain") digs; the "not-cheap" tabs are still a "square deal" when measured by quality.

☑ Sripraphai ⊄ *Thai*

26 | 13 | 16 | $28

Woodside | 64-13 39th Ave. (bet. 64th & 65th Sts.) | Queens | 718-899-9599 | www.sripraphairestaurant.com

Maybe even "better than Bangkok", this "wildly popular" 20-year-old Woodside Siamese is again voted NYC's Top Thai thanks to "real-deal" specialties with "three-alarm" spice levels; despite "nothing-fancy" decor, "poker-face" service and a "cash-only" rule, it's so "affordable" that few mind the usual "waiting in line."

Stage Deli ◐ *Deli*

21 | 10 | 15 | $30

W 50s | 834 Seventh Ave. (bet. 53rd & 54th Sts.) | 212-245-7850 | www.stagedeli.com

"Skyscraper" sandwiches "named after celebrities" and other "classic Jewish deli" items can cause eating "overload" at this Midtown "cholesterol heaven", now in its 75th year; between the "crusty" servers, "no-personality" decor and "throngs of tourists", "don't expect any bells or whistles."

Stamatis ◐ *Greek*

22 | 12 | 17 | $35

Astoria | 29-09 23rd Ave. (bet. 29th & 31st Sts.) | Queens | 718-932-8596

"As Greek as it gets", this "busy" Astoria taverna supplies "no-nonsense" Hellenica in a "friendly", "rough-and-tumble" style; the setting's "nothing special", but at least the experience "won't bankrupt you."

Stand ◐ *Burgers*

20 | 13 | 15 | $23

G Village | 24 E. 12th St. (bet. 5th Ave. & University Pl.) | 212-488-5900 | www.standburger.com

The "upscale burgers" are a "mouthful" at this Village "quickie", but the real stars of the show are the "adult" booze-spiked shakes in weird flavors (think "toasted marshmallow"); maybe the service and "industrial" decor need some work, but at least the "price is right."

Standard Grill ◐ *American*

21 | 22 | 19 | $58

Meatpacking | Standard Hotel | 848 Washington St. (bet. Little W. 12th & 13th Sts.) | 212-645-4100 | www.thestandardgrill.com

There's plenty of "buzz" at this "high-energy" Meatpacking "scene" where the "chic" and "good-looking" toy with "seriously good" American food "with all eyes on the front door"; both the "deafening" bar/cafe and less frenetic rear room provide "dinner and a show" – but the opening act includes a "snooty" reception and "long" waits to get in, while the last act costs slightly above standard.

St. Anselm *American*

– | – | – | M

Williamsburg | 355 Metropolitan Ave. (Havemeyer St.) | Brooklyn | 718-384-5054

The owners of Williamsburg's beer-focused bar Spuyten Duyvil have revamped its adjacent storefront into this hipster American chop shop

| | FOOD | DECOR | SERVICE | COST |

slinging a variety of steak, poultry and fish; the brick walls, wood-plank ceiling and rustic farm-tool decor match the just-folks vibe and no-beefs pricing.

Stanton Social ❶ *Eclectic*
23 | 22 | 20 | $55

LES | 99 Stanton St. (bet. Ludlow & Orchard Sts.) | 212-995-0099 | www.thestantonsocial.com

"Social is the key word" at this "exhilarating" LES Eclectic, where "tempting" small plates, "trendy" libations and "sexy" vibrations thrill "skinny people with fat wallets"; "stadium-concert" acoustics, "crazy-crowded" conditions and "bachelorettes" aplenty come with the territory.

STK ❷ *Steak*
22 | 24 | 19 | $72

Meatpacking | 26 Little W. 12th St. (bet. 9th Ave. & Washington St.) | 646-624-2444 | www.stkhouse.com

A steakhouse for "beautiful people" may sound like an "oxymoron", but this "nightclub"-ish Meatpacking chop shop seduces "Kim Kardashian" wannabes with "prime" cuts, "modern" looks and new roof-deck dining; still, critics say the "too expensive" food "doesn't measure up to the setting"; P.S. a spin-off near Bryant Park is in the works.

Stone Park Café *American*
25 | 21 | 22 | $48

Park Slope | 324 Fifth Ave. (3rd St.) | Brooklyn | 718-369-0082 | www.stoneparkcafe.com

"Who needs Manhattan?" ask devotees of this Park Slope American "standard-bearer" hailed for its "exceptional", "locally sourced" menu, "welcoming" service and "sweet", "understated" setting; "well-priced" given the "high quality", it predictably hosts a "busy brunch."

Strip House *Steak*
25 | 23 | 22 | $77

G Village | 13 E. 12th St. (bet. 5th Ave. & University Pl.) | 212-328-0000 | www.striphouse.com

Satisfying all your "prehistoric urges", this "edgy" Village steakhouse (now run by Steve Hanson) offers "super" chops and "sumptuous sides" in a "naughty", "red-lit" setting mimicking an "1890s bordello"; sure, it's "expensive", but those in the mood to "eat big and drink big" don't care.

Stuzzi *Italian*
20 | 17 | 18 | $43

Flatiron | 928 Broadway (bet. 21st & 22nd Sts.) | 212-780-5100 | www.stuzziristorante.com

Stuzzicheria *Italian*

TriBeCa | 305 Church St. (bet. Lispenard & Walker Sts.) | 212-219-4037 | www.stuzzicheriatribeca.com

"Appealing" small plates "go down smoothly" paired with "excellent" wines at this great "big" Flatiron Italian, formerly known as Bar Stuzzichini; it's an "after-work standby" for the youth brigade, while the separately owned TriBeCa satellite packs the same "hip" format into a tighter space.

Sueños Ⓜ *Mexican*
22 | 18 | 19 | $47

Chelsea | 311 W. 17th St. (bet. 8th & 9th Aves.) | 212-243-1333 | www.suenosnyc.com

Chef Sue Torres plies "a mix of the familiar and the innovative" at this "down-the-alley" Chelsea Mexican where the "upscale" chow plays well against the "smoking margaritas"; sure, it's "pricier than most" and service careens from "considerate" to "slow", but overall it's a "pleasant respite."

☑ Sugiyama ●🅰🅼 *Japanese*   27 | 21 | 26 | $90

W 50s | 251 W. 55th St. (bet. B'way & 8th Ave.) | 212-956-0670 | www.sugiyama-nyc.com

"Master" chef Nao Sugiyama takes "justifiable pride" in the "extraordinary" kaiseki meals tendered at this "small", "peaceful" Midtown Japanese where the "flawless" morsels and "unhurried" service add up to dining "perfection"; it helps to bring along your "rich uncle", however, since the "fixed menus" run $58 and up.

Sunburnt Cow ● *Australian*   17 | 13 | 19 | $29

E Village | 137 Ave. C (bet. 8th & 9th Sts.) | 212-529-0005 | www.thesunburntcow.com

Sunburnt Calf ● *Australian*

W 70s | 226 W. 79th St. (bet. Amsterdam Ave. & B'way) | 646-823-9255 | www.thesunburntcalf.com

"Decent" Australian pub grub for Down Under dough draws droves of "younger" yobbos to this "raucous" duo in the East Village and UWS; "binge drinkers" plug the $18 "all-you-can-drink" brunch that comes with a free side of "noise."

Superfine 🅼 *Mediterranean*   18 | 18 | 16 | $33

Dumbo | 126 Front St. (bet. Jay & Pearl Sts.) | Brooklyn | 718-243-9005

A "super find" in underserved Dumbo, this "quirky" spot purveys "good" enough Mediterranean cooking in a "big" former warehouse space with an "art bar" feel; it gets "boisterous" around the pool table and during Sunday's bluegrass brunch, but at least that distracts from the "slow service."

Supper ●≠ *Italian*   24 | 18 | 19 | $39

E Village | 156 E. Second St. (bet. Aves. A & B) | 212-477-7600 | www.supperrestaurant.com

They sure "know how to cook" at this "as-good-as-advertised" East Village Italian from the Frank folks that dispenses "superb" pastas and other "fresh"-flavored fare in "rustic" digs for good "value"; it's "beyond popular", despite "communal" seating and no-reservations, no-plastic policies.

Surya *Indian*   ∇ 21 | 18 | 19 | $37

W Village | 302 Bleecker St. (bet. Grove St. & 7th Ave. S.) | 212-807-7770 | www.suryany.com

This longtime West Village Indian is a bona fide "neighborhood" asset thanks to its "quality" eats, "helpful" staff and "decent" prices; since the "modern" interior is a bit "nondescript", aesthetes dine in the "lovely back garden."

SushiAnn 🅰 *Japanese*   24 | 17 | 23 | $65

E 50s | 38 E. 51st St. (bet. Madison & Park Aves.) | 212-755-1780 | www.sushiann.com

"Business" types wheel and deal over "power sushi" at this "civilized" Midtown Japanese, a "consistent" supplier of "top-quality" raw fish dispatched by a pro crew; given the "upscale" tabs, some suggest it's time to upgrade the "bright, boring" setting.

	FOOD	DECOR	SERVICE	COST

Sushiden *Japanese* — 25 | 18 | 22 | $58

E 40s | 19 E. 49th St. (bet. 5th & Madison Aves.) | 212-758-2700
W 40s | 123 W. 49th St. (bet. 6th & 7th Aves.) | 212-398-2800 ⱻ
www.sushiden.com

"Soothing" surroundings and "soft-spoken" servers set the "calm" mood at this Midtown Japanese twosome that lures a "corporate" crowd with "top-tier" sushi and other "reliable" items; it's "not cheap", but "yen for yen" you'd have trouble doing better in Japan.

Sushi Hana *Japanese* — 21 | 16 | 19 | $40

E 70s | 1501 Second Ave. (78th St.) | 212-327-0582
W 80s | 466 Amsterdam Ave. (bet. 82nd & 83rd Sts.) | 212-874-0369 ◐

Locals seeking a "neighborhood" Japanese "fix" turn to these separately owned crosstown sushi bars for "reliable" renditions of the "usual suspects" via an "accommodating" crew; the decor's "nothing to talk about", but fortunately the prices aren't either.

SushiSamba ◐ *Brazilian/Japanese* — 21 | 20 | 19 | $51

Flatiron | 245 Park Ave. S. (bet. 19th & 20th Sts.) | 212-475-9377
W Village | 87 Seventh Ave. S. (Barrow St.) | 212-691-7885
www.sushisamba.com

"Unique" Japanese-Brazilian fusion is the hook at this "playful" duo where the food is nearly overwhelmed by the "snazzy" cocktails and "loud music" (there's also a "remarkable roof" in the Village); still, some say these "aged starlets" are starting to "lose their luster."

☑ Sushi Seki ◐ⱻ *Japanese* — 27 | 13 | 21 | $72

E 60s | 1143 First Ave. (bet. 62nd & 63rd Sts.) | 212-371-0238

"Sushi snobs" are "wowed" by chef Seki's omakase "masterpieces" at this "top-of-the-heap" East Side Japanese that's a particular favorite of night owls given its 2:30 AM closing time; trade-offs include "shabby" looks, "serious" prices and "rush-you-through-dinner" service.

☑ Sushi Sen-nin ⱻ *Japanese* — 27 | 16 | 20 | $62

Murray Hill | 30 E. 33rd St. (bet. Madison Ave. & Park Ave. S.) | 212-889-2208 | www.sushisennin.com

Although "underutilized" due to a "hidden" location, this Murray Hill Japanese earns a "thumbs-up" from "picky sushi lovers" for its "awesome" slicing and "cordial" service; the decor's nothing much, but the prices are likely to make an impression.

☑ Sushi Yasuda ⱻ *Japanese* — 28 | 22 | 24 | $86

E 40s | 204 E. 43rd St. (bet. 2nd & 3rd Aves.) | 212-972-1001 | www.sushiyasuda.com

It's true, "chef Yasuda has left the building", but this Grand Central-area Japanese remains in "top form" with "ethereal" sushi sliced from the "freshest fish known to man"; the blond wood-lined, "island-of-serenity" setting distracts from the "skyrocketing" tabs, though the $23 prix fixe is a "steal"; P.S. "reservations are imperative."

Sushi Zen ⱻ *Japanese* — 26 | 20 | 23 | $69

W 40s | 108 W. 44th St. (bet. B'way & 6th Ave.) | 212-302-0707 | www.sushizen-ny.com

Somewhat "unassuming", this "small" Theater District Japanese is still a "first-class treat" for "superior" sushi that's "beautifully served" in a "spa-like" setting; though not cheap, aficionados say it's "more reasonably priced" than others in the "same league."

Suteishi *Japanese*   ▽ 25 | 20 | 23 | $46

Seaport | 24 Peck Slip (Front St.) | 212-766-2344 | www.suteishi.com

"Slightly hidden" from the South Street Seaport scrum, this "upscale" Japanese best-kept secret supplies "scrumptious" sushi and "accommodating" service at an inviting price; the "quiet sidestreet" locale features bonus outdoor tables and Brooklyn Bridge views.

Swagat Indian Cuisine *Indian*   ▽ 22 | 13 | 21 | $30

W 70s | 411A Amsterdam Ave. (bet. 79th & 80th Sts.) | 212-362-1400

They "try hard to satisfy" at this UWS Indian "local" with a "tasty" (albeit "typical") menu, "friendly service" and "cheap" rates; aesthetes put off by the "small", "plain" digs opt for "takeout"; editor's note: Swagat and Zagat are not related.

Sweet Melissa *Dessert/Sandwiches*   20 | 17 | 18 | $20

Cobble Hill | 276 Court St. (bet. Butler & Douglass Sts.) | Brooklyn | 718-855-3410

Park Slope | 175 Seventh Ave. (bet. 1st & 2nd Sts.) | Brooklyn | 718-788-2700

www.sweetmelissapatisserie.com

"How sweet it is" at these Cobble Hill/Park Slope patisseries, petite retreats for "decadent desserts", "lovely tea service" or a "light lunch"; a "relaxed" mood and "charming" back gardens offset the "stroller obstacle course" settings and slightly "expensive" pricing.

Swifty's *American*   18 | 17 | 18 | $69

E 70s | 1007 Lexington Ave. (bet. 72nd & 73rd Sts.) | 212-535-6000 | www.swiftysnyc.com

"Kiss your way through" this UES "bastion of the ladies who lunch" – and their spouses – where the pleasant American grub plays second fiddle to eyeballing "high-society" types between their trips to the Hamptons and Palm Beach; cynics who dub it "Snooty's" warn you'll "sit in Siberia" (the front room) if you're not a "dressed-up socialite" regular.

Sylvia's *Soul Food*   19 | 14 | 18 | $36

Harlem | 328 Lenox Ave. (bet. 126th & 127th Sts.) | 212-996-0660 | www.sylviasrestaurant.com

The "sweetheart of soul food", this 50-year-old Harlem "landmark" remains "sensibly busy" thanks to "classic" Southern home cooking and a "heavenly" Sunday gospel brunch; while some say it "ain't what it used to be", far more consider it "worth the pilgrimage" – as the "busloads of tourists" demonstrate.

Symposium *Greek*   ▽ 20 | 15 | 21 | $27

W 100s | 544 W. 113th St. (bet. Amsterdam Ave. & B'way) | 212-865-1011 | www.symposiumnyc.com

"Students and faculty" repose at this Morningside Heights Greek that's been a "Columbia standby" since 1969; it's distinctly "nontrendy" and certainly "not Astoria", but the traditional menu is "solid", the tabs "reasonable" and "you can sit around all night" if you want to.

Szechuan Gourmet *Chinese*   23 | 12 | 16 | $30

Garment District | 21 W. 39th St. (bet. 5th & 6th Aves.) | 212-921-0233 | www.szechuangourmetnyc.com

(continued)

Szechuan Gourmet

W 50s | 242 W. 56th St. (bet. B'way & 8th Ave.) | 212-265-2226 |
www.szechuangourmet56.com
Flushing | 135-15 37th Ave. (bet. Main & Prince Sts.) | Queens |
718-888-9388

"Not for the timid", this "real-deal", "lip-numbing" Sichuan threesome
dishes out "exhilarating" chow that just might "blow the top of your
head off"; despite "dour" service and "bland" digs, the "right-on" spicing and modest tabs keep them "crazy busy."

Table d'Hôte *French*   21 | 16 | 20 | $49

E 90s | 44 E. 92nd St. (bet. Madison & Park Aves.) | 212-348-8125 |
www.tabledhote.info

"*Très français*", this "charming" if "super-tight" Carnegie Hill bistro has
been a local "sweet spot" for "homey" country French cooking since
1978; it's "perfect" before the 92nd Street Y, but the "dinky" dimensions mean you'll have to "slim down" to squeeze in.

Taboon *Mediterranean/Mideastern*   24 | 20 | 21 | $55

W 50s | 773 10th Ave. (52nd St.) | 212-713-0271 | www.taboonnyc.com
A "real boon" in an "out-of-the-way" location, this West Hell's Kitchen
"trailblazer" is known for "terrific" Med-Mideastern food, starting with
the "addictive" fresh bread from its taboon oven; while "not inexpensive", it's ever "popular" thanks to those "wonderful aromas" alone.

Taci's Beyti *Turkish*   25 | 11 | 20 | $30

Midwood | 1955 Coney Island Ave. (bet. Ave. P & Kings Hwy.) | Brooklyn |
718-627-5750

"Russian immigrants" frequent this "friendly" Midwood BYO for "incredible" Turkish food in "generous portions"; it's a "looney bin on weekends"
and "Blanche DuBois" wouldn't dig the "killer fluorescent lighting", but
all is forgiven when the "extremely reasonable" check arrives.

☑ Taïm ⌖ *Israeli/Vegetarian*   26 | 8 | 15 | $13

W Village | 222 Waverly Pl. (bet. Perry & W. 11th Sts.) | 212-691-1287 |
www.taimfalafel.com

"Bliss in a pita" paired with "perfectly seasoned" fries makes for
"falafel perfection" at this "damn good" West Villager, a "cheap",
"cash-only" option for vegetarian Israeli eats; it's "closet-size" with a
"handful of stools", so "takeout is a must."

Takahachi *Japanese*   24 | 17 | 22 | $40

E Village | 85 Ave. A (bet. 5th & 6th Sts.) | 212-505-6524 ◑
TriBeCa | 145 Duane St. (bet. Church St. & W. B'way) | 212-571-1830
www.takahachi.net

Sushiphiles swear by this Japanese duo for "delicious" maki and "interesting daily specials" delivered by a "thoughtful" team; although
it's pretty "simple" in terms of decor, "well-priced" tabs "keep regulars
coming back" and back.

Takashi Ⓜ *Japanese*   ▽ 26 | 17 | 23 | $62

W Village | 456 Hudson St. (Barrow St.) | 212-414-2929 |
www.takashinyc.com

"Outstanding" yakiniku (i.e. "grill-it-yourself" Japanese BBQ) is the
"interesting twist" at this pricey West Village "carnivore heaven"; the

Latest openings, menus, photos and more - free at ZAGAT.com   253

"normal cuts are delish", while the more "exotic parts" – like stomach, tongue and intestines – are strictly for the "adventuresome", but either way "knowledgeable" servers will guide you.

Taksim Square *Turkish*

21 | 12 | 17 | $30

E 50s | 1030 Second Ave. (bet. 54th & 55th Sts.) | 212-421-3004 | www.taksimnyc.com

It's recently "changed hands", but this "unpretentious" Midtown Turk still supplies enough "reasonably priced" staples to keep it a "local standby"; not much decor leads many to opt for take-out.

☑ Tamarind ● *Indian*

25 | 24 | 23 | $58

Flatiron | 41-43 E. 22nd St. (bet. B'way & Park Ave. S.) | 212-674-7400

TriBeCa | 99 Hudson St. (bet. Franklin & Harrison Sts.) | 212-775-9000

www.tamarind22.com

Go "upper caste" at this "exceptional" Flatiron Indian where the "nuanced" cuisine (rated No. 1 in its genre) is enhanced by "first-class service" and "swanky" scenery – its bigger, "more corporate" TriBeCa follow-up features even "more bells and whistles" on the menu; granted, the tariffs may be "high end", but the $24 prix fixe lunch is a "bargain."

Tang Pavilion *Chinese*

22 | 17 | 21 | $41

W 50s | 65 W. 55th St. (bet. 5th & 6th Aves.) | 212-956-6888 | www.tangpavilionnyc.com

"Authentic" Shanghai cuisine comes with a "touch of refinement" at this "on-the-mark" Midtown Chinese near City Center; applauded for its "capable service" and "grown-up" mien, it's also remarkably "easy on the wallet" for the quality.

☑ Tanoreen Ⓜ *Mediterranean/Mideastern*

26 | 19 | 22 | $37

Bay Ridge | 7523 Third Ave. (76th St.) | Brooklyn | 718-748-5600 | www.tanoreen.com

"Distinctive" cooking that "puts Bay Ridge on the map" is the draw at this "memorable" Med-Mideastern where "hands-on" chef Rawia Bishara's "intoxicating" dishes are "served with love"; a "warm" setting and "price-is-right" tabs cement its "crowd-pleaser" rep.

Tanuki Tavern *Japanese*

∇ 20 | 19 | 19 | $53

Meatpacking | Gansevoort Hotel | 18 Ninth Ave. (enter on 13th St., bet. Hudson St. & 9th Ave.) | 212-660-6766 | www.chinagrillmgt.com

Jeffrey Chodorow's contemporary Japanese duplex in the Meatpacking's Gansevoort Hotel puts out "tasty" izakaya plates and "fresh sushi" in a "pink, girlie" setting; "trendy" types say it's "not bad" but waver at the "expensive" price tag.

Tao ● *Asian*

22 | 26 | 19 | $61

E 50s | 42 E. 58th St. (bet. Madison & Park Aves.) | 212-888-2288 | www.taorestaurant.com

There's "plenty of pow" at this "cavernous" Midtown Pan-Asian "hot spot" where the "flashy" attractions include "loud" music and a huge Buddha; "rushed" service doesn't detract from the "satisfying" chow, and "sticker shock" doesn't deter droves of "out-of-towners" and "under-35" folk from partying.

	FOOD	DECOR	SERVICE	COST

Tarallucci e Vino *Italian* | 20 | 16 | 16 | $38

E Village | 163 First Ave. (bet. 10th & 11th Sts.) | 212-388-1190
Flatiron | 15 E. 18th St. (bet. B'way & 5th Ave.) | 212-228-5400
NEW **W 80s** | 475 Columbus Ave. (83rd St.) | 212-362-5454
www.tarallucievino.net

"You'll think you're in Italy" sampling "solid" small plates and vinos at
this Flatiron Italian, a "comfortable", "conversation"-friendly stop; the
"small" East Village original and new UWS sibling are better known for
"sweet treats", espresso and panini, but all share "not-quick" service.

Tartine ⊄ *French* | 22 | 16 | 18 | $32

W Village | 253 W. 11th St. (4th St.) | 212-229-2611

The "waters of the Seine" don't seem far away at this West Village
"staple" offering "earthy" French bistro eats, "accommodating" service and "fair prices" (helped along by the BYO policy); given the
"postage-stamp" dimensions, there's often a "line on the street."

Taste *American* | ∇ 22 | 15 | 21 | $62

E 80s | 1413 Third Ave. (80th St.) | 212-717-9798 | www.elizabar.com
Eli Zabar's UES "neighborhood sleeper" converts from a self-service
daytime cafe to a "white-tablecloth" restaurant after dark with a
"fine", "constantly changing" American menu made from the freshest
possible ingredients; sure, it's "expensive", but its mature crowd
always leaves "satisfied."

Tatiana ● *Russian* | 21 | 19 | 18 | $54

Brighton Bch | 3152 Brighton 6th St. (Brightwater Ct.) | Brooklyn |
718-891-5151 | www.tatianarestaurant.com

"Like visiting the Russian Riviera", this "over-the-top" Brighton Beach
nightclub serves "tasty" Soviet staples that play second fiddle to its
"cheesy", "Vegas-style" floor show replete with "dancing girls in fur
bikinis"; "boardwalk seating" overlooking the Atlantic makes the
"brusque" service more tolerable.

☑ Taverna Kyclades *Greek/Seafood* | 26 | 12 | 18 | $36

Astoria | 33-07 Ditmars Blvd. (bet. 33rd & 35th Sts.) | Queens |
718-545-8666 | www.tavernakyclades.com

"Superb" renditions of the "freshest fish" surface at this "popular"
Astoria Greek, famed for its "cheap" tabs, "adequate" service and
"subway-at-rush-hour" ambiance; given the "no-reservations" policy,
"long waits for a table" are a given.

T-Bar Steak & Lounge *Steak* | 22 | 19 | 20 | $61

E 70s | 1278 Third Ave. (bet. 73rd & 74th Sts.) | 212-772-0404 |
www.tbarnyc.com

Owner Tony Fortuna "runs a good shop" at this "upbeat" UES "urban
reprieve" where "solid" steaks and "fine service" draw "mature" folks
who've had "some work done"; the "noisy bar" scene sends conversa-
tionalists to the "quiet" back room.

Tea & Sympathy *British* | 20 | 18 | 18 | $29

W Village | 108 Greenwich Ave. (bet. 12th & 13th Sts.) | 212-807-8329 |
www.teaandsympathynewyork.com

"Anglophiles and expats" tout this "novelty" West Village tearoom
that offers "English nursery food" on "mismatched china" in "seen-

better-days" digs; though the "tiny" dimensions and "cheeky" service are a bore, sympathists cite its "proper tea service."

ⓩ Telepan   American   26 | 22 | 25 | $72

W 60s | 72 W. 69th St. (bet. Columbus Ave. & CPW) | 212-580-4300 | www.telepan-ny.com

"Masterful" toque Bill Telepan "delights the palate" with some "serious" New American cooking at this UWS "farm-to-table winner" that's also lauded for its "polished service" and "civilized" setting; for "memorable" dining, it's "money well spent" – and an "outstanding" option before Lincoln Center from a chef who can really tell a pot from a pan.

Telly's Taverna ☻ Greek/Seafood   23 | 14 | 19 | $40

Astoria | 28-13 23rd Ave. (bet. 28th & 29th Sts.) | Queens | 718-728-9056 | www.tellystaverna.com

"Perfectly prepared fresh fish" is the calling card of this longtime Astoria Greek seafooder, "one of the best things about Queens"; "efficient" service trumps the "tired", "dinerlike" decor, though the cost-effective tabs are fine as is.

10 Downing   American   19 | 19 | 18 | $49

W Village | 10 Downing St. (6th Ave.) | 212-255-0300 | www.10downingnyc.com

Any parallels to the "U.K. prime minister's residence" end with the name at this "chic", "artwork"-filled West Villager, where the "hopping" vibe, "decent" (if "overpriced") New American fare and "sunny brunch" balance uneven service and "noisy" acoustics; "eat outdoors" for prime "people-watching."

🆕 Tenpenny   American   - | - | - | M

E 40s | Gotham Hotel | 16 E. 46th St. (bet. 5th & Madison Aves.) | 212-490-8300 | www.tenpennynyc.com

A fresh "find" in Midtown, this "tucked-away" newcomer near Grand Central offers a "tasty", "unusual" American menu with an Italian accent; the rough-hewn, brick-walled space exudes a "cozy" vibe, while "wonderful cocktails" and penny-wise pricing seal the deal.

Tenzan   Japanese   22 | 16 | 19 | $35

E 50s | 988 Second Ave. (bet. 52nd & 53rd Sts.) | 212-980-5900 | www.tenzanrestaurants.com ☻
E 80s | 1714 Second Ave. (89th St.) | 212-369-3600 | www.tenzansushi89.com
W 70s | 285 Columbus Ave. (73rd St.) | 212-580-7300 | www.tenzanrestaurants.com ☻
Bensonhurst | 7116 18th Ave. (71st St.) | Brooklyn | 718-621-3238 | www.tenzanrestaurants.com

These separately owned Japanese are "steady" sources of "top-notch" sushi that "don't skimp" on the portion size or freshness quotient; though the settings skew "utilitarian", "modest prices" make them a "real success story."

Teodora   Italian   21 | 16 | 20 | $53

E 50s | 141 E. 57th St. (bet. Lexington & 3rd Aves.) | 212-826-7101 | www.teodorarestaurant.com

Although "not well known", this "sleeper" trattoria remains a "satisfying standby" for pasta-centric Northern Italian plates served by a "cordial" crew; despite "not much atmosphere" and "somewhat expensive" tabs, it offers "quiet relief" in a "hectic" part of Midtown.

NEW Teqa ◐ Mexican
∇ 21 | 23 | 19 | $34

Murray Hill | 447 Third Ave. (bet. 30th & 31st Sts.) | 212-213-3223 | www.teqanyc.com

Muy "cool" for Murray Hill, this "swank" new taqueria dispenses "designer tacos" and various Mexican small plates for "surprisingly" modest sums; critics are peeved by *"pequeño portions"*, but thanks to a "sexy" scene stoked by "crafty cocktails", it's already a hit with "young professionals."

Teresa's Diner
18 | 12 | 16 | $24

Brooklyn Heights | 80 Montague St. (Hicks St.) | Brooklyn | 718-797-3996

This Brooklyn Heights "hangover helper" is an "unflagging" source of "passable" diner fare jazzed up with some "Polish delicacies"; "bargain" tabs make the generic decor and "surly Eastern bloc" service easier to swallow.

Terrace in the Sky Ⓜ French/Mediterranean
22 | 25 | 22 | $71

W 100s | 400 W. 119th St., 16th fl. (bet. Amsterdam Ave. & Morningside Dr.) | 212-666-9490 | www.terraceinthesky.com

Boasting wraparound views of the "twinkling city", this "upscale" Morningside Heights aerie follows through with "excellent" French-Med fare and "pro" service; its "old-school charm" (complete with a "harpist") makes for "memorable meals", but given equally "memorable tabs", many reserve it for "special celebrations."

Terroir ◐ Italian
20 | 17 | 22 | $40

E Village | 413 E. 12th St. (bet. Ave. A & 1st Ave.) | no phone
TriBeCa | 24 Harrison St. (bet. Greenwich & Hudson Sts.) | 212-625-9463
www.wineisterroir.com

Not just for "wine geeks", these "unpretentious" enotecas from the owners of Hearth pair an "impressive selection" of vinos with "on-the-money" Italian tapas; both are overseen by "engaged" staffers, though the East Village original is quite the "squeeze" compared to the airier TriBeCa offshoot; P.S. a new Murray Hill outpost is in the works.

NEW Tertulia ◐Ⓢ Spanish
- | - | - | M

W Village | 359 Sixth Ave. (Washington Pl.) | 646-559-9909 | www.tertulianyc.com

The first solo effort of chef Seamus Mullen (ex Boqueria), this West Village tapas specialist evokes the cider houses of Northern Spain, offering cured meats, cheeses and other dishes from that region; prices are moderate, and the food's served in a faux rustic setting.

Testaccio Italian
22 | 21 | 20 | $46

LIC | 47-30 Vernon Blvd. (47th Rd.) | Queens | 718-937-2900 | www.testacciony.com

"Surprisingly sophisticated" for LIC, this slick, multilevel Italian turns out "authentic Roman food" in a "beautiful" setting that combines elements of the "rustic" and the "high-tech"; moderate prices and "attentive" service make for "fully satisfying" dining – the only problem is what the name sounds like.

Thai Market *Thai*
24 | 19 | 20 | $25

W 100s | 960 Amsterdam Ave. (bet. 107th & 108th Sts.) | 212-280-4575 |
www.thaimarketny.com

The UWS Thai scene has a new "neighborhood leader" in this "dependable" Siamese offering "incendiary" specialties, "Bangkok street" vibes and "fast", "courteous" service; the portions may be "small-ish", but happily so are the prices.

Thalassa *Greek/Seafood*
24 | 24 | 23 | $65

TriBeCa | 179 Franklin St. (bet. Greenwich & Hudson Sts.) | 212-941-7661 |
www.thalassanyc.com

Hard-core Hellenists hail the "theatrical display" of "amazingly fresh fish" arranged on a "mountain of ice" at this "elite" TriBeCan; the "top-dollar" tabs are easier to digest thanks to "attentive" service and a "gorgeous", wide-open setting that feels like a "Greek isle escape."

Thalia ❷ *American*
20 | 20 | 19 | $49

W 50s | 828 Eighth Ave. (50th St.) | 212-399-4444 |
www.restaurantthalia.com

"Perfectly located for the theater", this "sure-bet" Hell's Kitchen American owes its "popularity" to "solid" food served by "friendly" folks for "reasonable costs"; if the "colorful" confines are too "busy", there's always outdoor seating with primo "Eighth Avenue people-watching."

This Little Piggy
Had Roast Beef ❷ *Sandwiches*
▽ 23 | 10 | 15 | $13

E Village | 149 First Ave. (bet. 9th & 10th Sts.) | 212-253-1500 |
www.thislittlepiggynyc.com

"Hefty", "juicy" roast beef sandwiches are the specialty of this "novel" East Village "hole-in-the-wall" that draws both "protein cravers" and the "budget-minded"; sure, it's a seatless "shoebox", but it stays open into the wee, wee, wee hours – 4 AM on weekends.

Thistle Hill Tavern *American*
23 | 19 | 21 | $38

Park Slope | 441 Seventh Ave. (15th St.) | Brooklyn | 347-599-1262 |
www.thistlehillbrooklyn.com

This year-old Park Slope American has such a "home-away-from-home" ambiance that it's already "crazy busy" (it "feels like it's been there forever"); credit also goes to its "locally grown", "seasonal" menu, "creative cocktails" and "modest" pricing.

Tía Pol *Spanish*
24 | 15 | 19 | $44

Chelsea | 205 10th Ave. (bet. 22nd & 23rd Sts.) | 212-675-8805 |
www.tiapol.com

"Every bite delivers" at this Chelsea Spaniard, an "unbeatable" source of "scrumptious" tapas and "smooth sangria" dispatched in a "tiny", "rough-and-ready" room; "cramped" quarters, "long lines" and checks that "get big fast" don't deter diehards from "taking a deep breath and squeezing in."

Tiella *Italian*
▽ 26 | 17 | 24 | $55

E 60s | 1109 First Ave. (bet. 60th & 61st Sts.) | 212-588-0100 |
www.tiellanyc.com

Eastsiders salute this Italian "hideaway" for its "creative" Neapolitan cooking, ranging from "superior pastas" to the "must-get", pan pizza–

like namesake dish; the food arrives in a "tight" "railroad" setting and is no bargain, but "eager-to-please" service distracts.

Tiffin Wallah *Indian/Kosher/Vegetarian* | 23 | 12 | 16 | $20 |

Murray Hill | 127 E. 28th St. (bet. Lexington Ave. & Park Ave S.) | 212-685-7301 | www.tiffindelivery.us

"Authentic" Southern Indian cooking that's both vegetarian and kosher – not to mention "one of the best values" around – is the draw at this "subdued" Curry Hill subcontinental; fans don't mind the sari decor and service given the "stellar" $7 lunch buffet.

NEW Tiny's ● *American* | - | - | - | M |

TriBeCa | 135 W. Broadway (bet. Duane & Thomas Sts.) | 212-374-1135

Aptly named, this compact new TriBeCan comes via nightlife kingpin Matt Abramcyk (Beatrice Inn, The Bunker) and NY Ranger Sean Avery; the equally compact American menu showcases a notable burger, served in an artfully distressed duplex setting comprised of scuffed tile, crumbling brick and pressed tin.

Tipsy Parson *Southern* | 20 | 19 | 18 | $46 |

Chelsea | 156 Ninth Ave. (bet. 19th & 20th Sts.) | 212-620-4545 | www.tipsyparson.com

"Southern comfort food done right" sums up this Chelsea charmer where the "butter-overload" cooking is as "delicious" as the name is "strange" and the drinks are "potent"; the "Low Country vibe" is reflected in its "cute" vintage tchotchkes and "helpful" but "slow" service.

Z Tocqueville ⊠ *American/French* | 25 | 25 | 26 | $78 |

Union Sq | 1 E. 15th St. (bet. 5th Ave. & Union Sq. W.) | 212-647-1515 | www.tocquevillerestaurant.com

All about "subdued elegance", this "tranquil" Union Square French-New American showcases the "brilliant" cooking of chef Marco Moreira served by a "first-class" team in a "lovely room"; of course, such "refinement" can be "expensive", but it's a natural for "sealing a deal" or popping the question – and the $29 prix fixe lunch is a "true bargain."

NEW Tolani ● *Eclectic* | 24 | 21 | 24 | $45 |

W 70s | 410 Amsterdam Ave. (bet. 79th & 80th Sts.) | 212-873-6252 | www.tolaninyc.com

Global small plates are paired with "excellent" wines at this "transporting" UWS newcomer offering an "original" but "accessible" roster in a "sexy" duplex setting; "warm" hospitality and a "pretty" garden make this "standout" "worth a visit from anywhere."

Toledo ⊠ *Spanish* | ▽ 24 | 23 | 24 | $62 |

Murray Hill | 6 E. 36th St. (bet. 5th & Madison Aves.) | 212-696-5036 | www.toledorestaurant.com

"Lesser known" but long frequented by an "old-fashioned" crowd, this circa-1975 Murray Hill Spaniard supplies "excellent" classic cooking and "A-plus service" in a "quiet" setting with "well-spaced" tables; though "consistently satisfying", holy Toledo, it's "high priced."

Toloache *Mexican* | 23 | 17 | 20 | $45 |

W 50s | 251 W. 50th St. (bet. B'way & 8th Ave.) | 212-581-1818
(continued)

(continued)

Toloache Taqueria 🗷 *Mexican*

NEW **Financial District** | 83 Maiden Ln. (bet. Gold & William Sts.) | 212-809-9800
www.toloachenyc.com

"Savory", "upscale" Mexican dishes are matched with "sublime" margaritas, a "cheerful" ambiance and "super-friendly" service at this "top-choice", tile-lined cantina in the Theater District; its new Maiden Lane spin-off feeds "street food" to the FiDi's "lunch-hour" masses, while an Upper East Side outlet is in the works.

Tommaso *Italian*

24 | 20 | 22 | $53

Dyker Heights | 1464 86th St. (bet. Bay 8th St. & 15th Ave.) | Brooklyn | 718-236-9883 | www.tommasoinbrooklyn.com

"Character oozes" out of this circa-1969 Dyker Heights "classic" where "wonderful" red-sauce dishes arrive along with an "aria or two" by "opera-singing" chef-owner Thomas Verdillo; it may be a tad "expensive", but "there's a lot of love behind the cooking" and the music.

🗷 Tomoe Sushi *Japanese*

26 | 9 | 16 | $43

G Village | 172 Thompson St. (bet. Bleecker & Houston Sts.) | 212-777-9346
The "long lines" outside speak volumes about the "oversized, lusciously fresh" sushi sliced at this Tokyo-style Village Japanese; sure, there's "zero ambiance" in the "postage-stamp" space and service is "not friendly", but no one cares what with its "good-value" tabs.

Tom's ⊅ *Diner*

21 | 17 | 23 | $18

Prospect Heights | 782 Washington Ave. (Sterling Pl.) | Brooklyn | 718-636-9738

"Deservedly a neighborhood institution", this '30s-era Prospect Heights diner slings "every kind of pancake imaginable" plus "forgettable coffee" in "wonderfully retro" digs; "long" weekend waits are a fact of life, but genuine "hospitality" and low tabs compensate.

Tony's Di Napoli ❶ *Italian*

21 | 16 | 20 | $41

W 40s | 147 W. 43rd St. (bet. B'way & 6th Ave.) | 212-221-0100 | www.tonysnyc.com

The food arrives "by the cubic yard" at this "family-style" Southern Italian, a "Carmine's wannabe" dishing out "reliable but not outstanding" grub; "typical Theater District chaos" detracts, but "great value" trumps the "noise" and "factory" atmosphere; sadly, the popular UES outlet has shuttered, "done in by the Second Avenue subway."

Topaz Thai *Thai*

21 | 12 | 16 | $30

W 50s | 127 W. 56th St. (bet. 6th & 7th Aves.) | 212-957-8020 | www.topazthai.com

Recently "doubled in size", this Midtown Thai near Carnegie Hall offers "vibrant" fare for "inexpensive" sums; the digs are "dated" and the service "utilitarian", but at least the "food arrives with speed."

🗷 Torrisi Italian Specialties *Italian*

27 | 15 | 20 | $78

NoLita | 250 Mulberry St. (bet. Prince & Spring Sts.) | 212-965-0955 | www.piginahat.com

Changes are afoot at this "must-try" NoLita Italian, formerly a deli-restaurant hybrid that's transitioning into a full-time dining room serving the same "virtuoso" dinners for a "reasonable" $60 set price (and now

Vote at ZAGAT.com

adding prix fixe lunches); the no-rez rule and "long waits" for a seat remain in place, though the revamp puts the Decor score in question.

Tortilleria Nixtamal ⊄ *Mexican* ▽ 24 | 10 | 18 | $15

Corona | 104-05 47th Ave. (bet. 104th & 108th Sts.) | Queens |
718-699-2434 | www.tortillerianixtamal.com

"They grind their own corn" at this Corona "storefront wonder" known for "homemade tortillas" as well as "expertly crafted" tacos and tamales; maybe the ultrasmall setting "could use an upgrade", but it's "cheap" and the mood's "happy."

Tosca Café ● *Italian* ▽ 21 | 19 | 16 | $36

Throgs Neck | 4038 E. Tremont Ave. (bet. Miles & Sampson Aves.) |
Bronx | 718-239-3300 | www.toscanyc.com

Pretty "cool" for Throgs Neck, this "club"-like Italian includes a "wonderful" sushi bar and "delicious" pizza on its "all-over-the-place" menu; service is only "fair", and regulars admit the "food is good, but the scene's better."

Z Totonno's Pizzeria Napolitano M⊄ *Pizza* 26 | 10 | 14 | $20

Coney Island | 1524 Neptune Ave. (bet. W. 15th & 16th Sts.) | Brooklyn |
718-372-8606

A "mandatory stop" in Coney Island, this "historic", circa-1924 venue slings "bubbly-crusted", "bucket list"–worthy pies so "special" that it's voted the No. 1 pizzeria in this year's Survey; "dated" decor and "Brooklynese curt" service buttress its "old-school" authenticity.

Totto Ramen ⊄ *Noodle Shop* 25 | 10 | 16 | $19

W 50s | 366 W. 52nd St. (bet. 8th & 9th Aves.) | 212-582-0052 |
www.tottoramen.com

"Luxurious" broths and "delicious" noodles render fans "speechless" at this Hell's Kitchen "total ramen experience" where "crazy lines" are part of the experience (blame the "affordable" tabs); as for its "impossible" dimensions – "if it were any smaller, it would be a food truck."

Tournesol *French* 25 | 17 | 22 | $42

LIC | 50-12 Vernon Blvd. (bet. 50th & 51st Aves.) | Queens | 718-472-4355 |
www.tournesolnyc.com

"Like Paris, only friendlier", this French bistro lures "loyal" neighbors with "outstanding" cooking served in a "Left Bank"-ish room; though somewhat "out-of-the-way" in "emerging LIC", it's "near *le métro*" and just "one stop from Grand Central."

Z Traif ●M *Eclectic* 27 | 18 | 22 | $40

Williamsburg | 229 S. Fourth St. (bet. Havemeyer & Roebling Sts.) |
Brooklyn | 347-844-9578 | www.traifny.com

Set on the edge of Hasidic Williamsburg, this "ironically named" Eclectic offers an "exciting" small-plates menu that's "as delicious as it is unkosher" (think lots of pork and shellfish); its "loud hipster" crowd says it "lives up to the hype" "hitting high notes" for a "terrific price."

Trattoria Alba *Italian* 21 | 18 | 21 | $41

Murray Hill | 233 E. 34th St. (bet. 2nd & 3rd Aves.) | 212-689-3200 |
www.trattoriaalba.com

Older diners escape the "young Murray Hill crowd" at this "longtime favorite" offering "leisurely" Northern Italian meals overseen by a "welcoming" crew; sure, the decor may be "tired" and the chow "inconsistent", but it's still a bona fide "neighborhood" destination.

Trattoria Cinque *Italian* | 21 | 22 | 22 | $44

TriBeCa | 363 Greenwich St. (bet. Franklin & Harrison Sts.) | 212-965-0555 | www.trattoriacinquenyc.com

"Quiet" and fairly "undiscovered", this "sprawling" TriBeCa Italian delivers "simplicity that satisfies" with a five-choices-for-each-course "gimmick", plus "addictive" thin-crust pizzas; "shareable" portions add to the "value", so locals label it their "ace-in-the-hole."

Trattoria Dell'Arte ● *Italian* | 23 | 21 | 21 | $58

W 50s | 900 Seventh Ave. (bet. 56th & 57th Sts.) | 212-245-9800 | www.trattoriadellarte.com

Whether for a "biz meeting" or before Carnegie Hall, this "perfect-location" Tuscan is always "buzzing" thanks to an "unbelievable" antipasti bar and "trademark paper-thin" pizza; the "fun '80s decor" includes a giant "body parts" sculpture, but the big tabs make it best on an "expense account."

⊠ Trattoria L'incontro Ⓜ *Italian* | 27 | 20 | 25 | $56

Astoria | 21-76 31st St. (Ditmars Blvd.) | Queens | 718-721-3532 | www.trattorialincontro.com

"As good as it gets" in Astoria and sometimes even "better than Manhattan", this "first-class" trattoria features the "Midas-touch" Italian cooking of chef-owner Rocco Sacramone; devotees don't notice the "Midtown prices" and "Queens decor", mesmerized by the waiters' "memorized recitation" of a "telephone-directory" list of specials.

Trattoria Pesce & Pasta *Italian/Seafood* | 19 | 14 | 18 | $38

E 80s | 1562 Third Ave. (bet. 87th & 88th Sts.) | 212-987-4696
W 90s | 625 Columbus Ave. (bet. 90th & 91st Sts.) | 212-579-7970
W Village | 262 Bleecker St. (bet. 6th Ave. & 7th Ave. S.) | 212-645-2993 | www.pesce-pasta.com ●

"Good value" seafood and other "straightforward" Italian eats turn up at this "red-sauce" "neighborhood" threesome; although it's "nothing exotic or particularly exciting", at least you "won't leave hungry" or impoverished.

Trattoria Romana *Italian* | 26 | 17 | 23 | $48

Dongan Hills | 1476 Hylan Blvd. (Benton Ave.) | Staten Island | 718-980-3113 | www.trattoriaromana.com

"Exceptionally good" cooking with "Roman flair" earns this Dongan Hills Italian "top"-choice status in Staten Island, while "personal attention" from the staff plays up the "family" vibe; "close quarters" and "no reservations" are downsides, but at least it "won't empty your wallet."

Trattoria Toscana Ⓜ *Italian* | ▽ 24 | 17 | 24 | $47

W Village | 64 Carmine St. (bet. Bedford St. & 7th Ave. S.) | 212-675-8736

"Excellent" traditional Tuscan cooking and "spot-on" service make this "calm" West Village Italian a natural for "unpretentious" dining; ok, it's "not glamorous", but locals say it's "just what you want in a neighborhood restaurant."

	FOOD	DECOR	SERVICE	COST

Trattoria Trecolori *Italian* | 23 | 19 | 23 | $43

W 40s | 254 W. 47th St. (bet. B'way & 8th Ave.) | 212-997-4540 |
www.trattoriatrecolori.com
They "make you feel like family" at this "upbeat" Theater District Italian
offering "thoughtfully prepared" grub for "decent" dough; a "spacious"
setting and service that's "never rushed" enhance the "comfy" feel.

Tre Dici 🖂 *Italian* | 23 | 20 | 21 | $52

Chelsea | 128 W. 26th St. (bet. 6th & 7th Aves.) | 212-243-8183
Tre Dici Steak 🖂 *Steak*
Chelsea | 128 W. 26th St., 2nd fl. (bet. 6th & 7th Aves.) | 212-243-2085
www.tredicinyc.com
Tucked away on a "quiet" Chelsea street, this "intimate" Italian pleases
with "creative" cooking, "pleasant" service and *"moderno"* decor; upstairs, a "solid", pricier steakhouse takes you "back to Prohibition"
days with its "unmarked" doors and New Orleans bordello looks.

Tree *French* | 20 | 17 | 20 | $42

E Village | 190 First Ave. (bet. 11th & 12th Sts.) | 212-358-7171 |
www.treebistro.com
Regulars are rooting for this "small" East Village French bistro where
the pricing offers "value" and the "simple yet satisfying" meals demonstrate "attention to detail"; for best results, "eat outside" in the all-
seasons back garden.

NEW Tremont *American* | - | - | - | E

W Village | 51 Bank St. (W. 4th St.) | 212-488-1019 | www.tremontnyc.com
Bringing a Hamptons feel to the West Village, this airy American newcomer exudes beachlike vibes via a white-on-white color scheme and
laid-back airs; the simple, seafood-heavy menu has Mediterranean
leanings and is priced for the South Fork set.

Tre Otto *Italian* | 20 | 15 | 16 | $44

E 90s | 1408 Madison Ave. (bet. 97th & 98th Sts.) | 212-860-8880 |
www.treotto.com
"Underserved" Carnegie Hill gets a lift from this "pleasant" Italian
yearling serving "basic", "delicious" eats for an "agreeable" price
point; "poor" service and a "small", "crowded" setting are forgotten in
its "adorable" garden.

Trestle on Tenth *American* | 21 | 17 | 20 | $49

Chelsea | 242 10th Ave. (24th St.) | 212-645-5659 | www.trestleontenth.com
"Gallery-hoppers" and "High Line" gawkers tout this "popular" West
Chelsea spot for its "lovingly prepared" New American food with a
pronounced Swiss accent; a "pleasant" staff and "soothing" garden
make the somewhat "pricey" tabs more tolerable.

Tribeca Grill *American* | 23 | 21 | 22 | $62

TriBeCa | 375 Greenwich St. (Franklin St.) | 212-941-3900 |
www.tribecagrill.com
Produced by Drew Nieporent and Robert De Niro, this longtime
TriBeCa "standard-bearer" still draws "interesting" locals and the
"tourist trade" with "quality" New American cooking and "kingly"
treatment; its "adult" following eats up its "old NYC charm" and overlooks the modern-day prices; check out the upstairs party space.

	FOOD	DECOR	SERVICE	COST

Triomphe *French*
25 | 23 | 25 | $69

W 40s | Iroquois Hotel | 49 W. 44th St. (bet. 5th & 6th Aves.) | 212-453-4233 | www.triompheny.com

To go "upscale" all the way, try this Theater District French sleeper that's praised for "cosmopolitan" cooking and a "tasteful", "grown-up" setting; "pampering", time-sensitive service makes it "ideal" for ticket-holders, leaving "too-high" prices as the only snag.

Tsampa ● *Tibetan*
▽ 20 | 17 | 20 | $28

E Village | 212 E. Ninth St. (bet. 2nd & 3rd Aves.) | 212-614-3226

A "little slice of Zen" in the East Village, this "unusual" spot offers a "healthy", vegetarian-centric Tibetan menu that's both "familiar and different at the same time"; a "dark", "calming" setting and "afford-ability" seal the deal for its "NYU" fan base.

Tse Yang *Chinese*
23 | 23 | 23 | $66

E 50s | 34 E. 51st St. (bet. Madison & Park Aves.) | 212-688-5447 | www.tseyangnyc.com

"Gourmet Chinese" food fit for a "royal dynasty" draws the "business" and "special-occasion" set to this 30-year-old Midtowner renowned for its "terrific" Peking duck; a "mesmerizing" fish tank and "old-school", "white-jacketed" waiters make the "upmarket" tabs more understandable.

Tuck Shop *Australian*
▽ 21 | 11 | 19 | $13

NEW Chelsea | Chelsea Mkt. | 75 Ninth Ave. (bet. 15th & 16th Sts.) | 212-255-2021
E Village | 115 St. Marks Pl. (bet. Ave. A & 1st Ave.) | 212-979-5200 ●
E Village | 68 E. First St. (bet. 1st & 2nd Aves.) | 212-979-5200 ●
www.tuckshopnyc.com

"Savory meat pies" are the "Down Under" specialty of this "easy" Aussie trio that "fills your belly" for a "frugal" price; the affable staff "makes you want to stay forever", despite "small", "greasy-hole" setups.

Tulcingo del Valle ⊘ *Mexican*
▽ 22 | 7 | 16 | $20

W 40s | 665 10th Ave. (bet. 46th & 47th Sts.) | 212-262-5510 | www.tulcingorestaurant.com

"Street-cart goodness" arrives in a sit-down "coffee-shop" setting at this Hell's Kitchen Mexican "find" touted for its "authentic" Puebla-style cooking; the "amateurish" service, "down 'n' dirty" decor and "cash-only" rule are forgotten when the ultra-"cheap" checks arrives.

NEW Tulsi *Indian*
21 | 22 | 20 | $55

E 40s | 211 E. 46th St. (bet. 2nd & 3rd Aves.) | 212-888-0820 | www.tulsinyc.com

"Passionate" chef Hemant Mathur (ex Dévi) is the mind behind this "modern Indian" newcomer near Grand Central serving "innovative", intricately spiced subcontinental fare; the "airy", "contemporary" setting and "superb" service are in keeping with the "luxury" pricing.

Turkish Cuisine ● *Turkish*
21 | 15 | 20 | $35

W 40s | 631 Ninth Ave. (bet. 44th & 45th Sts.) | 212-397-9650 | www.turkishcuisinenyc.com

Forget the "bland name", this "easygoing" Theater District "standby" comes across with "honest" Turkish cuisine that's "priced right" and

	FOOD	DECOR	SERVICE	COST

served by a "prompt" team; aesthetes avoid the "sparse" interior by dining in the "little back garden."

Turkish Grill | Turkish
23 | 16 | 21 | $33

Sunnyside | 42-03 Queens Blvd. (42nd St.) | Queens | 718-392-3838 | www.turkishgrillnyc.com

"Wonderful smells" emanate from the kitchen of this Sunnyside "gem" that rolls out a "plentiful" array of "delicious" Turkish items; a "spiffy" new redo may not be reflected in the ratings, but the "affable" service and "good-deal" pricing are readily apparent.

Turkish Kitchen | Turkish
22 | 18 | 20 | $42

Murray Hill | 386 Third Ave. (bet. 27th & 28th Sts.) | 212-679-6633 | www.turkishkitchen.com

There's "no istan-bull" about this "special" Murray Hill Turk, now in its 20th year and as "popular" as ever thanks to "flavorful" cooking, "designer martinis" and a "high-gloss", "red-walled" setting; prices are "reasonable" enough, particularly Sunday's $22 all-you-can-eat brunch.

Turkuaz | Turkish
19 | 20 | 20 | $39

W 100s | 2637 Broadway (100th St.) | 212-665-9541 | www.turkuazrestaurant.com

"Ali Baba"–worthy tents and "plush pillows" set the "exotic" mood at this UWS Turk where "bountiful mezes" and "superlative" kebabs win fans; "skilled" service and "reasonable" tabs draw huzzahs, though the "boogying belly dancers" are either "entertaining" or "unfortunate."

Tuscany Grill | Italian
23 | 19 | 22 | $49

Bay Ridge | 8620 Third Ave. (bet. 86th & 87th Sts.) | Brooklyn | 718-921-5633

Locals laud the "sumptuous" Tuscan fare plied by this longtime Bay Ridge Italian, a "friendly" joint with "gracious" service and pricing that "won't burn a hole in your pocket"; though some suggest a decor "update", others say it works fine for "date night."

12th St. Bar & Grill | American
21 | 20 | 21 | $40

Park Slope | 1123 Eighth Ave. (12th St.) | Brooklyn | 718-965-9526 | www.12thstreetbarandgrill.com

The "quintessential neighborhood" eatery, this "friendly, accommodating" Park Slope "standby" serves New American staples "with finesse" at "reasonable" rates; its "more casual" round-the-corner pub has the same menu, but lacks the "bonus" of validated parking.

12 Chairs | American/Mideastern
20 | 16 | 18 | $28

SoHo | 56 MacDougal St. (bet. Houston & Prince Sts.) | 212-254-8640

Though it "accommodates more" diners than its name suggests, "little" is the word for this "casual", "living room"–like SoHo vet cherished for its "tasty" American-Mideastern chow; any grumbles about "lowkey" (read: "slow") service are quelled by the "cheap" prices.

⮾ 21 Club ⧉ | American
22 | 24 | 24 | $73

W 50s | 21 W. 52nd St. (bet. 5th & 6th Aves.) | 212-582-7200 | www.21club.com

At this circa-1929 "icon" of "old NY" in Midtown, you can "rub elbows" with "influential" folk and be "treated like you belong" by a "first-class" tuxedoed staff in "former-speakeasy" digs, where the bar/dining room is hung with "toy cars, trains, planes" and other corporate memorabilia donated by its patrons; just "dress properly" (jackets required) and prepare to pay "big bucks" for "country club-style" American fare – or go for the "fab deal" of a $30 lunch prix fixe; P.S. the "refined" upstairs private rooms are "perfect" for parties.

26 Seats Ⓜ French
22 | 16 | 20 | $41

E Village | 168 Ave. B (bet. 10th & 11th Sts.) | 212-677-4787 | www.26seatsonb.com

"Holes-in-the-wall don't get any more charming" than this "tiny" East Village French bistro vending "reliable favorites" for a "reasonable price" *sans* attitude; "close-knit seating" lends an "intimate feel" perfect for kindling "romance" – or "hearing what's going on at the next table."

Two Boots Pizza
18 | 10 | 15 | $16

E 40s | Grand Central | lower level (42nd St. & Vanderbilt Ave.) | 212-557-7992 | www.twoboots.com
E 80s | 1617 Second Ave. (84th St.) | 212-734-0317 | www.twoboots.com ◐
E Village | 42 Ave. A (3rd St.) | 212-254-1919 | www.twoboots.com ◐
NoHo | 74 Bleecker St. (B'way) | 212-777-1033 | www.twoboots.com ◐
W 40s | 625 Ninth Ave. (bet. 44th & 45th Sts.) | 212-956-2668 | www.twoboots.com ◐
W 90s | 2547 Broadway (bet. 95th & 96th Sts.) | 212-280-2668 | www.twoboots.com ◐
W Village | 201 W. 11th St. (7th Ave. S.) | 212-633-9096 | www.twoboots.com ◐
Park Slope | 514 Second St. (bet. 7th & 8th Aves.) | Brooklyn | 718-499-3253 | www.twobootsbrooklyn.com

"Kids of all ages" frequent this "cute" pizza chain turning out "zany" specialty pies with "unique" cornmeal crusts, "Louisiana-inspired toppings" and "goofy" names; but party-poopers call it "middle-America quality" and wonder whether they're booting the "once fresh" concept.

2 West American
▽ 22 | 23 | 23 | $59

Financial District | Ritz-Carlton Battery Park | 2 West St. (Battery Pl.) | 917-790-2525 | www.ritzcarlton.com

You'll feel as "comfortable and welcome" as the "Wall Street titans" who just may be dining beside you at this "elegant" New American refuge in the out-of-the-way Ritz-Carlton Battery Park; "expensive" tabs feel a little less so when you factor in the Hudson River view.

Txikito Spanish
25 | 16 | 21 | $48

Chelsea | 240 Ninth Ave. (bet. 24th & 25th Sts.) | 212-242-4730 | www.txikitonyc.com

"Distinctive" pintxos matched with a "different" kind of sangria transport diners from Chelsea to "San Sebastián" at this "rustic" Basque small-plate specialist; the "tiny" setting is on par with the humble costs, though habitués warn that the bill tends to "add up quickly"; P.S. it's pronounced 'chic-kee-toe.'

Umberto's Clam House Italian/Seafood
20 | 14 | 18 | $37

Little Italy | 132 Mulberry St. (bet. Grand & Hester Sts.) | 212-431-7545 | www.umbertosclamhouse.com ◐
Fordham | 2356 Arthur Ave. (186th St.) | Bronx | 718-220-2526 | www.umbertosclamhousebronx.com

Reopened at a new Mulberry Street address, this "infamous" – remember Joey Gallo? – Italian seafooder still draws "touristy" types with its signature linguine with clam sauce and affordable pricing; its Arthur Avenue spin-off replicates the experience, right down to the "indifferent" service and "seen-better-days" decor.

Umi Nom 🅵 *Filipino/Thai* ▽ | 26 | 20 | 22 | $29 |

Clinton Hill | 433 DeKalb Ave. (Classon Ave.) | Brooklyn | 718-789-8806 | www.uminom.com

"Inventive", surprisingly "excellent" Thai-accented Filipino food lures locals to this "tiny" Clinton Hill BYO; "pleasant" digs, ultra-affordable tabs and welcoming service make up for the "nondescript" locale.

Uncle Jack's Steakhouse *Steak* 23 | 20 | 22 | $70 |

Garment District | 440 Ninth Ave. (bet. 34th & 35th Sts.) | 212-244-0005
W 50s | 44 W. 56th St. (bet. 5th & 6th Aves.) | 212-245-1550
Bayside | 39-40 Bell Blvd. (40th Ave.) | Queens | 718-229-1100
www.unclejacks.com

Forget the "folksy name", this serious chophouse trio seduces the "white-collar" crowd with "fine steaks" and "service with a capital 'S'"; some bemoan the "suburban attitude" and "expensive" pricing, but if "not quite top-of-the-class", it's still way up there.

Uncle Nick's *Greek* 20 | 12 | 18 | $37 |

Chelsea | 382 Eighth Ave. (29th St.) | 212-609-0500
W 50s | 747 Ninth Ave. (bet. 50th & 51st Sts.) | 212-245-7992
www.unclenicksgreekrestaurant.com

Workmanlike "alternatives to Astoria", these "unfussy" Greeks offer "solid" grilled fish and the "spectacle of flaming cheese" for "reasonable" sums; while the Chelsea outlet is the more spacious of the two, in "hectic" Hell's Kitchen an adjacent *ouzaria* helps ease the crush.

🅓 Union Square Cafe *American* 27 | 23 | 26 | $70 |

Union Sq | 21 E. 16th St. (bet. 5th Ave. & Union Sq. W.) | 212-243-4020 | www.unionsquarecafe.com

Diners have an "emotional connection" with Danny Meyer's "sentimental-favorite" flagship off Union Square that "never gets old, just better" thanks to its "full-flavored", "Greenmarket-fresh" American cooking, "on-the-ball" service, stylish surrounds and that "camaraderie" at the bar; it's "lasted an eternity in restaurant time" – 27 years – in part because "you can carry on a conversation" here.

Untitled *American* - | - | - | E |

E 70s | Whitney Museum | 945 Madison Ave., downstairs (75th St.) | 212-570-3670 | www.untitledatthewhitney.com

Like a piece of installation art, this new Whitney cafe from Danny Meyer is well integrated with its surroundings, from its starkly modern look that echoes the exterior architecture to the all-American menu reflecting the museum's all-American art collection; coffee-shop items like soups, sandwiches and omelets are offered for breakfast and lunch, while a limited, more ambitious dinner menu is served Friday–Sunday only.

Ushiwakamaru 🅵 *Japanese* ▽ | 26 | 18 | 22 | $85 |

G Village | 136 W. Houston St. (bet. MacDougal & Sullivan Sts.) | 212-228-4181

"Masterful" sushi chefs "dazzle" purists at this "unexpected" Village Japanese providing "exquisite" fish in a simple, "small" setting; yes, it's "expensive" (especially if you go omakase), but oh-so-"gratifying."

	FOOD	DECOR	SERVICE	COST

Uskudar *Turkish* `21` `12` `20` `$37`

E 70s | 1405 Second Ave. (bet. 73rd & 74th Sts.) | 212-988-4046 | www.uskudarnyc.com

"Deliciously seasoned" food seemingly straight off the "Bosphorus" turns up at this "terrific" UES Turk; sure, it's "tiny" with "unassuming" decor, but the "welcoming" mood and "inexpensive" tabs make for most "satisfying" dining.

Utsav *Indian* `21` `18` `20` `$43`

W 40s | 1185 Sixth Ave., 2nd fl. (enter on 46th St., bet. 6th & 7th Aves.) | 212-575-2525 | www.utsavny.com

"Proximity to the theaters" and a "fantastic" $19 lunch buffet are the key selling points of this "upscale" Midtown Indian that's somewhat "tucked away" but worth seeking out; the food is "above average", the service "caring" and overall mood "comfortable."

Uva ● *Italian* `22` `22` `20` `$42`

E 70s | 1486 Second Ave. (bet. 77th & 78th Sts.) | 212-472-4552 | www.uvawinebar.com

"Young" "pretty" folk flock to this "buzzy" UES wine bar for "tasty" Italiana and "fab" vinos at "moderate" tabs; it's renowned as a "first-date spot" thanks to a "lovely" back garden and "romantic", "rustic" interior that's "as attractive as the staff."

Uvarara Ⓜ *Italian* `▽` `26` `23` `22` `$37`

Middle Village | 79-28 Metropolitan Ave. (bet. 79th & 80th Sts.) | Queens | 718-894-0052 | www.uvararany.com

"Something special" in "middle-of-nowhere" Middle Village, this family-run Italian draws huzzahs for its "serious" wine list, "impressive" gnocchi and "surprisingly good" Italian menu; it's "small" and "quaint" with "old-world" decor and fair pricing.

Valbella Ⓩ *Italian* `26` `24` `25` `$81`

Meatpacking | 421 W. 13th St. (bet. 9th Ave. & Washington St.) | 212-645-7777 | www.valbellanyc.com

"Adult" dining is alive and well at this "classy" Meatpacking District Northern Italian that draws everyone from "Regis Philbin" to "Tony Soprano look-alikes" with its *bella* cooking, "blow-your-mind" wine list and "chic modern" setting (with "spectacular" private rooms upstairs); an "unlimited line of credit" helps when it's time to negotiate your exit visa.

NEW **Valentino's on the Green** Ⓜ *Italian*   `21` `23` `22` `$60`

Bayside | 201-10 Cross Island Pkwy. (bet. Clearview Expwy. & Utopia Pkwy.) | Queens | 718-352-2300 | www.valentinosonthegreen.com

Matinee idol Rudolph Valentino's former residence is home to this "elegant", expensive new Italian in Bayside (fka Caffé on the Green) that brings "fine dining to Queens"; a "romantic" setting with views of Little Bay and the Throgs Neck Bridge makes the *delizioso* food even tastier.

Vandaag *Danish/Dutch* `20` `18` `20` `$51`

E Village | 103 Second Ave. (6th St.) | 212-253-0470 | www.vandaagnyc.com

"Going Dutch" takes on a new meaning at this "adventurous" East Villager specializing in the cuisines of Denmark and Holland; while the

| | FOOD | DECOR | SERVICE | COST |

"creative" cooking and "well-crafted" cocktails outperform the "austere", "industrial" decor, some find it too "odd" and "pricey."

Vanderbilt, The ● American   23 | 20 | 20 | $44

Prospect Heights | 570 Vanderbilt Ave. (Bergen St.) | Brooklyn | 718-623-0570 | www.thevanderbiltnyc.com

"First-rate", "delicately flavored" New Americana via Saul Bolton draws "hipsters" and the "strollerati" to this "roomy" retreat on Prospect Heights' up-and-coming "Vanderbilt Avenue strip"; it's "even better for brunch", provided you can withstand the "impossible" decibels.

V&T ● Italian/Pizza   18 | 10 | 15 | $24

W 100s | 1024 Amsterdam Ave. (bet. 110th & 111th Sts.) | 212-666-8051 | www.vtpizzeriarestaurant.com

"Feeding Columbia University" since 1945, this "checkered-tablecloth" Italian "relic" slaps together "good sloppy pizza" and assorted "red-sauce" staples for low dough; it's "cheesy but endearing", despite "greasy-spoon" decor and often "incompetent" service.

Vanessa's Dumpling House ● Chinese   20 | 7 | 11 | $10

E Village | 220 E. 14th St. (bet. 2nd & 3rd Aves.) | 212-529-1329
LES | 118A Eldridge St. (bet. Broome & Grand Sts.) | 212-625-8008
One of the "few bargains left in NYC", this East Village–LES Chinese duo vends "tasty, filling" dumplings for "bargain-basement" rates; there's "zero atmo" and "even less service", so insiders frequently get it to go.

Vatan Indian/Vegetarian   ∇ 24 | 23 | 25 | $38

Murray Hill | 409 Third Ave. (29th St.) | 212-689-5666 | www.vatanny.com

"No one goes home hungry" from this Murray Hill Indian "getaway" where the "vegetarian's delight" menu is offered in an "all-you-can-eat" Thali format for $30; an "atmospheric village setting" overseen by an "excellent" crew enhances the feeling of "stepping into another world."

Veniero's ● Dessert   24 | 15 | 15 | $18

E Village | 342 E. 11th St. (bet. 1st & 2nd Aves.) | 212-674-7070 | www.venierospastry.com

"Sinful splendors" are the specialty of this "old-school" Italian bakery that's been vending "luscious" cannoli, cakes and coffee drinks in the East Village since 1894; it "may be showing its age" and "long lines" are a given, but ultimately its longevity is "well deserved."

☑ Veritas ● American   26 | 22 | 26 | $92

Flatiron | 43 E. 20th St. (bet. B'way & Park Ave. S.) | 212-353-3700 | www.veritas-nyc.com

Now in its "second coming", this Flatiron "oenophile mecca" uncorks an "impeccable" New American menu that manages to "stand up to the imposing wine list"; no longer prix fixe-only, it's still "very expensive", though "wine-cellar" decor and "outstanding" service compensate.

Vermicelli Vietnamese   19 | 15 | 19 | $32

E 70s | 1492 Second Ave. (bet. 77th & 78th Sts.) | 212-288-8868 | www.vermicellinyc.com

Despite the Italian-sounding moniker, this "bustling" UES "neighborhood" joint offers "dependable" Vietnamese items served by a "fast" team in "tired" digs; though the "Hanoi prices" "can't be beat", this "steady" performer is even more "affordable" for lunch.

Veselka *Ukrainian* 20 | 12 | 16 | $23

E Village | 144 Second Ave. (9th St.) | 212-228-9682 ●
NEW **E Village** | 9 E. First St. (bet. Bowery & 2nd Ave.) | 212-387-7000
www.veselka.com

For "blintzes and borscht at 2 AM", look no further than this 24/7 East Village "hoot" that's been slinging "gut-busting" Ukrainian food in a "coffee-shop atmosphere" since 1954; it supplies big-time "bang for the buck" to a diverse crowd, and the slick new upcoming First Street spin-off promises more of the same.

Vespa *Italian* 18 | 17 | 19 | $47

E 80s | 1625 Second Ave. (bet. 84th & 85th Sts.) | 212-472-2050 | www.vesparestaurant.us

At this longtime UES "neighborhood" Italian, the "old-world charm" is echoed in the "no-surprises" menu, "fair prices" and "friendly service"; for a "*laissez-faire*" attitude adjustment, regulars retreat to its "lovely" leafy patio.

Vesta *Italian* ∇ 25 | 20 | 25 | $38

Astoria | 21-02 30th Ave. (21st St.) | Queens | 718-545-5550 | www.vestavino.com

A "breath of fresh air for Astoria", this "rustic" Italian thrills locals with "seasonal", Greenmarket-inspired cooking (and "remarkable pizza") served in an "intimate", "East Village–esque" setting sans "Manhattan attitude"; "local wines on tap" and reassuring rates seal the deal.

Vezzo *Pizza* 23 | 15 | 15 | $27

Murray Hill | 178 Lexington Ave. (31st St.) | 212-839-8300 | www.vezzothincrust.com

"Thin is in" at this Murray Hill pizzeria turning out "crackerlike-crusted" pies with "fresh toppings" in "crowded", brick-walled digs; even though there's "no atmosphere", minimal service and "always a wait" to get in, that "Shroomtown pie is a thing of beauty."

Via Brasil *Brazilian/Steak* 21 | 15 | 20 | $43

W 40s | 34 W. 46th St. (bet. 5th & 6th Aves.) | 212-997-1158 | www.viabrasilrestaurant.com

Perhaps "not terribly original", this "down-to-earth" Midtown Brazilian is "reliable" enough for its "solid", meat-centric menu ferried by an "amenable" team; the circa-1978 digs may be "unprepossessing", but "mind-bending" caipirinhas, moderate prices and weekend live music are adequate offsets.

Via Emilia 🔝⌖ *Italian* 23 | 15 | 20 | $40

Flatiron | 47 E. 21st St. (bet. B'way & Park Ave. S.) | 212-505-3072 | www.viaemilia.us

This "everyday" Flatiron eatery features the "rich" cuisine of Italy's Emilia-Romagna region paired with an "extensive selection" of Lambruscos; "reasonable" rates make up for the "inconvenient" cash-only policy and "too-modern" decor.

Viand *Coffee Shop* 18 | 8 | 17 | $23

E 60s | 673 Madison Ave. (bet. 61st & 62nd Sts.) | 212-751-6622 ⌖

(continued)

Viand
E 70s | 1011 Madison Ave. (78th St.) | 212-249-8250
E 80s | 300 E. 86th St. (2nd Ave.) | 212-879-9425 ●

Viand Cafe ● *Coffeehouse*
W 70s | 2130 Broadway (75th St.) | 212-877-2888 |
www.viandnyc.com

For a "classic New York City luncheonette" experience straight out of a "Woody Allen" movie (with the mayor in attendance), drop by these coffee-shop exemplars of a "vanishing genre"; the "decent" offerings include a signature "white-meat" turkey sandwich, and service so "quick" you won't notice the diner decor.

Via Quadronno *Italian*   22 | 15 | 17 | $44
E 70s | 25 E. 73rd St. (bet. 5th & Madison Aves.) | 212-650-9880

Via Quadronno Cafe ⊠ *Italian*
E 50s | GM Bldg. | 767 Fifth Ave. (59th St.) | 212-421-5300
www.viaquadronno.com

"Well-heeled" Madison Avenue types hobnob at this "charming" but "crowded" UES Milanese for its "addictive" espresso, panini and "Euro" people-watching; the Fifth Avenue spin-off is strictly takeout, but either way they won't break the bank.

ViceVersa *Italian*   22 | 22 | 23 | $55
W 50s | 325 W. 51st St. (bet. 8th & 9th Aves.) | 212-399-9291 |
www.viceversarestaurant.com

Anyway you look at it, this "firing-on-all-cylinders" Theater District Italian is a "hit" with ticket-holders thanks to "delicious, plentiful" food, "sleek", "spacious" environs and staffers "at your beck and call"; creative cuisine and a "cool NY" patio ice the cake.

Vico *Italian*   22 | 15 | 21 | $67
E 90s | 1302 Madison Ave. (bet. 92nd & 93rd Sts.) | 212-876-2222

"Familiar faces" are "treated like royalty" at this Carnegie Hill "oldie but goodie" where "classic, well-prepared" Italiana appeals to both "club" members and outsiders; "stuck-in-the-'80s" decor and "quite expensive" tabs are the only downsides.

Victor's Cafe ● *Cuban*   23 | 20 | 22 | $50
W 50s | 236 W. 52nd St. (bet. B'way & 8th Ave.) | 212-586-7714 |
www.victorscafe.com

"Plentiful" plates of "fantastic" Cuban cuisine and waiters oozing "Latino charm" conjure up "1940s Havana" at this 1963-vintage Theater District "standby"; the "convivial" ambiance is lubricated by "flowing sangria" and "one, two, cha-cha-cha" music that keep the joint "hopping."

View, The *American*   18 | 24 | 19 | $103
W 40s | Marriott Marquis Hotel | 1535 Broadway, 47th fl. (bet. 45th & 46th Sts.) | 212-704-8880 | www.theviewny.com

For a "stunning", "360-degree" panorama of Times Square and beyond, it's hard to beat this "revolving" New American "tourist heaven" atop the Marriott Marquis; the high, prix fixe-only prices for only "adequate" food and service may leave you "spinning", but cocktails and Sunday brunch are worth a whirl.

	FOOD	DECOR	SERVICE	COST

Villa Berulia *Italian* — 24 | 20 | 26 | $50

Murray Hill | 107 E. 34th St. (bet. Lexington & Park Aves.) | 212-689-1970 | www.villaberulia.com

"Family-run with lots of pride", this Murray Hill Italian is known for "consistently good" cooking, "fair pricing" and "coddling service" ("no problem" is the answer to every request); though it may "need dusting", its "welcoming", "quiet" mien never goes out of style.

Villa Mosconi ⊠ *Italian* — 21 | 17 | 23 | $48

G Village | 69 MacDougal St. (bet. Bleecker & Houston Sts.) | 212-673-0390 | www.villamosconi.com

"Like an old friend" to its fans, this Italian red-sauce "institution" has been slinging "*tutto buono*" eats in the Village since 1976; "gracious" service, "relatively modest" tabs and a "lovely" back garden complete the overall "enjoyable" picture.

NEW Villa Pacri ●⊠Ⓜ *Italian* — ▽ 24 | 25 | 19 | $64

Meatpacking | 55 Gansevoort St., 2nd fl. (bet. Greenwich & Washington Sts.) | 212-924-5559 | www.villapacri.com

From the Bagatelle team comes this surprisingly "nonsceney" Meatpacking Italian serving "delicious" chow in a "stunning", brick-walled space formerly home to Merkato 55; like the St. Barts original, it's "high on pretense" and targeted toward the champagne-swilling set.

Vincent's ● *Italian* — 22 | 14 | 19 | $42

Little Italy | 119 Mott St. (Hester St.) | 212-226-8133

The spirit of "old Little Italy" endures at this "gingham-tableclothed" survivor that's been dishing out "reliable" Italian food since 1904; though a few claim it's "not as good as it used to be", its "famous" hot sauce remains a "favorite."

Vinegar Hill House *American* — 25 | 20 | 21 | $50

Vinegar Hill | 72 Hudson Ave. (bet. Front & Water Sts.) | Brooklyn | 718-522-1018 | www.vinegarhillhouse.com

Way "off the beaten track" in "unknown" Vinegar Hill, this "destination" New American wins over "hipster foodie" types with its "first-rate" cooking, "oh-so-cozy" ambiance and "magical" outdoor garden; but many say "it's time they consider taking reservations" given the "dollhouse" dimensions and no-man's-land neighborhood.

Virgil's Real Barbecue ● *BBQ* — 20 | 15 | 18 | $35

W 40s | 152 W. 44th St. (bet. B'way & 6th Ave.) | 212-921-9494 | www.virgilsbbq.com

"Rural Texas" by way of Times Square, this "touristy" roadhouse delivers "gut-busting BBQ" without the "hearty price tag"; the "convenient" location and "rushed" service mean you'll make the curtain – though "you may nod off during the first act."

Vivolo ⊠ *Italian* — 19 | 18 | 21 | $50

E 70s | 140 E. 74th St. (bet. Lexington & Park Aves.) | 212-737-3533

Cucina Vivolo ⊠ *Italian*

E 70s | 138 E. 74th St. (bet. Lexington & Park Aves.) | 212-717-4700 | www.vivolonyc.com

An "older set" touts this "civilized" UES Italian duplex, a "dependable" choice for "quality" items served in a "dark", "fireplace"-equipped

| | FOOD | DECOR | SERVICE | COST |

townhouse by "rise-to-the-occasion" staffers; those looking for a "quickie" head for the cheaper next-door cafe, which serves breakfast.

Wa Jeal *Chinese*
24 | 15 | 19 | $32

E 80s | 1588 Second Ave. (bet. 82nd & 83rd Sts.) | 212-396-3339 | www.wajealrestaurant.com

"Fire extinguishers" come in handy at this "upscale" UES Sichuan that turns up the heat with "authentic" specialties; there's no decor and service skews "spotty", but overall, this one's the "real deal."

Walker's ◑ *Pub Food*
19 | 15 | 19 | $31

TriBeCa | 16 N. Moore St. (Varick St.) | 212-941-0142

Far from "TriBeCa trendy", this "unassuming", circa-1987 "neighborhood" tavern is an "old-school" kind of joint where the "waiters know everyone's names"; though the setting's strictly "barroom", the "great-tasting" pub grub's modestly priced and the service "personable."

Wall & Water *American*
20 | 23 | 20 | $54

Financial District | Andaz Wall Street Hotel | 75 Wall St. (Water St.) | 212-699-1700 | www.wallandwaterny.com

"Fine dining–starved" Lower Manhattan gets a "chic" jolt via this "über-modern" venue in the Andaz Wall Street, offering "farm-to-table" New Americana that's "a cut above typical hotel dining"; "high prices" and a "beautiful" David Rockwell setting come with the territory.

NEW Walle ◑ *Chinese*
- | - | - | M

E 50s | 251 E. 53rd St., downstairs (bet. 2nd & 3rd Aves.) | 212-371-0888 | www.wallerestaurant.com

From a Chin Chin owner comes this upscale East Midtown Chinese geared toward the business crowd with a roster of small and large plates heavy on shellfish and steak; the slick, contemporary setting includes leather walls, low lights and loungelike vibrations.

☑ Wallsé *Austrian*
26 | 22 | 25 | $75

W Village | 344 W. 11th St. (Washington St.) | 212-352-2300 | www.kg-ny.com

A "classic that always pleases", this elevated Austrian imports a "slice of Vienna" to the West Village via Kurt Gutenbrunner's "glorious" food served in "understatedly elegant" environs hung with "stunning" Julian Schnabel artwork; it may be "pricey", but this "grown-up experience" has "special occasion" written all over it.

Walter Foods ◑ *American*
∇ 23 | 23 | 23 | $42

Williamsburg | 253 Grand St. (Roebling St.) | Brooklyn | 718-387-8783 | www.walterfoods.com

There's a "hip scene" with "no attitude" in progress at this "cool" Williamsburg American where the "haute comfort" chow is enhanced by an "amazing raw bar" and "killer" cocktails; aside from the "loud" decibels, it's "fine all-around", with affordable tabs to boot.

Watawa *Japanese*
∇ 24 | 17 | 20 | $28

Astoria | 33-10 Ditmars Blvd. (bet. 33rd & 35th Sts.) | Queens | 718-545-9596

"Delicious", "beautifully presented" sushi is sliced in a "simple, subdued" setting at this "dynamite" Astoria Japanese; given the "fair" prices and "friendly" staffers, "be ready to wait" at prime times.

Water Club *American* | 23 | 26 | 23 | $69 |
Murray Hill | East River & 30th St. (enter on 23rd St.) | 212-683-3333 | www.thewaterclub.com

Moored on an East River barge, this 30-year-old American makes a splash with its "outstanding" food and "sweeping views" of Brooklyn and Queens; though "hard to find", it's a bona fide "destination" for "sunset cocktails", "Sunday brunch" and "engagement-ring" presentations – provided you can handle the "special-occasion" price tag.

Water's Edge Ⓩ *American/Seafood* | 21 | 25 | 22 | $68 |
LIC | East River & 44th Dr. (Vernon Blvd.) | Queens | 718-482-0033 | www.watersedgenyc.com

"Eye-candy" panoramas of Midtown Manhattan are the calling card of this "romantic" LIC getaway that's a free water taxi ride away; "surprisingly good" New American seafood, "pro" service and "pretty" decor make for an "exceptional experience", the expense notwithstanding.

Watty & Meg *American* | 20 | 18 | 20 | $38 |
Cobble Hill | 248 Court St. (Kane St.) | Brooklyn | 718-643-0007 | www.wattyandmeg.com

Savor "archetypal Brooklyn" dining at this "cozy" Cobble Hill New American where the "local, sustainable" menu is "solid", the service "cheery" and the mahogany-lined, speakeasy-ish setting "quite engaging"; bargain-hunters say Monday night's $10 burger-and-beer special is "one of the best deals around."

Waverly Inn ❶ *American* | 21 | 22 | 19 | $73 |
W Village | 16 Bank St. (Waverly Pl.) | 917-828-1154

Although "not so exclusive anymore", Graydon Carter's West Village American still draws a "beautiful crowd" (and some random "celebs") with its "homey" cooking, "dim lighting" and ultra-"relaxed" ambiance; yes, prices are "high", but it sure feels like "classic NY" in the "dead of winter" with a table opposite the fireplace and that Edward Sorel mural.

Ⓩ WD-50 Ⓜ *American/Eclectic* | 25 | 20 | 24 | $92 |
LES | 50 Clinton St. (bet. Rivington & Stanton Sts.) | 212-477-2900 | www.wd-50.com

There's "never a dull moment" at this "envelope-pushing" LES American-Eclectic where "trailblazer" chef Wylie Dufresne "challenges the palate" with "out-there combinations" that make for "weird-sounding, good-tasting" dining; ok, "some of it works, some doesn't", but "smart" service and "hefty price tags" are constants.

West Bank Cafe ❶ *American* | 19 | 16 | 20 | $44 |
W 40s | Manhattan Plaza | 407 W. 42nd St. (bet. 9th & 10th Aves.) | 212-695-6909 | www.westbankcafe.com

Convenience to 42nd Street's Theater Row is the thing at this "adequate" American where "straightforward" cooking and "reasonable" tabs trump the "nondescript" decor; maybe it's "not very exciting" overall, but post-curtain "celeb" sightings add some jazz.

Westville *American* | 23 | 13 | 18 | $26 |
Chelsea | 246 W. 18th St. (bet. 7th & 8th Aves.) | 212-924-2223
W Village | 210 W. 10th St. (bet. Bleecker & W. 4th Sts.) | 212-741-7971

(continued)

Westville East *American*

E Village | 173 Ave. A (11th St.) | 212-677-2033
www.westvillenyc.com

"Veggies abound" at this crosstown American trio patronized for its "seasonal" cooking with a "healthy bent"; trade-offs include "cramped" quarters and "long waits", though "inexpensive" pricing and a "casual" mood keep regulars regular.

NEW White & Church Ⓜ *Italian* `- | - | - | M`

TriBeCa | 281 Church St. (White St.) | 212-226-1607 |
www.whiteandchurch.com

The team behind TriBeCa's shuttered Il Matto launches this new concept in the same airy space, now redone in muted gray tones; the Italian small-plate menu is more accessible than before, but the cocktails remain as wacky as ever, including several concoctions made with insects.

Whole Foods Café *Eclectic* `19 | 10 | 11 | $18`

LES | 95 E. Houston St., 2nd fl. (bet. Bowery & Chrystie St.) | 212-420-1320
TriBeCa | 270 Greenwich St., 2nd fl. (bet. Murray & Warren Sts.) |
212-349-6555
Union Sq | 4 Union Sq. S. (bet. B'way & University Pl.) | 212-673-5388
W 60s | Time Warner Ctr. | 10 Columbus Circle, downstairs
(60th St. at B'way) | 212-823-9600
W 90s | 808 Columbus Ave. (bet. 97th & 100th Sts.) | 212-222-6160
www.wholefoods.com

"Tons of choices" – from "prepared dishes" to a "huge salad bar" – lie ahead at these "busy", self-service cafes in "Whole Paycheck" catering to "on-the-run" types with an "interesting variety" of items mostly "sold by weight"; given "little atmosphere" and "hard-to-get" seats, most opt for takeout.

Whym *American* `20 | 18 | 20 | $42`

W 50s | 889 Ninth Ave. (bet. 57th & 58th Sts.) | 212-315-0088 |
www.whymnyc.com

"Down to earth" and within "easy walking distance of Lincoln Center", this "pleasant" Hell's Kitchen American suits Fordham students and theatergoers alike; alright, it's "not exciting", but the food's "tasty", the setting "roomy" and the pricing almost whymsical.

'Wichcraft *Sandwiches* `20 | 12 | 15 | $18`

Chelsea | 269 11th Ave. (bet. 27th & 28th Sts.) | 212-780-0577 🅂
E 40s | 245 Park Ave. (47th St.) | 212-780-0577 🅂
E 40s | 555 Fifth Ave. (46th St.) | 212-780-0577 🅂
Flatiron | 11 E. 20th St. (bet. B'way & 5th Ave.) | 212-780-0577
G Village | 60 E. Eighth St. (Mercer St.) | 212-780-0577
SoHo | Equinox | 568 Broadway (Prince St.) | 212-780-0577
TriBeCa | 397 Greenwich St. (Beach St.) | 212-780-0577
W 40s | 11 W. 40th St. (6th Ave.) | 212-780-0577
W 50s | 1 Rockefeller Plaza (49th St., bet. 5th & 6th Aves.) | 212-780-0577
W 60s | David Rubenstein Atrium at Lincoln Ctr. | 61 W. 62nd St.
(bet. B'way & Columbus Ave.) | 212-780-0577
www.wichcraftnyc.com
Additional locations throughout the NY area

Tom Colicchio provides the "pedigree" at these grab-and-go counters where the "artistry of the sandwich" is demonstrated with "fresh ingredients" and "unique flavor combinations"; granted, a few consider it "expensive for what it is", but most say "you get what you pay for" here.

Wild Ginger *Asian/Vegetarian* | 22 | 17 | 20 | $28 |

Little Italy | 380 Broome St. (Mott St.) | 212-966-1883 | www.wildgingeronline.com

Cobble Hill | 112 Smith St. (bet. Dean & Pacific Sts.) | Brooklyn | 718-858-3880 | www.wildgingeronline.com

Williamsburg | 212 Bedford Ave. (bet. 5th & 6th Sts.) | Brooklyn | 718-218-8828 | www.wildgingerny.com

Even carnivores "don't miss the meat" at these separately owned vegan "delights" that put a "healthy" spin on "familiar" Pan-Asian dishes – and are a "good value" to boot; "relaxed" settings and "friendly" service keep the trade brisk.

Wildwood Barbeque *BBQ* | 19 | 17 | 18 | $37 |

Flatiron | 225 Park Ave. S. (bet. 18th & 19th Sts.) | 212-533-2500 | www.wildwoodbbq.com

Bringing an "urban sensibility" to BBQ, Steve Hanson's "massive" Flatiron joint slings "serviceable" 'cue in a "lively" room; "loud" decibels, "indifferent" service and a "chain restaurant vibe" detract, but its "frat-boy" fan base finds the "fair" prices fine.

Wo Hop ●⊄ *Chinese* | 22 | 5 | 14 | $21 |

Chinatown | 17 Mott St., downstairs (bet. Chatham Sq. & Mosco St.) | 212-267-2536

"Time stopped long ago" at this circa-1938 cash-only Mott Street "bargain basement" where "tasty" if "not inspired" Cantonese chow is slung in "dank" "dumpy" digs; service is thankfully "fast" – it may be best to "linger elsewhere" – but late-night hours make it a natural for "alcohol absorption" after "too much partying."

⧉ Wolfgang's Steakhouse *Steak* | 26 | 21 | 22 | $77 |

E 50s | 200 E. 54th St. (3rd Ave.) | 212-588-9653
Murray Hill | 4 Park Ave. (33rd St.) | 212-889-3369
TriBeCa | 409 Greenwich St. (bet. Beach & Hubert Sts.) | 212-925-0350
www.wolfgangssteakhouse.net

These steakhouses supply "cooked-to-perfection" chops in "high-testosterone" settings that skew "loud" verging on "chaotic"; the Murray Hill original flaunts striking Oyster Bar–style tiles on the ceiling, but all outlets share "slick" service, "large tabs" and "businessmen" galore.

Wollensky's Grill ● *Steak* | 24 | 19 | 22 | $58 |

E 40s | 201 E. 49th St. (3rd Ave.) | 212-753-0444 | www.smithandwollensky.com

"Slightly cheaper" but just "as good as" its symbiotic sibling Smith & Wollensky, this "more relaxed" East Side steakhouse keeps its "boy's club" following loyal with "big, juicy" chops and "memorable burgers"; the "gregarious" atmo keeps carnivores content into the wee hours – at least until the kitchen closes at 2 AM.

Wondee Siam *Thai* | 21 | 10 | 17 | $24 |

W 40s | 641 10th Ave. (bet. 45th & 46th Sts.) | 212-245-4601 | www.wondeesiam3.com

W 50s | 792 Ninth Ave. (bet. 52nd & 53rd Sts.) | 212-459-9057 ⊄

(continued)

Wondee Siam

W 50s | 813 Ninth Ave. (bet. 53rd & 54th Sts.) | 917-286-1726 |
www.wondeesiam2.com

W 100s | 969 Amsterdam Ave. (bet. 107th & 108th Sts.) | 212-531-1788 |
www.wondeesiamv.com

"Eat-and-run" types hype this West Side Siamese quartet for its
"tasty" Thai food and dirt-"cheap" tabs rather than its "claustrophobia"-
inducing quarters and "lost-in-translation" service; fortunately, delivery is "lightning fast."

WonJo ● *Korean* | 21 | 14 | 17 | $35 |

Garment District | 23 W. 32nd St. (bet. B'way & 5th Ave.) | 212-695-5815 |
www.newwonjo.com

"Sizzling" Korean barbecue cooked tableside is the specialty of this
Garment District smokehouse with a 24/7 open-door policy; purists
say it "lost something" following an ownership change, but "efficient"
service and "reliable", cheap food keep "a line out the door."

Wright, The *American* | ▽ 22 | 25 | 20 | $63 |

E 80s | Guggenheim Museum | 1071 Fifth Ave. (88th St.) | 212-427-5690 |
www.thewrightrestaurant.com

Given the "artfully plated" menu and "stunning", "midcentury modern" design, aesthetes are amazed that this New American yearling in
the Guggenheim "hasn't been discovered" yet; for the moment, it's
only serving an expensive lunch, while "erratic hours" suggest it's best
to call ahead.

Wu Liang Ye *Chinese* | 24 | 12 | 16 | $36 |

W 40s | 36 W. 48th St. (bet. 5th & 6th Aves.) | 212-398-2308

"Not for the weak of tongue", this "terrific" Chinese on a funky block
near Rock Center slings "seriously spicy" Sichuan fare and is one of
"Midtown's best cost performers"; but while the "food is hot, service
is cold", and the "no-ambiance" room is getting "run-down."

Xi'an Famous Foods ⊄ *Chinese* | 23 | 5 | 13 | $12 |

NEW Chinatown | 67 Bayard St. (bet. Bowery & Mott St.) |
212-608-4170

Chinatown | 88 E. Broadway (Forsyth St.) | 212-786-2068

E Village | 81 St. Marks Pl. (1st Ave.) | 212-786-2068

Flushing | Golden Shopping Mall | 41-28 Main St., downstairs (41st Rd.) |
Queens | 212-786-2068

www.xianfoods.com

Experience a "Silk Road journey" for "rock-bottom" rates at this
"unique"mini-chain famous for its "fiery" Western Chinese cuisine
and Anthony Bourdain–approved lamb burgers; "paper plates", scarce
seats and "no decor to speak of" are all forgiven when those "to-die-
for noodles" arrive.

Yakitori Totto ● *Japanese* | 25 | 17 | 18 | $46 |

W 50s | 251 W. 55th St., 2nd fl. (bet. B'way & 8th Ave.) | 212-245-4555 |
www.tottonyc.com

"First-rate nibbles on a stick" turn up at this "tiny" Midtown yakitori
grill where meats, veggies and "more parts of a chicken than you can
imagine" get skewered; it's a real "Tokyo experience" in Midtown, so
be prepared for "long lines" and tabs that "mount up quickly."

Yama ⊠ *Japanese*

E 40s | 308 E. 49th St. (bet. 1st & 2nd Aves.) | 212-355-3370
Gramercy | 122 E. 17th St. (Irving Pl.) | 212-475-0969
W Village | 38-40 Carmine St. (bet. Bedford & Bleecker Sts.) | 212-989-9330

	FOOD	DECOR	SERVICE	COST
	24	14	18	$41

"Pristine", "full-figured" sushi and sashimi "like butter" are the hallmarks of this Japanese threesome where the "value" is on par with the "enormous" portions; "uncomfortable", "crowded" settings detract, though the East Midtowner is the most "visually appealing."

Yerba Buena *Pan-Latin*

23	18	21	$51

E Village | 23 Ave. A (bet. Houston & 2nd Sts.) | 212-529-2919
W Village | 1 Perry St. (Greenwich Ave.) | 212-620-0808
www.ybnyc.com

Chef Julian Medina puts a *"muy delicioso"* spin on Pan-Latin cooking at these crosstown Villagers where the "lick-the-plate-clean" dishes are matched with "potent", "sexy" cocktails; "cheerful" servers render the "loud" acoustics and "tight" layouts more tolerable.

York Grill *American*

21	20	22	$52

E 80s | 1690 York Ave. (bet. 88th & 89th Sts.) | 212-772-0261

Popular with the "boomer generation", this "old-fashioned" Yorkville New American keeps its "neighbors" loyal with a "conventional" menu served in "comfortable" digs; there's "no Manhattan glitz" in evidence, but "you will be well taken care of" nonetheless.

Yuca Bar ● *Pan-Latin*

22	17	18	$30

E Village | 111 Ave. A (7th St.) | 212-982-9533 |
www.yucabarnyc.com

Big windows overlooking Tompkins Square Park supply "fun" people-watching at this East Village Pan-Latin that "hits the right notes" with "excellent-value" grub chased with "lethal" cocktails; "rushed" service and not much decor go unnoticed in the "loud and crazy" scene.

Yuka ⊅ *Japanese*

23	12	20	$32

E 80s | 1557 Second Ave. (bet. 80th & 81st Sts.) | 212-772-9675

"Quantity and quality merge" at this "solid" little Yorkville Japanese offering all-you-can-eat sushi for an "amazing" $21 price; it "no longer accepts credit cards" and the "spartan" digs "aren't the loveliest", but "you can't beat the value" and its Food rating has soared since last year.

Yura on Madison *Sandwiches*

21	11	15	$21

E 90s | 1292 Madison Ave. (92nd St.) | 212-860-1598 |
www.yuraonmadison.com

"Private school kids" and "Lilly Pulitzer" moms patronize this "preppy" Carnegie Hill cafe for the "smell alone", though its "delicious sandwiches" and "excellent baked goods" aren't bad either; given limited seating and an "uncomfortable" ambiance, it's "basically for takeout."

Yuva *Indian*

23	19	21	$41

E 50s | 230 E. 58th St. (bet. 2nd & 3rd Aves.) | 212-339-0090 |
www.yuvanyc.com

Part of 58th Street's "Indian Restaurant Row", this "high-end" subcontinental uses "top-quality ingredients" in its "spicy", "outside-the-box" dishes; if the pricing seems too "upscale", there's always the $14 buffet lunch that will bang your buck out of the ballpark.

	FOOD	DECOR	SERVICE	COST

Zabar's Cafe *Deli* 20 | 8 | 12 | $19

W 80s | 2245 Broadway (80th St.) | 212-787-2000 |
www.zabars.com

You "bring the *Times*" and they'll "bring on the bagels" at this counter-service UWS adjunct to the famed market, where "outstanding" deli items can be had for a "good price"; sure, it can be a "zoo" with "zero ambiance" and "no-smiles" service, but its "central-casting", only-in-NY ambiance is a must-see.

Zabb Elee ◑ *Thai* ▽ 23 | 12 | 17 | $19

NEW **E Village** | 75 Second Ave. (bet. 4th & 5th Sts.) |
212-505-9533
Jackson Heights | 71-28 Roosevelt Ave. (72nd St.) | Queens |
718-426-7992 ⊟
www.zabbelee.com

With outposts in Jackson Heights and the East Village, this budget-friendly duo specializes in "killer", Laotian-leaning Siamese food from Thailand's Isan region; while the settings and service are utilitarian, the "spicy" dishes on the untypical menu supply the jazz.

Zaitzeff *Burgers* 21 | 13 | 17 | $21

E Village | 18 Ave. B (bet. 2nd & 3rd Sts.) | 212-477-7137 ◑
Financial District | 72 Nassau St. (John St.) | 212-571-7272
NEW **Murray Hill** | 711 Second Ave. (bet. 38th & 39th Sts.) | 212-867-3471
www.zaitzeffnyc.com

"Top-quality" burgers – made from sirloin, Kobe beef, turkey or veggies – come accompanied by "exalted fries" at this "tasty" chain-let; despite "bare-bones" settings and "erratic service", those patties are "worth it."

Zaytoons *Mideastern* 19 | 13 | 17 | $21

Carroll Gardens | 283 Smith St. (Sackett St.) | Brooklyn |
718-875-1880
Fort Greene | 472 Myrtle Ave. (bet. Hall St. & Washington Ave.) |
Brooklyn | 718-623-5522
Prospect Heights | 594 Vanderbilt Ave. (St. Marks Ave.) | Brooklyn |
718-230-3200 ⊟
www.zaytoonsrestaurant.com

"Tasty" Middle Eastern fare "hits the spot" at this "laid-back" Brooklyn trio, where the decor may be "lackluster", but the pricing's a "veritable bargain" especially at the BYO Carroll Gardens and Fort Greene outlets; there's also a "lovely garden" in Prospect Heights.

Za Za *Italian* 21 | 16 | 22 | $44

E 60s | 1207 First Ave. (bet. 65th & 66th Sts.) | 212-772-9997 |
www.zazanyc.com

"Leisurely" dining in "low-key" digs lures Eastsiders to this "tiny" "neighborhood" place that's rather "under the radar" despite "reliable" Florentine food and "solicitous" service; regulars bypass the so-so interior and head for the "hidden" garden "oasis" out back.

Zebú Grill *Brazilian* 20 | 14 | 19 | $43

E 90s | 305 E. 92nd St. (bet. 1st & 2nd Aves.) | 212-426-7500 |
www.zebugrill.com

"You get a lot for your money" at this UES "best-kept secret" where habitués savor "flavorful" Brazilian eats washed down with "fabulous" caipirinhas; "pleasant" service and a "cozy" (if "somewhat tired") setting complete the "relaxing" picture.

Ze Café   French/Italian
| 22 | 23 | 20 | $53 |

E 50s | 398 E. 52nd St. (bet. FDR Dr. & 1st Ave.) | 212-758-1944 | www.zecafe.com

"Civilized" is the word for this "upper-crust" Sutton Place "asset" offering "appealing" French-Italian fare in a "small" but "beautiful" room adorned with "fabulous" flowers and topiary; service is "attentive", the pricing "expensive" and the crowd mainly "never-can-be-too-thin" types who've "given the staff the night off."

Zengo   Pan-Latin
| 22 | 24 | 20 | $52 |

E 40s | 622 Third Ave. (40th St.) | 212-808-8110 | www.richardsandoval.com

With plenty of "NY swagger", this "ambitious" Pan-Latin near Grand Central offers chef Richard Sandoval's "zesty" menu in a "cavernous", AvroKO-designed tri-level setting; surveyors zing the "big prices", "skimpy portions" and sometimes "sporadic" service, but tout the "sexy" downstairs tequila bar as "super-cool."

⚡ Zenkichi ●Ⓜ Japanese
| 26 | 27 | 25 | $61 |

Williamsburg | 77 N. Sixth St. (Wythe Ave.) | Brooklyn | 718-388-8985 | www.zenkichi.com

"Exceptional" Japanese small plates await at this sushi-free Williamsburg izakaya, a "Zen", "mazelike" triplex where "private booths", "stone walkways" and muted lights set the stage for "romantic tête-à-têtes"; "buzzers" summon the servers, and the mood's "calm", save for when the bill arrives.

Zen Palate   Vegetarian
| 19 | 14 | 18 | $31 |

Gramercy | 115 E. 18th St. (bet. Irving Pl. & Park Ave. S.) | 212-387-8885 ●
W 40s | 663 Ninth Ave. (46th St.) | 212-582-1669 ●
🆕 **W 100s** | 239 W. 105th St. (B'way) | 212-222-2111
www.zenpalate.com

This "serviceable" vegetarian mini-chain vends a "straight-up" meat-free menu that fans call "delish" and skeptics find "more healthy than tasty"; there's consensus on the "decent" pricing, "efficient" service and "stark" settings.

Zero Otto Nove   Pizza
| 25 | 23 | 22 | $40 |

🆕 **Flatiron** | 15 W. 21st St. (bet. 5th & 6th Aves.) | 212-242-0899
Fordham | 2357 Arthur Ave. (186th St.) | Bronx | 718-220-1027 Ⓜ
www.roberto089.com

For a taste of "Arthur Avenue at its finest", check out this "more casual, less expensive" Roberto spin-off touted for its "light-as-air" brick-oven pizza, trompe l'oeil "opera-set" decor and "bend-over-backwards" service; P.S. the Flatiron satellite opened post-Survey.

Zest Ⓜ American
| ∇ 26 | 26 | 25 | $50 |

Rosebank | 977 Bay St. (Willow Ave.) | Staten Island | 718-390-8477 | www.zestaurant.com

"Manhattan sparkle" comes to Staten Island via this "intimate" place where "excellent" French-inspired New Americana is ferried by an "attentive" staff in "beautiful" digs; if it's "a bit expensive" for "not so cool" Rosebank, most "walk out satisfied", especially after experiencing the "fantastic garden."

Zoma *Ethiopian*

▽ 22 | 17 | 17 | $33

Harlem | 2084 Frederick Douglass Blvd. (113th St.) | 212-662-0620 | www.zomanyc.com

"Newly hip South Harlem" is home to this "modern" Ethiopian offering "authentic", "well-spiced" dishes meant to be "eaten with your fingers"; a "stylish" setting reminiscent of a "West Elm store" enhances the "sophisticated" mood, though "erratic" service detracts.

Zum Schneider ⊅ *German*

19 | 15 | 16 | $31

E Village | 107 Ave. C (7th St.) | 212-598-1098 | www.zumschneider.com

It's always "festive" at this "cash-only" East Village "suds-and-grub" dispenser where the "beer flows freely" and the "generous" plates are piled high with "unpronounceable" Bavarian eats; given its "frat boy" and "soccer fan" following, it gets "rowdy in the true *bierhaus* tradition."

Zum Stammtisch *German*

24 | 20 | 22 | $39

Glendale | 69-46 Myrtle Ave. (bet. 69th Pl. & 70th St.) | Queens | 718-386-3014 | www.zumstammtisch.com

"Tasty", "traditional" German grub washed down with "huge steins" of beer keeps this 40-year-old Glendale "throwback" going, even if the food – and the crowd – is "a little heavy"; "dirndl"-clad waitresses, "old-world" decor and a "gemütlich" vibe make it a hit with grown-ups and a "hoot" for younger folk.

Zuni ◗ *American*

19 | 14 | 20 | $38

W 40s | 598 Ninth Ave. (43rd St.) | 212-765-7626 | www.zuniny.com

A "safe bet" for "inexpensive" New Americana in Hell's Kitchen, this decidedly "unpretentious" spot is "rarely crowded" and admirers say it "deserves a greater buzz than it gets"; attention to "theatergoers' time frames" gets ticket-holders in and out "quick."

Zutto *Japanese*

21 | 16 | 18 | $43

TriBeCa | 77 Hudson St. (Harrison St.) | 212-233-3287

Long a "treasured" neighborhood "sleeper", this 1980-vintage TriBeCa Japanese provides "tasty" sushi and cooked dishes in "comfortable" environs; it's "not anywhere near Nobu – though physically close" to it – but then again, it's not that expensive either.

Zuzu Ramen ⊅ *Noodle Shop*

20 | 16 | 19 | $22

Park Slope | 173 Fourth Ave. (Degraw St.) | Brooklyn | 718-398-9898 | www.zuzuramen.com

Park Slopers relish this little "ramen haven" providing a "lightning-fast noodle fix" with choices of "nontraditional" broths; though "nothing to merit a river crossing", it's "laid-back, hip" and way "less expensive than comparable Manhattan joints."

INDEXES

Cuisines 284
Locations 309
Special Features 333

LOCATION MAPS

Brooklyn Detail 306
Manhattan Neighborhoods 308

Cuisines

Includes names, locations and Food ratings.

AFGHAN

Afghan Kebab | **multi.** 20

AFRICAN

(See also Egyptian, Ethiopian, Moroccan, North African, South African, Tunisian)

Ponty Bistro | **Gramercy** 23

AMERICAN

☷ ABC Kitchen | **Flatiron**	25
Abe/Arthur | **Meatpacking**	22
Algonquin | **W 40s**	18
Alias | **LES**	21
Anella | **Greenpt**	24
Angus McIndoe | **W 40s**	16
☷ Annisa | **W Vill**	28
Apiary | **E Vill**	25
NEW APL | **LES**	-
Applewood | **Park Slope**	25
Arabelle | **E 60s**	24
☷ Asiate | **W 60s**	25
NEW Astor Room | **Astoria**	22
☷ Aureole | **W 40s**	26
Back Forty | **E Vill**	21
NEW B&B | **SoHo**	24
Bar Americain | **W 50s**	23
Bar Henry | **G Vill**	21
Barmarché | **NoLita**	21
Battery Gdns. | **Financial**	19
Beacon | **W 50s**	23
NEW Beagle | **E Vill**	-
☷NEW Beauty & Essex | **LES**	22
NEW Beecher's | **Flatiron**	-
NEW Bell Book/Candle | **W Vill**	23
Benjamin | **Murray Hill**	18
Black Duck | **Murray Hill**	21
Black Whale | **City Is**	22
BLT B&G | **Financial**	22
BLT Market | **W 50s**	24
☷ Blue Hill | **G Vill**	27
☷ Blue Ribbon | **multi.**	25
Blue Ribbon Bakery | **W Vill**	25
Boathouse | **E 70s**	18
Bobo | **W Vill**	22
Bouchon Bakery | **multi.**	24
Bridge Cafe | **Financial**	21
Brooklyn Diner | **multi.**	18
Bryant Park | **W 40s**	18
Bubby's | **multi.**	20
Butter | **E Vill**	22

Buttermilk | **Carroll Gdns**	24
Cafe Cluny | **W Vill**	20
Cafeteria | **Chelsea**	19
CamaJe | **G Vill**	22
Casellula | **W 50s**	25
Caviar Russe | **E 50s**	24
Chadwick's | **Bay Ridge**	22
Chestnut | **Carroll Gdns**	23
Cibo | **E 40s**	21
Clinton St. Baking | **LES**	25
Coffee Shop | **Union Sq**	16
Colicchio/Sons | **Chelsea**	24
NEW Colonie | **Bklyn Hts**	26
Commerce | **W Vill**	23
Community Food | **W 100s**	23
Cookshop | **Chelsea**	22
NEW Co-op Food/Drink | **LES**	-
Cornelia St. Cafe | **W Vill**	19
Corner Bistro | **W Vill**	22
☷ Craft | **Flatiron**	26
Craftbar | **Flatiron**	23
NEW CrossBar | **Flatiron**	-
NEW Darby | **W Vill**	20
David Burke/Bloom. | **E 50s**	19
NEW David Burke Kitchen | **SoHo**	24
☷ David Burke Townhse. | **E 60s**	25
Del Frisco's | **W 50s**	25
Delicatessen | **NoLita**	18
NEW Desmond's | **E 60s**	22
Diner | **W'burg**	23
☷ Dovetail | **W 70s**	26
Dressler | **W'burg**	25
Duane Park | **TriBeCa**	22
DuMont | **W'burg**	23
NEW Duo | **Murray Hill**	-
☷NEW Dutch | **SoHo**	24
Dylan Prime | **TriBeCa**	24
NEW East End Kitchen | **E 80s**	-
E.A.T. | **E 80s**	20
Eatery | **W 50s**	19
EJ's Luncheon. | **E 70s**	16
NEW Ellabess | **NoLita**	-
Fairway Cafe | **multi.**	18
Farm/Adderley | **Ditmas Pk**	24
NEW Fat Goose | **W'burg**	-
NEW Fedora | **W Vill**	22
Fishtail | **E 60s**	24
5 & Diamond | **Harlem**	21
Five Leaves | **Greenpt**	25

5 9th | **Meatpacking**	19	Kenmare | **L Italy**	19
5 Points | **NoHo**	22	Kings' Carriage | **E 80s**	22
Fives | **W 50s**	22	Knickerbocker | **G Vill**	20
Flatbush Farm | **Park Slope**	21	Lambs Club | **W 40s**	21
Fort Defiance | **Red Hook**	21	**NEW** Left Bank | **W Vill**	-
44 & X/44½ | **W 40s**	21	Lion | **G Vill**	20
Z Four Seasons | **E 50s**	27	Little Giant | **LES**	22
Fraunces Tavern | **Financial**	17	Little Owl | **W Vill**	25
Fred's at Barneys | **E 60s**	20	**NEW** Little Town NYC | **Gramercy**	-
Freemans | **LES**	23	Mama's Food | **E Vill**	22
Friedman's Lunch | **Chelsea**	21	**Z** Marc Forgione | **TriBeCa**	26
Friend/Farmer | **Gramercy**	18	**Z** Mark | **E 70s**	22
Fulton | **E 70s**	23	Market Table | **W Vill**	24
Garden Café | **Inwood**	22	Marlow/Sons | **W'burg**	24
Z Gilt | **E 50s**	26	**Z** Mas | **W Vill**	27
Giorgio's | **Flatiron**	21	**NEW** Masten Lake | **W'burg**	-
Glass House | **W 40s**	20	Melba's | **Harlem**	20
Good | **W Vill**	20	Melt | **Park Slope**	20
Good Enough/Eat | **W 80s**	21	Mercer Kitchen | **SoHo**	22
Z Gotham B&G | **G Vill**	28	Mike's Bistro | **W 70s**	23
Z Gramercy Tavern | **Flatiron**	27	**Z** Modern | **W 50s**	26
Greenhouse | **Bay Ridge**	21	**Z** Momofuku Ko | **E Vill**	27
Z Grocery | **Carroll Gdns**	27	Momofuku Noodle | **E Vill**	24
Harrison | **TriBeCa**	24	**Z** Momofuku Ssäm | **E Vill**	25
Hearth | **E Vill**	24	Monkey Bar | **E 50s**	19
Heartland | **multi.**	15	**NEW** Monument Lane | **W Vill**	-
Henry Public | **Cobble Hill**	20	Morgan | **Murray Hill**	20
Henry's | **W 100s**	19	Morrell Wine | **W 40s**	19
Henry's End | **Bklyn Hts**	24	**NEW** National | **E 50s**	20
NEW Highliner | **Chelsea**	-	New Leaf | **Wash. Hts**	21
Highpoint | **Chelsea**	22	**NEW** 9 | **W 50s**	20
Hillstone | **multi.**	22	NoHo Star | **NoHo**	19
Home | **W Vill**	22	Norma's | **W 50s**	25
NEW Hotel Chantelle | **LES**	-	Northern Spy | **E Vill**	23
Hotel Griffou | **G Vill**	19	North Sq. | **G Vill**	23
House | **Gramercy**	21	No. 7 | **Ft Greene**	23
NEW Hudson Clearwater | **W Vill**	25	Oceana | **W 40s**	24
		Odeon | **TriBeCa**	19
Hudson Place | **Murray Hill**	19	**Z** One if by Land | **W Vill**	24
Hudson River | **Harlem**	21	101 | **Bay Ridge**	21
Hundred Acres | **SoHo**	20	**Z** Ouest | **W 80s**	24
Ici | **Ft Greene**	22	Palm Court | **W 50s**	20
NEW Isa | **W'burg**	-	**Z** Park Avenue | **E 60s**	25
Isabella's | **W 70s**	20	Patroon | **E 40s**	23
Jackson Hole | **multi.**	18	Peels | **E Vill**	20
Jack Horse | **Bklyn Hts**	23	Penelope | **Murray Hill**	21
James | **Prospect Hts**	23	**Z** Perilla | **W Vill**	26
Jane | **G Vill**	21	**Z** Perry St. | **W Vill**	26
NEW Jeffrey's Grocery | **W Vill**	21	**Z** Per Se | **W 60s**	28
Jimmy's | **E Vill**	21	Philip Marie | **W Vill**	20
Joe Allen | **W 40s**	18	Place | **W Vill**	25
JoeDoe | **E Vill**	24	Popover Cafe | **W 80s**	19
Joseph Leonard | **W Vill**	22	Prime Meat | **Carroll Gdns**	24

CUISINES

Print	**W 40s**	25
Prune	**E Vill**	25
NEW PSbklyn	**Park Slope**	-
Quaint	**Sunnyside**	22
Quality Meats	**W 50s**	24
Recette	**W Vill**	24
Recipe	**W 80s**	24
Red Cat	**Chelsea**	24
Redeye Grill	**W 50s**	20
Redhead	**E Vill**	23
Regency	**E 60s**	19
Z River Café	**Dumbo**	26
NEW Riverpark	**Murray Hill**	25
Riverview	**LIC**	20
Robert	**W 50s**	20
Rock Ctr.	**W 50s**	19
Rose Water	**Park Slope**	26
Rouge Tomate	**E 60s**	24
Rye	**W'burg**	24
Sanford's	**Astoria**	23
Sarabeth's	**multi.**	20
Z Saul	**Boerum Hill**	27
Schnipper's	**W 40s**	19
S'MAC	**E Vill**	22
Smith	**E Vill**	21
South Gate	**W 50s**	24
Spitzer's	**LES**	19
Square Meal	**E 90s**	23
Standard Grill	**Meatpacking**	21
St. Anselm	**W'burg**	-
Stone Park	**Park Slope**	25
Swifty's	**E 70s**	18
Taste	**E 80s**	22
T-Bar Steak	**E 70s**	22
Z Telepan	**W 60s**	26
10 Downing	**W Vill**	19
NEW Tenpenny	**E 40s**	-
Thalia	**W 50s**	20
Thistle Hill	**Park Slope**	23
NEW Tiny's	**TriBeCa**	-
Z Tocqueville	**Union Sq**	25
NEW Tremont	**W Vill**	-
Trestle on 10th	**Chelsea**	21
Tribeca Grill	**TriBeCa**	23
12th St. B&G	**Park Slope**	21
12 Chairs	**SoHo**	20
Z 21 Club	**W 50s**	22
2 West	**Financial**	22
Z Union Sq. Cafe	**Union Sq**	27
NEW Untitled	**E 70s**	-
Vanderbilt	**Prospect Hts**	23
Z Veritas	**Flatiron**	26
View	**W 40s**	18

Vinegar Hill Hse.	**Vinegar Hill**	25
Walker's	**TriBeCa**	19
Wall/Water	**Financial**	20
Walter Foods	**W'burg**	23
Water Club	**Murray Hill**	23
Water's Edge	**LIC**	21
Watty/Meg	**Cobble Hill**	20
Waverly Inn	**W Vill**	21
Z WD-50	**LES**	25
West Bank	**W 40s**	19
Westville	**multi.**	23
Whym	**W 50s**	20
Wright	**E 80s**	22
York Grill	**E 80s**	21
Zest	**Rosebank**	26
Zuni	**W 40s**	19

ARGENTINEAN

Buenos Aires	**E Vill**	23
Chimichurri Grill	**W 40s**	23
Novecento	**SoHo**	21
Sosa Borella	**W 50s**	20

ASIAN

Aja	**E 50s**	21
Amber	**multi.**	19
Aquamarine	**Murray Hill**	21
Z Asiate	**W 60s**	25
Betel	**W Vill**	22
Z Buddakan	**Chelsea**	24
Cafe Asean	**W Vill**	22
China Grill	**W 50s**	22
Citrus B&G	**W 70s**	20
East Buffet	**Flushing**	19
Fatty 'Cue	**multi.**	21
Fatty Fish	**E 60s**	21
Purple Yam	**Ditmas Pk**	21
Qi	**Union Sq**	20
Ruby Foo's	**W 40s**	18
NEW Social Eatz	**E 50s**	23
Z Spice Market	**Meatpacking**	23
Tao	**E 50s**	22
Wild Ginger	**multi.**	22
Zengo	**E 40s**	22

AUSTRALIAN

Sunburnt Cow/Calf	**multi.**	17
Tuck Shop	**multi.**	21

AUSTRIAN

Blaue Gans	**TriBeCa**	22
Café Katja	**LES**	24
NEW Café Kristall	**SoHo**	23
Café Sabarsky	**E 80s**	22
Cafe Steinhof	**Park Slope**	19

NEW Edi & the Wolf | E Vill	22
Mont Blanc | W 40s	21
NEW Schnitzel & Things | E 40s	20
Z Seäsonal | W 50s	25
Z Wallsé | W Vill	26

BAKERIES

Andre's Café | E 80s	20
Bouchon Bakery | multi.	24
City Bakery | Flatiron	22
Clinton St. Baking | LES	25
Z Eataly | Flatiron	23
Ferrara | L Italy	23
Kyotofu | W 40s	21
La Bergamote | multi.	24
La Flor | Woodside	25
Le Pain Q. | multi.	19
Momofuku Milk Bar | multi.	23
Once Upon a Tart . . . | SoHo	22
Provence/Boite | Carroll Gdns	20
Veniero's | E Vill	24

BARBECUE

Blue Smoke | multi.	22
Brother Jimmy's | multi.	17
Daisy May's | W 40s	23
Dallas BBQ | multi.	16
Dinosaur BBQ | Harlem	22
Fatty 'Cue | multi.	21
Z Fette Sau | W'burg	26
Hill Country | Flatiron	22
NEW Mable's Smoke Hse. | W'burg	-
NEW Mexicue | multi.	-
NEW Neely's BBQ | E 60s	-
Rack & Soul | W 100s	22
Rub BBQ | Chelsea	21
Smoke Joint | Ft Greene	22
Virgil's BBQ | W 40s	20
Wildwood BBQ | Flatiron	19

BELGIAN

B. Café | multi.	21
BXL | multi.	18
Le Pain Q. | multi.	19
Markt | Flatiron	18
Petite Abeille | multi.	19
Resto | Murray Hill	20

BRAZILIAN

Churrascaria | multi.	23
Circus | E 60s	20
Coffee Shop | Union Sq	16
Malagueta | Astoria	24
Rice 'n' Beans | W 50s	21
SushiSamba | multi.	21
Via Brasil | W 40s	21
Zebú Grill | E 90s	20

BRITISH

Z Breslin | Chelsea	22
ChipShop | multi.	21
NEW Fat Radish | LES	20
NEW Jones Wood Foundry | E 70s	23
Tea & Sympathy | W Vill	20

BURGERS

Back Forty | E Vill	21
NEW B&B | SoHo	24
BareBurger | multi.	23
Big Nick's | W 70s	18
Bill's Bar | multi.	19
Black Iron | E Vill	23
BLT Burger | G Vill	21
Brgr | multi.	19
Burger Heaven | multi.	17
Z Burger Joint/Le Parker | W 50s	24
Corner Bistro | W Vill	22
NEW Counter | W 40s	17
Z DB Bistro Moderne | W 40s	25
DuMont | W'burg	23
NEW Elevation Burger | Chelsea	20
Five Guys | multi.	20
5 Napkin Burger | multi.	21
NEW Go Burger | multi.	22
Goodburger | multi.	17
Heartland | W 40s	15
Island Burgers | multi.	21
Jackson Hole | multi.	18
J.G. Melon | E 70s	21
Z Minetta | G Vill	23
P.J. Clarke's | multi.	17
Pop Burger/Pub | multi.	17
Rare B&G | multi.	21
Schnipper's | W 40s	19
Shake Shack | multi.	22
67 Burger | Ft Greene	22
Stand | G Vill	20
Zaitzeff | multi.	21

CAJUN/CREOLE

Bayou | Rosebank	23
Bourbon St. Café | Bayside	18
Delta Grill | W 40s	19
Great Jones Cafe | NoHo	21

CALIFORNIAN

Z Michael's | W 50s	22

CUISINES

CAMBODIAN

Num Pang | **multi.**	26

CARIBBEAN

Don Pedro's | **E 90s**	21
NEW Nights and Weekends | **Greenpt**	-

CAVIAR

Caviar Russe | **E 50s**	24
Mari Vanna | **Flatiron**	20
Petrossian | **W 50s**	24
Russian Tea | **W 50s**	19

CHEESESTEAKS

Carl's Steaks | **multi.**	21
99 Mi. to Philly | **E Vill**	19
Shorty's | **W 40s**	21

CHICKEN

Bon Chon | **multi.**	20
Coco Roco | **multi.**	19
El Malecon | **multi.**	20
Flor/Mayo | **multi.**	20
NEW Hill Country Chicken | **Flatiron**	19
Kyochon | **multi.**	19
Pies-n-Thighs | **W'burg**	23
Pio Pio | **multi.**	22
Rack & Soul | **W 100s**	22

CHILEAN

Pomaire | **W 40s**	20

CHINESE

(* dim sum specialist)

Amazing 66 | **Chinatown**	21
Au Mandarin | **Financial**	19
BaoHaus | **multi.**	20
Big Wong | **Chinatown**	23
Bo-Ky | **multi.**	22
Café Evergreen* | **E 60s**	18
Chef Ho's | **E 80s**	22
China Chalet | **multi.**	19
Chinatown Brass.* | **NoHo**	22
Chin Chin | **E 40s**	23
Congee | **LES**	20
Dim Sum Go Go* | **Chinatown**	21
Dumpling Man | **E Vill**	21
East Manor* | **Flushing**	19
Empire Szechuan | **multi.**	17
Excellent Dumpling* | **Chinatown**	21
Flor/Mayo | **multi.**	20
Fuleen | **Chinatown**	22
Golden Unicorn* | **Chinatown**	21
Grand Sichuan | **multi.**	21
Great NY Noodle | **Chinatown**	23

Hop Kee | **Chinatown**	22
Hunan Kit./Grand Sichuan | **Flushing**	24
NEW Hung Ry | **NoHo**	20
Jing Fong* | **Chinatown**	20
Joe's Shanghai | **multi.**	22
Joe's | **Chinatown**	21
King Yum | **Fresh Meadows**	19
Lychee Hse.* | **E 50s**	23
Macao Trading | **TriBeCa**	19
Mandarin Court* | **Chinatown**	22
Mee Noodle | **multi.**	17
Mr. Chow | **multi.**	22
Mr. K's | **E 50s**	24
Nice Green Bo | **Chinatown**	23
NoHo Star | **NoHo**	19
Nom Wah Tea* | **Chinatown**	23
NEW Old Town Hot Pot | **W Vill**	-
Ollie's | **multi.**	16
Z Oriental Gdn.* | **Chinatown**	23
Our Place* | **E 70s**	18
Z Pacificana* | **Sunset Pk**	25
Peking Duck | **multi.**	23
Philippe | **E 60s**	23
Phoenix Gdn. | **Murray Hill**	23
Pig Heaven | **E 80s**	20
Ping's Sea.* | **multi.**	22
Red Egg* | **L Italy**	20
NEW RedFarm* | **W Vill**	-
Rickshaw Dumpling | **multi.**	18
Shang | **LES**	20
Shanghai Café | **L Italy**	22
Shanghai Cuisine | **Chinatown**	23
Shanghai Pavilion | **E 70s**	21
Shun Lee Cafe* | **W 60s**	21
Z Shun Lee Palace | **E 50s**	25
Shun Lee West | **W 60s**	23
Spicy & Tasty | **Flushing**	23
Szechuan Gourmet | **multi.**	23
Tang Pavilion | **W 50s**	22
Tse Yang | **E 50s**	23
Vanessa's Dumpling | **multi.**	20
Wa Jeal | **E 80s**	24
NEW Walle | **E 50s**	-
Wo Hop | **Chinatown**	22
Wu Liang Ye | **W 40s**	24
Xi'an | **multi.**	23

COFFEEHOUSES

Cafe Lalo | **W 80s**	19
Café Sabarsky | **E 80s**	22
Ferrara | **L Italy**	23
Le Pain Q. | **multi.**	19
Omonia | **Astoria**	19

Once Upon a Tart . . .	**SoHo**	22
NEW Untitled	**E 70s**	-
Yura on Madison	**E 90s**	21

COFFEE SHOPS/ DINERS

Brooklyn Diner	**multi.**	18
Burger Heaven	**multi.**	17
NEW Coppelia	**Chelsea**	20
Diner	**W'burg**	23
EJ's Luncheon.	**E 70s**	16
Junior's	**multi.**	19
La Taza de Oro	**Chelsea**	21
Schnipper´s	**W 40s**	19
Teresa's	**Bklyn Hts**	18
Tom's	**Prospect Hts**	21
Viand	**multi.**	18

CONTINENTAL

NEW Astor Room	**Astoria**	22
Cebu	**Bay Ridge**	21
Cole's Dock	**Great Kills**	21
NEW Crown	**E 80s**	-
Jack's Lux.	**E Vill**	26
Lake Club	**St. George**	21
Petrossian	**W 50s**	24
Russian Samovar	**W 50s**	20
Russian Tea	**W 50s**	19
Sardi's	**W 40s**	18

CUBAN

Café Habana/Outpost	**multi.**	22
Cuba	**G Vill**	23
Cubana Café	**multi.**	20
Guantanamera	**W 50s**	20
Havana Alma	**W Vill**	22
Havana Central	**multi.**	18
Victor's Cafe	**W 50s**	23

CZECH

| **NEW** Hospoda | **E 70s** | - |

DANISH

| Vandaag | **E Vill** | 20 |

DELIS

Artie's Deli	**W 80s**	18
Z Barney Greengrass	**W 80s**	24
Ben's Best	**Rego Pk**	23
Ben's Kosher	**multi.**	19
Z Carnegie Deli	**W 50s**	22
Eisenberg's Sandwich	**Flatiron**	18
Z Katz's Deli	**LES**	24
Leo's Latticini	**multi.**	27
Liebman's	**Riverdale**	22
Mile End	**Boerum Hill**	24

Mill Basin Deli	**Mill Basin**	23
Pastrami Queen	**E 70s**	22
Sarge's Deli	**Murray Hill**	21
2nd Ave Deli	**multi.**	23
Stage Deli	**W 50s**	21
Z Torrisi	**NoLita**	27
Zabar's Cafe	**W 80s**	20

DOMINICAN

| El Malecon | **multi.** | 20 |

DUTCH

| Vandaag | **E Vill** | 20 |

EASTERN EUROPEAN

(See also Czech, Hungarian, Polish, Russian, Ukrainian)

| Sammy's | **LES** | 20 |

ECLECTIC

Abigael's	**Garment**	20
Carol's	**Dongan Hills**	24
East Buffet	**Flushing**	19
NEW FoodParc	**Chelsea**	18
Z Good Fork	**Red Hook**	25
Graffiti	**E Vill**	25
Harry's Cafe/Steak	**Financial**	23
NEW Hotel Chantelle	**LES**	-
Josie's	**multi.**	19
La Flor	**Woodside**	25
Lake Club	**St. George**	21
NEW Mehtaphor	**TriBeCa**	25
NEW Milk St. Café	**Financial**	-
NEW Mussel Pot	**G Vill**	22
Nook	**W 50s**	22
Plaza Food Hall	**W 50s**	22
Public	**NoLita**	24
Rice	**multi.**	21
NEW Romera	**Chelsea**	-
Schiller's	**LES**	19
Sojourn	**E 70s**	23
Stanton Social	**LES**	23
NEW Tolani	**W 70s**	24
Z Traif	**W'burg**	27
Z WD-50	**LES**	25
Whole Foods	**multi.**	19

EGYPTIAN

| Kabab Café | **Astoria** | 24 |

ETHIOPIAN

Awash	**multi.**	23
Ghenet	**Park Slope**	24
Meskerem	**multi.**	21
Queen of Sheba	**W 40s**	22
Zoma	**Harlem**	22

EUROPEAN

August	**W Vill**	22
Belcourt	**E Vill**	20
NEW Boulud Sud	**W 60s**	23
Z Danny Brown	**Forest Hills**	27
Don Pedro's	**E 90s**	21
Le Caprice	**E 60s**	20
Radegast	**W'burg**	18
Z Spotted Pig	**W Vill**	23

FILIPINO

Kuma Inn	**LES**	23
Umi Nom	**Clinton Hill**	26

FONDUE

Artisanal	**Murray Hill**	23
Bourgeois Pig	**E Vill**	20
Chocolate Room	**multi.**	25
NEW Heartbreak	**E Vill**	24
Kashkaval	**W 50s**	23
La Bonne Soupe	**W 50s**	19
Mont Blanc	**W 40s**	21

FRENCH

Z Adour	**E 50s**	26
Arabelle	**E 60s**	24
Ayza Wine	**Garment**	20
NEW Bar Basque	**Chelsea**	19
Barbès	**Murray Hill**	20
Bouchon Bakery	**multi.**	24
Z Bouley	**TriBeCa**	28
Bourgeois Pig	**E Vill**	20
Breeze	**W 40s**	20
Brick Cafe	**Astoria**	22
Z Brooklyn Fare	**Downtown Bklyn**	29
NEW Buvette	**W Vill**	24
Z Café Boulud	**E 70s**	27
Café du Soleil	**W 100s**	19
Cafe Gitane	**multi.**	20
Café Henri	**multi.**	20
Z Carlyle	**E 70s**	24
Chez Lucienne	**Harlem**	20
Z Corton	**TriBeCa**	25
Z Daniel	**E 60s**	29
Z Degustation	**E Vill**	27
Z Eleven Madison	**Flatiron**	28
NEW Fedora	**W Vill**	22
Fives	**W 50s**	22
Gordon Ramsay	**W 50s**	23
Ici	**Ft Greene**	22
Indochine	**E Vill**	22
Jack's Lux.	**E Vill**	26
Z Jean Georges	**W 60s**	28
Z Jean Georges Noug.	**W 60s**	27

La Baraka	**Little Neck**	22
La Bergamote	**multi.**	24
La Boîte en Bois	**W 60s**	22
Z La Grenouille	**E 50s**	28
NEW La Petite Maison	**W 50s**	19
Z L'Atelier/Robuchon	**E 50s**	27
Z Le Bernardin	**W 50s**	29
Z Le Cirque	**E 50s**	25
L'Ecole	**SoHo**	25
Le Colonial	**E 50s**	21
Le Grainne Cafe	**Chelsea**	23
Le Marais	**W 40s**	22
Le Perigord	**E 50s**	24
Le Pescadeux	**SoHo**	23
Le Rivage	**W 40s**	21
NEW Lyon	**W Vill**	20
Má Pêche	**W 50s**	23
Maze	**W 50s**	22
Mercer Kitchen	**SoHo**	22
Z Modern	**W 50s**	26
NEW MPD	**Meatpacking**	20
Nizza	**W 40s**	19
Once Upon a Tart . . .	**SoHo**	22
Pascalou	**E 90s**	21
Z Per Se	**W 60s**	28
Petrossian	**W 50s**	24
Z Picholine	**W 60s**	27
Ponty Bistro	**Gramercy**	23
Z SHO Shaun	**Financial**	26
Terrace in Sky	**W 100s**	22
Z Tocqueville	**Union Sq**	25
Triomphe	**W 40s**	25
Ze Café	**E 50s**	22

FRENCH (BISTRO)

NEW Affaire	**E Vill**	-
Almond	**Flatiron**	20
Alouette	**W 90s**	20
A.O.C.	**multi.**	20
Bacchus	**Boerum Hill**	19
Z Bar Boulud	**W 60s**	24
Belleville	**Park Slope**	19
Benoit	**W 50s**	21
Bistro Cassis	**W 70s**	21
Bistro Chat Noir	**E 60s**	19
Bistro Citron	**W 80s**	19
Bistro Les Amis	**SoHo**	20
Bistro Le Steak	**E 70s**	18
Bistro 61	**E 60s**	20
Bistro Vendôme	**E 50s**	22
Cafe Cluny	**W Vill**	20
Cafe Joul	**E 50s**	19
Cafe Loup	**W Vill**	20

Vote at ZAGAT.com

Cafe Luluc	**Cobble Hill**	20
Cafe Luxembourg	**W 70s**	21
Cafe Un Deux	**W 40s**	17
CamaJe	**G Vill**	22
Capsouto Frères	**TriBeCa**	24
Chez Jacqueline	**G Vill**	20
Chez Josephine	**W 40s**	20
Chez Napoléon	**W 50s**	22
Cornelia St. Cafe	**W Vill**	19
Z DB Bistro Moderne	**W 40s**	25
Deux Amis	**E 50s**	19
Gascogne	**Chelsea**	21
Jean Claude	**SoHo**	22
JoJo	**E 60s**	25
Jubilee	**E 50s**	22
La Bonne Soupe	**W 50s**	19
La Lunchonette	**Chelsea**	22
La Mangeoire	**E 50s**	21
La Mirabelle	**W 80s**	22
Landmarc	**multi.**	21
La Petite Aub.	**Murray Hill**	22
La Ripaille	**W Vill**	22
Z NEW La Silhouette	**W 50s**	26
La Sirène	**Hudson Square**	25
Le Bilboquet	**E 60s**	21
Le Charlot	**E 60s**	21
Le Gigot	**W Vill**	24
Le Magnifique	**E 70s**	18
Le Monde	**W 100s**	18
Le Parisien	**Murray Hill**	22
Les Halles	**multi.**	20
Le Singe Vert	**Chelsea**	18
Le Veau d'Or	**E 60s**	20
L'Express	**Flatiron**	18
Lucien	**E Vill**	22
Lucky Strike	**SoHo**	17
Madison Bistro	**Murray Hill**	21
Z Minetta	**G Vill**	23
Mon Petit Cafe	**E 60s**	20
NEW Morgane	**W'burg**	-
Nice Matin	**W 70s**	20
Odeon	**TriBeCa**	19
Paradou	**Meatpacking**	22
Park Ave. Bistro	**Murray Hill**	21
Pastis	**Meatpacking**	21
Picnic	**W 100s**	21
Plein Sud	**TriBeCa**	20
Provence/Boite	**Carroll Gdns**	20
Quatorze Bis	**E 70s**	21
Quercy	**Cobble Hill**	21
Raoul's	**SoHo**	24
Saju Bistro	**W 40s**	21
Table d'Hôte	**E 90s**	21

Tartine	**W Vill**	22
Tournesol	**LIC**	25
Tree	**E Vill**	20
26 Seats	**E Vill**	22

FRENCH (BRASSERIE)

Artisanal	**Murray Hill**	23
Z Balthazar	**SoHo**	24
Bar Breton	**Chelsea**	18
NEW Beaumarchais	**Meatpacking**	-
Brasserie	**E 50s**	21
Brasserie Cognac	**W 50s**	19
Brasserie 8½	**W 50s**	21
Brass. Ruhlmann	**W 50s**	20
Café d'Alsace	**E 80s**	21
Ça Va	**W 40s**	22
DBGB	**E Vill**	23
Jacques	**multi.**	18
L'Absinthe	**E 60s**	22
Maison	**W 50s**	19
Marseille	**W 40s**	20
Orsay	**E 70s**	18
Pigalle	**W 40s**	18
Rue 57	**W 50s**	18
Serge	**Murray Hill**	22

GASTROPUB

NEW Beagle	Amer.	**E Vill**	-
NEW CrossBar	Amer.	**Flatiron**	-
NEW Fat Goose	Amer.	**W'burg**	-
NEW Mary Queen of Scots	Scottish	**LES**	21
NEW PSbklyn	Amer.	**Park Slope**	-
Resto	Belgian	**Murray Hill**	20
Spitzer's	Amer.	**LES**	19
Z Spotted Pig	Euro.	**W Vill**	23

GERMAN

NEW Berlyn	**Ft Greene**	19
Blaue Gans	**TriBeCa**	22
NEW Heartbreak	**E Vill**	24
Heidelberg	**E 80s**	19
Loreley	**multi.**	19
Nurnberger	**New Brighton**	21
Prime Meat	**Carroll Gdns**	24
Rolf's	**Gramercy**	13
Zum Schneider	**E Vill**	19
Zum Stammtisch	**Glendale**	24

GREEK

Aegean Cove	**Astoria**	22
Agnanti	**multi.**	23

Ammos | **E 40s**	21	
Avra | **E 40s**	25	
Cávo | **Astoria**	21	
Dafni Greek | **W 40s**	20	
Eliá | **Bay Ridge**	27	
Elias Corner | **Astoria**	23	
Ethos | **multi.**	21	
NEW FishTag | **W 70s**	22	
Greek Kitchen | **W 50s**	21	
Ithaka | **E 80s**	20	
Kefi | **W 80s**	22	
Kellari Tav./Parea | **W 40s**	23	
Z Milos, Estiatorio | **W 50s**	27	
Molyvos | **W 50s**	23	
Omonia | **Astoria**	19	
Periyali | **Flatiron**	24	
Persephone | **E 60s**	22	
Z Pylos | **E Vill**	26	
Snack | **multi.**	22	
Stamatis | **Astoria**	22	
Symposium | **W 100s**	20	
Z Taverna Kyclades | **Astoria**	26	
Telly's Taverna | **Astoria**	23	
Thalassa | **TriBeCa**	24	
Uncle Nick's | **multi.**	20	

HEALTH FOOD

(See also Vegetarian)

Qi | **multi.**	20
NEW Romera | **Chelsea**	-

HOT DOGS

Bark Hot Dogs | **Park Slope**	21
Crif Dogs | **multi.**	22
NEW Go Burger | **multi.**	22
Gray's Papaya | **multi.**	20
Z Katz's Deli | **LES**	24
Papaya King | **E 80s**	21
Shake Shack | **multi.**	22

HUNGARIAN

Andre's Café | **E 80s**	20

ICE CREAM PARLORS

L&B Spumoni | **Bensonhurst**	24
Serendipity 3 | **E 60s**	19

INDIAN

Amma | **E 50s**	24
Baluchi's | **multi.**	19
Banjara | **E Vill**	22
Bombay Palace | **W 50s**	19
Bombay Talkie | **Chelsea**	20
Brick Ln. Curry | **multi.**	22
Bukhara Grill | **E 40s**	22
Chennai Gdn. | **Murray Hill**	21

Chola | **E 50s**	24
Curry Leaf | **Murray Hill**	19
Darbar | **multi.**	21
Dawat | **E 50s**	23
Dévi | **Flatiron**	24
Dhaba | **Murray Hill**	24
Hampton Chutney | **multi.**	20
Haveli | **E Vill**	22
Indus Valley | **W 100s**	22
Jackson Diner | **multi.**	21
Jewel of India | **W 40s**	20
NEW Junoon | **Flatiron**	23
Kati Roll | **multi.**	21
Mint | **E 50s**	22
Mughlai | **W 70s**	20
Nirvana | **Murray Hill**	21
Pongal | **Murray Hill**	22
Salaam Bombay | **TriBeCa**	22
Sapphire | **W 60s**	21
Saravanaa Bhavan | **multi.**	24
Surya | **W Vill**	21
Swagat Indian | **W 70s**	22
Z Tamarind | **multi.**	25
Tiffin Wallah | **Murray Hill**	23
NEW Tulsi | **E 40s**	21
Utsav | **W 40s**	21
Vatan | **Murray Hill**	24
Yuva | **E 50s**	23

ISRAELI

Azuri Cafe | **W 50s**	26
Hummus Pl. | **multi.**	22
Miriam | **Park Slope**	22
Z Taïm | **W Vill**	26

ITALIAN

(N=Northern; S=Southern)

Abboccato | **W 50s**	21
Acappella | N | **TriBeCa**	24
Accademia/Vino | **multi.**	18
Acqua | S | **W 90s**	20
Z NEW Ai Fiori | **Garment**	27
Alberto | N | **Forest Hills**	24
Z Al Di La | N | **Park Slope**	27
Al Forno Pizza | **E 70s**	20
Alfredo/Rome | S | **W 40s**	21
Alloro | **E 70s**	25
Amarone | **W 40s**	20
Amorina | **Prospect Hts**	23
Angelina's | **Tottenville**	22
Angelo's/Mulberry | S | **L Italy**	23
Angelo's Pizza | **multi.**	20
Ann & Tony's | **Fordham**	20
Antica Venezia | **W Vill**	23

Antonucci | **E 80s**	23
Ápizz | **LES**	24
Areo | **Bay Ridge**	24
Armani Rist. | N | **E 50s**	21
Arno | N | **Garment**	20
Aroma Kitchen | **NoHo**	23
Arté Café | **W 70s**	18
Arturo's | **G Vill**	21
NEW Asellina | **Murray Hill**	19
Aurora | **multi.**	24
A Voce | **multi.**	23
🅩 Babbo | **G Vill**	27
Baci/Abbracci | **W'burg**	21
Bamonte's | **W'burg**	24
Baraonda | **E 70s**	18
Barbetta | N | **W 40s**	21
Barbone | **E Vill**	25
Barbuto | **W Vill**	25
Bar Italia | N | **multi.**	21
Barolo | **SoHo**	19
Barosa | **Rego Pk**	21
Bar Pitti | **G Vill**	22
Stuzzi | S | **multi.**	20
Basilica | **W 40s**	20
Basso56 | S | **W 50s**	23
Basta Pasta | **Flatiron**	23
Becco | **W 40s**	23
Beccofino | **Riverdale**	23
Bella Blu | N | **E 70s**	21
Bella Via | **LIC**	22
Bello | **W 50s**	22
NEW Betto | **W'burg**	–
Bettola | **W 70s**	21
Bianca | N | **NoHo**	24
Bice | N | **E 50s**	20
Bino | **Carroll Gdns**	24
Biricchino | N | **Chelsea**	21
NEW Birreria | **Flatiron**	21
Bistango | **Murray Hill**	22
Bistro Milano | N | **W 50s**	21
Bocca | S | **Flatiron**	22
Bocca/Bacco | **multi.**	22
Bocca Lupo | **Cobble Hill**	24
Bocelli | **Grasmere**	25
Bond 45 | **W 40s**	20
Bottega/Vino | **E 50s**	22
Bottino | N | **Chelsea**	19
Bread | **TriBeCa**	21
NEW Bread/Tulips | **Murray Hill**	–
Bricco | **W 50s**	20
Brick Cafe | N | **Astoria**	22
Brio | **multi.**	19
Brioso | **New Dorp**	23
Cacio e Pepe | S | **E Vill**	21
Cacio e Vino | S | **E Vill**	21
Cafe Fiorello | **W 60s**	20
Caffe Cielo | **W 50s**	21
Caffe e Vino | **Ft Greene**	24
Caffe Grazie | **E 80s**	20
Campagnola | **E 70s**	23
Canaletto | N | **E 60s**	20
Cara Mia | **W 40s**	21
Caravaggio | **E 70s**	23
Carmine's | S | **multi.**	21
NEW Carpe Diem | **E 70s**	22
Casa Lever | **E 50s**	23
NEW Casa Nonna | **Garment**	–
Celeste | S | **W 80s**	24
Cellini | N | **E 50s**	23
Centolire | N | **E 80s**	22
Centro Vinoteca | **W Vill**	20
'Cesca | S | **W 70s**	23
Chelsea Ristorante | N | **Chelsea**	20
🅩**NEW** Ciano | **Flatiron**	25
Cibo | N | **E 40s**	21
Cipriani Dolci | **E 40s**	21
Cipriani D'twn | **SoHo**	22
Cipriani Wall Street | **Financial**	23
Circo | N | **W 50s**	23
Coppola's | **multi.**	19
Corsino | **W Vill**	21
Covo | **Harlem**	22
Crispo | N | **W Vill**	24
Cucina/Pesce | **E Vill**	19
Da Andrea | N | **G Vill**	22
Da Ciro | **Murray Hill**	23
Da Nico | **L Italy**	20
Da Noi | N | **multi.**	23
Da Silvana | **Forest Hills**	22
🅩 Da Silvano | N | **G Vill**	22
Da Tommaso | N | **W 50s**	20
Da Umberto | N | **Chelsea**	24
Defonte's | **multi.**	24
DeGrezia | **E 50s**	23
🅩 Dell'anima | **W Vill**	25
🅩 Del Posto | **Chelsea**	27
Divino | N | **E 80s**	20
Dominick's | **Fordham**	24
Don Peppe | **Ozone Pk**	25
Due | N | **E 70s**	22
🅩 Eataly | **Flatiron**	23
Ecco | **TriBeCa**	24
🅩 Elio's | **E 80s**	24
Emilio's Ballato | **NoLita**	25
Emporio | **NoLita**	23
Enoteca Maria | **St. George**	25

Enzo's | **multi.**	23	Il Fornaio | **L Italy**	23
NEW Eolo | S | **Chelsea**	24	Il Gattopardo | S | **W 50s**	23
Erminia | S | **E 80s**	25	Il Giglio | N | **TriBeCa**	26
Z Esca | S | **W 40s**	25	**Z** Il Mulino | **G Vill**	27
Etcetera Etcetera | **W 40s**	22	Il Palazzo | **L Italy**	24
Fabio Piccolo | **E 40s**	23	Il Postino | **E 40s**	25
Falai | **multi.**	24	Il Riccio | S | **E 70s**	21
F & J Pine | **Morris Park**	21	**Z** Il Tinello | N | **W 50s**	26
Felice | **multi.**	24	Inatteso | **Financial**	24
Z Felidia | **E 50s**	26	'Ino | **W Vill**	24
Ferdinando's | S | **Carroll Gdns**	25	'Inoteca | **multi.**	22
Filippo's | **Dongan Hills**	25	I Sodi | **W Vill**	24
Fiorentino's | S | **Gravesend**	21	Italianissimo | **E 80s**	23
Fiorini | S | **E 50s**	21	I Trulli | **Murray Hill**	23
Firenze | N | **E 80s**	22	Joe & Pat's | **Castleton Corners**	24
NEW Forcella | S | **W'burg**	-	John's/12th St. | **E Vill**	22
Forlini's | N | **Chinatown**	19	La Carbonara | S | **W Vill**	20
Fornino | **multi.**	22	**NEW** La Follia | **Gramercy**	23
Fragole | **Carroll Gdns**	25	La Gioconda | **E 50s**	21
Frank | **E Vill**	24	La Lanterna | **G Vill**	20
Z Frankies | **multi.**	25	La Masseria | S | **W 40s**	23
Z Franny's | **Prospect Hts**	25	L&B Spumoni | **Bensonhurst**	24
Fratelli | **Pelham Gardens**	21	La Pizza Fresca | **Flatiron**	24
Fred's at Barneys | N | **E 60s**	20	La Rivista | N | **W 40s**	21
Fresco | N | **multi.**	23	L'Artusi | **W Vill**	26
Gabriel's | N | **W 60s**	23	Lasagna | **multi.**	18
Gargiulo's | S | **Coney Is**	22	Lattanzi | S | **W 40s**	22
Gemma | **E Vill**	20	Lavagna | **E Vill**	24
Gennaro | **W 90s**	24	La Vela | N | **W 70s**	20
Gigino | **multi.**	20	La Vigna | **Forest Hills**	24
Giorgione | **Hudson Square**	23	La Villa Pizzeria | **multi.**	21
Giovanni | N | **E 80s**	24	**NEW** Lavo | **E 50s**	21
Girasole | **E 80s**	22	**NEW** Leopard/des Artistes | S | **W 60s**	21
Gnocco | N | **E Vill**	23		
Gottino | **W Vill**	20	Leo's Latticini | **multi.**	27
Grace's Tratt. | **E 70s**	19	Le Zie 2000 | N | **Chelsea**	21
Gradisca | **W Vill**	23	**NEW** Lido | N | **Harlem**	26
Grand Tier | **W 60s**	21	Lil' Frankie | **E Vill**	23
Grano Tratt. | **W Vill**	23	**Z** Lincoln | **W 60s**	24
Greenwich Grill/Sushi Azabu | **TriBeCa**	25	Lisca | N | **W 90s**	20
		Locale | **Astoria**	23
Grifone | N | **E 40s**	24	**Z** Locanda Verde | **TriBeCa**	25
Gusto | **W Vill**	21	**Z** Locanda Vini | N | **Clinton Hill**	27
Harry Cipriani | N | **E 50s**	22	Lorenzo's | **Bloomfield**	21
Harry's Italian | **multi.**	21	Lumi | N | **E 70s**	20
Hearth | N | **E Vill**	24	Luna Piena | **E 50s**	21
I Coppi | N | **E Vill**	22	Lunetta | **Boerum Hill**	22
Il Bagatto | **E Vill**	23	Lupa | S | **G Vill**	25
Il Bambino | **Astoria**	26	Lusardi's | N | **E 70s**	24
Z Il Buco | **NoHo**	26	Luzzo's/Ovest | S | **E Vill**	25
Il Cantinori | N | **G Vill**	24	Macelleria | N | **Meatpacking**	22
Il Corallo | **SoHo**	23	Madison's | **Riverdale**	20
Il Cortile | **L Italy**	22	**Z** Maialino | S | **Gramercy**	25

Restaurant	Rating
NEW Malaparte | N | **W Vill**	–
Malatesta | N | **W Vill**	24
Manducatis | S | **LIC**	23
Manetta's | **LIC**	22
Manzo | **Flatiron**	24
Marcony | **Murray Hill**	25
Marco Polo | **Carroll Gdns**	21
⊠ Marea | **W 50s**	28
Maria Pia | **W 50s**	19
Marinella | **W Vill**	22
Mario's | S | **Fordham**	21
Maruzzella | N | **E 70s**	22
Max | **multi.**	22
Max SoHa/Caffe | **W 100s**	23
Mediterraneo | N | **E 60s**	19
Mercato | **Garment**	23
Mezzaluna/Pizza | **E 70s**	22
Mezzogiorno | N | **SoHo**	21
Mia Dona | **E 50s**	19
Miranda | **W'burg**	25
Montebello | N | **E 50s**	23
Morandi | **W Vill**	22
Nanni | N | **E 40s**	24
Naples 45 | S | **E 40s**	18
Nello | N | **E 60s**	17
Nicola's | **E 80s**	22
Nino's | N | **multi.**	22
Nizza | **W 40s**	19
Nocello | N | **W 50s**	22
Noi Due | **W 60s**	–
Noodle Pudding | **Bklyn Hts**	24
Nove | **Eltingville**	24
Novitá | N | **Gramercy**	25
Olio | S | **W Vill**	20
101 | **Bay Ridge**	21
⊠ Orso | N | **W 40s**	23
Osso Buco | **E 90s**	19
Osteria al Doge | N | **W 40s**	20
Osteria Laguna | **E 40s**	20
NEW Osteria Morini | N | **SoHo**	24
Otto | **G Vill**	23
Padre Figlio | **E 40s**	23
Palma | S | **W Vill**	22
Paola's | **E 90s**	23
Pappardella | **W 70s**	21
Park Side | **Corona**	24
Parma | N | **E 70s**	22
Pasquale's | **Fordham**	21
Patricia's | **Morris Park**	24
Patsy's | S | **W 50s**	22
Paul & Jimmy's | **Gramercy**	21
Peasant | **NoLita**	24
Pellegrino's | **L Italy**	23
Pepe | **multi.**	19
⊠ Pepolino | N | **TriBeCa**	26
Perbacco | **E Vill**	25
Per Lei | **E 70s**	20
Petaluma | **E 70s**	19
Petrarca Vino | **TriBeCa**	23
Piccola Venezia | **Astoria**	26
Piccolo Angolo | **W Vill**	26
Pietro's | **E 40s**	24
Pinocchio | **E 90s**	23
Pisticci | S | **W 100s**	24
NEW PizzArte | S | **W 50s**	–
Pó | **W Vill**	25
Pomodoro Rosso | **W 70s**	21
Ponte's | **TriBeCa**	25
Ponticello | N | **Astoria**	24
Porchetta | **E Vill**	24
NEW Porsena | **E Vill**	22
Portofino | N | **City Is**	21
Primola | **E 60s**	22
Puttanesca | **W 50s**	19
Quattro Gastro. | N | **Hudson Square**	23
Quattro Gatti | **E 80s**	21
Queen | **Bklyn Hts**	24
Rao's | S | **Harlem**	23
Regional | **W 90s**	21
Remi | **W 50s**	22
Re Sette | **W 40s**	21
Risotteria | **W Vill**	21
⊠ Roberto | **Fordham**	27
Roc | **TriBeCa**	21
Rocco | N | **G Vill**	22
Rossini's | N | **Murray Hill**	22
NEW Rubirosa | **NoLita**	25
Sac's Place | **Astoria**	24
Salumeria Rosi | N | **W 70s**	25
Salute! | **Murray Hill**	19
Sambuca | S | **W 70s**	19
Sandro's | S | **E 80s**	25
⊠ San Pietro | S | **E 50s**	26
Sant Ambroeus | N | **multi.**	21
Sapori D'Ischia | S | **Woodside**	24
Savoia | **Carroll Gdns**	20
Scaletta | N | **W 70s**	21
⊠ Scalinatella | **E 60s**	26
⊠ Scalini Fedeli | N | **TriBeCa**	27
Scarlatto | N | **W 40s**	21
⊠ Scarpetta | **Chelsea**	26
Scottadito | N | **Park Slope**	23
SD26 | **Murray Hill**	24
Serafina | **multi.**	19

CUISINES

Sette Mezzo | **E 70s**	23
Sfoglia | **N** | **E 90s**	23
❷ Sistina | **N** | **E 80s**	26
Sorella | **LES**	26
Sosa Borella | **W 50s**	20
NEW Spasso | **W Vill**	24
Spiga | **W 80s**	24
Spigolo | **E 80s**	25
Spina | **E Vill**	25
S.P.Q.R. | **S** | **L Italy**	19
Supper | **N** | **E Vill**	24
Tarallucci | **multi.**	20
Teodora | **N** | **E 50s**	21
Terroir | **multi.**	20
Testaccio | **S** | **LIC**	22
Tiella | **S** | **E 60s**	26
Tommaso | **Dyker Hts**	24
Tony's Di Napoli | **S** | **W 40s**	21
❷ Torrisi | **NoLita**	27
Tosca Café | **Throgs Neck**	21
Tratt. Alba | **N** | **Murray Hill**	21
Trattoria Cinque | **TriBeCa**	21
Tratt. Dell'Arte | **N** | **W 50s**	23
❷ Tratt. L'incontro | **Astoria**	27
Tratt. Pesce | **multi.**	19
Tratt. Romana | **Dongan Hills**	26
Trattoria Toscana | **N** | **W Vill**	24
Trattoria Trecolori | **W 40s**	23
Tre Dici/Steak | **Chelsea**	23
Tre Otto | **E 90s**	20
Tuscany Grill | **N** | **Bay Ridge**	23
Umberto's | **multi.**	20
Uva | **E 70s**	22
Uvarara | **Middle Vill**	26
Valbella | **N** | **Meatpacking**	26
NEW Valentino's/Green | **Bayside**	21
V&T | **W 100s**	18
Veniero's | **E Vill**	24
Vespa | **E 80s**	18
Vesta | **Astoria**	25
Vezzo | **Murray Hill**	23
Via Emilia | **N** | **Flatiron**	23
Via Quadronno | **N** | **multi.**	22
ViceVersa | **W 50s**	22
Vico | **E 90s**	22
Villa Berulia | **N** | **Murray Hill**	24
Villa Mosconi | **G Vill**	21
NEW Villa Pacri | **Meatpacking**	24
Vincent's | **L Italy**	22
Vivolo/Cucina | **E 70s**	19
NEW White & Church | **TriBeCa**	-
Za Za | **N** | **E 60s**	21

Ze Café | **E 50s**	22
Zero Otto | **S** | **multi.**	25

JAMAICAN

NEW Miss Lily's | **G Vill**	-
Negril | **G Vill**	21

JAPANESE

(* sushi specialist)

Aburiya Kinnosuke | **E 40s**	25
Aji Sushi* | **Murray Hill**	21
Aki* | **W Vill**	25
Arirang Hibachi | **multi.**	20
Blue Ginger* | **Chelsea**	21
❷ Blue Ribbon Sushi* | **multi.**	26
Blue Ribbon Sushi B&G* | **W 50s**	25
Bohemian | **NoHo**	27
Bond St.* | **NoHo**	25
❷**NEW** Brushstroke | **TriBeCa**	28
❷ Donguri | **E 80s**	27
EN Japanese | **W Vill**	25
❷ 15 East* | **Union Sq**	26
Fushimi* | **multi.**	24
❷ Gari/Sushi* | **multi.**	27
Geido* | **Prospect Hts**	25
Greenwich Grill/Sushi Azabu* | **TriBeCa**	25
Gyu-Kaku | **multi.**	21
Haru* | **multi.**	21
Hasaki* | **E Vill**	23
Hatsuhana* | **E 40s**	24
Hibino* | **Cobble Hill**	26
Hide-Chan | **E 50s**	21
Inakaya | **W 40s**	23
Ippudo | **E Vill**	25
Ise* | **multi.**	21
Japonica* | **G Vill**	23
❷ Jewel Bako* | **E Vill**	26
Kajitsu | **E Vill**	28
❷ Kanoyama* | **E Vill**	26
Katsu-Hama | **multi.**	20
Ki Sushi* | **Boerum Hill**	25
Koi* | **W 40s**	23
Ko Sushi* | **multi.**	20
Kouzan* | **W 90s**	21
❷ Kuruma Zushi* | **E 40s**	28
Kyotofu | **W 40s**	21
Kyo Ya | **E Vill**	26
❷ Masa/Bar Masa* | **W 60s**	27
Matsuri* | **Chelsea**	23
Megu | **multi.**	24
Menchanko-tei | **multi.**	21
Minca | **E Vill**	24
Mishima* | **Murray Hill**	24

Momo Sushi Shack* | **Bushwick**	⎯
Momoya* | **multi.**	23
Z Morimoto | **Chelsea**	26
NEW Mr. Robata | **W 50s**	⎯
Natsumi* | **W 50s**	22
NEW Niko* | **SoHo**	22
Ninja | **TriBeCa**	18
Z Nobu* | **multi.**	26
Omen | **SoHo**	24
1 or 8* | **W'burg**	24
Poke* | **E 80s**	25
Prime Grill/KO | **W 80s**	23
Rai Rai Ken | **E Vill**	22
Ramen Setagaya | **E Vill**	18
Robataya | **E Vill**	25
Rosanjin | **TriBeCa**	27
Sakagura | **E 40s**	25
Z Sasabune* | **E 70s**	29
Shabu-Shabu 70* | **E 70s**	21
Shabu-Tatsu | **E Vill**	22
Soba Nippon | **W 50s**	23
Soba Totto | **E 40s**	22
Soba-ya | **E Vill**	24
Z Soto* | **W Vill**	29
Z Sugiyama | **W 50s**	27
SushiAnn* | **E 50s**	24
Sushiden* | **multi.**	25
Sushi Hana* | **multi.**	21
SushiSamba* | **multi.**	21
Z Sushi Seki* | **E 60s**	27
Z Sushi Sen-nin* | **Murray Hill**	27
Z Sushi Yasuda* | **E 40s**	28
Sushi Zen* | **W 40s**	26
Suteishi* | **Seaport**	25
Takahachi* | **multi.**	24
Takashi | **W Vill**	26
Tanuki* | **Meatpacking**	20
Tenzan* | **multi.**	22
Z Tomoe Sushi* | **G Vill**	26
Totto Ramen | **W 50s**	25
Ushiwakamaru* | **G Vill**	26
Watawa* | **Astoria**	24
Yakitori Totto | **W 50s**	25
Yama* | **multi.**	24
Yuka* | **E 80s**	23
Z Zenkichi | **W'burg**	26
Zutto* | **TriBeCa**	21
Zuzu Ramen | **Park Slope**	20

JEWISH

Artie's Deli | **W 80s**	18
Z Barney Greengrass | **W 80s**	24
Ben's Best | **Rego Pk**	23
Ben's Kosher | **multi.**	19
Z Carnegie Deli | **W 50s**	22
Z Katz's Deli | **LES**	24
Lattanzi | **W 40s**	22
Liebman's | **Riverdale**	22
Mile End | **Boerum Hill**	24
Mill Basin Deli | **Mill Basin**	23
Pastrami Queen | **E 70s**	22
Sammy's | **LES**	20
Sarge's Deli | **Murray Hill**	21
2nd Ave Deli | **multi.**	23
Stage Deli | **W 50s**	21

KOREAN

(* barbecue specialist)

Bann | **W 50s**	22
Bon Chon | **multi.**	20
Cho Dang Gol | **Garment**	22
NEW Danji | **W 50s**	24
Do Hwa* | **W Vill**	21
Gahm Mi Oak | **Garment**	22
Z HanGawi | **Murray Hill**	25
Kang Suh* | **Garment**	23
Kum Gang San* | **multi.**	22
Kyochon | **multi.**	19
Madangsui* | **Garment**	22
Mandoo Bar | **Garment**	22
Moim | **Park Slope**	23
WonJo* | **Garment**	21

KOSHER/ KOSHER-STYLE

Abigael's | **Garment**	20
Azuri Cafe | **W 50s**	26
Ben's Best | **Rego Pk**	23
Ben's Kosher | **multi.**	19
Caravan/Dreams | **E Vill**	22
Chennai Gdn. | **Murray Hill**	21
Colbeh | **Garment**	21
Hummus Pl. | **multi.**	22
Le Marais | **W 40s**	22
Liebman's | **Riverdale**	22
Mike's Bistro | **W 70s**	23
NEW Milk St. Café | **Financial**	⎯
Mill Basin Deli | **Mill Basin**	23
Noi Due | **W 60s**	⎯
Pastrami Queen | **E 70s**	22
Peacefood Café | **W 80s**	22
Pongal | **Murray Hill**	22
Prime Grill/KO | **multi.**	23
2nd Ave Deli | **multi.**	23
Solo | **E 50s**	24
Tiffin Wallah | **Murray Hill**	23

LEBANESE

Al Bustan	**E 50s**	20
Ilili	**Chelsea**	25
Naya/Express	**multi.**	22

MALAYSIAN

Fatty Crab	**multi.**	20
Laut	**Union Sq**	22
Nyonya	**multi.**	22

MEDITERRANEAN

Alta	**G Vill**	25
Amaranth	**E 60s**	19
Anella	**Greenpt**	24
Ayza Wine	**Garment**	20
Balaboosta	**NoLita**	23
Barbounia	**Flatiron**	21
Beast	**Prospect Hts**	21
Bodrum	**W 80s**	20
NEW Boulud Sud	**W 60s**	23
Cafe Centro	**E 40s**	21
Café du Soleil	**W 100s**	19
Cafe Ronda	**W 70s**	20
Conviv. Osteria	**Park Slope**	25
Dee's	**Forest Hills**	22
Dervish	**W 40s**	19
Epices/Traiteur	**W 70s**	21
Extra Virgin	**W Vill**	23
Fig & Olive	**multi.**	20
5 Points	**NoHo**	22
Z Il Buco	**NoHo**	26
Isabella's	**W 70s**	20
Kashkaval	**W 50s**	23
Kenmare	**L Italy**	19
Little Owl	**W Vill**	25
Mangia	**multi.**	20
Marseille	**W 40s**	20
NEW Mémé	**W Vill**	24
Miriam	**Park Slope**	22
Nanoosh	**multi.**	18
Nice Matin	**W 70s**	20
Nick & Toni	**W 60s**	20
Olea	**Ft Greene**	22
Olives	**Union Sq**	23
Pera	**E 40s**	21
Peri Ela	**E 90s**	19
Z Picholine	**W 60s**	27
Place	**W Vill**	25
Red Cat	**Chelsea**	24
Sahara	**Gravesend**	23
Sezz Medi'	**W 100s**	21
Solo	**E 50s**	24
Superfine	**Dumbo**	18
Taboon	**W 50s**	24

Z Tanoreen	**Bay Ridge**	26
Terrace in Sky	**W 100s**	22

MEXICAN

Alma	**Carroll Gdns**	19
Blockhead Burrito	**multi.**	17
Café Frida	**multi.**	19
Café Habana/Outpost	**multi.**	22
Z Calexico	**multi.**	24
Cascabel/Cantina	**E 80s**	23
Centrico	**TriBeCa**	20
Crema	**Chelsea**	23
Dos Caminos	**multi.**	19
Dos Toros	**multi.**	23
El Centro	**W 50s**	22
El Parador Cafe	**Murray Hill**	23
El Paso Taqueria	**multi.**	23
NEW Empellón	**W Vill**	21
Fonda	**Park Slope**	23
Gabriela's	**W 90s**	19
Hecho en Dumbo	**NoHo**	23
Hell's Kitchen	**W 40s**	22
Itzocan	**E Vill**	24
La Esquina	**multi.**	23
La Flor	**Woodside**	25
La Palapa	**E Vill**	22
La Superior	**W'burg**	24
Mamá Mexico	**multi.**	19
Maya	**E 60s**	23
Maz Mezcal	**E 80s**	21
Mercadito	**multi.**	23
Mesa Coyoacan	**W'burg**	25
Mexicana Mama	**multi.**	24
Mexican Radio	**NoLita**	19
NEW Mexicue	**multi.**	-
Móle	**multi.**	23
Noche Mex.	**W 100s**	23
Oaxaca	**multi.**	20
Ofrenda	**W Vill**	20
Pampano	**E 40s**	24
Rocking Horse	**Chelsea**	21
Rosa Mexicano	**multi.**	22
Sinigual	**E 40s**	21
Sueños	**Chelsea**	22
NEW Teqa	**Murray Hill**	21
Toloache	**multi.**	23
Tortilleria Nixtamal	**Corona**	24
Tulcingo del Valle	**W 40s**	22

MIDDLE EASTERN

Balaboosta	**NoLita**	23
Chickpea	**multi.**	18
Gazala Place	**multi.**	21
Maoz Veg.	**multi.**	21

Mimi's Hummus | **Ditmas Pk**	24
Moustache | **multi.**	22
Taboon | **W 50s**	24
🄑 Tanoreen | **Bay Ridge**	26
12 Chairs | **SoHo**	20
Zaytoons | **multi.**	19

MOROCCAN

Barbès | **Murray Hill**	20
Cafe Gitane | **multi.**	20
Cafe Mogador | **E Vill**	22

NEW ENGLAND

Ed's Lobster | **multi.**	23
Mermaid | **multi.**	22
🄑 Pearl Oyster | **W Vill**	26

NOODLE SHOPS

Bao Noodles | **Gramercy**	19
Bo-Ky | **multi.**	22
🄑 Donguri | **E 80s**	27
Great NY Noodle | **Chinatown**	23
Hide-Chan | **E 50s**	21
NEW Hung Ry | **NoHo**	20
Ippudo | **E Vill**	25
Mee Noodle | **multi.**	17
Menchanko-tei | **multi.**	21
Minca | **E Vill**	24
Momofuku Noodle | **E Vill**	24
Noodle Bar | **multi.**	20
Pho Bang | **multi.**	21
Pho Viet Huong | **Chinatown**	22
Rai Rai Ken | **E Vill**	22
Ramen Setagaya | **E Vill**	18
Republic | **Union Sq**	19
Soba Nippon | **W 50s**	23
Soba Totto | **E 40s**	22
Soba-ya | **E Vill**	24
Totto Ramen | **W 50s**	25
Zuzu Ramen | **Park Slope**	20

NORTH AFRICAN

Nomad | **E Vill**	20

NUEVO LATINO

Cabana | **multi.**	21
Calle Ocho | **W 80s**	21
Citrus B&G | **W 70s**	20
NEW Copacabana | **W 40s**	-
NEW Coppelia | **Chelsea**	20
Luz | **Ft Greene**	22

PAN-LATIN

Boca Chica | **E Vill**	22
Bogota | **Park Slope**	21
Miranda | **W'burg**	25

Nuela | **Flatiron**	22
Palo Santo | **Park Slope**	23
Rayuela | **LES**	23
Yerba Buena | **multi.**	23
Yuca Bar | **E Vill**	22
Zengo | **E 40s**	22

PERSIAN

Colbeh | **Garment**	21
Persepolis | **E 70s**	22
Ravagh | **multi.**	22
Shalezeh | **E 80s**	22

PERUVIAN

Coco Roco | **multi.**	19
Flor/Mayo | **multi.**	20
🄑 Nobu | **multi.**	26
Pio Pio | **multi.**	22

PIZZA

Acqua | **W 90s**	20
Adrienne's | **Financial**	23
Al Forno Pizza | **E 70s**	20
Amorina | **Prospect Hts**	23
Angelo's Pizza | **multi.**	20
Ápizz | **LES**	24
Artichoke Basille | **multi.**	22
Arturo's | **G Vill**	21
Baci/Abbracci | **W'burg**	21
Bella Blu | **E 70s**	21
Bella Via | **LIC**	22
Bettola | **W 70s**	21
Big Nick's | **W 70s**	18
NEW Bread/Tulips | **Murray Hill**	-
Bricco | **W 50s**	20
Brio | **multi.**	19
Cacio e Vino | **E Vill**	21
Cafe Fiorello | **W 60s**	20
Co. | **Chelsea**	23
Covo | **Harlem**	22
Da Ciro | **Murray Hill**	23
Dee's | **Forest Hills**	22
🄑 Denino | **Port Richmond**	26
🄑 Di Fara | **Midwood**	26
NEW Donatella | **Chelsea**	21
🄑 Eataly | **Flatiron**	23
NEW Forcella | **W'burg**	-
Fornino | **multi.**	22
🄑 Franny's | **Prospect Hts**	25
Gigino | **multi.**	20
NEW Giuseppina's | **Greenwood Hts**	-
Grimaldi's | **multi.**	24
Gruppo | **E Vill**	26

Harry's Italian | multi.	21
Inatteso | Financial	24
Joe & Pat's | Castleton Corners	24
Joe's Pizza | multi.	23
John's Pizzeria | multi.	23
Keste Pizza | W Vill	25
L&B Spumoni | Bensonhurst	24
La Pizza Fresca | Flatiron	24
La Villa Pizzeria | multi.	21
Lazzara's | multi.	23
Lil' Frankie | E Vill	23
Lombardi's | NoLita	25
☑ Lucali | Carroll Gdns	26
Luzzo's/Ovest | E Vill	25
Mediterraneo | E 60s	19
Mezzaluna/Pizza | multi.	22
Motorino | E Vill	24
Naples 45 | E 40s	18
Nick's | multi.	24
NEW 900 Degrees | W Vill	-
Nino's | E 40s	22
No. 28 | multi.	25
Olio | W Vill	20
Otto | G Vill	23
Patsy's Pizzeria | multi.	20
Pintaile's Pizza | E 80s	20
NEW PizzArte | W 50s	-
Posto | Gramercy	24
Pulino's | NoLita	19
Rizzo's Pizza | multi.	23
☑ Roberta's | Bushwick	26
NEW Rubirosa | NoLita	25
Sac's Place | Astoria	24
Savoia | Carroll Gdns	20
Sezz Medi' | W 100s	21
☑ Totonno Pizza | Coney Is	26
Two Boots | multi.	18
V&T | W 100s	18
Vesta | Astoria	25
Vezzo | Murray Hill	23
Zero Otto | multi.	25

POLISH

Teresa's | Bklyn Hts	18

POLYNESIAN

Hurricane Club | Flatiron	20
King Yum | Fresh Meadows	19

PORTUGUESE

Aldea | Flatiron	25
NEW Alfama | E 50s	-
Macao Trading | TriBeCa	19

PUB FOOD

NEW B&B | SoHo	24
Donovan's | Woodside	20
Elephant & Castle | W Vill	19
Fort Defiance | Red Hook	21
Fraunces Tavern | Financial	17
Heartland | multi.	15
Henry Public | Cobble Hill	20
Jack Horse | Bklyn Hts	23
J.G. Melon | E 70s	21
Landmark Tavern | W 40s	17
Molly's | Gramercy	22
Neary's | E 50s	16
Pete's Tavern | Gramercy	15
P.J. Clarke's | multi.	17
Walker's | TriBeCa	19

PUERTO RICAN

La Taza de Oro | Chelsea	21
Sazon | TriBeCa	21
Sofrito | E 50s	23

RUSSIAN

FireBird | W 40s	20
Mari Vanna | Flatiron	20
Russian Samovar | W 50s	20
Russian Tea | W 50s	19
Tatiana | Brighton Bch	21

SANDWICHES

(See also Delis)	
An Choi | LES	21
Baoguette | multi.	21
NEW Beecher's | Flatiron	-
Bouchon Bakery | multi.	24
Bread | NoLita	21
Brennan | Sheepshead	22
Così | multi.	16
Defonte's | multi.	24
Dishes | multi.	21
DuMont | W'burg	23
E.A.T. | E 80s	20
Eisenberg's Sandwich | Flatiron	18
Friedman's Lunch | Chelsea	21
Hale/Hearty | multi.	19
Hanco's | multi.	21
Il Bambino | Astoria	26
NEW Jeffrey's Grocery | W Vill	21
Mangia | multi.	20
Meatball Shop | multi.	25
Nicky's | multi.	22
No. 7 | Chelsea	23
Num Pang | multi.	26
Peanut Butter Co. | G Vill	22
Porchetta | E Vill	24

Press 195	multi.	22	**NEW** Imperial No. Nine	SoHo	25
Pret A Manger	multi.	18	Ithaka	E 80s	20
Roll-n-Roaster	Sheepshead	21	Jack's Lux.	E Vill	26
Saltie	W'burg	23	**NEW** John Dory	Chelsea	23
sNice	multi.	20	Kellari Tav./Parea	W 40s	23
NEW Social Eatz	E 50s	23	☑ Le Bernardin	W 50s	29
Sweet Melissa	multi.	20	Le Pescadeux	SoHo	23
This Little Piggy	E Vill	23	Lobster Box	City Is	20
'Wichcraft	multi.	20	London Lennie	Rego Pk	23
Yura on Madison	E 90s	21	Luke's Lobster	multi.	23
Zabar's Cafe	W 80s	20	Lure Fishbar	SoHo	23
Zaitzeff	multi.	21	☑ Marea	W 50s	28

SCANDINAVIAN

☑ Aquavit	E 50s	25
Smorgas Chef	multi.	19

SCOTTISH

NEW Mary Queen of Scots	LES	21

SEAFOOD

Ammos	E 40s	21	Marina Cafe	Great Kills	22
☑ Aquagrill	SoHo	26	Mary's Fish	W Vill	25
Artie's	City Is	23	McCormick/Schmick	W 50s	20
Atlantic Grill	multi.	23	Mermaid	multi.	22
Avra	E 40s	25	**NEW** Millesime	Murray Hill	21
Black Duck	Murray Hill	21	☑ Milos, Estiatorio	W 50s	27
BLT Fish	Flatiron	24	**NEW** Mussel Pot	G Vill	22
Blue Fin	W 40s	22	Oceana	W 40s	24
☑ Blue Water	Union Sq	24	Ocean Grill	W 70s	24
Bocelli	Grasmere	25	☑ Oriental Gdn.	Chinatown	23
Brooklyn Fish	Park Slope	23	☑ Oyster Bar	E 40s	22
City Crab	Flatiron	19	Pampano	E 40s	24
City Hall	TriBeCa	21	Parlor Steak	E 90s	21
City Is. Lobster	City Is	19	☑ Pearl Oyster	W Vill	26
City Lobster	W 40s	19	Pearl Room	Bay Ridge	23
Cole's Dock	Great Kills	21	Periyali	Flatiron	24
Cowgirl	Seaport	17	Petite Crev.	Carroll Gdns	24
Cucina/Pesce	E Vill	19	**NEW** Pier 9	W 50s	23
Ditch Plains	multi.	18	Ping's Sea.	multi.	22
Docks Oyster	E 40s	21	Portofino	City Is	21
Ed's Chowder	W 60s	20	Redeye Grill	W 50s	20
Ed's Lobster	multi.	23	Red Hook Lobster Pound	Red Hook	24
Elias Corner	Astoria	23	Sammy's Fishbox	City Is	22
☑ Esca	W 40s	25	Sea Grill	W 40s	24
Fish	W Vill	23	☑ Taverna Kyclades	Astoria	26
NEW FishTag	W 70s	22	Telly's Taverna	Astoria	23
Fishtail	E 60s	24	Thalassa	TriBeCa	24
Flex Mussels	multi.	23	Tratt. Pesce	multi.	19
Francisco's	Chelsea	22	Umberto's	multi.	20
Fuleen	Chinatown	22	Water's Edge	LIC	21
Fulton	E 70s	23	
Hudson River	Harlem	21	

SMALL PLATES

(See also Spanish tapas specialist)

Alta	Med.	G Vill	25
Stuzzi	Italian	multi.	20
Beast	Med.	Prospect Hts	21
☑ **NEW** Beauty & Essex	Amer.	LES	22
Beyoglu	Turkish	E 80s	22
Bocca Lupo	Italian	Cobble Hill	24

NEW Buvette | French | **W Vill**	24
Casellula | Amer. | **W 50s**	25
Centro Vinoteca | Italian | **W Vill**	20
Corsino | Italian | **W Vill**	21
NEW Danji | Korean | **W 50s**	24
Z Degustation | French/Spanish | **E Vill**	27
EN Japanese | Japanese | **W Vill**	25
Enoteca Maria | Italian | **St. George**	25
Fig & Olive | Med. | **multi.**	20
Gottino | Italian | **W Vill**	20
Ilili | Lebanese | **Chelsea**	25
'Inoteca | Italian | **multi.**	22
Jimmy's | Amer. | **E Vill**	21
Kuma Inn | Asian | **LES**	23
Z L'Atelier/Robuchon | French | **E 50s**	27
Lunetta | Italian | **Boerum Hill**	22
Macao Trading | Chinese/Portuguese | **TriBeCa**	19
Marlow/Sons | Amer. | **W'burg**	24
Maze | French | **W 50s**	22
NEW Mehtaphor | Eclectic | **TriBeCa**	25
Mercadito | Mex. | **multi.**	23
Nuela | Pan-Latin | **Flatiron**	22
Olea | Med. | **Ft Greene**	22
Perbacco | Italian | **E Vill**	25
Prime Meat | Amer. | **Carroll Gdns**	24
Rayuela | Pan-Latin | **LES**	23
Recette | Amer. | **W Vill**	24
Robataya | Japanese | **E Vill**	25
Sakagura | Japanese | **E 40s**	25
Salumeria Rosi | Italian | **W 70s**	25
Sojourn | Eclectic | **E 70s**	23
Sorella | Italian | **LES**	26
Stanton Social | Eclectic | **LES**	23
Tanuki | Japanese | **Meatpacking**	20
Tarallucci | Italian | **multi.**	20
Terroir | Italian | **multi.**	20
Thistle Hill | Amer. | **Park Slope**	23
Z Traif | Eclectic | **W'burg**	27
Umi Nom | Asian | **Clinton Hill**	26
Uva | Italian | **E 70s**	22
Vanderbilt | Amer. | **Prospect Hts**	23
NEW White & Church | Italian | **TriBeCa**	–
Z Zenkichi | Japanese | **W'burg**	26

SOUL FOOD

Amy Ruth's | **Harlem**	21
Miss Mamie/Maude | **Harlem**	18
Pies-n-Thighs | **W'burg**	23
Rack & Soul | **W 100s**	22
Sylvia's | **Harlem**	19

SOUP

Hale/Hearty | **multi.**	19
La Bonne Soupe | **W 50s**	19
Original Soupman | **W 50s**	23

SOUTH AFRICAN

Braai | **W 50s**	20
Madiba | **Ft Greene**	20

SOUTH AMERICAN

(See also Argentinean, Brazilian, Chilean, Peruvian, Venezuelan)

Cafe Ronda | **W 70s**	20

SOUTHERN

Amy Ruth's | **Harlem**	21
Bourbon St. Café | **Bayside**	18
Brooklyn Star | **W'burg**	25
B. Smith's | **W 40s**	19
NEW Cardinal, The | **E Vill**	–
Char No. 4 | **Cobble Hill**	23
Commodore | **W'burg**	25
Egg | **W'burg**	23
NEW Gravy | **Flatiron**	–
NEW Hill Country Chicken | **Flatiron**	19
Kitchenette | **multi.**	19
NEW Lowcountry | **W Vill**	20
Miss Mamie/Maude | **Harlem**	18
Peaches | **Bed-Stuy**	23
Pink Tea Cup | **W Vill**	19
Rack & Soul | **W 100s**	22
Z NEW Red Rooster | **Harlem**	21
Seersucker | **Carroll Gdns**	21
Sylvia's | **Harlem**	19
Tipsy Parson | **Chelsea**	20

SOUTHWESTERN

Agave | **W Vill**	19
Canyon Rd. | **E 70s**	19
Cilantro | **multi.**	18
Cowgirl | **multi.**	17
Z Mesa Grill | **Flatiron**	24
Mojave | **Astoria**	21

SPANISH

(* tapas specialist)

NEW Bar Basque | **Chelsea**	19
Bar Carrera* | **G Vill**	21
Bar Jamon* | **Gramercy**	23

Vote at ZAGAT.com

Boqueria* | **multi.**	22
Cafe Español | **multi.**	20
Z Casa Mono* | **Gramercy**	25
Z Degustation | **E Vill**	27
El Charro | **W Vill**	23
El Faro* | **W Vill**	22
El Porrón* | **E 60s**	23
El Pote | **Murray Hill**	22
El Quijote | **Chelsea**	21
El Quinto Pino* | **Chelsea**	21
Euzkadi* | **E Vill**	20
Flor/Sol* | **TriBeCa**	21
Francisco's | **Chelsea**	22
NEW GastroArte* | **W 60s**	22
La Fonda/Sol | **E 40s**	21
Las Ramblas* | **W Vill**	23
Mercat* | **NoHo**	20
Nomad* | **E Vill**	20
Pipa* | **Flatiron**	21
Real Madrid | **Mariners Harbor**	24
Sala* | **Flatiron**	23
NEW Salinas* | **Chelsea**	-
Sevilla | **W Vill**	24
Socarrat* | **multi.**	23
Solera* | **E 50s**	22
NEW Tertulia* | **W Vill**	-
Tía Pol* | **Chelsea**	24
Toledo | **Murray Hill**	24
Txikito* | **Chelsea**	25

STEAKHOUSES

A.J. Maxwell's | **W 40s**	22
Angelo/Maxie's | **Flatiron**	21
Arirang Hibachi | **multi.**	20
Artie's | **City Is**	23
Ben & Jack's | **multi.**	23
Ben Benson's | **W 50s**	24
Benjamin Steak | **E 40s**	24
Bistro Le Steak | **E 70s**	18
Z BLT Prime | **Gramercy**	26
Z BLT Steak | **E 50s**	25
Bobby Van's | **multi.**	22
Buenos Aires | **E Vill**	23
Bull & Bear | **E 40s**	21
Capital Grille | **multi.**	24
Chimichurri Grill | **W 40s**	23
Christos | **Astoria**	23
Churrascaria | **multi.**	23
Circus | **E 60s**	20
City Hall | **TriBeCa**	21
Club A Steak | **E 50s**	24
Del Frisco's | **W 40s**	25
Delmonico's | **Financial**	24

Dylan Prime | **TriBeCa**	24
NEW E&E Grill House | **W 40s**	-
Embers | **Bay Ridge**	20
NEW Empire Steakhouse | **E 50s**	20
Fairway Cafe | **W 70s**	18
Frankie/Johnnie | **multi.**	23
Gallagher's | **W 50s**	21
Harry's Cafe/Steak | **Financial**	23
Jake's | **Riverdale**	24
Z Keens | **Garment**	25
NEW Lavo | **E 50s**	21
Le Marais | **W 40s**	22
Le Relais/Venise | **E 50s**	20
Les Halles | **multi.**	20
Macelleria | **Meatpacking**	22
Maloney/Porcelli | **E 50s**	23
Manzo | **Flatiron**	24
NEW Marble Lane | **Chelsea**	-
MarkJoseph | **Financial**	23
Michael Jordan | **E 40s**	20
Morton's | **multi.**	25
Novecento | **SoHo**	21
NYY Steak | **Yankee Stadium**	20
Old Homestead | **Meatpacking**	24
Padre Figlio | **E 40s**	23
Z Palm | **multi.**	25
Parlor Steak | **E 90s**	21
Z Peter Luger | **W'burg**	28
Pietro's | **E 40s**	24
Porter House | **W 60s**	24
Post House | **E 60s**	24
Prime Grill/KO | **multi.**	23
Primehouse | **Murray Hill**	24
Prime Meat | **Carroll Gdns**	24
Quality Meats | **W 50s**	24
Rothmann's | **E 50s**	23
Ruth's Chris | **W 50s**	24
Shula's | **W 40s**	20
Smith/Wollensky | **E 40s**	24
Z Sparks | **E 40s**	26
STK | **Meatpacking**	22
Strip House | **G Vill**	25
T-Bar Steak | **E 70s**	22
Tre Dici/Steak | **Chelsea**	23
Uncle Jack's | **multi.**	23
Via Brasil | **W 40s**	21
Z Wolfgang's | **multi.**	26
Wollensky's | **E 40s**	24

SWISS

Café Select | **SoHo**	19
NEW Heartbreak | **E Vill**	24
Mont Blanc | **W 40s**	21

CUISINES

TEAROOMS

Lady Mendl's	**Gramercy**	21
Sweet Melissa	**multi.**	20
Tea & Sympathy	**W Vill**	20

TEX-MEX

El Rio Grande	**Murray Hill**	18
Mary Ann's	**multi.**	16

THAI

Bann Thai	**Forest Hills**	21
Breeze	**W 40s**	20
Chai Home Kitchen	**multi.**	22
Erawan	**Bayside**	24
Holy Basil	**E Vill**	22
Jaiya Thai	**Murray Hill**	23
Joya	**Cobble Hill**	23
NEW Kin Shop	**W Vill**	24
Kittichai	**SoHo**	23
Kuma Inn	**LES**	23
Land	**multi.**	22
Lantern	**multi.**	18
Laut	**Union Sq**	22
Lemongrass	**multi.**	17
NEW Lotus of Siam	**G Vill**	20
Pam Real Thai	**W 40s**	22
Pongsri Thai	**multi.**	21
Pukk	**E Vill**	23
NEW Pure Thai Shop.	**W 50s**	24
Qi	**W 40s**	20
Room Service	**multi.**	20
Sala Thai	**E 80s**	20
Sea	**multi.**	21
Siam Sq.	**Riverdale**	24
Song	**Park Slope**	22
Sookk	**W 100s**	23
Spice	**multi.**	19
Z Sripraphai	**Woodside**	26
Thai Market	**W 100s**	24
Topaz Thai	**W 50s**	21
Umi Nom	**Clinton Hill**	26
Wondee Siam	**multi.**	21
Zabb Elee	**multi.**	23

TIBETAN

Tsampa	**E Vill**	20

TUNISIAN

Epices/Traiteur	**W 70s**	21

TURKISH

Akdeniz	**W 40s**	21
A La Turka	**E 70s**	19
Ali Baba	**multi.**	20
Bereket	**LES**	21
Beyoglu	**E 80s**	22

NEW Bi Lokma	**E 40s**	–
Bodrum	**W 80s**	20
Hanci	**W 50s**	22
Pasha	**W 70s**	21
Pera	**E 40s**	21
Peri Ela	**E 90s**	19
Sahara	**Gravesend**	23
Sahara's Turkish	**Murray Hill**	22
Sip Sak	**E 40s**	21
Taci's Beyti	**Midwood**	25
Taksim Square	**E 50s**	21
Turkish Cuisine	**W 40s**	21
Turkish Grill	**Sunnyside**	23
Turkish Kitchen	**Murray Hill**	22
Turkuaz	**W 100s**	19
Uskudar	**E 70s**	21

UKRAINIAN

Veselka	**E Vill**	20

VEGETARIAN

(* vegan)

Angelica Kit.*	**E Vill**	22
Blossom*	**multi.**	22
Candle Cafe*	**E 70s**	23
Candle 79*	**E 70s**	24
Caravan/Dreams*	**E Vill**	22
Chennai Gdn.	**Murray Hill**	21
Z Dirt Candy	**E Vill**	26
Gobo*	**multi.**	22
Z HanGawi	**Murray Hill**	25
Hummus Pl.	**multi.**	22
John's/12th St.*	**E Vill**	22
Kajitsu	**E Vill**	28
Maoz Veg.	**multi.**	21
Peacefood Café*	**W 80s**	22
Pongal	**Murray Hill**	22
Pukk	**E Vill**	23
Pure Food/Wine*	**Gramercy**	23
Quantum Leap	**multi.**	21
Saravanaa Bhavan	**multi.**	24
sNice	**multi.**	20
Z Taïm	**W Vill**	26
Tiffin Wallah	**Murray Hill**	23
Vatan	**Murray Hill**	24
Wild Ginger*	**multi.**	22
Zen Palate	**multi.**	19

VENEZUELAN

Arepas Café	**Astoria**	25
Caracas	**multi.**	24

VIETNAMESE

An Choi	**LES**	21
Baoguette	**multi.**	21

Bao Noodles | **Gramercy** 19
Bo-Ky | **multi.** 22
Hanco's | **multi.** 21
NEW Ha Noi | **Park Slope** -
Indochine | **E Vill** 22
Le Colonial | **E 50s** 21
Má Pêche | **W 50s** 23
Nam | **TriBeCa** 22

Nha Trang | **Chinatown** 22
Nicky's | **multi.** 22
Omai | **Chelsea** 23
Pho Bang | **multi.** 21
Pho Viet Huong | **Chinatown** 22
Saigon Grill | **W 90s** 21
Vermicelli | **E 70s** 19

CUISINES

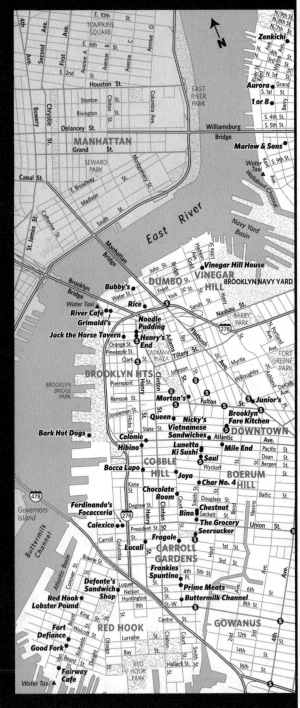

BROOKLYN

N. 9th St.
N. 8th St.
N. 7th St.
Zenkichi
N. 5th Ave.
N. 4th St.
Aurora Grand
S. 1st St.
1 or 8
S. 4th St.
S. 5th St.

Williamsburg Bridge

Marlow & Sons
Water Taxi
Wallabout Channel

Navy Yard Basin

East River

Vinegar Hill House
DUMBO **VINEGAR HILL**
BROOKLYN NAVY YARD
Bubby's
Rice
River Café Water Taxi
Grimaldi's
Noodle Pudding
Jack the Horse Tavern
Henry's End
BROOKLYN HTS.
Morton's
Queen **Nicky's**
Vietnamese Sandwiches
Bark Hot Dogs
Colonie
Hibino
Bocca Lupo
COBBLE HILL
Joya
Chocolate Room
Ferdinando's Focacceria
Calexico
Lucali
Fragole
CARROLL GARDENS
Frankies Spuntino
Defonte's Sandwich Shop
Prime Meats
Red Hook Lobster Pound
Buttermilk Channel
Fort Defiance
Good Fork
RED HOOK
Fairway Café
Water Taxi

Junior's
Brooklyn Fare Kitchen
DOWNTOWN
Lunetta **Mile End**
Ki Sushi
Saul
Char No. 4
BOERUM HILL
Chestnut
Bino
The Grocery
Seersucker

GOWANUS

Governors Island

Buttermilk Channel

RED HOOK PARK

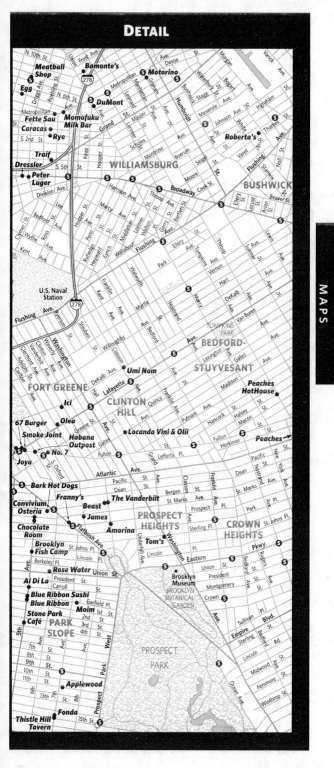

DETAIL

Meatball Shop
Bamonte's
Egg
Motorino
DuMont
Fette Sau
Caracas
Momofuku Milk Bar
Rye
Roberta's
Traif
Dressler
Peter Luger

WILLIAMSBURG

Broadway

BUSHWICK

U.S. Naval Station

BEDFORD-STUYVESANT

TOMPKINS PARK

Umi Nom
FORT GREENE
Ici
CLINTON HILL
Peaches HotHouse
Olea
67 Burger
Smoke Joint
Habana Outpost
Locanda Vini & Olii
Peaches
Joya
No. 7
Bark Hot Dogs
Convivium, Osteria
Franny's
The Vanderbilt
Beast
PROSPECT HEIGHTS
Chocolate Room
James
CROWN HEIGHTS
Amorina
Brooklyn Fish Camp
Tom's
Rose Water
Brooklyn Museum
Al Di La
BROOKLYN BOTANICAL GARDEN
Blue Ribbon Sushi
Blue Ribbon
Moim
Stone Park Café
PARK SLOPE
PROSPECT PARK
Applewood
Fonda
Thistle Hill Tavern

MAPS

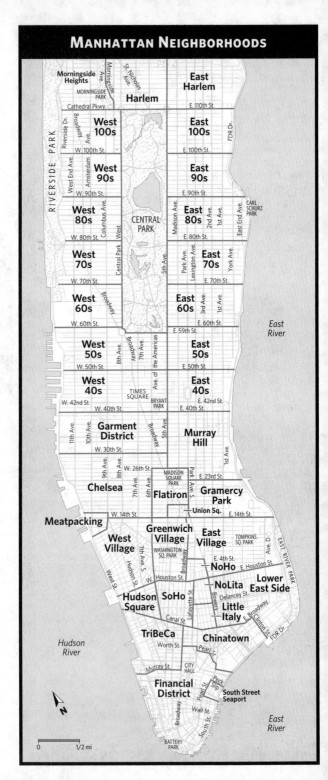

MANHATTAN NEIGHBORHOODS

Morningside Heights

MORNINGSIDE PARK

Cathedral Pkwy.

Harlem

East Harlem

E. 110th St.

West 100s

East 100s

W. 100th St.

E. 100th St.

West 90s

East 90s

W. 90th St.

E. 90th St.

West 80s

CENTRAL PARK

East 80s

W. 80th St.

E. 80th St.

CARL SCHURZ PARK

West 70s

East 70s

W. 70th St.

E. 70th St.

West 60s

East 60s

W. 60th St.

E. 60th St.

E. 59th St.

East River

West 50s

East 50s

W. 50th St.

E. 50th St.

West 40s

TIMES SQUARE

East 40s

W. 42nd St.

BRYANT PARK

E. 42nd St.

W. 40th St.

E. 40th St.

Garment District

Murray Hill

W. 30th St.

W. 26th St.

MADISON SQUARE PARK

E. 23rd St.

Chelsea

Flatiron

Gramercy Park

Union Sq.

W. 14th St.

E. 14th St.

Meatpacking

Greenwich Village

East Village

TOMPKINS SQ. PARK

West Village

WASHINGTON SQ. PARK

E. 4th St.

E. Houston St.

NoHo

Lower East Side

Houston St.

NoLita

Hudson Square

SoHo

Little Italy

Canal St.

TriBeCa

Chinatown

Worth St.

Pearl St.

Hudson River

Murray St.

CITY HALL

South Street Seaport

Financial District

Wall St.

BATTERY PARK

East River

0   1/2 mi

N

Locations

Includes names, street locations and Food ratings. Abbreviations key: (a=Avenue, s=Street, e.g. 1a/116s=First Ave. at 116th St.; 3a/82-83s=Third Ave. between 82nd & 83rd Sts.)

Manhattan

CHELSEA

(26th to 30th Sts., west of 5th; 14th to 26th Sts., west of 6th)

Artichoke Basille	10a/17s	22
NEW Bar Basque	6a/29-30s	19
Bar Breton	5a/28-29s	18
Biricchino	29s/8a	21
Blossom	9a/21-22s	22
Blue Ginger	8a/15-16s	21
Bombay Talkie	9a/21-22s	20
Bottino	10a/24-25s	19
☑ Breslin	29s/Bway-5a	22
Brgr	7a/26-27s	19
☑ Buddakan	9a/15-16s	24
Cafeteria	7a/17s	19
Chelsea Ristorante	8a/15-16s	20
Co.	9a/24s	23
Colicchio/Sons	10a/15-16s	24
Cookshop	10a/20s	22
NEW Coppelia	14s/7-8a	20
Crema	17s/6-7a	23
Dallas BBQ	8a/23s	16
Da Umberto	17s/6-7a	24
☑ Del Posto	10a/15-16s	27
NEW Donatella	8a/19-20s	21
NEW Elevation Burger	14s/6-7a	20
El Quijote	23s/7-8a	21
El Quinto Pino	24s/9-10a	21
NEW Eolo	7a/21-22s	24
NEW FoodParc	6a/29-30s	18
Francisco's	23s/6-7a	22
Friedman's Lunch	9a/15-16s	21
Gascogne	8a/17-18s	21
Grand Sichuan	multi.	21
Hale/Hearty	multi.	19
NEW Highliner	10a/22s	–
Highpoint	7a/22-23s	22
Ilili	5a/27-28s	25
NEW John Dory	Bway/29s	23
La Bergamote	9a/20s	24
La Lunchonette	10a/18s	22
Lasagna	8a/20s	18
La Taza de Oro	8a/14-15s	21
Le Grainne Cafe	9a/21s	23
Le Singe Vert	7a/19-20s	18
Le Zie 2000	7a/20-21s	21

NEW Marble Lane	16s/8-9a	–
Mary Ann's	8a/16s	16
Matsuri	16s/9a	23
NEW Mexicue	7a/29-30s	–
Momoya	7a/21s	23
☑ Morimoto	10a/15-16s	26
No. 7	Bway/28-29s	23
Omai	9a/19-20s	23
Patsy's Pizzeria	23s/8-9a	20
Pepe	10a/24-25s	19
Pongsri Thai	23s/6-7a	21
Rare B&G	26s/6-7a	21
Red Cat	10a/23-24s	24
Rocking Horse	8a/19-20s	21
NEW Romera	16s/8-9a	–
Room Service	8a/18-19s	20
Rub BBQ	23s/7-8a	21
NEW Salinas	9a/18-19s	–
Sarabeth's	9a/15-16s	20
☑ Scarpetta	14s/8-9a	26
Socarrat	19s/7-8a	23
Spice	multi.	19
Sueños	17s/8-9a	22
Tía Pol	10a/22-23s	24
Tipsy Parson	9a/19-20s	20
Tre Dici/Steak	26s/6-7a	23
Trestle on 10th	10a/24s	21
Tuck Shop	9a/15-16s	21
Txikito	9a/24-25s	25
Uncle Nick's	8a/29s	20
Westville	18s/7-8a	23
'Wichcraft	11a/27-28s	20

CHINATOWN

(Canal to Pearl Sts., east of B'way)

Amazing 66	Mott/Canal	21
Big Wong	Mott/Bayard-Canal	23
Bo-Ky	Bayard/Mott-Mulberry	22
Dim Sum Go Go	E Bway/Chatham	21
Excellent Dumpling	Lafayette/Canal-Walker	21
Forlini's	Baxter/Walker	19
Fuleen	Division/Bowery	22
Golden Unicorn	E Bway/Catherine	21
Grand Sichuan	Canal/Chrystie	21
Great NY Noodle	Bowery/Bayard	23

LOCATIONS

Hop Kee | *Mott/Chatham-Mosco* 22
Jing Fong | *Elizabeth/Bayard-Canal* 20
Joe's Shanghai | *Pell/Bowery* 22
Joe's | *Pell/Doyers* 21
Mandarin Court | *Mott/Bayard-Canal* 22
Nha Trang | *multi.* 22
Nice Green Bo | *Bayard/Elizabeth-Mott* 23
Nom Wah Tea | *Doyers/Bowery* 23
☑ Oriental Gdn. | *Elizabeth/Bayard-Canal* 23
Peking Duck | *Mott/Mosco-Pell* 23
Pho Viet Huong | *Mulberry/Bayard-Canal* 22
Ping's Sea. | *Mott/Chatham-Mosco* 22
Pongsri Thai | *Bayard/Baxter* 21
Shanghai Cuisine | *Bayard/Mulberry* 23
Wo Hop | *Mott/Canal* 22
Xi'an | *multi.* 23

EAST 40s

Aburiya Kinnosuke | *45s/2-3a* 25
Ali Baba | *2a/46s* 20
Ammos | *Vanderbilt/44-45s* 21
Avra | *48s/Lex-3a* 25
Ben & Jack's | *44s/2-3a* 23
Benjamin Steak | *41s/Mad-Park* 24
NEW Bi Lokma | *45s/2-3a* -
Bobby Van's | *Park/46s* 22
Bukhara Grill | *49s/2-3a* 22
Bull & Bear | *Lex/49s* 21
Burger Heaven | *multi.* 17
Cafe Centro | *Park/45s* 21
Capital Grille | *42s/Lex-3a* 24
Chin Chin | *49s/2-3a* 23
Cibo | *2a/41s* 21
Cipriani Dolci | *42s/Vanderbilt* 21
Così | *45s/Mad-Vanderbilt* 16
Darbar | *46s/Lex-3a* 21
Dishes | *multi.* 21
Docks Oyster | *3a/40s* 21
Fabio Piccolo | *44s/2-3a* 23
Five Guys | *3a/43-44s* 20
Goodburger | *2a/42s* 17
Grifone | *46s/2-3a* 24
Gyu-Kaku | *3a/49-50s* 21
Hale/Hearty | *3a/43-44s* 19
Haru | *48s/Mad-Park* 21
Hatsuhana | *multi.* 24
Il Postino | *49s/1-2a* 25
Ise | *49s/Lex-3a* 21
Junior's | *42s/Vanderbilt* 19
Katsu-Hama | *47s/5a-Mad* 20

☑ Kuruma Zushi | *47s/5a-Mad* 28
La Fonda/Sol | *Park/44s* 21
Mamá Mexico | *49s/2-3a* 19
Mangia | *48s/5a-Mad* 20
Mee Noodle | *2a/49s* 17
Megu | *1a/47s* 24
Menchanko-tei | *45s/Lex-3a* 21
Michael Jordan | *43s/Vanderbilt* 20
Morton's | *5a/45s* 25
Nanni | *46s/Lex-3a* 24
Naples 45 | *Park/45s* 18
Naya/Express | *3a/43s* 22
Nino's | *2a/47-48s* 22
Num Pang | *41s/Lex-3a* 26
Osteria Laguna | *42s/2-3a* 20
☑ Oyster Bar | *42s/Vanderbilt* 22
Padre Figlio | *44s/1-2a* 23
☑ Palm | *2a/44-45s* 25
Pampano | *49s/2-3a* 24
Patroon | *46s/Lex-3a* 23
Pepe | *42s/Vanderbilt* 19
Pera | *Mad/41-42s* 21
Pietro's | *43s/2-3a* 24
Pret A Manger | *multi.* 18
Prime Grill/KO | *49s/Mad-Park* 23
Rickshaw Dumpling | *Lex/45s* 18
Sakagura | *43s/2-3a* 25
NEW Schnitzel & Things | *3a/45-46s* 20
Sinigual | *3a/41s* 21
Sip Sak | *2a/49-50s* 21
Smith/Wollensky | *3a/49s* 24
Soba Totto | *43s/2-3a* 22
☑ Sparks | *46s/2-3a* 26
Sushiden | *49s/5a-Mad* 25
☑ Sushi Yasuda | *43s/2-3a* 28
NEW Tenpenny | *46s/5a-Mad* -
NEW Tulsi | *46s/2-3a* 21
Two Boots | *42s/Vanderbilt* 18
'Wichcraft | *multi.* 20
Wollensky's | *49s/3a* 24
Yama | *49s/1-2a* 24
Zengo | *3a/40s* 22

EAST 50s

☑ Adour | *55s/5a-Mad* 26
Aja | *1a/58s* 21
Al Bustan | *53s/1-2a* 20
NEW Alfama | *52s/2-3a* -
Amma | *51s/2-3a* 24
Angelo's Pizza | *2a/55s* 20
☑ Aquavit | *55s/Mad-Park* 25
Armani Rist. | *5a/56s* 21
Bice | *54s/5a-Mad* 20

Bistro Vendôme | 58s/1a-Sutton	22
Blockhead Burrito | 2a/50-51s	17
ⓩ BLT Steak | 57s/Lex-Park	25
Bobby Van's | 54s/Lex-Park	22
Bon Chon | 2a/51s	20
Bottega/Vino | 59s/5a-Mad	22
Brasserie | 53s/Lex-Park	21
Brick Ln. Curry | 53s/2-3a	22
Burger Heaven | 53s/5a-Mad	17
BXL | 51s/2-3a	18
Cafe Joul | 1a/58-59s	19
Casa Lever | 53s/Mad-Park	23
Caviar Russe | Mad/54-55s	24
Cellini | 54s/Mad-Park	23
Chola | 58s/2-3a	24
Club A Steak | 58s/2-3a	24
Così | 56s/Mad-Park	16
Darbar | 55s/Lex-3a	21
David Burke/Bloom. | 59s/Lex-3a	19
Dawat | 58s/2-3a	23
DeGrezia | 50s/2-3a	23
Deux Amis | 51s/1-2a	19
Dishes | Park/54s	21
Dos Caminos | 3a/50-51s	19
NEW Empire Steakhouse | 52s/5-6a	20
Ethos | 1a/51s	21
ⓩ Felidia | 58s/2-3a	26
Fig & Olive | 52s/5a-Mad	20
Fiorini | 56s/2-3a	21
ⓩ Four Seasons | 52s/Lex-Park	27
Fresco | 52s/Mad-Park	23
ⓩ Gilt | Mad/50-51s	26
Goodburger | Lex/54s	17
Grand Sichuan | 2a/55-56s	21
Harry Cipriani | 5a/59-60s	22
Hide-Chan | 52s/2-3a	21
Hillstone | 3a/54s	22
Jubilee | 54s/1-2a	22
La Gioconda | 53s/2-3a	21
ⓩ La Grenouille | 52s/5a-Mad	28
La Mangeoire | 2a/53-54s	21
Lasagna | 2a/50s	18
ⓩ L'Atelier/Robuchon | 57s/Mad-Park	27
NEW Lavo | 58s/Mad-Park	21
ⓩ Le Cirque | 58s/Lex-3a	25
Le Colonial | 57s/Lex-3a	21
Le Perigord | 52s/FDR-1a	24
Le Relais/Venise | Lex/52s	20
Luna Piena | 53s/2-3a	21
Lychee Hse. | 55s/Lex-3a	23

Maloney/Porcelli | 50s/Mad-Park	23
Mia Dona | 58s/2-3a	19
Mint | 50s/Lex-3a	22
Monkey Bar | 54s/Mad-Park	19
Montebello | 56s/Lex-Park	23
Mr. Chow | 57s/1-2a	22
Mr. K's | Lex/51s	24
NEW National | Lex/50s	20
Naya/Express | 2a/55-56s	22
Neary's | 57s/1a	16
Peking Duck | 53s/2-3a	23
P.J. Clarke's | 3a/55s	17
Pop Burger/Pub | 58s/5a-Mad	17
Pret A Manger | multi.	18
Rosa Mexicano | 1a/58s	22
Rothmann's | 54s/5a-Mad	23
ⓩ San Pietro | 54s/5a-Mad	26
Serafina | 58s/Mad-Park	19
ⓩ Shun Lee Palace | 55s/Lex-3a	25
NEW Social Eatz | 53s/2-3a	23
Sofrito | 57s/1a-Sutton	23
Solera | 53s/2-3a	22
Solo | Mad/55-56s	24
SushiAnn | 51s/Mad-Park	24
Taksim Square | 2a/54-55s	21
Tao | 58s/Mad-Park	22
Tenzan | 2a/52-53s	22
Teodora | 57s/Lex-3a	21
Tse Yang | 51s/Mad-Park	23
Via Quadronno | 5a/59s	22
NEW Walle | 53s/2-3a	-
ⓩ Wolfgang's | 54s/3a	26
Yuva | 58s/2-3a	23
Ze Café | 52s/FDR-1a	22

EAST 60s

Accademia/Vino | 3a/63-64s	18
Amaranth | 62s/5a-Mad	19
Arabelle | 64s/Mad-Park	24
Bar Italia | Mad/66s	21
Bistro Chat Noir | 66s/5a-Mad	19
Bistro 61 | 1a/61s	20
Brgr | 3a/60-61s	19
Brio | 61s/Lex	19
Burger Heaven | Lex/62s	17
Cabana | 3a/60-61s	21
Café Evergreen | 1a/69-70s	18
Canaletto | 60s/2-3a	20
Circus | 61s/Lex-Park	20
ⓩ Daniel | 65s/Mad-Park	29
ⓩ David Burke Townhse. | 61s/Lex-Park	25
NEW Desmond's | 60s/Lex-3a	22
El Porrón | 1a/61-62s	23

Restaurant	Score
Fatty Fish	64s/1a-York	21
Felice	1a/64s	24
Fig & Olive	Lex/62-63s	20
Fishtail	62s/Lex-Park	24
Fred's at Barneys	Mad/60s	20
Hale/Hearty	Lex/64-65s	19
Jackson Hole	64s/2-3a	18
John's Pizzeria	64s/1a-York	23
JoJo	64s/Lex-3a	25
L'Absinthe	67s/2-3a	22
Le Bilboquet	63s/Mad-Park	21
Le Caprice	61s/5a	20
Le Charlot	69s/Mad-Park	21
Le Pain Q.	Lex/63-64s	19
Le Veau d'Or	60s/Lex-Park	20
Maya	1a/64-65s	23
Mediterraneo	2a/66s	19
Mon Petit Cafe	Lex/62s	20
NEW Neely's BBQ	1a/62s	-
Nello	Mad/62-63s	17
Z Park Avenue	63s/Lex-Park	25
Patsy's Pizzeria	multi.	20
Persephone	60s/Lex-Park	22
Philippe	60s/Mad-Park	23
Post House	63s/Mad-Park	24
Primola	2a/64-65s	22
Ravagh	1a/66-67s	22
Regency	Park/61s	19
Rouge Tomate	60s/5a-Mad	24
Z Scalinatella	61s/3a	26
Serafina	61s/Mad-Park	19
Serendipity 3	60s/2-3a	19
Z Sushi Seki	1a/62-63s	27
Tiella	1a/60-61s	26
Viand	Mad/61-62s	18
Za Za	1a/65-66s	21

EAST 70s

Restaurant	Score
Afghan Kebab	2a/70-71s	20
A La Turka	2a/74s	19
Al Forno Pizza	2a/77-78s	20
Alloro	77s/1-2a	25
Atlantic Grill	3a/76-77s	23
Baraonda	2a/75s	18
Bar Italia	2a/77s	21
B. Café	75s/2-3a	21
Bella Blu	Lex/70-71s	21
Bistro Le Steak	3a/75s	18
Boathouse	Central Pk/72s	18
Bocca/Bacco	2a/78s	22
Brother Jimmy's	2a/77-78s	17
Z Café Boulud	76s/5a-Mad	27
Campagnola	1a/73-74s	23

Restaurant	Score
Candle Cafe	3a/74-75s	23
Candle 79	79s/Lex-3a	24
Canyon Rd.	1a/76-77s	19
Caravaggio	74s/5a-Mad	23
Z Carlyle	76s/Mad	24
NEW Carpe Diem	78s/Lex-3a	22
Cilantro	1a/71s	18
Dallas BBQ	3a/72-73s	16
Dos Toros	Lex/77-78s	23
Due	3a/79-80s	22
EJ's Luncheon.	3a/73s	16
Fulton	75s/2-3a	23
Z Gari/Sushi	78s/1a-York	27
NEW Go Burger	2a/75-76s	22
Grace's Tratt.	71s/2-3a	19
Haru	3a/76s	21
NEW Hospoda	73s/1-2a	-
Il Riccio	79s/Lex-3a	21
J.G. Melon	3a/74s	21
NEW Jones Wood Foundry	76s/1a-York	23
Ko Sushi	2a/70s	20
Le Magnifique	Lex/73s	18
Le Pain Q.	77s/2-3a	19
Lumi	Lex/70s	20
Lusardi's	2a/77-78s	24
Z Mark	77s/5a-Mad	22
Maruzzella	1a/77-78s	22
Mezzaluna/Pizza	3a/74-75s	22
Nino's	1a/72-73s	22
Orsay	Lex/75s	18
Our Place	79s/2-3a	18
Parma	3a/79-80s	22
Pastrami Queen	Lex/78-79s	22
Per Lei	2a/71s	20
Persepolis	2a/73-74s	22
Petaluma	1a/73s	19
Quatorze Bis	79s/1-2a	21
Sant Ambroeus	Mad/77-78s	21
Z Sasabune	73s/1a-York	29
2nd Ave Deli	1a/75s	23
Serafina	Mad/79s	19
Sette Mezzo	Lex/70-71s	23
Shabu-Shabu 70	70s/1-2a	21
Shanghai Pavilion	3a/78-79s	21
Sojourn	79s/2-3a	23
Spice	multi.	19
Sushi Hana	2a/78s	21
Swifty's	Lex/72-73s	18
T-Bar Steak	3a/73-74s	22
NEW Untitled	Mad/75s	-
Uskudar	2a/73-74s	21
Uva	2a/77-78s	22

Vermicelli | 2a/77-78s	19
Viand | Mad/78s	18
Via Quadronno | 73s/5a-Mad	22
Vivolo/Cucina | 74s/Lex-Park	19

EAST 80s

Amber | 3a/80s	19
Andre's Café | 2a/84-85s	20
Antonucci | 81s/Lex-3a	23
Baluchi's | 2a/89-90s	19
Beyoglu | 3a/81s	22
Blockhead Burrito | 2a/81-82s	17
Café d'Alsace | 2a/88s	21
Café Sabarsky | 5a/86s	22
Caffe Grazie | 84s/5a-Mad	20
Cascabel/Cantina | multi.	23
Centolire | Mad/85-86s	22
Chef Ho's | 2a/89-90s	22
Cilantro | 2a/88-89s	18
NEW Crown | 81s/Mad	-
Divino | 2a/80-81s	20
2 Donguri | 83s/1-2a	27
NEW East End Kitchen | 81s/E End-York	-
E.A.T. | Mad/80-81s	20
2 Elio's | 2a/84-85s	24
Erminia | 83s/2-3a	25
Fairway Cafe | 86s/2a	18
Felice | 1a/83s	24
Firenze | 2a/82-83s	22
Flex Mussels | 82s/Lex-3a	23
Giovanni | 83s/5a-Mad	24
Girasole | 82s/Lex-3a	22
Gobo | 3a/81s	22
Heidelberg | 2a/85-86s	19
Italianissimo | 84s/1-2a	23
Ithaka | 86s/1-2a	20
Jackson Hole | 2a/83-84s	18
Jacques | 85s/2-3a	18
Kings' Carriage | 82s/2-3a	22
Ko Sushi | York/85s	20
Land | 2a/81-82s	22
Le Pain Q. | Mad/84-85s	19
Luke's Lobster | 81s/2-3a	23
Maz Mezcal | 86s/1-2a	21
Nicola's | 84s/Lex-3a	22
Papaya King | 86s/3a	21
Pig Heaven | 2a/80-81s	20
Pintaile's Pizza | York/83-84s	20
Poke | 85s/1-2a	25
Quattro Gatti | 81s/2-3a	21
Sala Thai | 2a/89-90s	20
Sandro's | 81s/1-2a	25
Shake Shack | 86s/Lex-3a	22

Shalezeh | 3a/80-81s	22
2 Sistina | 2a/80-81s	26
Spigolo | 2a/81s	25
Taste | 3a/80s	22
Tenzan | 2a/89s	22
Tratt. Pesce | 3a/87-88s	19
Two Boots | 2a/84s	18
Vespa | 2a/84-85s	18
Viand | 86s/2a	18
Wa Jeal | 2a/82-83s	24
Wright | 5a/88s	22
York Grill | York/88-89s	21
Yuka | 2a/80-81s	23

EAST 90s & 100s

(90th to 110th Sts.)

Brother Jimmy's | 3a/92s	17
Don Pedro's | 2a/96s	21
El Paso Taqueria | multi.	23
Jackson Hole | Mad/91s	18
Moustache | Lex/102s	22
Nick's | 2a/94s	24
Osso Buco | 3a/93s	19
Paola's | Mad/92s	23
Parlor Steak | 3a/90s	21
Pascalou | Mad/92-93s	21
Peri Ela | Lex/90-91s	19
Pinocchio | 1a/90-91s	23
Pio Pio | 1a/90-91s	22
Rizzo's Pizza | Lex/93s	23
Sarabeth's | Mad/92	20
Sfoglia | Lex/92s	23
Square Meal | 92s/5a-Mad	23
Table d'Hôte | 92s/Mad-Park	21
Tre Otto | Mad/97-98s	20
Vico | Mad/92-93s	22
Yura on Madison | Mad/92s	21
Zebú Grill | 92s/1-2a	20

EAST VILLAGE

(14th to Houston Sts., east of B'way, excluding NoHo)

NEW Affaire | Ave B/3-4s	-
Angelica Kit. | 12s/1-2a	22
Apiary | 3a/10-11s	25
Artichoke Basille | 14s/1-2a	22
Awash | 6s/1-2a	23
Back Forty | Ave B/11-12s	21
Banjara | 1a/6s	22
Baoguette | St Marks/2a	21
BaoHaus | 14s/2-3a	20
Barbone | Ave B/11-12s	25
NEW Beagle | Ave A/10-11s	-
Belcourt | 4s/2a	20
Black Iron | 5s/Aves A-B	23

Restaurant	Rating
Boca Chica	*1a/1s*	22
Bon Chon	*St Marks/2-3a*	20
Bourgeois Pig	*7s/Ave A-1a*	20
Brick Ln. Curry	*6s/1-2a*	22
Buenos Aires	*6s/Aves A-B*	23
Butter	*Lafayette/Astor-4s*	22
Cacio e Pepe	*2a/11-12s*	21
Cacio e Vino	*2a/4-5s*	21
Cafe Mogador	*St Marks/Ave A-1a*	22
Caracas	*multi.*	24
Caravan/Dreams	*6s/1a*	22
NEW Cardinal, The	*4s/Aves A-B*	-
Chickpea	*14s/2-3a*	18
ChikaLicious	*10s/1-2a*	24
Crif Dogs	*St Marks/Ave A-1a*	22
Cucina/Pesce	*4s/Bowery-2a*	19
Dallas BBQ	*2a/St Marks*	16
DBGB	*Bowery/Houston*	23
Z Degustation	*5s/2-3a*	27
Z Dirt Candy	*9s/Ave A-1a*	26
Dos Toros	*4a/13s*	23
Dumpling Man	*St Marks/Ave A-1a*	21
NEW Edi & the Wolf	*Ave C/6-7s*	22
Euzkadi	*4s/1-2a*	20
Frank	*2a/5-6s*	24
Gemma	*Bowery/2-3s*	20
Gnocco	*10s/Aves A-B*	23
Graffiti	*10s/1-2a*	25
Grand Sichuan	*St Marks/2-3a*	21
Gruppo	*Ave B/11-12s*	26
Gyu-Kaku	*Cooper/Astor-4s*	21
Hasaki	*9s/2-3a*	23
Haveli	*2a/5-6s*	22
NEW Heartbreak	*2s/2a*	24
Hearth	*12s/1a*	24
Holy Basil	*2a/9-10s*	22
Hummus Pl.	*St Marks/Ave A-1a*	22
I Coppi	*9s/Ave A-1a*	22
Il Bagatto	*2s/Aves A-B*	23
Indochine	*Lafayette/Astor-4s*	22
Ippudo	*4a/9-10s*	25
Itzocan	*9s/Ave A-1a*	24
Jack's Lux.	*2a/5-6s*	26
Z Jewel Bako	*5s/2-3a*	26
Jimmy's	*7s/2-3a*	21
JoeDoe	*1s/1-2a*	24
John's/12th St.	*12s/2a*	22
Kajitsu	*9s/Ave A-1a*	28
Z Kanoyama	*2a/11-12s*	26
Kyo Ya	*7s/1a*	26
La Palapa	*St Marks/1-2a*	22
Lavagna	*5s/Aves A-B*	24
Lil' Frankie	*1a/1-2s*	23
Lucien	*1a/1s*	22
Luke's Lobster	*7s/Ave A-1a*	23
Luzzo's/Ovest	*1a/12-13s*	25
Mama's Food	*3s/Aves A-B*	22
Mary Ann's	*2a/4-5s*	16
Max	*Ave B/3-4s*	22
Mercadito	*Ave B/11-12s*	23
Mermaid	*2a/5-6s*	22
Minca	*5s/Aves A-B*	24
Z Momofuku Ko	*1a/10-11s*	27
Momofuku Milk Bar	*13s/2-3a*	23
Momofuku Noodle	*1a/10-11s*	24
Z Momofuku Ssäm	*2a/13s*	25
Motorino	*12s/1-2a*	24
Moustache	*10s/Ave A-1a*	22
Nicky's	*2s/Ave A*	22
99 Mi. to Philly	*3a/12-13s*	19
Nomad	*2a/4s*	20
Northern Spy	*12s/Aves A-B*	23
No. 28	*2a/11s*	25
Oaxaca	*Extra/Bowery-2a*	20
Peels	*Bowery/2s*	20
Perbacco	*4s/Aves A-B*	25
Porchetta	*7s/Ave A-1a*	24
NEW Porsena	*7s/2-3a*	22
Prune	*1s/1-2a*	25
Pukk	*1a/4-5s*	23
Z Pylos	*7s/Ave A-1a*	26
Quantum Leap	*1a/12-13s*	21
Rai Rai Ken	*10s/1-2a*	22
Ramen Setagaya	*St Marks/2-3a*	18
Redhead	*13s/1-2a*	23
Robataya	*9s/2-3a*	25
Shabu-Tatsu	*10s/1-2a*	22
S'MAC	*12s/1-2a*	22
Smith	*3a/10-11s*	21
Soba-ya	*9s/2-3a*	24
Spice	*multi.*	19
Spina	*Ave B/11s*	25
Sunburnt Cow/Calf	*Ave. C/8-9s*	17
Supper	*2s/Aves A-B*	24
Takahachi	*Ave A/5-6s*	24
Tarallucci	*1a/10-11s*	20
Terroir	*12s/Ave A-1a*	20
This Little Piggy	*1a/9-10s*	23
Tree	*1a/11-12s*	20
Tsampa	*9s/2-3a*	20

Tuck Shop	*multi.*	21
26 Seats	*Ave B/10-11s*	22
Two Boots	*Ave A/3s*	18
Vandaag	*2a/6s*	20
Vanessa's Dumpling	*14s/2-3a*	20
Veniero's	*11s/1-2A*	24
Veselka	*multi.*	20
Westville	*Ave A/11s*	23
Xi'an	*St Marks/1a*	23
Yerba Buena	*Ave A/Houston-2s*	23
Yuca Bar	*Ave A/7s*	22
Zabb Elee	*2a/4-5s*	23
Zaitzeff	*Ave B/2-3s*	21
Zum Schneider	*Ave C/7s*	19

FINANCIAL DISTRICT

(South of Murray St.)

Adrienne's	*Pearl/Coenties-Hanover*	23
Au Mandarin	*Vesey/West*	19
Baoguette	*Maiden/Bway*	21
Battery Gdns.	*Battery Pk*	19
Blockhead Burrito	*World Fin/North-Vesey*	17
BLT B&G	*Wash/Albany-Carlisle*	22
Bobby Van's	*Broad/Exchange*	22
Bon Chon	*John/Cliff*	20
Bridge Cafe	*Water/Dover*	21
Capital Grille	*Bway/Nassau-Pine*	24
Chickpea	*William/John*	18
China Chalet	*Bway/Exchange-Morris*	19
Cipriani Wall Street	*Wall/Hanover-William*	23
Così	*multi.*	16
Delmonico's	*Beaver/William*	24
Fraunces Tavern	*Pearl/Broad*	17
Fresco	*Pearl/Hanover*	23
Gigino	*Battery/West*	20
Goodburger	*Maiden/Pearl*	17
Hale/Hearty	*Broad/Beaver-Exchange*	19
Harry's Cafe/Steak	*multi.*	23
Harry's Italian	*Gold/Maiden-Platt*	21
Haru	*Wall/Beaver-Pearl*	21
Inatteso	*West/1pl*	24
Ise	*Pine/Pearl-William*	21
Lemongrass	*William/Maiden*	17
Les Halles	*John/Bway-Nassau*	20
Luke's Lobster	*William/Stone*	23
MarkJoseph	*Water/Dover-Peck*	23

NEW Milk St. Café	*Wall/William*	–
Nicky's	*Nassau/Ann-Fulton*	22
P.J. Clarke's	*World Fin/Vesey*	17
Pret A Manger	*Broad/Beaver*	18
Shake Shack	*Murray/N End-West*	22
Z SHO Shaun	*Broad/Beaver-Exchange*	26
Smorgas Chef	*Stone/William*	19
Toloache	*Maiden/Gold-William*	23
2 West	*West/Battery*	22
Wall/Water	*Wall/Water*	20
Zaitzeff	*Nassau/John*	21

FLATIRON

(14th to 26th Sts., 6th Ave. to
Park Ave. S., excluding Union Sq.)

Z ABC Kitchen	*18s/Bway-Park*	25
Aldea	*17s/5-6a*	25
Almond	*22s/Bway-Park*	20
Angelo/Maxie's	*Park/19s*	21
A Voce	*Mad/26s*	23
Barbounia	*Park/20s*	21
Basta Pasta	*17s/5-6a*	23
NEW Beecher's	*Bway/20s*	–
NEW Birreria	*5a/23-24s*	21
BLT Fish	*17s/5-6a*	24
Bocca	*19s/Bway-Park*	22
Boqueria	*19s/5-6a*	22
Brio	*Bway/21s*	19
Chickpea	*6a/21-22s*	18
Z NEW Ciano	*22s/Bway-Park*	25
City Bakery	*18s/5-6a*	22
City Crab	*Park/19s*	19
Così	*6a/22-23s*	16
Z Craft	*19s/Bway-Park*	26
Craftbar	*Bway/19-20s*	23
NEW CrossBar	*20s/5-6a*	–
Dévi	*18s/Bway-5a*	24
Z Eataly	*5a/23-24s*	23
Eisenberg's Sandwich	*5A/22-23s*	18
Z Eleven Madison	*Mad/24s*	28
Giorgio's	*21s/Bway-Park*	21
Goodburger	*Bway/17-18s*	17
Z Gramercy Tavern	*20s/Bway-Park*	27
NEW Gravy	*21s/Bway-Park*	–
Grimaldi's	*20s/6a*	24
Haru	*Park/18s*	21
Hill Country	*26s/Bway-6a*	22
NEW Hill Country Chicken	*Bway/25s*	19

Hurricane Club	*Park/26s*	20
NEW Junoon	*24s/5-6a*	23
La Pizza Fresca	*20s/Bway-Park*	24
Le Pain Q.	*19s/Bway-Park*	19
L'Express	*Park/20s*	18
Mangia	*23s/5-6a*	20
Manzo	*5a/23-24s*	24
Mari Vanna	*20s/Bway-Park*	20
Markt	*6a/21s*	18
Z Mesa Grill	*5a/15-16s*	24
Nuela	*24s/Bway-6a*	22
Periyali	*20s/5-6a*	24
Petite Abeille	*17s/5-6a*	19
Pipa	*19s/Bway-Park*	21
Rickshaw Dumpling	*23s/5-6a*	18
Rosa Mexicano	*18s/Bway-5a*	22
Sala	*19s/5-6a*	23
Shake Shack	*23s/Mad*	22
Stuzzi	*Bway/21-22s*	20
SushiSamba	*Park/19-20s*	21
Z Tamarind	*22s/Bway-Park*	25
Tarallucci	*18s/Bway-5a*	20
Z Veritas	*20s/Bway-Park*	26
Via Emilia	*21s/Bway-Park*	23
'Wichcraft	*20s/Bway-5a*	20
Wildwood BBQ	*Park/18-19s*	19
Zero Otto	*21s/5-6a*	25

GARMENT DISTRICT

(30th to 40th Sts., west of 5th)

Abigael's	*Bway/38-39s*	20
Z NEW Ai Fiori	*39s/5-6a*	27
Arno	*38s/Bway-7a*	20
Ayza Wine	*31s/Bway-5a*	20
Ben's Kosher	*38s/7-8a*	19
Bon Chon	*38s/7-8a*	20
Brother Jimmy's	*8a/31s*	17
NEW Casa Nonna	*38s/8-9a*	-
Cho Dang Gol	*35s/5-6a*	22
Colbeh	*39s/5-6a*	21
Frankie/Johnnie	*37s/5-6a*	23
Gahm Mi Oak	*32s/Bway-5a*	22
NEW Go Burger	*38s/8-9a*	22
Hale/Hearty	*7a/35s*	19
Heartland	*5a/34s*	15
Kang Suh	*Bway/32s*	23
Kati Roll	*39s/5-6a*	21
Z Keens	*36s/5-6a*	25
Kum Gang San	*32s/Bway-5a*	22
Lazzara's	*38s/7-8a*	23
Madangsui	*35s/5-6a*	22
Mandoo Bar	*32s/Bway-5a*	22
Mangia	*39s/5-6a*	20

Mercato	*39s/8-9a*	23
Pret A Manger	*7a/38-39s*	18
Sarabeth's	*5a/38-39s*	20
Szechuan Gourmet	*39s/5-6a*	23
Uncle Jack's	*9a/34-35s*	23
WonJo	*32s/Bway-5a*	21

GRAMERCY PARK

(14th to 23rd Sts., east of
Park Ave. S.)

Bao Noodles	*2a/22-23s*	19
Bar Jamon	*17s/Irving*	23
Z BLT Prime	*22s/Lex-Park*	26
Brother Jimmy's	*16s/Irving-Union Sq*	17
Z Casa Mono	*Irving/17s*	25
Defonte's	*3a/21s*	24
Friend/Farmer	*Irving/18-19s*	18
House	*17s/Irving-Park*	21
Lady Mendl's	*Irving/17-18s*	21
NEW La Follia	*3a/19s*	23
Lantern	*2a/18s*	18
NEW Little Town NYC	*15s/Irving*	-
Z Maialino	*Lex/21s*	25
Molly's	*3a/22-23s*	22
Novitá	*22s/Lex-Park*	25
Paul & Jimmy's	*18s/Irving-Park*	21
Pete's Tavern	*18s/Irving*	15
Petite Abeille	*20s/1a*	19
Ponty Bistro	*3a/18-19s*	23
Posto	*2a/18s*	24
Pure Food/Wine	*Irving/17s*	23
Rolf's	*3a/22s*	13
Yama	*17s/Irving*	24
Zen Palate	*18s/Irving-Park*	19

GREENWICH VILLAGE

(Houston to 14th Sts., west of
B'way, east of 6th Ave.)

Alta	*10s/5-6a*	25
Amber	*6a/9-10s*	19
Artichoke Basille	*MacDougal/Blkr-3s*	22
Arturo's	*Houston/Thompson*	21
Z Babbo	*Waverly/MacDougal-6a*	27
Bar Carrera	*Houston/MacDougal*	21
BareBurger	*Laguardia/Blkr-3s*	23
Bar Henry	*Houston/La Guardia-Thompson*	21
Bar Pitti	*6a/Blkr-Houston*	22
BLT Burger	*6a/11-12s*	21
Z Blue Hill	*Wash pl/MacDougal-6a*	27

Cafe Español | *Blkr/MacDougal-Sullivan* | 20

CamaJe | *MacDougal/Blkr-Houston* | 22

Chez Jacqueline | *MacDougal/Blkr-Houston* | 20

Così | *multi.* | 16

Cuba | *Thompson/Blkr-3s* | 23

Cubana Café | *Thompson/Prince-Spring* | 20

Da Andrea | *13s/5-6a* | 22

Ⓩ Da Silvano | *6a/Blkr* | 22

Five Guys | *La Guardia/Blkr-Houston* | 20

Ⓩ Gotham B&G | *12s/5a-Uni* | 28

Gray's Papaya | *6a/8s* | 20

Hotel Griffou | *9s/5-6a* | 19

Il Cantinori | *10s/Bway-Uni* | 24

Ⓩ Il Mulino | *3s/Sullivan-Thompson* | 27

Jackson Diner | *Uni/10-11s* | 21

Jane | *Houston/La Guardia-Thompson* | 21

Japonica | *Uni/12s* | 23

Kati Roll | *MacDougal/Blkr-3s* | 21

Knickerbocker | *Uni/9s* | 20

La Lanterna | *MacDougal/3-4s* | 20

Le Pain Q. | *multi.* | 19

Lion | *9s/5-6a* | 20

ⁿᵉʷ Lotus of Siam | *5a/9s* | 20

Lupa | *Thompson/Blkr-Houston* | 25

Maoz Veg. | *8s/Bway-Uni* | 21

Max Brenner | *Bway/13-14s* | 20

Mermaid | *MacDougal/Blkr-Houston* | 22

Meskerem | *MacDougal/Blkr-3s* | 21

Mexicana Mama | *12s/Bway-Uni* | 24

Mezzaluna/Pizza | *Houston/MacDougal* | 22

Ⓩ Minetta | *MacDougal/Blkr-3s* | 23

ⁿᵉʷ Miss Lily's | *Houston/Sullivan* | -

ⁿᵉʷ Mussel Pot | *Blkr/MacDougal-Sullivan* | 22

Nanoosh | *Uni/12-13s* | 18

Negril | *3s/La Guardia-Thompson* | 21

North Sq. | *Waverly/MacDougal* | 23

Num Pang | *12s/5a-Uni* | 26

Otto | *8s/5a-Uni* | 23

Patsy's Pizzeria | *Uni/10-11s* | 20

Peanut Butter Co. | *Sullivan/3s* | 22

Pop Burger/Pub | *Uni/11-12s* | 17

Quantum Leap | *Thompson/Blkr-3s* | 21

Rocco | *Thompson/Houston* | 22

Spice | *13s/Bway-Uni* | 19

Stand | *12s/5a-Uni* | 20

Strip House | *12s/5a-Uni* | 25

Ⓩ Tomoe Sushi | *Thompson/Blkr-Houston* | 26

Ushiwakamaru | *Houston/MacDougal-Sullivan* | 26

Villa Mosconi | *MacDougal/Blkr-Houston* | 21

'Wichcraft | *8s/Mercer* | 20

HARLEM/ EAST HARLEM

(110th to 155th Sts., excluding Columbia U. area)

Amy Ruth's | *116s/Lenox-7a* | 21

Chez Lucienne | *Lenox/125-126s* | 20

Covo | *135s/12a* | 22

Dinosaur BBQ | *125s/12a* | 22

El Paso Taqueria | *116s/3a* | 23

5 & Diamond | *Douglass/112s* | 21

Hudson River | *133s/12a* | 21

ⁿᵉʷ Lido | *Douglass/117s* | 26

Melba's | *114s/Douglass* | 20

Miss Mamie/Maude | *multi.* | 18

Patsy's Pizzeria | *1a/117-118s* | 20

Rao's | *114s/Pleasant* | 23

Ⓩⁿᵉʷ Red Rooster | *Lenox/125s* | 21

Sylvia's | *Lenox/126-127s* | 19

Zoma | *Douglass/113s* | 22

HUDSON SQUARE

(Canal to Houston Sts., west of 6th Ave.)

Giorgione | *Spring/Greenwich s-Hudson* | 23

La Sirène | *Broome/Varick* | 25

Quattro Gastro. | *Spring/6a-Varick* | 23

LITTLE ITALY

(Canal to Kenmare Sts., Bowery to Lafayette St.)

Angelo's/Mulberry | *Mulberry/Grand-Hester* | 23

Bo-Ky | *Grand/Elizabeth* | 22

Da Nico | *Mulberry/Broome-Grand* | 20

Ferrara | *Grand/Mott-Mulberry* | 23

Il Cortile | *Mulberry/Canal-Hester* | 22

Il Fornaio | *Mulberry/Grand-Hester* | 23

Il Palazzo | *Mulberry/Grand-Hester* | 24

Kenmare | *Kenmare/Lafayette-Mulberry* | 19

La Esquina | _Kenmare/Cleveland-Lafayette_ — 23

Nyonya | _Grand/Mott-Mulberry_ — 22

Pellegrino's | _Mulberry/Grand-Hester_ — 23

Pho Bang | _Mott/Broome-Grand_ — 21

Red Egg | _Centre/Howard_ — 20

Shanghai Café | _Mott/Canal_ — 22

S.P.Q.R. | _Mulberry/Grand-Hester_ — 19

Umberto's | _Mulberry/Grand-Hester_ — 20

Vincent's | _Mott/Hester_ — 22

Wild Ginger | _Broome/Mott_ — 22

LOWER EAST SIDE

(Houston to Canal Sts., east of Bowery)

Alias | _Clinton/Riv_ — 21

An Choi | _Orchard/Broome_ — 21

Ápizz | _Eldridge/Riv-Stanton_ — 24

NEW APL | _Orchard/Riv-Stanton_ — -

BaoHaus | _Riv/Norfolk-Suffolk_ — 20

Z NEW Beauty & Essex | _Essex/Riv-Stanton_ — 22

Bereket | _Houston/Orchard_ — 21

Café Katja | _Orchard/Broome-Grand_ — 24

Clinton St. Baking | _Clinton/Houston-Stanton_ — 25

Congee | _multi._ — 20

NEW Co-op Food/Drink | _Riv/Essex-Ludlow_ — -

Ed's Lobster | _Clinton/Houston-Stanton_ — 23

Falai | _multi._ — 24

NEW Fat Radish | _Orchard/Canal-Hester_ — 20

Z Frankies | _Clinton/Houston-Stanton_ — 25

Freemans | _Riv/Bowery-Chrystie_ — 23

NEW Hotel Chantelle | _Ludlow/Broome-Delancey_ — -

'Inoteca | _Riv/Ludlow_ — 22

Z Katz's Deli | _Houston/Ludlow_ — 24

Kuma Inn | _Ludlow/Delancey-Riv_ — 23

Little Giant | _Orchard/Broome_ — 22

Loreley | _Riv/Bowery-Chrystie_ — 19

NEW Mary Queen of Scots | _Allen/Delancey_ — 21

Meatball Shop | _Stanton/Allen-Orchard_ — 25

NEW Mexicue | _Forsyth/Broome-Grand_ — -

Móle | _Allen/Houston_ — 23

Noodle Bar | _Orchard/Stanton_ — 20

Rayuela | _Allen/Riv-Stanton_ — 23

Sammy's | _Chrystie/Delancey_ — 20

Schiller's | _Riv/Norfolk_ — 19

Shang | _Orchard/Houston-Stanton_ — 20

Sorella | _Allen/Broome-Delancey_ — 26

Spitzer's | _Riv/Ludlow_ — 19

Stanton Social | _Stanton/Ludlow-Orchard_ — 23

Vanessa's Dumpling | _Eldridge/Broome-Grand_ — 20

Z WD-50 | _Clinton/Riv-Stanton_ — 25

Whole Foods | _Houston/Bowery-Chrystie_ — 19

MEATPACKING

(Gansevoort to 15th Sts., west of 9th Ave.)

Abe/Arthur | _14s/9a-Wash_ — 22

NEW Beaumarchais | _13/9a-Wash_ — -

Bill's Bar | _9a/13s_ — 19

Dos Caminos | _Hudson/14s_ — 19

Fig & Olive | _13s/9a-Wash_ — 20

5 9th | _9a/Gansevoort-Little W 12s_ — 19

Macelleria | _Gansevoort/Greenwich s-Wash_ — 22

NEW MPD | _Gansevoort/Wash_ — 20

Old Homestead | _9a/14-15s_ — 24

Paradou | _Little W 12s/Greenwich s-Wash_ — 22

Pastis | _9a/Little W 12s_ — 21

Pop Burger/Pub | _9a/14-15s_ — 17

Sea | _Wash/Little W 12s_ — 21

Z Spice Market | _13s/9a_ — 23

Standard Grill | _Wash/Little W 12-13s_ — 21

STK | _Little W 12s/9a-Wash_ — 22

Tanuki | _13s/Hudson-9a_ — 20

Valbella | _13s/9a-Wash_ — 26

NEW Villa Pacri | _Gansevoort/Greenwich s-Wash_ — 24

MURRAY HILL

(26th to 40th Sts., east of 5th; 23rd to 26th Sts., east of Park Ave. S.)

Aji Sushi | _3a/34-35s_ — 21

Ali Baba | _34s/2-3a_ — 20

Amber | _3a/27-28s_ — 19

Aquamarine | _2a/38-39s_ — 21

Artisanal | _32s/Mad-Park_ — 23

NEW Asellina | _Park/29s_ — 19

Baluchi's | _3a/24-25s_ — 19

Baoguette | _Lex/25-26s_ — 21

Barbès | _36s/5a-Mad_ — 20

BareBurger | _3a/34-35s_ — 23

Ben & Jack's | _5a/28-29s_ — 23

Benjamin | _2a/33s_ — 18

Bistango	*3a/29s*	22
Black Duck	*28s/Lex-Park*	21
Blockhead Burrito	*3a/33-34s*	17
Blue Smoke	*27s/Lex-Park*	22
Bon Chon	*5a/32-33s*	20
NEW Bread/Tulips	*Park/26s*	-
Brother Jimmy's	*Lex/31s*	17
Carl's Steaks	*3a/34s*	21
Chennai Gdn.	*27s/Park*	21
Coppola's	*3a/27-28s*	19
Così	*Park/31s*	16
Curry Leaf	*Lex/27s*	19
Da Ciro	*Lex/33-34s*	23
Dhaba	*Lex/27-28s*	24
Dos Caminos	*Park/26-27s*	19
NEW Duo	*Mad/27-28s*	-
El Parador Cafe	*34s/1-2a*	23
El Pote	*2a/38-39s*	22
El Rio Grande	*38s/Lex-3a*	18
Ethos	*3a/33-34s*	21
Grand Sichuan	*Lex/33-34s*	21
Z HanGawi	*32s/5a-Mad*	25
Hillstone	*Park/27s*	22
Hudson Place	*3a/36s*	19
'Inoteca	*3a/24s*	22
I Trulli	*27s/Lex-Park*	23
Jackson Hole	*3a/35s*	18
Jaiya Thai	*3a/28s*	23
Josie's	*3a/37s*	19
Kyochon	*5a/32-33s*	19
La Petite Aub.	*Lex/27-28s*	22
Lemongrass	*34s/Lex-3a*	17
Le Parisien	*33s/Lex-3a*	22
Les Halles	*Park/28-29s*	20
Madison Bistro	*Mad/37-38s*	21
Marcony	*Lex/31-32s*	25
Mee Noodle	*2a/30-31s*	17
NEW Millesime	*Mad/29s*	21
Mishima	*Lex/30-31s*	24
Morgan	*Mad/36-37s*	20
Nanoosh	*Mad/33-34s*	18
Nirvana	*Lex/39-40s*	21
Park Ave. Bistro	*Park/26-27s*	21
Patsy's Pizzeria	*3a/34-35s*	20
Penelope	*Lex/30s*	21
Phoenix Gdn.	*40s/2-3a*	23
Pio Pio	*34s/2-3a*	22
Pongal	*Lex/27-28s*	22
Primehouse	*Park/27s*	24
Rare B&G	*Lex/37s*	21
Ravagh	*30s/5a-Mad*	22
Resto	*29s/Lex-Park*	20
NEW Riverpark	*29s/1a-FDR*	25

Rossini's	*38s/Lex-Park*	22
Sahara's Turkish	*2a/28-29s*	22
Salute!	*Mad/39s*	19
Saravanaa Bhavan	*Lex/26s*	24
Sarge's Deli	*3a/36-37s*	21
SD26	*26s/5a-Mad*	24
2nd Ave Deli	*33s/Lex-3a*	23
Serge	*Mad/32-33s*	22
Smorgas Chef	*Park/37-38s*	19
Z Sushi Sen-nin	*33s/Mad-Park*	27
NEW Teqa	*3a/30-31s*	21
Tiffin Wallah	*28s/Lex-Park*	23
Toledo	*36s/5a-Mad*	24
Tratt. Alba	*34s/2-3a*	21
Turkish Kitchen	*3a/27-28s*	22
Vatan	*3a/29s*	24
Vezzo	*Lex/31s*	23
Villa Berulia	*34s/Lex-Park*	24
Water Club	*E River/23s*	23
Z Wolfgang's	*Park/33s*	26
Zaitzeff	*2a/38-39s*	21

NOHO

(Houston to 4th Sts., Bowery to B'way)

Aroma Kitchen	*4s/Bowery-Lafayette*	23
Bianca	*Blkr/Bowery-Elizabeth*	24
Bohemian	*Gr Jones/Bowery-Lafayette*	27
Bond St.	*Bond/Bway-Lafayette*	25
Chinatown Brass.	*Lafayette/Gr Jones*	22
5 Points	*Gr Jones/Bowery-Lafayette*	22
Great Jones Cafe	*Gr Jones/Bowery-Lafayette*	21
Hecho en Dumbo	*Bowery/4s-Gr Jones*	23
NEW Hung Ry	*Bond/Bowery-Lafayette*	20
Z Il Buco	*Bond/Bowery-Lafayette*	26
Mercat	*Bond/Bowery-Lafayette*	20
NoHo Star	*Lafayette/Blkr*	19
Rice	*Elizabeth/Blkr-Houston*	21
Two Boots	*Blkr/Bway*	18

NOLITA

(Houston to Kenmare Sts., Bowery to Lafayette St.)

Balaboosta	*Mulberry/Prince-Spring*	23
Barmarché	*Spring/Elizabeth*	21
Bread	*Spring/Elizabeth-Mott*	21
Cafe Gitane	*Mott/Prince*	20

Café Habana/Outpost | *Prince/Elizabeth* | 22

Delicatessen | *Prince/Lafayette* | 18

Ed's Lobster | *Lafayette/Kenmare-Spring* | 23

NEW Ellabess | *Elizabeth/Kenmare* | -

Emilio's Ballato | *Houston/Mott* | 25

Emporio | *Mott/Prince-Spring* | 23

Jacques | *Prince/Elizabeth-Mott* | 18

Lombardi's | *Spring/Mott* | 25

Mexican Radio | *Cleveland/Kenmare-Spring* | 19

Peasant | *Elizabeth/Prince-Spring* | 24

Public | *Elizabeth/Prince-Spring* | 24

Pulino's | *Bowery/Houston* | 19

NEW Rubirosa | *Mulberry/Prince-Spring* | 25

Socarrat | *Mulberry/Houston-Prince* | 23

Z Torrisi | *Mulberry/Prince-Spring* | 27

SOHO

(Canal to Houston Sts., west of Lafayette St.)

Z Aquagrill | *Spring/6a* | 26

Aurora | *Broome/Thompson-Bway* | 24

Z Balthazar | *Spring/Bway-Crosby* | 24

NEW B&B | *Houston/Greene-Mercer* | 24

Barolo | *W Bway/Broome-Spring* | 19

Bistro Les Amis | *Spring/Thompson* | 20

Z Blue Ribbon | *Sullivan/Prince-Spring* | 25

Z Blue Ribbon Sushi | *Sullivan/Prince-Spring* | 26

Boqueria | *Spring/Thompson-W Bway* | 22

NEW Café Kristall | *Mercer/Broome-Spring* | 23

Café Select | *Lafayette/Broome-Spring* | 19

Cipriani D'twn | *W Bway/Broome-Spring* | 22

NEW David Burke Kitchen | *Grand/6a* | 24

Dos Caminos | *W Bway/Houston-Prince* | 19

Z NEW Dutch | *Sullivan/Prince* | 24

Falai | *Lafayette/Prince* | 24

Hampton Chutney | *Prince/Crosby-Lafayette* | 20

Hundred Acres | *MacDougal/Prince* | 20

Il Corallo | *Prince/Sullivan-Thompson* | 23

NEW Imperial No. Nine | *Crosby/Grand-Howard* | 25

Jean Claude | *Sullivan/Houston-Prince* | 22

Kittichai | *Thompson/Broome-Spring* | 23

L'Ecole | *Bway/Grand* | 25

Le Pain Q. | *Grand/Greene-Mercer* | 19

Le Pescadeux | *Thompson/Prince-Spring* | 23

Lucky Strike | *Grand/W Bway-Wooster* | 17

Lure Fishbar | *Mercer/Prince* | 23

Mercer Kitchen | *Prince/Mercer* | 22

Mezzogiorno | *Spring/Sullivan* | 21

NEW Niko | *Mercer/Houston-Prince* | 22

No. 28 | *Spring/Sullivan-Thompson* | 25

Novecento | *W Bway/Broome-Grand* | 21

Omen | *Thompson/Prince-Spring* | 24

Once Upon a Tart . . . | *Sullivan/Houston-Prince* | 22

NEW Osteria Morini | *Lafayette/Broome-Spring* | 24

Pepe | *Sullivan/Houston-Prince* | 19

Raoul's | *Prince/Sullivan-Thompson* | 24

Snack | *Thompson/Prince-Spring* | 22

sNice | *Sullivan/Houston-Prince* | 20

12 Chairs | *MacDougal/Houston-Prince* | 20

'Wichcraft | *Bway/Prince* | 20

SOUTH STREET SEAPORT

Cabana | *South/Fulton* | 21

Cowgirl | *Front/Dover* | 17

Heartland | *South/Fulton* | 15

Suteishi | *Peck/Front* | 25

TRIBECA

(Canal to Murray Sts., west of B'way)

Acappella | *Hudson/Chambers* | 24

Baluchi's | *Greenwich s/Warren* | 19

Stuzzi | *Church/Lispenard-Walker* | 20

Blaue Gans | *Duane/Church-W Bway* | 22

Z Bouley | *Duane/Greenwich s-Hudson* | 28

Bread | *Church/Walker* | 21

Z NEW Brushstroke | *Hudson/Duane* | 28

Bubby's | *Hudson/N Moore* 20

Capsouto Frères | *Wash/Watts* 24

Carl's Steaks | 21
Chambers/Bway-Church

Centrico | *W Bway/Franklin* 20

Churrascaria | 23
W Bway/Franklin-White

City Hall | 21
Duane/Church-W Bway

☑ Corton | 25
W Bway/Walker-White

Duane Park | 22
Duane/Hudson-W Bway

Dylan Prime | 24
Laight/Greenwich s

Ecco | *Chambers/Church-W Bway* 24

Flor/Sol | 21
Greenwich s/Franklin-Harrison

Gigino | 20
Greenwich s/Duane-Reade

Greenwich Grill/Sushi Azabu | 25
Greenwich s/Laight-Vestry

Harrison | *Greenwich s/Harrison* 24

Il Giglio | 26
Warren/Greenwich s-W Bway

Kitchenette | 19
Chambers/Greenwich a-W Bway

Landmarc | 21
W Bway/Leonard-Worth

☑ Locanda Verde | 25
Greenwich s/N Moore

Macao Trading | 19
Church/Lispenard-Walker

☑ Marc Forgione | 26
Reade/Greenwich s-Hudson

Mary Ann's | 16
Greenwich s/Harrison

Max | *Duane/Greenwich s-Hudson* 22

Megu | 24
Thomas/Church-W Bway

NEW Mehtaphor | *Duane/Church* 25

Mr. Chow | *Hudson/N Moore* 22

Nam | *Reade/W Bway* 22

Ninja | *Hudson/Duane-Reade* 18

☑ Nobu | *Hudson/Franklin* 26

Odeon | *W Bway/Duane-Thomas* 19

☑ Palm | *West/Chambers-Warren* 25

☑ Pepolino | 26
W Bway/Canal-Lispenard

Petite Abeille | 19
W Bway/Duane-Thomas

Petrarca Vino | *White/Church* 23

Plein Sud | 20
W Bway/Chambers-Warren

Ponte's | *Desbrosses/Wash-West* 25

Roc | *Duane/Greenwich s* 21

Rosanjin | 27
Duane/Church-W Bway

Salaam Bombay | 22
Greenwich s/Duane-Reade

Sarabeth's | 20
Greenwich s/Harrison-Jay

Sazon | *Reade/Church-W Bway* 21

☑ Scalini Fedeli | 27
Duane/Greenwich s-Hudson

Takahachi | 24
Duane/Church-W Bway

☑ Tamarind | 25
Hudson/Franklin-Harrison

Terroir | 20
Harrison/Greenwich s-Hudson

Thalassa | 24
Franklin/Greenwich s-Hudson

NEW Tiny's | -
W Bway/Duane-Thomas

Trattoria Cinque | 21
Greenwich s/Franklin-Harrison

Tribeca Grill | 23
Greenwich s/Franklin

Walker's | *N Moore/Varick* 19

NEW White & Church | -
Church/White

Whole Foods | 19
Greenwich s/Murray-Warren

'Wichcraft | *Greenwich s/Beach* 20

☑ Wolfgang's | 26
Greenwich s/Beach-Hubert

Zutto | *Hudson/Harrison* 21

UNION SQUARE

(14th to 17th Sts., 5th Ave. to
Union Sq. E.)

☑ Blue Water | *Union sq/16s* 24

Coffee Shop | *Union sq/16s* 16

☑ 15 East | *15s/5a-Union sq* 26

Heartland | *Union sq/16-17s* 15

Laut | *17s/Bway-5a* 22

Maoz Veg. | *Union sq/16-17s* 21

Olives | *Park/17s* 23

Qi | *14s/5-6a* 20

Republic | *Union sq/16-17s* 19

☑ Tocqueville | *15s/5a-Union sq* 25

☑ Union Sq. Cafe | 27
16s/5a-Union sq

Whole Foods | 19
Union sq/Bway-Uni

WASHINGTON HTS./ INWOOD

(North of W. 155th St.)

Dallas BBQ | *Bway/165-166s* 16

El Malecon | *Bway/175s* 20

Empire Szechuan | 17
Bway/170-171s

Garden Café | *Bway/Isham-207s*	22
New Leaf | *Corbin/190s*	21

WEST 40s

A.J. Maxwell's | *48s/5-6a*	22	Goodburger | *45s/5-6a*	17
Akdeniz | *46s/5-6a*	21	Grand Sichuan | *46s/8-9a*	21
Alfredo/Rome | *49s/5-6a*	21	Hale/Hearty | *multi.*	19
Algonquin | *44s/5-6a*	18	Harry's Italian | *6a/49-50s*	21
Amarone | *9a/47-48s*	20	Haru | *43s/Bway-8a*	21
Angus McIndoe | *44s/Bway-8a*	16	Havana Central | *46s/6-7a*	18
☷ Aureole | *42s/Bway-6a*	26	Heartland | *multi.*	15
Barbetta | *46s/8-9a*	21	Hell's Kitchen | *9a/46-47s*	22
Basilica | *9a/46-47s*	20	Inakaya | *40s/7-8a*	23
Becco | *46s/8-9a*	23	Jewel of India | *44s/5-6a*	20
Blue Fin | *Bway/47s*	22	Joe Allen | *46s/8-9a*	18
Bobby Van's | *45s/6-7a*	22	John's Pizzeria | *44s/Bway-8a*	23
Bond 45 | *45s/6-7a*	20	Junior's | *45s/Bway-8a*	19
Bouchon Bakery | *48s/5-6a*	24	Kellari Tav./Parea | *44s/5-6a*	23
Breeze | *9a/45-46s*	20	Koi | *40s/5-6a*	23
Brooklyn Diner | *43s/Bway-6a*	18	Kyotofu | *9a/48-49s*	21
Bryant Park | *40s/5-6a*	18	La Masseria | *48s/Bway-8a*	23
B. Smith's | *46s/8-9a*	19	Lambs Club | *44s/6-7a*	21
BXL | *43s/Bway-6a*	18	Landmark Tavern | *11a/46s*	17
Cafe Un Deux | *44s/Bway-6a*	17	La Rivista | *46s/8-9a*	21
Cara Mia | *9a/45-46s*	21	Lattanzi | *46s/8-9a*	22
Carmine's | *44s/Bway-8a*	21	Lazzara's | *9a/43-44s*	23
Ça Va | *44s/8a*	22	Le Marais | *46s/6-7a*	22
Chez Josephine | *42s/9-10a*	20	Le Rivage | *46s/8-9a*	21
Chimichurri Grill | *9a/43-44s*	23	Maoz Veg. | *multi.*	21
Churrascaria | *49s/8-9a*	23	Marseille | *9a/44-45s*	20
City Lobster | *49s/6a*	19	Meskerem | *47s/9-10a*	21
☷ Copacabana | *47s/8a*	–	Mont Blanc | *48s/8-9a*	21
Così | *42s/5-6a*	16	Morrell Wine | *49s/5-6a*	19
☷ Counter | *Bway/41s*	17	Nizza | *9a/44-45s*	19
Dafni Greek | *42s/8-9a*	20	Oceana | *49s/6-7a*	24
Daisy May's | *11a/46s*	23	Ollie's | *42s/9-10a*	16
Dallas BBQ | *42s/7-8a*	16	☷ Orso | *46s/8-9a*	23
☷ DB Bistro Moderne | *44s/5a*	25	Osteria al Doge | *44s/Bway-6a*	20
Del Frisco's | *6a/48-49s*	25	Pam Real Thai | *multi.*	22
Delta Grill | *9a/48s*	19	Pigalle | *8a/48s*	18
Dervish | *47s/6-7a*	19	Pio Pio | *10a/43-44s*	22
☷ E&E Grill House | *49s/Bway-8a*	–	Pomaire | *46s/8-9a*	20
☷ Esca | *43s/9a*	25	Pongsri Thai | *48s/Bway-8a*	21
Etcetera Etcetera | *44s/8-9a*	22	Pret A Manger | *multi.*	18
FireBird | *46s/8-9a*	20	Print | *11a/47-48s*	25
Five Guys | *48s/5-6a*	20	Qi | *8a/43s*	20
5 Napkin Burger | *9a/44-45s*	21	Queen of Sheba | *10a/45-46s*	22
44 & X/44½ | *multi.*	21	Re Sette | *45s/5-6a*	21
Frankie/Johnnie | *45s/Bway-8a*	23	Room Service | *9a/47-48s*	20
☷ Gari/Sushi | *46s/8-9a*	27	Ruby Foo's | *Bway/49s*	18
Gazala Place | *9a/48-49s*	21	Saju Bistro | *44s/Bway-6a*	21
Glass House | *47s/Bway-8a*	20	Sardi's | *44s/Bway-8a*	18
		Scarlatto | *47s/Bway-8a*	21
		Schnipper's | *8a/41s*	19
		Sea Grill | *49s/5-6a*	24
		Serafina | *49s/Bway-8a*	19
		Shake Shack | *44s/8a*	22

Shorty's | 9a/41-42s 21
Shula's | 43s/Bway-8a 20
Sushiden | 49s/6-7a 25
Sushi Zen | 44s/Bway-6a 26
Tony's Di Napoli | 43s/Bway-6a 21
Trattoria Trecolori | 47s/Bway-8a 23
Triomphe | 44s/5-6a 25
Tulcingo del Valle | 10a/46-47s 22
Turkish Cuisine | 9a/44-45s 21
Two Boots | 9a/44-45s 18
Utsav | 46s/6-7a 21
Via Brasil | 46s/5-6a 21
View | Bway/45-46s 18
Virgil's BBQ | 44s/Bway-6a 20
West Bank | 42s/9-10a 19
'Wichcraft | 40s/6a 20
Wondee Siam | 10a/45-46s 21
Wu Liang Ye | 48s/5-6a 24
Zen Palate | 9a/46s 19
Zuni | 9a/43s 19

WEST 50s

Abboccato | 55s/6-7a 21
Afghan Kebab | 9a/51-52s 20
Angelo's Pizza | multi. 20
Azuri Cafe | 51s/9-10a 26
Baluchi's | 56s/Bway-8a 19
Bann | 50s/8-9a 22
Bar Americain | 52s/6-7a 23
Basso56 | 56s/Bway-8a 23
Beacon | 56s/5-6a 23
Bello | 9a/56s 22
Ben Benson's | 52s/6-7a 24
Benoit | 55s/5-6a 21
Bill's Bar | 51s/5-6a 19
Bistro Milano | 55s/5-6a 21
Blockhead Burrito | 50s/8-9a 17
BLT Market | 6a/CPS 24
Blue Ribbon Sushi B&G | 58s/8-9a 25
Bobby Van's | 50s/6-7a 22
Bocca/Bacco | 9a/54-55s 22
Bombay Palace | 52s/5-6a 19
Braai | 51s/8-9a 20
Brasserie Cognac | Bway/55s 19
Brasserie 8½ | 57s/5-6a 21
Brass. Ruhlmann | 50s/5-6a 20
Bricco | 56s/8-9a 20
Brooklyn Diner | 57s/Bway-7a 18
Z Burger Joint/Le Parker | 56s/6-7a 24
Caffe Cielo | 8a/52-53s 21
Capital Grille | 51s/6-7a 24
Z Carnegie Deli | 7a/55s 22

Casellula | 52s/9-10a 25
Chai Home Kitchen | 8a/55s 22
Chez Napoléon | 50s/8-9a 22
China Grill | 53s/5-6a 22
Circo | 55s/6-7a 23
Così | Bway/50s 16
NEW Danji | 52s/8-9a 24
Da Tommaso | 8a/53-54s 20
Del Frisco's | 51s/5-6a 25
Eatery | 9a/53s 19
El Centro | 9a/54s 22
Empanada Mama | 9a/51-52s 22
Five Guys | 55s/5-6a 20
Fives | 5a/55s 22
Gallagher's | 52s/Bway-8a 21
Goodburger | 8a/57-58s 17
Gordon Ramsay | 54s/6-7a 23
Greek Kitchen | 10a/58s 21
Guantanamera | 8a/55-56s 20
Hale/Hearty | 56s/5-6a 19
Hanci | 10a/56-57s 22
Heartland | 6a/51s 15
Il Gattopardo | 54s/5-6a 23
Z Il Tinello | 56s/5-6a 26
Ise | 56s/5-6a 21
Island Burgers | 9a/51-52s 21
Joe's Shanghai | 56s/5-6a 22
Kashkaval | 9a/56s 23
Katsu-Hama | 55s/5-6a 20
La Bergamote | 52s/10-11a 24
La Bonne Soupe | 55s/5-6a 19
NEW La Petite Maison | 54s/5-6a 19
Z NEW La Silhouette | 53s/8-9a 26
Z Le Bernardin | 51s/6-7a 29
Le Pain Q. | 7a/58s 19
Maison | Bway/53s 19
Mangia | 57s/5-6a 20
Má Pêche | 56s/5-6a 23
Z Marea | CPS/Bway-7a 28
Maria Pia | 51s/8-9a 19
Maze | 54s/6-7a 22
McCormick/Schmick | 52s/6-7a 20
Mee Noodle | 9a/53s 17
Menchanko-tei | 55s/5-6a 21
Z Michael's | 55s/5-6a 22
Z Milos, Estiatorio | 55s/6-7a 27
Z Modern | 53s/5-6a 26
Molyvos | 7a/55-56s 23
Momofuku Milk Bar | 56s/5-6a 23
NEW Mr. Robata | Bway/52-53s -
Natsumi | 50s/Bway-8a 22

NEW 9	*9a/53s*	20
Nino's	*58s/6-7a*	22
Z Nobu	*57s/5-6a*	26
Nocello	*55s/Bway-8a*	22
Nook	*9a/50-51s*	22
Norma's	*56s/6-7a*	25
Original Soupman	*55s/Bway-8a*	23
Z Palm	*50s/Bway-8a*	25
Palm Court	*5a/59s*	20
Patsy's	*56s/Bway-8a*	22
Petrossian	*58s/7a*	24
NEW Pier 9	*9a/53-54s*	23
NEW PizzArte	*55s/5-6a*	-
Plaza Food Hall	*59s/5a*	22
Pret A Manger	*multi.*	18
NEW Pure Thai Shop.	*9a/51-52s*	24
Puttanesca	*9a/56s*	19
Quality Meats	*58s/5-6a*	24
Redeye Grill	*7a/56s*	20
Remi	*53s/6-7a*	22
Rice 'n' Beans	*9a/50-51s*	21
Robert	*Bway/8a*	20
Rock Ctr.	*50s/5-6a*	19
Rue 57	*57s/6a*	18
Russian Samovar	*52s/Bway-8a*	20
Russian Tea	*57s/6-7a*	19
Ruth's Chris	*51s/6-7a*	24
Sarabeth's	*CPS/5-6a*	20
Z Seäsonal	*58s/6-7a*	25
Serafina	*55s/Bway*	19
Soba Nippon	*52s/5-6a*	23
Sosa Borella	*8a/50s*	20
South Gate	*CPS/6-7a*	24
Stage Deli	*7a/53-54s*	21
Z Sugiyama	*55s/Bway-8a*	27
Szechuan Gourmet	*56s/Bway-8a*	23
Taboon	*10a/52s*	24
Tang Pavilion	*55s/5-6a*	22
Thalia	*8a/50s*	20
Toloache	*50s/Bway-8a*	23
Topaz Thai	*56s/6-7a*	21
Totto Ramen	*52s/8-9a*	25
Tratt. Dell'Arte	*7a/56-57s*	23
Z 21 Club	*52s/5-6a*	22
Uncle Jack's	*56s/5-6a*	23
Uncle Nick's	*9a/50-51s*	20
ViceVersa	*51s/8-9a*	22
Victor's Cafe	*52s/Bway-8a*	23
Whym	*9a/57-58s*	20
'Wichcraft	*Rock plz/49s*	20

Wondee Siam	*multi.*	21
Yakitori Totto	*55s/Bway-8a*	25

WEST 60s

Z Asiate	*60s/Bway*	25
Atlantic Grill	*64s/Bway-CPW*	23
A Voce	*60s/Bway*	23
Z Bar Boulud	*Bway/63-64s*	24
Bouchon Bakery	*60s/Bway*	24
NEW Boulud Sud	*64s/Bway-CPW*	23
Cafe Fiorello	*Bway/63-64s*	20
Ed's Chowder	*63s/Bway-Colum*	20
Empire Szechuan	*Colum/68-69s*	17
Gabriel's	*60s/Bway-Colum*	23
NEW GastroArte	*69s/Bway-Colum*	22
Grand Tier	*Lincoln Ctr/63-65s*	21
Z Jean Georges	*CPW/60-61s*	28
Z Jean Georges Noug.	*CPW/60-61s*	27
La Boîte en Bois	*68s/Colum-CPW*	22
Landmarc	*60s/Bway*	21
NEW Leopard/des Artistes	*67s/Colum-CPW*	21
Le Pain Q.	*65s/Bway-CPW*	19
Z Lincoln	*65s/Amst-Bway*	24
Z Masa/Bar Masa	*60s/Bway*	27
Nanoosh	*Bway/68-69s*	18
Nick & Toni	*67s/Bway-Colum*	20
Noi Due	*69s/Bway*	-
Ollie's	*Bway/67-68s*	16
Z Per Se	*60s/Bway*	28
Z Picholine	*64s/Bway-CPW*	27
P.J. Clarke's	*63s/Colum*	17
Porter House	*60s/Bway*	24
Rosa Mexicano	*Colum/62s*	22
Sapphire	*Bway/60-61s*	21
Shun Lee Cafe	*65s/Colum-CPW*	21
Shun Lee West	*65s/Colum-CPW*	23
Z Telepan	*69s/Colum-CPW*	26
Whole Foods	*60s/Bway*	19
'Wichcraft	*62s/Bway-Colum*	20

WEST 70s

Amber	*Colum/70s*	19
Arté Café	*73s/Amst-Colum*	18
Bettola	*Amst/79-80s*	21
Big Nick's	*multi.*	18
Bistro Cassis	*Colum/70-71s*	21
Café Frida	*Colum/77-78s*	19
Cafe Luxembourg	*70s/Amst-W End*	21
Cafe Ronda	*Colum/71-72s*	20

'Cesca | 75s/Amst — 23

Citrus B&G | Amst/75s — 20

Coppola's | 79s/Amst-Bway — 19

Dallas BBQ | 72s/Colum-CPW — 16

❷ Dovetail | 77s/Colum — 26

Epices/Traiteur | 70s/Colum — 21

Fairway Cafe | Bway/74s — 18

Fatty Crab | Bway/77s — 20

NEW FishTag | 79s/Amst-Bway — 22

❷ Gari/Sushi | Colum/77-78s — 27

Gazala Place | Colum/78s — 21

Grand Sichuan | Amst/74-75s — 21

Gray's Papaya | Bway/72s — 20

Hummus Pl. | Amst/74-75s — 22

Isabella's | Colum/77s — 19

Josie's | Amst/74s — 20

La Vela | Amst/77-78s — 19

Le Pain Q. | 72s/Colum-CPW — 21

Maoz Veg. | Amst/70-71s — 23

Mike's Bistro | 72s/Bway-W End — 20

Mughlai | Colum/75s — 20

Nice Matin | 79s/Amst — 24

Ocean Grill | Colum/78-79s — 21

Pappardella | Colum/75s — 21

Pasha | 71s/Colum-CPW — 20

Patsy's Pizzeria | 74s/Colum-CPW — 21

Pomodoro Rosso | Colum/70-71s —

Salumeria Rosi | Amst/73-74s — 25

Sambuca | 72s/Colum-CPW — 19

Saravanaa Bhavan | Amst/79-80s — 24

Scaletta | 77s/Colum-CPW — 21

Shake Shack | Colum/77s — 22

Sunburnt Cow/Calf | 79s/Amst-Bway — 17

Swagat Indian | Amst/79-80s — 22

Tenzan | Colum/73s — 22

NEW Tolani | Amst/79-80s — 24

Viand | Bway/75s — 18

WEST 80s

Accademia/Vino | Bway/89-90s — 18

Artie's Deli | Bway/82-83s — 18

❷ Barney Greengrass | Amst/86-87s — 24

B. Café | Amst/87-88s — 21

Bistro Citron | Colum/82-83s — 19

Blossom | Colum/82-83s — 22

Bodrum | Amst/88-89s — 20

Brother Jimmy's | Amst/80-81s — 17

Cafe Lalo | 83s/Amst-Bway — 19

Calle Ocho | 81s/Colum-CPW — 21

Celeste | Amst/84-85s — 24

Cilantro | Colum/83-84s — 18

Ditch Plains | 82s/Amst-Colum — 18

5 Napkin Burger | Bway/84s — 21

Flor/Mayo | Amst/83-84s — 20

Good Enough/Eat | Amst/83s-84s — 21

Hampton Chutney | Amst/82-83s — 20

Haru | Amst/80-81s — 21

Island Burgers | Amst/80s — 21

Jackson Hole | Colum/85s — 18

Kefi | Colum/84-85s — 22

La Mirabelle | 86s/Amst-Colum — 22

Land | Amst/81-82s — 22

Luke's Lobster | Amst/80-81s — 23

Mermaid | Amst/87-88s — 22

Momoya | Amst/80-81s — 23

Ollie's | Bway/89-90s — 16

❷ Ouest | Bway/84s — 24

Peacefood Café | Amst/82a — 22

Popover Cafe | Amst/86-87s — 19

Prime Grill/KO | 85s/Amst-Bway — 23

Recipe | Amst/81-82s — 24

Sarabeth's | Amst/80-81s — 20

Spice | Amst/81s — 19

Spiga | 84s/Amst-Bway — 24

Sushi Hana | Amst/82-83s — 21

Tarallucci | Colum/83s — 20

Zabar's Cafe | Bway/80s — 20

WEST 90s

Acqua | Amst/95s — 20

Alouette | Bway/97-98s — 20

Café Frida | Amst/97-98s — 19

Carmine's | Bway/90-91s — 21

El Malecon | Amst/97-98s — 20

Gabriela's | Colum/93-94s — 19

Gennaro | Amst/92-93s — 24

Hummus Pl. | Bway/98-99s — 22

Kouzan | Amst/93s — 21

Lisca | Amst/92-93s — 20

Pio Pio | Amst/94s — 22

Regional | Bway/98-9s — 21

Saigon Grill | Amst/90s — 21

Tratt. Pesce | Colum/90-91s — 19

Two Boots | Bway/95-96s — 18

Whole Foods | Colum/97-100 — 19

WEST 100s

(See also Harlem/East Harlem)

Awash | Amst/106-107s — 23

Blockhead Burrito | Amst/106-107s — 17

L
O
C
A
T
I
O
N
S

Café du Soleil | Bway/104s	19	Cafe Loup | 13s/6-7a	20
Community Food | Bway/112-113s	23	Centro Vinoteca | 7a/Barrow	20
Empire Szechuan | Bway/100-101s	17	Commerce | Commerce/Barrow	23
Flor/Mayo | Bway/100-101s	20	Cornelia St. Cafe | Cornelia/Blkr-4s	19
Havana Central | Bway/113-114s	18	Corner Bistro | 4s/Jane	22
Henry's | Bway/105s	19	Corsino | Hudson/Horatio	21
Indus Valley | Bway/100s	22	Cowgirl | Hudson/10s	17
Kitchenette | Amst/122-123s	19	Crispo | 14s/7-8a	24
Le Monde | Bway/112-113s	18	NEW Darby | 14s/7-8a	20
Mamá Mexico | Bway/102s	19	☑ Dell'anima | 8a/Jane	25
Maoz Veg. | Bway/110-111s	21	Ditch Plains | Bedford/Downing	18
Max SoHa/Caffe | multi.	23	Do Hwa | Carmine/Bedford	21
Noche Mex. | Amst/101-102s	23	Dos Toros | Carmine/Blkr-6a	23
Ollie's | Bway/116s	16	El Charro | Charles/Greenwich-7a	23
Picnic | Bway/101-102s	21	Elephant & Castle | Greenwich a/Perry-7a	19
Pisticci | La Salle/Bway	24	El Faro | Greenwich s/Horatio-Jane	22
Rack & Soul | 109s/Bway	22	NEW Empellón | 4s/10s	21
Sezz Medi' | Amst/122s	21	Empire Szechuan | 7a/Perry-11s	17
Sookk | Bway/102-103s	23	EN Japanese | Hudson/Leroy	25
Symposium | 113s/Amst-Bway	20	Extra Virgin | 4s/Perry	23
Terrace in Sky | 119s/Amst-Morn	22	Fatty Crab | Hudson/Gansevoort-Horatio	20
Thai Market | Amst/107-108s	24	Fatty 'Cue | Carmine/Bedford-Blkr	21
Turkuaz | Bway/100s	19	NEW Fedora | 4s/Charles-10s	22
V&T | Amst/110-111s	18	Fish | Blkr/Jones	23
Wondee Siam | Amst/107-108s	21	Five Guys | Blkr/7a	20
Zen Palate | 105s/Bway	19	Flex Mussels | 13s/6-7s	23

WEST VILLAGE

(Houston to 14th Sts., west of 6th Ave., excluding Meatpacking)

Agave | 7a/Charles-10s	19	☑ Frankies | Hudson/11s	25
Aki | 4s/Barrow-Jones	25	Gobo | 6a/8s-Waverly	22
☑ Annisa | Barrow/7a-4s	28	Good | Greenwich a/Bank-12s	20
Antica Venezia | West/10s	23	Gottino | Greenwich a/Charles-Perry	20
A.O.C. | Blkr/Grove	20	Gradisca | 13s/6-7a	23
August | Blkr/Charles-10s	22	Grand Sichuan | 7a/Carmine-Leroy	21
Baoguette | Christopher/Bedford	21	Grano Tratt. | Greenwich a/10s	23
Barbuto | Wash/Jane-12s	25	Gusto | Greenwich a/Perry	21
NEW Bell Book/Candle | 10s/Greenwich a-Waverly	23	Havana Alma | Christopher/Bedford-Blkr	22
Betel | Grove/Blkr-7a	22	Home | Cornelia/Blkr-4s	22
Blue Ribbon Bakery | Downing/Bedford	25	NEW Hudson Clearwater | Hudson/Morton	25
Bobo | 10s/7a	22	Hummus Pl. | 7a/Barrow-Blkr	22
NEW Buvette | Grove/Bedford-Blkr	24	'Ino | Bedford/Downing-6a	24
Cafe Asean | 10s/Greenwich-6a	22	I Sodi | Christopher/Blkr-Hudson	24
Cafe Cluny | 12s/4s	20	NEW Jeffrey's Grocery | Waverly/Christopher	21
Cafe Español | Carmine/Bedford-7a	20	Joe's Pizza | Carmine/Blkr-6a	23
Cafe Gitane | Jane/Wash-West	20	John's Pizzeria | Blkr/6-7a	23
Café Henri | Bedford/Downing	20	Joseph Leonard | Waverly/Grove	22
		Keste Pizza | Blkr/Morton	25

NEW Kin Shop | *6a/11-12s* 24
La Carbonara | *14s/7-8a* 20
La Ripaille | *Hudson/Bethune-12s* 22
L'Artusi | *10s/Blkr-Hudson* 26
Las Ramblas | *4s/Cornelia-Jones* 23
NEW Left Bank | *Perry/Greenwich s* -
Le Gigot | *Cornelia/Blkr-4s* 24
Little Owl | *Bedford/Grove* 25
NEW Lowcountry | *10s/Greenwich a-Waverly* 20
NEW Lyon | *Greenwich a/13s* 20
NEW Malaparte | *Wash/Bethune* -
Malatesta | *Wash/Christopher* 24
Marinella | *Carmine/Bedford* 22
Market Table | *Carmine/Bedford* 24
Mary's Fish | *Charles/4s* 25
Z Mas | *Downing/Bedford-Varick* 27
NEW Mémé | *Hudson/Bank* 24
Mercadito | *7a/Blkr-Grove* 23
Mexicana Mama | *Hudson/Charles-10s* 24
Móle | *Jane/Hudson* 23
NEW Monument Lane | *Greenwich a/12s* -
Morandi | *Waverly/Charles* 22
Moustache | *Bedford/Grove* 22
NEW 900 Degrees | *7a/Leroy-Morton* -
Noodle Bar | *Carmine/Bedford* 20
No. 28 | *Carmine/Bedford-Blkr* 25
Ofrenda | *7a/Christopher-10s* 20
NEW Old Town Hot Pot | *7a/Commerce* -
Olio | *Greenwich a/Christopher-6a* 20
Z One if by Land | *Barrow/7a-4s* 24
Palma | *Cornelia/Blkr-4s* 22
Z Pearl Oyster | *Cornelia/Blkr-4s* 26
Pepe | *Hudson/Perry-11s* 19
Z Perilla | *Jones/Blkr-4s* 26
Z Perry St. | *Perry/West* 26
Petite Abeille | *Hudson/Barrow* 19
Philip Marie | *Hudson/11s* 20
Piccolo Angolo | *Hudson/Jane* 26
Pink Tea Cup | *7a/Barrow-Grove* 19
Place | *4s/Bank-12s* 25
Pó | *Cornelia/Blkr-4s* 25
Recette | *12s/Greenwich s* 24
NEW RedFarm | *Hudson/Charles-10s* -
Risotteria | *Blkr/Morton* 21
Sant Ambroeus | *4s/Perry* 21
Sevilla | *Charles/4s* 24
Smorgas Chef | *12s/4s* 19

Snack | *Bedford/Morton* 22
sNice | *8a/Horatio-Jane* 20
Z Soto | *6a/4s-Wash* 29
NEW Spasso | *Hudson/Perry* 24
Z Spotted Pig | *11s/Greenwich s* 23
Surya | *Blkr/Grove-7a* 21
SushiSamba | *7a/Barrow* 21
Z Taïm | *Waverky/11s-Perry* 26
Takashi | *Hudson/Barrow* 26
Tartine | *11s/4s* 22
Tea & Sympathy | *Greenwich a/12-13s* 20
10 Downing | *Downing/6a* 19
NEW Tertulia | *6a/Wash* -
Tratt. Pesce | *Blkr/6-7a* 19
Trattoria Toscana | *Carmine/Bedford-7a* 24
NEW Tremont | *Bank/4s* -
Two Boots | *11s/7a* 18
Z Wallsé | *11s/Wash* 26
Waverly Inn | *Bank/Waverly* 21
Westville | *10s/Blkr-4s* 23
Yama | *Carmine/Bedford-Blkr* 24
Yerba Buena | *Perry/Greenwich a* 23

Bronx

CITY ISLAND

Artie's | *City Is/Ditmars* 23
Black Whale | *City Is/Hawkins* 22
City Is. Lobster | *Bridge/City Is* 19
Lobster Box | *City Is/Belden-Rochelle* 20
Portofino | *City Is/Cross* 21
Sammy's Fishbox | *City Is/Rochelle* 22

FORDHAM

Ann & Tony's | *Arthur/187-188s* 20
Dominick's | *Arthur/Crescent-187s* 24
Enzo's | *Arthur/Crescent-186s* 23
Mario's | *Arthur/184-186s* 21
Pasquale's | *Arthur/Crescent* 21
Z Roberto | *Crescent/Hughes* 27
Umberto's | *Arthur/186s* 20
Zero Otto | *Arthur/186s* 25

KINGSBRIDGE

El Malecon | *Bway/231s* 20

MORRIS PARK

Enzo's | *Williamsbridge/Neill* 23
F & J Pine | *Bronxdale/Matthews-Muliner* 21
Patricia's | *Morris Pk/Haight-Lurting* 24

LOCATIONS

MOTT HAVEN

Pio Pio | *Cypress/138-139s* 22

PELHAM GARDENS

Fratelli | *Eastchester/Mace* 21

RIVERDALE

Beccofino | 23
Mosholu/Fieldston-Spencer
Jake's | *Bway/242s* 24
Liebman's | *235s/Johnson* 22
Madison's | *Riverdale/259s* 20
Siam Sq. | *Kappock/Henry* 24

THROGS NECK

Tosca Café | 21
Tremont/Miles-Sampson

UNIVERSITY HEIGHTS

Dallas BBQ | *Fordham/Deegan* 16

YANKEE STADIUM

NYY Steak | *161s/River* 20

Brooklyn

BAY RIDGE

Agnanti | *5a/78s* 23
Areo | *3a/84-85s* 24
Arirang Hibachi | *4a/88-89s* 20
Cebu | *3a/88s* 21
Chadwick's | *3a/89s* 22
Eliá | *3a/86-87s* 27
Embers | *3a/95-96s* 20
Five Guys | *5a/85-86s* 20
Fushimi | *4a/93-94s* 24
Greenhouse | *3a/77-78s* 21
101 | *4a/101s* 21
Pearl Room | *3a/82s* 23
Z Tanoreen | *3a/76s* 26
Tuscany Grill | *3a/86-87s* 23

BEDFORD-STUYVESANT

Peaches | *multi.* 23

BENSONHURST

L&B Spumoni | *86s/10-11s* 24
Nyonya | *86s/23-24a* 22
Tenzan | *18a/71s* 22

BOERUM HILL

Bacchus | *Atlantic/Bond-Nevins* 19
Hanco's | *Bergen/Hoyt-Smith* 21
Ki Sushi | *Smith/Dean-Pacific* 25
Lunetta | *Smith/Dean-Pacific* 22
Mile End | *Hoyt/Atlantic-Pacific* 24

Nicky's | *Atlantic/Hoyt-Smith* 22
Z Saul | *Smith/Bergen-Dean* 27

BOROUGH PARK

Nyonya | *8a/53-54s* 22

BRIGHTON BEACH

Tatiana | 21
Brighton 6s/Brightwater

BROOKLYN HEIGHTS

ChipShop | 21
Atlantic/Clinton-Henry
NEW Colonie | 26
Atlantic/Clinton-Henry
Five Guys | 20
Montague/Clinton-Henry
Hale/Hearty | *Court/Remsen* 19
Henry's End | 24
Henry/Cranberry-Middagh
Jack Horse | *Hicks/Cranberry* 23
Lantern | 18
Montague/Henry-Hicks
Noodle Pudding | 24
Henry/Cranberry-Middagh
Queen | 24
Court/Livingston-Schermerhorn
Teresa's | *Montague/Hicks* 18

BUSHWICK

Momo Sushi Shack | -
Bogart/Moore
Z Roberta's | *Moore/Bogart* 26

CARROLL GARDENS

Alma | *Columbia/Degraw* 19
Bino | *Smith/Degraw* 24
Buttermilk | *Court/Huntington* 24
Z Calexico | *Union/Hicks* 24
Chestnut | 23
Smith/Degraw-Sackett
Cubana Café | 20
Smith/Degraw-Sackett
Ferdinando's | *Union/Col.-Hicks* 25
Fragole | *Court/Carroll-1pl* 25
Z Frankies | *Court/4pl-Luquer* 25
Z Grocery | 27
Smith/Sackett-Union
Z Lucali | *Henry/Carroll-1pl* 26
Marco Polo | *Court/Union* 21
Petite Crev. | 24
Hicks/President-Union
Prime Meat | *Court/Luquer* 24
Provence/Boite | *Smith/Degraw* 20
Savoia | *Smith/Degraw-Sackett* 20
Seersucker | 21
Smith/Carroll-President
Zaytoons | *Smith/Sackett* 19

CLINTON HILL

⚡ Locanda Vini | *Gates/Cambridge-Grand*	27
Umi Nom | *DeKalb/Classon*	26

COBBLE HILL

Bocca Lupo | *Henry/Warren*	24
Cafe Luluc | *Smith/Baltic*	20
Char No. 4 | *Smith/Baltic-Warren*	23
Chocolate Room | *Court/Butler-Douglass*	25
Coco Roco | *Smith/Bergen-Dean*	19
Henry Public | *Henry/Atlantic-Pacific*	20
Hibino | *Henry/Pacific*	26
Joya | *Court/Warren-Wyckoff*	23
Lemongrass | *Court/Dean-Pacific*	17
Oaxaca | *Smith/Degraw-Douglass*	20
Quercy | *Court/Baltic-Kane*	21
Sweet Melissa | *Court/Butler-Douglass*	20
Watty/Meg | *Court/Kane*	20
Wild Ginger | *Smith/Dean-Pacific*	22

CONEY ISLAND

Gargiulo's | *15s/Mermaid-Surf*	22
⚡ Totonno Pizza | *Neptune/15-16s*	26

DITMAS PARK

Farm/Adderley | *Cortelyou/Stratford-Westmin*	24
Mimi's Hummus | *Cortelyou/Westmin*	24
Purple Yam | *Cortelyou/Argyle-Rugby*	21

DOWNTOWN BROOKLYN

⚡ Brooklyn Fare | *Schermerhorn/Hoyt*	29
Dallas BBQ | *Livingston/Hoyt-Smith*	16
Five Guys | *Metrotech/Bridge-Lawrence*	20
Junior's | *Flatbush/DeKalb*	19
Morton's | *Adams/Tillary-Willoughby*	25

DUMBO

Bubby's | *Main/Plymouth-Water*	20
Grimaldi's | *Old Fulton/Front-Water*	24
Rice | *Wash/Front-York*	21
⚡ River Café | *Water/Furman-Old Fulton*	26
Superfine | *Front/Jay-Pearl*	18

DYKER HEIGHTS

Tommaso | *86s/Bay 8s-15a*	24

FORT GREENE

NEW Berlyn | *Lafayette/Ashland*	19
Café Habana/Outpost | *Fulton/Portland*	22
Caffe e Vino | *Dekalb/Ashland-St Felix*	24
Ici | *DeKalb/Clermont-Vanderbilt*	22
Luz | *Vanderbilt/Myrtle-Willoughby*	22
Madiba | *DeKalb/Carlton*	20
No. 7 | *Greene/Cumberland-Fulton*	23
Olea | *Lafayette/Adelphi*	22
67 Burger | *Lafayette/Fulton*	22
Smoke Joint | *Elliott/Lafayette*	22
Zaytoons | *Myrtle/Hall-Wash*	19

GRAVESEND

Fiorentino's | *Ave U/McDonald-West*	21
Sahara | *Coney Is/Aves T-U*	23

GREENPOINT

Anella | *Franklin/Green-Huron*	24
⚡ Calexico | *Manhattan/Bedford*	24
Five Leaves | *Bedford/Lorimer-Manhattan*	25
NEW Nights and Weekends | *Bedford/Manhattan*	-

GREENWOOD HEIGHTS

NEW Giuseppina's | *6a/20s*	-

MIDWOOD

⚡ Di Fara | *Ave J/15s*	26
Taci's Beyti | *Coney Is/Ave P-Kings*	25

MILL BASIN

La Villa Pizzeria | *Ave U/66-67s*	21
Mill Basin Deli | *Ave T/59s*	23

PARK SLOPE

⚡ Al Di La | *5a/Carroll*	27
A.O.C. | *5a/Garfield*	20
Applewood | *11s/7-8a*	25
Baluchi's | *5a/2-3s*	19
BareBurger | *7a/1s*	23
Bark Hot Dogs | *Bergen/5a-Flatbush*	21
Belleville | *5s/5a*	19
⚡ Blue Ribbon | *5a/1s-Garfield*	25
⚡ Blue Ribbon Sushi | *5a/1s-Garfield*	26
Bogota | *5a/Lincoln-St Johns*	21

Brooklyn Fish | *5a/Degraw-Douglass*	23
Cafe Steinhof | *7a/14s*	19
ChipShop | *5a/6-7s*	21
Chocolate Room | *5a/Propsect-St Marks*	25
Coco Roco | *5a/6-7s*	19
Conviv. Osteria | *5a/Bergen-St Marks*	25
Cubana Café | *6a/St Marks*	20
Five Guys | *7a/6-7s*	20
Flatbush Farm | *St Marks/Flatbush*	21
Fonda | *7a/14-15s*	23
Fornino | *5a/Carroll-Garfield*	22
Ghenet | *Douglass/4-5a*	24
Hanco's | *7a/10s*	21
NEW Ha Noi | *9s/7a*	-
Joe's Pizza | *7a/Carroll-Garfield*	23
La Villa Pizzeria | *5a/1s-Garfield*	21
Melt | *Bergen/5s-Flatbush*	20
Miriam | *5a/Prospect*	22
Moim | *Garfield/7-8a*	23
Oaxaca | *4a/Carroll-President*	20
Palo Santo | *Union/4-5a*	23
Press 195 | *5a/Berkeley-Union*	22
NEW PSbklyn | *Union/6-7a*	-
Rose Water | *Union/6a*	26
Scottadito | *Union/6-7a*	23
sNice | *5a/2-3s*	20
Song | *5a/1-2s*	22
Spice | *7a/Berkeley-Lincoln*	19
Stone Park | *5a/3s*	25
Sweet Melissa | *7a/1-2s*	20
Thistle Hill | *7a/15s*	23
12th St. B&G | *8a/12s*	21
Two Boots | *2s/7-8a*	18
Zuzu Ramen | *4a/Degraw*	20

PROSPECT HEIGHTS

Amorina | *Vanderbilt/Prospect*	23
Beast | *Bergen/Vanderbilt*	21
Z Franny's | *Flatbush/Prospect-St Marks*	25
Geido | *Flatbush/7a*	25
James | *Carlton/St Marks*	23
Tom's | *Wash/Sterling*	21
Vanderbilt | *Vanderbilt/Bergen*	23
Zaytoons | *Vanderbilt/St Marks*	19

RED HOOK

Defonte's | *Columbia/Luquer*	24
Fairway Cafe | *Van Brunt/Reed*	18
Fort Defiance | *Van Brunt/Coffey-Dikeman*	21

Z Good Fork | *Van Brunt/Coffey-Van Dyke*	25
Red Hook Lobster Pound | *Van Brunt/Verona-Visitation*	24

SHEEPSHEAD BAY

Brennan | *Nostrand/Ave U*	22
Roll-n-Roaster | *Emmons/Nostrand-29s*	21

SUNSET PARK

Z Pacificana | *55s/8a*	25

VINEGAR HILL

Vinegar Hill Hse. | *Hudson/Front-Water*	25

WILLIAMSBURG

Aurora | *Grand/Wythe*	24
Baci/Abbracci | *Grand/Bedford-Driggs*	21
Bamonte's | *Withers/Lorimer-Union*	24
NEW Betto | *8s/Bedford/Berry*	-
Brooklyn Star | *Lorimer/Conselyea*	25
Caracas | *Grand/Havemeyer*	24
Chai Home Kitchen | *6s/Berry*	22
Commodore | *Metro/Havemeyer*	25
Crif Dogs | *Driggs/7s*	22
Diner | *Bway/Berry*	23
Dressler | *Bway/Bedford-Driggs*	25
DuMont | *multi.*	23
Egg | *N 5s/Bedford-Berry*	23
NEW Fat Goose | *Wythe/8s*	-
Fatty 'Cue | *S 6s/Berry*	21
Z Fette Sau | *Metro/Havemeyer-Roebling*	26
NEW Forcella | *Lorimer/Grand-Powers*	-
Fornino | *Bedford/6-7s*	22
NEW Isa | *Wythe/S 2s*	-
La Esquina | *Wythe/3s*	23
La Superior | *Berry/S 2-3s*	24
Loreley | *Frost/Leonard-Lorimer*	19
NEW Mable's Smoke Hse. | *11s/Berry-Wythe*	-
Marlow/Sons | *Bway/Berry-Whythe*	24
NEW Masten Lake | *Bedford/Grand-S 1s*	-
Meatball Shop | *Bedford/7-8s*	25
Mesa Coyoacan | *Graham/Conselyea-Skillman*	25
Miranda | *Berry/N 9s*	25
Móle | *Kent/4s*	23
Momofuku Milk Bar | *Matro/Havemeyer-Marcy*	23

Vote at ZAGAT.com

NEW Morgane	*Bedford/2-3s*	-
1 or 8	*2s/Kent-Wythe*	24
Z Peter Luger	*Bway/Driggs*	28
Pies-n-Thighs	*4s/Driggs*	23
Radegast	*N 3s/Berry*	18
Rye	*S 1s/Havemeyer-Roebling*	24
Saltie	*Metro/Havemeyer-Marcy*	23
Sea	*N 6s/Berry*	21
St. Anselm	*Metro/Havemeyer*	-
Z Traif	*S 4s/Havemeyer-Roebling*	27
Walter Foods	*Grand/Roebling*	23
Wild Ginger	*Bedford/5-6s*	22
Z Zenkichi	*N 6s/Wythe*	26

Queens

ASTORIA

Aegean Cove	*Steinway/20a*	22
Afghan Kebab	*Steinway/28a*	20
Agnanti	*Ditmars/19s*	23
Arepas Café	*36a/34s*	25
NEW Astor Room	*36s/35-36a*	22
BareBurger	*31a/34s*	23
Brick Cafe	*33s/31a*	22
Cávo	*31a/42-43s*	21
Christos	*23a/41s*	23
Elias Corner	*31s/24a*	23
5 Napkin Burger	*36s/35a*	21
Il Bambino	*31a/34-35s*	26
Kabab Café	*Steinway/25a*	24
Locale	*34a/33s*	23
Malagueta	*36a/28s*	24
Mojave	*31s/Ditmars-23a*	21
Omonia	*Bway/33s*	19
Piccola Venezia	*28a/42s*	26
Ponticello	*Bway/46-47s*	24
Rizzo's Pizza	*Steinway/30-31a*	23
Sac's Place	*Bway/29s*	24
Sanford's	*Bway/30-31s*	23
Stamatis	*23a/29-31s*	22
Z Taverna Kyclades	*Ditmars/33-35s*	26
Telly's Taverna	*23a/28-29s*	23
Z Tratt. L'incontro	*31s/Ditmars*	27
Vesta	*30a/21s*	25
Watawa	*Ditmars/33-35s*	24

BAYSIDE

Ben's Kosher	*26a/Bell*	19
Bon Chon	*Bell/45dr-45r*	20
Bourbon St. Café	*Bell/40-41a*	18
Erawan	*Bell/42-43a*	24
Jackson Hole	*Bell/35a*	18
Press 195	*Bell/40-41a*	22
Uncle Jack's	*Bell/40a*	23

NEW Valentino's/Green	*Cross Is/Clear-Utopia*	21

CORONA

Leo's Latticini	*104s/46a*	27
Park Side	*51a/108s*	24
Tortilleria Nixtamal	*47a/104-108s*	24

DOUGLASTON

Grimaldi's	*61a/Douglaston-244s*	24

ELMHURST

Pho Bang	*Bway/Elmhurst*	21
Ping's Sea.	*Queens/Goldsmith*	22

FLUSHING

Blue Smoke	*126s/Roosevelt*	22
East Buffet	*Main/Franklin-Maple*	19
East Manor	*Kissena/Kalmia-Lanburnum*	19
Hunan Kit./Grand Sichuan	*Main/Franklin*	24
Joe's Shanghai	*37a/Main-Union*	22
Kum Gang San	*Northern/Bowne-Union*	22
Kyochon	*Northern/156-157s*	19
Leo's Latticini	*126s/Roosevelt*	27
Pho Bang	*Kissena/Main*	21
Shake Shack	*126s/Roosevelt*	22
Spicy & Tasty	*Prince/39a*	23
Szechuan Gourmet	*37a/Main-Prince*	23
Xi'an	*Main/41r*	23

FOREST HILLS

Alberto	*Metro/69-70a*	24
Baluchi's	*Queens/76a-76r*	19
Bann Thai	*Austin/69r-Yellowstone*	21
Cabana	*70r/Austin-Queens*	21
Z Danny Brown	*Metro/71dr*	27
Da Silvana	*Yellowstone/Clyde-Dartmouth*	22
Dee's	*Metro/74a*	22
La Vigna	*Metro/70a*	24
Nick's	*Ascan/Austin-Burns*	24

FRESH MEADOWS

King Yum	*Union/181s*	19

GLENDALE

Five Guys	*Woodhaven/74a-Rutledge*	20
Zum Stammtisch	*Myrtle/69pl-70s*	24

LOCATIONS

HOWARD BEACH

La Villa Pizzeria | 153a/82s 21

JACKSON HEIGHTS

Afghan Kebab | 37a/74-75s 20
Jackson Diner | 21
  74s/Roosevelt-37a
Jackson Hole | Astoria/70s 18
Pio Pio | Northern/84-85s 22
Zabb Elee | Roosevelt/72s 23

JAMAICA

Bobby Van's | JFK/Amer. Air. 22

LITTLE NECK

La Baraka | Northern/Little Neck 22

LONG ISLAND CITY

Bella Via | Vernon/48a 22
Café Henri | 20
  50a/Jackson-Vernon
Manducatis | multi. 23
Manetta's | Jackson/49a 22
Riverview | 49a/Ctr. 20
Testaccio | Vernon/47r 22
Tournesol | Vernon/50-51a 25
Water's Edge | E River/44dr 21

MIDDLE VILLAGE

Uvarara | Metro/79-80s 26

OZONE PARK

Don Peppe | Lefferts/135-149a 25

REGO PARK

Barosa | Woodhaven/62r 21
Ben's Best | Queens/63r-64a 23
Dallas BBQ | Junction/I-495 16
Grand Sichuan | Queens/66r-67a 21
London Lennie | 23
  Woodhaven/Fleet-Penelope
Pio Pio | Woodhaven/62r 22

SUNNYSIDE

Quaint | Skillman/46-47s 22
Turkish Grill | Queens/42s 23

WOODSIDE

Donovan's | Roosevelt/58s 20
La Flor | Roosevelt/53s 25
Sapori D'Ischia | 37a/56s 24
🅩 Sripraphai | 39a/64-65s 26

Staten Island

BLOOMFIELD

Lorenzo's | South/Lois 21

CASTLETON CORNERS

Joe & Pat's | Victory/Manor 24

DONGAN HILLS

Carol's | 24
  Richmond/Four Crnrs-Seaview
Filippo's | 25
  Richmond/Buel-Seaver
Tratt. Romana | Hylan/Benton 26

ELTINGVILLE

China Chalet | 19
  Amboy/Armstrong-Rich
Nove | Richmond/Amboy 24

GRANT CITY

Fushimi | Richmond/Lincoln 24

GRASMERE

Bocelli | 25
  Hylan/Old Town-Parkinson

GREAT KILLS

Arirang Hibachi | Nelson/Locust 20
Cole's Dock | Cleveland/Hylan 21
Marina Cafe | Mansion/Hillside 22

MARINERS HARBOR

Real Madrid | Forest/Union 24

NEW BRIGHTON

Nurnberger | 21
  Castleton/Davis-Pelton

NEW DORP

Brioso | New Dorp/9s 23

PORT RICHMOND

🅩 Denino | 26
  Port Richmond/Hooker-Walker

ROSEBANK

Bayou | Bay/Chestnut-St Mary 23
Zest | Bay/Willow 26

SHORE ACRES

Da Noi | Fingerboard/Tompkins 23

ST. GEORGE

Enoteca Maria | Hyatt/Central 25
Lake Club | Clove/Victory 21

TOTTENVILLE

Angelina's | Ellis/Arthur Kill 22

TRAVIS

Da Noi | Victory/Service 23

Special Features

Listings cover the best in each category and include names, locations and Food ratings. Multi-location restaurants' features may vary by branch.

BAR/SINGLES SCENES

Abe/Arthur	**Meatpacking**	22
Angelo/Maxie's	**Flatiron**	21
Atlantic Grill	**E 70s**	23
Baraonda	**E 70s**	18
🆕 Bar Basque	**Chelsea**	19
🅉🆕 Beauty & Essex	**LES**	22
Betel	**W Vill**	22
Bill's Bar	**Meatpacking**	19
🅉 Blue Ribbon	**multi.**	25
🅉 Blue Water	**Union Sq**	24
Bobo	**W Vill**	22
Boca Chica	**E Vill**	22
🅉 Breslin	**Chelsea**	22
Brother Jimmy's	**multi.**	17
Bryant Park	**W 40s**	18
🅉 Buddakan	**Chelsea**	24
Butter	**E Vill**	22
Cabana	**multi.**	21
Café Select	**SoHo**	19
Canyon Rd.	**E 70s**	19
Chinatown Brass.	**NoHo**	22
Citrus B&G	**W 70s**	20
Coffee Shop	**Union Sq**	16
DBGB	**E Vill**	23
Del Frisco's	**W 40s**	25
Delicatessen	**NoLita**	18
Dos Caminos	**multi.**	19
🅉🆕 Dutch	**SoHo**	24
Freemans	**LES**	23
Heartland	**multi.**	15
Hillstone	**multi.**	22
Hotel Griffou	**G Vill**	19
🆕 Hudson Clearwater	**W Vill**	25
Hurricane Club	**Flatiron**	20
'Inoteca	**LES**	22
Joya	**Cobble Hill**	23
Kenmare	**L Italy**	19
Koi	**W 40s**	23
La Esquina	**L Italy**	23
🆕 Lavo	**E 50s**	21
Lion	**G Vill**	20
Lure Fishbar	**SoHo**	23
Macao Trading	**TriBeCa**	19
🆕 Miss Lily's	**G Vill**	-
🆕 Niko	**SoHo**	22
Otto	**G Vill**	23

Pastis	**Meatpacking**	21
Peels	**E Vill**	20
Pete's Tavern	**Gramercy**	15
Pulino's	**NoLita**	19
Schiller's	**LES**	19
Smith	**E Vill**	21
🆕 Social Eatz	**E 50s**	23
🅉 Spice Market	**Meatpacking**	23
Standard Grill	**Meatpacking**	21
Stanton Social	**LES**	23
STK	**Meatpacking**	22
SushiSamba	**multi.**	21
Tanuki	**Meatpacking**	20
Tao	**E 50s**	22

BREAKFAST

(See also Hotel Dining)

🅉 Balthazar	**SoHo**	24
🅉 Barney Greengrass	**W 80s**	24
Brasserie	**E 50s**	21
Brooklyn Diner	**multi.**	18
Bubby's	**TriBeCa**	20
🆕 Buvette	**W Vill**	24
🆕 Café Kristall	**SoHo**	23
Cafe Luxembourg	**W 70s**	21
Cafe Mogador	**E Vill**	22
Café Sabarsky	**E 80s**	22
🅉 Carnegie Deli	**W 50s**	22
Casa Lever	**E 50s**	23
City Bakery	**Flatiron**	22
City Hall	**TriBeCa**	21
Clinton St. Baking	**LES**	25
🆕 Coppelia	**Chelsea**	20
E.A.T.	**E 80s**	20
Egg	**W'burg**	23
EJ's Luncheon.	**E 70s**	16
Good Enough/Eat	**W 80s**	21
🆕 Jeffrey's Grocery	**W Vill**	21
Joseph Leonard	**W Vill**	22
🅉 Katz's Deli	**LES**	24
Kitchenette	**multi.**	19
Landmarc	**W 60s**	21
Le Pain Q.	**multi.**	19
Marlow/Sons	**W'burg**	24
🅉 Michael's	**W 50s**	22
Morandi	**W Vill**	22
🆕 Morgane	**W'burg**	-
Naples 45	**E 40s**	18
Nice Matin	**W 70s**	20

NoHo Star | **NoHo**	19
Pastis | **Meatpacking**	21
Peels | **E Vill**	20
Penelope | **Murray Hill**	21
Popover Cafe | **W 80s**	19
Prime Meat | **Carroll Gdns**	24
Pulino's | **NoLita**	19
Rue 57 | **W 50s**	18
Sant Ambroeus | **multi.**	21
Sarabeth's | **multi.**	20
Tartine | **W Vill**	22
Taste | **E 80s**	22
Teresa's | **Bklyn Hts**	18
NEW Untitled | **E 70s**	-
Veselka | **E Vill**	20

BRUNCH

NEW Affaire | **E Vill**	-
NEW Alfama | **E 50s**	-
Alias | **LES**	21
Almond | **Flatiron**	20
Amy Ruth's | **Harlem**	21
Anella | **Greenpt**	24
A.O.C. | **W Vill**	20
Applewood | **Park Slope**	25
Z Aquagrill | **SoHo**	26
Arté Café | **W 70s**	18
Artisanal | **Murray Hill**	23
NEW Astor Room | **Astoria**	22
Atlantic Grill | **multi.**	23
Back Forty | **E Vill**	21
Balaboosta | **NoLita**	23
Z Balthazar | **SoHo**	24
Beast | **Prospect Hts**	21
NEW Beaumarchais | **Meatpacking**	-
Belcourt | **E Vill**	20
Belleville | **Park Slope**	19
Black Whale | **City Is**	22
Blue Ribbon Bakery | **W Vill**	25
Z Blue Water | **Union Sq**	24
Bocca Lupo | **Cobble Hill**	24
Brasserie 8½ | **W 50s**	21
Bridge Cafe | **Financial**	21
Bubby's | **multi.**	20
Buttermilk | **Carroll Gdns**	24
Cafe Cluny | **W Vill**	20
Cafe Loup | **W Vill**	20
Cafe Luluc | **Cobble Hill**	20
Cafe Luxembourg | **W 70s**	21
Cafe Mogador | **E Vill**	22
Cafe Ronda | **W 70s**	20
Cafeteria | **Chelsea**	19
Caffe Cielo | **W 50s**	21

Calle Ocho | **W 80s**	21
Capsouto Frères | **TriBeCa**	24
Z Carlyle | **E 70s**	24
Carmine's | **W 40s**	21
NEW Carpe Diem | **E 70s**	22
Cebu | **Bay Ridge**	21
Celeste | **W 80s**	24
Z NEW Ciano | **Flatiron**	25
Clinton St. Baking | **LES**	25
Colicchio/Sons | **Chelsea**	24
NEW Colonie | **Bklyn Hts**	26
Community Food | **W 100s**	23
Cookshop | **Chelsea**	22
Cornelia St. Cafe | **W Vill**	19
Z David Burke Townhse. | **E 60s**	25
Delicatessen | **NoLita**	18
Z Dell'anima | **W Vill**	25
Delta Grill | **W 40s**	19
Diner | **W'burg**	23
Dressler | **W'burg**	25
E.A.T. | **E 80s**	20
Eatery | **W 50s**	19
Ed's Chowder | **W 60s**	20
Elephant & Castle | **W Vill**	19
NEW Empellón | **W Vill**	21
Extra Virgin | **W Vill**	23
NEW Fat Radish | **LES**	20
Fatty Crab | **multi.**	20
NEW FishTag | **W 70s**	22
Five Leaves | **Greenpt**	25
5 Points | **NoHo**	22
44 & X/44½ | **W 40s**	21
Friend/Farmer | **Gramercy**	18
Good | **W Vill**	20
Good Enough/Eat | **W 80s**	21
Great Jones Cafe | **NoHo**	21
NEW Heartbreak | **E Vill**	24
Home | **W Vill**	22
Hundred Acres | **SoHo**	20
Ilili | **Chelsea**	25
NEW Isa | **W'burg**	-
Isabella's | **W 70s**	20
Jack Horse | **Bklyn Hts**	23
Jane | **G Vill**	21
JoeDoe | **E Vill**	24
JoJo | **E 60s**	25
Joseph Leonard | **W Vill**	22
Kitchenette | **multi.**	19
NEW La Follia | **Gramercy**	23
Z NEW La Silhouette | **W 50s**	26
NEW Lavo | **E 50s**	21
Le Caprice | **E 60s**	20
Le Gigot | **W Vill**	24

NEW Leopard/des Artistes | W 60s	21
Les Halles | multi.	20
Lion | G Vill	20
Little Giant | LES	22
Locale | Astoria	23
Z Locanda Verde | TriBeCa	25
Lorenzo's | Bloomfield	21
NEW Lyon | W Vill	20
Z Mark | E 70s	22
Melt | Park Slope	20
Mercadito | multi.	23
Z Mesa Grill | Flatiron	24
Z Minetta | G Vill	23
Miriam | Park Slope	22
NEW Miss Lily's | G Vill	-
Miss Mamie/Maude | Harlem	18
Mon Petit Cafe | E 60s	20
Nice Matin | W 70s	20
Norma's | W 50s	25
No. 7 | Ft Greene	23
Ocean Grill | W 70s	24
Odeon | TriBeCa	19
Ofrenda | W Vill	20
Olea | Ft Greene	22
Z Ouest | W 80s	24
Palm Court | W 50s	20
Paradou | Meatpacking	22
Pastis | Meatpacking	21
Penelope | Murray Hill	21
Z Perilla | W Vill	26
Petrossian | W 50s	24
Pipa | Flatiron	21
Plein Sud | TriBeCa	20
Popover Cafe | W 80s	19
Prune | E Vill	25
NEW PSbklyn | Park Slope	-
Public | NoLita	24
Puttanesca | W 50s	19
Z NEW Red Rooster | Harlem	21
Z River Café | Dumbo	26
NEW Riverpark | Murray Hill	25
Rocking Horse | Chelsea	21
Rose Water | Park Slope	26
Sanford's | Astoria	23
Sarabeth's | multi.	20
Schiller's | LES	19
Scottadito | Park Slope	23
Seersucker | Carroll Gdns	21
NEW Spasso | W Vill	24
Z Spotted Pig | W Vill	23
Square Meal | E 90s	23
Stanton Social | LES	23

Stone Park | Park Slope	25
Sunburnt Cow/Calf | E Vill	17
Superfine | Dumbo	18
Sylvia's | Harlem	19
Tartine | W Vill	22
Taste | E 80s	22
Z Telepan | W 60s	26
10 Downing | W Vill	19
Thistle Hill | Park Slope	23
Tipsy Parson | Chelsea	20
Tom's | Prospect Hts	21
Tribeca Grill | TriBeCa	23
Turkish Kitchen | Murray Hill	22
Z Union Sq. Cafe | Union Sq	27
Vanderbilt | Prospect Hts	23
View | W 40s	18
Z Wallsé | W Vill	26
Water Club | Murray Hill	23
Waverly Inn | W Vill	21

BUFFET

(Check availability)

Z Aquavit | E 50s	25
Black Whale | City Is	22
Bombay Palace | W 50s	19
Bombay Talkie | Chelsea	20
Brasserie 8½ | W 50s	21
Brick Ln. Curry | E Vill	22
Bukhara Grill | E 40s	22
Chennai Gdn. | Murray Hill	21
Chola | E 50s	24
Darbar | multi.	21
Dhaba | Murray Hill	24
East Buffet | Flushing	19
Indus Valley | W 100s	22
Jackson Diner | multi.	21
Jewel of India | W 40s	20
La Baraka | Little Neck	22
Lake Club | St. George	21
Lorenzo's | Bloomfield	21
Mangia | multi.	20
Mari Vanna | Flatiron	20
Meatball Shop | multi.	25
Mughlai | W 70s	20
Nirvana | Murray Hill	21
Palm Court | W 50s	20
Riverview | LIC	20
Salaam Bombay | TriBeCa	22
Sapphire | W 60s	21
South Gate | W 50s	24
Taste | E 80s	22
Tiffin Wallah | Murray Hill	23
Tosca Café | Throgs Neck	21
Turkish Kitchen | Murray Hill	22

SPECIAL FEATURES

Turkuaz	**W 100s**	19
2 West	**Financial**	22
Utsav	**W 40s**	21
Water Club	**Murray Hill**	23
Yuva	**E 50s**	23

BYO

Afghan Kebab	**multi.**	20
Amy Ruth's	**Harlem**	21
Angelica Kit.	**E Vill**	22
Baluchi's	**Murray Hill**	19
☒ Brooklyn Fare	**Downtown Bklyn**	29
☒ Di Fara	**Midwood**	26
Gazala Place	**multi.**	21
Kabab Café	**Astoria**	24
Kuma Inn	**LES**	23
La Sirène	**Hudson Square**	25
☒ Lucali	**Carroll Gdns**	26
Mama's Food	**E Vill**	22
Mezzaluna/Pizza	**G Vill**	22
Nook	**W 50s**	22
Oaxaca	**multi.**	20
Peking Duck	**Chinatown**	23
Petite Crev.	**Carroll Gdns**	24
Phoenix Gdn.	**Murray Hill**	23
Poke	**E 80s**	25
Sweet Melissa	**Cobble Hill**	20
Taci's Beyti	**Midwood**	25
Tartine	**W Vill**	22
Tea & Sympathy	**W Vill**	20
Umi Nom	**Clinton Hill**	26
Wondee Siam	**W 50s**	21
Zaytoons	**multi.**	19

CELEBRATIONS

(Special prix fixe meals offered at major holidays)

☒ Adour	**E 50s**	26
☒ Aureole	**W 40s**	26
Beacon	**W 50s**	23
BLT Fish	**Flatiron**	24
☒ BLT Prime	**Gramercy**	26
☒ Blue Hill	**G Vill**	27
Bond 45	**W 40s**	20
☒ Bouley	**TriBeCa**	28
'Cesca	**W 70s**	23
☒ Daniel	**E 60s**	29
Duane Park	**TriBeCa**	22
FireBird	**W 40s**	20
☒ Four Seasons	**E 50s**	27
Fresco	**E 50s**	23
Gallagher's	**W 50s**	21
☒ Gotham B&G	**G Vill**	28
Home	**W Vill**	22

☒ La Grenouille	**E 50s**	28
Lambs Club	**W 40s**	21
☒ Le Bernardin	**W 50s**	29
☒ Le Cirque	**E 50s**	25
☒ Maialino	**Gramercy**	25
☒ Marc Forgione	**TriBeCa**	26
☒ Marea	**W 50s**	28
☒ Mas	**W Vill**	27
Mercer Kitchen	**SoHo**	22
☒ Minetta	**G Vill**	23
☒ Modern	**W 50s**	26
Molyvos	**W 50s**	23
Olives	**Union Sq**	23
☒ One if by Land	**W Vill**	24
☒ Ouest	**W 80s**	24
☒ Palm	**multi.**	25
☒ Park Avenue	**E 60s**	25
☒ Peter Luger	**W'burg**	28
Petrossian	**W 50s**	24
Raoul's	**SoHo**	24
Redeye Grill	**W 50s**	20
☒ River Café	**Dumbo**	26
Rock Ctr.	**W 50s**	19
☒ Scarpetta	**Chelsea**	26
Sea Grill	**W 40s**	24
☒ SHO Shaun	**Financial**	26
Terrace in Sky	**W 100s**	22
Tratt. Dell'Arte	**W 50s**	23
View	**W 40s**	18
Water Club	**Murray Hill**	23
Water's Edge	**LIC**	21

CELEBRITY CHEFS

Dan Barber
| ☒ Blue Hill | **G Vill** | 27 |

Lidia Bastianich
☒ Del Posto	**Chelsea**	27
☒ Eataly	**Flatiron**	23
☒ Felidia	**E 50s**	26
Manzo	**Flatiron**	24

Mario Batali
☒ Babbo	**G Vill**	27
☒ Casa Mono	**Gramercy**	25
☒ Del Posto	**Chelsea**	27
☒ Eataly	**Flatiron**	23
☒ Esca	**W 40s**	25
Lupa	**G Vill**	25
Manzo	**Flatiron**	24
Otto	**G Vill**	23

Jonathan Benno
| ☒ Lincoln | **W 60s** | 24 |

April Bloomfield
| ☒ Breslin | **Chelsea** | 22 |
| **NEW** John Dory | **Chelsea** | 23 |

Ⓩ Spotted Pig | **W Vill** | 23

Saul Bolton
Ⓩ Saul | **Boerum Hill** | 27
Vanderbilt | **Prospect Hts** | 23

David Bouley
Ⓩ Bouley | **TriBeCa** | 28
Ⓩ NEW Brushstroke | **TriBeCa** | 28

Daniel Boulud
Ⓩ Bar Boulud | **W 60s** | 24
NEW Boulud Sud | **W 60s** | 23
Ⓩ Café Boulud | **E 70s** | 27
Ⓩ Daniel | **E 60s** | 29
Ⓩ DB Bistro Moderne | **W 40s** | 25
DBGB | **E Vill** | 23

Antoine Bouterin
Le Perigord | **E 50s** | 24

Jimmy Bradley
Harrison | **TriBeCa** | 24

Terrance Brennan
Artisanal | **Murray Hill** | 23
Ⓩ Picholine | **W 60s** | 27

Scott Bryan
Apiary | **E Vill** | 25

David Burke
David Burke/Bloom. | **E 50s** | 19
NEW David Burke Kitchen | **SoHo** | 24
Ⓩ David Burke Townhse. | **E 60s** | 25
Fishtail | **E 60s** | 24

Marco Canora
Hearth | **E Vill** | 24
Terroir | **multi.** | 20

Andrew Carmellini
Ⓩ NEW Dutch | **SoHo** | 24
Ⓩ Locanda Verde | **TriBeCa** | 25

Michael Cetrulo
Ⓩ Scalini Fedeli | **TriBeCa** | 27

David Chang
Má Pêche | **W 50s** | 23
Ⓩ Momofuku Ko | **E Vill** | 27
Momofuku Milk Bar | **E Vill** | 23
Momofuku Noodle | **E Vill** | 24
Ⓩ Momofuku Ssäm | **E Vill** | 25

Rebecca Charles
Ⓩ Pearl Oyster | **W Vill** | 26

Tom Colicchio
Colicchio/Sons | **Chelsea** | 24
Ⓩ Craft | **Flatiron** | 26
Craftbar | **Flatiron** | 23
NEW Riverpark | **Murray Hill** | 25
'Wichcraft | **multi.** | 20

Scott Conant
Ⓩ Scarpetta | **Chelsea** | 26

Christian Delouvrier
La Mangeoire | **E 50s** | 21

John DeLucie
NEW Crown | **E 80s** | -
Lion | **G Vill** | 20

Alain Ducasse
Ⓩ Adour | **E 50s** | 26
Benoit | **W 50s** | 21

Wylie Dufresne
Ⓩ WD-50 | **LES** | 25

Todd English
Ça Va | **W 40s** | 22
NEW CrossBar | **Flatiron** | -
Olives | **Union Sq** | 23
Plaza Food Hall | **W 50s** | 22

Sandro Fioriti
Sandro's | **E 80s** | 25

Bobby Flay
Bar Americain | **W 50s** | 23
Ⓩ Mesa Grill | **Flatiron** | 24

Shea Gallante
Ⓩ NEW Ciano | **Flatiron** | 25

Kurt Gutenbrunner
Blaue Gans | **TriBeCa** | 22
NEW Café Kristall | **SoHo** | 23
Café Sabarsky | **E 80s** | 22
Ⓩ Wallsé | **W Vill** | 26

Gabrielle Hamilton
Prune | **E Vill** | 25

Kerry Heffernan
South Gate | **W 50s** | 24

Shaun Hergatt
Ⓩ SHO Shaun | **Financial** | 26

Peter Hoffman
Back Forty | **E Vill** | 21

Daniel Humm
Ⓩ Eleven Madison | **Flatiron** | 28

Michael Huynh
Baoguette | **multi.** | 21

Sara Jenkins
Porchetta | **E Vill** | 24
NEW Porsena | **E Vill** | 22

Thomas Keller
Bouchon Bakery | **multi.** | 24
Ⓩ Per Se | **W 60s** | 28

Gabriel Kreuther
Ⓩ Modern | **W 50s** | 26

Susur Lee
Shang | **LES** | 20

Paul Liebrandt
Ⓩ Corton | **TriBeCa** | 25

SPECIAL FEATURES

Anita Lo	
Z Annisa | **W Vill**	28
Michael Lomonaco	
Porter House | **W 60s**	24
Pino Luongo	
Centolire | **E 80s**	22
Waldy Malouf	
Beacon | **W 50s**	23
Nobu Matsuhisa	
Z Nobu | **multi.**	26
Marco Moreira	
Z 15 East | **Union Sq**	26
Z Tocqueville | **Union Sq**	25
Masaharu Morimoto	
Z Morimoto | **Chelsea**	26
Tadashi Ono	
Matsuri | **Chelsea**	23
Charlie Palmer	
Z Aureole | **W 40s**	26
David Pasternack	
Z Esca | **W 40s**	25
Zak Pelaccio	
Fatty Crab | **multi.**	20
Fatty 'Cue | **multi.**	21
Alfred Portale	
Z Gotham B&G | **G Vill**	28
Michael Psilakis	
NEW FishTag | **W 70s**	22
Kefi | **W 80s**	22
Mary Redding	
Brooklyn Fish | **Park Slope**	23
Mary's Fish | **W Vill**	25
Eric Ripert	
Z Le Bernardin | **W 50s**	29
Missy Robbins	
A Voce | **multi.**	23
Joël Robuchon	
Z L'Atelier/Robuchon | **E 50s**	27
Miguel Sanchez Romera	
NEW Romera | **Chelsea**	-
Marcus Samuelsson	
Z NEW Red Rooster | **Harlem**	21
Richard Sandoval	
Maya | **E 60s**	23
Pampano | **E 40s**	24
Zengo | **E 40s**	22
Suvir Saran	
Dévi | **Flatiron**	24
Gari Sugio	
Z Gari/Sushi | **multi.**	27
Nao Sugiyama	
Z Sugiyama | **W 50s**	27

Masayoshi Takayama	
Z Masa/Bar Masa | **W 60s**	27
Bill Telepan	
Z Telepan | **W 60s**	26
Sue Torres	
Sueños | **Chelsea**	22
Laurent Tourondel	
BLT Market | **W 50s**	24
Tom Valenti	
Z Ouest | **W 80s**	24
Jean-Georges Vongerichten	
Z ABC Kitchen | **Flatiron**	25
Z Jean Georges | **W 60s**	28
JoJo | **E 60s**	25
Z Mark | **E 70s**	22
Mercer Kitchen | **SoHo**	22
Z Perry St. | **W Vill**	26
Z Spice Market | **Meatpacking**	23
Jonathan Waxman	
Barbuto | **W Vill**	25
Michael White	
Z NEW Ai Fiori | **Garment**	27
Z Marea | **W 50s**	28
NEW Osteria Morini | **SoHo**	24
Jody Williams	
NEW Buvette | **W Vill**	24
Geoffrey Zakarian	
Lambs Club | **W 40s**	21
NEW National | **E 50s**	20
Galen Zamarra	
Z Mas | **W Vill**	27

CHEESE SPECIALISTS

Z Adour | **E 50s**	26
Artisanal | **Murray Hill**	23
Z Babbo | **G Vill**	27
Z Bar Boulud | **W 60s**	24
NEW Beecher's | **Flatiron**	-
Casellula | **W 50s**	25
Celeste | **W 80s**	24
Z Craft | **Flatiron**	26
Z Daniel | **E 60s**	29
Z Eataly | **Flatiron**	23
Z Eleven Madison | **Flatiron**	28
Gordon Ramsay | **W 50s**	23
Z Gramercy Tavern | **Flatiron**	27
'Inoteca | **multi.**	22
Z Jean Georges | **W 60s**	28
Z La Grenouille | **E 50s**	28
Z Maialino | **Gramercy**	25
Z Modern | **W 50s**	26
Otto | **G Vill**	23
Z Per Se | **W 60s**	28
Z Picholine | **W 60s**	27

Plaza Food Hall | **W 50s**	22
Terroir | **E Vill**	20

CHEF'S TABLE

Abigael's | **Garment**	20
Acappella | **TriBeCa**	24
Aldea | **Flatiron**	25
🔁 Aquavit | **E 50s**	25
Avra | **E 40s**	25
NEW Bar Basque | **Chelsea**	19
🔁 Bar Boulud | **W 60s**	24
Barbuto | **W Vill**	25
NEW Bread/Tulips | **Murray Hill**	-
🔁 Breslin | **Chelsea**	22
Café Select | **SoHo**	19
🔁 NEW Ciano | **Flatiron**	25
Gordon Ramsay | **W 50s**	23
NEW Gravy | **Flatiron**	-
Hearth | **E Vill**	24
Hecho en Dumbo | **NoHo**	23
House | **Gramercy**	21
🔁 Il Buco | **NoHo**	26
NEW John Dory | **Chelsea**	23
Kyo Ya | **E Vill**	26
Macelleria | **Meatpacking**	22
Maloney/Porcelli | **E 50s**	23
Marina Cafe | **Great Kills**	22
Mari Vanna | **Flatiron**	20
Maze | **W 50s**	22
Mercat | **NoHo**	20
Mercer Kitchen | **SoHo**	22
Mezzogiorno | **SoHo**	21
Mia Dona | **E 50s**	19
Molyvos | **W 50s**	23
NEW Mr. Robata | **W 50s**	-
Oceana | **W 40s**	24
Olives | **Union Sq**	23
🔁 Park Avenue | **E 60s**	25
Patroon | **E 40s**	23
NEW Porsena | **E Vill**	22
Remi | **W 50s**	22
SD26 | **Murray Hill**	24
Smith/Wollensky | **E 40s**	24
Sojourn | **E 70s**	23
Solo | **E 50s**	24
Tosca Café | **Throgs Neck**	21
Valbella | **Meatpacking**	26
Wall/Water | **Financial**	20
Yuva | **E 50s**	23

CHILD-FRIENDLY

(* children's menu available)

Amorina* | **Prospect Hts**	23
Amy Ruth's | **Harlem**	21

Arirang Hibachi* | **multi.**	20
Artie's Deli* | **W 80s**	18
Bamonte's | **W'burg**	24
Beacon* | **W 50s**	23
NEW Beecher's | **Flatiron**	-
Belleville* | **Park Slope**	19
BLT Burger* | **G Vill**	21
🔁 Blue Ribbon* | **multi.**	25
Blue Smoke* | **Murray Hill**	22
Boathouse* | **E 70s**	18
Bocca Lupo* | **Cobble Hill**	24
Brennan | **Sheepshead**	22
Brooklyn Fish* | **Park Slope**	23
Bubby's* | **multi.**	20
Buttermilk* | **Carroll Gdns**	24
Café Habana/Outpost | **Ft Greene**	22
Cafe Un Deux* | **W 40s**	17
Carmine's* | **W 40s**	21
ChipShop* | **multi.**	21
Cowgirl* | **W Vill**	17
Dallas BBQ | **multi.**	16
DBGB* | **E Vill**	23
EJ's Luncheon.* | **E 70s**	16
Farm/Adderley* | **Ditmas Pk**	24
Fatty Crab* | **multi.**	20
Five Guys* | **multi.**	20
Friend/Farmer* | **Gramercy**	18
Gabriela's* | **W 90s**	19
Gargiulo's | **Coney Is**	22
Good Enough/Eat* | **W 80s**	21
Jackson Hole* | **multi.**	18
Joe & Pat's | **Castleton Corners**	24
Junior's* | **multi.**	19
L&B Spumoni* | **Bensonhurst**	24
Landmarc* | **multi.**	21
La Villa Pizzeria | **multi.**	21
London Lennie* | **Rego Pk**	23
Max* | **multi.**	22
Max Brenner* | **G Vill**	20
Miss Mamie/Maude* | **Harlem**	18
Nick's | **multi.**	24
Ninja* | **TriBeCa**	18
Noodle Pudding | **Bklyn Hts**	24
Osso Buco | **E 90s**	19
Otto | **G Vill**	23
Peanut Butter Co. | **G Vill**	22
Petite Abeille* | **multi.**	19
Pig Heaven | **E 80s**	20
NEW PSbklyn* | **Park Slope**	-
Pulino's* | **NoLita**	19

Rack & Soul*	**W 100s**	22
Riverview*	**LIC**	20
Rock Ctr.*	**W 50s**	19
Ruby Foo's*	**W 40s**	18
Sambuca*	**W 70s**	19
Sarabeth's	**multi.**	20
Serendipity 3	**E 60s**	19
Shake Shack	**multi.**	22
Sylvia's*	**Harlem**	19
Tony's Di Napoli	**W 40s**	21
Two Boots*	**multi.**	18
View*	**W 40s**	18
Virgil's BBQ*	**W 40s**	20
Whole Foods	**multi.**	19
Zero Otto	**Fordham**	25
Zum Stammtisch*	**Glendale**	24

COLLEGE-CENTRIC

Columbia
Community Food	**W 100s**	23
Havana Central	**multi.**	18
Kitchenette	**multi.**	19
Le Monde	**W 100s**	18
Maoz Veg.	**W 100s**	21
Max SoHa/Caffe	**W 100s**	23
Miss Mamie/Maude	**Harlem**	18
Pisticci	**W 100s**	24
Rack & Soul	**W 100s**	22
Sezz Medi'	**W 100s**	21
Symposium	**W 100s**	20
V&T	**W 100s**	18

NYU
Angelica Kit.	**E Vill**	22
Artichoke Basille	**E Vill**	22
Café Habana/Outpost	**NoLita**	22
Café Henri	**W Vill**	20
Caracas	**E Vill**	24
Crif Dogs	**E Vill**	22
Dos Toros	**E Vill**	23
Gyu-Kaku	**E Vill**	21
Ippudo	**E Vill**	25
John's/12th St.	**E Vill**	22
La Esquina	**L Italy**	23
99 Mi. to Philly	**E Vill**	19
Num Pang	**G Vill**	26
Otto	**G Vill**	23
Republic	**Union Sq**	19
S'MAC	**E Vill**	22
Smith	**E Vill**	21
Spice	**G Vill**	19
Tsampa	**E Vill**	20
Vanessa's Dumpling	**E Vill**	20
Veselka	**E Vill**	20

COMMUTER OASES

Grand Central
Ammos	**E 40s**	21
Benjamin Steak	**E 40s**	24
NEW Bi Lokma	**E 40s**	-
Bobby Van's	**E 40s**	22
Burger Heaven	**E 40s**	17
Cafe Centro	**E 40s**	21
Capital Grille	**E 40s**	24
Cipriani Dolci	**E 40s**	21
Dishes	**E 40s**	21
Docks Oyster	**E 40s**	21
Fabio Piccolo	**E 40s**	23
Hatsuhana	**E 40s**	24
Junior's	**E 40s**	19
La Fonda/Sol	**E 40s**	21
Menchanko-tei	**E 40s**	21
Michael Jordan	**E 40s**	20
Morton's	**E 40s**	25
Nanni	**E 40s**	24
Naples 45	**E 40s**	18
Naya/Express	**E 40s**	22
Num Pang	**E 40s**	26
☑ Oyster Bar	**E 40s**	22
Patroon	**E 40s**	23
Pepe	**E 40s**	19
Pera	**E 40s**	21
Pietro's	**E 40s**	24
Sakagura	**E 40s**	25
NEW Schnitzel & Things	**E 40s**	20
Sinigual	**E 40s**	21
Soba Totto	**E 40s**	22
☑ Sparks	**E 40s**	26
☑ Sushi Yasuda	**E 40s**	28
NEW Tenpenny	**E 40s**	-
NEW Tulsi	**E 40s**	21
Two Boots	**E 40s**	18
Zengo	**E 40s**	22

Penn Station
Brother Jimmy's	**Garment**	17
NEW Casa Nonna	**Garment**	-
☑ Keens	**Garment**	25
Lazzara's	**Garment**	23
Uncle Jack's	**Garment**	23

Port Authority
Angus McIndoe	**W 40s**	16
Chez Josephine	**W 40s**	20
Chimichurri Grill	**W 40s**	23
Dafni Greek	**W 40s**	20
Dallas BBQ	**W 40s**	16
☑ Esca	**W 40s**	25
Etcetera Etcetera	**W 40s**	22

Vote at ZAGAT.com

Heartland	**W 40s**	15
John's Pizzeria	**W 40s**	23
Marseille	**W 40s**	20
Mercato	**Garment**	23
Schnipper´s	**W 40s**	19
Shorty's	**W 40s**	21
Shula's	**W 40s**	20
West Bank	**W 40s**	19

CRITIC-PROOF

(Gets lots of business despite so-so food)

Blockhead Burrito	**multi.**	17
Burger Heaven	**multi.**	17
Dallas BBQ	**multi.**	16
Heartland	**multi.**	15
Mary Ann's	**multi.**	16
Ollie's	**multi.**	16

DANCING/ ENTERTAINMENT

(Call for days and times of performances)

Blue Fin	jazz	**W 40s**	22
Blue Smoke	jazz	**Murray Hill**	22
☑ Blue Water	jazz	**Union Sq**	24
Cafe Steinhof	live music	**Park Slope**	19
Cávo	belly dancing	**Astoria**	21
Chez Josephine	piano	**W 40s**	20
⚠ Copacabana	Latin	**W 40s**	–
Cornelia St. Cafe	varies	**W Vill**	19
Delta Grill	live music	**W 40s**	19
Flor/Sol	dancing/live music	**TriBeCa**	21
Knickerbocker	jazz	**G Vill**	20
La Lanterna	jazz	**G Vill**	20
☑ River Café	piano	**Dumbo**	26
Sofrito	dancing	**E 50s**	23
Sylvia's	live music	**Harlem**	19
Tommaso	piano/vocalist	**Dyker Hts**	24
Walker's	jazz	**TriBeCa**	19

DESSERT SPECIALISTS

☑ Blue Hill	**G Vill**	27
Bouchon Bakery	**multi.**	24
Cafe Lalo	**W 80s**	19
Café Sabarsky	**E 80s**	22
ChikaLicious	**E Vill**	24
Chocolate Room	**multi.**	25
City Bakery	**Flatiron**	22
☑ Daniel	**E 60s**	29

Ferrara	**L Italy**	23
Junior's	**multi.**	19
Kyotofu	**W 40s**	21
La Bergamote	**multi.**	24
Lady Mendl's	**Gramercy**	21
La Lanterna	**G Vill**	20
L&B Spumoni	**Bensonhurst**	24
Max Brenner	**G Vill**	20
Momofuku Milk Bar	**multi.**	23
Omonia	**Astoria**	19
Once Upon a Tart . . .	**SoHo**	22
Orsay	**E 70s**	18
Osteria al Doge	**W 40s**	20
Sant Ambroeus	**multi.**	21
Serendipity 3	**E 60s**	19
Sweet Melissa	**multi.**	20
Veniero's	**E Vill**	24

FIREPLACES

Aegean Cove	**Astoria**	22
Alberto	**Forest Hills**	24
Ali Baba	**E 40s**	20
Alta	**G Vill**	25
Antica Venezia	**W Vill**	23
Applewood	**Park Slope**	25
⚠ Asellina	**Murray Hill**	19
Battery Gdns.	**Financial**	19
Benjamin Steak	**E 40s**	24
Black Duck	**Murray Hill**	21
Boathouse	**E 70s**	18
☑ Bouley	**TriBeCa**	28
Bourbon St. Café	**Bayside**	18
Ça Va	**W 40s**	22
Cebu	**Bay Ridge**	21
Christos	**Astoria**	23
☑⚠ Ciano	**Flatiron**	25
Club A Steak	**E 50s**	24
Cornelia St. Cafe	**W Vill**	19
⚠ Crown	**E 80s**	–
Cucina/Pesce	**E Vill**	19
Dawat	**E 50s**	23
Delta Grill	**W 40s**	19
Donovan's	**Woodside**	20
⚠ Duo	**Murray Hill**	–
☑⚠ Dutch	**SoHo**	24
⚠ E&E Grill House	**W 40s**	–
F & J Pine	**Morris Park**	21
FireBird	**W 40s**	20
5 9th	**Meatpacking**	19
Frankie/Johnnie	**Garment**	23
Friend/Farmer	**Gramercy**	18
Giorgione	**Hudson Square**	23
Glass House	**W 40s**	20

Greenhouse | **Bay Ridge**	21
House | **Gramercy**	21
Hudson Place | **Murray Hill**	19
Ici | **Ft Greene**	22
I Trulli | **Murray Hill**	23
Z Keens | **Garment**	25
Lady Mendl's | **Gramercy**	21
Lake Club | **St. George**	21
La Lanterna | **G Vill**	20
Lambs Club | **W 40s**	21
NEW La Petite Maison | **W 50s**	19
La Ripaille | **W Vill**	22
Lattanzi | **W 40s**	22
Lobster Box | **City Is**	20
Lorenzo's | **Bloomfield**	21
Lumi | **E 70s**	20
Manducatis | **LIC**	23
Manetta's | **LIC**	22
Marco Polo | **Carroll Gdns**	21
McCormick/Schmick | **W 50s**	20
Moim | **Park Slope**	23
Molly's | **Gramercy**	22
NEW Neely's BBQ | **E 60s**	–
NEW 9 | **W 50s**	20
Nurnberger | **New Brighton**	21
Z One if by Land | **W Vill**	24
Pearl Room | **Bay Ridge**	23
Z Per Se | **W 60s**	28
Piccola Venezia | **Astoria**	26
Place | **W Vill**	25
Public | **NoLita**	24
Quality Meats | **W 50s**	24
Sac's Place | **Astoria**	24
NEW Salinas | **Chelsea**	–
Scottadito | **Park Slope**	23
South Gate | **W 50s**	24
STK | **Meatpacking**	22
Telly's Taverna | **Astoria**	23
Terrace in Sky | **W 100s**	22
Tosca Café | **Throgs Neck**	21
Trattoria Cinque | **TriBeCa**	21
Triomphe | **W 40s**	25
Z 21 Club | **W 50s**	22
NEW Villa Pacri | **Meatpacking**	24
Vivolo/Cucina | **E 70s**	19
Water Club | **Murray Hill**	23
Waverly Inn | **W Vill**	21
Z WD-50 | **LES**	25

GLUTEN-FREE OPTIONS

(Call to discuss specific needs)

Bistango | **Murray Hill**	22
Caracas | **multi.**	24

Friedman's Lunch | **Chelsea**	21
Hill Country | **Flatiron**	22
Hummus Pl. | **multi.**	22
Keste Pizza | **W Vill**	25
Lumi | **E 70s**	20
Nice Matin | **W 70s**	20
Nizza | **W 40s**	19
Risotteria | **W Vill**	21
NEW Rubirosa | **NoLita**	25
Sambuca | **W 70s**	19
S'MAC | **E Vill**	22

GREEN/LOCAL/ ORGANIC

Z ABC Kitchen | **Flatiron**	25
Aldea | **Flatiron**	25
Alias | **LES**	21
Angelica Kit. | **E Vill**	22
Applewood | **Park Slope**	25
Arabelle | **E 60s**	24
Aroma Kitchen | **NoHo**	23
Z Aureole | **W 40s**	26
Aurora | **multi.**	24
Z Babbo | **G Vill**	27
Back Forty | **E Vill**	21
Barbetta | **W 40s**	21
Z Bar Boulud | **W 60s**	24
Barbuto | **W Vill**	25
BareBurger | **multi.**	23
Bark Hot Dogs | **Park Slope**	21
Belcourt | **E Vill**	20
NEW Bell Book/Candle | **W Vill**	23
Blossom | **Chelsea**	22
BLT Market | **W 50s**	24
Z Blue Hill | **G Vill**	27
NEW Bread/Tulips | **Murray Hill**	–
Buttermilk | **Carroll Gdns**	24
Café Habana/Outpost | **Ft Greene**	22
Candle Cafe | **E 70s**	23
Candle 79 | **E 70s**	24
Caravan/Dreams | **E Vill**	22
Chennai Gdn. | **Murray Hill**	21
Chestnut | **Carroll Gdns**	23
City Bakery | **Flatiron**	22
Clinton St. Baking | **LES**	25
Community Food | **W 100s**	23
Cookshop | **Chelsea**	22
Z Craft | **Flatiron**	26
Z Degustation | **E Vill**	27
Z Dell'anima | **W Vill**	25
Diner | **W'burg**	23
Z Dirt Candy | **E Vill**	26

Vote at ZAGAT.com

☑ Dovetail | **W 70s**	26
☑ Eataly | **Flatiron**	23
Egg | **W'burg**	23
NEW Elevation Burger | **Chelsea**	20
☑ Eleven Madison | **Flatiron**	28
☑ Esca | **W 40s**	25
Falai | **LES**	24
Farm/Adderley | **Ditmas Pk**	24
☑ Fette Sau | **W'burg**	26
5 Points | **NoHo**	22
Flatbush Farm | **Park Slope**	21
Fornino | **W'burg**	22
☑ Frankies | **multi.**	25
☑ Franny's | **Prospect Hts**	25
Gobo | **multi.**	22
Good Enough/Eat | **W 80s**	21
☑ Good Fork | **Red Hook**	25
☑ Gotham B&G | **G Vill**	28
☑ Gramercy Tavern | **Flatiron**	27
☑ Grocery | **Carroll Gdns**	27
Harrison | **TriBeCa**	24
Hearth | **E Vill**	24
Highpoint | **Chelsea**	22
Home | **W Vill**	22
Hundred Acres | **SoHo**	20
Ici | **Ft Greene**	22
☑ Il Buco | **NoHo**	26
Isabella's | **W 70s**	20
James | **Prospect Hts**	23
☑ Jewel Bako | **E Vill**	26
Jimmy's | **E Vill**	21
Josie's | **multi.**	19
L'Artusi | **W Vill**	26
Le Pain Q. | **Flatiron**	19
☑ Lincoln | **W 60s**	24
Little Giant | **LES**	22
☑ Locanda Verde | **TriBeCa**	25
Lunetta | **Boerum Hill**	22
Lupa | **G Vill**	25
☑ Marc Forgione | **TriBeCa**	26
Market Table | **W Vill**	24
Marlow/Sons | **W'burg**	24
☑ Mas | **W Vill**	27
☑ Momofuku Ko | **E Vill**	27
Momofuku Milk Bar | **multi.**	23
Momofuku Noodle | **E Vill**	24
☑ Momofuku Ssäm | **E Vill**	25
New Leaf | **Wash. Hts**	21
Northern Spy | **E Vill**	23
Palo Santo | **Park Slope**	23
Peaches | **Bed-Stuy**	23
☑ Pearl Oyster | **W Vill**	26
☑ Per Se | **W 60s**	28
Picnic | **W 100s**	21
Prime Meat | **Carroll Gdns**	24
Print | **W 40s**	25
Prune | **E Vill**	25
Pure Food/Wine | **Gramercy**	23
Quaint | **Sunnyside**	22
Recipe | **W 80s**	24
☑ Roberta's | **Bushwick**	26
Rose Water | **Park Slope**	26
Rouge Tomate | **E 60s**	24
☑ Saul | **Boerum Hill**	27
Seersucker | **Carroll Gdns**	21
Sfoglia | **E 90s**	23
☑ Telepan | **W 60s**	26
Tortilleria Nixtamal | **Corona**	24
☑ Union Sq. Cafe | **Union Sq**	27
Vesta | **Astoria**	25
Watty/Meg | **Cobble Hill**	20
Whole Foods | **multi.**	19
Zen Palate | **W 40s**	19

GROUP DINING

Accademia/Vino | **multi.**	18
Alta | **G Vill**	25
Angelo/Maxie's | **Flatiron**	21
Arirang Hibachi | **multi.**	20
Artisanal | **Murray Hill**	23
Atlantic Grill | **multi.**	23
☑ Balthazar | **SoHo**	24
Bar Americain | **W 50s**	23
Beacon | **W 50s**	23
☑ **NEW** Beauty & Essex | **LES**	22
Becco | **W 40s**	23
Blaue Gans | **TriBeCa**	22
☑ BLT Prime | **Gramercy**	26
☑ BLT Steak | **E 50s**	25
Blue Fin | **W 40s**	22
Blue Smoke | **multi.**	22
☑ Blue Water | **Union Sq**	24
Boathouse | **E 70s**	18
Bond 45 | **W 40s**	20
Brasserie 8½ | **W 50s**	21
☑ Breslin | **Chelsea**	22
Brioso | **New Dorp**	23
☑ Buddakan | **Chelsea**	24
Cabana | **multi.**	21
Calle Ocho | **W 80s**	21
Capital Grille | **multi.**	24
Carmine's | **multi.**	21
NEW Casa Nonna | **Garment**	–
China Grill | **W 50s**	22
Chinatown Brass. | **NoHo**	22
Churrascaria | **multi.**	23

SPECIAL FEATURES

Cilantro | **multi.**	18
Citrus B&G | **W 70s**	20
Colicchio/Sons | **Chelsea**	24
Congee | **LES**	20
Craftbar | **Flatiron**	23
Crispo | **W Vill**	24
Dallas BBQ | **multi.**	16
DBGB | **E Vill**	23
Del Frisco's | **W 40s**	25
Dinosaur BBQ | **Harlem**	22
Dominick's | **Fordham**	24
Don Peppe | **Ozone Pk**	25
Dos Caminos | **multi.**	19
East Manor | **Flushing**	19
F & J Pine | **Morris Park**	21
Z Fette Sau | **W'burg**	26
Fig & Olive | **multi.**	20
Flor/Sol | **TriBeCa**	21
Golden Unicorn | **Chinatown**	21
Gyu-Kaku | **multi.**	21
Havana Central | **multi.**	18
Heartland | **multi.**	15
NEW Hill Country Chicken | **Flatiron**	19
Hurricane Club | **Flatiron**	20
Ilili | **Chelsea**	25
Jing Fong | **Chinatown**	20
Kefi | **W 80s**	22
Kuma Inn | **LES**	23
Kum Gang San | **multi.**	22
L&B Spumoni | **Bensonhurst**	24
Landmarc | **multi.**	21
Mamá Mexico | **multi.**	19
Mandarin Court | **Chinatown**	22
Má Pêche | **W 50s**	23
Z Momofuku Ssäm | **E Vill**	25
Z Morimoto | **Chelsea**	26
Ninja | **TriBeCa**	18
Z Nobu | **multi.**	26
Nuela | **Flatiron**	22
Osso Buco | **E 90s**	19
Otto | **G Vill**	23
Z Oyster Bar | **E 40s**	22
Z Pacificana | **Sunset Pk**	25
Z Palm | **multi.**	25
Pastis | **Meatpacking**	21
Peking Duck | **multi.**	23
Z Peter Luger | **W'burg**	28
Pipa | **Flatiron**	21
Public | **NoLita**	24
Quality Meats | **W 50s**	24
Redeye Grill | **W 50s**	20
Z NEW Red Rooster | **Harlem**	21

Republic | **Union Sq**	19
Rosa Mexicano | **multi.**	22
Ruby Foo's | **W 40s**	18
Saigon Grill | **W 90s**	21
Sambuca | **W 70s**	19
Sammy's | **LES**	20
Smith/Wollensky | **E 40s**	24
Z Sparks | **E 40s**	26
Z Spice Market | **Meatpacking**	23
Standard Grill | **Meatpacking**	21
Stanton Social | **LES**	23
Z Tamarind | **multi.**	25
Z Tanoreen | **Bay Ridge**	26
Tao | **E 50s**	22
Tony's Di Napoli | **W 40s**	21
Tribeca Grill | **TriBeCa**	23
Victor's Cafe | **W 50s**	23
Wildwood BBQ | **Flatiron**	19
Z Wolfgang's | **multi.**	26
Zengo | **E 40s**	22

HIPSTER

Z Breslin | **Chelsea**	22
Brooklyn Star | **W'burg**	25
Commodore | **W'burg**	25
DuMont | **W'burg**	23
Egg | **W'burg**	23
Fatty 'Cue | **multi.**	21
NEW Fedora | **W Vill**	22
Z Fette Sau | **W'burg**	26
Five Leaves | **Greenpt**	25
Freemans | **LES**	23
Hecho en Dumbo | **NoHo**	23
Henry Public | **Cobble Hill**	20
NEW Isa | **W'burg**	-
Jimmy's | **E Vill**	21
La Superior | **W'burg**	24
Marlow/Sons | **W'burg**	24
Meatball Shop | **multi.**	25
Mile End | **Boerum Hill**	24
Momo Sushi Shack | **Bushwick**	-
Motorino | **E Vill**	24
NEW Nights and Weekends | **Greenpt**	-
No. 7 | **multi.**	23
Peels | **E Vill**	20
Pies-n-Thighs | **W'burg**	23
Prime Meat | **Carroll Gdns**	24
Z Roberta's | **Bushwick**	26
Saltie | **W'burg**	23
Spitzer's | **LES**	19
St. Anselm | **W'burg**	-
Z Traif | **W'burg**	27
Vanderbilt | **Prospect Hts**	23

Vinegar Hill Hse. | **Vinegar Hill** 25
Walter Foods | **W'burg** 23

HISTORIC PLACES

(Year opened; * building)

1787 | One if by Land* | **W Vill** 24
1794 | Bridge Cafe* | **Financial** 21
1837 | Delmonico's | **Financial** 24
1864 | Pete's Tavern | **Gramercy** 15
1868 | Landmark Tavern* | **W 40s** 17
1868 | Old Homestead | **Meatpacking** 24
1880 | Veniero's* | **E Vill** 24
1884 | P.J. Clarke's | **E 50s** 17
1885 | Keens | **Garment** 25
1887 | Peter Luger | **W'burg** 28
1888 | Katz's Deli | **LES** 24
1892 | Ferrara | **L Italy** 23
1896 | Rao's | **Harlem** 23
1900 | Bamonte's | **W'burg** 24
1900 | El Parador Cafe* | **Murray Hill** 23
1900 | Le Rivage* | **W 40s** 21
1902 | Algonquin | **W 40s** 18
1902 | Angelo's/Mulberry | **L Italy** 23
1904 | Ferdinando's | **Carroll Gdns** 25
1904 | Vincent's | **L Italy** 22
1905 | Bottino* | **Chelsea** 19
1905 | Morgan* | **Murray Hill** 20
1906 | Barbetta | **W 40s** 21
1907 | Gargiulo's | **Coney Is** 22
1908 | Barney Greengrass | **W 80s** 24
1908 | John's/12th St. | **E Vill** 22
1910 | Miranda* | **W'burg** 25
1910 | Totonno Pizza* | **Coney Is** 26
1910 | Wolfgang's* | **Murray Hill** 26
1911 | Commerce* | **W Vill** 23
1913 | Oyster Bar | **E 40s** 22
1919 | Mario's | **Fordham** 21
1920 | Leo's Latticini | **Corona** 27
1920 | Nom Wah Tea | **Chinatown** 23
1920 | Umberto's* | **Fordham** 20
1920 | Waverly Inn | **W Vill** 21
1921 | Sardi's | **W 40s** 18
1922 | Defonte's | **Red Hook** 24
1922 | Rocco | **G Vill** 22
1922 | Sanford's | **Astoria** 23
1925 | El Charro | **W Vill** 23
1926 | Frankie/Johnnie | **W 40s** 23

1926 | Palm | **E 40s** 25
1927 | Ann & Tony's | **Fordham** 20
1927 | Diner* | **W'burg** 23
1927 | El Faro | **W Vill** 22
1927 | Gallagher's | **W 50s** 21
1927 | Highliner* | **Chelsea** -
1929 | Eisenberg's Sandwich | **Flatiron** 18
1929 | Eleven Madison* | **Flatiron** 28
1929 | John's Pizzeria | **W Vill** 23
1929 | Russian Tea* | **W 50s** 19
1929 | 21 Club | **W 50s** 22
1930 | Carlyle | **E 70s** 24
1930 | El Quijote | **Chelsea** 21
1931 | Heartland* | **Garment** 15
1932 | Pietro's | **E 40s** 24
1933 | New Leaf* | **Wash. Hts** 21
1933 | Patsy's Pizzeria | **Harlem** 20
1934 | Papaya King | **E 80s** 21
1935 | Del Frisco's* | **W 50s** 25
1936 | Monkey Bar* | **E 50s** 19
1936 | Tom's | **Prospect Hts** 21
1937 | Carnegie Deli | **W 50s** 22
1937 | Denino | **Port Richmond** 26
1937 | Le Veau d'Or | **E 60s** 20
1937 | Minetta* | **G Vill** 23
1937 | Stage Deli | **W 50s** 21
1938 | Brennan | **Sheepshead** 22
1938 | Heidelberg | **E 80s** 19
1938 | Wo Hop | **Chinatown** 22
1939 | L&B Spumoni | **Bensonhurst** 24
1941 | Sevilla | **W Vill** 24
1943 | Burger Heaven | **multi.** 17
1944 | Patsy's | **W 50s** 22
1945 | Ben's Best | **Rego Pk** 23
1945 | Forlini's | **Chinatown** 19
1945 | V&T | **W 100s** 18
1946 | Lobster Box | **City Is** 20
1950 | Junior's | **Downtown Bklyn** 19
1950 | Paul & Jimmy's | **Gramercy** 21
1953 | King Yum | **Fresh Meadows** 19
1953 | Liebman's | **Riverdale** 22
1954 | Serendipity 3 | **E 60s** 19
1954 | Veselka | **E Vill** 20
1956 | Emilio's Ballato | **NoLita** 25
1957 | Arturo's | **G Vill** 21
1957 | La Taza de Oro | **Chelsea** 21
1958 | Queen | **Bklyn Hts** 24
1959 | Brasserie | **E 50s** 21

1959	Four Seasons	**E 50s**	27
1959	London Lennie	**Rego Pk**	23
1959	Rizzo's Pizza	**Astoria**	23
1960	Bull & Bear	**E 40s**	21
1960	Chez Napoléon	**W 50s**	22
1960	Joe & Pat's	**Castleton Corners**	24
1960	Molly's	**Gramercy**	22
1961	Corner Bistro	**W Vill**	22
1962	Big Nick's	**W 70s**	18
1962	La Grenouille	**E 50s**	28
1962	Sylvia's	**Harlem**	19

HOTEL DINING

Ace Hotel
  Ⓩ Breslin | **Chelsea** — 22
  🆕 John Dory | **Chelsea** — 23
  No. 7 | **Chelsea** — 23

Algonquin Hotel
  Algonquin | **W 40s** — 18

Amsterdam Court Hotel
  Natsumi | **W 50s** — 22

Andaz Wall Street Hotel
  Wall/Water | **Financial** — 20

Benjamin Hotel
  🆕 National | **E 50s** — 20

Blakely Hotel
  Abboccato | **W 50s** — 21

Bowery Hotel
  Gemma | **E Vill** — 20

Bryant Park Hotel
  Koi | **W 40s** — 23

Carlton Hotel
  🆕 Millesime | **Murray Hill** — 21

Carlyle Hotel
  Ⓩ Carlyle | **E 70s** — 24

Chambers Hotel
  Má Pêche | **W 50s** — 23
  Momofuku Milk Bar | **W 50s** — 23

Chatwal Hotel
  Lambs Club | **W 40s** — 21

City Club Hotel
  Ⓩ DB Bistro Moderne | **W 40s** — 25

Dream Downtown Hotel
  🆕 Marble Lane | **Chelsea** — –
  🆕 Romera | **Chelsea** — –

Dream Hotel
  Serafina | **W 50s** — 19

Duane Street Hotel
  🆕 Mehtaphor | **TriBeCa** — 25

Dylan Hotel
  Benjamin Steak | **E 40s** — 24

Elysée Hotel
  Monkey Bar | **E 50s** — 19

Empire Hotel
  Ed's Chowder | **W 60s** — 20

Eventi Hotel
  🆕 Bar Basque | **Chelsea** — 19
  🆕 FoodParc | **Chelsea** — 18

Excelsior Hotel
  Calle Ocho | **W 80s** — 21

Fashion 26 Hotel
  Rare B&G | **Chelsea** — 21

Four Seasons Hotel
  Ⓩ L'Atelier/Robuchon | **E 50s** — 27

Gansevoort Hotel
  Tanuki | **Meatpacking** — 20

Gansevoort Park Avenue Hotel
  🆕 Asellina | **Murray Hill** — 19

Giraffe Hotel
  🆕 Bread/Tulips | **Murray Hill** — –

Gotham Hotel
  🆕 Tenpenny | **E 40s** — –

Gramercy Park Hotel
  Ⓩ Maialino | **Gramercy** — 25

Greenwich Hotel
  Ⓩ Locanda Verde | **TriBeCa** — 25

Hilton Garden Inn
  Pigalle | **W 40s** — 18

Hotel on Rivington
  🆕 Co-op Food/Drink | **LES** — –

Ink48 Hotel
  Print | **W 40s** — 25

Inn at Irving Pl.
  Lady Mendl's | **Gramercy** — 21

InterContinental NY Times Sq.
  Ça Va | **W 40s** — 22
  Shake Shack | **W 40s** — 22

Iroquois Hotel
  Triomphe | **W 40s** — 25

James Hotel
  🆕 David Burke Kitchen | **SoHo** — 24

Jane Hotel
  Cafe Gitane | **W Vill** — 20

Jumeirah Essex Hse.
  South Gate | **W 50s** — 24

Le Parker Meridien
  Ⓩ Burger Joint/Le Parker | **W 50s** — 24
  Norma's | **W 50s** — 25

Loews Regency Hotel
  Regency | **E 60s** — 19

London NYC Hotel	
Gordon Ramsay | **W 50s**	23
Maze | **W 50s**	22
Lowell Hotel	
Post House | **E 60s**	24
Mandarin Oriental Hotel	
⚡ Asiate | **W 60s**	25
Maritime Hotel	
Matsuri | **Chelsea**	23
Mark Hotel	
⚡ Mark | **E 70s**	22
Marriott Marquis Hotel	
View | **W 40s**	18
Mela Hotel	
Saju Bistro | **W 40s**	21
Mercer Hotel	
Mercer Kitchen | **SoHo**	22
Mondrian Hotel	
NEW Imperial No. Nine | **SoHo**	25
Nolitan Hotel	
NEW Ellabess | **NoLita**	-
NY Marriott Brooklyn	
Morton's | **Downtown Bklyn**	25
NY Palace Hotel	
⚡ Gilt | **E 50s**	26
Park South Hotel	
Black Duck | **Murray Hill**	21
Pearl Hotel	
NEW E&E Grill House | **W 40s**	-
Peninsula Hotel	
Fives | **W 50s**	22
Pierre Hotel	
Le Caprice | **E 60s**	20
Plaza Athénée Hotel	
Arabelle | **E 60s**	24
Plaza Hotel	
Palm Court | **W 50s**	20
Plaza Food Hall | **W 50s**	22
Ritz-Carlton Battery Park	
2 West | **Financial**	22
Ritz-Carlton Central Park	
BLT Market | **W 50s**	24
San Carlos Hotel	
Mint | **E 50s**	22
Setai Fifth Avenue Hotel	
⚡NEW Ai Fiori | **Garment**	27
Shelburne Murray Hill Hotel	
Rare B&G | **Murray Hill**	21
Sherry-Netherland Hotel	
Harry Cipriani | **E 50s**	22

6 Columbus Hotel	
Blue Ribbon Sushi B&G | **W 50s**	25
60 Thompson	
Kittichai | **SoHo**	23
Smyth Hotel	
Plein Sud | **TriBeCa**	20
Standard Hotel	
Standard Grill | **Meatpacking**	21
St. Regis Hotel	
⚡ Adour | **E 50s**	26
Surrey Hotel	
⚡ Café Boulud | **E 70s**	27
Thompson LES Hotel	
Shang | **LES**	20
Time Hotel	
Serafina | **W 40s**	19
Trump Int'l Hotel	
⚡ Jean Georges | **W 60s**	28
⚡ Jean Georges Noug. | **W 60s**	27
Trump SoHo Hotel	
Quattro Gastro. | **Hudson Square**	23
Waldorf-Astoria	
Bull & Bear | **E 40s**	21
Wales Hotel	
Paola's | **E 90s**	23
Washington Square Hotel	
North Sq. | **G Vill**	23
Westin Times Sq. Hotel	
Shula's | **W 40s**	20
W Hotel Downtown	
BLT B&G | **Financial**	22
W Hotel Times Sq.	
Blue Fin | **W 40s**	22
W Hotel Union Sq.	
Olives | **Union Sq**	23

HOT SPOTS

Abe/Arthur | **Meatpacking**	22
NEW Bar Basque | **Chelsea**	19
⚡NEW Beauty & Essex | **LES**	22
NEW Crown | **E 80s**	-
DBGB | **E Vill**	23
⚡NEW Dutch | **SoHo**	24
⚡ Eataly | **Flatiron**	23
NEW Fedora | **W Vill**	22
NEW Hudson Clearwater | **W Vill**	25
Hurricane Club | **Flatiron**	20
NEW Lavo | **E 50s**	21
Lion | **G Vill**	20
⚡ Minetta | **G Vill**	23

SPECIAL FEATURES

NEW Miss Lily's | **G Vill**	⌐	
NEW Nights and Weekends | **Greenpt**	⌐	
Peels | **E Vill**	20	
Z NEW Red Rooster | **Harlem**	21	
NEW Rubirosa | **NoLita**	25	
Standard Grill | **Meatpacking**	21	
Stanton Social | **LES**	23	
Tao | **E 50s**	22	

JACKET REQUIRED

Z Carlyle | **E 70s**	24
Z Daniel | **E 60s**	29
Z Four Seasons | **E 50s**	27
Z Jean Georges | **W 60s**	28
Z La Grenouille | **E 50s**	28
Z Le Bernardin | **W 50s**	29
Z Le Cirque | **E 50s**	25
Le Perigord | **E 50s**	24
Z Per Se | **W 60s**	28
Z River Café | **Dumbo**	26
Z 21 Club | **W 50s**	22

JURY DUTY

(Near Foley Sq.)

Acappella | **TriBeCa**	24
Big Wong | **Chinatown**	23
Blaue Gans | **TriBeCa**	22
Bo-Ky | **Chinatown**	22
Z Bouley | **TriBeCa**	28
Bread | **TriBeCa**	21
Carl's Steaks | **TriBeCa**	21
Centrico | **TriBeCa**	20
City Hall | **TriBeCa**	21
Dim Sum Go Go | **Chinatown**	21
Ecco | **TriBeCa**	24
Excellent Dumpling | **Chinatown**	21
Forlini's | **Chinatown**	19
Fuleen | **Chinatown**	22
Golden Unicorn | **Chinatown**	21
Great NY Noodle | **Chinatown**	23
Jing Fong | **Chinatown**	20
Joe's | **Chinatown**	21
Mandarin Court | **Chinatown**	22
Nam | **TriBeCa**	22
Nha Trang | **Chinatown**	22
Nice Green Bo | **Chinatown**	23
Odeon | **TriBeCa**	19
Z Oriental Gdn. | **Chinatown**	23
Peking Duck | **Chinatown**	23
Petite Abeille | **TriBeCa**	19
Petrarca Vino | **TriBeCa**	23
Pho Viet Huong | **Chinatown**	22
Ping's Sea. | **Chinatown**	22

Pongsri Thai | **Chinatown**	21
Red Egg | **L Italy**	20
Shanghai Cuisine | **Chinatown**	23
Takahachi | **TriBeCa**	24
Wo Hop | **Chinatown**	22

LATE DINING

(Weekday closing hour)

Artichoke Basille | varies | **multi.**	22
Arturo's | 1 AM | **G Vill**	21
Baraonda | 1 AM | **E 70s**	18
Bar Carrera | 2 AM | **G Vill**	21
Bar Jamon | 2 AM | **Gramercy**	23
NEW Beagle | varies | **E Vill**	⌐
Z NEW Beauty & Essex | 1 AM | **LES**	22
Bereket | 24 hrs. | **LES**	21
NEW Betto | 1 AM | **W'burg**	⌐
Big Nick's | varies | **W 70s**	18
NEW Birreria | 2 AM | **Flatiron**	21
Black Iron | varies | **E Vill**	23
Z Blue Ribbon | varies | **SoHo**	25
Z Blue Ribbon Sushi | varies | **SoHo**	26
Blue Ribbon Sushi B&G | 2 AM | **W 50s**	25
Bocca/Bacco | varies | **W 50s**	22
Bohemian | 1 AM | **NoHo**	27
Bon Chon | varies | **multi.**	20
Bourgeois Pig | 2 AM | **E Vill**	20
Brennan | 1 AM | **Sheepshead**	22
Brooklyn Star | 2 AM | **W'burg**	25
Bubby's | 24 hrs. | **TriBeCa**	20
NEW Buvette | 2 AM | **W Vill**	24
Cafe Lalo | 2 AM | **W 80s**	19
Cafeteria | 24 hrs. | **Chelsea**	19
Z Carnegie Deli | 3:30 AM | **W 50s**	22
Casellula | 2 AM | **W 50s**	25
Cebu | 3 AM | **Bay Ridge**	21
Chickpea | varies | **Flatiron**	18
Coffee Shop | varies | **Union Sq**	16
NEW Coppelia | 24 hrs | **Chelsea**	20
Corner Bistro | 3:30 AM | **W Vill**	22
Crif Dogs | varies | **multi.**	22
Z Dell'anima | 2 AM | **W Vill**	25
Ditch Plains | 2 AM | **multi.**	18
DuMont | 2 AM | **W'burg**	23
Z NEW Dutch | 2 AM | **SoHo**	24
El Malecon | varies | **Wash. Hts**	20
Empanada Mama | 1 AM | **W 50s**	22

Restaurant	Rating
Empire Szechuan | varies | **multi.**	17
NEW Fedora | varies | **W Vill**	22
Frank | 1 AM | **E Vill**	24
Fraunces Tavern | 1 AM | **Financial**	17
Fuleen | 2:30 AM | **Chinatown**	22
Gahm Mi Oak | 24 hrs. | **Garment**	22
Gottino | 2 AM | **W Vill**	20
Gray's Papaya | 24 hrs. | **multi.**	20
Great NY Noodle | 4 AM | **Chinatown**	23
NEW Heartbreak | varies | **E Vill**	24
Henry Public | 1 AM | **Cobble Hill**	20
Hide-Chan | 2 AM | **E 50s**	21
Hunan Kit./Grand Sichuan | 2 AM | **Flushing**	24
NEW Hung Ry | 3 AM | **NoHo**	20
'Ino | 2 AM | **W Vill**	24
'Inoteca | 3 AM | **multi.**	22
Jackson Hole | varies | **multi.**	18
J.G. Melon | 2:30 AM | **E 70s**	21
Joe's Pizza | 5 AM | **W Vill**	23
Joseph Leonard | 2 AM | **W Vill**	22
Kang Suh | 24 hrs. | **Garment**	23
Kati Roll | varies | **G Vill**	21
Kenmare | 1 AM | **L Italy**	19
Knickerbocker | 1 AM | **G Vill**	20
Kum Gang San | 24 hrs. | **multi.**	22
La Esquina | 2 AM | **multi.**	23
La Lanterna | 3 AM | **G Vill**	20
Landmarc | 2 AM | **multi.**	21
NEW Lavo | 1 AM | **E 50s**	21
L'Express | 24 hrs. | **Flatiron**	18
Lil' Frankie | 2 AM | **E Vill**	23
Lucky Strike | varies | **SoHo**	17
Macao Trading | 4 AM | **TriBeCa**	19
Maison | 24 hrs. | **W 50s**	19
Maoz Veg. | varies | **W 40s**	21
Mari Vanna | 1 AM | **Flatiron**	20
Z Mark | 1 AM | **E 70s**	22
Meatball Shop | varies | **multi.**	25
Mercato | 1 AM | **Garment**	23
NEW Mexicue | 2 AM | **LES**	–
Z Minetta | 2 AM | **G Vill**	23
NEW Miss Lily's | varies | **G Vill**	–
Z Momofuku Ko | 1 AM | **E Vill**	27
Z Momofuku Ssäm | 2 AM | **E Vill**	25
NEW Mr. Robata | 3 AM | **W 50s**	–
NEW Mussel Pot | 2 AM | **G Vill**	22
NEW National | 1 AM | **E 50s**	20
NEW Nights and Weekends | 2 AM | **Greenpt**	–
NEW Niko | 2 AM | **SoHo**	22
NEW 900 Degrees | 1 AM | **W Vill**	–
99 Mi. to Philly | 1 AM | **E Vill**	19
Ollie's | varies | **W 100s**	16
Omonia | 4 AM | **Astoria**	19
NEW Osteria Morini | 1 AM | **SoHo**	24
Pastis | varies | **Meatpacking**	21
P.J. Clarke's | varies | **multi.**	17
Pop Burger/Pub | varies | **multi.**	17
Redhead | 1 AM | **E Vill**	23
Roll-n-Roaster | 1 AM | **Sheepshead**	21
NEW Rubirosa | 1 AM | **NoLita**	25
Russian Samovar | 2 AM | **W 50s**	20
Sammy's Fishbox | 2 AM | **City Is**	22
Sanford's | 24 hrs. | **Astoria**	23
Sarge's Deli | 24 hrs. | **Murray Hill**	21
Schiller's | 1 AM | **LES**	19
Shorty's | varies | **W 40s**	21
Sorella | 2 AM | **LES**	26
Z Spotted Pig | 2 AM | **W Vill**	23
Stage Deli | 2 AM | **W 50s**	21
Standard Grill | 4 AM | **Meatpacking**	21
Stanton Social | 3 AM | **LES**	23
SushiSamba | varies | **multi.**	21
Z Sushi Seki | 2:30 AM | **E 60s**	27
Tatiana | 1 AM | **Brighton Bch**	21
Terroir | varies | **E Vill**	20
Thalia | 12 AM | **W 50s**	20
This Little Piggy | 5 AM | **E Vill**	23
NEW Tolani | 2 AM | **W 70s**	24
Tosca Café | 1 AM | **Throgs Neck**	21
Z Traif | 2 AM | **W'burg**	27
Tratt. Dell'Arte | 1:30 AM | **W 50s**	23
Tuck Shop | varies | **E Vill**	21
Two Boots | varies | **multi.**	18
Umberto's | 4 AM | **L Italy**	20
Uva | 2 AM | **E 70s**	22
Veselka | varies | **E Vill**	20
Viand | varies | **multi.**	18
Vincent's | 1:30 AM | **L Italy**	22
Walker's | 1 AM | **TriBeCa**	19
Walter Foods | varies | **W'burg**	23
Wo Hop | 7 AM | **Chinatown**	22
Wollensky's | 2 AM | **E 40s**	24

SPECIAL FEATURES

WonJo | 24 hrs. | **Garment**	21
Zabb Elee | varies | **multi.**	23

MEET FOR A DRINK

(Most top hotels, bars and the following standouts)

Algonquin | **W 40s**	18
Amaranth | **E 60s**	19
Artisanal | **Murray Hill**	23
Atlantic Grill | **multi.**	23
Aurora | **W'burg**	24
☑ Balthazar | **SoHo**	24
NEW Bar Basque | **Chelsea**	19
☑ Bar Boulud | **W 60s**	24
Barbounia | **Flatiron**	21
Betel | **W Vill**	22
Blue Fin | **W 40s**	22
☑ Blue Water | **Union Sq**	24
Bond St. | **NoHo**	25
Boqueria | **Flatiron**	22
Brick Cafe | **Astoria**	22
Bryant Park | **W 40s**	18
☑ Buddakan | **Chelsea**	24
Bull & Bear | **E 40s**	21
Cafe Luxembourg | **W 70s**	21
Cafe Steinhof | **Park Slope**	19
Casa Lever | **E 50s**	23
Centro Vinoteca | **W Vill**	20
City Hall | **TriBeCa**	21
Colicchio/Sons | **Chelsea**	24
NEW Crown | **E 80s**	-
☑ Daniel | **E 60s**	29
Del Frisco's | **W 40s**	25
Dos Caminos | **multi.**	19
Dressler | **W'burg**	25
El Rio Grande | **Murray Hill**	18
Five Leaves | **Greenpt**	25
Flatbush Farm | **Park Slope**	21
☑ Four Seasons | **E 50s**	27
Freemans | **LES**	23
Glass House | **W 40s**	20
☑ Gotham B&G | **G Vill**	28
☑ Gramercy Tavern | **Flatiron**	27
Harry's Cafe/Steak | **Financial**	23
Henry's | **W 100s**	19
Hillstone | **multi.**	22
Hotel Griffou | **G Vill**	19
House | **Gramercy**	21
Hudson River | **Harlem**	21
'Inoteca | **LES**	22
☑ Jean Georges | **W 60s**	28
J.G. Melon | **E 70s**	21
☑ Keens | **Garment**	25
Kellari Tav./Parea | **W 40s**	23

Koi | **W 40s**	23
La Fonda/Sol | **E 40s**	21
Landmarc | **W 60s**	21
☑ Le Cirque | **E 50s**	25
Le Colonial | **E 50s**	21
Lucky Strike | **SoHo**	17
Macao Trading | **TriBeCa**	19
Maloney/Porcelli | **E 50s**	23
Mari Vanna | **Flatiron**	20
☑ Mark | **E 70s**	22
Markt | **Flatiron**	18
☑ Masa/Bar Masa | **W 60s**	27
Matsuri | **Chelsea**	23
Maze | **W 50s**	22
Michael Jordan | **E 40s**	20
☑ Minetta | **G Vill**	23
☑ Modern | **W 50s**	26
Monkey Bar | **E 50s**	19
☑ Morimoto | **Chelsea**	26
Natsumi | **W 50s**	22
☑ Nobu | **W 50s**	26
Odeon | **TriBeCa**	19
Orsay | **E 70s**	18
☑ Ouest | **W 80s**	24
Pastis | **Meatpacking**	21
Patroon | **E 40s**	23
Pera | **E 40s**	21
Pies-n-Thighs | **W'burg**	23
P.J. Clarke's | **multi.**	17
Pop Burger/Pub | **E 50s**	17
Quaint | **Sunnyside**	22
Rayuela | **LES**	23
☑ NEW Red Rooster | **Harlem**	21
SD26 | **Murray Hill**	24
☑ SHO Shaun | **Financial**	26
South Gate | **W 50s**	24
☑ Spice Market | **Meatpacking**	23
Standard Grill | **Meatpacking**	21
Stanton Social | **LES**	23
STK | **Meatpacking**	22
Stone Park | **Park Slope**	25
Tao | **E 50s**	22
☑ 21 Club | **W 50s**	22
Wollensky's | **E 40s**	24
Zengo | **E 40s**	22

NEWCOMERS

Affaire | **E Vill**	-
☑ Ai Fiori | **Garment**	27
Alfama | **E 50s**	-
APL | **LES**	-
Asellina | **Murray Hill**	19
Astor Room | **Astoria**	22

B&B	**SoHo**	24	Ha Noi	**Park Slope**	-
Bar Basque	**Chelsea**	19	Heartbreak	**E Vill**	24
Beagle	**E Vill**	-	Highliner	**Chelsea**	-
Beaumarchais	**Meatpacking**	-	Hill Country Chicken	**Flatiron**	19
☑ Beauty & Essex	**LES**	22	Hospoda	**E 70s**	-
Beecher's	**Flatiron**	-	Hotel Chantelle	**LES**	-
Bell Book/Candle	**W Vill**	23	Hudson Clearwater	**W Vill**	25
Berlyn	**Ft Greene**	19	Hung Ry	**NoHo**	20
Betto	**W'burg**	-	Imperial No. Nine	**SoHo**	25
Bi Lokma	**E 40s**	-	Isa	**W'burg**	-
Birreria	**Flatiron**	21	Jeffrey's Grocery	**W Vill**	21
Boulud Sud	**W 60s**	23	John Dory	**Chelsea**	23
Bread/Tulips	**Murray Hill**	-	Jones Wood Foundry	**E 70s**	23
Brooklyn Star	**W'burg**	25	Junoon	**Flatiron**	23
☑ Brushstroke	**TriBeCa**	28	Kin Shop	**W Vill**	24
Buvette	**W Vill**	24	La Follia	**Gramercy**	23
Café Kristall	**SoHo**	23	La Petite Maison	**W 50s**	19
Cardinal, The	**E Vill**	-	☑ La Silhouette	**W 50s**	26
Carpe Diem	**E 70s**	22	Lavo	**E 50s**	21
Casa Nonna	**Garment**	-	Left Bank	**W Vill**	-
☑ Ciano	**Flatiron**	25	Leopard/des Artistes	**W 60s**	21
Colonie	**Bklyn Hts**	26	Lido	**Harlem**	26
Co-op Food/Drink	**LES**	-	Little Town NYC	**Gramercy**	-
Copacabana	**W 40s**	-	Lotus of Siam	**G Vill**	20
Coppelia	**Chelsea**	20	Lowcountry	**W Vill**	20
Counter	**W 40s**	17	Lyon	**W Vill**	20
CrossBar	**Flatiron**	-	Mable's Smoke Hse.	**W'burg**	-
Crown	**E 80s**	-	Malaparte	**W Vill**	-
Danji	**W 50s**	24	Marble Lane	**Chelsea**	-
Darby	**W Vill**	20	Mary Queen of Scots	**LES**	21
David Burke Kitchen	**SoHo**	24	Masten Lake	**W'burg**	-
Desmond's	**E 60s**	22	Mehtaphor	**TriBeCa**	25
Donatella	**Chelsea**	21	Mémé	**W Vill**	24
Duo	**Murray Hill**	-	Mexicue	**multi.**	-
☑ Dutch	**SoHo**	24	Milk St. Café	**Financial**	-
E&E Grill House	**W 40s**	-	Millesime	**Murray Hill**	21
East End Kitchen	**E 80s**	-	Miss Lily's	**G Vill**	-
Edi & the Wolf	**E Vill**	22	Monument Lane	**W Vill**	-
Elevation Burger	**Chelsea**	20	Morgane	**W'burg**	-
Ellabess	**NoLita**	-	MPD	**Meatpacking**	20
Empellón	**W Vill**	21	Mr. Robata	3 AM	**W 50s**	-
Empire Steakhouse	**E 50s**	20	Mussel Pot	**G Vill**	22
Eolo	**Chelsea**	24	National	**E 50s**	20
Fat Goose	**W'burg**	-	Neely's BBQ	**E 60s**	-
Fat Radish	**LES**	20	Nights and Weekends	**Greenpt**	-
Fedora	**W Vill**	22	Niko	**SoHo**	22
FishTag	**W 70s**	22	9	**W 50s**	20
FoodParc	**Chelsea**	18	900 Degrees	**W Vill**	-
Forcella	**W'burg**	-	Old Town Hot Pot	**W Vill**	-
GastroArte	**W 60s**	22	Osteria Morini	**SoHo**	24
Giuseppina's	**Greenwood Hts**	-	Pier 9	**W 50s**	23
Go Burger	**multi.**	22	PizzArte	**W 50s**	-
Gravy	**Flatiron**	-	Porsena	**E Vill**	22

PSbklyn | **Park Slope**	-
Pure Thai Shop. | **W 50s**	24
RedFarm | **W Vill**	-
ⓩ Red Rooster | **Harlem**	21
Riverpark | **Murray Hill**	25
Romera | **Chelsea**	-
Rubirosa | **NoLita**	25
Salinas | **Chelsea**	-
Schnitzel & Things | **E 40s**	20
Social Eatz | **E 50s**	23
Spasso | **W Vill**	24
Tenpenny | **E 40s**	-
Teqa | **Murray Hill**	21
Tertulia | **W Vill**	-
Tiny's | **TriBeCa**	-
Tolani | **W 70s**	24
Tremont | **W Vill**	-
Tulsi | **E 40s**	21
Untitled | **E 70s**	-
Valentino's/Green | **Bayside**	21
Villa Pacri | **Meatpacking**	24
Walle | **E 50s**	-
White & Church | **TriBeCa**	-

NEWCOMERS ON TAP

(keep posted at ZAGAT.com)

Aamanns | *Danish* | **TriBeCa**
Alison 18 | *American* | **Flatiron**
Alls Well | *American* | **W'burg**
Al Mayass | *Armenian* | **Flatiron**
Atera | *American* | **TriBeCa**
Bao & Bunny | *Chicken* | **E Vill**
Barraca | *Spanish* | **W Vill**
Basik | *Am./Sm. Plates* | **W'burg**
Bevacco | *Italian* | **Bklyn Hts**
BLT Am. Brasserie | *American* | **W 40s**
Bowery Diner | *American* | **LES**
Café Comptoir Royere | *Fr.* | **Carroll Gdns.**
Café Pushkin | *Russian* | **W 50s**
Casa Enrique | *Guatemalan* | **LIC**
Catch | *Seafood* | **Meatpacking**
Center Bar | *Sm. Plates* | **W 60s**
Clyde's | *American* | **Garment**
Dans le Noir | *French* | **Garment**
Da Giovanni of Rome | *Italian* | **Chelsea**
Empellón Cocina | *Mexican* | **E Vill**
Family Recipe | *Eclectic* | **LES**
Fighting Chair | *Steak* | **Seaport**
Fratelli la Bufala | *Italian* | **UWS**
Greenwich Gardens | *Am.* | **W Vill**

Hakkasan | *Chinese* | **W 40s**
Hillside | *Sm. Plates* | **Vinegar Hill**
Il Tesoro | *Italian* | **E 80s**
Indie Food & Wine | *Am./Italian* | **W 60s**
Jung Sik | *Korean* | **TriBeCa**
Kimchi Grill | *Mex./Kor.* | **Prospect Hts**
Kutsher's | *American* | **TriBeCa**
La Mar Cebicheria | *Peruvian* | **Flatiron**
La Prom. des Anglais | *French* | **Chelsea**
Lexington Brass | *American* | **E 40s**
Loi | *Greek* | **W 70s**
Marca | *Argentine* | **Flatiron**
Mas (La Grillade) | *American* | **W Vill**
Melibea | *Spanish* | **W Vill**
Morso | *Italian* | **E 50s**
Moscow 57 | *Russian* | **W 50s**
NoMad | *American* | **Chelsea**
North End Grill | *American* | **Financial**
Onegin | *Russian* | **W Vill**
Parm | *Sandwiches* | **NoLita**
Pier A | *Seafood* | **Financial**
Pig & Khao | *Asian* | **E Vill**
Pillar & Plough | *American* | **W'burg**
Red Gravy | *Italian* | **Bklyn Hts**
Sauce | *Italian* | **LES**
Saxon & Parole | *Eclectic* | **NoHo**
Sen | *Japanese* | **Flatiron**
Speedy Romeo | *Italian* | **Clinton Hill**
Steak 'n Shake | *Burgers* | **W 50s**
STK Grace | *Steak* | **W 40s**
Taka Taka | *Japan./Mex.* | **SoHo**
Talde | *Thai* | **Park Slope**
Tappo | *Pizza* | **Flatiron**
Tribeca Canvas | *Am./Japan* | **TriBeCa**
Whitehall | *British* | **W Vill**
Wong | *Asian* | **G Vill**
Zi Pep | *Italian* | **E Vill**

NOTEWORTHY CLOSINGS (65)

Agua Dulce
Allegretti
Alto
Anthos

Austin's Steakhouse
Bay Leaf
Bello Sguardo
Bliss Bistro
Blu
Braeburn
Bravo Gianni
Bread and Butter
Cabrito
Chiam Chinese Cuisine
Choptank
Chow Bar
Collective, The
Compass
Convivio
Cru
Danal
Double Crown
Earthen Oven
East Side Social Club
Elaine's
Elephant, The
Elizabeth
Faustina
Hello Pasta
Il Matto
Japonais
Jolie
Josephina
Klee Brasserie
Le Jardin Bistro
Long Tan
Los Dos Molinos
Mara's Homemade
Matsugen
Meltemi
Metrazur
Montenapo
M. Wells
One 83
Orchard, The
Patty & Bun
Philoxenia
Piano Due
Q Thai Bistro
Rabbit in the Moon
Rughetta
Savoy
718
South Houston
Sweetiepie
Tabla
Takesushi

Thomas Beisl
202 Cafe
Union Smith Cafe
Village Tart
Woo Lae Oak
Xiao Ye
Zarela
Zeytin

OFFBEAT

Bohemian	**NoHo**	27
Crif Dogs	**multi.**	22
Grand Tier	**W 60s**	21
Hurricane Club	**Flatiron**	20
Ninja	**TriBeCa**	18
Peanut Butter Co.	**G Vill**	22
Rolf's	**Gramercy**	13
Romera	**Chelsea**	-
Sammy's	**LES**	20
Serendipity 3	**E 60s**	19
S'MAC	**E Vill**	22
Tatiana	**Brighton Bch**	21
Tea & Sympathy	**W Vill**	20
☑ WD-50	**LES**	25

OUTDOOR DINING

(G=garden; P=patio; R=rooftop;
S=sidewalk; T=terrace)

Alma	R	**Carroll Gdns**	19
Anella	P	**Greenpt**	24
A.O.C.	G	**W Vill**	20
☑ Aquagrill	T	**SoHo**	26
Aurora	G	**W'burg**	24
Avra	G, P	**E 40s**	25
Bacchus	G	**Boerum Hill**	19
Barbetta	G	**W 40s**	21
Barolo	G	**SoHo**	19
Bar Pitti	S	**G Vill**	22
Battery Gdns.	G, P, T	**Financial**	19
☑ Blue Water	T	**Union Sq**	24
Boathouse	P	**E 70s**	18
Bobo	T	**W Vill**	22
Bogota	P	**Park Slope**	21
Bottino	G	**Chelsea**	19
Brass. Ruhlmann	P	**W 50s**	20
Bryant Park	G, R	**W 40s**	18
Cabana	T	**Seaport**	21
Cacio e Pepe	G, S	**E Vill**	21
Cafe Centro	S	**E 40s**	21
Cafe Fiorello	S	**W 60s**	20
Cávo	G, P	**Astoria**	21
Coffee Shop	S	**Union Sq**	16
Conviv. Osteria	G	**Park Slope**	25
Da Nico	G, S	**L Italy**	20

SPECIAL FEATURES

☑ Da Silvano	S	**G Vill**	22
☑ Esca	P	**W 40s**	25
Farm/Adderley	G	**Ditmas Pk**	24
5 9th	G	**Meatpacking**	19
Flatbush Farm	G	**Park Slope**	21
Fonda	P	**Park Slope**	23
Gascogne	G	**Chelsea**	21
Gemma	S	**E Vill**	20
Gigino	P, S	**multi.**	20
Gnocco	G	**E Vill**	23
Gottino	G	**W Vill**	20
☑ Grocery	G	**Carroll Gdns**	27
Home	G	**W Vill**	22
I Coppi	G	**E Vill**	22
Il Gattopardo	P	**W 50s**	23
Il Palazzo	S	**L Italy**	24
Isabella's	S	**W 70s**	20
I Trulli	G, S	**Murray Hill**	23
Lake Club	P	**St. George**	21
La Lanterna	G	**G Vill**	20
La Mangeoire	S	**E 50s**	21
L&B Spumoni	G	**Bensonhurst**	24
Lattanzi	G, T	**W 40s**	22
Marina Cafe	T	**Great Kills**	22
Markt	S	**Flatiron**	18
NEW Morgane	G, P, S	**W'burg**	-
•New Leaf	P	**Wash. Hts**	21
Ocean Grill	S	**W 70s**	24
Pampano	T	**E 40s**	24
Pastis	S	**Meatpacking**	21
Pete's Tavern	S	**Gramercy**	15
Portofino	T	**City Is**	21
Primehouse	S	**Murray Hill**	24
Pure Food/Wine	G	**Gramercy**	23
Riverview	P	**LIC**	20
Rock Ctr.	T	**W 50s**	19
Sahara	G	**Gravesend**	23
NEW Salinas	G, P	**Chelsea**	-
☑ San Pietro	T	**E 50s**	26
Sea Grill	G	**W 40s**	24
Shake Shack	G	**Flatiron**	22
☑ Sripraphai	G	**Woodside**	26
Surya	G	**W Vill**	21
Sweet Melissa	G	**Cobble Hill**	20
Tartine	S	**W Vill**	22
Terrace in Sky	T	**W 100s**	22
Tree	G	**E Vill**	20
Trestle on 10th	G	**Chelsea**	21
ViceVersa	G, P	**W 50s**	22
Water Club	P	**Murray Hill**	23
Water's Edge	P	**LIC**	21

Wollensky's	S	**E 40s**	24
Zum Schneider	S	**E Vill**	19

PEOPLE-WATCHING

Amaranth	**E 60s**	19
☑ Balthazar	**SoHo**	24
Barolo	**SoHo**	19
Bice	**E 50s**	20
☑ Breslin	**Chelsea**	22
☑ Café Boulud	**E 70s**	27
Cafe Fiorello	**W 60s**	20
Cafe Gitane	**NoLita**	20
☑ Carnegie Deli	**W 50s**	22
Casa Lever	**E 50s**	23
Cipriani D'twn	**SoHo**	22
NEW Crown	**E 80s**	-
☑ Da Silvano	**G Vill**	22
☑ David Burke Townhse.	**E 60s**	25
NEW Desmond's	**E 60s**	22
☑ Elio's	**E 80s**	24
☑ Four Seasons	**E 50s**	27
Fred's at Barneys	**E 60s**	20
Freemans	**LES**	23
☑ Gilt	**E 50s**	26
Harry Cipriani	**E 50s**	22
Indochine	**E Vill**	22
Isabella's	**W 70s**	20
Joe Allen	**W 40s**	18
☑ Katz's Deli	**LES**	24
NEW Lavo	**E 50s**	21
Le Bilboquet	**E 60s**	21
Le Caprice	**E 60s**	20
☑ Le Cirque	**E 50s**	25
NEW Leopard/des Artistes	**W 60s**	21
Lion	**G Vill**	20
Maison	**W 50s**	19
☑ Marea	**W 50s**	28
☑ Michael's	**W 50s**	22
☑ Minetta	**G Vill**	23
Morrell Wine	**W 40s**	19
Nello	**E 60s**	17
Nicola's	**E 80s**	22
NEW Niko	**SoHo**	22
Orsay	**E 70s**	18
☑ Orso	**W 40s**	23
Pastis	**Meatpacking**	21
Philippe	**E 60s**	23
Rao's	**Harlem**	23
☑**NEW** Red Rooster	**Harlem**	21
Sant Ambroeus	**multi.**	21
Sette Mezzo	**E 70s**	23
☑ Sparks	**E 40s**	26
☑ Spice Market	**Meatpacking**	23

🄩 Spotted Pig | **W Vill**	23
Standard Grill | **Meatpacking**	21
Swifty's | **E 70s**	18
🄩 21 Club | **W 50s**	22
Via Quadronno | **multi.**	22
Ze Café | **E 50s**	22

POWER SCENES

Bar Americain | **W 50s**	23
Ben Benson's | **W 50s**	24
Bobby Van's | **E 40s**	22
🄩 Carlyle | **E 70s**	24
Casa Lever | **E 50s**	23
China Grill | **W 50s**	22
Cipriani Wall Street | **Financial**	23
City Hall | **TriBeCa**	21
Del Frisco's | **W 40s**	25
Delmonico's | **Financial**	24
🄩 Del Posto | **Chelsea**	27
🄩 Four Seasons | **E 50s**	27
Fresco | **E 50s**	23
Gallagher's | **W 50s**	21
🄩 Gotham B&G | **G Vill**	28
Harry's Cafe/Steak | **Financial**	23
🄩 Jean Georges | **W 60s**	28
🄩 Keens | **Garment**	25
🄩 La Grenouille | **E 50s**	28
🄩 Le Bernardin | **W 50s**	29
🄩 Le Cirque | **E 50s**	25
🄩 Marea | **W 50s**	28
🄩 Michael's | **W 50s**	22
Morton's | **E 40s**	25
🄩 Nobu | **multi.**	26
Norma's | **W 50s**	25
Patroon | **E 40s**	23
🄩 Peter Luger | **W'burg**	28
Regency | **E 60s**	19
Russian Tea | **W 50s**	19
🄩 San Pietro | **E 50s**	26
Sant Ambroeus | **multi.**	21
Smith/Wollensky | **E 40s**	24
Solo | **E 50s**	24
🄩 Sparks | **E 40s**	26
Tse Yang | **E 50s**	23
🄩 21 Club | **W 50s**	22

PRIVATE ROOMS/ PARTIES

(Capacity figures following name are approximate; call venue for details)

Arabelle | 24 | **E 60s**	24
A Voce | 66 | **W 60s**	23
Barbetta | 120 | **W 40s**	21
Battery Gdns. | 300 | **Financial**	19

Beacon | 90 | **W 50s**	23
Ben & Jack's | 250 | **E 40s**	23
BLT Fish | 66 | **Flatiron**	24
🄩 BLT Prime | 50 | **Gramercy**	26
🄩 BLT Steak | 20 | **E 50s**	25
🄩 Blue Hill | 16 | **G Vill**	27
Blue Smoke | 45 | **Murray Hill**	22
🄩 Blue Water | 35 | **Union Sq**	24
🄩 Breslin | 225 | **Chelsea**	22
🄩 Buddakan | 40 | **Chelsea**	24
Capital Grille | 40 | **E 40s**	24
Casa Lever | 20 | **E 50s**	23
Cellini | 100 | **E 50s**	23
Centolire | 28 | **E 80s**	22
City Hall | 110 | **TriBeCa**	21
🄩 Craft | 40 | **Flatiron**	26
🄩 Daniel | 90 | **E 60s**	29
Del Frisco's | 80 | **W 40s**	25
Delmonico's | 70 | **Financial**	24
🄩 Del Posto | 200 | **Chelsea**	27
🄩 Eleven Madison | 50 | **Flatiron**	28
EN Japanese | 25 | **W Vill**	25
🄩 Felidia | 45 | **E 50s**	26
FireBird | 250 | **W 40s**	20
🄩 Four Seasons | 300 | **E 50s**	27
Fresco | 45 | **E 50s**	23
Gabriel's | 36 | **W 60s**	23
🄩 Gramercy Tavern | 22 | **Flatiron**	27
Harry's Cafe/Steak | 80 | **Financial**	23
Hurricane Club | 80 | **Flatiron**	20
🄩 Il Buco | 25 | **NoHo**	26
Il Cortile | 120 | **L Italy**	22
Ilili | 42 | **Chelsea**	25
'Inoteca | 30 | **LES**	22
🄩 Jean Georges | 35 | **W 60s**	28
🄩 Keens | 85 | **Garment**	25
🄩 La Grenouille | 70 | **E 50s**	28
Landmark Tavern | 50 | **W 40s**	17
🄩 Le Bernardin | 80 | **W 50s**	29
🄩 Le Cirque | 90 | **E 50s**	25
Le Perigord | 35 | **E 50s**	24
Le Zie 2000 | 22 | **Chelsea**	21
🄩 Lincoln | 16 | **W 60s**	24
🄩 Maialino | 22 | **Gramercy**	25
Maloney/Porcelli | 110 | **E 50s**	23
🄩 Marea | 16 | **W 50s**	28
Matsuri | 60 | **Chelsea**	23
Megu | 50 | **TriBeCa**	24
🄩 Michael's | 75 | **W 50s**	22
🄩 Milos, Estiatorio | 24 | **W 50s**	27

SPECIAL FEATURES

🅩 Modern | 64 | **W 50s**	26
Mr. Chow | 35 | **E 50s**	22
Mr. K's | 50 | **E 50s**	24
🅩 Nobu | 36, 66 | **multi.**	26
Oceana | 50 | **W 40s**	24
Palma | 20 | **W Vill**	22
Parlor Steak | 50 | **E 90s**	21
Patroon | 150 | **E 40s**	23
Periyali | 45 | **Flatiron**	24
🅩 Per Se | 65 | **W 60s**	28
🅩 Picholine | 22 | **W 60s**	27
Ponte's | 150 | **TriBeCa**	25
Raoul's | 35 | **SoHo**	24
Redeye Grill | 80 | **W 50s**	20
Remi | 80 | **W 50s**	22
Re Sette | 40 | **W 40s**	21
🅩 River Café | 100 | **Dumbo**	26
Rock Ctr. | 30 | **W 50s**	19
Sambuca | 150 | **W 70s**	19
🅩 Shun Lee Palace | 30 | **E 50s**	25
Solo | 26 | **E 50s**	24
🅩 Sparks | 250 | **E 40s**	26
🅩 Spice Market | 22 | **Meatpacking**	23
Tao | 26 | **E 50s**	22
Terrace in Sky | 80 | **W 100s**	22
Thalassa | 200 | **TriBeCa**	24
🅩 Tocqueville | 80 | **Union Sq**	25
Tribeca Grill | 350 | **TriBeCa**	23
🅩 21 Club | 200 | **W 50s**	22
Valbella | 100 | **Meatpacking**	26
Water Club | 210 | **Murray Hill**	23

QUICK BITE

Azuri Cafe | **W 50s**	26
Baoguette | **multi.**	21
Bark Hot Dogs | **Park Slope**	21
Bereket | **LES**	21
Brennan | **Sheepshead**	22
Carl's Steaks | **Murray Hill**	21
City Bakery | **Flatiron**	22
Così | **multi.**	16
Crif Dogs | **multi.**	22
Daisy May's | **W 40s**	23
David Burke/Bloom. | **E 50s**	19
Defonte's | **multi.**	24
Dishes | **E 40s**	21
Dos Toros | **multi.**	23
Dumpling Man | **E Vill**	21
🅩 Eataly | **Flatiron**	23
Empanada Mama | **W 50s**	22
NEW FoodParc | **Chelsea**	18
Fresco | **multi.**	23
Gray's Papaya | **multi.**	20

Hale/Hearty | **multi.**	19
Hampton Chutney | **SoHo**	20
Hummus Pl. | **multi.**	22
Island Burgers | **multi.**	21
Joe's Pizza | **multi.**	23
Kati Roll | **multi.**	21
Kyochon | **multi.**	19
La Esquina | **L Italy**	23
Leo's Latticini | **Corona**	27
Meatball Shop | **LES**	25
Momofuku Milk Bar | **multi.**	23
Momofuku Noodle | **E Vill**	24
🅩 Momofuku Ssäm | **E Vill**	25
Nicky's | **multi.**	22
99 Mi. to Philly | **E Vill**	19
Noodle Bar | **W Vill**	20
No. 7 | **Chelsea**	23
Num Pang | **G Vill**	26
Oaxaca | **multi.**	20
Once Upon a Tart . . . | **SoHo**	22
Papaya King | **E 80s**	21
Pastrami Queen | **E 70s**	22
Porchetta | **E Vill**	24
Press 195 | **multi.**	22
Rickshaw Dumpling | **Flatiron**	18
Schnipper´s | **W 40s**	19
Shake Shack | **multi.**	22
Two Boots | **multi.**	18
Whole Foods | **multi.**	19
'Wichcraft | **multi.**	20
Zabar's Cafe | **W 80s**	20

QUIET CONVERSATION

🅩 Adour | **E 50s**	26
🅩 Annisa | **W Vill**	28
Arabelle | **E 60s**	24
Aroma Kitchen | **NoHo**	23
🅩 Asiate | **W 60s**	25
🅩 Aureole | **W 40s**	26
Basso56 | **W 50s**	23
Bombay Palace | **W 50s**	19
🅩 Brooklyn Fare | **Downtown Bklyn**	29
Caffe Cielo | **W 50s**	21
Canaletto | **E 60s**	20
Cellini | **E 50s**	23
Circus | **E 60s**	20
Da Umberto | **Chelsea**	24
EN Japanese | **W Vill**	25
Fiorini | **E 50s**	21
Fives | **W 50s**	22
Giovanni | **E 80s**	24

Henry's | **W 100s**	19
Il Gattopardo | **W 50s**	23
☑ Il Tinello | **W 50s**	26
☑ Jean Georges | **W 60s**	28
Jewel of India | **W 40s**	20
Kings' Carriage | **E 80s**	22
Kyotofu | **W 40s**	21
La Gioconda | **E 50s**	21
☑ La Grenouille | **E 50s**	28
☑ Le Bernardin | **W 50s**	29
NEW Left Bank | **W Vill**	-
Lumi | **E 70s**	20
☑ Marea | **W 50s**	28
☑ Masa/Bar Masa | **W 60s**	27
Mint | **E 50s**	22
Montebello | **E 50s**	23
Mr. K's | **E 50s**	24
Nam | **TriBeCa**	22
North Sq. | **G Vill**	23
Palm Court | **W 50s**	20
Paul & Jimmy's | **Gramercy**	21
☑ Perry St. | **W Vill**	26
☑ Per Se | **W 60s**	28
Petite Crev. | **Carroll Gdns**	24
Petrarca Vino | **TriBeCa**	23
Petrossian | **W 50s**	24
☑ Picholine | **W 60s**	27
Provence/Boite | **Carroll Gdns**	20
Remi | **W 50s**	22
Rosanjin | **TriBeCa**	27
Salaam Bombay | **TriBeCa**	22
Sfoglia | **E 90s**	23
Square Meal | **E 90s**	23
Teodora | **E 50s**	21
Terrace in Sky | **W 100s**	22
☑ Tocqueville | **Union Sq**	25
Toledo | **Murray Hill**	24
Trattoria Cinque | **TriBeCa**	21
Tree | **E Vill**	20
Tsampa | **E Vill**	20
12 Chairs | **SoHo**	20
Villa Berulia | **Murray Hill**	24
Ze Café | **E 50s**	22
☑ Zenkichi | **W'burg**	26

RAW BARS

Ammos | **E 40s**	21
☑ Aquagrill | **SoHo**	26
Atlantic Grill | **multi.**	23
☑ Balthazar | **SoHo**	24
Bar Americain | **W 50s**	23
BLT Fish | **Flatiron**	24
Blue Fin | **W 40s**	22

☑ Blue Ribbon | **multi.**	25
☑ Blue Water | **Union Sq**	24
Brasserie Cognac | **W 50s**	19
City Crab | **Flatiron**	19
City Hall | **TriBeCa**	21
City Lobster | **W 40s**	19
NEW Darby | **W Vill**	20
Docks Oyster | **E 40s**	21
☑ NEW Dutch | **SoHo**	24
East Buffet | **Flushing**	19
Ed's Chowder | **W 60s**	20
Ed's Lobster | **multi.**	23
☑ Esca | **W 40s**	25
NEW Fedora | **W Vill**	22
Fig & Olive | **multi.**	20
Fish | **W Vill**	23
Fishtail | **E 60s**	24
Flex Mussels | **multi.**	23
Flor/Sol | **TriBeCa**	21
Fulton | **E 70s**	23
Giorgione | **Hudson Square**	23
NEW Imperial No. Nine | **SoHo**	25
Jack's Lux. | **E Vill**	26
NEW Jeffrey's Grocery | **W Vill**	21
NEW John Dory | **Chelsea**	23
London Lennie | **Rego Pk**	23
Lure Fishbar | **SoHo**	23
Macao Trading | **TriBeCa**	19
Má Pêche | **W 50s**	23
Marina Cafe | **Great Kills**	22
☑ Mark | **E 70s**	22
Markt | **Flatiron**	18
Marlow/Sons | **W'burg**	24
McCormick/Schmick | **W 50s**	20
Mercer Kitchen | **SoHo**	22
Mermaid | **multi.**	22
NEW Millesime | **Murray Hill**	21
Oceana | **W 40s**	24
Ocean Grill | **W 70s**	24
Olea | **Ft Greene**	22
☑ Oyster Bar | **E 40s**	22
Parlor Steak | **E 90s**	21
☑ Pearl Oyster | **W Vill**	26
Pearl Room | **Bay Ridge**	23
NEW Pier 9 | **W 50s**	23
P.J. Clarke's | **multi.**	17
Plaza Food Hall | **W 50s**	22
Primehouse | **Murray Hill**	24
Riverview | **LIC**	20
Standard Grill | **Meatpacking**	21
SushiSamba | **multi.**	21
Tosca Café | **Throgs Neck**	21
☑ 21 Club | **W 50s**	22

Umberto's | **Fordham**	20	James | **Prospect Hts**	23
Uncle Jack's | **multi.**	23	JoJo | **E 60s**	25
Wall/Water | **Financial**	20	Kings' Carriage | **E 80s**	22
Walter Foods | **W'burg**	23	Kyotofu | **W 40s**	21
Water's Edge | **LIC**	21	L'Absinthe | **E 60s**	22
		Lady Mendl's | **Gramercy**	21

ROMANTIC PLACES

		◪ La Grenouille | **E 50s**	28
Algonquin | **W 40s**	18	Lake Club | **St. George**	21
Alma | **Carroll Gdns**	19	La Lanterna | **G Vill**	20
Alta | **G Vill**	25	La Mangeoire | **E 50s**	21
Antica Venezia | **W Vill**	23	Lambs Club | **W 40s**	21
◪ Asiate | **W 60s**	25	La Ripaille | **W Vill**	22
August | **W Vill**	22	Le Gigot | **W Vill**	24
◪ Aureole | **W 40s**	26	Locale | **Astoria**	23
Aurora | **multi.**	24	Maria Pia | **W 50s**	19
◪ Balthazar | **SoHo**	24	Mari Vanna | **Flatiron**	20
Barbetta | **W 40s**	21	◪ Mas | **W Vill**	27
Barmarché | **NoLita**	21	Mercat | **NoHo**	20
Barolo | **SoHo**	19	Mr. K's | **E 50s**	24
Battery Gdns. | **Financial**	19	Nino's | **E 70s**	22
◪ Blue Hill | **G Vill**	27	Olea | **Ft Greene**	22
Blue Ribbon Bakery | **W Vill**	25	◪ One if by Land | **W Vill**	24
Boathouse | **E 70s**	18	Paola's | **E 90s**	23
Bottino | **Chelsea**	19	Pasha | **W 70s**	21
◪ Bouley | **TriBeCa**	28	Peasant | **NoLita**	24
Bourgeois Pig | **E Vill**	20	Periyali | **Flatiron**	24
CamaJe | **G Vill**	22	◪ Perry St. | **W Vill**	26
Capsouto Frères | **TriBeCa**	24	Petrossian | **W 50s**	24
Caviar Russe | **E 50s**	24	Philip Marie | **W Vill**	20
Chez Josephine | **W 40s**	20	Piccola Venezia | **Astoria**	26
Conviv. Osteria | **Park Slope**	25	Pinocchio | **E 90s**	23
◪ Daniel | **E 60s**	29	Place | **W Vill**	25
◪ David Burke Townhse. | **E 60s**	25	Quercy | **Cobble Hill**	21
◪ Del Posto | **Chelsea**	27	Raoul's | **SoHo**	24
Dressler | **W'burg**	25	◪ River Café | **Dumbo**	26
Duane Park | **TriBeCa**	22	Riverview | **LIC**	20
Dylan Prime | **TriBeCa**	24	Roc | **TriBeCa**	21
◪ Eleven Madison | **Flatiron**	28	Rye | **W'burg**	24
Erminia | **E 80s**	25	◪ Saul | **Boerum Hill**	27
FireBird | **W 40s**	20	◪ Scalini Fedeli | **TriBeCa**	27
Firenze | **E 80s**	22	◪ Sistina | **E 80s**	26
Flor/Sol | **TriBeCa**	21	◪ Spice Market | **Meatpacking**	23
◪ Four Seasons | **E 50s**	27	Spiga | **W 80s**	24
◪ Frankies | **LES**	25	Teodora | **E 50s**	21
Gascogne | **Chelsea**	21	Terrace in Sky | **W 100s**	22
Gigino | **Financial**	20	◪ Tocqueville | **Union Sq**	25
Holy Basil | **E Vill**	22	Tre Dici/Steak | **Chelsea**	23
Hotel Griffou | **G Vill**	19	26 Seats | **E Vill**	22
House | **Gramercy**	21	Uva | **E 70s**	22
I Coppi | **E Vill**	22	**NEW** Valentino's/Green | **Bayside**	21
◪ Il Buco | **NoHo**	26		
I Trulli | **Murray Hill**	23	View | **W 40s**	18
Jack's Lux. | **E Vill**	26	◪ Wallsé | **W Vill**	26

Vote at ZAGAT.com

Water Club | **Murray Hill**	23
Water's Edge | **LIC**	21
☑ Zenkichi | **W'burg**	26

SENIOR APPEAL

Arabelle | **E 60s**	24
Artie's Deli | **W 80s**	18
☑ Aureole | **W 40s**	26
Bamonte's | **W'burg**	24
Barbetta | **W 40s**	21
☑ Barney Greengrass | **W 80s**	24
Campagnola | **E 70s**	23
Capsouto Frères | **TriBeCa**	24
Chadwick's | **Bay Ridge**	22
Chez Napoléon | **W 50s**	22
Dawat | **E 50s**	23
DeGrezia | **E 50s**	23
☑ Del Posto | **Chelsea**	27
Due | **E 70s**	22
Eisenberg's Sandwich | **Flatiron**	18
Embers | **Bay Ridge**	20
☑ Felidia | **E 50s**	26
Fiorini | **E 50s**	21
Gallagher's | **W 50s**	21
Giovanni | **E 80s**	24
Grifone | **E 40s**	24
☑ Il Tinello | **W 50s**	26
☑ Jean Georges | **W 60s**	28
Jubilee | **E 50s**	22
La Bonne Soupe | **W 50s**	19
☑ La Grenouille | **E 50s**	28
La Mangeoire | **E 50s**	21
La Mirabelle | **W 80s**	22
La Petite Aub. | **Murray Hill**	22
Lattanzi | **W 40s**	22
Le Caprice | **E 60s**	20
☑ Le Cirque | **E 50s**	25
Le Marais | **W 40s**	22
NEW Leopard/des Artistes | **W 60s**	21
Le Perigord | **E 50s**	24
Lusardi's | **E 70s**	24
☑ Mark | **E 70s**	22
Mr. K's | **E 50s**	24
Nicola's | **E 80s**	22
Palm Court | **W 50s**	20
Pastrami Queen | **E 70s**	22
Paul & Jimmy's | **Gramercy**	21
Piccola Venezia | **Astoria**	26
Pietro's | **E 40s**	24
Ponticello | **Astoria**	24
Primola | **E 60s**	22
Quatorze Bis | **E 70s**	21

Quattro Gatti | **E 80s**	21
Rao's | **Harlem**	23
☑ River Café | **Dumbo**	26
Rossini's | **Murray Hill**	22
Russian Tea | **W 50s**	19
☑ San Pietro | **E 50s**	26
Sardi's | **W 40s**	18
☑ Saul | **Boerum Hill**	27
Scaletta | **W 70s**	21
Shun Lee West | **W 60s**	23
Teresa's | **Bklyn Hts**	18
12 Chairs | **SoHo**	20

SLEEPERS

(Fine food, but little known)

Anella | **Greenpt**	24
Bohemian | **NoHo**	27
Commodore | **W'burg**	25
Emilio's Ballato | **NoLita**	25
Ferdinando's | **Carroll Gdns**	25
Filippo's | **Dongan Hills**	25
Geido | **Prospect Hts**	25
Ghenet | **Park Slope**	24
Gruppo | **E Vill**	26
Hunan Kit./Grand Sichuan | **Flushing**	24
Il Bambino | **Astoria**	26
Kabab Café | **Astoria**	24
La Superior | **W'burg**	24
La Vigna | **Forest Hills**	24
Locale | **Astoria**	23
Mesa Coyoacan | **W'burg**	25
Miranda | **W'burg**	25
Nom Wah Tea | **Chinatown**	23
Nove | **Eltingville**	24
Palo Santo | **Park Slope**	23
Peaches | **Bed-Stuy**	23
Petite Crev. | **Carroll Gdns**	24
Place | **W Vill**	25
Pukk | **E Vill**	23
Real Madrid | **Mariners Harbor**	24
Rizzo's Pizza | **multi.**	23
Rosanjin | **TriBeCa**	27
Sac's Place | **Astoria**	24
Saltie | **W'burg**	23
Scottadito | **Park Slope**	23
Shanghai Cuisine | **Chinatown**	23
Siam Sq. | **Riverdale**	24
Solo | **E 50s**	24
Sorella | **LES**	26
Takashi | **W Vill**	26
Umi Nom | **Clinton Hill**	26
Uvarara | **Middle Vill**	26

Walter Foods | **W'burg**	23
Zest | **Rosebank**	26

STARGAZING

Abe/Arthur | **Meatpacking**	22
Angus McIndoe | **W 40s**	16
Z Balthazar | **SoHo**	24
Bar Pitti | **G Vill**	22
Cafe Luxembourg | **W 70s**	-
NEW Crown | **E 80s**	-
NEW Darby | **W Vill**	20
Z Da Silvano | **G Vill**	22
Z Elio's | **E 80s**	24
Joe Allen | **W 40s**	18
NEW Leopard/des Artistes | **W 60s**	21
Lion | **G Vill**	20
Z Minetta | **G Vill**	23
Philippe | **E 60s**	23
Rao's | **Harlem**	23
Z Spotted Pig | **W Vill**	23
Waverly Inn | **W Vill**	21

SUNDAY BEST BETS

(See also Hotel Dining)

Z Aquagrill | **SoHo**	26
Z Aquavit | **E 50s**	25
Artisanal | **Murray Hill**	23
Z Balthazar | **SoHo**	24
Bar Americain | **W 50s**	23
Z Blue Hill | **G Vill**	27
Z Blue Ribbon | **SoHo**	25
Z Blue Water | **Union Sq**	24
Z Bouley | **TriBeCa**	28
Z David Burke Townhse. | **E 60s**	25
5 Points | **NoHo**	22
Z Gotham B&G | **G Vill**	28
Z Gramercy Tavern | **Flatiron**	27
Lucky Strike | **SoHo**	17
Lupa | **G Vill**	25
Z Mesa Grill | **Flatiron**	24
Odeon | **TriBeCa**	19
Z Ouest | **W 80s**	24
Z Peter Luger | **W'burg**	28
Piccolo Angolo | **W Vill**	26
Z Picholine | **W 60s**	27
Pomaire | **W 40s**	20
Prune | **E Vill**	25
Z River Café | **Dumbo**	26
Solo | **E 50s**	24
Tratt. Dell'Arte | **W 50s**	23
Tribeca Grill | **TriBeCa**	23
Z Union Sq. Cafe | **Union Sq**	27
Water Club | **Murray Hill**	23

TEA SERVICE

Abigail's | **Garment**	20
Arabelle | **E 60s**	24
Z Asiate | **W 60s**	25
Darbar | **multi.**	21
Duane Park | **TriBeCa**	22
Kings' Carriage | **E 80s**	22
Lady Mendl's | **Gramercy**	21
Maze | **W 50s**	22
Megu | **multi.**	24
Mercer Kitchen | **SoHo**	22
Morgan | **Murray Hill**	20
North Sq. | **G Vill**	23
Palm Court | **W 50s**	20
Robert | **W 50s**	20
Russian Tea | **W 50s**	19
Sant Ambroeus | **multi.**	21
Sarabeth's | **multi.**	20
Sweet Melissa | **multi.**	20
Z Tamarind | **Flatiron**	25
Tea & Sympathy | **W Vill**	20

THEME RESTAURANTS

Cowgirl | **W Vill**	17
Hurricane Club | **Flatiron**	20
Ninja | **TriBeCa**	18
Ruby Foo's | **W 40s**	18

TOUGH TICKETS

Z ABC Kitchen | **Flatiron**	25
NEW Birreria | **Flatiron**	21
Z Brooklyn Fare | **Downtown Bklyn**	29
NEW Crown | **E 80s**	-
Z NEW Dutch | **SoHo**	24
Lion | **G Vill**	20
Z Minetta | **G Vill**	23
Z Momofuku Ko | **E Vill**	27
Z NEW Red Rooster | **Harlem**	21
Z Torrisi | **NoLita**	27

TRANSPORTING EXPERIENCES

Z Asiate | **W 60s**	25
Z Balthazar | **SoHo**	24
Z NEW Beauty & Essex | **LES**	22
Boathouse | **E 70s**	18
Z Buddakan | **Chelsea**	24
Chez Josephine | **W 40s**	20
FireBird | **W 40s**	20
Z Il Buco | **NoHo**	26
Ilili | **Chelsea**	25
Z Keens | **Garment**	25
Z La Grenouille | **E 50s**	28

Lambs Club | **W 40s**	21
Le Colonial | **E 50s**	21
Mari Vanna | **Flatiron**	20
⊠ Masa/Bar Masa | **W 60s**	27
Matsuri | **Chelsea**	23
Megu | **TriBeCa**	24
Monkey Bar | **E 50s**	19
Ninja | **TriBeCa**	18
⊠ One if by Land | **W Vill**	24
⊠ Per Se | **W 60s**	28
Qi | **Union Sq**	20
Rao's | **Harlem**	23
⊠ Spice Market | **Meatpacking**	23
Tao | **E 50s**	22
Vatan | **Murray Hill**	24
Water's Edge | **LIC**	21

VIEWS

Alma | **Carroll Gdns**	19
Angelina's | **Tottenville**	22
Antica Venezia | **W Vill**	23
⊠ Asiate | **W 60s**	25
A Voce | **W 60s**	23
Battery Gdns. | **Financial**	19
Boathouse | **E 70s**	18
Bouchon Bakery | **W 60s**	24
Bryant Park | **W 40s**	18
Bubby's | **Dumbo**	20
Cabana | **Seaport**	21
Cipriani Dolci | **E 40s**	21
City Is. Lobster | **City Is**	19
Cole's Dock | **Great Kills**	21
Fairway Cafe | **Red Hook**	18
Gigino | **Financial**	20
Heartland | **Seaport**	15
NEW Hotel Chantelle | **LES**	-
Hudson River | **Harlem**	21
Lake Club | **St. George**	21
Landmarc | **W 60s**	21
⊠ Lincoln | **W 60s**	24
Lobster Box | **City Is**	20
Marina Cafe | **Great Kills**	22
Michael Jordan | **E 40s**	20
⊠ Modern | **W 50s**	26
Morrell Wine | **W 40s**	19
⊠ Per Se | **W 60s**	28
P.J. Clarke's | **Financial**	17
Ponte's | **TriBeCa**	25
Porter House | **W 60s**	24
Portofino | **City Is**	21
⊠ River Café | **Dumbo**	26
NEW Riverpark | **Murray Hill**	25
Riverview | **LIC**	20

Robert | **W 50s**	20
Rock Ctr. | **W 50s**	19
Sea Grill | **W 40s**	24
Suteishi | **Seaport**	25
Terrace in Sky | **W 100s**	22
2 West | **Financial**	22
View | **W 40s**	18
Water Club | **Murray Hill**	23
Water's Edge | **LIC**	21

VISITORS ON EXPENSE ACCOUNT

⊠ Adour | **E 50s**	26
⊠ **NEW** Ai Fiori | **Garment**	27
⊠ Aureole | **W 40s**	26
⊠ Babbo | **G Vill**	27
⊠ Bouley | **TriBeCa**	28
⊠ Café Boulud | **E 70s**	27
Colicchio/Sons | **Chelsea**	24
⊠ Corton | **TriBeCa**	25
⊠ Craft | **Flatiron**	26
⊠ Daniel | **E 60s**	29
Del Frisco's | **W 40s**	25
⊠ Del Posto | **Chelsea**	27
⊠ Eleven Madison | **Flatiron**	28
⊠ Four Seasons | **E 50s**	27
⊠ Gari/Sushi | **W 40s**	27
Gordon Ramsay | **W 50s**	23
⊠ Gramercy Tavern | **Flatiron**	27
⊠ Il Mulino | **G Vill**	27
⊠ Jean Georges | **W 60s**	28
⊠ Keens | **Garment**	25
⊠ Kuruma Zushi | **E 40s**	28
⊠ La Grenouille | **E 50s**	28
Lambs Club | **W 40s**	21
⊠ Le Bernardin | **W 50s**	29
⊠ Le Cirque | **E 50s**	25
⊠ Marea | **W 50s**	28
⊠ Masa/Bar Masa | **W 60s**	27
⊠ Milos, Estiatorio | **W 50s**	27
⊠ Modern | **W 50s**	26
Montebello | **E 50s**	23
⊠ Nobu | **multi.**	26
⊠ Palm | **multi.**	25
⊠ Per Se | **W 60s**	28
⊠ Peter Luger | **W'burg**	28
⊠ Picholine | **W 60s**	27
⊠ River Café | **Dumbo**	26
⊠ Scarpetta | **Chelsea**	26
⊠ SHO Shaun | **Financial**	26
⊠ Spice Market | **Meatpacking**	23
⊠ Sushi Yasuda | **E 40s**	28
⊠ Union Sq. Cafe | **Union Sq**	27
⊠ Veritas | **Flatiron**	26

SPECIAL FEATURES

WATERSIDE

Angelina's | **Tottenville**	22
Battery Gdns. | **Financial**	19
Boathouse | **E 70s**	18
Bubby's | **Dumbo**	20
Cabana | **Seaport**	21
City Is. Lobster | **City Is**	19
Cole's Dock | **Great Kills**	21
Gigino | **Financial**	20
Lake Club | **St. George**	21
Lobster Box | **City Is**	20
Marina Cafe | **Great Kills**	22
Portofino | **City Is**	21
☑ River Café | **Dumbo**	26
NEW Riverpark | **Murray Hill**	25
Riverview | **LIC**	20
Tatiana | **Brighton Bch**	21
Water Club | **Murray Hill**	23
Water's Edge | **LIC**	21

WINNING WINE LISTS

Accademia/Vino | **multi.**	18
☑ Adour | **E 50s**	26
Aldea | **Flatiron**	25
Alta | **G Vill**	25
☑ Annisa | **W Vill**	28
Artisanal | **Murray Hill**	23
☑ Asiate | **W 60s**	25
☑ Aureole | **W 40s**	26
A Voce | **Flatiron**	23
☑ Babbo | **G Vill**	27
Bacchus | **Boerum Hill**	19
☑ Balthazar | **SoHo**	24
Barbetta | **W 40s**	21
☑ Bar Boulud | **W 60s**	24
Barolo | **SoHo**	19
Becco | **W 40s**	23
Benoit | **W 50s**	21
BLT Fish | **Flatiron**	24
BLT Market | **W 50s**	24
☑ BLT Prime | **Gramercy**	26
☑ BLT Steak | **E 50s**	25
Blue Fin | **W 40s**	22
☑ Blue Hill | **G Vill**	27
Bobby Van's | **multi.**	22
Bottega/Vino | **E 50s**	22
☑ Bouley | **TriBeCa**	28
Buttermilk | **Carroll Gdns**	24
☑ Café Boulud | **E 70s**	27
Café d'Alsace | **E 80s**	21
Café Select | **SoHo**	19
Capital Grille | **E 40s**	24

☑ Casa Mono | **Gramercy**	25
'Cesca | **W 70s**	23
City Hall | **TriBeCa**	21
☑ Craft | **Flatiron**	26
☑ Daniel | **E 60s**	29
☑ David Burke Townhse. | **E 60s**	25
☑ DB Bistro Moderne | **W 40s**	25
Del Frisco's | **W 40s**	25
☑ Dell'anima | **W Vill**	25
Delmonico's | **Financial**	24
☑ Del Posto | **Chelsea**	27
☑ Eataly | **Flatiron**	23
☑ Eleven Madison | **Flatiron**	28
☑ Esca | **W 40s**	25
☑ Felidia | **E 50s**	26
☑ Frankies | **multi.**	25
☑ Franny's | **Prospect Hts**	25
☑ Gilt | **E 50s**	26
☑ Gotham B&G | **G Vill**	28
☑ Gramercy Tavern | **Flatiron**	27
Harry's Cafe/Steak | **Financial**	23
Hearth | **E Vill**	24
☑ Il Buco | **NoHo**	26
'Ino | **W Vill**	24
'Inoteca | **LES**	22
I Trulli | **Murray Hill**	23
☑ Jean Georges | **W 60s**	28
NEW Junoon | **Flatiron**	23
Landmarc | **multi.**	21
La Pizza Fresca | **Flatiron**	24
☑ Le Bernardin | **W 50s**	29
Le Charlot | **E 60s**	21
☑ Le Cirque | **E 50s**	25
Lupa | **G Vill**	25
☑ Maialino | **Gramercy**	25
☑ Marea | **W 50s**	28
☑ Mas | **W Vill**	27
Megu | **TriBeCa**	24
☑ Michael's | **W 50s**	22
☑ Milos, Estiatorio | **W 50s**	27
☑ Modern | **W 50s**	26
Morrell Wine | **W 40s**	19
Motorino | **E Vill**	24
Nice Matin | **W 70s**	20
Oceana | **W 40s**	24
NEW Osteria Morini | **SoHo**	24
Otto | **G Vill**	23
☑ Ouest | **W 80s**	24
☑ Per Se | **W 60s**	28
☑ Picholine | **W 60s**	27
Pomaire | **W 40s**	20
Porter House | **W 60s**	24
Post House | **E 60s**	24

Vote at ZAGAT.com

Primehouse | **Murray Hill** | 24
Raoul's | **SoHo** | 24
Z River Café | **Dumbo** | 26
Rothmann's | **E 50s** | 23
Rouge Tomate | **E 60s** | 24
Salumeria Rosi | **W 70s** | 25
Z San Pietro | **E 50s** | 26
Z Scalini Fedeli | **TriBeCa** | 27
Z Scarpetta | **Chelsea** | 26
SD26 | **Murray Hill** | 24
Z SHO Shaun | **Financial** | 26
Smith/Wollensky | **E 40s** | 24
Solera | **E 50s** | 22
Z Sparks | **E 40s** | 26
Z Telepan | **W 60s** | 26
Terroir | **multi.** | 20

Thalassa | **TriBeCa** | 24
Tía Pol | **Chelsea** | 24
Tommaso | **Dyker Hts** | 24
Trestle on 10th | **Chelsea** | 21
Tribeca Grill | **TriBeCa** | 23
Tse Yang | **E 50s** | 23
Z 21 Club | **W 50s** | 22
Txikito | **Chelsea** | 25
Z Union Sq. Cafe | **Union Sq** | 27
Uva | **E 70s** | 22
Valbella | **Meatpacking** | 26
Z Veritas | **Flatiron** | 26
Vinegar Hill Hse. | **Vinegar Hill** | 25
Z Wallsé | **W Vill** | 26
Water's Edge | **LIC** | 21

Wine Vintage Chart

This chart is based on a 30-point scale. The ratings (by U. of South Carolina law professor **Howard Stravitz**) reflect vintage quality and the wine's readiness to drink. A dash means the wine is past its peak or too young to rate. Loire ratings are for dry whites.

Whites

	95	96	97	98	99	00	01	02	03	04	05	06	07	08	09	10
France:																
Alsace	24	23	23	25	23	25	26	22	21	22	23	21	26	26	23	26
Burgundy	27	26	22	21	24	24	23	27	23	26	26	25	26	25	25	–
Loire Valley	–	–	–	–	–	–	–	25	20	22	27	23	24	24	24	25
Champagne	26	27	24	25	25	25	21	26	21	–	–	–	–	–	–	–
Sauternes	21	23	25	23	24	24	29	24	26	21	26	25	27	24	27	–
California:																
Chardonnay	–	–	–	–	22	21	24	25	22	26	29	24	27	23	27	–
Sauvignon Blanc	–	–	–	–	–	–	–	–	25	24	27	25	24	25	–	–
Austria:																
Grüner V./Riesl.	22	–	25	22	26	22	23	25	25	24	23	26	25	24	25	–
Germany:	22	26	22	25	24	–	29	25	26	27	28	26	26	26	26	–

Reds

	95	96	97	98	99	00	01	02	03	04	05	06	07	08	09	10
France:																
Bordeaux	25	25	24	25	24	29	26	24	26	25	28	24	24	25	27	–
Burgundy	26	27	25	24	27	22	23	25	25	23	28	24	24	25	27	–
Rhône	26	22	23	27	26	27	26	–	26	25	27	25	26	23	27	–
Beaujolais	–	–	–	–	–	–	–	–	–	–	27	25	24	23	28	25
California:																
Cab./Merlot	27	24	28	23	25	–	27	26	25	24	26	24	27	26	25	–
Pinot Noir	–	–	–	–	–	–	26	25	24	25	26	24	27	24	26	–
Zinfandel	–	–	–	–	–	–	25	24	26	24	23	21	26	23	25	–
Oregon:																
Pinot Noir	–	–	–	–	–	–	–	26	24	25	24	25	24	27	24	–
Italy:																
Tuscany	25	24	29	24	27	24	27	–	24	27	25	26	25	24	–	–
Piedmont	21	27	26	25	26	28	27	–	24	27	26	26	27	26	–	–
Spain:																
Rioja	26	24	25	22	25	24	28	–	23	27	26	24	24	25	26	–
Ribera del Duero/Priorat	25	26	24	25	25	24	27	–	24	27	26	24	25	27	–	–
Australia:																
Shiraz/Cab.	23	25	24	26	24	24	26	26	25	25	26	21	23	26	24	–
Chile:	–	–	–	–	24	22	25	23	24	24	27	25	24	26	24	–
Argentina:																
Malbec	–	–	–	–	–	–	–	–	–	25	26	27	26	26	25	–

ZAGATMAP

Manhattan Subway Map

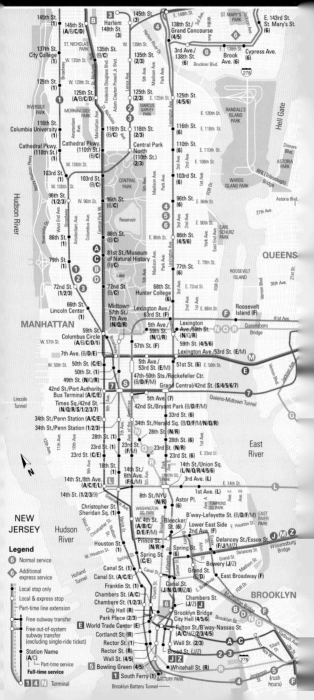

Most Popular Restaurants

Map coordinates follow each name. Sections A–H lie south of 34th Street (see adjacent map). Sections I–P lie north of 34th Street (see reverse side of map).

1 Le Bernardin (O-3)

2 Gramercy Tavern (B-4)

3 Peter Luger Steak House (E-7)

4 Union Square Cafe (B-4)

5 Eleven Madison Park (B-4)

6 Daniel (M-4)

7 Babbo (C-3)

8 Gotham Bar & Grill (C-4)

9 Jean Georges (N-3)

10 Balthazar (E-4)

11 Del Posto (C-2)

12 Bouley (F-4)

13 Atlantic Grill (L-5, N-3)

14 Per Se (N-3)

15 Café Boulud (L-4)

16 Nobu (F-3, N-4)

17 5 Napkin Burger (K-2, N-7, P-3)

18 ABC Kitchen (B-4)

19 Aureole (P-4)

20 Four Seasons* (O-5)

21 21 Club (O-4)

22 La Grenouille (O-4)

23 Blue Water Grill (B-4)

24 Modern (O-4)

25 Palm (F-3, O-3, P-5)

26 Del Frisco's (O-4)

27 Marea (N-3)

28 Becco (O-3)

29 Rosa Mexicano (B-4, N-3, N-6)

30 Il Mulino (D-4)

31 Aquagrill (E-3)

32 A Voce (B-4, N-3)

33 Shake Shack (B-4, G-3, K-5, L-2, P-3)

34 Jean Georges' Nougatine (N-3)

35 Blue Hill (D-3)

36 Carmine's (K-2, P-3)

37 Bar Boulud (N-3)

38 Bar Americain (O-3)

39 Aquavit (N-4)

40 Katz's Delicatessen (D-5)

41 Picholine (N-3)

42 Buddakan (C-2)

43 Maialino (B-4)

44 Artisanal (A-4)

45 Telepan (M-3)

46 David Burke Townhouse (N-5)

47 Spice Market (C-2)

48 River Café (G-6)

49 Blue Smoke (A-4, P-7)

50 Felidia (N-5)

*Indicates tie with above